Expert Systems

DESIGN AND DEVELOPMENT

John Durkin

UNIVERSITY OF AKRON

Macmillan Publishing Company
NEW YORK

Maxwell Macmillan Canada
TORONTO

Maxwell Macmillan International
NEW YORK   OXFORD   SINGAPORE   SYDNEY

In memory of my sons David and Michael
whose fires flared only briefly,
but enough to light my memories for a lifetime.
And to my daughters Kira and Kristi,
who I will cherish always
for the joy that they brought into my life.

Editor: John Griffin
Production Supervisor: John Travis
Production Manager: Su Levine
Text and cover designer: Natasha Sylvester
Cover illustration: Dave Brown
Illustrations: Academy ArtWorks, Inc.

This book was set in Times Roman by BiComp Inc.
and was printed and bound by Book Press.
The cover was printed by Phoenix Color Corp.

Macmillan Publishing Company
866 Third Avenue, New York, New York 10022

Macmillan Publishing Company is part
of the Maxwell Communication Group of Companies.

Maxwell Macmillan Canada, Inc.
1200 Eglinton Avenue East
Suite 200
Don Mills, Ontario M3C 3N1

Library of Congress Cataloging in Publication Data
Durkin, John,
    Expert systems : design and development / John Durkin.
      p. cm.
    Includes bibliographical references and index.
    ISBN 0-02-330970-9
    1. Expert systems (Computer science) I. Title.
QA76.76.E95D87 1994
006.3'3—dc20

                                        93-2508
                                          CIP

Printing: 1 2 3 4 5 6 7 8   Year: 4 5 6 7 8 9 0 1 2 3

Foreword

Artificial Intelligence may be defined as: The study of the mechanisms underlying intelligent behavior through the construction and evaluation of artifacts that enact those mechanisms.

Artificial Intelligence is both a science and an engineering discipline. It is a science in that it seeks explication of the nature of knowledge, understanding, and skill. AI also offers a paradigm for testing our understanding of and interaction with the world. We design experiments and run them. The results of our experiments demonstrate our understanding of the world; our revised experiments show our improved comprehension. Artificial Intelligence is engineering in that its practice requires appropriate, flexible, and timely solutions: the design and building of programs and applications that work.

AI has now successfully delivered to the user community many successful design and programming tools; these include algorithms for machine learning, planning and robotics, including the building of closed loop control systems for manufacturing processes. Above all else the Artificial Intelligence research community has developed and delivered expert system or "knowledge-based" programming techniques and applications.

Expert systems encode a human expert's knowledge for a computer in such a fashion that this expert program can be run and the knowledge applied where needed. The expert program is built from explicit pieces of knowledge extracted from the human expert. It is modular and can be easily changed when humans discover new approaches to the problem solving or when the needs of the problem solver change. This expert program can explain itself, by describing why some line of questioning is relevant as well as presenting a proof for how it arrived at some conclusion. The program is also heuristic in that it seldom relies on exhaustive search methods but rather considers the data and knowledge of the application much as the human expert does: with confidences, rules of thumb, and encoded experience of the problem application.

John Durkin's book offers one of the best guides available for the design and building of expert systems. John introduces knowledge-based programming techniques as practical, useful, application-oriented tools. His approach presents expert systems as a natural evolution of AI concepts, thus integrating AI theory with the practice and delivery of quality software.

Figure 1 and some text taken with permission from *Artificial Intelligence: Structures and Strategies for Complex Problem Solving*, George F. Luger and William A. Stubblefield, Benjamin Cummings, 1993.

Durkin's approach to expert system software is founded on the use of a "conceptual model" to drive his software development. Figure 1 shows how this conceptual model stands between experience in the world and the creation of code for a computer. A good part of Durkin's book describes AI data structures and shows how they are important conceptual tools for problem solving.

To build an expert system we address a domain of knowledge and skill in an application area; this knowledge is often vague or only partially articulated. The knowledge engineer must translate this into a formal language. This process brings with it several important problems:

1. Human skill is practice based. As Aristotle points out in his *Ethics,* "what we have to learn to do, we learn by doing." Skills such as those possessed by medical doctors are learned as much through years of internship and residency, with their constant focus on patients, as they are in anatomy or physiology lectures, where emphasis is on experiment and theory. Delivery of medical care is to a great extent practice driven. And after years of performance, these skills are highly integrated and often not explicitly retrievable.

2. Human expertise often takes the form of knowing *how* to cope in a situation rather than knowing *what* a rational characterization of the situation might be, of developing skilled performance mechanisms rather than a fundamental understanding of what these mechanisms are. An obvious example of this is riding a unicycle: the successful rider is not, in real time, consciously solving multiple sets of simultaneous differential equations to keep in

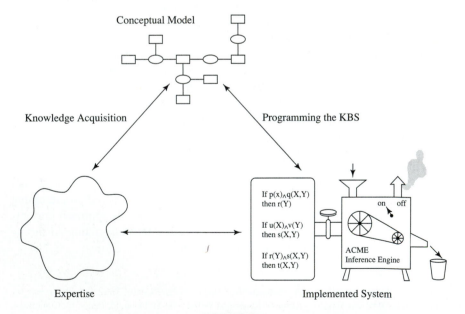

FIGURE 1

balance; rather she is using an intuitive combination of feelings of "gravity," "momentum," and "inertia" to form a usable control procedure. In fact, we find a huge gap often exists between human expertise in an application area and any precise accounting of this skill.
3. We often think of knowledge acquisition as gaining factual knowledge of an objective reality, the so-called "real world." As both theory and practice have shown, there is no immediate access to some "real" world; rather human expertise represents an individual's or community's model of the world. Such models are as influenced by convention, social processes, and hidden agendas as they are by empirical methodologies.
4. Expertise changes. Not only do human experts gain new knowledge, but also existing knowledge may be subject to radical reformulation, as evidenced by ongoing controversies in both scientific and nonscientific fields.

Consequently, knowledge engineering is difficult and should be viewed as spanning the life cycle of any expert system. To simplify this task, it is useful to have, as in Figure 1, a *conceptual* or *mental* model that lies between human expertise and the implemented program. The conceptual model is the knowledge engineer's evolving conception of the domain knowledge. Although this is undoubtedly different from the domain expert's, it is this model that actually underlies the construction of the formal knowledge base.

Because of the complexity and multiple sources of ambiguity in the problem, we should not take this intermediate stage for granted. Expert system builders should document and make public their assumptions about the domain through common software engineering methodologies. A knowledge based system should include a requirements document; however, because of the constraints of exploratory programming, expert system requirements should be treated as co-evolving with the prototype. Data dictionaries, graphic representations of state spaces, and comments in the code itself are all part of this model. By publicizing these design decisions, we reduce errors in both the implementation and the maintenance of the knowledge base.

Knowledge engineers should save recordings of interviews with domain experts. Often, as the knowledge engineer's understanding of the domain grows, she may form a new interpretation or discover new information in one of these sessions. The recordings, along with documentation of the interpretation given them, play a valuable role in reviewing design decisions and testing prototypes.

Finally, this model serves an intermediate role in the formalization of knowledge. The choice of a representation language exerts a strong influence on a knowledge engineer's model of the domain. The model is usually based on one of the AI representation languages, either the predicate calculus, or frames, objects, or hybrid designs.

The conceptual model is not formal or directly executable on a computer. It is an intermediate design construct, a template to begin to constrain and codify human skill. It can, for instance, if the knowledge engineer uses a predicate calculus model, begin as a number of simple networks representing the expert's states of reasoning through typical problem-solving situations. Only after further refinement does this network become explicit if . . . then . . . rules.

Questions often worked through in the context of a conceptual model include: Is the problem solving deterministic or search based? Is it data-driven, perhaps with a generate-and-test flavor? Is problem solving goal-driven, based on a small set of hypotheses about situations? Are there stages of reasoning? Is it exact or fuzzy? Is it nonmonotonic, with the need of a truth maintenance system?

The eventual users' needs should also be addressed in the context of the conceptual model: What are their expectations of the eventual program? Where is their level of expertise: novice, intermediate, or expert? What levels of explanation are appropriate? What interface best serves their needs?

To accomplish this concept based development process requires:

- Knowledge acquisition, understanding its stages and techniques,
- Tool selection, understanding the many powerful tools available to expert system designers and builders,
- Building the system with steps and cross checks, often employing the exploratory programming methodology,
- Verification and Validation,
- Documentation, and
- Maintenance.

Durkin's book presents excellent suggestions and guidance for performing these tasks.

George F. Luger
Albuquerque

Preface

*When we seek knowledge
we are bounded by only our imagination*

The Purpose of this Book

This book is a comprehensive introduction to the design and development of expert systems. In writing it, my goal has been to place expert systems within the larger context of knowledge evolution. The subject of expert systems is not about computer programming. It is about developing tools that enable us to make better use of our knowledge.

Knowledge is our first frontier. Man has always sought to obtain knowledge, use it, and expand it to improve his world. It has been man's pursuit of knowledge that has taken us from kneeling over a fire in our first cave to walking on the moon. We are a product of an evolutionary process that has been fueled by knowledge. Throughout this evolution man has developed many tools to push the knowledge frontier. One of the more recent developments, the computer, offers a tool of enormous value for expanding our knowledge.

Early computers were wonderful machines. They could process large amounts of data quickly and provide an accuracy far beyond their human counterpart. Today computers not only store, manipulate, and retrieve data, they are increasingly taking on the role of making decisions. In a very short period, the technology moved from the data crunching age, through the information manipulation era, into our present world of knowledge processing. An area of study that hastened this change is *artificial intelligence* (AI).

The primary goal of AI is to develop computer programs that "think" like humans. Success in this endeavor would provide intelligent machines that could assist humans with decision-making tasks. A secondary goal of AI, but of equal importance to the primary, is to better understand how humans reason. Developing an intelligent program requires an understanding of how a human stores and manipulates knowledge. Success here may point to better ways of using and discovering knowledge—further pushing our frontier.

One of the major contributions that AI has made to our quest of knowledge is *expert systems*. An expert system is a computer program that emulates the decision making of a human expert. It is designed to work in a narrow area, similar to the focus of an expert, such as medical diagnosis, computer configuration, and work personnel scheduling. Through marrying the power of computers to the richness of human experience, we can enhance the value of human expertise by making it readily and widely available. Though the technology is enthusiastically accepted today, it had a very quiet birth.

I can still recall the many claims made by AI researchers about the potential of expert systems, but, I can also remember how they fell on deaf ears. As with most new technologies, unless you can pinpoint and demonstrate their real-world value you are inviting disinterest. Computer "games" were the focus of early AI researchers. They knew that even though the programs were games, experimenting with them would produce the insight needed to develop meaningful systems. However, outsiders wanted proof that the technology had value. Let's explore the history that led to its acceptance.

During the 1970s expert systems was mostly a laboratory curiosity. Researchers were focused on developing ways of representing and reasoning about knowledge in a computer, and not on designing actual systems. Very few applications were developed, explaining to a large degree why individuals outside the AI community were disinterested. During the early 1980s the number of developed systems rose modestly, with a report of 50 deployed systems by 1985. The scene changed dramatically after this date when success stories of the technology began to spread. Most importantly—from a pragmatic point of view—these stories told of commercial organizations who used expert systems and realized increased profits. These developments led others to *quickly* pursue the technology, resulting in an estimated 12,500 systems developed by 1992—a remarkable record for any new technology. We can find their application today in such diverse areas as helping a mine manager control dust levels within a mine, aiding a farmer with pest infestation problems, and assisting astronauts with the operation of space vehicles. As shown in Appendix C, these systems can improve productivity, safety, and enhance our understanding of a topic area—those who would not listen to our shouts about the technology earlier, now strain to hear our whispers.

What about the future? Researchers will obviously continue looking for improved ways of capturing and using human knowledge to permit our "machine," the computer, to better solve problems. This activity is a part of our makeup—we are driven by our nature to improve things. However, much of the future of expert systems will rest in the hands of the practitioner. The technology has now matured to the point where we have enough understanding of it to put it into place. The key to opening the door to future benefits of expert systems will be our understanding of where, when, and how to appropriately utilize the technology. The value we receive from expert systems will depend as much on how wise we are in appropriately applying the technology as on the technology itself.

The goal of this book is to produce an educated practitioner of expert systems—a *craftsman*—one who not only knows how to use the tools of the trade but also knows when to apply them.

The book was designed to serve both new students to the field and practicing knowledge engineers. For use in an instructional setting, the book should serve the needs of an instructor of upper-level undergraduates and graduate students in the areas of business, computer science, engineering, and the social sciences.

For the established knowledge engineer, the text provides design suggestions for developing such systems as rule-based, frame-based, and fuzzy logic. It also provides insight into how to manage an expert system project. All of this information should be of value to the professional who wants to sharpen his or her skills.

One particular point should be mentioned concerning reader prerequisites. This text was written to teach the reader expert system design concepts that can most easily be implemented using commercially available expert system development software (a shell). As such, there are no prerequisites on the part of the reader to the exposure to any programming languages; including ones traditionally associated with AI such as LISP and PROLOG.

This book presents technical issues in a progressive fashion. It introduces the reader to the important concepts of expert system development, then builds on the reader's understanding of these concepts by introducing more advanced topics. Progressively, the book builds the reader's competence in designing expert systems. Each step is accomplished by first introducing the reader to a specific theoretical concept in expert system design, then is followed by one or more examples which illustrate this theory in operation. Through these examples, the student sees not only the correct approach to be taken, but also problems that can be expected if an incorrect approach is taken. By working through the examples, the end-of-chapter exercises, and most importantly by being challenged to build an expert system as part of a term project, the student learns.

> *What we have to learn to do*
> *we learn by doing.*
> ——Aristotle, Ethics

Book Contents

Body

Chapter 1 **introduces** the field of expert systems. It explains *what* an expert system is and *why* the technology is valuable. Later chapters provide instruction on *how* to build various types of expert systems, while this chapter provides the motivation for the effort.

Chapter 2 explores the **major characteristics** of an expert system. It also discusses the basic differences between conventional programs and expert systems, and introduces the major players involved in an expert system project.

Chapter 3 presents techniques for **representing knowledge** in an expert system. Unlike procedures found in a conventional computer program which processes *data,* an expert system must process *symbols* that represent a problem's knowledge. Chapter 3 reviews the popular symbolic knowledge representation methods while Chapter 4 shows how these symbols can be manipulated to simulate human reasoning.

Chapter 5 reviews one of the classic expert systems—**MYCIN.** I believe the student should appreciate the contributions that the MYCIN team made to our understanding of both the design and development of an expert system.

Chapter 6 provides an overview of **rule-based expert systems,** including a history of its development. The chapter also reviews the advantages and limitations of rule-based systems.

Chapters 7 and 8 cover **backward-chaining rule-based systems.** Through several examples, Chapter 7 shows how these types of system work. This chapter also introduces advanced features of a backward-chaining system which provides insight into its effective design. Chapter 8 provides a design methodology for developing a backward-chaining system.

Chapters 9 and 10 focus on **forward-chaining rule-based systems.** Chapter 9 uses several examples to provide an in-depth look at the operation of this type of system. Chapter 10 provides a step-by-step process for designing a forward-chaining rule-based system.

Chapters 11 12, and 13 cover the important topic of inexact reasoning in an expert system. Chapter 11 reviews the subject from a basic probability viewpoint by presenting the **Bayesian** approach. This chapter also includes a detailed look at another classic expert system—PROSPECTOR—that uses a Bayesian-like method for inexact reasoning. Chapter 12 introduces the **certainty theory** approach. This technique grew out of the work on MYCIN and relies on defining judgmental measures of belief rather than adhering to strict probability estimates. It is perhaps the most popular approach used today in expert system design. Chapter 13 covers **fuzzy logic,** a subject that has only recently captured the attention of expert system designers. Fuzzy logic relies on representing vague terms in mathematical forms called fuzzy sets, then performs inexact reasoning using fuzzy logic inference operations. This approach to inexact reasoning has been gaining popularity rapidly, and should attract even more interest during the 1990s.

Chapters 14 and 15 focus on **frame-based expert systems.** A frame-based system is considerably different from a rule-based one. When developing a frame-based system we consider the entire problem as being composed of objects. Our role becomes that of a teacher rather than a programmer. Chapter 14 shows how we can describe what objects exist, how they are related, and how they behave. Chapter 15 offers a structured methodology for building a frame-based system.

Machine learning has been a hot topic for many years in the field of artificial intelligence. Many theories have been offered and several experimental systems developed. To this point, however, only a few techniques have evolved to the point where expert system designers can make effective use of them. Chapter 16 presents the most popular one called **induction.** This technique relies upon a set of examples to induce decision-making rules that act as the basis of the expert system. This chapter reviews the theory behind the technique, provides example systems, and offers a methodology for designing an induction-based expert system.

Chapter 17 covers, in a very comprehensive fashion, what has long been recognized as the most difficult challenge when developing an expert system—**knowledge acquisition.** This chapter discusses the most commonly used knowledge acquisition techniques and provides guidelines for effectively conducting each technique.

Chapter 18 brings together the key ideas raised throughout the book related to expert system design and development under the subject of **knowledge engineering.** This subject is concerned with the complete picture of an expert system project. That is, after the student has learned about the expert system tools and how to use them (as provided in earlier chapters), he or she must now be taught how to bring them together to effectively plan and manage the project. This chapter provides this instruction through a six phase process, beginning with assessing the applicability of the technology, and continuing through maintaining a completed system.

Appendices

The appendices have been written to serve both the student and the practicing knowledge engineer.

Appendix A is a **glossary** that contains the definitions of over 300 AI and expert system terms. This information is of value when the reader wants a quick and clear definition of a term used within a given chapter.

Appendix B provides a list of over 100 commercially available **expert system development software products.** Each product description includes the product name, price, development platform, knowledge representation and inference techniques, and ordering information.

Appendix C contains brief **synopses of over 200 developed expert systems** from a variety of application areas. Also provided is a reference for each system, permitting access to more detailed information on a system of interest.

Appendix D provides a **bibliography of expert systems.** It offers a valuable list of references categorized into various expert system subject areas (such as building an expert system, frame-based expert systems, induction systems, etc.).

Appendix E provides a list of references for **additional information on expert systems** (e.g., books, journals, magazines, etc.)

Using This Book

Expert systems is a broad field. It covers a variety of knowledge processing techniques, each of which offers a way of emulating human reasoning. This book covers all of the most popular techniques used today by professionals in the field; consequently, it was written to serve several courses.

For an **introductory course on expert systems,** I recommend you cover the basics of the technology and teach the students how to develop rule-based systems. This approach provides the student with the essential understanding of the technology, and provides instruction for him or her to develop the simplest but most popular type of expert system: the rule-based system.

The basics are covered in Chapters 1 through 5. These chapters cover the important issues of WHAT the technology is, WHY it is important, and insight into the various ways we can process knowledge to provide human-like reasoning.

Chapters 6 through 10 cover rule-based design issues. The student is shown in detail how these types of systems work and how to develop them.

An additional point you should consider in an introductory course is to teach the student how to incorporate **inexact reasoning** within an expert system. Chapters 11 through 13 cover this topic. I suggest you cover Chapter 11 (basic probability approach) to show the student the pros and cons of this well-founded approach. I would also suggest you cover Chapter 12 whose subject is the certainty theory. It contains the most popular technique for incorporating inexact reasoning in an expert system.

If you follow these suggestions for an introductory course on expert systems you will create a student who has a basic understanding of the technology and who has insight into building an intelligent system. Hopefully, you will have also created a student who wants to learn more about the technology. Chapters 13 through 18 provide material that you can use in advanced courses for teaching these students.

Chapter 13 covers the subject of **fuzzy logic.** This topic has been of great interest during the past decade in Japan and is rapidly gaining the attention of expert system developers within the U.S. Chapter 13 introduces the student to the mathematics of fuzzy logic, teaches him or her how to design a fuzzy logic expert system, and illustrates the process through a design example.

I would highly suggest you dedicate one course for instructing a student on **frame-based expert system design.** There has been a major swing towards this type of system during recent years and the trend should continue during the 1990s. Chapters 14 and 15 provide all of the necessary material you will need for this course.

After the student has been taught about all of the tools of the trade (e.g., rule-based systems, frame-based systems, fuzzy logic systems, etc.), you should consider a separate course that instructs the student how, where, and when they should be used—an ability that is a trademark of a craftsman. In the field of expert systems this is the subject of **knowledge engineering.** Chapters 17 and 18 cover this subject. Chapter 17 goes into detail on how to manage the most difficult challenge when developing an expert system: **knowledge acquisition** and Chapter 18 provides the basic material needed for this course.

The Project

Molding a student into the form where he or she can be productive in a given field takes time and effort. It also requires the educator to know *how* this job can be best accomplished. There is an old but wise proverb that I have found to be an invaluable guide:

> *I hear and I forget*
> *I see and I remember*
> *I do and I understand*

This book provides a comprehensive coverage of the major AI tools that the student needs to effectively build an expert system. It introduces the theory behind each tool, illustrates the operation of the tool through examples, and builds the reader's competency in the technology by progressively leading him or her through more advanced examples. To complete the picture, create a competent and productive student, you should require the students to complete a project in which they build an expert system that addresses a problem of their choosing—*I do and I understand.*

The Pseudocode

Most of the examples presented in this book use a natural language pseudocode. That is, they are presented in a style that is easy to follow and conveys to the reader the important ideas behind the theory being described, without adhering to the syntax of a specific language or shell that might only serve to confuse the reader. However, the pseudocode is presented in such a fashion that it should be easy for the student to code in his or her language or shell of choice.

Some examples follow the syntax of specific shells: LEVEL5, LEVEL5 Object, 1STCLASS, Kappa PC, and CubiCalc. The choice of the shell to illustrate an example was based on two points: 1.) it had the functionality to demonstrate the theory being presented, and 2.) it was easy to follow and thus easy to convert to a language or another shell.

Acknowledgments

Edited books always owe whatever success they enjoy to the contributors. It is no different for this book.

I want to first extend my appreciation to the many reviewers of the book. Their suggestions and criticisms helped to improve the book immensely. The remaining flaws belong only to me.

In particular, I want to acknowledge the support and guidance provided by Dr. George Luger. His insight into the field of expert systems makes it easier to understand the technology when everyone else is trying to make it more difficult.

Finally, I want to acknowledge the biggest contributors of all, my family. Writing a book is an enormous undertaking. It requires patience, dedication, and energy. Most of all, however, it requires time. My wife Lucy, and our two daughters Kira and Kristi, patiently gave me the time but at a sacrifice to us all. I can't undo the past and regain the lost time, but now understanding the cost of the loss, I have a better view of my priorities.

J.D.

Contents

CHAPTER 1

Introduction to Expert Systems

INTRODUCTION

This chapter introduces you to expert systems and explains *what* they are and *why* they are valuable. It also places their development within the historic perspective of machine evolution. You will also see how they have been put to use across many application areas. The major objective of this chapter is to show you the value of these systems, while later chapters teach you *how* to build them.

INTELLIGENT MACHINES

The wealth of a nation once arose from the physical labors of its people. For centuries, this wealth was limited by the size and stamina of the work force. With the dawn of the industrial revolution came a new direction for increasing national wealth. Machines fueled by steam and oil were developed to assist labor-intensive tasks, providing dramatic increases in productivity. History shows us that leading nations today are ones that earlier embraced such technology.

Today, national wealth arises from intellectual resources. Nations possessing skillful people in such diverse areas as science, medicine, business, and engineering, produce innovations that drive the nation towards a higher quality of life. To better exploit these resources, we are now looking for new machines that can capture the expertise of these talented people. This quest has placed us in search of machines powered not by steam but by *knowledge*, and into the *knowledge revolution* era.

Success in this endeavor would provide an enormous benefit to mankind. Nations lacking the expertise could use these machines to improve their medical care, advance their engineering technology, or increase their manufacturing productivity. Companies could use them to assist decision making or to proliferate throughout their organization the skills of a scarce number of experts. Researchers could also use them to better understand how humans reason. They would serve us today with meeting our mental challenges and provide a vehicle for discovering tomorrow's technology.

THE QUEST FOR AN INTELLIGENT MACHINE

The quest for the holy grail of an intelligent machine is not new. For the past several centuries the search has been on, motivated in part by the practical benefits offered with success, and in part by the fascination of the effort. Let's briefly review some of the highlights of this quest leading up to the present efforts.

During the late 1700s and early 1800s, a group toured Europe and America demonstrating a device called the "Chess Automation," which was advertised to be able to play chess on a par with humans. This device contained a box full of gears and levers, but also included one of the better chess players of the day.

This famous hoax illustrates man's fascination with intelligent machines even in those early times.

In 1834, Charles Babbage designed and developed the first mechanical computer called the "Analytical Engine" (McCorduck 1977) This machine could make mathematical computations and print its results. Babbage proposed developing this machine further to enable it to play chess, with the vision that such a machine could potentially compete favorably with humans. He never pursued this proposed effort due to the skepticism at the time that a machine could compete intellectually with a human—a sentiment shared by many today about intelligent computers.

Up to the first half of this century, the desire for an intelligent machine remained an elusive dream, a dream that was waiting for technology to catch up to it. The technology that could make this dream a reality came with the development of the computer.

The early computers were high-speed data processors that used programs written to perform a series of tasks following a prescribed algorithm. Programs were written to solve equations, process a list of data, or scan databases in search of needed information. However, as well as they were able to process data, they were not able to reason about the information provided to them. Problems requiring human reasoning were left to humans.

The turning point came when researchers began coding *knowledge* about a problem into the computer. Problem facts, rules, and structures were coded into the computer in "symbolic" form. Symbols are simply alphanumeric characters that we can use to represent pieces of problem knowledge. New symbolic processing languages were also developed, such as LISP and PROLOG, that could encode and search through symbolic information.

Armed with symbolic knowledge representation and search methods and symbolic programming languages, researchers took aim at developing programs that exhibited intelligent behavior. The quest for an intelligent machine found a different direction and a new field of study called *artificial intelligence* (AI) was born.

ARTIFICIAL INTELLIGENCE

In 1956, a small group of computer scientists attended a summer workshop sponsored by IBM at Dartmouth College. Their discussion focused on their present research efforts in automatic theorem proving and new programming languages. They also discussed ways that this work might be directed for developing a computer that could simulate human reasoning. This conference marked the birth of **artificial intelligence.**

DEFINITION 1.1: Artificial Intelligence
A field of study in computer science that pursues the goal of making a computer reason in a manner similar to humans.

Artificial intelligence (AI) is an intimidating term. It brings forth images as threatening to us as the cotton gin was to farm laborers during the Industrial Revolution. The fear of displacement by automated machines with superior brute force has now been replaced by anxiety caused by the perceived risk of the loss to machines of our basic human trait: our intelligence. However, when we look beyond the alarming label to see what this field is about, a far less ominous picture is painted.

In the simplest sense, AI is the study of developing computer programs that exhibit human-like intelligence. This represents an abstract and elusive goal, since it is difficult to even define intelligence. Competent reasoning is one measure of human intelligence, but the knowledge one has on a given topic represents another.

From a practical standpoint, the goal of AI is to make computers more useful for humans. This can be achieved by producing computer programs that assist humans in decision making, intelligent information search, or simply by making computers easier to use with natural language interfaces. A second goal of AI, but an equally important one, is to better understand human intelligence. Building an intelligent computer system requires us to understand how humans capture, organize, and use knowledge during their problem solving.

—————— THE RISE, FALL AND REBIRTH OF AI ——————

The Rise

Most of the early work in AI was academic in nature where programs were developed for playing games. Good examples are Shannon's (1955) chess-playing program and the checkers program developed by Samuel (1963). Though these efforts produced some interesting toys, their real purpose was to obtain a better understanding of how to encode into a computer human reasoning capability.

Another important area of study during this early period was in computational logic. In 1957, one of the first programs for automatic theorem proving was developed called the Logic Theorist (Newell and Simon 1972). Using resolution (an automatic technique for proving a hypothesis from available information), Green (1969) developed QA3, a general-purpose question-answering system that could solve simple problems in such areas as puzzles and chemistry.

One of the more ambitious projects of this early era involved the development of the General Problem Solver (GPS) (Newell et al. 1960). GPS was a general-purpose problem-solving technique, developed to solve a variety of problems ranging from games to symbolic integration. GPS was the first attempt to separate the problem solving methods from the knowledge of the problem.

The approach taken by GPS was to first define the problem in terms of "states" which represented different stages of the problem solving. In a chess game, for example, a given board configuration of chess pieces would be a state. GPS relied on a technique known as "means-end analysis," which would try to determine a difference between the "current problem state" and the "goal state," such as checkmate. Appropriate "operators" (such as legal chess moves) would then be chosen and applied to the current state, resulting in new problem states hopefully closer to the goal state. This procedure would then be repeated until the goal state was reached. The set of operators found would then form the solution plan.

One difficulty with GPS was with determining the differences between the states and finding appropriate operators for complex problems. Another practical problem found was that computer time and memory requirements would not support a GPS approach for complex problems. It was soon recognized that this general-purpose problem-solving strategy was too weak for complex problems.

By 1970, the early euphoria surrounding AI was replaced with the sobering realization that building intelligent programs to solve real-world problems was a difficult challenge. This point was underscored by the Lighthill report (Lighthill 1972).

The Fall

In 1971, the Science Research Council (principal government agency responsible for financing research in British universities) commissioned Sir James Lighthill of Cambridge University to review the accomplishments in the field of AI. With the promises made and funding expended, the Council wanted to know if continued funding was advisable. Lighthill reported, "In no part of the field have the discoveries made so far produced the major impact that was promised." He also reported that researchers at the time were predicting that ". . . possibilities in the 1980s include an all-purpose intelligence on a human-scale knowledge-base; that awe-inspiring possibilities suggest themselves based on machine intelligence exceeding human intelligence by the year 2000"—the same predictions made in the mid-fifties. In conclusion, he saw no need for a separate AI field and felt that an intelligent computer would eventually be a natural offspring of the combined efforts from the fields of automation and computer science.

The immediate impact of the Lighthill report was highly damaging to the AI efforts in England and abroad. However, to the credit of a few researchers at the time who continued to labor within the shadow of this damning report, the field experienced a rebirth with a new direction.

The Rebirth

On hindsight, the findings of the Lighthill report are highly debatable. We generally overestimate what a technology can do for us in a few years and underestimate what it can do in a few decades. When the report was written, AI was still a relatively new and emerging field with very few practical systems to show for the effort. To the outsider, the results would appear as toys with no real relevance to practical problems, rather than their real intent as testbeds to study the theories of intelligent machine design. However, the report was right on one important point; no system at that time had been created that could manage a real-world problem. The question that remained was, What new direction needed to be taken to achieve this goal and win back support for the efforts in the field?

To answer this question it is best first to reflect on the past work. A common theme found in most of the prior research efforts was the emphasis on search techniques. At the time, researchers believed that intelligent behavior was primarily based on smart reasoning techniques and that clever search algorithms could be devised that would emulate human problem solving. However, since earlier programs failed to produce meaningful systems, researchers began to realize that search techniques alone would not be enough to produce an intelligent machine.

The beacon that would guide researchers in the right direction was a program called DENDRAL, whose development began in 1965 at Stanford University at the request of NASA (Buchanan and Feigenbaum 1978). NASA was planning to send an unmanned spacecraft to Mars and wanted a computer program that could perform chemical analysis of the Martian soil. Given mass spectral data of the soil, the program needed to determine its molecular structure.

In a chemistry laboratory, the traditional method of solving this problem is through a generate-and-test technique. Possible structures that could account for the mass spectrogram data are first generated and then each is tested to see if it matches the data. The basic difficulty facing the Stanford team was that there are millions of possible structures that might first be generated. They needed to find a way to reduce this to a more manageable number.

The Stanford team found in practice that there were knowledgeable chemists who first used rules-of-thumb (heuristics) to weed-out structures that are unlikely to account for the data. They decided to capture these heuristics within their program to constrain the number of structures generated. The result was a computer program that operated as well as an expert chemist in recognizing molecular structures of unknown compounds. More important, it was the first program whose success was attributed to what it knew about the problem, rather than complex search techniques.

The pioneering work on DENDRAL led AI researchers to realize that intelligent behavior is dependent not so much on the methods of reasoning as on the knowledge one has to reason with. This emphasis on knowledge led Ed Feigenbaum at Stanford to claim "In the knowledge lies the power," and the process of building such systems as **knowledge engineering.** It also led to the concept of a **knowledge-based system** or **expert system**—the era of the expert system had begun.

EXPERT SYSTEMS

The early stages of the field of expert systems were aided by two major lessons learned from the work on AI and DENDRAL. The first was the importance of encoding a rich source of knowledge within the program. General-purpose reasoning techniques were now recognized as being too limited to solve real problems. The second lesson was related to the scope of the system's knowledge. Systems that were designed for well-focused issues fared far better than ones that addressed broad problems.

These two lessons naturally lead us toward one source when building an expert system: an expert on the problem. An expert is an individual who possesses a superior understanding of the problem. Through experience, the expert develops the skills that enable him or her to effectively and efficiently solve the problem. Our job is to "clone" this expert in our expert system.

> **DEFINITION 1.2:** Expert System
> **A computer program designed to model the problem-solving ability of a human expert.**

There are two major traits of an expert we attempt to model in our system: the expert's knowledge and reasoning. To accomplish this, the system must have two principal modules: a knowledge base and an inference engine. This simple view of an expert system is illustrated in Figure 1.1.

The **knowledge base** contains highly specialized knowledge on the problem area as provided by the expert. It includes problem facts, rules, concepts, and relationships. For example, it might contain knowledge provided by a physician for diagnosing blood diseases, portfolio planning knowledge provided by an investment counselor, or knowledge for interpreting geophysical survey data provided by a petroleum engineer. How we code this knowledge in the knowledge base is the subject of **knowledge representation** and is covered in Chapter 3.

The **inference engine** is the knowledge processor which is modeled after the expert's reasoning. The engine works with available information on a given problem, coupled with the knowledge stored in the knowledge base, to draw conclusions or recommendations. How we design this engine is the subject of **inference techniques** and is covered in Chapter 4. The next chapter introduces you to more details about the operation of an expert system.

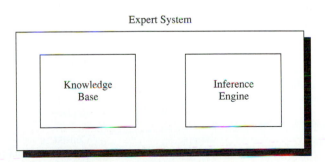

FIGURE 1.1 Expert system block diagram.

WHY BUILD AN EXPERT SYSTEM?

Experts represent a valuable resource for any organization. They can offer creative ideas, solve difficult problems, or efficiently perform routine tasks. Their contributions can enhance the productivity of the organization, which in turn can improve its competitive position within the marketplace. But what is the value of capturing this talent in an expert system? One way we can answer this question is by comparing an expert system with a human expert as illustrated in Table 1.1.

Like any machine, an expert system continues to churn long after the expert's workday. Like any computer program, we can cheaply duplicate it and disperse it geographically to locations lacking the expert's talents. We can also send our system into hostile environments, and sleep soundly at night knowing that the source of our system's skills is out of harm's way.

Human expertise is perishable. Through death, retirement, or job transfer, an organization can lose the talents of an expert. Once captured in an expert system, the organization retains this expertise, permitting continued support. The organization might also be able to use the system in a training role, to pass the expertise along to novices.

An expert system produces more consistent results than a human expert. Human decision making is influenced by many factors that might impact performance. For example, personal problems may preoccupy an expert, preventing productive results. In an emergency situation, the expert might forget some important piece of knowledge because of time pressures or stress. In its unemotional world of 1's and 0's, the expert system is not susceptible to these distractions.

The speed at which an expert solves a problem is also influenced by many factors. By contrast, an expert system performs at a consistent speed, and in many cases, can perform the task much more quickly than the expert. For example, an expert system called CCH was developed to assist in assigning client credit ratings and dollar-specific credit limit recommendations in the apparel industry for the Credit Clearing House (CCH) (Jambor, R. et al. 1991). The system processes an application within 10 seconds, a task that previously required three days to complete.

TABLE 1.1 Comparison of a Human Expert and an Expert System

Factor	Human Expert	Expert System
Time availability	Workday	Always
Geographic	Local	Anywhereavailability
Safety	Irreplaceable	Replaceable
Perishable	Yes	No
Performance	Variable	Consistent
Speed	Variable	Consistent (usually faster)
Cost	High	Affordable

Human experts tend to be expensive. They command high salaries or service fees, and have little difficulty with obtaining their demands due to their scarcity. By contrast, expert systems are relatively inexpensive. Development cost can be high, but in many cases, it can be recovered quickly following the system's deployment. For example, an expert system called AUTHORIZER'S ASSIS-TANT (AA) was developed to aid in credit card application processing for American Express (Rothi and Yen 1990). It helps credit authorizers sort through 12 databases to determine whether or not to approve individual charges. The system cuts the time needed to process credit card customers' purchase authorization requests, minimizes losses from bad credit decisions, and improves human authorizers' overall business performance. American Express found a 20% increase in productivity when using the system, an amount that would provide a payback within two years.

From the comparison shown in Table 1.1, there appear to be two general reasons why we might want to build an expert system: replace an expert or assist an expert. In a survey conducted of the expert system literature (discussed in detail later in the chapter), these two reasons also appear to be the motivation of most organizations who reported on developed systems. The next several sections discuss each area and provides a brief description of example systems.

Replacement of Expert

Stating that you are developing an expert system to replace a human produces ominous overtones. It brings forth the same resentful images envisioned by our forefathers, as they watched the march of the industrial revolution—machine replacing man. Though the potential exists, in practice the use of an expert system in place of a human has played a less foreboding role.

Some of the principal reasons expert systems are developed to replace an expert are:

- Make available expertise after hours or in other locations.
- Automate a routine task requiring an expert.
- Expert is retiring or leaving.
- Expert is expensive.
- Expertise is needed in a hostile environment.

To illustrate how some organizations have used expert systems to their advantage for replacing an expert, consider the following examples.

Drilling Advisor

The oil exploration company Elf-Aquitaine of France maintains a number of oil wells, and like many oil companies, will often experience problems with drill bits becoming stuck. Drill sticking occurs when the drill bit has struck something that prevents the drill from turning, which prevents any further drilling or necessitates the return of the drill bit to the surface. It is not unusual for drilling-related expenses to exceed $100,000 per day, and shutdowns due to drilling problems to last for several weeks until an expert can be brought to the site.

A limited number of causes of sticking drill bits have been identified, such as debris plugging the hole or the existence of a conical hole. However, it is very difficult to determine the cause because no subsurface information is available about the location and condition of the end of the drill; the expert must rely upon simple, crude, and often limited information to determine the cause of the problem. The expert is somewhat like an archaeologist who will examine rock pieces, mud, and the lubricant brought up from the drilling, in order to determine the cause of the problem. Unfortunately, very few experts exist in this area, and when a problem occurs, the firm must locate one and have him or her transported as quickly as possible to the drilling site.

Because of the scarcity of experts in this field, Elf-Aquitaine contracted with the California-based company Teknowledge to develop an expert system that would serve in the place of the human expert. This system was aptly called the "Drilling Advisor" (Elf-Aquitane 1983), and was developed within nine months. The system uses information about the geological formations at the site, conditions of the current problem, and historical information about other problems experienced in the past. It produces a recommendation to correct the problem and provides advice for changes to current practices to avoid the problem in the future.

Cooker Advisor

The Campbell Soup Company uses and maintains large food product sterilizers, commonly referred to as "cookers." They are expensive and important pieces of equipment used in Campbell's food production process, and are installed in their plants throughout the world. Downtime costs caused by malfunctions in a cooker are very expensive, and the complexity of the equipment presents a diagnostic challenge.

At most plant locations, cooker problems can be handled by local maintenance personnel. On occasion, however, problems occur that require the experience of an expert on the equipment. The expert who is usually called upon to aid in solving the problem is production engineer Aldo Cimino; an expert on the company's cookers with over 44 years of experience. Mr. Cimino was nearing retirement age and Campbell wanted to capture his cooker diagnostic expertise in a computer program before it was lost through retirement. Campbell wanted the program to be used for both diagnosing cooker problems and for training new maintenance personnel.

To accomplish this task, a joint development effort between Texas Instruments' Industrial Systems Division and Campbell was established. A decision was made early in the study that a PC based expert system offered the most practical approach to the problem. Campbell had installed at most of their plants a number of IBM PCs and considered it a practical delivery machine. The system development time took approximately six months, and the final version of the system became known as the COOKER ADVISOR (Herrod and Smith 1986).

The major benefit of the system is that it allows Campbell to retain the expertise of an employee with years of experience in solving problems with one of the company's critical pieces of equipment. During actual in-place operation, the system was found to correctly identify about 95% of all cooker malfunctions.

Assisting an Expert

Assisting a human expert is the most commonly found application of expert systems. In this type of application, the system aids the expert in a routine or mundane task. For example, a physician may have knowledge of most diseases, but, due to the extensive number of diseases, could benefit from the support provided by an expert system to quickly isolate the disease. A bank loan officer could benefit by being able to process quickly and effectively the numerous loan applications that cross his desk daily. In both applications, the expert is fully capable of performing the task, but obtains additional support from the expert system. In this type of application, the objective is to improve the overall productivity of the current practice.

Some of the principal reasons expert systems are developed to assist an expert are:

- Aiding expert in some routine task to improve productivity.
- Aiding expert in some difficult task to effectively manage the complexities.
- Making available to the expert information that is difficult to recall.

R1/XCON

Digital Equipment Company (DEC) offers a variety of computer system components that can be configured to offer a fully functional system to their customers. A customer places an order that includes as many as 30 to 40 different components such as the central processor, disk drives, printers, cabinets, etc. Given this order, DEC personnel must first make sure that the component list is complete, or whether other components must be added. They must also make sure the configuration of these components can be manufactured. Performing these tasks is both time consuming and complex. It takes about 25 minutes to configure a system manually and DEC receives about 10,000 orders a year.

In an attempt to make this configuration task more efficient, DEC developed a conventional computer program that automated the task. However, they met with very limited success. They next turned to researchers at Carnegie Mellon University (CMU) to see if expert systems could help. Though many at DEC were skeptical of the new technology (a point we will discuss in more detail in Chapter 18), they were willing to try anything to solve the problem. After discussions focused on the potential of the technology, DEC was convinced enough to fund a program at CMU. Under the direction of John McDermott, an expert system was developed called R1 (later named XCON) that was capable of assisting in the configuration of VAX-11 and some PDP-11 computer systems (McDermott 1980).

XCON successfully configures a system in approximately 2 minutes, and produces configuration layout sheets that can be used by technicians to assemble the system. It has proven to be a valuable tool for DEC, with estimates of savings of $25 million per year. The system is also a good example of how an expert system can improve the productivity of an organization through assisting present expertise. For an excellent review on the operation and the trials and tribulations of building XCON, see Rauch-Hindin (1988).

Lending Advisor

During the past several years, the business sectors have been a major target for expert system developers. This should not be surprising. Good business decisions translates into dollars, and expert systems offer the potential to improve decision making.

One such application that has proven profitable is called the LENDING ADVISOR—an expert system that assists banks and other lending institutions with the processing of loan applications (Hart, et al. 1986). The system evaluates commercial loan applications, defines the level of potential risk, and helps in forming loan approval decisions. The systems considers the nature of the loan request along with the applicant's past and present financial situation and credit rating. Credit managers use the system for loan applications in the $5 million to $100 million range. The system allows for consistent decision making while adhering to the company's policies for loan application processing.

LENDING ADVISOR was developed in 1984 as a commercial venture by Syntelligence, a California-based company. The program was developed in cooperation with the help of Wells Fargo Bank and First Walchovia Bank of Wisconsin. The system is presently commercially available from Syntelligence.

——————— WHERE HAVE EXPERT SYSTEMS BEEN BUILT? ———————

In 1979, a group of individuals who were intimately involved with the development of earlier expert systems met at a workshop chaired by Don Waterman and Frederick Hayes-Roth to exchange ideas about the field and to formulate a way of developing such systems. This workshop lead to a landmark text, *Building Expert Systems* (Hayes-Roth et al. 1983), that laid a foundation for developing future systems.

Viewing the developments of the last decade, and with an understanding of the capability and potential of the technology, they predicted;

"Over time, the knowledge engineering field will have an impact on all areas of human activity where knowledge provides the power for solving important problems."

In 1992, I conducted a survey of the literature in search of developed systems. I was curious to see where they were being developed and their number. This search took me through a variety of sources: journals, books, conference proceedings, and vendors of expert system development tools. The time period covered was the entire history of expert systems. The result of this survey was astounding and confirmed the earlier prediction.

The survey first categorized (as best as possible) each discovered system into an application area. Table 1.2 shows those areas that seem to naturally develop—the breadth of the applications is remarkable. Figure 1.2 shows the number of systems developed in each area. The total number of systems uncovered during the survey was approximately 2500. Though the survey was extensive, it was by no means comprehensive. I "believe" the number uncovered represents about 20% of the total population—12,500 developed systems, also remarkable. A sample of the survey is given in Appendix C. The entire survey, which includes reports on over 2500 developed expert systems, can be found in Durkin (1993).

The distribution of Figure 1.2 reveals the major directions that the technology has taken. A 1986 survey conducted by Waterman (1986) showed that the majority (30%) of the applications were in the field of medicine. Figure 1.2 shows that this field remains attractive to expert system developers (12%). Even more revealing is the activity in the business and industrial areas over recent years. According to Waterman's survey, about 10% of the applications were in these areas in 1986. Today, these areas account for approximately 60% of the applications. This is a sign that expert systems are merging with the mainstream of information processing that was previously dominated by conventional data processors. It also attests to the maturity of the field by revealing the acceptance of the technology by the commercial sectors.

TABLE 1.2 Major Application Areas of Expert Systems

Agriculture	Law
Business	Manufacturing
Chemistry	Mathematics
Communications	Medicine
Computer Systems	Meteorology
Education	Military
Electronics	Mining
Engineering	Power Systems
Environment	Science
Geology	Space Technology
Image Processing	Transportation
Information Management	

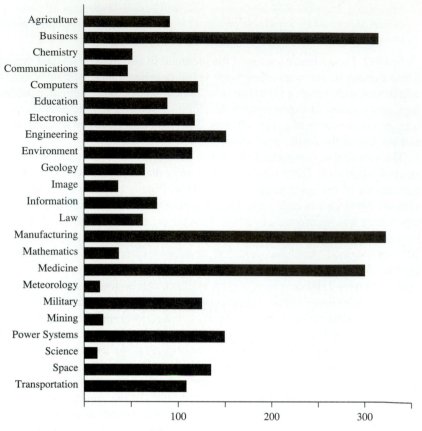

FIGURE 1.2   Number of developed expert systems in various application areas.

In the future, the opportunity for the technology in these areas is enormous. According to Joe Carter, a partner with Andersen Consulting Inc., 70% of the development costs in manufacturing and 90% of the service costs in such endeavors as financial counseling are attributed to human decision making (Business Week, 1992).

It is also interesting to follow the growth rate of the technology. During the 1970s, when researchers were focusing on developing intelligent programming techniques, only a handful of systems were built. During the 1980s, with a better understanding of the technology, the situation changed dramatically. To illustrate, consider a report by Paul Harmon.

In 1990, along with Brian Sawyer, Harmon published *Creating Expert Systems for Business and Industry* (Harmon and Sawyer 1990). The book included estimates of the number of developed expert systems between 1985 and 1988.

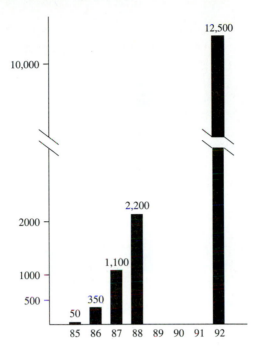

FIGURE 1.3   Number of developed expert systems per year.

These estimates are shown in Figure 1.3 along with the result from the 1992 survey. The impressive growth rate of expert systems is an indicator of the acceptance of the technology by industry and a testament to the labors of earlier researchers.

We can also attribute the large growth rate in developed systems in part to the new hardware and software technologies of the 80s. During the 70s, most expert systems were developed on powerful workstations, using languages such as LISP, PROLOG, and OPS. This left the challenge of developing systems in the hands of the select few who could afford the platforms and had the patience to learn the complexities of the available languages.

During the 80s, we witnessed the proliferation of personal computers, PCs, and the introduction of easy-to-use expert system software development tools called "shells." A shell is a programming environment that contains all of the necessary utilities for both developing and running an expert system. During the last decade, a large number of shells were marketed running on platforms ranging from the PC to the mainframe (see Appendix B). The opportunity to develop an expert system was now in the hands of many individuals from all disciplines.

Figures 1.4 and 1.5 show the percentage of applications from the 1992 survey that were developed on different platforms and with different software tools. The "other" software category of Figure 1.5 includes the languages C, Pascal,

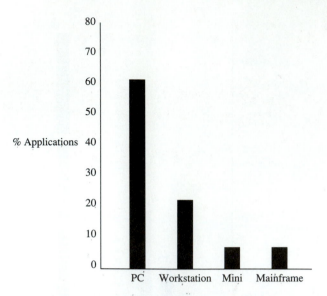

FIGURE 1.4   Platforms used in expert system development.

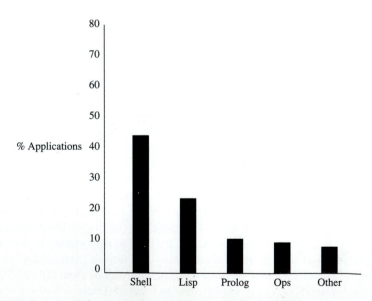

FIGURE 1.5   Software used in expert system development.

LOOPS, Fortran, Smalltalk, and Basic. As these figures illustrate, the vast majority of systems have been developed on a PC with the aid of a shell.

—————— HOW ARE EXPERT SYSTEMS USED? ——————

In the last section, we categorized expert system applications by problem areas (see Table 1.2). Another way we can sort the applications is by *problem-solving paradigms*. Experts perform a generic set of tasks when solving certain types of problems such as diagnosis or planning. Regardless of the application area, given the type of problem, the expert collects and reasons with information in similar ways. Expert systems likewise are designed to accomplish generic tasks on the basis of the problem type as illustrated in Table 1.3 (adapted from Hayes-Roth et al. 1983).

Control

Control systems adaptively govern the behavior of a given system. For example, controlling a manufacturing process or the treatment of a patient in the hospital. An expert control system obtains data on the system's operation, interprets the data to form an understanding of the state of the system or a prediction its future state, and determines and executes needed adjustments. Control systems must also perform monitoring and interpretation tasks to track system behavior over time. Some systems include prediction and planning tasks that allow them to formulate plans to avoid anticipated problems.

VM (Fagan 1978) monitors a patient in an intensive care unit and controls the patient's treatments. The system characterizes the patient's state from sensory data, identifies any alarms, and suggests useful therapies. The system measures the

TABLE 1.3   Types of Problems Solved by Expert Systems

Problem-Solving Paradigm	Description
Control	Governing system behavior to meet specifications
Design	Configuring objects under constraint
Diagnosis	Inferring system malfunctions from observables
Instruction	Diagnosing, debugging, and repairing student behavior
Interpretation	Inferring situation description from data
Monitoring	Comparing observations to expectations
Planning	Designing actions
Prediction	Inferring likely consequences of given situations
Prescription	Recommending solution to system malfunction
Selection	Identifying best choice from a list of possibilities
Simulation	Modeling the interaction between system components

patient's heart rate, blood pressure, and the state of the operation of a mechanical ventilator that assists the patient's breathing. Working with this information, coupled with information on the medical history of the patient, the system makes the needed adjustments to the ventilator.

Design

Design systems configure objects under a set of problem constraints. For example, designing a computer system under user-defined constraints of needed memory, speed, etc. These systems usually perform their tasks following a series of steps, each with its own specific constraints. Complicating matters, these steps are usually dependent upon each other, which makes it difficult to assess the impact a change in one step will have on the other steps. Because of this complication, these types of systems are often built using a *non-monotonic reasoning* technique, discussed in Chapter 4.

PEACE (Dincbas 1980) is an expert system developed to assist engineers in the design of electronic circuits. The system is an intelligent computer-assisted design (CAD) tool that performs both synthesis and analysis of passive and digital circuits. The system uses knowledge on the functional description of the basic circuit components, coupled with topological structural constraints. The system can synthesize the circuit in defined steps, which fulfill the design specification under the problem constraints.

Diagnosis

Diagnosis systems infer system malfunctions or faults from observable information. Most diagnosis systems have knowledge of possible fault conditions with means to infer whether the fault exists from information on the system observable behavior. For example, diagnosing a given disease from the patient's symptoms, or locating malfunctions in an electronic circuit from test results. A more recent trend in the field relies on a *model-based reasoning* approach, which models the system's normal behavior, and detects and diagnoses faults (not known a-priori) from deviations in expectations (Fulton and Pepe 1990). Most diagnosis systems include a prescription task that offers a remedy to the detected fault.

NEAT (MIS Week 1989) assists nontechnical staff at a help desk troubleshoot data processing and telecommunications network equipment. NEAT isolates, diagnoses, and resolves problems phoned in by users having difficulty with a terminal or application. It first prompts the help desk operator for the identification number of the malfunctioning terminal. By consulting its knowledge base, the system determines the configuration of the terminal in question. Prompts from NEAT ask the user several questions and NEAT then suggests a few simple diagnostic procedures. The help desk user enters the results into the expert system, which immediately generates a repair recommedation.

Instruction

Instruction systems guide the education of a student in a given topic. They treat the student as a system that must be diagnosed and repaired. Typically they begin by interacting with the student to form a model of the student's understanding of the topic. They then compare this student model with an ''ideal'' model to uncover weaknesses in the student's understanding. This task is then followed by remedial instruction to correct any misunderstandings.

GUIDON (Clancey 1979) instructs students in the treatment of patients with bacterial infections by teaching them to properly select the antimicrobial therapy. The system begins with a solved case and presents it to the student to solve. The system analyzes the student's solutions and answers to queries during the session. The system then compares the student's problem solving approach with its own. Differences found are used to instruct the student.

Interpretation

Interpretation systems produce an understanding of a situation from available information. Typically this information consists of data from such sources as sensors, instruments, test results, etc. For example, machine monitoring sensors, imaging systems, or speech analysis results. These systems translate the raw data into symbolic form that describes the situation. These systems often need to work with noisy, incomplete, or unreliable data that requires inexact or statistical reasoning.

FXAA (AI WEEK 1988) provides auditing assistance in foreign exchange trading for the Chemical Bank, a Manhattan-based money center bank. This bank performs thousands of transactions a day. FXAA was designed to identify those transactions that are irregular. In the past, Chemical Bank used a manual audit system that involved electronically recording all trades on the trading room floor. Each printout consolidated 3 months of transactions. Auditors manually reviewed entries and spot-checked them in an attempt to identify suspect trades. FAXX automatically selects transactions that need to be examined by the auditors.

Monitoring

Monitoring systems compare observable information on the behavior of a system with system states that are considered crucial to its operation. Monitoring systems will usually interpret signals from sensors and compare the information with known crucial states. When a crucial state is detected, an established sequence of tasks is performed.

NAVEX (Marsh 1984) monitors radar data and estimates the velocity and position of the space shuttle. The system detects any errors and predicts if a problem may occur. If an error is detected, the system further recommends the appropriate actions.

Planning

Planning systems form actions to achieve a given goal under problem constraints. For example, planning the different tasks performed by a robot to accomplish a given work function. Some planning systems must have the flexibility to change the series of planned tasks when they obtain new problem information. To accomplish this, they need the ability to backtrack and reject a current line of reasoning in favor of exploring a better one. As in the case of systems built for design applications, planning systems usually require non-monotonic reasoning.

PLANPOWER (Stansfield and Greenfield 1987) provides a wide range of financial plans for households in the areas of cash management, tax planning, investment, risk management, etc. PlanPower addresses the financial needs for individuals with a high annual income (above $75,000). The system covers a range of financial products including securities, fixed income assets, insurance, real estate, and tax incentive partnerships. PLANPOWER generates individualized financial plans, which include specific recommendations for a client's financial situation over a five-year period.

Prediction

Prediction systems infer likely consequences from a given situation. These systems attempt to predict future events using available information and a model of the problem. Prediction systems often must be able to reason about time or ordered events. Models must be available to infer how some given action influences future events. For example, predicting the expected damage to a crop from an invading insect. Intelligent simulation models are often used in these types of systems.

PLANT (Boulanger 1983) predicts the damage to corn caused by the invasion of black cutworms. The system first obtains information on the current corn field situation, including such information as the amount of weeds present, soil condition, and corn variety being grown. This information, coupled with black worm simulation programs, is used to predict the expected level of damage from this pest.

Prescription

Prescription systems recommend solutions to a given system malfunction. These types of systems usually first incorporate a diagnostic task to determine the nature of the malfunction. Most rely on a ''canned'' prescription for each known fault. More advanced systems incorporate planning and prediction techniques for creating tailored remedies.

BLUE BOX (Mulsant and Servan-Schreiber 1984) recommends an appropriate therapy for patients suffering from depression. The system uses information on the patient's symptoms and the patient's history to diagnose the type and extent of the depression. From this information, the system formulates a prescription for controlling the depression.

Selection

Selection systems identify the best choice from a list of possibilities. They work from problem specifications defined by the user and attempt to find a solution that most closely matches these specifications. These systems usually employ an inexact reasoning technique or a matching evaluation function when forming their selections.

IREX (Gardone and Ragade 1990) assists in the selection of industrial robots in a work environment. The system is comprised of three basic parts. The first part examines several proposed applications where automation is desired and chooses the one best suited for automation using a robot. The second part uses rules to select the configuration, drive, programming type, and playback type. The third section of the expert system examines a database of robots and selects the best five robots for the application on the basis of the user's specifications of that job.

Simulation

Simulation systems model a process or system to permit operational studies under various conditions. They model the various components of the system and their interactions. Users are usually permitted to make adjustments to the model to account for either existing or hypothetical conditions. Using the model along with the user-supplied information, these systems can be used to predict operating conditions for the real system.

STEAMER (Williams et al. 1983) simulates and explains the operation of the Navy's 1078-class frigate steam propulsion plant to aspiring naval engineers. The system simulates various plant components, such as valves, switches, etc., that the user can adjust and observe the impact on the plant's overall operation by observing changes in such items as pressures, temperatures, etc.

SURVEY OF PROBLEM-SOLVING
APPROACHES

From the survey of approximately 2500 expert system applications discussed earlier in the chapter, Figure 1.6 shows the percentage of applications for each type of activity. It should be recognized that many applications employ more than one activity. For example, a diagnostic system might first perform interpretation of available data, and later prescribe a remedy to the recognized fault.

As Figure 1.6 illustrates, the predominant role of expert systems has been diagnosis. One reason for this result is that this is the same role most experts play. In fields such as medicine, engineering, and manufacturing, we find many individuals who provide assistance with diagnosing problems. Another reason for the large number of diagnostic systems is due to their relative ease of development. Most diagnostic problems have a finite list of possible solutions and a limited amount of information needed to reach a solution. These bounds provide an environment which is conducive to effective system design.

Another explanation for the large percentage of diagnostic expert systems can

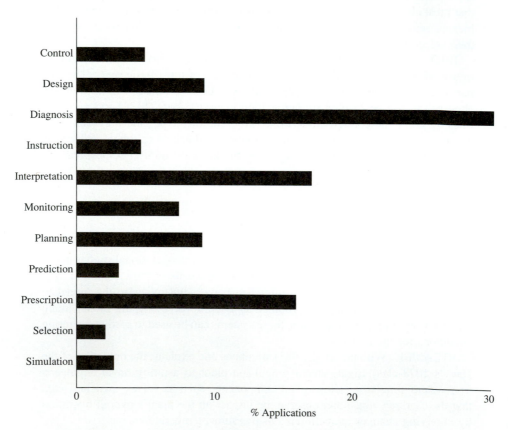

FIGURE 1.6 Applications of expert systems by problem type.

be traced to the practical considerations of introducing a new technology into an organization. Most organizations prefer to take a low-risk position when considering a new technology. As such, projects that require the minimum resources and have the maximum likelihood of success are preferred. Since these systems are relatively easy to build, they are attractive candidates to firms venturing into the field.

The drop-off in the number of applications from diagnosis to some of the other areas is dramatic. Two reasons might help explain this result. First, tasks such as design and planning are difficult to implement in an expert system because their steps vary to a great degree between application areas and it is often hard to precisely define these steps. Second, tasks such as instruction, control, and simulation, though they are excellent areas for expert system applications, are relatively new ventures of the technology, giving rise to the few number of systems.

SUMMARY

During the past several decades, we have seen a technology mature from a laboratory curiosity into a valuable tool for assisting human decision making. We have witnessed its application over a wide range of tasks: from assisting mine managers with planning mining activities, helping farmers avoid pest infestations, to controlling life support systems aboard the space station. It is in the area of business, however, that we find the major reason for the technology's success. In the highly competitive environment of today's business sectors, organizations realize that good decision making quickly translates into profit. As shown in this chapter, many business organizations have come to recognize the potential of expert systems and have adopted them for routine use. As the history of the industrial revolution has shown us, those with the insight to quickly adopt a promising new technology were the ones to prosper the most later. We may someday trace the success of tomorrow's leading organizations to today's decision to embrace expert systems—only in fairy tales do we find turtles beating hares. The major lessons learned in this chapter were:

- The technology of expert systems is the present stage in the history of man's quest for an intelligent machine.
- Expert systems model the problem-solving ability of a human expert.
- Expert systems have been developed in a wide range of application areas.
- The growth rate of developed expert systems over the last decade has been geometric.

REFERENCES

AI WEEK, Chemical Bank Develops Foreign Trading ES, pp. 8–9, Sept. 15, 1988.
Boulanger, A.G., The Expert System PLANT/CD: A Case Study in Applying the General Purpose Inference System ADVISE to Predicting Black Cutworm Damage in Corn,

M.S. Thesis, Computer Science Dept., University of Illinois at Champaign-Urbana, July 1983.

Buchanan, B. and E. Feigenbaum, DENDRAL and Meta-DENDRAL: Their Applications Dimension, Artificial Intelligence, vol. 11, 1978.

Business Week, Smart Programs Go to Work, pp. 97–105, Mar. 2, 1992.

Clancey, W.J., Tutoring Rules for Guiding a Case Method Dialog, International Journ. of Man-Machine Studies, vol. 11, pp. 25–49, 1979.

Dincbas, M., A Knowledge-Based Expert System for Automatic Analysis and Synthesis in CAD, Information Processing 80, IFIPS Proceedings, pp. 705–710, 1980.

Durkin, John, Expert Systems: Catalog of Applications, Intelligent Computer Systems, P.O. Box 4117, Akron, Ohio 44321-0117, 1993.

Elf-Aquitane and Teknowledge, The Drilling Advisor, Fundamentals of Knowledge Engineering, Teknowledge Report, 1983.

Fagan, L.M., Ventilator Manager: A Program to Provide On-Line Consultative Advice in the Intensive Care Unit, Report HPP-78-16, Computer Science Dept., Stanford University, Stanford, Calf., Sept. 1978.

Fulton, S.L. and C.O. Pepe, An Introduction to Model-Based Reasoning, AI Expert, pp. 48–55, Jan. 1990.

Gardone, B.A. and R.K. Ragade, IREX. An Expert System for the Selection of Industrial Robots and its Implementation in Two Environments, Proceedings of the 3rd International Conference on Industrial and Engineering Applications of Artificial Intelligence and Expert Systems, IEA/AIE 90, Charleston, S.C., pp. 1086–1095, July 15–18, 1990.

Green, C.C., The Application of Theorem-Proving to Question Answering Systems, IJCAI-1, pp. 219–237, 1969.

Harmon, P. and B. Sawyer, Creating Expert Systems for Business and Industry, John Wiley, New York, 1990.

Hart, P., A. Barzily, and R. Duda, Qualitative Reasoning for Financial Assessments: A Prospectus, AI Magazine, vol. 7, no. 1, pp. 62–68, Spring 1986.

Hayes-Roth, F., D.A. Waterman, and D.B. Lenat, Building Expert Systems, Addison-Wesley, Reading, Mass., 1983.

Herrod, R. and M. Smith, The Campbell Soup Story: An Application of AI Technology in the Food Industry, TI Engineering Journal, Jan./Feb. 1986.

Jambor, R., et al., CCH: The Credit Clearing House Expert System, The 1991 Third Annual Conference on Innovative Applications of Artificial Intelligence, 1991.

Lighthill, J., Artificial Intelligence: A General Survey, Scientific Research Council of Britian, SRC 72–72, Mar. 1972.

Marsh, A.K., Pace of Artificial Intelligence Research Shows Acceleration, Aviation Week & Space Technology, Dec. 10, 1984.

McCorduck, P., History of Artificial Intelligence, IJCAI-77, pp. 951–954, 1977.

McDermott, J., R1: An Expert System in the Computer Systems Domain, Proceedings AAAI-80, 1980.

MIS Week, Aug. 28, 1989.

Mulsant, B. and D. Servan-Schreiber, Knowledge Engineering: A Daily Activity on a Hospital Ward, Computers and Biomedical Research, vol. 17, pp. 71–91, 1984.

Newell, A. and H.A. Simon, Human Problem Solving, Prentice Hall, Englewood Cliffs, N.J., 1972.

Newell, A., J.C. Shaw, and H.A. Simon, A Variety of Intelligent Learning in a General Problem Solver, in Self Organizing Systems, M.C. Yovits and S. Cameron, eds., Pergamon Press, New York, pp. 153–189, 1960.

Rauch-Hindin, W. B., A Guide to Commercial Artificial Intelligence, Prentice Hall, Englewood Cliffs, N.J., 1988.

Rothi, J.A. and D.C. Yen, Why American Express Gambled on an Expert Data Base, Information Strategy: The Executive's Journal, vol. 6, no. 3, pp. 16–22, Spring 1990.

Samuel, A.L., Some Studies in Machine Learning Using the Game of Checkers, in Computers and Thought, E.A. Feigenbaum and J. Feldman, eds., McGraw-Hill, New York, 1963.

Shannon, C.E., A Chess Playing Machine, in The World of Mathematics, vol. 4, J.R. Newman, ed., Simon and Schuster, New York, 1955.

Stansfield, J.L. and N.R. Greenfield, PlanPower: A Comprehensive Financial Planner, IEEE Expert, vol. 2, no. 3, pp. 51–60, Fall 1987.

Waterman, D.A., A Guide to Expert Systems, Addison-Wesley, Reading, Mass., 1986.

Williams, M.D., J.D. Hollan, and A.L. Stevens, Human Reasoning About a Simple Physical System, in Mental Models, D. Genter and A. Stevens, eds., Erlbaum, Hillsdale, N.J., pp. 131–153, 1983.

CHAPTER 2

Major Characteristics of Expert Systems

INTRODUCTION

In this chapter we explore the major characteristics of an expert system. We take our first look at the basic structure of an expert system and compare it with the problem-solving methods of human experts. We also review the differences between conventional programs and expert systems. Finally, this chapter introduces the major players involved in an expert system project.

Later chapters will introduce you to expert system design techniques. However, it is important that you first understand the basic characteristics of an expert system before you attempt to design one.

EXPERT SYSTEM STRUCTURE

We consider someone an expert on a problem when he or she has specialized knowledge about the problem. In the field of expert systems, we call this type of knowledge *domain knowledge*. We use the word "domain" to emphasize that the knowledge pertains to a specific problem. An expert stores the domain knowledge in his long-term memory (LTM).

When providing advice to someone (an advisee), an expert first obtains facts about the problem (case facts), and stores them in his short-term memory (STM). The expert then reasons about the problem by combining the STM facts with the LTM knowledge. Using this process, the expert infers new problem information and eventually arrives at conclusions about the problem. Figure 2.1 shows a block diagram of the problem-solving approach used by an expert.

To illustrate this process, consider a problem of automobile diagnostics. Assume you have a problem with your car. A reasonable action is to take it to an auto mechanic (an expert). Through years of experience with working on cars, the mechanic stores knowledge in his LTM needed for diagnosing a variety of problems with cars. Further assume you tell the mechanic that your "car won't start." The mechanic stores this information in his STM and begins to reason with it.

Using the information you provided, along with his domain knowledge, the mechanic might infer that the "problem may be in the electrical system." He then adds this belief to his STM and continues to reason about the problem.

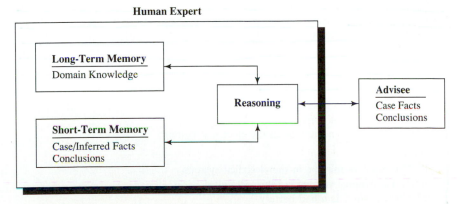

FIGURE 2.1   Human expert problem solving.

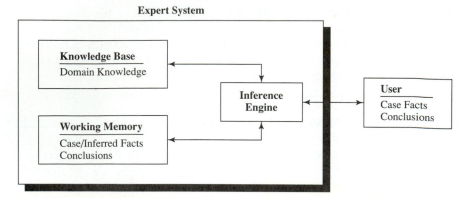

FIGURE 2.2   Expert system problem solving.

Battery tests might then be conducted that could lead the mechanic to conclude, "the fault is a bad battery." The mechanic cannot only solve the problem using this approach, he can also explain the reasoning behind his findings.

Expert systems solve problems using a process that is very similar to the methods used by a human expert, using a structure shown in Figure 2.2.

Knowledge Base

An expert system maintains the expert's domain knowledge in a module known as the **knowledge base.** The knowledge base is a model for the LTM block of Figure 2.1.

> **DEFINITION 2.1:** Knowledge Base
> **Part of an expert system that contains the domain knowledge.**

Your job, as a knowledge engineer, is to obtain the knowledge from the expert and code it in the knowledge base using one of several techniques that are discussed in Chapter 3. One typical way of representing knowledge in an expert system is *rules*. A rule is an IF/THEN structure that logically relates information contained in the IF part to other information contained in the THEN part. For example, we could use the following two rules to represent the knowledge for our automobile diagnostics problem:

> **RULE 1**
> IF The car will not start
> THEN The problem may be in the electrical system
>
> **RULE 2**
> IF The problem may be in the electrical system
> AND The battery voltage is below 10 volts
> THEN The fault is a bad battery

Working Memory

The **working memory** contains the facts about a problem that are discovered during a consultation. The working memory is a model for the STM block of Figure 2.1.

> **DEFINITION 2.2: Working Memory**
> Part of an expert system that contains the problem facts that are discovered during the session.

During a consultation with an expert system, the user enters information on a current problem into the working memory. The system matches this information with knowledge contained in the knowledge base to infer new facts. The system then enters these new facts into the working memory and the matching process continues. Eventually the system reaches some conclusion that it also enters into the working memory.

The working memory contains all the information about the problem that is either supplied by the user or inferred by the system. The entire information gained during the consultation is often called the session's *context*.

Many expert system applications can benefit from information contained in external storage such as databases, spreadsheets, or sensors. The system can load this information into the working memory at the beginning of the session or access it on a as-needed basis as the consultation proceeds. The system may conduct the entire session exclusively using this information or use it to augment the information supplied by the user.

Inference Engine

The expert system models the process of human reasoning with a module known as the **inference engine**.

> **DEFINITION 2.3: Inference Engine**
> Processor in an expert system that matches the facts contained in the working memory with the domain knowledge contained in the knowledge base, to draw conclusions about the problem.

The inference engine works with the facts contained in the working memory and the domain knowledge contained in the knowledge base to derive new information. It searches the rules for a match between their premises and information contained in the working memory. When the inference engine finds a match, it adds the rule's conclusion to the working memory and continues to scan the rules looking for new matches.

To illustrate the operation of the inference engine, consider the two rules given earlier with the following system questions and user answers:

STEP 1

EXPERT SYSTEM: Does the car not start?
USER: TRUE

Comment: *The user asserts this fact into the working memory. Since this new fact supports RULE 1, the expert system asserts into the working memory the rule's conclusion:*

USER ASSERTS: The car will not start
SYSTEM ASSERTS: The problem may be in the electrical system

STEP 2

EXPERT SYSTEM: Is the battery voltage below 10 volts?
USER: TRUE

Comment: *The working memory now contains the facts that supports RULE 2 and the expert system asserts its conclusion into the working memory.*

USER ASSERTS: The battery voltage is below 10 volts
SYSTEM ASSERTS: The fault is a bad battery

Comment: *The session now stops because there are no further rules to consider.*

This example illustrates a simple form of the inference process performed in an expert system. Chapter 4 explores the subject of inference in detail, and also introduces you to more advanced inference techniques.

Explanation Facility

A trademark of expert systems is their ability to explain their reasoning. Though not shown in Figure 2.2, an expert system has an additional module called the **explanation facility.** Using this facility, an expert system can provide an explanation to the user about *why* it is asking a question and *how* it reached some conclusion.

The explanation facility provides a benefit to both the system's developer and user. The developer can use it to uncover errors in the system's knowledge. The user benefits from the transparency provided into the system's reasoning.

Explaining HOW

Besides providing a final result, both human experts and expert systems can explain *how* they arrived at a result. This capability is very important in an expert system. Unlike a conventional program which works on a well-defined problem, an expert system usually works on a problem that lacks the same structure. This situation often brings into question the validity of the system's findings, which requires that a justification be given to support the results.

From the prior example, a typical explanation provided by a human expert for the final result might be:

EXPERT: The battery is bad.

PERSON: HOW

EXPERT: *"Since your car won't start, I assumed there was a problem with the electrical system. Once I found the battery voltage was below 10 volts, I knew the battery was bad."*

This type of explanation follows the reasoning process used by the expert. Expert systems respond to a HOW query in a similar fashion by tracing back through the rules that established the conclusion. This tracing is a map of the system's line of reasoning. The user will be more confident in the result when he or she can see the rationale behind the recommendation.

Explaining WHY

An expert system can also explain *why* it is asking a given question. When an individual consults with a human expert, the conversation is highly interactive. On occasion, the individual may ask the expert *why* he is pursing a certain line of reasoning. The explanation given can make the user feel more comfortable with the line of questioning and can also provide insight into what issues the expert believes are important. Again, considering the prior example:

EXPERT: Will the car not start?

PERSON: WHY

EXPERT: *"If I know that the car won't start, then I usually assume the problem is in the electrical system."*

When asked why some question is posed, experts respond by describing what they might conclude from the answer. Most expert systems respond to a WHY query by displaying the rule it is currently pursuing.

Interface

The interaction between an expert system and user is conducted in a natural language style. The interaction is also highly interactive and follows closely the conversation found between humans. To conduct this process in a manner that is acceptable to the user places special demands on you when designing the **user interface.**

A basic design requirement of the interface is to ask questions. To obtain reliable information from the user, you will need to pay particular attention to the question's design. This may require you to design the interface using menus, graphics, or tailor-made screens. The user may also request the ability to explore or change information contained in the working memory. This feature can be important in applications where the user may want to change the answer to some prior question. You must be aware of the requirements of the user and design the interface to meet them in an accommodating manner.

CHARACTERISTICS OF AN EXPERT SYSTEM

Separates Knowledge from Control

As illustrated in Figure 2.2, the knowledge base and inference engine are separate modules in an expert system. Separating the system's knowledge from its control is a valuable feature of an expert system. This separation is also a characteristic of an expert system that distinguishes it from a conventional program. Conventional computer programs intermix the program's knowledge with the control of this knowledge. The major result of this mixing is that changes to the code impact both the knowledge and the processing. It can also be difficult to review the code and understand what knowledge is being used and how it is used.

Since an expert system's knowledge and control are separate, the tasks of modifying and maintaining the system are made easier. You can easily locate and change some particular piece of knowledge, or add new knowledge at any location within the knowledge base. If changes in the control of this knowledge are needed, you can make the necessary adjustments to the inference engine's algorithm. Duda (1981) comments on this important expert system feature:

> "There is a clear separation of general knowledge about the problem (the rules forming the knowledge base) from information about the current problem (the input data) and methods for applying the general knowledge to the problem (the rule interpreter) ... the program itself is only an interpreter (or general reasoning mechanism) and ideally the system can be changed by simply adding or subtracting rules in the knowledge base."

Possesses Expert Knowledge

An important feature of the knowledge used in an expert system is that it embodies the expertise of a human expert. It is this expertise that we try to capture and encode in an expert system. It includes both domain knowledge and problem-solving skills.

Expertise is a resource held by a few individuals who can successfully apply it to solve problems that are out of reach of others. It is not necessarily unique or brilliant, but it is special, and valuable to capture in an expert system.

The label *expert* is really meant to describe someone who is *skillful* in solving a problem in an effective and efficient manner. A doctor diagnosing a disease, a bank loan manager reviewing mortgage applications, or a technician repairing some system, may all be considered experts within their fields. We label them experts when they exhibit reasoning abilities that are superior to others in their profession.

Focuses Expertise

Most experts are skillful at solving problems within their narrow area of expertise, but have limited ability outside this area. Like their human counterparts, expert systems are adept at what they know but perform poorly outside their area of expertise.

To some extent this issue should be obvious. For example, we wouldn't expect an expert system designed for automobile diagnostics to be effective when applied to financial planning. However, another more subtle difficulty surfaces when the designer tries to encode broad knowledge in the expert system.

A common difficulty encountered by expert system developers, one that has burdened the development process and added frustration to the effort, can be traced to the issue of the problem's scope. The most successful expert system projects have been ones that have directed their effort towards a well-focused problem. Designers who have attacked broad topics have often achieved limited success (Ham 1984).

The following example will help to illustrate this point. Suppose we want to develop an expert system to diagnose all possible problems with an automobile. This would not only be a complex problem, but possibly an unmanageable one due to its broad scope. We might feel more comfortable by first dividing the problem into diagnosing the major subsystems, such as the electrical system and the fuel system. This might be a good starting point, since we divided the problem into two areas. However, building an expert system for either area may still pose some major difficulties because of their large scope.

In general, you should try to divide the problem into smaller areas until the scope within each area is at a manageable level. To illustrate, consider Figure 2.3 which shows a natural division of our automobile diagnostic problem. A more manageable initial step might be for you to design an expert system to diagnose problems with the carburetor's choke. You will find this approach makes it far easier to both design and maintain the system. You could later design systems for the other components of the car and integrate them using techniques that will be introduced in later chapters.

Reasons with Symbols

Expert systems represent knowledge in symbolic form. We can use symbols to represent a variety of types of knowledge, such as facts, concepts, or rules. For example:

- Jack has a fever.
- People.
- People with a fever should take a couple of aspirin.

Much of the early work in AI focused on developing programming techniques that could effectively encode and process symbols. This area of study is formally known as *knowledge representation* (subject of Chapter 3). Each knowledge representation technique begins with the problem's knowledge expressed in symbolic form. For example, using a knowledge representation technique known as the *predicate calculus,* we could represent the statement ''Jack has a fever'' as

$$fever(jack)$$

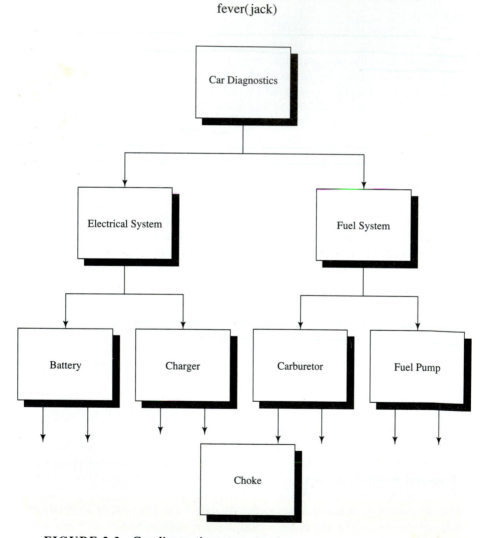

FIGURE 2.3   Car diagnostic system structure.

Besides representing statements in symbolic form, expert systems manipulate these symbols when solving a problem. For example, assume we have the following rule, "People with a fever should take a couple of aspirin." Given the assertion that Jack has a fever, we might then logically conclude that Jack should be taking aspirin:

Assert:	Jack has a fever	fever(jack)
Rule:	IF Person has fever	fever(X) $\rightarrow$ takes(X,aspirin)
	THEN Take aspirin	
Conclusion:	Jack takes aspirin	takes(jack,aspirin)

The predicate calculus uses an operator known as *implies* "$\rightarrow$" to represent a rule structure. This representation technique also permits the use of variables such as "X" that permit implications to be drawn for several objects.

You can see by this example that expert systems solve problems by manipulating symbols rather than performing numeric processing. Tasks that primarily work with information in data form are better solved using conventional programs. In general, you can view conventional programs as *data processors* and expert systems as *knowledge processors*.

Reasons Heuristically

Experts are adept at drawing on their experiences to help them efficiently solve some current problem. Through their experiences, they form a practical understanding of the problem and retain it in the form of rules-of-thumb or *heuristics*. Typical heuristics used by experts during problem solving are:

- I always check the electrical system first.
- People rarely get a cold during the summer.
- If I suspect cancer, then I always check the family history.

Much of the early AI work looked at applying heuristic search techniques for solving problems. Minksy refers to heuristic search in computers by stating (Baraiko 1982);

> *"If you can't tell a computer how best to do something, program it to try many approaches."*

Experts use heuristics to find short cuts to a solution. To replicate this reasoning strategy in an expert system, you use methods that are unlike the strict procedures found in conventional programs. Conventional programs process data using algorithms, but an expert system will often use heuristic reasoning techniques. An algorithm represents a series of well-defined tasks to perform. For example:

Algorithm: 1. Get the temperature and pressure values
                      2. Multiply them together with some constant
                      3. Compute the flow rate
                      4. If flow rate > 100, then ....

This algorithm will always perform the same operations and in the same order. It is this exactness that makes conventional programs attractive in performing numeric processing.

Heuristic reasoning works with the available information to draw conclusions about the problem, but doesn't follow a prescribed sequence of steps. Attempting to determine whether a low flow rate exists, a heuristic program can make use of different methods. For example:

Heuristic: Old pipes often vibrate under low flow rates.
Heuristic reasoning: IF   Pipes are vibrating
                           AND   The pipes are old
                           THEN Suspect low flow rate

The expert system could use this heuristic rule to guide the reasoning and determine the cause of the vibrating pipes. This rule provides no guarantee that the problem is with a low flow rate, but it provides a reasonable place to start. If this method fails, the system might then rely upon more basic methods such as those used in the conventional program.

Permits Inexact Reasoning

Expert systems have demonstrated considerable success in applications that require inexact reasoning. These types of applications are characterized by information that is uncertain, ambiguous or unavailable, and by domain knowledge that is inherently inexact. For example, a physician diagnosing problems with a patient in an emergency room may have to work under time constraints that prevent access to more exhaustive test information. This situation happens daily in most hospitals, yet the attending physician can still make life-saving decisions by using good judgments.

Consider for example the following statements that illustrate inexactness in information and knowledge:

INEXACT INFORMATION
- I will *probably* buy a hamburger from Bob.
- I *don't have* the EKG test results.
- The motor is running *hot*.

INEXACT KNOWLEDGE
- Bob's hamburgers are *usually* good.
- If EKG test results aren't available, but the patient is suffering chest pains, I *might* still suspect a heart problem.
- Add a *little* oil to a motor that is running *hot*.

You will be introduced to methods for managing inexact information and knowledge within an expert system in Chapters 11 through 13.

Is Limited to Solvable Problems

Before an expert system project begins, you must first determine if the problem is solvable. This may surprise newcomers to the field of expert systems who might initially feel that AI can solve any problem; a belief possibly rooted in viewing one too many science fiction movies. The reality is, if an expert doesn't exist who can solve the problem, there is little hope that the expert system will do any better. If the problem is too new or changes too quickly, there may be no real expert who can solve the problem. Expert systems should not be designed to address new or novel research issues. They apply only to problems that can currently be solved by human experts.

Thrives on Reasonable Complexity

The problem should be reasonably complex, not too easy or too difficult. In general, if the task is too easy, requiring the expert only a few minutes to solve, justifying the effort may be difficult. However, some simple tasks may exist where an expert system may still be of value, even if it takes the expert only a few minutes to solve. For example, a secretary who verifies travel expenses may only spend a few minutes on any one. However, there may be a large number of expense forms to verify, each requiring similar decision making. An expert system could ease this task by providing the same decision-making effort for each travel expense.

The problem must not be so complex that it results in a situation that is unmanageable with an expert system approach. If the task requires the expert several hours to solve, then it is likely beyond the capability of an expert system. A problem that requires an expert around fifteen minutes to solve is a reasonable problem for an expert system. If the problem is more complex, try to break it into sub-topics, each of which you could solve with a single expert system.

Makes Mistakes

As brilliant as some experts are, they share one shortcoming with the rest of us; they are only human and can make mistakes. We recognize this possibility any time we consult with an expert, but still trust their best judgment. Since your task is to capture as closely as possible the knowledge of the expert, you should recognize that your system, like its human counterpart, can make mistakes.

Since expert systems can err, you may believe that conventional programs offer an advantage over expert systems. However, this perception of an advantage is only an illusion. To compare the two fairly, you must consider the difference in the types of problems each address.

TABLE 2.1   Expert Systems versus Conventional Programs

Conventional Programs	Expert Systems
Numeric	Symbolic
Algorithmic	Heuristic
Information and control integrated	Knowledge separate from control
Difficult to modify	Easy to modify
Precise information	Uncertain information
Command interface	Natural dialogue with explanations
Final result given	Recommendation with explanation
Optimal solution	Acceptable solution

Conventional programs address problems where the information is complete and exact, such as database management systems or accounting programs. However, if data are faulty or missing, a conventional program may provide no results—an "all or nothing" situation.

As previously discussed, the types of problems that expert systems work on are less structured than conventional programs. The information available may not be sufficient to arrive at an exact solution. However, an expert system may still arrive at some reasonable conclusion—even if it is not optimal. This is possible if you employ some inexact reasoning technique. Some differences between expert systems and conventional programs are shown in Table 2.1.

PROGRAMMING vs. KNOWLEDGE ENGINEERING

Since the arrival of the first computer, individuals have been developing programs to perform rapid calculations, access information, or perform modeling of complex processes. Through the experience gained from building many systems, programmers have developed well-established techniques for building their programs. Expert systems are a somewhat recent addition to the field of computer programming. They have not matured to the point where we can describe an established methodology for building them. However, we can discuss the major steps involved and show how this process differs from building a conventional program.

Conventional Programming

A characteristic of conventional programming is that it is a sequential process. Conventional programmers follow a three-step development process of design, code, and debug. The program is deliverable only after the programmer has completed the final step.

A conventional computer program project begins with establishing the functional requirements of the program. This is the design phase where the programmer determines the informational needs and the necessary calculations. The programmer should also have a good idea of what the finished program will look like. At this point, the program's specifications are defined and the coding can begin.

During the coding phase, the programmer will usually work alone. The specifications defined during the design phase are assumed to be fixed and no changes are expected. The user of the system doesn't reenter the picture until the time arrives for system evaluation.

During the debugging phase, the programmer tests the program to see if it meets the original specifications. Any errors discovered are corrected by changing the source code. Following these corrections, the program should meet the initial specifications and the project is complete.

Knowledge Engineering

The conventional programmers' world of interest is *data*. Their focus is on the problem's data where they try to find ways to process it to reach a solution. The interest of expert system designers lies in the problem's *knowledge*. They acquire, organize, and study the knowledge to gain an understanding of the problem. They also build and test the system to enhance their understanding. The final solution becomes a natural by-product of this understanding. Expert system designers have termed the process of building the system **knowledge engineering**.

DEFINITION 2.4: Knowledge Engineering
The process of building an expert system.

Unlike conventional programming, developing an expert system is a highly iterative process. The designer partially builds the system, tests it, then modifies the system's knowledge. This process is repeated throughout the project where the system's knowledge and the designer's understanding grow with each test. Figure 2.4 illustrates this style of development.

Phase 1—Assessment

During the *assessment* phase, studies are conducted to determine the feasibility and justification of the candidate problem. Following this study, the problem is further examined to define the overall goals of the project. This effort specifies the important features and scope of the project, and also establishes the needed resources including project personnel. Sources of needed knowledge, including experts and various reports, are also identified. After this initial phase of the project, the principal project requirements are defined.

Phase 2—Knowledge Acquisition

The objective of the *knowledge acquisition* phase is to acquire the knowledge on the problem that is used to guide the development effort. This knowledge is used to provide both insight into the problem and the material for the design of

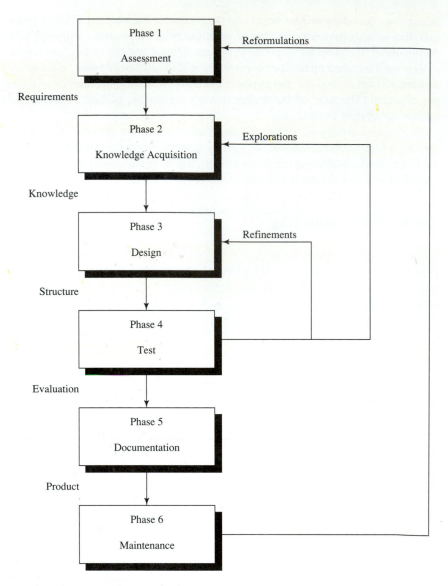

FIGURE 2.4   Phases in expert system development.

the expert system. The process of acquiring knowledge from the expert is formally known as **knowledge acquisition.**

DEFINITION 2.5: Knowledge Acquisition
The process of acquiring, organizing, and studying knowledge.

This phase of study involves meetings held with the expert where some aspect of the problem is discussed. In early stages of the project, the material covered is of a general nature. The objective is to uncover key concepts and general problem-solving methods used by the expert. Later sessions take advantage of information gained from system testing to explore for more detailed information.

Knowledge acquisition has long been recognized as the *bottleneck* in expert system development (Feigenbaum and McCorduck 1983). Due to its importance, Chapter 17 is dedicated to the subject.

Phase 3—Design

Following the knowledge acquisition phase, insight is gained on the best approach for representing the expert's knowledge and problem-solving strategies in the expert system. During the *design* phase, the overall structure and organization of the system's knowledge are defined. Methods are also defined for processing the knowledge. A software tool is chosen that can represent and reason with the system's knowledge in a manner that is similar to the approach taken by the human expert.

During the design phase, an initial prototype system is built. The purpose of the prototype is to provide a vehicle for obtaining a better understanding of the problem. By first building a small system, and reviewing the test results with the domain expert, insight is gained into additional system requirements. The prototype also serves as the focal point for further interviews with the expert. System design is inherently an iterative process where findings from system testing are used to refine the system's knowledge and structure.

Phase 4—Testing

The *testing* phase is not a separate task, but rather a continual process throughout the project. Following each interview with the domain expert, new knowledge is added to the system. This is followed by additional testing where again the system's knowledge may be modified. The major objective of testing is to validate the overall structure of the system and its knowledge. In addition, this phase studies the acceptability of the system by the end-user. Throughout the testing, the designer works closely with both the domain expert who serves to guide the growth of the knowledge and the end-user who provides guidance to the development of the system's interface.

Phase 5—Documentation

The *documentation* phase addresses the need to compile all of the project's information into a document that can meet the requirements of both the user and developer of the expert system. Accommodating the user requires that the documentation meets requirements found in most software projects. That is, it explains how to operate the system and possibly provides a tutorial that steps through the major operational features of the system. The documentation must also support the knowledge engineer during the development of the system. In particular, the documentation must contain a *knowledge dictionary* that provides a well-organized presentation of the system's knowledge and problem-solving procedures. It is augmented throughout the project as new knowledge is obtained.

Phase 6—Maintenance

After the system is deployed in the work environment, it will need to be periodically *maintained*. Like a child, an expert system continues to grow and learn. Knowledge isn't static, it grows, evolves, and matures. The system's knowledge may need to be refined or updated to meet current needs. Major system requirement changes may also occur that would require a reformulation of system specifications. Therefore, it is important that an effective maintenance program be established for an expert system project.

These are the major steps you can expect to perform during the development of an expert system. Though they were discussed separately, there is considerable overlap in their execution. They are not necessarily performed in the sequence given. However, you will need to perform each step (usually many times) during the course of the project. At best these steps characterize roughly the complex process of knowledge engineering (the subject of Chapter 18).

Programming vs. Expert System Development

The major differences between conventional programming and expert system development are highlighted in Table 2.2.

Development Focus

A conventional programmer first attempts to obtain a complete understanding of the problem before proceeding. When this is accomplished, the programmer can often envision the final solution and spends most of the time developing algorithms to solve the problem. An expert system designer follows a less strict process. The designer develops the system in parallel with obtaining a better understanding of the problem, with far less vision of the finished product than the conventional programmer. The development is an exploratory process accomplished through a series of iterative steps. The designer uses each piece of knowledge to improve

TABLE 2.2   Major Differences between Conventional Programming and Expert System Development

Conventional Programming	Expert System Development
Focus on solution	Focus on problem
Programmer works alone	Team effort
Sequential development	Iterative development

both the system's and his own understanding of the problem. The solution gracefully evolves during the development of the expert system through the introduction of additional knowledge.

Programming Effort

During the development of a conventional program, the programmer works largely alone, interacting with others only when difficulties arise or new directions are needed. An expert system designer works closely with the expert throughout the project. They work together to uncover the key pieces of knowledge, how they are naturally related, and strategies for solving the problem. They also collaborate during system testing to uncover deficiencies in the system's knowledge and problem-solving methods. Together, they shape the system into a form that models the expert's problem-solving talents. The success of the project depends on a strong team effort between the expert and the designer.

Program Development

A conventional program is not deliverable until the programmer has completed the three primarily tasks of design, code, and debug. At this point, the program's performance level should have reached original expectations. An expert system designer develops a program in an iterative fashion. A little amount of knowledge is added to the system and then tested to evaluate the system's understanding of the problem. The system's performance level continues to grow as the designer adds new knowledge. Developing an expert system is similar to teaching a small child about some new concept. A small amount of knowledge about the concept is first given to the child, then the child's understanding of the concept is tested and reviewed. Shortcomings found are usually addressed by providing the child new knowledge to strengthen the child's understanding of the concept.

The important point raised in this section is that a conventional program is *built*, while an expert system is *grown*.

PEOPLE INVOLVED IN AN EXPERT SYSTEM PROJECT

The main players on an expert system project are the **domain expert,** the **knowledge engineer,** and the **end-user.** Each plays a key role in the development of the system. Table 2.3 lists the important qualifications needed by each individual to contribute effectively to a successful project.

In the next few sections we review the qualifications needed by each of these individuals that you should consider when putting together a good team. Chapter 18 explores these same points in more detail, and also places them within a framework for assessing the overall feasibility and risk of the chosen project.

TABLE 2.3   Qualifications Needed by
People Working on an Expert System Project

Domain Expert
- Has expert knowledge
- Has efficient problem-solving skills
- Can communicate the knowledge
- Can devote time
- Is not hostile

Knowledge Engineer
- Has knowledge engineering skills
- Has good communication skills
- Can match problem to software
- Has expert system programming skills

End-User
- Can help define interface specifications
- Can aid in knowledge acquisition
- Can aid in system development

Domain Expert

The term *expert* can have several definitions. In the world of expert systems, the word *domain* is attached to provide the following definition:

DEFINITION 2.6: Domain Expert
A person who possesses the skill and knowledge to solve a specific problem in a manner superior to others.

The word "domain" has special significance in the context of expert systems. We build expert systems to solve a specific problem in a given area or domain. The individual with the expertise to solve a specific problem is therefore aptly named the **domain expert.**

Expert Knowledge

The major difference between an expert and a nonexpert is the knowledge the expert possesses on a problem. Davis (1983) puts this point in an interesting way. He states that "the absolute value of an expert is the knowledge that he or she possesses on a given problem."

$$| \text{ Expert } | = \text{Expert} - \text{Nonexpert} = \text{Knowledge}$$

Likewise, the absolute value of the expert system relates directly to the value of the knowledge it contains on a given problem.

The term *expert* is often used erroneously to describe someone who possesses knowledge on some complex subject. For example, most of us would acknowledge a Ph.D. in geophysics as an expert. However, you should recognize that a secretary may also be an expert on some problem. For example, reviewing and approving a set of travel expense reports submitted by a firm's salespersons requires expertise.

When building an expert system, look for an individual who has a talent for solving the problem of interest. There may be several individuals who have the responsibility for solving the problem within an organization. However, locate one who exhibits a capability that is superior to others—the expert on the problem.

Efficient Problem-Solving Skills

Another factor that sets an expert apart from nonexperts is his or her problem solving skills. An expert can often recognize important pieces of information and use them to her advantage to arrive efficiently at a solution. For example, a new intern at a hospital may request several tests on a patient before arriving at a diagnosis, while an established physician may have the insight to arrive at a solution following only a few select tests. An expert not only has expert knowledge, but efficient problem-solving skills as well.

Communication Skills

Domain experts gain their expertise through years of solving similar problems. Through this experience, they *compile* their knowledge and problem-solving skills into a compact form that enables them to solve problems efficiently. Often, they use this compiled knowledge in an *intuitive* fashion, without being aware of the details of the knowledge they used. They will seek the obvious from a complicated situation and derive a solution that may not be obvious to the layman.

One of your important tasks is to *decompile* this knowledge so that it can be coded into the expert system. This can be a challenge if the expert has difficulty in verbalizing the problem-solving knowledge.

When choosing an expert for a project, it seems only reasonable to choose the person most talented in solving the problem. However, if this individual has difficulty in communicating the knowledge, you should seek someone who might be less talented, but better able to explain the knowledge.

Availability

Within an organization, an expert's time is usually very valuable. This is the individual the organization counts on for solving problems that require the expert's special skills. Therefore, a conflict often arises over the expert devoting time to solving immediate problems or contributing to the development of the expert system.

Developing an expert system can be a lengthy process. A small prototype system is built, tested, then revised by modifying or adding knowledge. This process is repeated several times throughout the project, with the domain expert involved in each step. Given these demands, it is important that the expert has the time to devote to the project.

Cooperativeness

The expert's cooperation is vital for the success of the project. If the expert is resentful or hostile to the effort, attempts to acquire knowledge from the individual will fail. It is important that you learn how to win over an initially hostile expert. This is a particular problem for expert system developers, who are offering technology that comes under the eye-opening label of "artificial intelligence."

Winning over an initially hostile domain expert presents you with an important challenge. Convincing the domain expert that the system is meant to serve as an assistant and not a replacement, is one of the more important issues you must address. Chapter 17 discusses other techniques for addressing a hostile expert.

Knowledge Engineer

The expert system designer plays several roles during the project. He or she must be a psychologist, a diplomat, a researcher, as well as an individual versed in technical computer skills. Designers must be capable in each of these roles because their primary responsibilities are to acquire, process, and encode *knowledge*.

Since the designer's main focus throughout the project is on the problem's *knowledge,* the title given to the developer of an expert system is **knowledge engineer.**

> **DEFINITION 2.7: Knowledge Engineer**
> **A person who designs, builds, and tests an expert system.**

In one sense, a knowledge engineer is similar to a conventional programmer in that they both develop computer code. However, a knowledge engineer is also responsible for tasks that are quite unlike those of the conventional programmer. To accomplish these tasks, the knowledge engineer must be skillful in the area of *knowledge engineering*.

Knowledge Engineering Skills

Knowledge engineering is the art of building an expert system. It is considered an artform because the process is complex and few guidelines exist that can guarantee success. Due to its complexity and importance, Chapter 18 is devoted to the subject.

In this section, we review the major responsibilities of the knowledge engineer listed in Table 2.4.

Knowledge engineers must first determine whether it is both feasible and desirable to solve a problem using an expert system. These tasks are often subjective. Feasibility assessment involves studying the characteristics of the problem to determine if an expert system solution is possible. Some problems are well-suited to an expert system approach, whereas others may be difficult to address. Assessing the desirability of an expert system project will often lack

TABLE 2.4   Knowledge Engineer's Major Responsibilities

Problem assessment
Interviewing the expert
Concept identification
Knowledge organization
Problem-solving method identification
Choosing the software
Coding the system
Testing the system
Revising the system
Integrating the system into workplace
Maintaining the system

the rigid cost/benefit analysis found in conventional projects. Projects may be judged desirable on such intangible issues as an interest to explore the applicability of the technology or to expose individuals within the organization to expert systems.

During knowledge acquisition, the knowledge engineer's major goal is to uncover the expert's knowledge. Through interviews, the knowledge engineer seeks to reveal the problem's key concepts and the problem-solving methods used by the expert. During the interviews, the expert might also work through a few test cases while explaining the solution process. The knowledge engineer must have some basic interpersonal skills to guide the interview in a manner that will effectively uncover the expert's knowledge. This is a challenging task for the knowledge engineer and is discussed in Chapter 17.

The knowledge engineer also must organize the knowledge collected from the expert in a form that can effectively be mapped into the expert system. In particular, the knowledge engineer must structure the knowledge and problem-solving methods in a fashion that allows the expert system to solve the problem in a manner similar to the human expert. The knowledge engineer must then choose the proper software package that can best represent the expert's knowledge and inference strategies.

The knowledge engineer is also responsible for coding, testing, and revising the system, until the system has matured to the point where it demonstrates expert performance. After the project is completed, the knowledge engineer may also be responsible for maintaining the system.

Good Communication Skills

A large amount of the knowledge engineer's effort will involve eliciting knowledge from the expert. As previously discussed, experts have a tendency to compile their knowledge into a form that makes problem-solving a quick and efficient process. They will make seemingly quantum leaps in reasoning, taking elementary pieces of information and rapidly arriving at a solution. For an expert system to perform at the same level as the expert, the knowledge hidden between these leaps must be uncovered.

This difficult task is called *knowledge decompilation* and requires special training in the area of knowledge acquisition. Knowledge acquisition requires structuring the interview process in a manner that promotes the exchange of knowledge. Good communication skills can guide the expert in a manner that exposes the hidden knowledge (discussed in Chapter 17).

Ability to Match Problem to Software

There are many programming languages and expert system development tools called *shells* available for developing an expert system. Each has features important for solving a given type of problem, while lacking features important for other problems. A responsibility of the knowledge engineer is to choose the proper software for the application.

The knowledge engineer attempts to form a good marriage between the problem and the software. Experts use different types of knowledge, organize the knowledge in different ways, and use different reasoning methods to solve the problem. Likewise, various languages and shells can represent, organize, and process the knowledge in different ways. It is therefore important that the knowledge engineer match the problem's requirements to the software's capabilities.

Expert System Programming Skills

The knowledge engineer is responsible for coding into the expert system the knowledge uncovered during the interviews with the expert. This requires that he or she be skillful in expert system programming. Providing this skill is one of the major objectives of this book.

To become a skillful expert system programmer, you must first know how to represent and process knowledge. Chapter 3 reviews knowledge representation and Chapter 4 the processing of this knowledge. Most expert systems built today are classified as either rule-based or frame-based systems. Chapters 8 and 10 will introduce you to developing rule-based systems and Chapter 15 to the design of frame-based systems. Chapter 18 covers the topics of testing and maintaining these systems.

End-User

The end-user is the individual who will eventually be working with the system. Final acceptance of the system will depend to a large degree on how well the system meets the needs of the end-user. The history of expert systems is filled with systems that were a technical success but were never used because the end-user's needs were never considered.

Defines Interface Specifications

To effectively aid the end-user, the expert system must meet interface specifications defined by the end-user. Specifically, the end-user is usually responsible for specifying:

- System access
- Information entry
- System explanations
- Form of final results
- Utility needs

End-users can describe how the expert system should be accessed. Typical requests call for the system to be accessed from a batch file, a front-end menu, or another program. The end-user may request a "turn-key" approach that runs the expert system when the computer is powered.

Information is entered into an expert system in a variety of ways. Questions may be asked that require the user to answer true or false, select an appropriate answer from a menu list, or type the answer. The end-user must feel comfortable with the manner in which the system gives the answer, and can help you with choosing the most appropriate method.

The end-user may require the system to provide explanations of its line of reasoning. This is particularly important in those applications where the user needs a justification for the system's final recommendation. The end-user can provide guidance with designing the specifications of the explanation facility.

The user may also require some additional utilities to support the application. For example, the user may want the system to access or update information in external databases or spreadsheets, alleviating the need for the user to perform the task.

The design of the system's interface can be a complex task, and can consume half of the budget of the project. This work is crucial to the success of the project, and the end-user's input on this phase is vital. Without the support of the end-user on this effort, no matter how powerful the expert system, the project is likely to fail the ultimate test: *will it be used?*

Aids Knowledge Acquisition

The end-user can be a valuable aid during the knowledge acquisition task. In the beginning of the project, the knowledge engineer may have little or no knowledge of the problem, or insight into the final solution. Most new knowledge engineers will address this difficulty by initially consulting with the domain expert—a situation that may only compound the problem.

When asked to discuss a problem, experts will usually dwell on the details of the problem. You do not need problem details at the beginning of the project. You initially need a broad understanding of the problem that can best be provided by the end-user. The domain expert can fill in the details later.

SUMMARY ON EXPERT SYSTEM CHARACTERISTICS

This chapter reviewed the basic characteristics of expert systems. The structure and operation of an expert system were introduced, and shown to be a model of human problem solving. The characteristics of the primary individuals involved in an expert system project were reviewed. Understanding the characteristics of both an expert system and the people involved in the project is a prerequisite for effectively designing the system.

The major lessons learned in this chapter were:

- The essential components of an expert system structure are the knowledge base, inference engine, and working memory.
- The knowledge base contains the domain knowledge.
- The inference engine is the knowledge processor.
- The working memory contains case-specific information, supplied by the user and inferred by the expert system.
- An expert system can explain *how* it arrived at a solution and *why* it asks a question.
- An expert system embodies expertise on some well-focused problem.
- Conventional programs manipulate data and can be viewed as *data processors,* while expert systems manipulate symbols and can be thought of as *knowledge processors.*
- Expert systems use *heuristic* reasoning to efficiently solve problems.
- Expert systems can work under the constraints of uncertain or unknown information using inexact reasoning techniques.
- Expert systems, like their human counterparts, can make mistakes.
- Expert system development is called *knowledge engineering.*
- Developing an expert system is an iterative process.
- The process of acquiring, organizing, and studying knowledge from a domain expert is known as *knowledge acquisition.*
- The main players in an expert system project are the *domain expert, knowledge engineer,* and *end-user.*

REFERENCES

Baraiko, A.A., The Chip, National Geographic, pp. 421–456, Oct. 1982.

Davis, R., Video Course Manual: Artificial Intelligence, MIT Center for Advanced Engineering Study, 1983.

Duda, R.O., Knowledge-Based Expert Systems Come of Age, Byte, vol. 6, no. 9, pp. 238–281, Sept. 1981.

Feigenbaum, E. and P. McCorduck, The Fifth Generation, Addison Wesley, Reading, Mass., 1983.

Ham, M., Playing by the Rules, PC World, pp. 34–41, Jan. 1984.

_____ **EXERCISES**

1. List and define the major components of an expert system.
2. What is the value of having the knowledge of an expert system separate from its control?
3. Discuss the ways an expert system can explain its reasoning and further discuss the value of this capability.
4. Provide three examples of an expert system application that require a "HOW" explanation. Also provide a justification for your selections.
5. An expert system embodies expert knowledge obtained from a human expert. Explain what is meant by the term *expert knowledge*.
6. Why is it important that an expert system be designed for a well-focused problem?
7. List three problems that would be a good application of an expert system, and three which would be inappropriate. Discuss in detail your selection decisions.
8. Why can we view conventional programs as *data processors* and expert systems as *knowledge processors?*
9. Explain what is a heuristic and the various ways it can be used in an expert system.
10. Expert systems can perform inexact reasoning. Explain why this is important for the types of problems for which expert systems are applied.
11. List three problems that would be a good application of an expert system because of the inexact nature of either the available information or domain knowledge.
12. Discuss why expert systems can make mistakes and why we are willing to accept this situation.
13. Discuss the major differences between conventional programming and expert system development.
14. Describe an application where an expert system and a conventional program can work together to solve the problem.
15. What makes an expert an expert?
16. Discuss the *knowledge compilation* problem.
17. You have been instructed to build an expert system to model a grand chess master. What difficulties can you expect?
18. List the primary people on an expert system project and discuss their roles.
19. Discuss how an expert system project might fail.
20. A computer programmer, a philosopher, and a business manager, all want to become expert system designers. Which one do you believe will have the least difficulty with attaining their goal? Provide reasons for your choice.

Knowledge Representation

INTRODUCTION

In this chapter we consider techniques for encoding knowledge in an expert system. These techniques are considerably different from the procedures found in a conventional program. A program must process data, but an expert system must process knowledge. To accomplish this, the knowledge is represented in some symbolic form that can be manipulated by the expert system. This chapter reviews several of the popular methods for representing knowledge in symbolic form. Since no one technique is suited for every application, this chapter also provides insight into choosing the best one.

OVERVIEW

Knowledge is power. This short phrase is often used to emphasize the importance of knowledge to an expert system. It has long been recognized that the performance of an expert system is directly related to the quality of knowledge the system has on a given problem.

But what is knowledge? Knowledge is an abstract term that attempts to capture an individual's understanding of a given subject. To define knowledge in a manner that allows us to discuss it in terms of an expert system, we will take a more practical perspective.

DEFINITION 3.1: Knowledge
Understanding of a subject area.

For example, the understanding of the area of medicine. However, when building an expert system, we don't attempt to capture all of the expert's knowledge. Rather, we target on the expert's knowledge of a well-focused topic from the subject area. For example, the understanding of infectious blood diseases. In the world of expert systems, we call this **domain**-specific knowledge.

DEFINITION 3.2: Domain
A well-focused subject area.

A key point for the successful development of an expert system is the focusing of the domain. When the subject area is broad, requiring knowledge on a number of topics, the performance of the expert system will suffer.

After you acquire knowledge from the expert on some well-focused domain, you will want to encode it in the expert system. To do this, you will need to find a way of structuring the knowledge in the system that allows the system to solve the problem in a manner similar to that followed by the expert. This is the subject of the chapter and is formally known as **knowledge representation.**

DEFINITION 3.3: Knowledge Representation
The method used to encode knowledge in an expert system's knowledge base.

——————— TYPES OF KNOWLEDGE ———————

Cognitive psychologists have formed a number of theories to explain how humans solve problems. This work uncovered the types of knowledge humans commonly use, how they mentally organize this knowledge, and how they use it efficiently to solve a problem.Researchers in artificial intelligence have used the results of these studies to develop techniques to best represent these different knowledge types in the computer.

Just as there is no single theory to explain human knowledge organization or a best technique for structuring data in a conventional computer program, no single knowledge representation structure is ideal. One of your more important responsibilities as a knowledge engineer is to choose the knowledge representation technique best suited for the given application. To accomplish this, you must have an understanding of the various knowledge representation techniques and the types of knowledge that they can best represent. Figure 3.1 lists the different types of knowledge.

Procedural knowledge describes *how* a problem is solved. This type of knowledge provides direction on how to do something. Rules, strategies, agendas and procedures, are the typical type of procedural knowledge used in expert systems.

Declarative knowledge describes *what* is known about a problem. This includes simple statements that are asserted to be either true or false. This also includes a list of statements that more fully describes some object or concept.

Meta-knowledge describes *knowledge about knowledge*. This type of knowledge is used to pick other knowledge that is best suited for solving a problem. Experts use this type of knowledge to enhance the efficiency of problem solving by directing their reasoning into the most promising areas.

Heuristic knowledge describes a *rule-of-thumb* that guides the reasoning process. Heuristic knowledge is often called *shallow knowledge*. It is empirical and represents the knowledge compiled by an expert through the experience of solving past problems. Experts will often take fundamental knowledge about the problem (called *deep knowledge*), such as fundamental laws, functional relationships, etc., and compile it into simple heuristics to aid their problem solving.

Structural knowledge describes knowledge *structures*. This type of knowledge describes an expert's overall mental model of the problem. The expert's mental model of concepts, subconcepts, and objects is typical of this type of knowledge.

KNOWLEDGE REPRESENTATION TECHNIQUES

Through the efforts of researchers in artificial intelligence, a number of effective ways of representing knowledge in a computer were developed. An excellent review of these techniques is given by Barr and Feigenbaum (1981). In this chapter, we consider five of the most common techniques used in the development of an expert system:

- Object–attribute–value triplets
- Rules
- Semantic networks
- Frames
- Logic

Each representation technique emphasizes certain information about a problem while ignoring other information. Each technique also has advantages and disadvantages for capturing efficiently the different types of knowledge given in Figure 3.1. Choosing the correct representation for a given application produces a structure that supports effective problem solving. The following sections reviews each of these techniques.

Object–Attribute–Value Triplets

All the cognitive theories of human knowledge organization use *facts* as basic building blocks. A fact is a form of *declarative knowledge*. It provides some understanding of an event or problem.

Types of Knowledge	
Procedural Knowledge	Rules Strategies Agendas Procedures
Declarative Knowledge	Concepts Objects Facts
Meta-Knowledge	Knowledge About the Other Types of Knowledge and How to Use Them
Heuristic Knowledge	Rules of Thumb
Structural Knowledge	Rule sets Concept Relationships Concept to Object Relationships

FIGURE 3.1   Different types of knowledge.

In expert systems, facts are used to help describe parts of frames, semantic networks or rules. They are also used to describe relationships between more complex knowledge structures and to control the use of these structures during problem solving. In artificial intelligence and expert systems, a fact is often referred to as a **proposition.**

DEFINITION 3.4: Proposition
A statement that is either true or false.

A proposition can be a simple phrase such as

proposition: It is raining

In an expert system we assert into the working memory the Boolean truth value of this statement, i.e., **TRUE** or **FALSE,** and use this assertion in processing other knowledge.

A fact may also be used to assert a particular property value of some object. For example, the statement "the ball's color is red" assigns the value "red" to the ball's color. This type of fact is known as an **object–attribute–value** (O-A-V) triplet.

An O-A-V is a more complex type of proposition. It divides a given statement into three distinct parts: object, attribute, and attribute value. Consider for example the statement, "The chair's color is brown." We can represent this statement in an O-A-V structure by defining the *object* as "chair," the *attribute* as "color," and the *value* as "brown." This O-A-V structure is further illustrated in Figure 3.2.

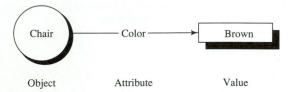

FIGURE 3.2   Object–attribute–value.

The object represented in an O-A-V can be a physical item, such as a car or a ball, or an abstract item, such as love or a mortgage. The attribute is a property or feature of the object that is an important problem consideration. The value specifies the attribute's assignment. This value can be Boolean, numeric, or string.

For most problems addressed by an expert system, objects have more than one important feature. In these instances, multiple attributes are defined for the object, with corresponding attribute values. Figure 3.3 shows an example of a multi-attribute O-A-V structure. You will see later in this chapter that frames and semantic networks both use multiple attributes to better describe objects.

Single Versus Multiple-Valued Facts

Some attributes can logically have only one value, while others can naturally have multiple values. These are often called *single-valued* and *multi-valued* facts. During the design of an expert system, you can designate whether an O-A-V attribute is either single- or multi-valued. This provides you with additional flexibility in representing the problem's knowledge.

Consider for example using an O-A-V to represent a statement about a barometer's pressure reading. The object would be "barometer" and the attribute "pressure reading." Possible values for the attribute might be falling, steady, or rising.

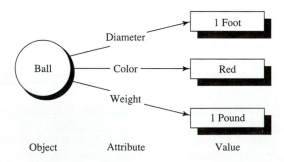

FIGURE 3.3   Object with multiple attributes.

If the expert system needs information on the barometric pressure, it would ask the following question:

Q: Please tell me if the barometric pressure is
   Falling
   Steady
   Rising

A: Falling

Logically, the barometric pressure can be in only one of the three states. You would then need to designate this O-A-V as *single-valued*.

Next consider an example on the issue of a person's education level. The object would be "person" and the attribute "education level." However, a person might have multiple degrees, e.g., high school, college, etc. Therefore, you would want to designate the O-A-V as *multi-valued*. A question now posed by the expert system would permit the user to select several items from a list. For example:

Q: Please select the level of education
   High school
   College
   Graduate school

A: High school
   College

Both single- and multi-valued O-A-V facts share an important feature. When the user selects a value from a list, the system asserts this value into the working memory as **TRUE**, and all other values as **FALSE**. Consider the barometric pressure question. If the user selects "falling," the system now not only knows this fact, but it also knows that the pressure is **not** rising and **not** steady. This feature of an O-A-V makes it more attractive than a simple propositional representation approach that asserts only a single fact.

Uncertain Facts

Our world is not black or white. That is, we don't always know if some event is true or false with complete certainty. Rather, we have some *degree of belief* in the event. This qualification can be heard in normal conversations with the use of the words "may," "likely," "very likely," and so on. For example, a person might say "It *probably* will rain today." Humans have little difficulty with interpreting such statements. Fortunately, expert systems can be provided the same ability.

A conventional method used in expert systems for managing uncertain information is called the **certainty factor**. A certainty factor (CF) is a numeric value assigned to a statement that represents the degree of belief in the statement.

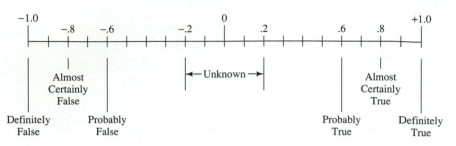

FIGURE 3.4   Certainty factor used in MYCIN.

Figure 3.4 shows how this value maps into a qualitative description of the statement. The CF concept originated during the work on MYCIN, and was formalized in an inexact reasoning technique known as the **certainty theory** (Shortliffe 1975).

As shown in Figure 3.4, a CF value ranges from -1, indicating the statement is "definitely false," to a value of +1, which indicates the statement is "definitely true." Between the two extremes, the value ascribes a degree of belief or disbelief in the statement. For example, to qualify the prior statement, "It *probably* will rain today," you could assign a CF value of 0.6 to the statement (see Figure 3.5).

Using CF values, an expert system can maintain a level of belief in both the user's answers and information it derives. These points are covered in detail in Chapter 12.

Fuzzy Facts

Another area where uncertainty enters the world of expert systems is the need to represent ambiguous terms commonly found in natural languages. For example, consider the statement "The person is *tall*." This statement is ambiguous because of the use of the word *tall*. Humans have little difficulty in interpreting and reasoning with ambiguous terms, however, computers need some help.

Fortunately, help is available in an area of study known as **fuzzy logic** (Zadeh 1965). Fuzzy logic provides methods for both representing and reasoning with

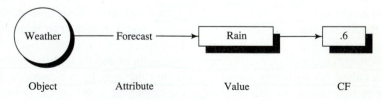

FIGURE 3.5   Weather forecast certainty factor.

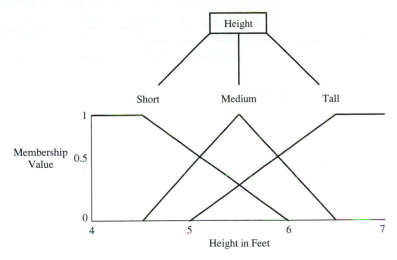

FIGURE 3.6 Fuzzy sets on height.

ambiguous terms. Ambiguous terms are represented in *fuzzy sets,* which capture quantitatively the human interpretation of the terms. For example, Figure 3.6 shows fuzzy sets that represent different adjectives that describe a person's height.

This figure shows three fuzzy sets mapping the domain of height into a number called the *membership value* (also called *membership grade*). The membership value is a number between 0 and 1 that reflects the level of belief that a given height belongs to a given fuzzy set. For example, an individual of a height of 5.5 feet would be said to a member of "medium" persons with a membership value of 1, and at the same time, a member of "short" and "tall" persons with a value of 0.25.

In addition to creating fuzzy sets, fuzzy logic permits you to write *fuzzy rules.* A fuzzy rule contains fuzzy sets in both its IF and THEN parts. Consider for example the following fuzzy rule:

IF   The person's height is *tall*
THEN The person's weight is *heavy*

By first forming a belief or membership grade in the rule's premise, this rule can infer the corresponding grade in the fuzzy set *heavy* defined on the domain *weight.* In effect, a fuzzy rule maps fuzzy sets to fuzzy sets. Chapter 13 explores further the subject of fuzzy logic and its role in the design of an expert system.

Rules

User-supplied facts are important to the operation of an expert system. They allow the system to understand the current state of the world. However, the system must have additional knowledge that allows it to work intelligently with these facts to solve a given problem. One knowledge structure commonly used in the design of an expert system that provides this additional knowledge is a **rule.**

> **DEFINITION 3.5: Rule**
> **A knowledge structure that relates some known information to other information that can be concluded or inferred to be known.**

A rule is a form of *procedural knowledge*. It associates given information to some action. This action may be the assertion of new information or some procedure to perform. In this sense, a rule describes how to solve a problem.

The rule's structure logically connects one or more **antecedents** (also called *premises)* contained in the **IF** part, to one or more **consequents** (also called *conclusions*) contained in the **THEN** part. For example:

IF   The ball's color is red
THEN I like the ball

For this simple example, if a given ball is red, then the rule infers that I like the ball.

In general, a rule can have multiple premises joined with AND statements (conjunctions), OR statements (disjunctions), or a combination of both. Its conclusion can contain a single statement or a combination joined with an AND. The rule can also contain an ELSE statement, that is inferred to be **TRUE** if one or more of its premises are **FALSE.** The following is an example of a general rule structure:

IF   Today's time is after 10 am
AND Today is a weekday
AND I am at home
OR   My boss called and said that I am late for work
THEN I am late for work
ELSE I am not late for work

In a rule-based expert system, domain knowledge is captured in a set of rules and entered in the system's knowledge base. The system uses these rules along with information contained in the working memory to solve a problem. When the **IF** portion of the rule matches the information contained in the working memory, the system performs the action specified in the **THEN** part of the rule. When this occurs, the rule *fires* and its **THEN** statements are added to the working memory. The new statements added to the working memory can also cause other rules to fire. Figure 3.7 shows an example of this process.

The process begins with the system asking the user for the ball's color. The system then takes the answer of "Red" and enters this fact into the working memory (Step 1). This assertion matches the premise of the first rule (Step 2). The match causes the rule to fire and its conclusion "I like the ball" is added to the working memory (Step 3). This new information matches the premise of

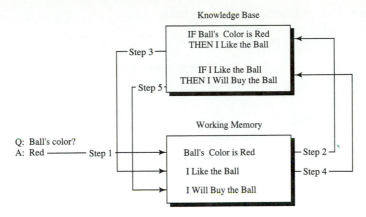

FIGURE 3.7 Rule-based system operation.

the second rule (Step 4). This causes the rule to fire and the fact "I will buy the ball" is also added to the working memory (Step 5). At this point, no other rules exist for the system to consider, so the processing stops.

The processing of rules in a rule-based expert system is managed by a module known as the *inference engine*. You have just seen a simple example of this module in action. Chapter 4 discusses more advanced ways this module can process a set of rules.

Executing a Procedure

Besides concluding new information, a rule can perform some operation. This operation can be a simple calculation as illustrated by the following example:

IF   The area of the square is needed
THEN AREA = LENGTH*WIDTH

This rule would fire when the information shown in its premise is added to the working memory. This firing results in the area computation.

In order to perform more complex operations, most rule-based systems are designed to access an external program. This program can be almost any type of traditional software, e.g., database, C program, etc. Consider for example the following rules. Note however, these rules are not coded in any language or shell; they are offered only as illustration.

1. PROCEDURAL PROGRAM

Rule 1
IF   The design requires a new box
AND   NUMBER = Number of items to pack
AND   SIZE = Size of item

THEN CALL COMPUTE_BOX_VOLUME
AND   SEND NUMBER, SIZE
AND   RETURN VOLUME

2. SPREADSHEET

Rule 2
IF   January sales needed
THEN OPEN SALES
AND   JANUARY_SALES = B7

3. DATABASE

Rule 3
IF   There is a plant emergency
AND   NAME = Smith
THEN OPEN TELEPHONE
AND   FIND NAME, NAME-FIELD
AND   TELEPHONE = TELEPHONE-FIELD

RULE 1 determines the volume of a box when a new box is required during a design task. The rule executes the program COMPUTE_BOX_VOLUME that calculates and returns the volume of the box, given the number and size of the items to be packed in the box. You could code this program in any conventional language such as Pascal, Fortran, etc.

RULE 2 determines the January sales amount. The rule obtains this information from cell B7 of spreadsheet SALES.

RULE 3 obtains the telephone number of the plant supervisor, Mr. Smith, when an emergency exists. It obtains this information from the database TELEPHONE by first locating the record containing the name Smith in the field NAME-FIELD. It then assigns to the variable TELEPHONE the value contained in the field TELEPHONE-FIELD.

In general, you can access or change information in external programs. This capability greatly enhances your flexibility in designing an expert system. You can make use of vast amounts of information contained in existing databases and spreadsheets, or alternatively change the information through the intelligent decision making of the expert system.

Types of Rules

Rules can represent various forms of knowledge as the following list illustrates:

Relationship
IF   The battery is dead
THEN The car will not start

Recommendation
IF   The car will not start
THEN Take a cab

Directive
IF   The car will not start
AND   The fuel system is ok
THEN Check out the electrical system

Strategy
IF   The car will not start
THEN First check out the fuel system then check out the electrical system

Heuristic
IF   The car will not start
AND   The car is a 1957 Ford
THEN Check the float

Rules can also be categorized according to the nature of the problem solving strategy—often called the *problem solving paradigm*. The following list shows typical rules found in some of the common paradigms:

Interpretation problem
IF   Voltage of resistor R1 is greater than 2.0 volts
AND   The collector voltage of Q1 is less than 1.0 volts
THEN The pre-amp section is in the normal range

Diagnosis problem
IF   The stain of the organism is grampos
AND   The morphology of the organism is coccus
AND   The growth of the organism is chains
THEN There is evidence that the organism is streptococcus

Design problem
IF   Current task is assigning a power supply
AND   The position of the power supply in the cabinet is known
AND   There is space available in the cabinet for the power supply
THEN Put the power supply in the cabinet

Variable Rules

In some applications, you will need to perform the same operation on a set of similar objects. You could write a single rule for each object, but, this approach is inefficient and makes it difficult to maintain the system. Consider for example the following rule that concludes whether John Smith can retire:

IF   John Smith is an employee
AND   John Smith's age is greater than 65
THEN John Smith can retire

This rule checks if John Smith is an employee of the company and is over the age of 65 before concluding he can retire. If you wanted the system to perform the same check for other individuals, you would need to write a similar rule for each person—an inefficient process. In addition, if the basic knowledge changes, for example if the retirement age changes from 65 to 60 years, you would need to make the appropriate change to every rule—a maintenance problem.

To avoid these types of problems, you can choose one of the computer languages or available shells that offer powerful **pattern-matching** rules. These rules include variables that you can use to match similar problem statements. Consider for example our retirement rule again, but this time with a variable:

```
IF      ?X is EMPLOYEE
AND     ?X AGE > 65
THEN    ?X can retire
```

This rule scans the working memory looking for matches to the two premises. If matches are found, then the rule concludes that the person can retire. Let's see how this rule works.

Assume the following information is in the working memory:

Smith is EMPLOYEE	Jones is EMPLOYEE	Miller is EMPLOYEE
Smith AGE = 67	Jones AGE = 70	Miller AGE = 60

The first premise scans this list of information and assigns the individual's name to the variable ?X if the person is an employee. The second premise checks to see if this same person, instantiated in ?X, is over the age of 65. If matches are found for both premises, the rule concludes that the person can retire and asserts this new information into the working memory. For the given contents in the working memory, two new assertions occur:

Smith can retire   Jones can retire

A pattern-matching rule offers you an efficient way to process information. You can write one rule instead of many, which eases both system coding and maintenance. It also permits you to directly capture general directions obtained from an expert. For example, the prior rule captures the following statement that might have come from the expert:

"If any employee is over the age of sixty-five, then he or she can retire."

Frame-based systems employ pattern-matching rules extensively: a subject discussed further in Chapter 14.

Uncertain Rules

Just as you can have uncertain facts, you can have uncertain rules. An expert will often provide a rule that establishes an inexact association between the premise and conclusion. For example:

```
IF      Inflation is high
THEN    Almost certainly interest rates are high
```

In this example, the expert believes "almost certainly" that if inflation is high then interest rates are also high. To capture the confidence that the expert has on this association, you can use certainty factors. For example, you could write the prior rule as follows:

IF Inflation is high
THEN Interest rates are high CF=0.8

Here, if it is found that inflation is definitely high, the system would conclude that interest rates are "almost certainly" high, by assigning this fact a CF value of 0.8.

 This example illustrates the simplest use of an uncertain rule. It works like the prior rules we have reviewed, with the exception that the conclusion is now asserted with a degree of belief. There are many other more complex aspects of processing uncertain rules that are explored in Chapter 12.

Meta-Rules

Often when solving a problem an expert will use knowledge that directs the problem solving. This knowledge is different from the type we have been looking at, which is used to characterize the domain. Rather, this new type of knowledge uses the existing domain knowledge to determine how to best solve the problem. This type of knowledge is called **meta-knowledge**.

> **DEFINITION 3.6:** Meta-knowledge
> **Knowledge about the use and control of domain knowledge.**

Meta-knowledge is often represented in a **meta-rule** to direct the consultation.

> **DEFINITION 3.7:** Meta-rule
> **A rule that describes how other rules should be used.**

A meta-rule establishes strategies for the use of domain-specific rules, instead of concluding new information. For example:

IF The car will not start
AND The electrical system is operating normally
THEN Use rules concerning the fuel system

This automobile diagnostic meta-rule directs the system to check the fuel system if no problems have been found in the electrical system.

 Meta-rules provide direction to the expert system during the session. You can use them to enhance the system's efficiency by directing its reasoning into the most promising areas.

Rule Sets

Through experience, an expert forms several sets of rules to apply to a given problem. One set of rules may be applicable to a given problem, while being useless for another problem. For example, an automobile mechanic may have separate sets of rules for the electrical and fuel systems. When he encounters an electrical problem, he uses only those rules formed from past experiences when working on the automobile's electrical system.

A given set of rules reflects the skill the expert has on the given topic. The choice and use of the different rule sets reflect the reasoning competence of the expert. Rules alone are not sufficient for expert reasoning. A strategy is also needed for knowing when and how to apply them.

To illustrate the organization and use of rule sets, consider Figure 3.8. This figure shows various rule sets that an automobile mechanic might use. They are organized in a hierarchical fashion—a style typically found in cognitive studies on human problem solving.

Each block of Figure 3.8 represents a set of rules related to the block's label. Upper level blocks contain a set of abstract rules for general problem solving.

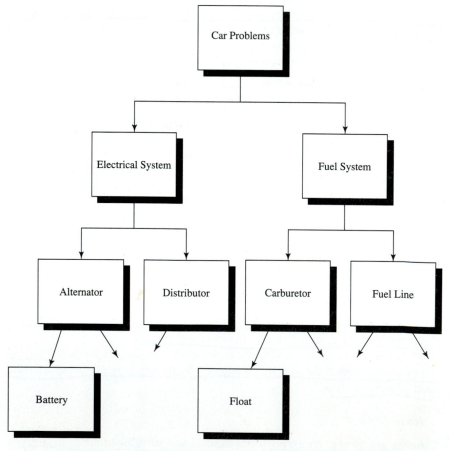

FIGURE 3.8   Automobile diagnostic rule sets.

They serve to direct the system's reasoning toward a more detailed investigation accomplished by the rule sets in the lower blocks.

The top level block "Car Problems" contains a set of rules that directs the system to investigate either the car's "Electrical System" or "Fuel System." This set of rules would work with car symptoms that could discriminate between electrical and fuel type problems. Under each of these subcategories, a more detailed category of rules exist, e.g., "Alternator" or "Distributor." The rules in the "Electrical System" module would be responsible for determining which of these two to pursue. The lower level blocks "Battery" and "Float" would contain rules to diagnose specific car problems by working with very specific test information on each unit.

This type of modular structure provides a natural ordering of the domain's rule sets. It also proposes a top-down approach to problem solving, where specific rule sets are used only when appropriate. The expert system could pass control to a given rule set using a meta-rule as discussed in the previous section.

The principal advantage of this design is that it represents a natural approach to solving complex problems. Humans generally attempt to dissect a complex problem into smaller more manageable subproblems—divide and conquer approach.

Another advantage of this approach is that it eases the system's development and maintenance. During the development of the expert system, you can focus your attention on one module at a time. You can build and test the module independently of the other modules. This allows you to focus your attention on one issue at a time. Also, since a large amount of your effort on the project will be devoted to modifying and maintaining the knowledge base, the modular aspect of the design greatly aids this effort.

A technical advantage is also offered with this approach. Since each module may be a separate expert system, it allows you to integrate different knowledge representation techniques and inferencing strategies into the system.

Blackboards

The last section discussed the importance of generating separate rule sets, but said nothing about how these different sets can communicate information with one another. This section addresses this point from the viewpoint of cooperating expert systems.

Complex problems may require knowledge from several human experts. For example, a problem of forming marketing strategies in the business world might be solved by forming a committee of company specialists. Each specialist would bring to this committee expertise on one aspect of marketing. Working together, this committee could then form an effective marketing plan. This approach to the problem is often referred to as *distributed problem solving*. In expert systems, distributed problem solving is accomplished through communicating rule sets.

One of the first expert systems developed that used a communicating rule set approach was the HEARSAY-II speech understanding system (Erman 1980).

This system interprets continuous speech drawn from a 1000-word vocabulary. To accomplish this goal, HEARSAY used 12 expert modules each of which performed a separate task. These modules worked collectively by exchanging information with each other through a structure known as a **blackboard.**

DEFINITION 3.8: Blackboard
A design in which several expert systems share information contained in a common source.

The architecture of an expert system employing a blackboard structure contains three major components:

1. Community of different expert systems
2. Blackboard
3. Scheduler

Each expert system module is uniquely different and addresses one subproblem. However, each shares and uses information with the other expert modules to accomplish its task. Expert system modules communicate by writing information on the blackboard and reading information from other modules. Typical information would be a module's findings or hypotheses that the other modules use to aid their problem solving. The scheduler maintains control over all the modules and guides the overall reasoning strategy.

This system architecture is similar to the marketing planning committee analogy. You could represent each committee member in a single expert system. The blackboard serves to model the conversation of the committee meeting. The scheduler models the committee chairperson who would be responsible for steering the meeting. This architecture also permits the expert modules to work concurrently, in a parallel processing mode.

Semantic Networks

One of the earliest attempts in AI to represent knowledge in a computer relied on a **semantic network.**

DEFINITION 3.9: Semantic Network
A method of knowledge representation using a graph made up of nodes and arcs where the nodes represent objects and the arcs the relationships between the objects.

A semantic network provides a graphical view of a problem's important objects, properties and relationships. It contains nodes and arcs that connect the nodes. The nodes can represent objects, object properties or property values. The arcs represent the relationships between the nodes. Both the nodes and arcs have labels that clearly describe the objects represented and their natural relationships.

A node for example might have the name "Bird" or "Jack." Arcs are commonly labeled with terms such as "IS-A," "HAS," etc., that clearly define the relationships between connected nodes.

Example of a Semantic Network

Figure 3.9 shows a simple example of a semantic network. This figure has two nodes that represent objects, and two representing properties. The "Bird" node is connected to both property nodes, providing the interpretation "a bird has wings and can fly." The "Canary" node is linked to the "Bird" node via an IS-A arc, i.e., "a canary is a bird."

By virtue of linking the "Canary" node to the "Bird" node through an IS-A link, an important feature of a semantic network is working behind the scene. Since birds have wings and can fly, and canaries are a type of bird, it seems only reasonable that they also have wings and can fly. When you code into a computer the semantic network shown in Figure 3.9, the computer obtains the same understanding. It knows not only about objects and their properties, it can infer information about related objects in the hierarchy.

Expanding the Network

You can easily expand a semantic network by simply adding nodes and linking them to their related nodes currently in the network. These new nodes represent

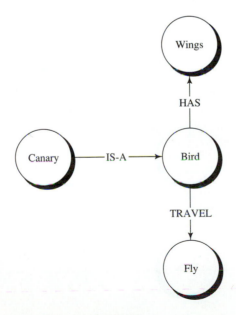

FIGURE 3.9   Semantic network of bird.

additional objects or properties. You will usually add a new object node in one
of three ways: (1) a similar object, (2) a more specific object, or (3) a more
general object. Consider Figure 3.10 which shows all three expansion approaches
for our bird network.

The network in Figure 3.9 represents only one type of bird, i.e., "Canary."
However, there are many other types, such as robins, penguins, etc. As shown
in Figure 3.10, you can easily add nodes to the network that represent these new
bird types. Here a "Penguin" node was added and linked to the "Bird" node
through an IS-A arc.

The IS-A link between the "Canary" and "Bird" nodes in Figure 3.9 defines
a specific-to-general relationship between the two. That is, a canary is a specific
type of bird. Using this idea, the second way you can expand a semantic network
is to add a node that represents a more specific object. For example, as shown
in Figure 3.10, the node "Tweety" was added and linked to the "Bird" node
through an IS-A arc. This figure not only tells you that Tweety is a canary, but
you can also infer that Tweety is a bird, simply by following the IS-A links.

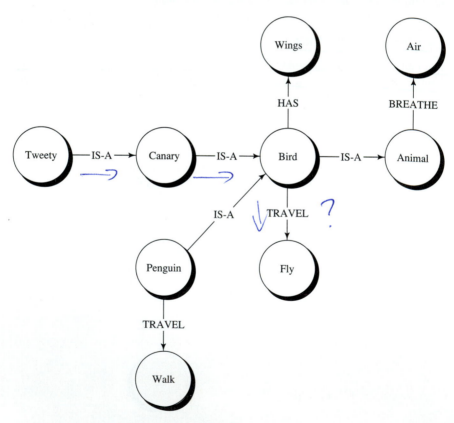

FIGURE 3.10   Expanded semantic network.

The third way you can expand the network follows the previous idea. You can add a node that represents a more general object, and link it using an IS-A arc to the appropriate node. For example, as shown in Figure 3.10, the node "Animal" was added and linked to the "Bird" node through an IS-A arc. This additional node adds a considerable amount of information to the network. You not only know that "a bird is an animal," but by tracing through the network you also know that "Tweety is an animal and breathes air."

Inheritance in Semantic Networks

The last section illustrated how nodes added to a semantic network automatically inherit information from the network. For example, "Tweety" breathes air because it is an "Animal." This is an important feature of a semantic network and is formally called **inheritance.**

The inheritance feature of a semantic network eases the task of coding knowledge. For example, if you add some specific object node to the network (e.g., "Tweety"), it inherits information throughout the network via the IS-A links. In addition, if you add a general object node (e.g., "Animal"), other nodes inherit its properties. It is this ability of a semantic network that made it an attractive knowledge representation technique to AI researchers (Quillian 1968).

Semantic Network Operation

To illustrate the benefit of inheritance to a semantic network, let's look at one in action. Assume we coded into a computer the network of Figure 3.10.

One simple way to use a semantic network is to ask some node a question. For example, you could ask the "Bird" node, "How do you *travel?*" To answer the question, the node first looks for an arc labeled "travel." In this case, that arc exists. The node then uses the information in the attached node as the answer, namely "Fly." Figure 3.11 illustrates this example as CASE 1.

If the node is unable to locate the answer via a local arc, it then searches for an answer via its IS-A links. In a sense, the nodes related through IS-A links pass the question along until one of the nodes can provide an answer. Consider for example the same question posed to the "Tweety" node illustrated in Figure 3.11 as CASE 2.

The "Tweety" node has no way to answer the question so it asks the "Canary" node. Likewise, this node passes the question along to the "Bird" node. Here, as in the previous example, an answer of "Fly" is found, and is sent back along the links finally arriving at the user.

As this last example illustrates, a semantic network equipped with an inheritance feature provides an efficient way to process information.

Exception Handling

Inheritance is a powerful feature in a semantic network, but it can cause problems. Consider for example the "Penguin" node in Figure 3.10. Since this node is

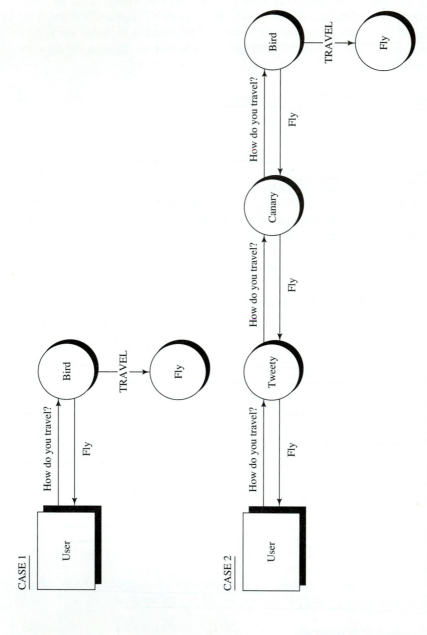

FIGURE 3.11 Semantic network operation.

linked to the "Bird" node, it inherits the information "TRAVEL—Fly." In other words, we would expect that a penguin, by virtue of being a bird, can fly. This is obviously a mistake; one that you can correct using a technique known as **exception handling.**

This technique requires you to account for exceptions on a local basis. When a node inherits incorrect information, you must link a new node to it with information that can effectively over-ride the inherited information.

Consider again our problem with the earth-bound penguin and Figure 3.10. As shown in this figure, a "Walk" node is attached to the "Penguin" node using a "Travel" link. Therefore, since a node first looks locally for an answer to a question, an answer of "Walk" is provided to a travel question posed to the penguin.

Exception handling is a simple technique used to avoid problems with a semantic network. However, the subject highlights an inherent weakness of semantic networks. If you fail to account for a necessary exception, obvious problems occur; you now have a flying penguin.

Frames

A natural extension of the semantic network is a *schema,* first proposed by Barlett (1932). A schema is a unit that contains typical knowledge about some concept or object, and includes both declarative and procedural knowledge. For example, the schema of a bird might include knowledge that it has wings and legs, and how it hunts for food. A schema holds stereotypical information about a concept that can be applied to a specific situation for study.

Expert system designers use this same idea to capture and represent conceptual knowledge in an expert system, but will usually refer to the schema as a **frame,** first proposed by Minsky (1975).

DEFINITION 3.10: Frame
A data structure for representing stereotypical knowledge of some concept or object.

Minsky described a frame in the following fashion:

"When one encounters a new situation (or makes a substantial change in one's view of a problem) one selects from memory a structure called a "frame." This is a remembered framework to be adapted to fit reality by changing details as necessary."

Basic Frame Design

A frame is similar in appearance to many forms, such as the student's report card shown in Figure 3.12. This form has a name "Report Card," fields such as "Student Name," and slots for entering field values. It provides the general type of information you can use to characterize each student in a school.

REPORT CARD

Student Name: [   ]

Address: [   ]

Course	Grade
Chemistry	
Math	
English	
•••	
•••	

FIGURE 3.12   Report card form.

The basic structure of a frame is shown in Figure 3.13. Like a form, it has a name "Object1," that is the name of the object represented by the frame. For example, if you wanted to represent a person named Bob, you could use his name. A frame also has fields, "Property1," "Property2," etc., that are features or attributes that describe the object represented. For our Bob frame, these

Frame Name:	Object1	
Class:	Object2	
Properties:	Property1	Value1
	Property2	Value2
	•••	•••
	•••	•••

FIGURE 3.13   General frame structure.

properties might be items such as his address, age, etc. Each property has a slot for entering a specific value, i.e., "Value1." For example, in Bob's age slot, you might put a value of 30. These properties and property values form a list of O-A-V type statements that provide a rich representation of the object. Property values are of three general types: Boolean, string, or numeric.

A frame also includes an optional field called "Class." You can enter a value (i.e., "Object2") that is the name of another frame related to "Object1." This relationship is usually of the "IS-A" type, discussed in the semantic network section. That is, you can form an "Object1 IS-A Object2" relationship. For example, by placing the name "Human" in the "Class" slot of "Bob," you represent the relationship "Bob is a human." The value of establishing this link between the two frames is similar to that obtained when two semantic network nodes are linked together; "Object1" inherits information from "Object2."

Class Frame

A **class frame** represents the general characteristics of some set of common objects. For example, you could create a class frame that describes such objects as cars, boats, or even intangible objects such as line pressures or temperatures. In each class frame you define those properties that are common to all the objects within the class, and possibly default property values. Properties are of two general types: static or dynamic. A static property describes an object feature whose value doesn't change. A dynamic property is a feature whose value is likely to change during the operation of the system.

Figure 3.14 shows an example of a class frame. The frame name "Bird" describes the object represented. The properties shown describe the general characteristics of most birds. Properties such as "Color" and "No._Wings" are

Frame Name:	Bird	
Properties:	Color	Unknown
	Eats	Worms
	No._Wings	2
	Flies	True
	Hungry	Unknown
	Activity	Unknown

FIGURE 3.14   Bird frame.

static. They describe nonchanging features of the bird. The properties "Hungry" and "Activity" are dynamic. During the operation of the system it is likely that these values will change.

The property values shown in the figure are also typical for most birds. For example, most birds have two wings and can fly. A value of "Unknown" means that we can't ascribe a value to the property. For example, even though we know that all birds have a color, its not logical to assign a value to the "Color" property until we are representing a specific bird.

Instance Frame

You use a different type of frame to describe a specific instance of a class frame and—not surprisingly—it is called an **instance frame.** When you create an instance of some class, the frame inherits both properties and property values from the class. You can then change the property values to tailor the description of the object represented in the instance frame. You could even add additional properties to the instance if necessary. Figure 3.15 shows an example of an instance frame. Details of this frame are discussed in the next section.

In general, you can create many instances of the same class. You simply assert that the new frame is an instance of the class, and it immediately inherits the class information. This approach greatly speeds system coding, especially when there are many instances to code.

Frame Name:	Tweety	
Class:	Bird	
Properties:	Color	Yellow
	Eats	Worms
	No._Wings	1
	Flies	False
	Hungry	Unknown
	Activity	Unknown
	Lives	Cage

FIGURE 3.15   Tweety frame.

Frame Inheritance

Just as a node in a semantic network can inherit information from other nodes, an instance frame inherits information from its class frame. When you create an instance frame, you begin by asserting that the frame is an instance of some class. This assertion causes the instance frame to inherit all of the information from its class frame.

Consider Figure 3.15 which shows the frame of "Tweety," an instance of a "Bird." Since Tweety is a bird, it inherits the information from Figure 3.14. Like most birds, Tweety eats worms. However, Tweety has only one wing and thus can't fly. In general, you can allow an instance to accept the class default values or provide values unique to the instance. You can also provide unique properties in the instance. For example, if it is known that Tweety lives in a cage, you can insert this information directly into the instance frame.

Inheriting Behavior

Besides inheriting descriptive information from its class, an instance also inherits its behavior. To accomplish this, you need to first include within a class frame a procedure (often called a *method*), that defines some action the frame performs. For example, in the class frame "Bird" of Figure 3.14, you could write a method that tells every bird what to do if it becomes hungry. Each instance of this class would then inherit the method and know how to respond when its property "Hungry" is set to "True." We explore this point further later in the chapter under the topic of *facets*.

Hierarchical Structure

Besides having only a single class and its associated instances, you can create complex frame structures. Consider for example Figure 3.16 which shows the world of birds arranged in a hierarchical structure.

This structure organizes the concept of a bird at different levels of abstraction. The top level frame contains information common to all birds. The middle-level frames (called *subclasses*) contain information more specific to their individual category. That is, though robins and canaries share features common to all birds, each possess some unique features that serve to discriminate between the two. The bottom frames are the specific bird instances. Each instance inherits information from the top level "Bird" frame, and also features from their associated subclass. In general, an instance inherits information from its parent, grandparent, etc.

Facets

Frame-based systems also offer a feature called **facets** that provide you additional control over property values. One way you can use a facet is to define a constraint

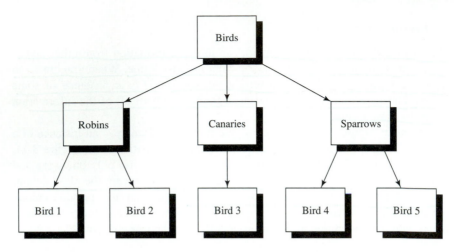

FIGURE 3.16   Frame world of birds.

on a property value. For example, you can limit a numeric property value to some set range or a string value to one of a few possible values. You can also use a facet to restrict the type of data that can be stored in a property value: i.e., string, numeric, or Boolean.

Another very powerful way you can use a facet is to instruct a property how to obtain its value or what to do if its value changes. These are formally called IF-NEEDED and IF-CHANGED facets.

IF-NEEDED Facet

In some applications you will need to define a procedure or *method* that executes whenever a property value is needed. This is typically the case where the property value is obtained through a series of computations, or from an external database or spreadsheet. It is also the case when the value depends on other property values that dynamically change during the session. The method is typically written in the procedural language of the chosen development shell, and attached to the property's IF-NEEDED facet. To illustrate how you can use an IF-NEEDED facet to obtain a property value, consider the following example.

Consider the property "Flies" in the "Tweety" frame of Figure 3.15. Assume this property value is initially unknown and you want the system to determine if Tweety can fly. Most birds can fly because most have two wings; the default property values in the "Bird" class frame of Figure 3.14. However, if Tweety has less than two wings, then it is reasonable to assume it can't fly. The following method, shown in general form, accomplishes this task:

IF   Tweety has less than two wings
THEN Tweety can't fly

IF   Tweety has two wings
THEN Tweety can fly

To implement this method within the chosen shell, you first need a way to obtain the property value of "No._Wings" in the "Tweety" frame. Shells differ slightly in the code they use for obtaining a frame's property value. The shell Kappa PC, for example, uses the following code:

Frame:Property

Using this code on the "Tweety" frame of Figure 3.15, we have

Tweety:No._Wings = 1

Next, you need to be able to assert a value of **True** or **False** to the "Flies" property, depending on Tweety's wing count. Again, shells differ slightly on this procedure. Kappa PC uses the following code:

Frame:Property = Value

Now, equipped with the general method and the syntax for writing the method, you can use the following code:

IF   Tweety:No_Wings < 2
THEN Tweety:Flies = False

IF   Tweety:No_Wings = 2
THEN Tweety:Flies = True

This method would next be given some name (e.g., Tweety_Fly) and attached to the IF-NEEDED facet of property "Flies" of the frame "Tweety."

Though this approach is effective in determining if Tweety can fly or not, it is not very efficient in large applications. Consider the case where many birds exist. You would need to write similar methods for each bird, where the name Tweety is replaced with the corresponding bird name.

Fortunately, most shells permit you to use a variable in place of the frame's name. For example, Kappa PC uses the variable *Self*. You can use this variable within the method and attach the method at the class level. Upon inheriting this method, each instance assigns its own name to the variable. This permits you to write one general method at the class level that accommodates any number of instance frames. Consider the use of this variable in our previous method:

IF   Self:No_Wings < 2
THEN Self:Flies = False

IF   Self:No_Wings = 2
THEN Self:Flies = True

Each bird instance frame can now use this method to determine whether it can fly.

IF-CHANGED Facet

A method can also be attached to a property's IF-CHANGED facet that performs some action whenever its value changes. You will need this type of method when a frame's property value impacts the property value of another frame, as in simulation or control applications. It can also be used to change a property value within its own frame; the example we consider in this section.

Assume you want each bird represented as an instance of the "Bird" class shown in Figure 3.14 to know what to do if it becomes hungry. A reasonable instruction is to tell the bird to eat what it normally eats, using the "Eats" property value. To maintain an account of what the bird is doing, you might also want to post the results in the "Activity" property value, e.g., "Eating worms."

To accomplish each of these points, you need to write a method (we will call it "Hungry_Action") and attach it to the IF-CHANGED facet of the "Hungry" property of the "Bird" class frame. This method executes within each instance whenever its "Hungry" property changes. So that each instance can use the method, the method must include the *Self* variable introduced in the last section. Consider the following method (written in Kappa PC code) that accomplishes all of these requirements:

```
IF      Self:Hungry = True
THEN  Self:Activity = Eating # Self:Eats
```

When the "Hungry" property of any instance frame changes, this method first checks to see if the value of this property is equal to "True." If found, this method sets the "Activity" property value to eating whatever the bird represented in the instance frame normally eats. The "Tweety" frame of Figure 3.15 for example, would have an "Activity" property value of "EatingWorms." Note that the "#" sign used in the method appends two strings.

Using an IF-CHANGED method in the class level provides a generality to the system. Each frame is taught the same type of general behavior. However, each frame can tailor the behavior to suit its own needs. For example, if we introduced a frame that represented a parrot that normally eats crackers, the result of the "Hungry_Action" method would be "EatingCrackers."

Logic

The oldest form of knowledge representation in a computer is **logic.** Over the years, several logic representation techniques have been suggested and studied. The ones most often linked with intelligent systems have been **propositional logic** and **predicate calculus.** Both techniques use symbols to represent knowledge and operators applied to the symbols to produce logical reasoning. They offer a formal well-founded approach to knowledge representation and reasoning.

Though expert system designers rarely use a classical logical knowledge representation approach, it forms the basis upon which most AI programming languages and shells are built. PROLOG for example is one of the key AI programming languages and is based on the predicate calculus. The predicate

TABLE 3.1 Logic operators and symbols

Operator	Symbol
AND	$\land$, &, $\cap$
OR	$\lor$, $\cup$, +
NOT	$\neg$, ~
IMPLIES	$\supset$, $\rightarrow$
EQUIVALENCE	$\equiv$

calculus is like the assembly language of knowledge representation. An understanding of it provides insight into higher level representation techniques.

Propositional Logic

Propositional logic represents and reasons with *propositions*; statements that are either true or false. Propositional logic assigns a symbolic variable to a proposition, such as

A = The car will start

The symbolic variable chosen could be of any form, such as

A,M,K,TEMP,CAR_STATE

In proposition logic, if we were concerned with the truth of the statement ''The car will start,'' we would check the truth of the variable **A.**

For many problems we are concerned with the truth of logically related propositions. Consider for example the following rule:

IF	The car will not start	$\rightarrow$	**A**
AND	It is too far to walk to work	$\rightarrow$	**B**
THEN	I will miss work today	$\rightarrow$	**C**

Propositional logic provides logical operators, such as AND, OR, NOT, IMPLIES, EQUIVALENCE, that allow us to reason with various rule structures. Table 3.1 lists the propositional logic operators and their common symbols.

Using the symbols of Table 3.1, we can write the rule as:

$A \land B \rightarrow C$

The first three operations of Table 3.1 are similar to those found in Boolean logic, as shown in the following truth tables:

AND

A	B	A AND B
F	F	F
F	T	F
T	F	F
T	T	T

OR

A	B	A OR B
F	F	F
F	T	T
T	F	T
T	T	T

NOT

A	NOT A
T	F
F	T

The EQUIVALENCE operator returns a T only when both propositions have the same truth assignment:

EQUIVALENCE

A	B	A ≡ B
F	F	T
F	T	F
T	F	F
T	T	T

$\overline{XOR}$

The IMPLIES operator is handled in a special manner. This function defines an *implication* between propositions of the form:

$C = A \rightarrow B$

That is for the implication **C,** if **A** is true, then **B** is implied to be true. The following truth table illustrates the operation of implication:

IMPLIES

A	B	C
F	F	T
F	T	T
T	F	F
T	T	T

→ T can not → F

The IMPLIES or implication operator returns an F when **A** is T and **B** is F, otherwise it returns a T. Another way of viewing this is that **C** is true if **A** is false OR **B** is true, and **C** is false only when **A** is true and **B** is false. That is, the following two statements are equivalent:

$A \rightarrow B \equiv \neg A \vee B$

To better illustrate the operation of the implication operator, it is valuable to view the implication in the form of a rule such as:

IF   The battery is dead
THEN The car won't start

From the first row in the implication truth table (**A**=F, **B**=F), our example rule could be interpreted:

> battery **not** dead $\rightarrow$ car **will** start; implication **T**

From the second row:

> battery **not** dead $\rightarrow$ car **won't** start; implication **T**

Believing this implication may seem strange, but it allows for the possibility that the car may not start even with a good battery because something else may be wrong with the car.

From the third row:

> battery **is** dead $\rightarrow$ car **will** start; implication **F**

Notice this is the only implication we don't believe, and we shouldn't.

From the fourth row we derive the simple implication:

> battery **is** dead $\rightarrow$ car **won't** start; implication **T**

Propositional logic offers techniques for capturing facts or rules in symbolic form and then operates on them through the use of logical operators. This formal logical approach provides an exact method for managing statements that are either true or false. However, for many problems, it can be difficult to assert a truth value to an entire statement. What is needed is a way for dissecting the statement into a finer granularity, where elements of the statement can be represented and reasoned with logically. For these applications, **predicate calculus** may provide more flexibility to representation.

Predicate Calculus

Predicate calculus, also called predicate logic, is an extension of propositional logic that provides a finer representation of the knowledge. For example, instead of representing an entire proposition with a single symbol, such as **A** = ball's color is red, the predicate calculus permits a representation that describes the relationship of the knowledge in a form of **color(ball,red)**. This representation enhances knowledge processing by allowing the use of variables and functions.

The predicate calculus, like propositional logic, uses symbols to represent knowledge. These symbols may represent either **constants, predicates, variables,** or **functions.** Predicate calculus also permits you to operate on these symbols using the propositional logic operators.

Constants

Constants are used to name specific objects or properties about the problem. In general, constants are symbols that begin with a lowercase letter. For example, **john, mary,** and **temperature** are valid constants. The constant **john** may have been chosen to represent the object **John,** a person in the domain. You could use ''**x**'' to represent the same object, however, it would make it difficult to interpret the knowledge represented.

Predicates

In predicate calculus, a fact or proposition is divided into two parts: a predicate and an argument. The argument represents the object or objects of the proposition and the predicate an assertion about the object. For example, to represent the proposition ''John likes Mary,'' you would write:

likes(john,mary)

In predicate calculus representation, the first word of each expression (i.e., likes) is a **predicate** denoting some relationship between the arguments within the parentheses. The arguments are symbols denoting objects within the problem. The standard convention represents predicates with the first character in lowercase.

Variables

Variables are used to represent general classes of objects or properties. Variables are written as symbols beginning with an uppercase letter. For example, to capture the propositions ''John likes Mary'' and ''Bob likes Judy,'' you can write:

likes(X,Y)

In this case, variables assume or *instantiate* the values X = john, bob, Y = mary, judy. In predicate calculus, variables can be used as arguments in a predicate expression or a function.

Functions

Predicate calculus also permits symbols to be used to represent a function. A function denotes a mapping from entities of a set to a unique element of another set. For example, the following functions might be defined to return the designated values:

father(jack) = bob   mother(judy) = kathy

Functions can also be used within predicates. For example, the following predicate indicates that Bob and Kathy are friends:

friends(father(jack),mother(judy)) = friends(bob,kathy)

Operations

Predicate calculus uses the same operators found in propositional logic. To illustrate their use, consider the following:

proposition: John likes Mary   likes(john,mary) proposition:

Bob likes Mary   likes(bob,mary)

These two predicates indicate that two different men like Mary. To account for the obvious jealousy that might occur, you could write:

likes(X,Y) AND likes(Z,Y) IMPLIES NOT likes(X,Z)

or

likes(X,Y) $\wedge$ likes(Z,Y) $\rightarrow$ $\neg$ likes(X,Z)

This is a general implication that captures the knowledge:

"If two different individuals like the same person, then they dislike each other."

Applying the implication produces the result:

$\neg$ likes(john,bob)

The predicate calculus also introduces two other symbols called **variable quantifiers** that you can use to define the range or scope of the variables in a logical expression. The two quantifiers are $\forall$, the universal quantifier, and $\exists$, the existential quantifier.

The universal quantifier $\forall$ indicates that the expression is **TRUE** for **all** values of the designated variable. For example, the following indicates that for all values of **X,** the statement is true, that is, everybody likes Mary:

$\forall$X likes(X,mary)   → UNIVERSAL

The existential quantifier $\exists$ indicates that the expression is **TRUE** for **some** values of the variable, i.e., at least one value "exists" that makes the statement true. Consider the statement at least someone likes Mary:

$\exists$X likes(X,mary)   EXISTANTIAL

Parentheses are used to indicate the *scope* of quantification, that is, the range over which the instances of the variable hold. For example:

$\forall$X (likes(X,mary) $\wedge$ nice(mary) $\rightarrow$ nice(X))

This logical expression determines all instances of **X** who like Mary, and if Mary is nice, then it is implied that those who like Mary are also nice.

Reasoning with Logic

The prior sections illustrated how you can use the predicate calculus to represent factual knowledge in symbolic form. However, an intelligent system also needs a way to reason with this knowledge. Through the use of the predicate calculus operators, you can provide this reasoning ability to the system. Reasoning requires the ability to infer conclusions from available facts. The process of reasoning in an expert system is called inferencing, the subject of Chapter 4.

One simple form of inference is **modus ponens.** Modus ponens states that if some proposition **A** is true, and **A IMPLIES B** is true, then proposition **B** is true.

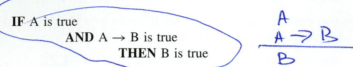

> **IF** A is true
>   **AND** A → B is true
>   **THEN** B is true

$$\frac{\begin{array}{l} A \\ A \to B \end{array}}{B}$$

This simple idea of inferring new information from known information using an implication or rule is central to reasoning in intelligent systems.

Robot Control Example

To illustrate reasoning with logic, we will consider a robot control problem. Assume that the function of the robot is to move a specified block to some specified location. Figure 3.17 illustrates the world in which the robot must operate. Our task is to provide the robot with an understanding of its world using the predicate calculus so that it can perform its function.

To accomplish this task, we would first need to provide the robot with an understanding about what objects exist and how they are arranged. Using the predicate calculus we can describe the blocks world by the following logical assertions:

1. cube(a) cube(b) cube(d) pyramid(c) sphere(e) hand(hand) table(table1)

2. on(a,table1) on(b,table1) on(d,a) on(c,b)

3. holding(hand,nothing)

Line 1 defines the types of objects within the blocks world. Line 2 describes the current relationship between the various objects. For example, "Block **a** is on

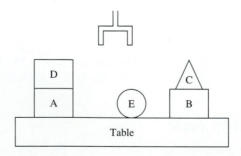

FIGURE 3.17   Blocks world.

table1.'' Line 3 describes the current state of the robot's hand: ''Robot's hand is holding nothing.''

The goal of the robot might be to put some block onto some other block, for example put block **b** onto block **a.** This goal could be expressed as:

$$put\_on(b,a)$$

To accomplish this goal the robot would have to obtain block **b** and make certain that block **a** is clear. Or in other words, if the robot is holding block **b** and block **a** is clear, then put block **b** onto block **a.** These tasks can be related to the goal by the following implication:

$$hand\_holding(b) \land clear(a) \rightarrow put\_on(b,a)$$

Since we may also want the robot to move other blocks, we can write this implication in variable form:

$$\forall X \ \exists Y \ (hand\_holding(X) \land clear(Y) \rightarrow put\_on(X,Y))$$

where the block to be moved is set to X and the target block to Y.

One of the first tasks that the robot would need to perform when instructed to pick up and move some block is to determine if it is clear. If the block is not clear, then the robot would need to first remove any items resting on the block. The following implication would provide this information:

$$\forall X \ (\neg \exists Y \ on(Y,X) \rightarrow clear(X))$$

This implication states that, for all X, X is clear if there does not exist a Y such that Y is on X, and for the example would produce the following assertions:

$$clear(c) \ clear(d) \ clear(e)$$

This step also illustrates how one implication can be used to support another. Obtaining information on which blocks are clear is needed by the implication directed at the goal of putting one block on another. Writing implications that support one another is the subject of inferencing, explored in Chapter 4.

New information from old information—a key to reasoning. This simple example illustrates how you can use the predicate calculus to create an intelligent system.

—————— SUMMARY ON KNOWLEDGE
REPRESENTATION ——————————

This chapter reviewed the subject of knowledge representation. The most popular current techniques were discussed in detail. Later chapters show how these techniques are used in the design of an expert system. The important issues covered in this chapter were:

- An O-A-V triplet fact represents an object's attribute value.
- An uncertain fact can be represented in an expert system using a confidence factor.
- An ambiguous fact can be represented in an expert system using a fuzzy set.
- Rules infer new information from known information—a key to reasoning.
- A pattern-matching rule contains a variable that can be used to match a large number of similar objects.
- Rules can represent uncertain or fuzzy inferences.
- A semantic network represents objects and their relationships.
- An object node in a semantic network inherits information from its parent node.
- A frame represents an object's declarative and procedural knowledge.
- An instance frame inherits both declarative and procedural knowledge from its class frame.
- A facet can be used to represent additional knowledge or control over an object's property.
- Logic offers a formal well-founded approach to knowledge representation and reasoning.
- Predicate calculus represents the qualitative aspects of a proposition symbolically either through constants or variables.
- Predicate calculus operators can be used to form complex implications.

━━━━━━━ R E F E R E N C E S

Barlett, F.C., Remembering, CUP, Cambridge, Mass., 1932.

Barr, A. and E.A. Feigenbaum (eds.), The Handbook of Artificial Intelligence, vol. 1, William Kaufman, 1981.

Erman, L.D., The HEARSAY-II Speech Understanding System: Integrating Knowledge to Resolve Uncertainties, Computing Surveys, vol. 12, no. 2, pp. 213–253, June 1980.

Minsky, M.L., Frame System Theory, Thinking: Readings in Cognitive Science, CUP, P.N. Johnson-Laird and P.C. Watson (eds.), Cambridge, Mass., 1975.

Quillian, M.R., Semantic Memory, Semantic Information Processing, M.L. Minsky (ed.), MIT Press, Cambridge, Mass., 1968.

Shortliffe E. and B.G. Buchanan, A Model of Inexact Reasoning in Medicine, Mathematical Biosciences, vol. 23, pp. 351–379, 1975.

Zadeh, L.A., Fuzzy Sets, Information and Control, vol. 8, 1965.

━━━━━━━ E X E R C I S E S

1. Knowledge can be categorized as either declarative or procedural. Describe the various types of knowledge within each of these categories and give examples for each type.

2. An object-attribute-value triplet can be used to represent a single- or multi-valued fact. Give an example that is appropriate for each type.

3. Provide an example of a fact that might logically change during a session because of changes to other facts.

4. The following statements express a degree of uncertainty. Determine the CF value that should be ascribed to each.
   "I really believe it will rain today."
   "It rarely rains on Tuesday."
   "I think Kathy likes Bob."

5. Choose some subject that can be described in ambiguous or fuzzy terms and draw fuzzy sets that represent the terms.

6. Define a set of rules that are related to automobile diagnostics. At least three rules should be written in a form that allows for inferencing.

7. Describe an application where a variable rule would be appropriate.

8. Write three rules that describe an uncertain relationship and determine the appropriate CF values for each.

9. Describe the value of each of the following. Also, describe a problem that can incorporate each and explain how each is implemented:
   Rule-sets
   Meta-rules
   Blackboard

10. Create a frame structure about an automobile. The upper level class should be AUTOS with subclasses of LUXURY_CARS and SPORT_CARS. Individual instances would be specific cars. Slots in each frame should be defined as appropriate. Discuss the inheritance capability of your structure and discuss the slot values for the instances.

11. Represent each of following statements in the predicate calculus:
    "Popeye loves spinach."
    "Football players are strong."
    "Girls who like strong men like football players."

12. For the blocks world example discussed in this chapter, determine what assertions would be made following the execution of the following implication.

$$\forall X\ \forall Y\ (on(Y,X) \rightarrow above(Y,X))$$

Inference Techniques

MONOTONIC AND NON-MONOTONIC INFERENCE
SUMMARY ON INFERENCE

_____ **INTRODUCTION** _____

Chapter 3 described how knowledge is represented in an expert system. In this chapter, we consider how the system reasons with this knowledge to solve a problem. Reasoning within an expert system is performed using inference techniques and control strategies. Inference techniques guide the system as it combines knowledge contained in its knowledge base with problem facts contained in its working memory. Control strategies establish the goals for the system and also guide its reasoning.

_____ **REASONING** _____

Humans solve problems by combining facts with knowledge. They take facts about a specific problem and use them with their general understanding of the problem domain to derive logical conclusions. This process is called **reasoning.**

DEFINITION 4.1: Reasoning
The process of working with knowledge, facts, and problem solving strategies to draw conclusions.

Understanding how humans reason, how they work with information on a given problem coupled with their general knowledge of the domain, provides insight into how to guide knowledge processing in an expert system.

Deductive Reasoning

Humans use deductive reasoning to deduce new information from logically related known information. Sherlock Holmes, for example, would inspect the evidence at the scene of the crime and form a chain of assertions that leads him to the identity of the criminal.

Deductive reasoning uses problem facts or *axioms* and related general knowledge in the form of rules or *implications*. The process begins with comparing the axioms with a set of implications to conclude new axioms. For example:

Implication: I will get wet if I am standing in the rain $A \rightarrow B$ Modus
Axiom: I am standing in the rain A
Conclusion: I will get wet B ponent

Deductive reasoning is logically appealing and one of the most common problem solving techniques used by humans. The **modus ponens** rule of inference is the basic form of deductive reasoning:

If A is true and if A implies B is true, then B is true

Inductive Reasoning

Humans use inductive reasoning to arrive at a general conclusion from a limited set of facts by the process of *generalization*. Consider the following example:

Premise: Monkeys in the Pittsburgh zoo eat bananas
Premise: Monkeys in the Cleveland zoo eat bananas
Conclusion: In general, all monkeys eat bananas

Through inductive reasoning, we form a generalization which we believe applies to *all* cases of a certain type, on the basis of a *limited* number of cases. It is the transition from *a few* to *all* that contains the heart of inductive reasoning. The induction process is described by Firebaugh (1988):

For a set of objects, X = {a,b,c,d,...}, if property P is true for a, and if P is true for b, and if P is true for c, ..., then P is true for all X.

Abductive Reasoning

Deduction is exact in the sense that inferences drawn from established facts and valid implications are logically correct. Abduction is a form of deduction that allows for *plausible inference*. By ''plausible'' it is meant that the conclusion might follow from the available information, but it might be wrong. For example:

If B is true and if A implies B is true, then A is true ?

To illustrate abduction, consider the following:

Implication: Ground is wet if it is raining $A \rightarrow B$
Axiom: Ground is wet $\dfrac{A}{B\ ?}$
Conclusion: It is raining ?

Given that the only information we have is ''ground is wet,'' a plausible inference might be ''it is raining.'' However, this conclusion could be wrong since there are other ways that the ground could become wet, such as someone watering the grass.

Analogical Reasoning

Humans form a mental model of some concept through their experiences. They use this model through analogical reasoning to help them to understand some situation or object. They draw analogies between the two, looking for similarities and differences to guide their reasoning.

To illustrate analogical reasoning, consider the following frame:

TIGER Frame
    Specialization-of: ANIMALS
    Number-of-legs: 4
    Eats: meat
    Lives: India and Southeast Asia
    Color: tawny with stripes

A frame provides a natural way of capturing stereotypical information. We can use it to represent the typical features of some set of similar objects. For example, in this frame we list several features common to all tigers. If we next state that a lion is like a tiger, we would naturally assume that they then share many of the same features. For example, both eat meat and live in India. However, there are differences. For example, they have different colors and live in different locations. In this fashion, we can use analogical reasoning to obtain some understanding of a new object, and refine this understanding by addressing any specific differences.

Common-Sense Reasoning

Through experience, humans learn to solve problems efficiently. They use their common sense to quickly derive a solution. Common sense reasoning relies more on good judgments than on exact logic. Consider an example drawn from an automobile diagnostic problem:

> *A loose fan belt usually causes strange noises.*

A mechanic might have formed this piece of common sense knowledge from his experience with working on many automobiles. He could then use it to immediately suspect a loose fan belt when working on a car creating strange noises. This type of knowledge is also referred to as a **heuristic;** a rule-of-thumb.

When heuristics are used to guide the problem solving in an expert system, it is called **heuristic search** or **best-first search.** This type of search looks for solutions in the most likely places. It provides no guarantee that a solution will be found in the direction taken; only that the direction taken is a reasonable one. Heuristic search is valuable in applications that require quick solutions.

Non-Monotonic Reasoning

For many situations, we reason about a problem using information that is static. That is, during the course of solving the problem, the state (i.e., true or false) of the various facts remains constant. This type of reasoning is known as **monotonic reasoning.**

In some problems, however, the state of facts changes. To illustrate, we will borrow a passage from a nursery rhyme and represent it in a rule:

When the wind blows, the cradle will rock.

IF   The wind blows
THEN   The cradle will rock

Next, and with another borrow, consider what happens with our rule:

Auntie Em, its a twister! → Wind blows → Cradle rocks

With the passing of the twister we would expect our cradle to rock. However, after the twister is gone we would expect the cradle to stop rocking. A system using monotonic reasoning would retain a rocking cradle.

Humans have little difficulty in keeping track of changing information. When something changes, they can easily adjust other dependent events. This style of reasoning is known as **non-monotonic reasoning.**

An expert system can perform non-monotonic reasoning if it has a **truth maintenance system.** A truth maintenance system maintains a record on *what* caused a fact to be asserted. Therefore, if the cause is removed the fact is likewise retracted. A system using non-monotonic reasoning on the prior example would retract the rocking cradle.

— LOGICALLY (NOT PHYSICALLY!)

―――――――――― **INFERENCE** ――――――――――

Expert systems model the reasoning process of humans using a technique called **inference.**

> **DEFINITION 4.2:** Inference
> **The process used in an expert system of deriving new information from known information.**

An expert system performs inference using a module called the **inference engine.** Chapter 2 defined an inference engine as a processor that works with current information to derive further conclusions. It combines facts contained in the working memory with knowledge contained in the knowledge base. From this action it is able to infer new information that it then adds to the working memory. Figure 4.1 illustrates this process.

The foregoing description of how inference works in an expert system is highly simplified. This discussion overlooks many of the other features of inference. For example, how does the inference engine know:

- What questions to ask the user?
- How to search through the knowledge base?
- How to pick a rule to fire from a number of rules that can fire?
- How does the concluded information influence the search?

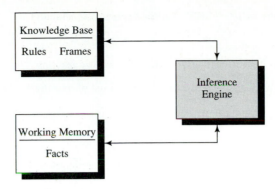

FIGURE 4.1 Inference process in an expert system.

We will answer these questions later in the chapter when we introduce forward and backward inference techniques. Since both techniques have a basis in logical inference, we will review this subject first.

Modus Ponens

Chapter 3 introduced propositional logic and the predicate calculus as formal methods of knowledge representation. Reasoning in logic was also introduced with the simple rule of inference called **modus ponens.**

> **IF** A is true
> **AND** A $\rightarrow$ B is true
> **THEN** B is true

DEFINITION 4.3: Modus Ponens
Rule of logic that asserts that if we know A is true and that A implies B is also true, then we can assume that B is true.

Modus ponens works with axioms (truth statements) to infer new facts. For example, if there is an axiom of the form $E^1 \rightarrow E^2$, and there is another one of the form E^1, then E^2 is logically inferred to be **TRUE.** The axioms can be compiled into a list as follows where axiom 3 follows from 1 and 2:

1. E^1
2. $E^1 \rightarrow E^2$
3. E^2

If another axiom exists of the form $E^2 \rightarrow E^3$, then E^3 would also be added to the list. To better illustrate modus ponens, consider the following two implications expressed as rules:

1. $E^1 \rightarrow E^2$

IF Temperature > 102   THEN Patient has high temperature

$$2. \ E^2 \rightarrow E^3$$

IF Patient has high temperature   THEN Advise two aspirins

These two implications represent the initial list of axioms as shown in STATE-0.

STATE-0

1. $E^1 \rightarrow E^2$
2. $E^2 \rightarrow E^3$

Next assume that some patient has a temperature greater than 102 degrees. We can then add this new axiom to the list creating STATE-1.

STATE-1

1. $E^1 \rightarrow E^2$
2. $E^2 \rightarrow E^3$
3. E^1—"Temperature > 102"

This new axiom causes axiom 1 to assert E^2 which is added to the list, as shown in STATE-2.

STATE-2

1. $E^1 \rightarrow E^2$
2. $E^2 \rightarrow E^3$
3. E^1—"Temperature > 102"
4. E^2—"Patient has high temperature"

Finally, this new information causes axiom 2 to assert E^3:

STATE-3

1. $E^1 \rightarrow E^2$
2. $E^2 \rightarrow E^3$
3. E^1—"Temperature > 102"
4. E^2—"Patient has high temperature"
5. E^3—"Advise two aspirins"

Working with a set of implications (rules) and initial data, modus ponens forms a series of logical assertions. In this fashion, the inference process is driven by asserted information. This style of inference is the basis of data-driven or forward-chaining expert systems.

Resolution

Modus ponens derives new information from initial problem data. This is the inference process of choice in applications where it is important to learn as much as possible from available information. However, in other applications we need to gather specific information to prove some goal. For example, a doctor attempting to prove that a patient has strep throat would run the appropriate lab tests to obtain supporting evidence. This style of inference is the basis of **resolution;** first introduced by Robinson (1965) and the basic algorithm used in the Prolog language.

DEFINITION 4.4: Resolution
Inference strategy used in logical systems to determine the truth of an assertion.

The resolution method attempts to prove that some theorem or goal expressed as proposition **P** is **TRUE,** given a set of axioms about the problem. This method actually attempts to prove that the negation of the goal ¬**P** cannot be **TRUE,** a technique known as *proof by refutation*. The resolution method involves producing new expressions called *resolvents* from the union of existing axioms and the negated theorem.

To illustrate resolution, assume there exist two axioms of the form A $\lor$ B (A is true or B is true) and ¬B $\lor$ C (B is not true or C is true). The resolution method forms the resolvent of these two axioms by joining them with a logical AND:

$$(A \lor B) \land (\neg B \lor C) = A \lor C$$

We obtain this result by means of logical addition:

A $\lor$ B
¬B $\lor$ C

giving   A $\lor$ C   since   B AND ¬B   cancel

These resolvents are then added to the list of axioms and new resolvents are derived. This process continues until a *contradiction* is produced. A contradiction is simply two axioms that are logically contradictory, such as **P** and ¬**P.** A contradiction implies that the proposition is **TRUE,** that is, **P** is **TRUE.**

The resolution algorithm is summarized in the following steps:

1. Assume ¬P is **TRUE.**
2. Show that the axioms and ¬P lead to a contradiction.
3. Conclude that ¬P is **FALSE** since it leads to a contradiction.
4. Conclude that P is **TRUE,** since ¬P is **FALSE.**

Before introducing an example of resolution, recall from the discussion given in Chapter 3 that an implication can be written two ways that are logically equivalent:

A $\rightarrow$ B i.e., IF A THEN B
¬A $\lor$ B i.e., either A is not true or B is true

To better illustrate resolution, consider the following axioms used earlier in the modus ponens example:

1. $\neg E^1 \vee E^2$—IF   Temperature > 102
            THEN   Patient has high temperature

2. $\neg E^2 \vee E^3$—IF   Patient has high temperature
            THEN   Advise two aspirins

3. E^1—Temperature > 102

We want to prove that E^3 (Advise two aspirins) is **TRUE.** According to the resolution algorithm, we first assume that the negation of the proposition is **TRUE,** namely $\neg E^3$. We then add this to our list of axioms as shown in STATE-0.

STATE-0

1. $\neg E^1 \vee E^2$
2. $\neg E^2 \vee E^3$
3. E^1
4. $\neg E^3$

We next resolve the axioms 1 and 2:

$$\frac{\neg E^1 \vee E^2}{\neg E^2 \vee E^3}$$
$$\neg E^1 \vee E^3$$

Adding this resolvant to the list produces STATE-1:

STATE-1

1. $\neg E^1 \vee E^2$
2. $\neg E^2 \vee E^3$
3. E^1
4. $\neg E^3$
5. $\neg E^1 \vee E^3$

Resolving axioms 3 with 5 results in:

$$\frac{E^1}{\neg E^1 \vee E^3}$$
$$E^3$$

Adding the result to the axiom list produces STATE-2:

STATE-2

1. $\neg E^1 \vee E^2$
2. $\neg E^2 \vee E^3$
3. E^1
4. $\neg E^3$
5. $\neg E^1 \vee E^3$
6. E^3

This final result reveals a contradiction between axioms 4 and 6. Therefore, we conclude that $\neg E^3$ is **FALSE** since it leads to a contradiction (Step 3 of algorithm). We also conclude that E^3 is **TRUE,** since $\neg E^3$ is **FALSE** (Step 4 of algorithm). For our problem, the initial goal "Advise two aspirins" is established. This is the same result that was obtained earlier using modus ponens. However, the approach taken is considerably different.

In modus ponens, the data in the form of asserted information initiated the search and the result was found through the use of logical implications. If the problem had many implications, then the result might have been "stumbled across" in the process of inferring all possible information. Resolution maintains a focus on the goal it is attempting to establish. It considers only those implications that are relevant to the task.

The resolution style of inference illustrated here is based in propositional logic. One based in the predicate calculus would be similar but more complex, requiring procedures for working with variables and quantifiers. This involves operations known as the *unification algorithm* and the introduction of *Skolem functions* (Luger and Stubblefield 1989).

Nonresolution

In resolution, no distinction is made between goals, premises, or rules. They are all added to a list of axioms and then processed with the resolution rule of inference. This style of processing can be confusing since we loose sight of what we are attempting to prove. A **nonresolution** or **natural-deduction** technique attempts to overcome this problem by proving some statement in a goal-directed manner. To accomplish this, natural-deduction uses a *back-chain* rule of inference in the following form (Cohen and Feigenbaum 1982):

$$\text{To prove } [H \wedge (A \rightarrow B) \rightarrow C]:$$
$$\text{If } (B \rightarrow C), \text{ then prove } (H \rightarrow A).$$

To illustrate this approach, consider the following problem. Assume we want to prove that Jack likes the Pittsburgh Steelers football team. Further assume that everyone who lives in Pittsburgh likes the Steelers. Therefore, if we can determine that Jack lives in Pittsburgh, then we could prove our goal. We can represent this problem as follows:

Antecedents:

[Lives-Pittsburgh(Jack) $\wedge$ (Lives-Pittsburgh(X) $\rightarrow$ Likes-Steelers(X))

Goal:

$\rightarrow$ Likes-Steelers(Jack)]:

To prove **Likes-Steelers(Jack),** the antecedents are scanned for something that allows for the conclusion of **Likes-Steelers(Jack),** and if found, it becomes a new subgoal to prove. In this example, we see that we can prove the goal if(**Lives-Pittsburgh(X)** $\rightarrow$ **Likes-Steelers(X)**)), and (**Lives-Pittsburgh(Jack)**). Therefore, the new subgoal would be to prove (**Lives-Pittsburgh(Jack)**).

Natural resolution is appealing because it allows the user to follow the progress of the search and interact with it occasionally to help with the proof. Natural resolution was successfully demonstrated in a system called IMPLY (Bledsoe 1977). It also has some of the same features seen in goal-driven or backward-chaining expert systems, as shown later in the chapter.

FORWARD-CHAINING

The solution process for some problems naturally begins by collecting information. This information is then reasoned with to infer logical conclusions. For example, a doctor normally begins patient diagnosis by first asking the patient about his or her symptoms. Sore throat, high temperature, or coughing are typical responses. The doctor then uses this information to infer a reasonable conclusion or to establish a hypothesis to further explore. This style of reasoning is modeled in an expert system using data-driven search; it is also called **forward-chaining**. Forward-chaining is similar to modus ponens discussed earlier.

> **DEFINITION 4.5**: Forward-Chaining
> **Inference strategy that begins with a set of known facts, derives new facts using rules whose premises match the known facts, and continues this process until a goal state is reached or until no further rules have premises that match the known or derived facts.**

The simplest application of forward-chaining in a rule-based expert system proceeds as follows. The system first obtains problem information from the user and places it in the working memory. The inference engine then scans the rules in some predefined sequence looking for one whose premises match the contents in the working memory. If it finds a rule, it adds the rule's conclusion to the working memory (called *firing* the rule) then cycles and checks the rules again looking for new matches. On the new cycle, rules that previously fired are ignored. This process continues until no matches are found. At this point the working memory contains information supplied by the user and inferred by the system. Figure 4.2 shows a flowchart of this simple form of forward-chaining. Later in this chapter you will see more advanced ways of using forward-chaining.

Forward-Chaining Example

To illustrate this simple style of forward-chaining consider the following example. Assume a patient comes into a doctor's office complaining about certain aliments. The doctor's job is to determine what is wrong with the patient using her general

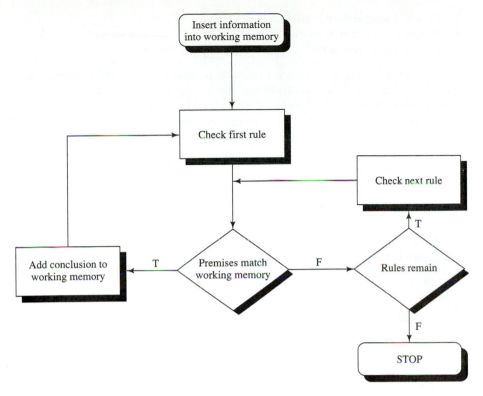

FIGURE 4.2   Forward chaining inference process.

medical knowledge coupled with information supplied by the patient. In this example, we want to model the doctor's diagnostic procedure in a forward-chaining rule-based expert system. To keep the example simple, we will limit the problem to diagnosing strep throat. Our system's rules are as follows:

Rule 1

IF	The patient has a sore throat
AND	We suspect a bacterial infection
THEN	We believe the patient has strep throat

Rule 2

IF	The patient's temperature is > 100
THEN	The patient has a fever

Rule 3

IF	The patient has been sick over a month
AND	The patient has a fever
THEN	We suspect a bacterial infection

We next assert the following facts into the working memory as supplied by the patient:

[Handwritten margin notes:]

WORKING Memory

- TEMP = 102
- SICK FOR 2 Mo
- Sore Throat

① We start with Premises

② IF PREMISE → CONCLUSION IS ADDED TO THE WORKING MEMORY

Patient's temperature = 102
Patient has been sick for two months
Patient has a sore throat

Figure 4.3 illustrates the forward-chaining processing of this information with our three rules. As shown in this figure, the system takes each rule in turn and checks to see if its premises are listed in the working memory. When the system finds matches for all the premises, it places the rule's conclusion in the working memory. It then cycles and repeats the process. In this fashion, the system gains new problem information that it uses for further reasoning. When no new rules emerge that can fire, the system stops.

From the initial information entered into the working memory, the system concludes three new pieces of information from the rules:

1. The patient has a fever
2. We suspect a bacterial infection
3. We believe the patient has strep throat

Forward-chaining systems conclude everything possible from available information. In some applications this approach is appropriate. However, in other applications it may produce unnecessary information. Consider for instance what happens if we add the following two rules to the prior example:

Rule 4
IF   The patient has a fever
THEN   The patient can't go out on a date

Rule 5
IF   The patient cannot go out on a date
THEN   The patient should stay home and read a book

In the prior example the system was able to determine that the patient has a fever. This information would cause both RULE 4 and RULE 5 to fire. This results in the conclusion that the patient cannot go out on a date but should stay home and read a book. This new information may be important to the patient, but the patient's social life is probably not a major concern of the doctor. However, the forward-chaining inference engine had no way of knowing that this information was not important.

In general, a forward-chaining system has no way of knowing if some information might be more important than others. Therefore, it spends as much time gathering trivial evidence as it does gathering crucial facts.

Conflict Resolution

In the prior example of forward-chaining, the system checked the rules in order and immediately fired a rule when its premises matched the contents of the working memory. It then cycled and repeated the process. However, there may have been other rules that could have fired, but were not considered by the system

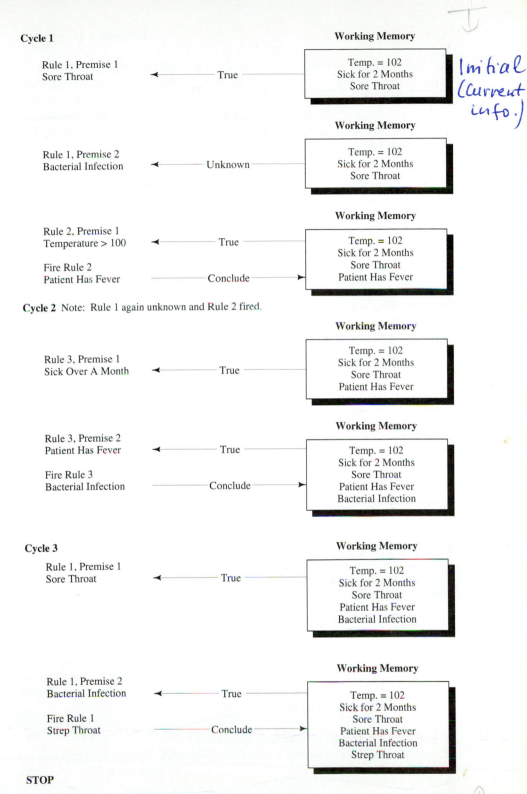

Cycle 1

Rule 1, Premise 1
Sore Throat
◄— True —— Working Memory: Temp. = 102 / Sick for 2 Months / Sore Throat

Initial (current info.)

Rule 1, Premise 2
Bacterial Infection
◄— Unknown —— Working Memory: Temp. = 102 / Sick for 2 Months / Sore Throat

Rule 2, Premise 1
Temperature > 100
◄— True

Fire Rule 2
Patient Has Fever
—— Conclude —► Working Memory: Temp. = 102 / Sick for 2 Months / Sore Throat / Patient Has Fever

Cycle 2 Note: Rule 1 again unknown and Rule 2 fired.

Rule 3, Premise 1
Sick Over A Month
◄— True —— Working Memory: Temp. = 102 / Sick for 2 Months / Sore Throat / Patient Has Fever

Rule 3, Premise 2
Patient Has Fever
◄— True

Fire Rule 3
Bacterial Infection
—— Conclude —► Working Memory: Temp. = 102 / Sick for 2 Months / Sore Throat / Patient Has Fever / Bacterial Infection

Cycle 3

Rule 1, Premise 1
Sore Throat
◄— True —— Working Memory: Temp. = 102 / Sick for 2 Months / Sore Throat / Patient Has Fever / Bacterial Infection

Rule 1, Premise 2
Bacterial Infection
◄— True

Fire Rule 1
Strep Throat
—— Conclude —► Working Memory: Temp. = 102 / Sick for 2 Months / Sore Throat / Patient Has Fever / Bacterial Infection / Strep Throat

STOP

FIGURE 4.3 Trace of forward-chaining example.

because of the cyclic action. Therefore, since the inference engine processes the rules in order, it follows that rule order may be important. This approach can cause difficulties in some applications as illustrated by the following example.

Consider the problem of determining what I should do tonight. Assume two choices are available: go to a ballgame or go to the theater. The following two rules aid in the selection:

Rule 1
IF　　　The Steelers are playing today
AND　　I have at least $20
THEN　I should go to the ballgame

Rule 2
IF　　　My favorite movie is playing today
AND　　I have at least $20
THEN　I should go to the theater

Assume that the premises of these two rules are true. Using the conventional forward-chaining approach, both rules will fire and conclude that I should go both to the ballgame and the theater. Obviously a conflict exists between these two recommendations.

To resolve conflicts in an expert system, designers use some conflict resolution strategy. One simple strategy is to first establish a goal and stop the system when the goal is attained. In our problem for example, we might define a goal "I should go to the ?X." When the system determines a value for ?X, such as ballgame or theater, it stops and presents this recommendation. Using this strategy, the ordering of the rules that conclude the goal is important. In the example given, the system would recommend going to the ballgame, even though I may now miss my favorite movie.

A different type of strategy relies on rule priorities. A rule priority is simply a number assigned to a rule that represents its importance. Using this strategy during forward-chaining, the system checks all the rules during one cycle and identifies those that can fire given the contents of the working memory. It then fires the rule with the highest priority.

Consider using this strategy for our example, along with stopping the system when it establishes our previous goal. Assume we assign RULE 2 a higher priority than RULE 1. This simply means that I prefer the theater over a ballgame. In this case, the system fires RULE 2 recommending a ballgame and stops. Using this strategy, rule order is not important.

The prior discussion illustrates that the simple form of forward-chaining shown in Figure 4.3 may not be appropriate for all problems. You may want to use some strategy for choosing a rule to fire when several compete. This issue is formally called **conflict resolution.**

DEFINITION 4.6: Conflict Resolution
Strategy used for choosing a rule-firing sequence when more than one rule can fire.

In systems that use conflict resolution, the inference engine follows a three-step *recognize–resolve–act* process when cycling through the rules.

1. *Recognize.* Match the premises of all the rules to the facts listed in the working memory, and identify those rules that can fire.
2. *Resolve.* If more than one rule can fire, choose one rule to fire according to some strategy.
3. *Act.* Fire the rule and add its conclusion to the working memory.

The *recognize* step identifies the rules that can fire and places them in a *conflict set*. The *resolve* step uses some strategy to choose a rule from the conflict set. Typical conflict resolution strategies used are:

1. First rule that matches contents of working memory.
2. Highest priority rule.
3. Most specific rule.
4. Rule that refers to the element most recently added to the working memory.
5. Don't fire a rule that has already fired.
6. Fire all rules with separate line of reasoning.

The first strategy uses a first come first served technique and relies on rule order. In many simple applications, this strategy will work and not cause a problem. However, as our earlier example illustrated, this strategy can lead to problems in some applications.

The second strategy uses rule priorities that place an emphasis on the more important rules. This strategy directs the system to reason with information in order of importance.

The third strategy assumes that a more specific rule is preferable to a general rule. A rule is more specific than another if it has more premises. The philosophy behind this strategy is that it ''seems'' more reasonable to select the rule that processes the most information.

The fourth strategy prefers rules whose premises were most recently added to the working memory. It relies on time tags assigned to each fact in the working memory. This strategy directs the system to reason with information most recently obtained during the session.

The fifth strategy prevents looping. It is an added strategy used by the other strategies.

The sixth strategy fires all the rules in a conflict set but adds their conclusions to separate working memories. This permits the system to maintain separate lines of reasoning and to consider alternative solutions. This advanced strategy is called ''Viewpoints'' in ART and ''Worlds'' in KEE.

Each conflict resolution strategy provides control over the firing of rules. You can use them to add to the system a *heuristic search* ability (discussed later), that directs it to search the rules intelligently. The choice of which one (or more than one) to use depends on the needs of the application.

FORWARD

Back WARD

BACKWARD-CHAINING

Forward-chaining is a good inference technique if we are working with a problem that requires us to begin with information and then derive logical conclusions. In other problems, we begin with a hypothesis and then attempt to prove it by gathering supporting information. For example, a doctor may suspect some problem with a patient, which he then attempts to prove by looking for certain symptoms. This style of reasoning is modeled in an expert system using goal-driven search; it is also called **backward-chaining.**

> **DEFINITION 4.7:** Backward-Chaining
> **Inference strategy that attempts to prove a hypothesis by gathering supporting information.**

A backward-chaining system begins with a goal to prove. It first checks the working memory to see if the goal has been previously added. This step is necessary since another knowledge base may have already proven the goal. If the goal has not been previously proven, the system searches its rules looking for one (or more) that contains the goal in its THEN part. This type of rule is called a *goal rule*. The system then checks to see if the goal rule's premises are listed in the working memory. Premises not listed then become new goals (also called *subgoals*) to prove, that may be supported by other rules. This process continues in this recursive manner, until the system finds a premise that is not supported by any rule—a **primitive.**

> **DEFINITION 4.8:** Primitive
> Premise of a rule that is not concluded by any rule.

When a primitive is found, the system asks the user for information about it. The system then uses this information to help prove both the subgoals and the original goal. The backward-chaining process is similar to hypothesis testing in human problem solving.

Backward-Chaining Example

To illustrate the backward-chaining process consider the following example. Assume a patient comes into a doctor's office and, after listening to the patient discuss her problem, the doctor believes the patient has strep throat. The doctor's job now is to prove this belief. In this example, we want to model the doctor's diagnostic procedure in a backward-chaining rule-based expert system. To keep the example simple, we will limit the problem to diagnosing strep throat. Our system's rules are as follows:

Rule 1
IF   There are signs of throat infection
AND   There is evidence that the organism is streptococcus
THEN Patient has strep throat

Step 1

Goal-Patient has strep-throat

Working Memory

Step 2

Goal known ◄────── No ──────

Step 3

Find rules with goal in then Part -Rule 1

Step 4

No

See if Rule 1, Premise 1 is known "There are signs of throat infection" ◄────┘ No

Step 5

Find rules with this Premise in then Part-Rule 2

Step 6

See if Rule 2, Premise 1 is known "The patient's throat is red"

Step 7

Find Rule with this Premise in then Part-None

Step 8

This Premise is a "Primitive" resulting in the following question and answer, and the firing of Rule 2:

Q: Is the patient's throat red?

Working Memory

A: True ────────────►

Patient's Throat Red

Rule 2 fires ────────────►

Throat Infection

"There are signs of throat infection"

No

Step 9

See if Rule 1, Premise 2 is known "There is evidence that the organism is streptococcus" ◄─┘

Step 10

Find rules with his premise in then Part-Rule 3

Step 11

The next series of steps follow that demonstrated above. All three premises of Rule 3 are primitives resulting in questions to the user. Assume the answer to each question is true. The system adds this new information to the working memory along with the fact "there is evidence that the organism is streptococcus," which is added by the firing of Rule 3.

Step 12

Working Memory

Since we were able to prove the premises of our original goal rule, i.e., Rule 1, it fires and adds its conclusion to the working memory.

Patient's Throat Red
Throat Infection
Stain is Grampos
Morphology is Coccus

"Patient has strep throat" ────────────►

Growth is Chains
Patient has Strep Throat

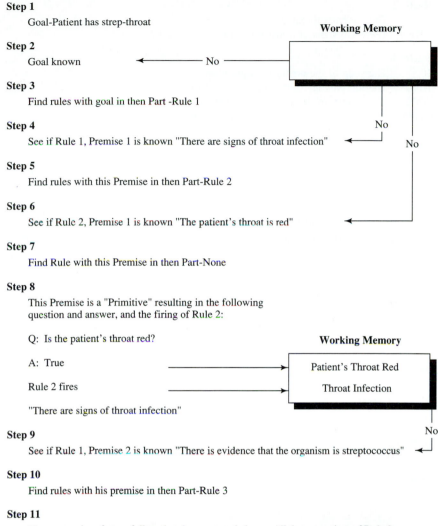

FIGURE 4.4   Trace of backward-chaining example.

Rule 2
IF   The patient's throat is red
THEN   There are signs of throat infection

Rule 3
IF   The stain of the organism is grampos
AND   The morphology of the organism is coccus
AND   The growth of the organism is chains
THEN   There is evidence that the organism is streptococcus

The objective of our system is to prove the goal "Patient has strep throat," the conclusion of RULE 1. Figure 4.4 shows an account of the backward-chaining process followed in this example. Figure 4.5 illustrates the process as a search through a tree structure that graphically shows the logical relationships between the rules.

To prove this goal, the backward-chaining inference engine processes these rules by first selecting the goal rule RULE 1. It then attempts to prove the

Rule 1
If There are signs of throat infection
And There is evidence that the organism is streptococcus
Then Patient has strep throat ——————————— GOAL ———

Rule 2
If The patient's throat is red
Then There are signs of throat infection

Rule 3
If The stain of the organism is grampos
And The morphology of the organism is coccus
And The growth of the organism is chains
Then There is evidence that the organism is streptococcus

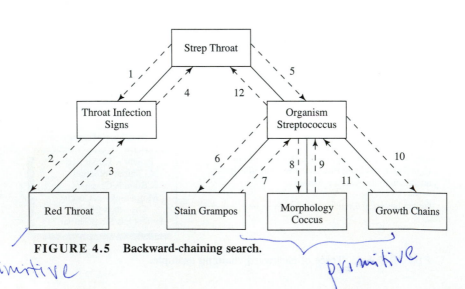

FIGURE 4.5   Backward-chaining search.

premises of this rule. Since both premises are conclusions of other rules, each premise becomes a subgoal to prove. To prove "There are signs of throat infection," the system checks the premises of RULE 2. To prove "There is evidence that the organism is streptococcus," the system checks the premises of RULE 3. All of these premises are primitives requiring the user to supply information. Since in this example the system was able to prove these two rules, the premises of the goal rule were also proven, along with the initial goal that the patient has strep throat.

Goal Agenda

Simple backward-chaining begins with the system having a given goal to prove. Every backward-chaining system needs at least one goal to begin the session. However, in many applications the system needs to pursue a series of goals in an established sequence. This is called a **goal agenda.**

> **DEFINITION 4.9:** Goal Agenda
> **A series of goals to pursue in a prescribed sequence.**

A goal agenda can be a simple ordered list of goals, such as:

1. Goal1
2. Goal2
3. Goal3

The system would pursue the goals in the order they appear on the agenda. You can use this type of goal agenda if the problem naturally follows a sequential process.

You can also instruct the system on what to do when a goal is proven. That is, you may want the system to try to prove every goal on the agenda, or to stop after it has successfully proven only one goal. Consider for example the following list of goals:

1. Recommend you purchase a television
2. Recommend you purchase a radio
3. Recommend you purchase a computer

Using this goal agenda, the system tries to determine a purchase for the user. If the user can purchase only one item, then you can instruct the system to stop after proving one goal. If the user wants a list of everything he or she should consider purchasing, you can permit the system to pursue every goal.

You can use a more complex agenda to instruct the system what to do in the event a goal is found true or false. Consider for example a problem of identifying an unknown animal. You could use the following agenda to refine the animal's identity:

1. The animal is a bird
    1.1 The bird is a robin
    1.2 The bird is a finch
        1.2.1 It is a golden finch
        1.2.2 It is a brown finch
2. The animal is a mammal
    2.1 The mammal is a horse
    2.2 The mammal is a cow
3. The animal is a reptile

In this example, the system first tries to prove that the animal is a bird, mammal, or reptile. If the animal is identified as a bird, the system continues in an attempt to prove whether it is a robin or a finch. If it finds the animal to be a finch, the system next tries to prove whether it is a golden or brown finch. If the system is unable to prove that the animal is a bird, it moves on to the second goal and follows the same procedure. The system stops when no further goals exist along its outlined search.

This type of goal agenda offers a natural approach for solving many problems. An expert often attempts to solve a complex problem by first obtaining a general understanding of the problem. The expert then refines this understanding by collecting more specific information.

This type of goal agenda also allows the expert system to play the role of an expert in another important way. At times, an expert will fail to solve a problem. However, he or she may still be able to produce some useful information about the problem. Consider for example our animal identification problem. The expert may fail to identify the exact animal (e.g., golden or brown finch), but might be able to at least tell us the general type of animal (e.g., a bird and finch). By using a goal outline structure, you can instruct the expert system to report high-level findings even if it fails to produce detailed solutions.

User-Established Goals

When you design a goal agenda you define the order in which the system will pursue its goals. At times, this ordered list is too rigid and prevents the system from taking advantage of specific information about the problem under consideration. This situation can lead to problems as illustrated in the following example.

Assume you were developing an expert system to diagnose problems with a large telecommunications switching system composed of ten different modules. You might define a goal agenda that has ten diagnostic goals, one for each module. Also, since there may be no reason for you to believe that one module is more likely to fail than the others, you might elect to order these goals consecutively on the agenda:

GOAL AGENDA

1. Determine fault with Module 1
2. Determine fault with Module 2
   .
   .
   .
10. Determine fault with Module 10

Now consider an application of this system. Assume a technician notices smoke coming from the tenth module and immediately runs to your expert system for help. The system begins its diagnosis by asking a question related to module one, item 1 on the agenda. This process continues until the system concludes there are no problems with units one through nine. At this point, the system begins to ask questions about a module that has very likely by now melted into the ground.

To avoid this type of problem, you should design the system to work with an **intelligent user.** By "intelligent" it is meant that the user has information that can help guide the system. One simple way you can accomplish this is to present the user with a menu of goals to pursue at the beginning of the session. Using this approach in our prior example, the user would direct the system immediately to module ten diagnosis. If the user has no information to direct the search, the system will default back to its prescribed goal outline.

You can also use this same idea during the session, when the system is pursuing subgoals. Consider for example the animal identification problem. If the system has established that the animal is a bird, you could present the user with the list of birds that the system could identify, such as goals 1.1 and 1.2. If the user knows the specific type of bird, such as finch, the system could avoid unneeded search and proceed to try to identify what type of finch.

Rule-Established Goals

In some applications, it is valuable to establish goals through the firing of rules. This approach permits the system to adapt its search according to problem findings. To illustrate this approach, consider an amplifier design problem.

One design issue the expert system would need to consider is the choice of the amplifier's output power transistors. These devices are chosen on the basis of the required output power of the unit. An additional part called a "heat sink" might be needed if the required output power exceeds a certain level. A heat sink dissipates heat from a transistor which prolongs its life. Since a heat sink might be needed, but not always, you could include the following rule that changes the system's goal:

IF   The output of the amplifier is above 10 watts
THEN   We must use high power output transistors
AND   Set new goal to design transistor heat sink

Allowing an expert system to control the order of search on the basis of discovered information is an important feature of intelligent systems. As illustrated in this example, one way you can accomplish this is to include a rule that changes the system's goal. This special type of rule is called a **meta-rule.**

ADVANTAGES AND DISADVANTAGES OF CHAINING TECHNIQUES

Forward and backward-chaining are the two basic inference techniques used in expert systems. Each technique has advantages and disadvantages.

Advantages of Forward-Chaining

- A major advantage of forward-chaining is that it works well when the problem naturally begins by gathering information and then seeing what can be inferred from it, such as

      Patient has a high temperature and a sore throat . . .

- Forward-chaining can provide a considerable amount of information from only a small amount of data:

DATA		NEW INFORMATION
Raining →	Grass is wet →	Can't mow grass
	Game cancelled →	Go to theater

- Forward-chaining is an excellent approach for certain types of problem solving tasks, such as planning, monitoring, control, and interpretation.

Disadvantages of Forward-Chaining

- One of the major disadvantages of a forward-chaining system is that it may have no means of recognizing that some evidence might be more important than others. The system will ask all possible questions, even though it may only need to ask a few questions to arrive at a conclusion.

      Q. Do you believe you are suffering a heart attack?
      A. YES . . . YES . . . YES

      Q. Is your nose running?
      A. WHAT!

- The system may also ask unrelated questions. Though the answers to these questions may be important, it is disconcerting to users to answer questions on unrelated subjects.

Q. Do you have a high temperature?

Q. Have you visited England lately?

Advantages of Backward-Chaining

- One of the major advantages of a backward-chaining system is that it works well when the problem naturally begins by forming a hypothesis and then seeing if it can be proven:

  "I believe the patient has strep throat."

- Backward-chaining remains focused on a given goal. This produces a series of questions on related topics, a situation that is comfortable for the user:

IF	Patient's symptoms indicate strep throat
AND	Patient's tests indicate strep throat
THEN	Conclude that the patient has strep throat

  Note: Line of questioning will concentrate first on "patient's symptoms" then on "patient's tests."

- Whereas a forward-chaining system attempts to infer everything possible from available information, a backward-chaining system searches only that part of the knowledge base that is relevant to the current problem.
- Backward-chaining is an excellent approach for certain types of problem solving tasks, such as diagnostics, prescription, and debugging.

Disadvantages of Backward-Chaining

- The principal disadvantage of a backward-chaining system is that it will continue to follow a given line of reasoning even if it should drop it and switch to a different one. The use of confidence factors and meta-rules can help this problem and are discussed in Chapter 12.

——————— CHOOSING BETWEEN FORWARD AND BACKWARD-CHAINING ———————

Now that we have reviewed both backward and forward-chaining and seen how they work and some of their advantages and limitations, the question is, When should we use one or the other? The short answer is **know your problem!**

Simply listening to or watching an expert solve a problem will provide insight into the proper choice. An expert at times will collect some basic information on the problem and use it to direct his or her problem solving. Other times, the expert will begin with a very specific goal to prove and gather evidence to support his or her belief.

The task of considering the search space looks at the number of possible conclusions or data that are available. For example, a doctor may know of hundreds of possible problems that can occur with an individual. It would be foolish for the doctor to try to prove one of these without first obtaining some preliminary data from the patient. In this case, you would employ forward-chaining. If the problem was to prove or disprove strep throat, you would have only two goals but would need to obtain a considerable amount of data to prove either one. In this case, you would use a backward-chaining technique.

Another practical recommendation is to review what others have done in the past for applications similar to yours. In particular, review past projects that use similar problem solving tasks such as planning, diagnosis, and so forth. Expert system designers traditionally use the same inference technique for a given problem solving task, regardless of the application area.

Finally, don't worry if you make the wrong choice. When you evaluate the prototype system you will know if the chosen inference technique suits the problem. In general, it is easy to change the technique early in the project.

In summary, when making a choice between the two techniques, consider the following:

- How does the expert solve it?
- Does he or she first collect data and then see what can be inferred from it?—**FORWARD-CHAINING**
- Does he/she hypothesize a solution and then sees if it can be proven?—**BACKWARD-CHAINING**
- Consider the search space
  —More data needed than conclusions?—**BACKWARD**
  —More conclusions than data?—**FORWARD**

- See what others have done in past applications similar to yours.
- Prototype the system early and evaluate the choice of the inference technique.

———— COMBINING FORWARD AND
BACKWARD-CHAINING ————

Many expert systems use both forward and backward-chaining. This is typically seen in applications where different tasks are naturally performed in either a data-driven or goal-driven fashion. Consider for example a medical diagnosis problem. A doctor will first obtain patient symptom information to form some hypothesis. The doctor would then test the hypothesis by searching for supporting information. An expert system built to model the doctor would use forward-chaining for the first task and backward-chaining for the second.

Expert system designers typically combine forward and backward-chaining techniques using one of two methods. The first method relies on separate systems, each with its own inference strategy. The second method incorporates *demons* within a backward-chaining system that act in a forward-chaining fashion.

Separate Systems

For complex problems, expert system designers often first divide the problem into subtasks, then design a separate expert system to address each subtask. Each system solves one part of the problem, then passes control on to another system. One advantage to this approach is each system can have its own inference technique. To illustrate this approach, consider again the medical diagnosis problem discussed in the prior section.

To address the first task, you could write a forward-chaining system that takes the patient information and infers a likely hypothesis. This system could then, through the action of a meta-rule, turn control over to the proper system that would try to prove the hypothesis through backward-chaining.

Assume for example that the forward-chaining system had the following rule:

RULE Suspect meningitis
IF   Patient is suffering persistent headaches
AND   Patient is suffering dizziness
THEN   There is evidence of meningitis

If after gathering information from the patient this rule-fires, the following meta-rule would also fire, turning control over to the "Meningitis_Expert" expert system:

RULE Meta-rule for meningitis study
IF   There is evidence of meningitis
THEN   LOAD **Meningitis_Expert**

This new expert system would attempt to prove meningitis in a backward-chaining fashion.

Demon Rules

Another way expert system designers combine forward and backward-chaining is through the use of **demon rules.**

DEFINITION 4.10: Demon Rule
A rule that fires whenever its premises match the contents of the working memory.

A demon rule sits among other backward-chaining rules, but it does not participate in the backward-chaining process. Rather, it remains dormant until information contained in its premises appears in the working memory. When this occurs, the demon fires and enters its conclusion into the working memory. This new information might support the backward-chaining rules, or it might set into motion other demon rules that collectively act like a series of forward-chaining rules. A demon rule allows the system to be self-modifying, which is essential for applications that need to adapt to new situations.

To illustrate the use of demon rules, consider the problem area of factory diagnostics. Assume the factory has several machines that work together in the fabrication of some product. Also assume that if one machine has a problem, the fabrication process must be shut down while machine diagnostics is performed. We will further assume that an expert system performs the diagnostics using backward-chaining inference.

During diagnosis, the system would first need to perform several standard steps such as shutting the power, releasing tank pressures, etc. It would next need to gather information to determine the cause of the fault and then take steps to correct the fault. However, consideration should also be given to the possibility of some unusual event, one that would cause the system to break off the normal diagnostic steps and address the event immediately. To accommodate this possibility, assume the following demon rules were embedded in the diagnostic system:

Demon 1 Tank Pressure Problem
IF Power is off
AND Tank pressure > 1000
THEN PROBLEM = Tank Pressure Problem

Demon 2 Emergency Situation
IF PROBLEM = TANK PRESSURE PROBLEM
THEN SITUATION = EMERGENCY

Demon 3 Evacuate
IF SITUATION = EMERGENCY
THEN RESPONSE = EVACUATE PERSONNEL

DEMON 1 fires if the normal procedure of shutting the power off is accomplished but the tank pressure remains high. The firing of this demon causes DEMON 2 to also fire asserting that a plant emergency exists. You could write other demons that are similar to DEMON 2, which would classify the plant's situation into other categories such as NORMAL, ALERT, and so forth. DEMON 3 forms the appropriate response to the emergency situation. You could also write other demons to respond to different situations.

This example illustrates how you can embed demons within a backward-chaining system that can respond to changing conditions. You can use them to adapt the system's reasoning according to current events. This ability is important in real-time systems and is called *event-driven inference*.

──────────── **BASIC SEARCH TECHNIQUES** ────────────

AI researchers like to view a problem's knowledge represented graphically in a **problem space,** through which problem solving proceeds as a search for a solution to the problem.

DEFINITION 4.11: Problem Space
Tree or graph containing nodes that represent problem states and branches that represent paths or relationships between states.

Nodes represent problem states and branches the possible paths between the nodes. Using this style of problem representation, problem solving can be viewed as navigating between the nodes over the branches in search of a solution node.

We can extend this view to the world of expert systems. We can use nodes to represent premises and conclusions of rules, and branches for their relationships. The graphical problem space created using this approach is often called an **inference network.**

To illustrate the way an expert system searches through a problem space to solve a problem, we will consider a small wine selection example. The problem is to pick the right type of wine to serve with a meal: red or white. We will use the following list of rules to make this decision, along with their problem space representation shown in Figure 4.6.

Rule 1
IF   You purchase meat—P1
THEN   You should serve red wine—C1

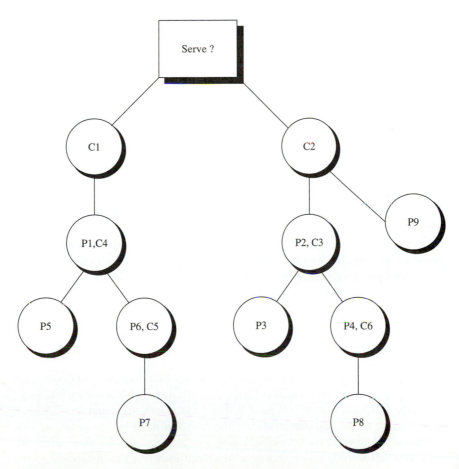

FIGURE 4.6   Wine selection problem space.

Rule 2
IF   You purchase fish—P2
THEN   You should serve white wine—C2

Rule 3
IF   The store has fish—P3
AND   You have enough money to buy fish—P4
THEN   You purchase fish—C3

Rule 4
IF   The store has meat—P5
AND   You have enough money to buy meat—P6
THEN   You purchase meat—C4

Rule 5
IF   You have greater than or equal to $10—P7
THEN   You have enough money to buy meat—C5

Rule 6
IF   You have between $5 and $10—P8
THEN   You have enough money to buy fish—C6

Rule 7
IF   You really like white wine—P9
THEN   You should serve white wine—C2

In any expert system application, the problem is to search through the problem space and locate a solution. In a backward-chaining system, the system begins the search at one of the possible solutions, that is, nodes C1 or C2. It continues the search down through the branches to the other nodes looking for supporting information. In a forward- chaining system, the system begins the search at one of the primitives or leaf nodes of the network, namely nodes P3, P5, P7, P8, or P9. It then searches up through the branches to the other nodes to see if it can locate a goal node.

In the sections on forward and backward-chaining, simple algorithms were given for each that showed how they search through knowledge. However, expert system designers have additional control over both chaining techniques that come in the form of depth-first search, breadth-first search and best-first search.

Depth-First Search

In depth-first search, the search begins at some starting node and continues until either a "dead-end" or the goal is found. At each node some arbitrary rule (e.g., "take the left most branch") is used to direct the search. If a dead-end is found, the search is backed up one level, and the next left most branch is taken. This operation is known as *backtracking*. Using a convention that the alternatives are tried in a left-to-right order, this type of search makes a headlong dash to the bottom of the search space along the left-most branches. This is the essence of **depth-first search.**

DEFINITION 4.12: Depth-First Search
Search technique that looks for a solution along each branch of a problem space to its full vertical length, then proceeds in some defined order, such as from left to right.

Figure 4.7 illustrates a backward-chaining depth-first search for the problem space of Figure 4.6. The search begins with trying to determine what wine to serve with the meal; the goal of the system. It chooses node C1 first, then searches down through the connected nodes looking for supporting information. If it finds support the search stops. Otherwise, the search continues in a left-to-right fashion.

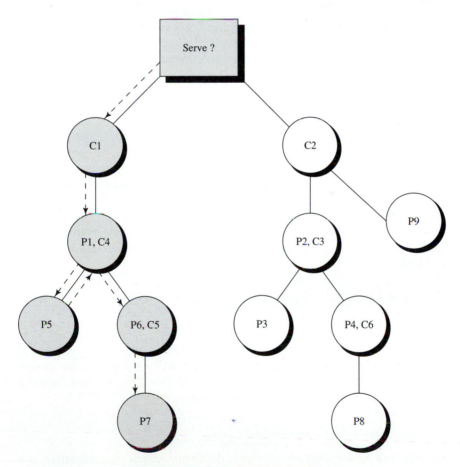

FIGURE 4.7   Depth-first search of wine selection rules.

As shown in Figure 4.7, the problem was solved after examining the five shaded nodes. A recommendation of "red wine" (C1) was made because the "store has meat" (P5) and "money was greater than or equal to $10" (P7). Since the system was able to find a solution in C1, node C2 and all of its descendants were not searched.

Advantages of Depth-First Search

Guarantees Solution

Depth-first search performs an exhaustive exploration of the problem space in an attempt to find a solution. Given that at least one solution exists, a depth-first search technique is guaranteed to find it.

Gets Quickly into Deep Problem Spaces

Depth-first search quickly searches deeply into a problem space. If it is known that the solution path will be long, then depth-first search is a good choice. For example, a game such as chess would require a deep search. Depth-first search will not waste time searching for shallow solutions as is the case with breadth-first search.

Maintains Focus

Depth-first search maintains a focus on a given issue during the search. Consider for instance our wine selection example. Beginning with the goal "serve red wine" (C1), depth-first search pursues the issues of whether you purchased meat (P1), the store has meat (P5), and whether you have enough money to buy meat (P6,C5). In this sense, the search maintains a focus on the issue of "meat."

Maintaining a focus is an advantage in an expert system application that interacts with humans. Humans feel more comfortable when the questions follow a related issue.

Disadvantages of Depth-First Search

Uninformed

Depth-first search blindly explores the problem space looking for a solution. It proceeds along a set path uninformed of any information that might help it move toward a solution. Constrained to follow its rigid algorithm, it could choose a bad starting point, or "shoot on by" a solution.

Inappropriate for Large Problem Spaces

For problems with a large search space, depth-first search may not arrive at a solution in a reasonable amount of time. Applying a depth-first search technique to a complex problem such as chess would require the computer to search through all the possible moves to find the optimal solution, resulting in a combinatorial explosion. To illustrate, consider a chess game with about 10^{70} possible board configurations. Assuming a computer could check each node in a microsecond, it would take approximately 10^{56} years to search completely the problem space!

Inefficient for Shallow Solutions

A depth-first search technique may overlook shallow solutions that can reduce its search effort. It searches along one branch of the tree as deeply as possible before searching another one. This is efficient if a branch containing a shallow solution is considered later during the search.

We can illustrate this point with the help of Figure 4.7. Assume the only information known is "You really like white wine" (P9). Also assume the search begins as before with C1. Depth-first search would exhaustively check the C1 branch before turning its attention to C2. It would also check the path along P2,C3 before arriving at the P9 node.

Breadth-First Search

An alternative search technique is **breadth-first search.**

DEFINITION 4.13: Breadth-First Search
Search technique that looks for a solution along all of the nodes on one level of a problem space before considering nodes at the next lower level.

A breadth-search technique begins searching across the first level of the problem space using some arbitrary rule (e.g., "left to right"). If it is unable to find a solution within this level, it drops down to the next level and searches in the same manner. It repeats this process at each level, probing deeper into the problem space until it can locate a solution.

Figure 4.8 illustrates a breadth-first search for the problem space of Figure 4.6. The problem was solved after examining the five shaded nodes. A recommendation of "white wine" (C2) was made because "You really like white wine" (P9).

Advantages of Breadth-First Search

Guarantees Solution

Like depth-first, one advantage of breadth-first is that the search is exhaustive and will find a solution if one exists.

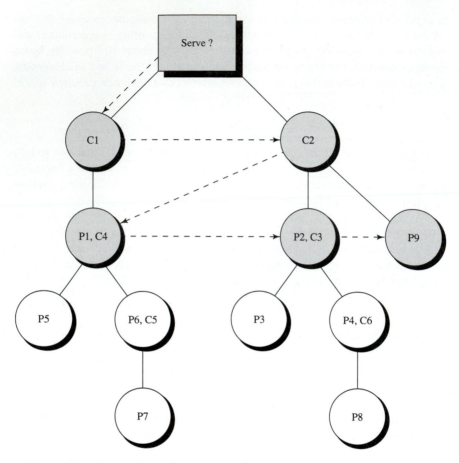

FIGURE 4.8   Breadth-first search of wine selection rules.

D O E S N ' T   M I S S   E A S Y   S O L U T I O N S   Another advantage of a breadth-first search is that it will not miss shallow or easy solutions. This was illustrated in our wine selection example.

Disadvantages of Breadth-First Search

Uninformed

Breadth-first search (like depth-first) is a rigid algorithm that blindly searches the problem space looking for a solution. Without information to help guide the search, it can easily miss a solution.

Inappropriate for Large Search Space

Like depth-first search, a breadth-first search suffers the same difficulty of not being able to realistically search through a large search space.

Inefficient for Deep Solutions

If the solution is located deep in the search space, then the breadth-first search technique is inefficient, since it spends effort looking for shallow solutions first.

Provides Poor User Interaction

Another disadvantage of this search technique rests with its interaction with a human user. Questions asked jump from one issue to another. Unrelated questions on different issues can be unnerving to the user.

Best-First Search

Both depth-first and breadth-first search techniques are basic methods for exploring a problem space. Each exhaustively searches the space for a solution to the problem using a well-defined search procedure. However, both techniques use no knowledge about the state of the problem to help guide their search. They follow their search procedures blindly, even if a better approach might be taken. Because of this, depth-first and breadth-first are often classified as *blind* or *uninformed* search techniques.

An alternative search technique, one that uses knowledge to guide its search (*informed*), is called **best-first search.**

> **DEFINITION 4.14:** **Best-First Search**
> **Search technique that uses knowledge about the problem to guide the search. It guides the search towards the solution nodes of the problem space.**

During the search of a problem space, at each node a best-search technique makes a "judgment" call on which branch to take. That is, it chooses the one it believes will lead to the "best" solution. Understand that the word "best" is open to the interpretation of the designer, and it usually boils down to choosing the path that meets the needs of the problem.

In AI programs, best-first search is implemented using an *evaluation function* (Cohen and Feigenbaum 1982). This function uses current information on important problem issues to assign a numeric to each node under consideration during the search. The node with the highest number is then chosen to search next.

In expert systems, best-first search is implemented using a *heuristic* (a rule of thumb). On the basis of discovered information, a heuristic can choose which system knowledge to process next. Because a heuristic is used to guide the search, it is often called *heuristic search*. Some of the typical ways you can use heuristics in an expert system to guide its search are:

- **Ordering the goals**—Place the goals in an order that best suits the needs of the application. You could place important goals first, or ones that might derive a solution quickly.

- **Ordering the premises**—Place the premises in some preferable order. As in goal ordering, you can use this approach to direct the search towards either important issues or ones that may result in the shortest search effort.
- **Using meta-rules**—Use a meta-rule to redirect the search toward a more productive area. Like a demon, a meta-rule monitors problem information via its premises. When it fires, you can use it to establish new system goals or to load a new knowledge base.
- **Using rule priorities**—Ascribe a priority number to a rule that reflects the importance of the rule. The system's search is directed toward rules with the higher priority numbers.
- **Using confidence factors**—Ascribe a confidence factor to each problem issue, which is a number that reflects the system's belief in the issue. You can further permit the system to pursue those issues with high confidence factors that guide it toward the most likely solutions.

Advantages of Best-First Search

Informed

The principal advantage of a best-first search technique is that it uses knowledge to guide the search. It uses knowledge to know where to best begin and how to best proceed in search of a solution.

Models Human Reasoning

Best-first search follows the reasoning process of a human expert. Humans apply knowledge to aid their reasoning and rarely rely on blind techniques such as seen in the depth-first and breadth-first search methods.

Disadvantages of Best-First Search

No Guarantee of Finding a Solution

The main disadvantage of best-first search is that it may fail to find a solution to the problem. While depth-first and breadth-first search techniques are exhaustive, the best-first technique is guided to that part of the problem space that "appears" promising. The exhaustive techniques are guaranteed to find a solution if one exists, but the best-first technique might never reach the solution.

———————— MONOTONIC INFERENCE ————————

In the types of problems we have been looking at in this chapter, we have assumed that the various facts found during the consultation do not change as the session proceeds. That is, once a fact is placed in the working memory by either the user or the firing of a rule, it remains there. For example, consider a problem of electronic diagnosis:

Assertion: Transistor Q1 is bad

RULE: IF   Transistor Q1 is bad
               THEN   Replace transistor Q1

Conclusion: Replace transistor Q1

Given the assertion, we would expect that both it and the conclusion are valid throughout the session. Systems that retain facts as unchanging assertions use **monotonic reasoning.**

DEFINITION 4.15: Monotonic Reasoning
Method of reasoning that assumes once a fact is asserted it cannot be altered during the course of the reasoning.

_____ **NON-MONOTONIC INFERENCE** _____

Some expert system applications work with facts whose state can change during the session. In addition, other information logically dependent on this fact also changes. To illustrate, consider the following example:

Assertion: It is raining—**FACT1**

RULE: IF   It is raining
               THEN   Carry an umbrella

Conclusion: Carry an umbrella—**FACT2**

Given the assertion and rule, we would conclude that we should carry an umbrella. However, if before we get the umbrella it stops raining, we might choose to leave the umbrella at home. In this sense, the retraction of **FACT1** also retracts **FACT2**. Systems relying on this style of knowledge processing use **non-monotonic reasoning.**

DEFINITION 4.16: Non-Monotonic Reasoning
Method of reasoning that allows changes in reasoning for changes in a given fact. It allows for both the retraction of the given fact and all the conclusions formed from the fact.

Retracting a single fact from the working memory is an easy task. We might employ some function to perform this task such as **RETRACT(FACT1).** However, retracting other facts that are logically dependent upon the retracted fact, such as **FACT2,** is more difficult and requires additional bookkeeping. This is particularly important when changes in one fact cause a ripple effect through a long inference chain, and require the retraction of several facts.

Expert systems perform non-monotonic reasoning by associating with each fact two pieces of information: *what* state it is in, and *how* it got into that state. The *what* is the value of the fact, such as true or false. The *how* is the way the fact was established, that is, its logical dependence on other facts. If the fact was dependent upon another fact that is now retracted, the *how* information allows for the retraction of the dependent fact. Maintaining the bookkeeping that links together logically dependent facts allows for the truth maintenance of all of the facts in working memory. In expert system design, the record keeping for non-monotonic reasoning is the task of a **truth maintenance system** (Doyle 1979; de Kleer 1986).

Non-monotonic reasoning is an important feature of expert systems applied to planning or design tasks. Early decisions on how to formulate the plan or design may later appear poor. These early decisions can be retracted with the corresponding retraction of later logically dependent decisions.

MONOTONIC AND NON-MONOTONIC INFERENCE

Some problems require both forms of reasoning. Consider a darkroom situation. Assume you walk into the room during film processing and turn on the light switch—you have now successfully ruined the film. Upon realizing your mistake, you are likely to react by immediately turning the switch off. However—too late—the damage is done and the film is ruined.

This example includes spots where both monotonic and non-monotonic reasoning are needed. Consider first the light switch. When you turned the switch off, the light would also turn off. This is a simple form of non-monotonic reasoning. Now consider the ruined film. Even though you shut off the light, it doesn't alter the fact that the film is ruined. This is a form of monotonic reasoning.

SUMMARY ON INFERENCE

This chapter introduced the subject of inference in an expert system. It reviewed the basic ways that humans reason and the techniques used in the design of expert systems that model human reasoning. The important points raised in this chapter were:

- Reasoning is the process of inferring new information from known information.

- Inference is the process used by an expert system that models human reasoning.

- The inference engine combines information contained in the working memory with knowledge contained in the knowledge base to derive conclusions.

- The two basic inference techniques used in an expert system are forward and backward-chaining.

- Forward-chaining works with available information on the problem to derive additional information.
- Forward-chaining is a good inference technique for problems that begin with problem data.
- Conflict resolution strategies offer an approach to choose one rule to fire from several competing rules.
- Backward-chaining tries to prove a goal by obtaining supporting information.
- Backward-chaining is a good inference technique for problems that begin with a goal or a hypothesis.
- Goal agendas provide further control over backward-chaining search.
- Depth-first and breadth-first search techniques are simple but uninformed methods for searching through the knowledge base.
- Best-first search uses knowledge to help guide the search.
- Monotonic reasoning assumes that asserted facts remain valid throughout the problem session.
- Non-monotonic reasoning allows for the retraction of both a given fact and other logically dependent facts.

REFERENCES

Bledsoe, W.W., Non-Resolution Theorem Proving, Artificial Intelligence, vol. 9, pp. 1–35, 1977.

Cohen, P.R. and E.A. Feigenbaum (eds.), The Handbook of Artificial Intelligence, vol. III, William Kaufmann, Inc., Los Altos, CA, 1982.

de Kleer, J., An Assumption Based Truth Maintenance System, Artificial Intelligence, vol. 28, 1986.

Doyle, J., A Truth Maintenance System, Artificial Intelligence, vol. 12, 1979.

Firebaugh, M.W., Artificial Intelligence: A Knowledge-Based Approach, Boyd & Fraser Publishing Co., Boston, Mass., 1988.

Luger, G.F. and W.A. Stubblefield, Artificial Intelligence and the Design of Expert Systems, Benjamin/Cummings, Redwood City, Calif., 1989.

Robinson, J.A., A Machine-Oriented Logic Based on the Resolution Principle, J. ACM, vol. 12, pp. 23–41, 1965.

EXERCISES

1. Name the principal techniques humans use in reasoning and give an example of each.
2. Human experts are experts because they possess both knowledge and problem solving skills on a particular subject. Consider a problem of designing a deck for a house. Discuss how successful you might expect the following individuals to be in accomplishing this task.
   Doctor
   Engineer
   Carpenter

3. Assume the present set of axioms are as shown in STATE-0, and list the other states that would develop using modus ponens.

STATE-0

1. $E^1 \rightarrow E^2$
2. $E^2 \rightarrow E^4$
3. $E^5 \rightarrow E^3$
4. $E^4 \rightarrow E^5$
5. $E^6 \rightarrow E^1$
6. $E^7 \rightarrow E^2$
7. E^6

4. From the list of axioms given in problem 3, use resolution to prove whether E^5 is true.

5. Given that you have only \$8 and the following rules, use forward-chaining to determine what you should buy and what wine you should serve. Provide a full trace of the session.

Rule 1
IF   You purchase meat
THEN   You should serve red wine

Rule 2
IF   You purchase fish
THEN   You should serve white wine

Rule 3
IF   The store has fish
AND   You have enough money to buy fish
THEN   You purchase fish

Rule 4
IF   The store has meat
AND   You have enough money to buy meat
THEN   You purchase meat

Rule 5
IF   You have greater than or equal to \$10
THEN   You have enough money to buy meat

Rule 6
IF   You have between \$5 and \$10
THEN   You have enough money to buy fish

6. If the following two rules were added to problem 5, determine what conclusions would be drawn and explain what is wrong with the addition of the rules.

Rule 7
IF   You should serve white wine
THEN   You should wear a white coat

Rule 8
IF   You purchase meat
THEN   You should wear a red coat

7. Discuss the potential value of conflict resolution and describe a small problem where this technique could help.

8. You have noticed that the U.S. currency exchange rate has decreased on the international market. You want to know if this would be a good time to invest in long-term treasury notes. Use the following set of rules in a backward-chaining fashion to determine your answer. Provide a full trace of the session.

Rule 1
IF   Bond prices are decreasing
THEN   Invest in long-term treasury notes

Rule 2
IF   Interest rates are increasing
THEN   Bond prices are decreasing

Rule 3
IF   Interest rates are decreasing
THEN   Bond prices are increasing

Rule 4
IF   Exchange rate has increased
THEN   Interest rates are decreasing

Rule 5
IF   Exchange rate has decreased
THEN   Interest rates are increasing

9. You have some money you want to invest and need some advice. Assume that you have a steady job, your yearly income is $50,000 and your savings is $20,000. Your expenses each year total $10,000. Use the following set of rules to determine your answer:
   a. In a backward-chaining fashion providing a full trace of the session. Also, how would you generate a goal agenda for the problem?
   b. In a forward-chaining fashion providing a full trace of the session.

Rule Advise Investment in Stocks
IF   The client's income is good
AND   The client's savings is good
THEN   Advice is invest money in stocks

Rule Advise Savings Account Investment
IF   The client's savings is not good
THEN   Advice is invest money in a savings account

Rule Advise Splitting Money Between Savings Account and Stocks
IF   The client's savings is good
AND   The client's income is not good
THEN   Advice is invest money in both a savings account and stocks

Rule Determine if Client is a Good Saver
IF   Client's total savings $> 0.5 *$ INCOME
THEN   The client's savings is good
ELSE   The client's savings is not good

Rule Client's Income is Not Good Based on Not Having a Steady Job
IF   The client's job is not steady
THEN   The client's income is not good

Rule Client's Income is Not Good Based on Small Income
IF   INCOME < EXPENSES
THEN   The client's income is not good

Rule Client's Income is Good
IF   The client's job is steady
AND   INCOME > EXPENSES
THEN   The client's income is good

10. Describe an application where demon rules would be of value and write the rules.

11. Explain the differences in the performance of an expert system when using depth-first, breadth-first, and best-first search techniques on problem 9.

12. Describe a problem that would be appropriate for each of the following reasoning techniques:
    Deduction
    Induction
    Abduction
    Analogical
    Common sense
    Monotonic
    Non-monotonic
    Monotonic and non-monotonic

CHAPTER 5

MYCIN

INTRODUCTION

In this chapter we examine the major features of MYCIN. MYCIN is a benchmark for today's rule-based expert systems. Many of the features commonplace in today's systems were first developed during the MYCIN project. A review of these features provides insight into developing a rule-based system. The major objective of this chapter is not primarily concerned with *what* MYCIN is, but rather *why* it is important to expert system development in general.

────────────── **BACKGROUND** ──────────────

MYCIN (Shortliffe 1976) was developed at Stanford University to aid physicians in diagnosing and treating patients with infectious blood diseases caused by bacteremia (bacteria in the blood) and meningitis (bacterial disease that causes inflammation of the membrane surrounding the brain and spinal cord). These diseases can be fatal if not recognized and treated quickly. The system was developed during the mid-1970s and took approximately 20 person-years to complete. MYCIN is a rule-based expert system that uses backward chaining and incorporates approximately 500 rules. The system was written in INTERLISP, a dialect of the LISP programming language.

The domain of infectious diseases was chosen by the Stanford researchers for several reasons. One of the primary motivations was that the need to react quickly to a possibly life-threatening situation caused several difficulties for the physician. To verify the presence and identity of the bacteremia, blood samples are taken and tests are conducted. Some tests may take up to two days to provide accurate results. Because of the need to react quickly, the physician may elect to begin treatment immediately with only partial or inexact information available. Due to the serious nature of the problem and the limited available information, the physician might often seek the advice of an expert on the problem.

During the 1970s, the field of AI was moving toward knowledge-based systems: systems that contain and emphasize expert knowledge. Since the physician sought the aid of an expert on infectious blood diseases to help solve the problem, this problem was a prime candidate for a knowledge-based approach.

Another aspect of the problem that intrigued the researchers was that if the system was going to be accepted by the physician, it had to pattern itself closely after the way physicians interact with resident blood disease experts. The system had to be interactive in a human like fashion and have the capability of answering any queries the physician might have. In general, the system had to be designed to be unobtrusive and accommodating to the physician.

Another interesting aspect of the problem was related to the present treatment procedures that often led to the misuse or overuse of antibiotics. An earlier study of hospital patients (Roberts and Visconti 1972) suggested that 66% of therapies selected by physicians were inadvisable and of these, over 62% used inappropriate combinations of antibiotics.

Following the introduction of penicillin, there have been a large number of other effective and powerful antibiotics produced. Though effective if used correctly, these drugs can have potentially serious side effects in certain individuals, and if given in an improper combination, can cause a toxic interaction. The problem for the physician is to remember what a given antibiotic is good for, and how to avoid its misuse. A standard reference manual, called the Physician's Desk Reference, is used by physicians for determining the applicability of various drugs and their possible contraindications.

The final interesting aspect of the problem was related to the shortage of expertise in diagnosing and treating infectious blood disease. In many major hospitals an expert might be available; however, in smaller hospitals in more remote sections of the country, this expertise is likely to be rare. The Stanford researchers were intrigued by the ability to develop a computer system that captured the expertise of some blood specialist from a large hospital, and have it made readily available to other smaller hospitals.

In summary, some of the primary motivating factors for building MYCIN were:

- An expert was required to solve the problem.
- Experts on the problem were scarce or unavailable because of time constraints.
- Immediate expertise was needed in a possibly life threatening situation.
- Time constraints required decisions to be made with limited or inexact information.
- The computer solution needed to be accommodating to the user, who may have limited experience with computers.
- Existing solutions may be irrational in cases where drug recommendations were inappropriate for the problem.
- Remembering the appropriateness and possible contraindications of a large number of drugs was a challenge for the physician.

On any new expert system project, one of your first concerns will be to provide a justification for the project. Chapter 2 discussed some of the more common reasons put forth for the appropriateness of this technology. This section listed those found by the MYCIN development team. You should note the similarity between the two.

MAJOR FEATURES OF MYCIN

In the following sections we review the major features of MYCIN. This review not only provides you insight into the workings of MYCIN, but also an understanding of the characteristics of today's rule-based systems.

Utilizes a Backward-Chaining System

MYCIN has about 500 rules and works in a backward chaining fashion to identify the nature of the infection. It can also identify the suspected invading organisms and their classes. The system also employs a backward-chaining technique when forming a suggested therapeutic remedy. The following is a rule from MYCIN in English and LISP form:

IF   The stain of the organism is gram negative
AND   The morphology of the organism is rod

AND   The aerobicity of the organism is anaerobic
THEN   There is strongly suggestive evidence (0.8) that the class of the
       organism is enterobacteriaceae

IF: (AND   (SAME CNTEXT GRAM GRAMNEG)
                 (SAME CNTEXT MORPH ROD)
                 (SAME CNTEXT AIR AEROBIC))
THEN: (CONCLUDE   CNTEXT   CLASS   ENTEROBACTERIACEAE
        TALLY .8)

To prove the conclusion of the rule, MYCIN works backward through other
rules that support each premise, searching for confirming evidence. These other
rules provide this evidence by working with information obtained from clinical
observations and laboratory test results.

Using this simple backward-chaining process, MYCIN was found to perform
at a level of human experts. This result illustrates that expert performance from
an expert system comes not from some clever algorithm, but from the system's
knowledge about the problem. This observation underscores the belief held in
the expert system community that expert systems attain their power from their
knowledge.

Separates Knowledge from Control

A trademark of all expert systems is the separation of the system's knowledge
from its control. MYCIN was one of the first systems developed that illustrated
the value of this separation. By maintaining the knowledge separate from its
control, the MYCIN development team found that they could easily modify the
system's knowledge. Adding new knowledge or modifying existing knowledge
became a simple task, requiring changes only to the knowledge base. This is
possible because rules are independent pieces of knowledge that are used on an
as-needed basis. Therefore, the addition or deletion of a rule does not require
changes to other rules in the system.

This style of programming is unlike that found in conventional programs such
as Fortran, which integrates the problem's knowledge and control in each line
of code. In a conventional program, changing a single line of code changes both
the program's knowledge and control.

Incorporates Meta-Rules

The MYCIN team found at times the simple backward-chaining search scheme
to be inadequate. For example, they would see the program exploring an issue
that is obviously fruitless, when it should be considering other potentially more

valuable areas. To enable the system to redirect its search, they incorporated **meta-rules.** The following is an example meta-rule from MYCIN:

> IF   The infection is a pelvic-abscess
> AND   There are rules that mention in their premise Enterobacteriaceae
> AND   There are rules that mention in their premise gram positive rods
> THEN There is suggestive evidence that the rules dealing with Enterobacteriaceae should be evoked before those dealing with gram positive rods

This rule suggests that, since enterobacteria are commonly associated with a pelvic abscess, then it is reasonable to try rules about them first, before the less promising rules dealing with gram positive rods.

A meta-rule permits the system to search intelligently for a solution. It also gives the system a behavior that more closely follows human problem solving. It is also one way you can incorporate *best-first* search into the system, as described in Chapter 4.

Employs Inexact Reasoning

MYCIN can also work with inexact or incomplete information—a common problem for many domains. This problem was of particular concern to the MYCIN team since the physician may have to make decisions under the life-threatening constraint of limited time. This situation could give rise to incomplete or uncertain information.

If MYCIN asks for information that is unknown to the physician, a simple response of UNKNOWN can be given. If the information is known but uncertain, then the physician can provide a numeric value called a **certainty factor** (CF), reflecting his degree of belief in the answer. This numeric is based on a scale of -1 to $+1$, where -1 represents definitely false and $+1$ definitely true (see Figure 3.4 in Chapter 3). For example, if the physician believes some evidence *may* be true, then he can enter a value of 0.7.

MYCIN can also work with inexact inference. The MYCIN team found when interviewing the expert that he might say, "If I see certain evidence, then I believe something *may* be true." To accommodate inexact inference, MYCIN incorporates certainty factors with the rules. For example:

> IF Evidence   THEN   Conclusion CF 0.7

In this fashion, given that the evidence is known, then the conclusion is asserted with a degree of belief reflected in the rule's CF value.

MYCIN can work under the constraints of unknown or uncertain information and with inexact rules. Even under these constraints, MYCIN is still able to derive solutions that may not always be completely precise but like those determined by the human expert, are usually acceptable. The methods developed to permit this style of inexact reasoning in expert systems, have their origin in the area of study known as the **certainty theory**—the subject of Chapter 12.

Remembers Prior Session

MYCIN remembers information from a prior session concerning a given patient. This includes data provided by the patient, conclusions drawn by MYCIN, and findings such as the identities of the suspected invading organisms and the therapeutic recommendations. This capability is important in those situations where new information may become available at a later time. The following discussion illustrates this point.

Recall from an earlier discussion that MYCIN works under time constraints that may prevent it from obtaining complete information. For example, if test results are not available, the user would respond with an UNKNOWN to a question related to the test. Without complete information, MYCIN's resultant findings may not be optimal. It could for example recommend a drug that is later found to be ineffective, causes side effects, etc. However, if later test information becomes available, MYCIN can add this new information to what it learned before and derive new findings. It might for example design a new drug regime that avoids earlier problems.

Like an expert, an expert system can make mistakes. However, also like a human expert, the system should be able to respond intelligently to its own mistakes.

Accommodates the User

The MYCIN team was quick to realize that for its system to be accepted by the physician, it had to be accommodating. The team members understood that many physicians are unaccustomed to working with a computer. In MYCIN's domain, the physician sought the advice of an expert on infectious diseases, not a computer. To perform the function of the expert in an acceptable manner, MYCIN had to be easy to use and present itself in a manner that was natural to the physician. Davis et al. (1977) report on this issue by stating

> *"The systems's acceptance (especially to a medical audience) will be strongly dependent upon the extent to which its performance is natural (i.e., human-like) and transparent. Lack of acceptance of some applications programs can be traced to their obscure reasoning mechanisms which leave the user forced to accept or reject advice without a chance to discover its basis."*

Natural Language Interaction

MYCIN interacts with the physician in English, making it easy to understand and use. This is important since a physician with limited experience with computers might be using MYCIN. Consider for example the following typical exchange:

MYCIN: What is the patient's race?
USER: CAUCASIAN

This approach presents MYCIN to the physician in a natural fashion. That is, the physician is accustomed to discussing an infectious disease problem with the expert using a normal conversational style.

Spelling Checker

The language of the physician includes complex terms. Since the typing of these terms is error-prone, the MYCIN team decided to help the physician by providing a spelling checker. The question facing the developers was how to best design a utility that would accommodate the user while maintaining the appearance of an intelligent system.

To appreciate the importance of this point, consider the following question and answer:

MYCIN: What is the infection?
USER: Endurteritis

Here the user has misspelled the word "Endarteritis." The question now is how should the system respond? If we were designing a conventional computer program and this problem occurred, the likely response might be:

Fatal error 6B4A program aborted

Aborting a program because of a typing error is very likely to make it difficult to convince the user that this is an **intelligent** system. How much belief will the physician have in the decisions made by the system if it can't recognize a simple spelling mistake?

Consider the following alternative:

Invalid response, please retype

Though this response is an improvement over the first, you could imagine the frustration a physician might feel seeing this message after misspelling a 30-character word by only one character. In addition, the retype might only lead to other mistakes.

To avoid the user's obvious negative reaction to either of these responses, the MYCIN team approached the problem in a very simple but effective manner. With each question, the system has a list of possible legal answers. Using this list, the system can determine the closest match between the physician's response and the answers on the list. If a typing problem occurs, the system displays to the physician its best guess. This approach is similar to the spelling checkers of today's word processors. Now consider the following response:

Q: Did you mean to type Endarteritis.
A: YES

Most expert systems built today use a menu selection approach for questioning. Rather than type an answer, the user selects the appropriate response from the menu. This approach avoids the need for any type of spelling checker. However, there is still a valuable lesson you can learn from the work performed on developing MYCIN's spelling checker—always make an effort to accommodate the user.

Provides Explanations

MYCIN can explain *why* it is asking a question and *how* it derived a conclusion. MYCIN can also explain *why* it found other results implausible. These features provide a more natural interaction and a transparency to the system's reasoning. Being able to explain its reasoning adds to the system's credibility.

Explains Why

When we discuss a problem with an expert, we may at times become curious *why* some question is asked; what is the expert trying to prove? We use the expert's explanation to better answer the question, as well as to get a feel for the overall approach the expert is taking to the problem.

The MYCIN team wanted their system to interact in a similar manner. To accomplish this, they designed a *why* explanation utility that presents to the physician the current rule under consideration by the system. Since the rule is an easily readable piece of knowledge, this approach was felt to provide the physician insight into the system's reasoning.

To illustrate this approach, consider the following example drawn from a problem on automobile diagnostics:

SYSTEM: How old is the car's battery
USER: WHY
SYSTEM: This will aid in determining the battery's condition:

RULE 037
IF   The car battery's age is over five years
AND   The car battery's voltage is below 10 volts
THEN   The battery's condition is probably bad

Provided this display, a user can see that the system is attempting to determine the condition of the battery. The user can also see that knowing the age of the battery is an important consideration when assessing a battery's condition.

MYCIN also allows for a second *why* request that prompts the system to explain why determining the rule's conclusion is important. Consider a second *why* to the battery issue:

USER: WHY
SYSTEM: This will aid in determining the proper recommendation:

RULE 044

IF   The battery's condition is probably bad
THEN   Recommend replacing the battery

This example illustrates how the system provides the user with a more global picture of the problem-solving strategy. The user now knows that the age of the battery is not only important for assessing the condition of the battery, but also for providing a final recommendation related to the battery.

A *why* explanation provides the user with an understanding of the question's relevance. It also provides transparency into the system's reasoning and better models the normal interaction between the user and a human expert.

Explains How

When using a conventional computer program we usually accept the results without question. In most cases this is acceptable because this type of program is normally written for a well-defined problem for which the programming solution is exact and repeatable. However, the types of problems solved by expert systems are usually far less exact, which often leaves the user with some degree of concern about the results. To help alleviate this concern, an expert system must be able to explain *how* it derived its results. To appreciate the importance of this point, consider MYCIN's domain.

MYCIN first determines the infecting organism and then recommends a series of drugs to eliminate the organism. Before a physician would accept MYCIN's drug recommendation, he might demand a justification. To accommodate this request, MYCIN shows the logic behind its reasoning. It does this by providing the physician a trace of the rules it used to reach its decision. To illustrate this *how* explanation utility, consider the following explanation drawn from the automobile diagnostic example:

SYSTEM: I recommend that you replace the battery.
USER: HOW
SYSTEM: I used rule 044 to conclude that the recommendation is to replace the battery:

RULE 044
IF   The battery's condition is probably bad
THEN   Recommend replacing the battery

I used rule 037 to conclude the condition of the battery:

RULE 037
IF   The car battery's age is over five years
AND   The car battery's voltage is below 10 volts
THEN   The battery's condition is probably bad

You told me:
1. The car battery's age is over five years
2. The car battery's voltage is below 10 volts

A *how* explanation provides the user with a justification of the system's findings. It makes the system's reasoning transparent, which increases the user's confidence in the findings.

Provides Alternative Recommendations

Many people have come to resent computers as mindless boxes that attempt to direct their behavior. This situation has always plagued designers of conventional programs, but when the software comes under the label of "artificial intelligence," the problem is magnified. The MYCIN team was aware of this potential situation and took steps to help avoid it.

In principle, the MYCIN team wanted the physician to feel in control and have the final say on the subject. They recognized that the series of drugs recommended by the system may not be acceptable to the physician for a variety of reasons. Therefore, the system needed to work further with the physician to formulate a new and acceptable list of drugs.

To illustrate, consider the following typical recommendation following a consultation with MYCIN:

[REC-1] My preferred therapy recommendation is as follows:
In order to cover the items <1 2 3>:
Give the following combination:

1.) AMPICILLIN Dose 2.5 g (30 ml) for 10 days
2.) GENTAMICIN Dose 131 mg (3.2 ml, 80 mg/2 ml ampule) for 10 days.

This recommendation is an explicit directive to the physician on what drugs and dosage levels to administer to the patient. However, the physician may want to avoid one of these recommended drugs for personal reasons.

To accommodate this possibility, MYCIN allows the physician to choose those drugs from the list that he would like the system to provide an alternative for. MYCIN then formulates a new drug list, and compares it to the old one and presents the comparison to the physician for further consideration. Details on how this is done are given later in the chapter.

The underlying lesson you should learn from this feature of MYCIN is that you build an expert system to help a user and not to replace him. The system should provide recommendations, not firm directives. Whether or not you build a utility that can consider alternative findings is secondary to conveying to the user that the final call is his.

Summary on Features

Prior sections of this chapter discussed the major features of MYCIN. Each of these features was required not only to solve the problem of treating a patient with an infectious blood disease, but also to accommodate the needs of the physician. Most rule-based systems developed today incorporate many of these same features. The major features of MYCIN are:

- Contains knowledge in the form of rules that aids a physician in diagnosing infectious blood diseases.
- Allows its knowledge to be easily modified by editing, deleting, or adding rules.
- Uses simple backward-chaining processor.
- Separates knowledge from control.
- Incorporates meta-rules to control search.
- Conducts session in English.
- Performs inexact reasoning.
  —Works with inexact or incomplete information.
  —Uses inexact inference.
- Remembers prior session.
- Explains *why* a question is being asked.
- Explains *how* a result was obtained.
- Can explain *why* a result was **not** obtained.
- Provides alternative solutions if requested.

MYCIN'S PROBLEM-SOLVING APPROACH

MYCIN is knowledgeable about many possible infections and infecting organisms. Its first task is to use information about a case supplied by the physician to determine the nature of the infection and the identity of the infecting organisms. This is called the **diagnosis** phase.

The system is also knowledgeable about drugs that could be used to combat the identified organisms. Its next task is to formulate a list of drugs that should eliminate the suspected infecting organisms while also assuring that the drugs are safe for the patient. This is called the **prescription** phase. In performing these two tasks, MYCIN answers the following questions:

PHASE 1: Diagnosis
—What is the nature of the infection?
—What organisms are causing the infection?

PHASE 2: Prescription
—What drugs should eliminate the infecting organism?
—What drugs should be safe for the patient?

Diagnosis

During the diagnosis phase, MYCIN first asks questions to obtain general background information on the patient including the patient's age, sex and symptoms.

MYCIN then asks for available results from laboratory tests. With each answer, MYCIN directs the line of questioning toward the suspected infection or infecting organisms. It asks questions that are consistent with suspicions formed from earlier information, while avoiding questions related to problems that it should have ruled out. This intelligent sequence of questions establishes in the mind of the physician a sense of credibility for the program.

Before trying to identify the infecting organism, MYCIN first asks the physician if he can perform the identification. This might be possible if laboratory test results are available. This approach avoids unnecessary search. It also offers a cooperative style of interaction, where the physician helps the system perform its tasks.

Classification Approach

MYCIN attempts to identify an organism using a *classification* approach. Each organism known to MYCIN can be classified according to a set of properties. For example, as Figure 5.1 illustrates, the identity of the organism might be determined from information on such properties as its gram stain, its morphology, and its aerobicity.

Each property is addressed in a premise of a rule designed to identify a given organism. The following is a typical rule from MYCIN in English form that illustrates this organism identification approach:

IF   The stain of the organism is gram negative
AND   The morphology of the organism is rod
AND   The aerobicity of the organism is anaerobic
THEN There is suggestive evidence (0.7) that the identity of the organism
          is bacteroides

This rule concludes that the organism is bacteroides, when evidence is found to support the various property values shown in the premises. Other organisms are identified in a similar classification manner, using various properties and property values.

MYCIN contains about 500 rules that work together to solve the problem. Each rule is somewhat of an independent piece of knowledge that the physician can inspect to confirm its correctness. Rules then add to the transparency of the system's knowledge, which greatly enhances the system's development and maintenance.

Inexact Diagnosis

MYCIN performs inexact diagnosis using rules of the form shown in the previous example. Assume, for example, that evidence is available that supports the rule's premises. MYCIN then believes the organism is bacteroides to a degree of 0.7 on a scale of -1 to 1. This is a form of inexact inference as discussed earlier.

The figure of 0.7 represents the belief in the rule's conclusion only if all three premises are absolutely true. However, in general, premises also have a degree

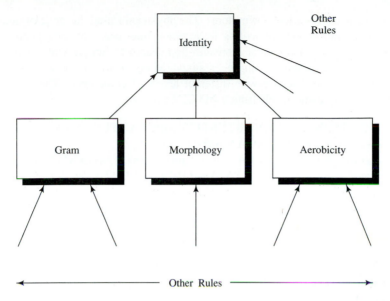

FIGURE 5.1   Bacteria identity.

of belief. MYCIN accounts for this possibility when establishing a belief in the rule's conclusion using a technique known as **certainty factor propagation,** a subject addressed in Chapter 12.

One final point on inexact reasoning is worth noting. As Figure 5.1 illustrates, there may be more than one rule that concludes with the same identity. Each of these rules in turn may have different CF values associated with them. The question then facing the MYCIN team was how to determine the overall level of belief of some conclusion that is supported by multiple rules.

The MYCIN team approached this problem in an intuitive fashion. They felt that if support for some conclusion comes from multiple sources, then the belief in the conclusion should be incrementally increased. Therefore, they wanted MYCIN to believe some conclusion a little more when it obtains additional proof via different rules. To accomplish this, they incorporated into MYCIN a technique known as **incrementally acquired evidence:** discussed in Chapter 12.

Depth-First Search

Through backward-chaining, MYCIN pursues each premise of a rule in a depth-first fashion. Consider the prior example rule. MYCIN would first search those rules that can establish one of the premises (e.g., organism's gram stain) before searching rules related to the issues addressed in the other premises.

One advantage the MYCIN team found in using this search approach is that the system would ask the physician a series of questions that maintained a common theme. For example, MYCIN asks several general questions about the patient, such as age, sex, etc., then another series of questions on a different subject, such as the patient's symptoms. The physician found this style of interaction natural, and was more willing to accept it than one that jumped between subjects, which would occur if a breadth-first search technique was used.

Following the diagnosis phase of study, MYCIN will have identified the suspected infecting bacteria with different levels of confidence. The following is a typical diagnostic result from a MYCIN session:

INFECTION-1 IS ENDARTERITIS with BACTEREMIA
<item1> E.COLI [ORGANISM-1] (.71)
<item2> SALMONELLA (species unknown) [ORGANISM-1] (.60)
<item3> KLEBSIELLA-PNEUMONIA [ORGANISM-1] (.25)

Prescription

MYCIN's next task is to prescribe a set of drugs to give to the patient that will eliminate each organism identified during the diagnostic study. You might at first think this is an easy task. It seems that MYCIN only needs to find in a table the name of the drug that is effective for each organism, then add it to the prescribed set of drugs. Unfortunately, the combination of various drugs can create a toxic mixture. Therefore, though this approach may be effective in eliminating the infecting organisms, it may be just as effective in eliminating the patient.

To avoid recommending a prescription that could be harmful to the patient, MYCIN contains knowledge on the proper combinations of various drugs. It uses this knowledge when prescribing the series of drugs to produce a recommendation that is both effective and safe. The prescription task of MYCIN addresses the following objectives:

- Prescription must eliminate the suspected infecting organisms.
- Prescription should minimize the number of recommended drugs.
- Prescription must be safe for the patient.

To achieve these objectives, MYCIN uses a plan-generate-test method as shown in Figure 5.2 (Buchanan and Shortliffe 1984).

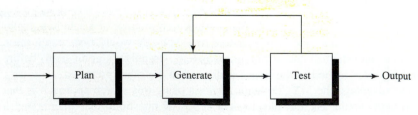

FIGURE 5.2   Therapy selection.

TABLE 5.1   Rank-Ordered Listing of Recommended Drugs

	ORGANISM-1	*ORGANISM-2*	*ORGANISM-3*
RANK-1	Drug-A	Drug-B	Drug-C
RANK-2	Drug-D	Drug-A	Drug-E
RANK-3	Drug-C	Drug-C	Drug-F

Plan

For each suspected organism identified during the diagnosis task, MYCIN forms a list of potentially effective drugs. The system also orders the drugs on the list according to their likely effectiveness in combating the organism. For example, given that three organisms were identified, the drug ranking shown in Table 5.1 might be produced.

Ideally it would be hoped that all three organisms might be eliminated with only one drug. For example, if all three would have Drug-A in rank-1, then it would be reasonable to prescribe this single drug. However, if rank-1 drugs are different, then prescribing all of them may be inappropriate because of considerations of overprescribing and potential toxic drug combinations.

A more reasonable approach taken by MYCIN is to see if one or two of the drugs listed may be effective for eliminating all of the organisms. For example, Drug-C appears under each column and shows some promise in a final recommendation. In general, however, attempting to find a reasonable recommendation that would be both effective and safe requires additional effort by MYCIN. This effort begins with the next step, generating a series of potential recommendations.

Generate

The objective of this task is to generate from the ordered list of drugs as shown in Table 5.1 a series of possible recommendations. This task is strictly procedural—it simply selects from the three columns one or two drugs for testing. This procedure is accomplished through a set of instructions such as those shown in Table 5.2 (Buchanan and Shortliffe 1984, Figure 5-2).

A listing of the possible result from this effort might be:

> Drug prescription 1: Drug-A
> Drug prescription 2: Drug-A and Drug-B
> Drug prescription 3: Drug-C and Drug-E
> Drug prescription 4: Drug-B and Drug-F

As can be seen from this listing, only one or two drugs would be recommended, consistent with the objective of avoiding over prescribing the number of drugs. To fulfill the other two objectives, namely making certain that the recommendation is both effective and safe, requires the final step of testing each prescription.

TABLE 5.2 Instructions for Generating
Potential Therapies

Instruction	*Number of Drugs of Each Rank*		
	FIRST	SECOND	THIRD
1	1	0	0
2	2	0	0
3	1	1	0
4	1	0	1
.			
.			
.			

Test

The first task of the testing step is to consider each drug prescription established in the generate step and determine if it should be effective in eliminating all of the suspected infecting organisms. This task screens out a number of the recommendations. The second task is to ensure that those recommendations remaining after the first task do not include drugs from the same drug class. The assumption here is that drugs from the same class cover essentially the same organisms and the strategy should be to select only one of them based on ranking. For example, if the recommendation contains the drugs ampicillin and penicillin—both from the same drug class—then the one with the higher rank will be selected.

The final task is to select from those recommendations remaining after the first two tasks one drug that is safe for the patient. This includes considering such factors as drug interactions and information about the patient such as age, sex, allergic reactions, etc.

Note: *MYCIN remembers from a vast assortment of antibiotics their effectiveness against various bacteria and their safe combination. Simply remembering all of this information can be difficult for the physician.*

The first recommendation that meets these requirements is selected as the therapy of choice. Final decisions on drug dosages are obtained through algorithmic procedures. A typical final result from this effort is as follows:

**[REC-1] My preferred therapy recommendation is as follows:
In order to cover the items <1 2 3>:
Give the following combination:**

1.) **AMPICILLIN Dose 2.5 g (30 ml)**
2.) **GENTAMICIN Dose 131 mg (3.2 ml, 80 mg/2 ml ampule) for 10 days.**

MYCIN can also accommodate the user who may be dissatisfied with the list of prescribed drugs. The system can eliminate at the physician's request certain prescribed drugs, and formulate alternative recommendations by repeating the plan-generate-test process.

SAMPLE MYCIN SESSION

The last few sections discussed the major features of MYCIN, most of which can be found in today's expert systems. To better appreciate some of these features, we now review parts of a short consultation with MYCIN. The session shows an interactive dialogue between MYCIN and the physician, where the physician is questioned about a given patient. MYCIN attempts to determine the nature of the infection and the organisms causing the infection, then follows with presenting a drug therapy recommendation. Comments are dispersed throughout in italic to highlight MYCIN's major features.

Mycin–Physician Dialogue

COMMENT: *MYCIN begins the session by asking for general information about the patient.*

STEPS

1. **MYCIN: What is the patient's name?**
   User: JACK DURKIN
2. **MYCIN: What is the patient's age?**
   User: 35
3. **MYCIN: What is the patient's sex?**
   User: MALE
4. **MYCIN: What is the patient's race?**
   User: CAUCASIAN

COMMENT: *After obtaining background information, MYCIN attempts to determine the nature of the infection. It first seeks help from the user to see if this information is known from test results that produced positive cultures.*

5. **MYCIN: Are there any cultures for JACK DURKIN which may be related to the present illness, and from which organisms have been grown successfully in the microbiology laboratory?**
   User: YES
6. **MYCIN: From what site was the specimen for the culture taken?**
   User: CSF

7. **MYCIN: Please give the date and time when the pending CSF culture was obtained.**
   User: 7-JULY-7:00
8. **MYCIN: Was a smear examined at the time the specimen was obtained?**
   User: YES
9. **MYCIN: Were any cultures seen on the smear of the specimen?**
   User: YES
10. **MYCIN: Have you been able to obtain positive microbiological information about infection of JACK DURKIN?**
    User: YES
11. **MYCIN: What is the infection?**
    User: End*u*rteritis

COMMENT: *To accommodate the user, MYCIN can recognize misspelled words and make a guess at the correct answer.*

12. **MYCIN: Did you mean to type ENDARTERITIS?**
    User: YES

COMMENT: *In the absence of positive test data, MYCIN would ask for other information related to the patient's symptoms to establish a general understanding of the problem leading to the following step. For example, MYCIN might ask questions related to the suspicion of meningitis as follows:*

MYCIN: Has JACK DURKIN recently had symptoms of persistent headache or other abnormal neurological symptoms (dizziness, lethargy, etc.)?
User: YES

MYCIN: Has JACK DURKIN recently had objective evidence of abnormal neurologic signs (rigidity, coma, seizures, etc.) documented by a physician?
User: YES

MYCIN: The CSF cultures will be considered to be associated with MENINGITIS.

COMMENT: *In the absence of positive test information, MYCIN would now suspect a meningitis infection and display this result to the user. However, since another infection has been identified, MYCIN now attempts to determine the identity of the infecting organisms for this infection. A number of questions would be ask to help in this identification beginning with asking the physician if he can identify the organism from past tests.*

13. **MYCIN: Enter the identity of ORGANISM-1**
    User: UNKNOWN

COMMENT: *The system wants to know if the user can identify the organism. However, in this case the organism is unknown to the user. We want the system* *to continue to reason even though some information may not be available. MYCIN will now attempt to identify the unknown organism from other available information.*

    14. **MYCIN: Is ORGANISM-1 a rod or coccus (etc.)**
        User: ROD
    15. **MYCIN: The gram stain of ORGANISM-1?**
        User: GRAMNEG
    16. **MYCIN: What is the aerobicity of ORGANISM-1?**
        User: FACUL
    17. **MYCIN: Is the patient's illness with ORGANISM-1 a hospital-acquired infection?**
        User: WHY

COMMENT: *User wants to know WHY this question is being asked.*

MYCIN:
[2.0] This will aid in determining the identity of ORGANISM-1 that might be infecting JACK DURKIN

[RULE 92]
It has already been established that
    [2.1] the morphology of ORGANISM-1 is rod, and
    [2.2] the gram stain of ORGANISM-1 is gramneg, and
    [2.3] the aerobicity of ORGANISM-1 is facul
Therefore, if
    [2.4] the infection with ORGANISM-1 was acquired while the patient was hospitalized
Then
    there is weakly suggestive evidence (.2) that the identity of ORGANISM-1 is pseudomonas

COMMENT: *MYCIN displays the rule that it is pursuing in response to the WHY question, providing the physician with a view of the reasoning approach. The display shows what was proven and what is being sought. If the user would ask WHY again, the system would explain why it is pursuing the identity of this particular organism. MYCIN then asks the question again.*

    18. **MYCIN: Is the patient's illness with ORGANISM-1 a hospital-acquired infection?**
        User: NO
    19. **MYCIN: Have there been POSITIVE cultures yielding organisms about which you will NOT be seeking advice?**
        User: YES
    20. **MYCIN: Enter the identity of ORGANISM-2**
        User: SALMONELLA (.4) E.COLI (.3)

COMMENT: *The user qualifies the belief in this answer, i.e., I believe it is Salmonella with a degree of belief of 0.4 and I also believe it might be E.Coli with a degree of belief of 0.3.*

The session would continue in this fashion, asking in total anywhere between 20 and 100 questions, and then finally arrive at the following listing of suspected organisms with corresponding levels of belief expressed numerically:

21. **MYCIN:**
    INFECTION-1 IS ENDARTERITIS with BACTEREMIA
    <item1> E.COLI [ORGANISM-1] (.71)
    <item2> SALMONELLA (species unknown) [ORGANISM-1] (.60)
    <item3> KLEBSIELLA-PNEUMONIA [ORGANISM-1] (.25)

MYCIN concludes that the infection is endarteritis, and lists three possible bacteremia organisms that might be causing the infection. The listing is also rank ordered with corresponding beliefs represented numerically for each organism suspected. The therapy selection would then have to address all three suspected organisms.

After reviewing the results, the physician may want to know *how* a given conclusion was derived.

22. **User: HOW DID YOU DECIDE THAT ORGANISM-1 WAS AN E.COLI?**
    MYCIN:
    I used rule 084 to conclude that the identity of ORGANISM-1 is e.coli. This gave a cumulative c.f. of (.71)

    RULE 084
    If 1) The site of the culture is one of those sites that are normally sterile, and
    2) This organism has at least one of the likely pathogens associated with the portal of entry of the organism agree with respect to the following properties: gram morph air
    Then There is strongly suggestive evidence (.8) that each of them is the identity of the organism

COMMENT: *MYCIN provides a list of rules that led to the conclusion. In most rule-based systems today, answering a query of HOW would provide a full trace of all the evidence that led to the final result.*

The physician can also ask the system *why* something was **not** found to be true.

23. **User: WHY DIDN'T YOU THINK THAT ORGANISM-1 WAS NEISSERIA?**
    MYCIN:
    The following rules could have been used to determine that the identity of ORGANISM-1 is neisseria—RULE 9. However, none of these suc-

ceeded in the context of ORGANISM-1. If you would like an explanation for why any of these rules failed, please enter their numbers:

24. User: 9
    MYCIN:
    Clause 2 of RULE 009 ["the morphology of the organism is coccus"] was already known to be false for ORGANISM-1, so the rule was never fired.

COMMENT: *MYCIN demonstrates a simple capability of introspection by being able to explain WHY and WHY NOT something was found to be true. It is capable of performing this introspection using the set of rules as a model through which it can trace back along its reasoning path to provide an answer to the query.*

COMMENT: *MYCIN would now proceed in an attempt to form a recommendation for the best treatment to eliminate the suspected infection. This is accomplished through a plan-generate-test cycle of various candidate drug therapy recommendations. The system would also ask for personal information about the patient to assure a safe final recommendation.*

25. MYCIN: Does JACK DURKIN have a clinically significant allergic reaction to any antimicrobial agent?
    User: NO

COMMENT: *Other personal questions might be asked leading to the following recommendation that meets the specific needs of the patient.*

26. MYCIN:
    [REC-1] My preferred therapy recommendation is as follows:
    In order to cover the items <1 2 3>:
    Give the following combination:

    1.) AMPICILLIN Dose 2.5 g (30 ml)
    2.) GENTAMICIN
    Dose 131 mg (3.2 ml, 80 mg/2 ml ampule) for 10 days.
    Comments: Monitor serum concentrations.
    Since high concentrations of penicillins can interact aminoglycosides, do not mix these two antibiotics in the same IV bottle.

COMMENT: *MYCIN provides a recommendation for the treatment. It also provides information in the form of comments for administering the drugs.*

COMMENT: *The system then proceeds to see if the physician agrees with the recommendation or wants to consider some alternative. If the answer is YES, MYCIN asks which drugs should be eliminated from the present prescription and again goes through the plan-generate-test cycle.*

27. MYCIN: Do you wish to see the next choice therapy?
    User: YES

28. **MYCIN: Which, if any, of the above drugs do you wish eliminated from consideration?**
    User: AMPICILLIN
    MYCIN:
    [REC-2] Next best therapy recommendation:
    In order to cover the items <2 3>:
    Give GENTAMICIN
    Dose 131 mg (3.2 ml, 80 mg/2 ml ampule) for 10 days
    Comments: Monitor serum concentrations.

    In order to cover the items <1>:
    2.) PENICILLIN
    Dose 4 million units (7.8 ml) for 14 days

    RECOMMENDATION-2 is substantially inferior to RECOMMENDATION-1

29. **MYCIN: Would you like to see details of this comparison?**
    User: NO

COMMENT: *MYCIN can provide further explanation that compares different recommendations.*

Session Review

The partial listing of a consultation with MYCIN given in the last section provides insight into its design and operation. It also illustrates some of MYCIN's major capabilities. The following review of this example session highlights the system's principal features.

Problem-Solving Approach

The session begins by asking routine questions about the patient (steps 1–4). This approach was taken by the MYCIN team because it follows the normal beginning interaction between the physician and the expert.

> **Note:** *Expert system designers attempt to model all aspects of the consultation as it normally occurs in practice.*

The system then enters into the diagnostic phase by first attempting to establish the global problem, namely, the nature of the infection. MYCIN knows about a large number of possible infections and attempts to determine which one is present for the current problem. The system first determines if the physician performed laboratory tests that could help identify the infection (steps 5–7). It then asks the physician if the infection could be identified from the test results (steps 8–11). If the physician could not identify the infection, MYCIN would attempt to perform the identification using the patient's symptoms.

The system accomplishes this by hypothesizing a particular infection, then attempts to prove or disprove it by asking questions guided by the backward-chaining process. MYCIN's knowledge includes rules that can restrict the hypothesis to be tested on the basis of information found earlier, where it may rule out certain hypotheses while suspecting others. This pruning of unsuspected hypotheses produces later questions that are related only to what is actually suspected.

Note: *This point is important because the system never asks questions related to infections that should have been ruled out. This in turn exhibits a higher degree of intelligence in the consultation.*

Following the identity of the suspected infection, MYCIN proceeds in an attempt to identify which organisms are the likely cause of the infection. In a fashion similar to the identification of the infection, MYCIN first asks the physician if he can perform the organism identification (steps 13 and 20) before attempting to infer this identification from other information (steps 14–18). MYCIN also knows about a large number of organisms, and since more than one organism may be causing the infection, it exhaustively searches for all possible ones that can cause the suspected infection.

Note: *This style of reasoning runs from the general to the specific. The system first attempts to establish the nature of the problem—the infection—then the cause of the problem—the organisms. This approach characterizes most diagnostic expert systems found today.*

MYCIN is seen to go through its two major phases of diagnosis followed by prescription. The system uses a backward-chaining technique to determine the identity of the infecting organism. Questions are asked and the answers are used to direct the system's search. After identifying the suspected organisms, the system formulates a set of recommended drugs that should be both effective and safe (step 26).

Accommodations

To accommodate the user, the system incorporates a number of helpful utilities.

Note: *It was mentioned earlier that accommodating a user—particularly one who has little experience with a computer—is important for the system's acceptance.*

MYCIN uses a spelling checker to detect user typing mistakes (step 12). It does it in an accommodating fashion by making a guess on what answer it believes the user meant to type.

MYCIN can also explain its reasoning. It can respond to a query of *why* it asked a question (step 17), and also to a query on *how* it arrived at a given result (step 22). It can also explain why some evidence was not found to be true given the context of the session (step 23).

The system can also cooperate with the user to form new recommendations in the event the user is not satisfied with the results (steps 27–29).

Inexact Reasoning

To form its findings, MYCIN works with inexact inference in its rules (step 22) and can also work with uncertainty in the information supplied by the user (steps 13 and 20). Its results are also presented with a level of belief, captured numerically with confidence factor values (step 21).

> **Note:** *Many problems are not black and white. The knowledge used to solve the problem is uncertain, as well as the information gathered to work on the problem. This leads to results that represent a "best" guess.*

Being able to work in an inexact world was of particular importance for MYCIN. Physicians often make intelligent decisions using their experience to guide them toward the most likely solution. Even under the constraint of limited time, which prevents them from having a complete picture of the problem that might be provided from clinical tests, they can make life-saving decisions.

—————— EVALUATION OF MYCIN ——————

In many instances, evaluating an expert system is a difficult challenge. Even knowing what to evaluate can be difficult for designers. This difficulty is not unique to expert systems but plagues the designers of conventional programs (Denning 1981). Denning reports that most designers evaluate their system on the basis of performance alone, while overlooking other important issues. In Chapter 18, we will explore the major issues you should consider when evaluating an expert system. In this section, we review how the MYCIN team evaluated the performance of their system.

When evaluating the performance of an expert system, many designers rely on the help of an expert. They ask the expert to solve some testcase problem, then compare the expert's solution to that derived by the expert system for the same problem. The MYCIN team took the same approach but extended this idea and included several experts during the evaluation (Buchanan and Shortliffe 1984).

For this evaluation study, ten case histories of meningitis were diagnosed by MYCIN and by eight individuals from the Stanford School of Medicine. These individuals included five faculty members, one research fellow in infectious diseases, one resident physician, and one medical student. The prior findings made by the earlier physicians on the cases were also included in the study, for a total of ten diagnoses for each case.

These ten diagnoses for each case (100 prescriptions, 10 each by 10 prescribers) were then evaluated by eight other individuals outside of Stanford who were experts on infectious diseases. These eight individuals, called the "evaluators," were asked to form their own recommendation for each case and then to assess the ten prescriptions provided by the eight individuals from Stanford, the prior findings by the physicians on the cases and the findings provided by MYCIN.

The assessment was based on classifying the given prescription into one of three categories (Buchanan and Shortliffe 1984):

Equivalent: recommendation was identical to or equivalent to that given by the evaluator.

Acceptable alternative: recommendation was different from the evaluator, but considered to be an acceptable alternative.

Not acceptable: recommendation was considered unacceptable or inappropriate by the evaluator.

During the assessment of the prescriptions, the evaluators were given the prescriptions with no knowledge of their source. That is, they didn't know if a given prescription came from MYCIN or one of the human prescribers. This approach was intended to remove any bias that might occur if the evaluators knew that a given prescription came from a specific prescriber.

The MYCIN team found this approach to be important following earlier evaluation studies. During these earlier studies, expert physicians who were asked to assess MYCIN knew they were reviewing the output of a computer program. Many of the criticisms raised reflected their own biases toward the application of computers in the medical domain, as demonstrated by the following statement made by one of the evaluators: "I don't think the computer has an adequate sense of how sick this patient is. You'd have to see a patient like this in order to judge." (Hayes–Roth et al. 1983).

Another point that should be mentioned about this evaluation approach is that the evaluators were *blind* to the knowledge about infectious diseases contained in MYCIN. In addition, since the test cases chosen represented new tests for MYCIN, MYCIN was also *blind* to this new information. In effect, this arrangement produced a *double-blind* test.

Note: *A double-blind test offers a credible unbiased evaluation of an expert system that is often used today when evaluating an expert system.*

The results of this evaluation are shown in Table 5.3. Column 2 of the table lists the scores on the basis of the percentage of prescriptions found acceptable by the majority of the eight evaluators, where "acceptable" is interpreted as a prescription that is either *equivalent* or an *acceptable alternative.*

Another issue studied during the evaluation was whether the recommended treatment failed to prescribe the correct drugs to treat the infection. Column 3 of Table 5.3 shows the results of this study.

Review of MYCIN Evaluation

We can make several observations from the results listed in Table 5.3. First, on the issue of providing an acceptable therapy (column 2), MYCIN's score of 70% is equal to or higher than that found for the human prescribers. This is an

TABLE 5.3   Evaluation of MYCIN and Nine Other Individuals (Buchanan and Shortliffe 1984)

Prescriber	Score (%) in Which Therapy was Rated as Acceptable by Majority of Evaluators	No. of Cases in Which Therapy Failed to Cover Treatable Pathogen
MYCIN	70	0
Prior Rx	70	0
Faculty-1	50	1
Faculty-2	50	1
Fellow	50	1
Faculty-4	50	0
Faculty-3	40	0
Resident	30	1
Faculty-5	30	0
Student	10	3

encouraging result, since it illustrates that the program outperformed the majority of human test subjects. However, would a correct score of 70% be acceptable?

When evaluating the performance of an expert system, it is first necessary to define acceptable performance specifications that can be used in judging the acceptability of the system. During the evaluation of MYCIN, the experts felt that the system should be capable of performing the correct diagnosis in at least 90% of the cases. However, before accepting this as a realistic figure, it seems only reasonable to first measure the performance of actual experts in the field.

The Stanford infectious disease specialists represent a high standard of excellence. Three of the Stanford physicians would have qualified as experts in the management of meningitis by the criteria used for the selection of the national evaluators (Buchanan and Shortliffe 1984). Yet, these three Stanford experts scored less than MYCIN and less than the original desired score of 90%. Therefore, the 90% figure originally sought may have been unrealistic, as reflected by the evidence of disagreement among the experts in the study. It follows that a better measure of an expert system's performance might be a comparison of its performance with other experts.

From the evaluation of MYCIN, the researchers formed a better understanding of establishing an acceptable performance criteria. They argued that it was reasonable to suggest that an expert system was acceptable if it performed at a level of a human expert, even if at times both prescribe the wrong remedy. This argument is consistent with one of the features of an expert system mentioned in Chapter 2, that stated expert systems **can make mistakes** just like their human counterparts. The axiom you draw from this is that an expert system provides an *expert opinion* rather than a guaranteed result.

The results of Table 5.3 (column 2) also illustrate that MYCIN did not fail to prescribe the correct treatment, a situation that could have been catastrophic if the correct treatment was not administered and the patient had died. It was also found during this study that MYCIN recommended fewer drugs than the other test individuals, and therefore didn't overprescribe for the infection.

EMYCIN

During the work on MYCIN, a large amount of LISP code was written for different modules:

- Knowledge base
- Inference engine
- Working memory
- Explanation facility
- End-user interface

Toward the end of the project, the MYCIN developers realized that because the knowledge on infectious diseases was separate from its control, then the code written for the other modules should be portable to other applications. Bill van Melle wrote (1979)

"One ought to be able to take out the clinical knowledge and plug in knowledge about some other domain."

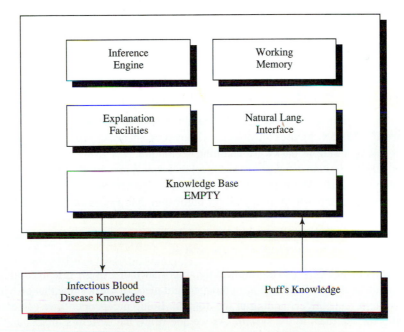

FIGURE 5.3 Block diagram of EMYCIN with PUFF knowledge.

By removing the knowledge about infectious blood diseases, a system known as EMYCIN (van Melle 1979) was formed. EMYCIN is a domain-independent version of MYCIN that contains all of MYCIN except its knowledge about infectious blood disease. EMYCIN facilitated the development of other expert systems, such as PUFF (Aikens et al. 1983), an application for the diagnosis of pulmonary problems. This process of removing MYCIN's knowledge and replacing it with knowledge from another domain is illustrated in Figure 5.3 which shows a stage of building PUFF.

The separation of knowledge from its processing is a powerful feature of expert systems that permits the reuse of existing code and greatly reduces the development time for other systems. For example, PUFF was produced in about 5 person-years, a considerable saving over the 20 person-years required to develop MYCIN. This capability of isolating an expert system's knowledge is also the basis of today's expert system development software tools, more commonly referred to as *shells*.

SUMMARY ON MYCIN

MYCIN was one of the first expert systems built that heralded in a new generation of computer programs that could reason at the level of human experts. It provided a well-defined benefit by assisting physicians in the diagnosis of infectious blood diseases. Beyond the success it achieved in its application area, lies an even more important value of the project.

The development effort on MYCIN laid the groundwork for designing expert systems today. It taught us many lessons that are summarized in this section. Later chapters refer often to these lessons, when arguing for the need to design specific features into an expert system.

Lesson 1: Knowledge is power.

One of the primary lessons MYCIN taught us is **"in the knowledge lies the power."** MYCIN captures the domain's knowledge in a set of rules and processes them using a simple backward-chaining technique. Yet even with this simple approach, the system can perform at a level that equals or exceeds the performance of human experts. We can therefore attribute its performance to the quality of its knowledge rather than to any clever algorithm that processed the knowledge.

Lesson 2: Rules are powerful independent pieces of knowledge that can be easily added to the system.

The work on MYCIN also highlighted the importance of a single rule in capturing domain knowledge. Each rule is an independent piece of knowledge that provides the system some understanding of the domain. Being independent, we can easily modify or add rules to the system. As we add rules, the system's understanding and performance improves. The rule's independence also permits us to easily inspect and verify the system's knowledge.

Lesson 3: Separation of knowledge from control permits the system to be used for other problems.

Since an expert system separates domain knowledge from its control, we can use the system for other problems by simply removing the knowledge and replacing it with knowledge on some other problem. This observation motivated the creation of EMYCIN (van Melle 1979), a skeletal system of MYCIN without the knowledge on infectious blood diseases. EMYCIN was used to create PUFF (Aikens et al. 1983), an expert system on pulmonary problems. EMYCIN provided the foundation for today's rule-based expert system shells.

Lesson 4: Expert systems can be built to manage inexact reasoning.

The world is not black and white. We often confront a problem where the available information is uncertain or incomplete, yet we are still able to make intelligent "guesses" to solve the problem. MYCIN also had to work within an inexact world. It would often be working in a life-threatening situation where time did not permit complete laboratory testing, leaving some degree of uncertainty in the available information. Through the efforts of developing MYCIN, a methodology evolved called the *certainty theory* that provides an expert system with techniques for managing inexact information.

Lesson 5: Accommodate the user.

MYCIN provides us insight into ways of developing an expert system that is accommodating to the user. The MYCIN team recognized that the user may be unaccustomed to working with a computer, or worse, may be skeptical of its value. To win over a convert, MYCIN was designed to operate in an interactive fashion that as closely as possible modeled the normal human consultation interaction. It converses in English, and can recognize and correct simple spelling mistakes.

Lesson 6: Maintain system transparency.

MYCIN provides the user transparency to its reasoning. MYCIN can respond to a question about *why* it needs some information, and to one about *how* it reached a conclusion. The ability to explain its reasoning adds to the system's credibility. Both types of explanations were found easy to implement in MYCIN because of the rigid syntax of a rule-based system. For example, to decide *how* it derived a conclusion, MYCIN looks for the conclusion in some rule that fired, then traces back through the other rules which supported the premises in the rule.

Lesson 7: Meta-rules can be used to provide better control over the search.

In a simple backward-chaining system, the inference engine exhaustively searches through the knowledge base in an attempt to prove some goal. This style of search is oblivious to information being gathered that may lead the system into unproductive areas, resulting in a decrease in search efficiency. MYCIN uses meta-rules to avoid this problem by redirecting the search into other potentially more productive areas.

Lesson 8: Depth-first backward chaining provides a more natural interaction with the user.

Using a depth-first search technique, MYCIN pursues each issue exhaustively before considering other issues. The principal advantage found with this approach was that a series of questions posed to the physician maintained a common theme, a situation that was more appealing to the physician. A forward-chaining system poses questions that seem random and unconnected, a style of questioning that is irritating to a user. Expert systems must do more than provide a correct answer—they must present themselves throughout the session in an intelligent fashion.

Lesson 9: The expert system makes only a recommendation; the user has the final say.

When designing an expert system we want the user to feel that she is in control and has the last say on the subject. As such, we must not only convey to the user that the results of the system are recommendations and not directives, but we should also build control features into the system that will allow the user to seek alternative results. MYCIN accomplishes this by allowing the user to question it on *why* other solutions were not found, and to prompt it to formulate other recommendations.

Lesson 10: Report intermediate important findings.

A subtle but significant feature of MYCIN is its presentation of intermediate important findings. In most conventional programs, we are accustomed to receiving only the final results, with no presentation of any intermediate findings. However, expert systems are designed to model the dialogue of a human expert, who will often report findings on important issues as they are discovered. For example, MYCIN reports both the identity of the infection and the infecting organisms, which are highly important issues, before deriving a final therapeutic recommendation. This feature, like others previously discussed, adds transparency to the system and presents the system in a more natural manner.

Lesson 11: Design system for the intelligent user.

In some cases, the user may already know the answer to some question that the expert system was designed to derive. In these situations, it is better to have the system first ask the user for the needed information, before trying to derive it.

This approach is not only efficient, it allows the system to work with the user in a cooperative fashion.

Lesson 12:   Evaluate system using a double-blind test.

One difficulty when evaluating an expert system is to set up a fair test. In particular, it is important we choose test conditions that avoid any appearance of bias. The approach taken by the MYCIN team to avoid this problem was the *double-blind* test. In this test, an expert not associated with the project chooses new test cases for the system evaluation. The new expert is *blind* since she is unaware of the system's knowledge on the subject, and the system is *blind* since the cases represent new information. This approach offers a fair assessment of the system and is acceptable in most applications.

Lesson 13:   Evaluate the system by comparison with expert performance.

When evaluating an expert system, we should judge its performance on the basis of a comparison of the system's findings with the findings of the other experts. This approach is more reasonable than setting specifications that are unrealistic and beyond the ability of the human experts. This argument was made during the evaluation of MYCIN, where outside experts disagreed with the prescriptions of MYCIN no more than they did with the recommendations of experts from Stanford's School of Medicine.

REFERENCES

Aikens, J.S., J.C. Kunz, and E.H. Shortliffe, PUFF: An Expert System for Interpretation of Pulmonary Function Data, Computers and Biomedical Research, vol. 16, pp. 199–208, 1983.

Buchanan, B.G. and E.H. Shortliffe (eds.), Rule-Based Expert Systems: The MYCIN Experiments of the Stanford Heuristic Programming Project. Addison-Wesley, Reading Mass., 1984.

Davis, R., B. Buchanan, and E. Shortliffe, Production Rules as a Representation for a Knowledge-Based Consultation Program, Artificial Intelligence, vol. 8, pp. 15–45, 1977.

Denning, P.J., Performance Analysis: Experimental Computer Science at Its Best, Communications of the ACM, vol. 24, pp. 725–727, 1981.

Hayes–Roth, F., D.A. Waterman, and D.B. Lenat, Building Expert Systems, Addison-Wesley, Reading Mass., 1983.

Roberts, A.W. and J.A. Visconti, The Rational and Irrational Use of Systemic Microbial Drugs, American Journal of Hospital Pharmacy, vol. 29, pp. 828–834, 1972.

Shortliffe, E.H., Computer-Based Medical Consultation, MYCIN, American Elsevier, New York, 1976.

van Melle, W., A Domain-Independent Production-Rule System for Consultation Programs, Proceedings IJCAI-79, pp. 923–925, 1979.

EXERCISES

1. Every expert system project must have some justification. Discuss the primary justifications for MYCIN.

2. MYCIN is a backward-chaining system. Discuss why this is the proper inference technique for this project and describe why a forward-chaining approach would be inappropriate.

3. MYCIN, like all expert systems, separates the knowledge from its control. Discuss the value of this arrangement.

4. MYCIN employs inexact reasoning in two major ways: representing uncertain information and uncertain rules. Describe some other problem that would require inexact reasoning and provide examples where both information and rules are inexact.

5. MYCIN can remember a session with a given patient that could be valuable if at a later time new information surfaces. Describe some other problem where this utility might be of value.

6. The MYCIN development team recognized the importance of accommodating the user. List the principal features designed into MYCIN to accomplish this and describe the value of each.

7. A trademark of today's expert systems is their ability to explain their reasoning. Discuss the value of this ability and describe how explanations were implemented in MYCIN.

8. Describe the double-blind test used in evaluating MYCIN and discuss its value for evaluating expert systems in general.

9. How can one establish a criteria for judging the performance of an expert system?

10. Discuss the value in using a depth-first search technique.

Rule-Based Expert Systems

INTRODUCTION

Rule-based systems are currently the most popular choice of knowledge engineers for building an expert system. This popularity has grown out of the large number of successful rule-based systems built and from the abundance of available rule-based expert system development software.

This chapter provides a brief overview of this type of system. In particular, it provides a review of the advantages and limitations of rule-based systems. The chapter serves as a starting point for material in the next several chapters that discuss in detail the operation and design of rule-based expert systems.

EVOLUTION OF RULE-BASED SYSTEMS

The rule-based systems that you see today are a product of an evolutionary process that has taken place over the past 30 years. Earlier studies broke ground

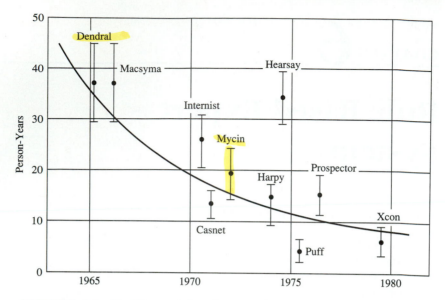

FIGURE 6.1   Development time for several expert system projects (from Hayes-Roth et al. 1984).

for the technology and pioneered techniques that evolved through trial-and-error into established methods for designing effective systems. A tour of the history of rule-based systems actually follows the path of expert systems in general, since most of the early systems were rule-based. Figure 6.1 shows some the major systems (the "classics") developed over this time period and the length of time required to developed them measured in person-years (Hayes–Roth et al. 1984).

The 1960s

Systems developed during the 1960s were more of a probing effort. Developers were learning their way in designing systems whose power came from the problem's knowledge, rather than from clever processing techniques. Because of the emphasis on knowledge, these systems were often called **knowledge-based systems.**

Most noteworthy of the developments during the 1960s was DENDRAL (Buchanan and Feigenbaum 1978). DENDRAL was developed at Stanford University in support of NASA's Mars exploration program. The system was designed to perform chemical analyses of the Martian soil. The developers encoded in the program the knowledge of a chemist who specialized in organic chemistry.

The success of DENDRAL demonstrated that intelligent systems could be built by capturing the knowledge of human experts. Researchers in AI vigorously began to look for better ways of representing and searching knowledge in computer systems—their heritage to later expert system developers.

The 1970s

Armed with better representation and search techniques, and inspired by the successes of knowledge-based systems developed during the 1960s, expert system developers during the 1970s sought to define effective design techniques. At this point, the feasibility of developing such systems was proven. It was now time to develop a number of systems and learn from the experience. It was also time to produce systems that provided real benefits.

No other system contributed more to our understanding of building rule-based systems than MYCIN (Shortliffe 1976). The objective of MYCIN was to diagnose infectious blood diseases. Its technical successes on this problem were discussed in Chapter 5. However, through the eyes of the expert system developer, the real success story of MYCIN was measured by the insight it provided into rule-based system design.

In terms of developing systems that produced real benefits, two systems stand out from the 1970s—XCON and PROSPECTOR. XCON, originally called R1, was developed at Carnegie Mellon and was designed to aid Digital Equipment Company (DEC) in the configuration of their VAX computer systems (McDermott 1980). XCON was developed using OPS, a rule-based programming language. XCON has proven to be a valuable tool for DEC, with estimates of savings up to $20 million dollars per year.

PROSPECTOR was an expert system developed at the Stanford Research Institute to aid geologists in the exploration of ore deposits (Duda et al. 1977). PROSPECTOR was field tested at a site near Mount Tolman, located in eastern Washington, where it predicted the existence of a molybdenum deposit. Subsequent drilling confirmed this prediction with the discovery of a $100 million molybdenum deposit.

At the close of the '70s, expert systems were an established technology. The understanding of rule-based systems provided by the work on MYCIN and the dramatic successes of XCON and PROSPECTOR lead to the development of a large number of systems during the '80s.

The 1980s

During the 1980s, many universities and companies turned their attention toward expert systems. Systems were built for applications ranging from aiding miners a mile below the earth's surface to helping astronauts aboard the space station. Over two thirds of the Fortune 1000 companies also became involved in applying the technology in daily business activities. The interest in the field also gave birth to a large number of companies that marketed expert system development software—expert system shells.

The credit for this success story should go to two sources: the people and the technology. From the time the developers of DENDRAL first met with the expert chemist, through the time PROSPECTOR discovered a valuable mineral deposit, the developers of these systems labored to make this new and sometimes fragile technology work. We often take for granted today the techniques first pioneered by these individuals.

Up to the mid-80s, the field was dominated by rule-based systems. Through experience with developing many early rule-based systems came a better understanding for their development. This brought about an explosion of applications, as discussed in Chapter 1. However, during the latter part of the '80s, there was a shift toward object-oriented systems. The additional power offered by these systems was recognized to be capable of solving problems that were beyond the reach of rule-based systems. We will review this technology in Chapter 14.

The Time Line

One final point is worthy of note on the history of expert system development. As shown in Figure 6.1, the number of person-years required for the development of expert systems dramatically decreased with the progression of time. One obvious explanation for this decrease is the experience gained by developers in designing these systems. However, there is another reason that is not as obvious. For insight, consider the work on PUFF.

An offspring of MYCIN was PUFF (Aikens et al. 1983), an application for the diagnosis of pulmonary problems. The developers of PUFF were the same as those that developed MYCIN. In taking on the new project, they ask a reasonable question: "What coding from MYCIN can we use on this new project?" After consideration, they found that all of the code could be used, minus the knowledge on infectious diseases. That is, they had already created an environment for the development of a rule-based system; all that needed to be changed was the problem's knowledge. The environment left over they called EMYCIN, the forerunner of today's expert system shells.

Having an established environment (a shell) for the creation of an expert system had a major impact on the time required to develop the system. For example, PUFF was produced in about 5 person-years, a considerable saving over the 20 person-years required to develop MYCIN.

The availability today of easy-to-use rule-based shells, has attracted a wider gathering of people willing to become involved in the effort. This situation should serve as a catalyst in the development of future systems.

─────────── PRODUCTION SYSTEMS ───────────

A study of the history of rule-based systems would not be complete without a discussion of the **production system.** The production system is the basis of today's rule-based system. Its basic architecture was used by all the previously discussed systems.

During the 1960s, Newell and Simon at Carnegie-Mellon University (CMU) studied the application of information-processing techniques for the modeling of human problem solving (Newell and Simon, 1972). In their work they represented a human's long-term memory as a set of situation-action rules called **productions** and the short-term memory as a set of situations or specific information about some problem.

DEFINITION 6.1: Production
Term used in cognitive psychology to describe the relationship between situations and actions, and more commonly referred to today as a rule.

The original concept of a production was first proposed by Post (Post 1943). The basic structure of a production consists of an antecedent or IF part describing the situation and a consequent or THEN part describing some action to be taken in the event that the situation exists.

ANTECEDENT		CONSEQUENT
Situation	$\rightarrow$	Action

or

IF Situation   THEN Action

Newell and Simon argued that when solving some problem humans use a set of productions from their long-term memory that apply to a given situation that is stored in their short-term memory. The situation causes some production to *fire* resulting in its action being added to their short-term memory. This process is similar to human reasoning: inferring new information from known information. With this additional information added to the short-term memory, the situation changes which could cause other productions to fire. This human problem solving model of evoking productions from long-term memory and changing the content of the short-term memory became known as the **production system** and is illustrated in Figure 6.2.

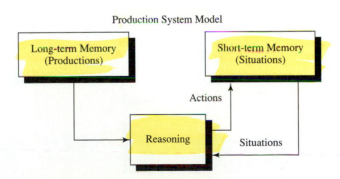

FIGURE 6.2 Production system model.

DEFINITION 6.2: Production System
A model of human problem solving where problem situations contained in the short-term memory are combined with productions in the long-term memory to infer new information which is added to the short-term memory.

RULE-BASED SYSTEMS

The idea behind the production system is simple but effective. It offers the argument that humans solve problems by combining problem-specific information contained in their short-term memory with a set of productions representing problem solving knowledge contained in their long-term memory. The production system became the foundation of today's **rule-based expert system** which is illustrated in Figure 6.3.

DEFINITION 6.3: Rule-Based Expert System
A computer program that processes problem-specific information contained in the working memory with a set of rules contained in the knowledge base, using an inference engine to infer new information.

A rule-based expert system models the production system using the following modules:

- **Knowledge base:** models a human's long-term memory as a set of rules.
- **Working memory:** models a human's short-term memory and contains problem facts both entered and inferred by the firing of the rules.
- **Inference engine:** models human reasoning by combining problem facts contained in the working memory with rules contained in the knowledge base to infer new information.

In the rule-based system, the rules contained in the knowledge base represent the productions contained in the long-term memory and the facts contained in

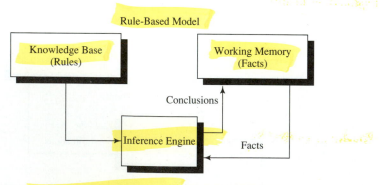

FIGURE 6.3   Rule-based model.

the working memory represent the situations in the short-term memory. The inference engine acts as the reasoning module of the production system model and compares the facts with the antecedents or premises of the rules to see which ones can fire. Those rules that can fire have their conclusions added to the working memory and the process continues until no other rules have antecedents that match the facts contained in the working memory. Rule-based expert systems are not necessarily an exact match for human problem solving, but they provide a reasonable model for replicating this behavior with a computer.

RULE-BASED SYSTEM ARCHITECTURE

The last section described a rule-based system as being composed of three modules: knowledge base, inference engine, and a working memory. These three components comprise the heart of the system, but there are other subsystems that you will find in any real system. The complete architecture of a rule-based system is shown in Figure 6.4. The additional subsystems are as follows:

- **User interface:** the vehicle through which the user views and interacts with the system.
- **Developer interface:** the vehicle through which the knowledge engineer develops the system.
- **Explanation facility:** the subsystem responsible for providing explanations on the reasoning of the system.
- **External programs:** programs such as databases, spreadsheets, algorithms, etc, that work in a support role for the system.

User/developer interface   All of the expert system development software, including both the shells and base languages, will offer different faces to the user and the developer of the system. The user may be exposed to simple textual displays or interactive graphics. The developer might develop the system using a source code approach or be led through a smart editor during system development.

Explanation facility   The nature of the explanation facility will depend on the choice of the development software. Most shells provide a limited capability for providing explanations of *why* some question is being asked and *how* some conclusion is reached. The types of explanations found are usually adequate for the developer during the debugging of the system but are too cryptic for the user. If a base language approach is taken for system development, you will have better control over the explanations and can tailor them to meet the needs of the user.

External programs   Most of the shells on the market offer an open architecture that permits you to interface the expert system with a variety of external programs. This capability adds to the utility of the system, so that information naturally stored in external sources can be easily accessed and used by the expert system.

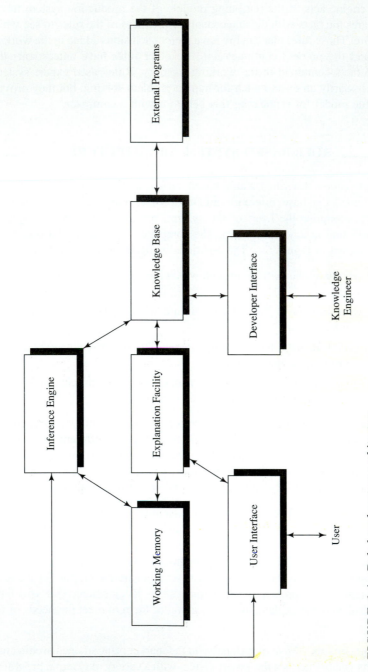

FIGURE 6.4 Rule-based system architecture.

ADVANTAGES OF RULE-BASED SYSTEMS

Natural Expression

For many problems, humans naturally express their problem solving knowledge in IF . . . THEN type statements. The ease of capturing this knowledge in a rule makes a rule-based approach an attractive choice for the design of the expert system.

Separation of Control From Knowledge

The work by Newell and Simon (1972) on the production system model implied that the human's knowledge about a problem was separate from the reasoning with that knowledge. Likewise, the rule-based system separates the knowledge contained in the knowledge base from its control performed by the inference engine. This feature is not unique to rule-based systems but is a trademark of all expert systems. This valuable feature permits you to change the system's knowledge or control separately.

Modularity of Knowledge

A rule is an independent chunk of knowledge. It logically derives facts that can be concluded about the problem contained in its THEN part from facts that are established in its IF part. Since it is an independent piece of knowledge, you can easily review it and verify its correctness.

Ease of Expansion

The separation of the system's knowledge from its control permits you to easily add additional rules allowing for a graceful expansion of the system's knowledge. As long as you adhere to the syntax requirements of the chosen software to assure the necessary logical relationships between rules, you can add the new rule anywhere in the knowledge base.

Proportional Growth of Intelligence

Even one rule can be a valuable piece of knowledge. It is capable of telling the system something new about the problem from established evidence. As the number of rules increase, the system's level of intelligence about the problem likewise increases. This situation is like a young child gaining more knowledge about her world and using this knowledge to solve future problems more intelligently.

Use of Relevant Knowledge

The system will use only the rules that are relevant to the problem. A rule-based system is likely to have many rules that can address a number of problem issues.

However, the system can decide on the basis of discovered information which ones should be pursued in order to solve the current problem. This situation is again like a young child who may know about a number of topics about her world, but applies only the knowledge that is important for the current problem.

Derivation of Explanations from Rigid Syntax

Since the problem solving model depends upon the rules matching various facts in the working memory, it offers an opportunity to determine *how* some piece of information came to be placed in the working memory. Since the information may have been placed by the firing of some rule, which itself depended upon other facts in the working memory, you can obtain a trace of the rules fired leading to the information. This capability allows the system to explain its reasoning for questions such as "How did you arrive at the recommendation of . . . ?"

Consistency Checking

The rigid structure of the rule also allows for consistency checking of the system to assure that the same situations do not lead to different actions. For example consider the following two rules:

| IF | Container contains acid | THEN | Don't drink the contents |
| IF | Container contains acid | THEN | Drink the contents |

Many shells can take advantage of the rule's rigid structure to automatically check the consistency of the rules and alert the developer of possible conflicts. As this example illustrates, this may not be a bad utility to have.

Utilization of Heuristic Knowledge

A typical trait of human experts is that they are particularly adept at using "rules of thumb" or "heuristics" to help them to solve a problem efficiently. These heuristics are "tricks of the trade" that they learn from experience and are often more valuable to them than fundamental principles that might be learned in a classroom setting. Rule-based systems are well suited for working with these heuristics. You can write heuristic rules that work in a common-sense fashion to draw conclusions or to efficiently control the search of the knowledge base.

Utilization of Uncertain Knowledge

For many problems, available information will only establish a level of *belief* on some issue rather than assert it with complete certainty. Rules can easily be written that capture this uncertain relationship. For example, given the following statement, you could write the rule that captures the uncertainty in the statement:

"If it looks like rain then I should *probably* carry an umbrella"

IF   Weather looks like rain
THEN   Carry an umbrella CF 80

This rule represents the uncertainty expressed in the use of the word "probably" by a number called the **certainty factor** (CF). In this fashion the system can establish a level of belief in the rule's conclusion. This topic is covered in more detail in Chapter 12.

Can Incorporate Variables

Variables can be used in the rules which greatly enhances the efficiency of the system. The variables can be bound to a number of instances in the working memory and tested by the rule. For example:

IF   ?Student GPA is adequate
THEN   ?Student can graduate

This rule will first scan all the facts in the working memory looking for a match for its premise, such as **Bob** GPA is adequate. Then assert into working memory: **Bob** can graduate. In general, through the use of variables you can write general rules that can be applied across a number of similar objects.

—————— DISADVANTAGES OF RULE-BASED SYSTEMS ——

Require Exact Matching

The rule-based system attempts to match the antecedents of the available rules with the facts in the working memory. For this process to be effective, this match must be exact, which in turn requires a strict adherence to consistent coding. Consider for example the following rule:

IF   The motor is hot
THEN   Shut the motor down

If we were to place in the short-term memory either of the following two statements:

> The motor is running hot
> The motor's temperature is hot

we would not have an exact match and the rule would not fire. As humans we can easily interpret these two statements as meaning the same thing as the antecedent of the example, but the computer is unforgiving of differences in the statement's syntax.

Have Opaque Rule Relationships

Although an individual rule may be easy to interpret, it is often difficult to determine how rules are logically related through an inference chain. For example:

IF C THEN D, IF B THEN C, IF A THEN B

The first rule is dependent on the other two, and the second on the third rule. During testing and debugging, it is important to be able to locate these related rules. Since the rules can be placed anywhere in the knowledge base, and the number of rules can be large, it is often difficult to locate and trace through the related rules.

Can Be Slow

Systems with a large set of rules can be slow. This difficulty occurs because when the inference engine is deciding which rules to apply, it must scan the entire set of rules. This can result in slow processing times, which can be detrimental in real-time applications.

Are Inappropriate for Some Problems

Another shortcoming of the rule-based system occurs when rules do not efficiently or naturally capture the representation of the domain's knowledge. Davis and King (1977) comment on this deficiency:

> *"Program designers have found that production systems easily model problems in some domains, but are awkward for others."*

Rules provide only one choice for representing the problem's knowledge in the expert system. Other techniques include frames, semantic networks, decision tables, etc. One of your jobs as the knowledge engineer is to choose the representation technique that is best suited for the problem.

———— SUMMARY ON RULE-BASED EXPERT SYSTEMS ——

This chapter provided an overview of rule-based expert systems. A brief discussion of the history of these systems was given that illustrated the progressive understanding in their design during the past several decades. Finally, the advantages and limitations of these systems were listed.

The major lessons learned in this chapter were:

- The capability of building today's rule-based systems is a product of the efforts performed during the past several decades.
- The dramatic decrease in the development time in building rule-based systems can mostly be attributed to the availability of shells.

- During the 1990s the movement will be towards object- oriented design but rule-based systems will continue to play an important role.
- A rule-based system is a tool that has several advantages and disadvantages. Like any other tool, it is important that you match the tool to the problem.

REFERENCES

Aikens, J.S., J.C. Kunz, and E.H. Shortliffe, PUFF: An Expert System for Interpretation of Pulmonary Function Data, Computers and Biomedical Research, vol. 16, pp. 199–208, 1983.

Buchanan, B. and E. Feigenbaum, DENDRAL and Meta-DENDRAL: Their Applications Dimension, Artificial Intelligence, vol. 11, 1978.

Davis, R. and J. King, An Overview of Production Systems, Machine Intelligence, vol. 8, pp. 300–322, 1977.

Duda, R., P.E. Hart, N.J. Nilsson, R. Reboh, J. Slocum, and G. Sutherland, Development of a Computer-Based Consultant for Mineral Exploration, SRI Report, Stanford Research Institute, 333 Ravenswood Avenue, Menlo Park, CA, Oct. 1977.

Hayes–Roth, F., D. Waterman, and D. Lenat, Building Expert Systems, Addison-Wesley, Reading, MA, 1984.

McDermott, J., R1: An Expert System In the Computer Systems Domain, Proceedings AAAI-80, 1980.

Newell, A. and H.A. Simon, Human Problem Solving, Prentice Hall, Englewood Cliffs, N.J., 1972.

Post, E., Formal Reductions of the General Combinational Problem, American Journal of Mathematics, vol. 65, pp. 197–268, 1943.

Shortliffe, E.H., Computer-Based Medical Consultation, MYCIN, American Elsevier, New York, 1976.

CHAPTER 7

Backward-Chaining Rule-Based Systems

INTRODUCTION

REVIEW OF BACKWARD-CHAINING INFERENCING

MEDICAL CONSULTATION SYSTEMS
    Example 1: Meningitis Diagnosis Expert System
    Example 2: Meningitis Prescription Expert System
    Example 3: Alternative Prescription Expert System

AUTOMOBILE DIAGNOSTIC SYSTEM
    Example 4: Automobile Diagnostics via a Blackboard

SUMMARY ON BACKWARD-CHAINING EXPERT SYSTEMS

INTRODUCTION

Chapter 4 introduced the backward-chaining inferencing technique. The backward-chaining algorithm was described and illustrated by several small examples. This chapter explores this style of reasoning further with several additional examples. The examples introduce advanced features of backward-chaining systems. They also provide insight into the effective design of backward-chaining systems that better prepares you for Chapter 8, which describes a design methodology for these systems.

REVIEW OF BACKWARD-CHAINING INFERENCING

The principal objective of a backward-chaining system is to prove some goal or hypothesis. The process begins by collecting a set of rules that contain the goal in their THEN part. These rules are called **goal rules** by which the goal can be proven if one of these goal rules fire. A goal rule, like any other rule, will fire only if its premises are true. The premises of the goal rule may themselves be supported by other rules, which requires the inference engine to establish them as subgoals that in turn must be proven. Following this process, the inference engine searches through the system's rules in a recursive fashion, attempting to acquire supporting evidence for both the subgoals and the original goal.

The backward-chaining inference engine will eventually reach some premise that is not supported by any of the system's rules—a **primitive.** The system then asks the user a question and the answer is placed in the working memory. The answer may also cause the firing of rules, which then add their conclusions to the working memory.

This process continues until all the goals and subgoals have been searched. At this point the working memory will contain all of the information provided by the user and inferred by the system. Part of this information will be an understanding of the state of the original goal, namely it is true or false.

The next several sections review several backward-chaining expert system examples. Each example is a small system designed to illustrate the operation of a backward-chaining system. Each also highlights important issues on expert system design in the form of "design suggestions."

MEDICAL CONSULTATION SYSTEM

The first example system follows the work of MYCIN. Like MYCIN, the system is designed to perform diagnosis and prescription for infectious blood diseases. Unlike MYCIN, the system doesn't identify the infecting organisms but rather simply the nature of the infection.

The example system includes three different expert systems designed for the tasks of diagnosis, prescription, and prescription changes. Many diagnostic problems follow the task sequence of diagnosis, repair recommendation, and repair guidance. By reviewing the three systems independently, various design issues related to each specific task can be highlighted.

Reviewing the three systems separately also provides insight into a development strategy inherent in good expert system design. Many complex problems can be divided into several smaller subtasks. An expert system can then be designed for each subtask which eases the development, testing and maintenance of each system.

DESIGN SUGGESTION: Divide complex problems into smaller tasks and design systems for each task.

To keep the example systems small, we will assume the only infection of interest is meningitis. The three systems address the following objectives:

- Determine if the patient has meningitis.
- Determine a prescription that should be given to a patient with meningitis.
- Formulate a different prescription if the recommended one is not acceptable to the user.

Example 1: Meningitis Diagnosis Expert System

The objective of this example expert system is to diagnose a patient suspected of having meningitis. In general, diagnosis is concerned with determining the cause of some system fault. Faulty transistor Q1 of some circuit or a malfunction of a pump, are typical faults of concern of a diagnostic system. For a problem on medical diagnosis, the fault is usually some infection and the first task is to determine the identity of the infection before proceeding to form a therapeutic recommendation. In this example, we assume that the presense of meningitis can be determined from information supplied from tests or from observable patient symptoms.

The objectives of reviewing this example are:

- Review the backward-chaining process.
- See how to design the system for an intelligent user.
- Introduce the importance of rule documentation.
- View the system's response to a **WHY** query.
- See how to effectively display the system's findings.
- Introduce the use of a **safety net.**
- Introduce an **inference network.**

Problem-Solving Approach

The rules used in the expert system are shown in Figure 7.1. The system has only one goal—to prove or disprove ''Infection is meningitis'' and one goal rule—RULE 1. This goal can be proven either if the user already knows that the patient has meningitis (avoiding unnecessary questioning) or the system can infer the infection. Meningitis is assumed if test results confirm it or the patient's symptoms indicate it—RULE 2. RULES 3 and 4 search the test results, while RULE 5 searches the area of patient symptoms.

Medical Diagnosis Example Session

We will now review the interaction between the system and the user and note the internal processing of the backward-chaining algorithm. The session begins with an empty working memory.

WORKING MEMORY

STEP 1
Find rules with hypothesis in ''THEN'' part—RULE 1

STEP 2
Look at first premise in RULE 1 and see if it is listed in working memory—NO

```
GOAL 1. Infection is meningitis

RULE 1   MENINGITIS INFECTION
IF       The physician knows the patient has meningitis
OR       We suspect meningitis
THEN     Infection is meningitis
AND      DISPLAY Infection
Note; information to be displayed must be designed and accessed by this statement
ELSE     DISPLAY No infection found

RULE 2   SUSPECT MENINGITIS FROM TESTS OR SYMPTOMS
IF       We suspect meningitis from test results
OR       We suspect meningitis from patient symptoms
THEN     We suspect meningitis

RULE 3   WE SUSPECT MENINGITIS FROM TESTS
IF       Tests were run
AND      Cultures were seen
AND      Cultures look like meningitis
THEN     We suspect meningitis from test results

RULE 4   CULTURES LOOK LIKE MENINGITIS
IF       The appearance of the culture is coccus
AND      The stain of the culture is grampos
THEN Cultures look like meningitis

RULE 5   WE SUSPECT MENINGITIS FROM SYMPTOMS
IF       The patient is suffering persistent headaches
AND      The patient is suffering dizziness
AND      The patient has been lethargic
THEN     We suspect meningitis from patient symptoms
```

FIGURE 7.1 Meningitis diagnosis rules.

STEP 3

See if this premise exists in ''THEN'' part of any rule—NO

STEP 4

This premise is a primitive generating the following question.

SYSTEM: Do you know if the patient has meningitis?
User: NO

WORKING MEMORY

Patient known to have meningitis—FALSE

COMMENT: *System begins the session by asking if the infection is known to be meningitis—accommodating the intelligent user. Since the answer was ''NO'', the system next attempts to prove meningitis from test results.*

STEP 5

Look at second premise in RULE 1 and see if it is listed in working memory—
NO

STEP 6

See if this premise exists in ''THEN'' part of any rule—RULE 2

STEP 7
Look at first premise in RULE 2 and see if it is listed in working memory—
NO

STEP 8
See if this premise exists in "THEN" part of any rule—RULE 3

COMMENT: *The first two premises of RULE 3 are unknown and are primitives, causing the following questions to be asked.*

STEP 9
SYSTEM: Were tests run?
User: YES

STEP 10
SYSTEM: Were cultures seen?
User: YES

COMMENT: *The third premise of RULE 3 is unknown and supported by RULE 4, leading to the following question in the pursuit of premise 1 of RULE 4.*

STEP 11
SYSTEM: The appearance of the culture is coccus?
User: WHY

COMMENT: *The user wants to know why this question is important. The system responds by displaying the current rule being pursued.*

SYSTEM: This will aid in determining if "CULTURES LOOK LIKE MENINGITIS".

> **[RULE 4]**
> **IF   The appearance of the culture is coccus   [4.1]**
> **AND   The stain of the culture is grampos   [4.2]**
> **THEN Cultures look like meningitis   [4.0]**

COMMENT: *The user might now ask why it is important to determine if the cultures look like meningitis. The system would respond by displaying the rule that needs this information, then asks the question again.*

STEP 12
User: WHY 4.0

SYSTEM: This will aid in determining if "WE SUSPECT MENINGITIS FROM TEST RESULTS".

> **[RULE 3]**
> **It has already been established that**
> > **Tests were run   [3.1]**
> > **Cultures were seen   [3.2]**

Therefore, if
    Cultures look like meningitis   **[3.3]**
Then We suspect meningitis from test results   **[3.0]**

STEP 13

SYSTEM: The appearance of the culture is coccus?
User: NO

WORKING MEMORY

Patient known to have meningitis—FALSE
Tests run—TRUE
Cultures seen—TRUE
Appearance of culture is coccus—FALSE

COMMENT: *The system was unsuccessful in establishing meningitis from test results (premise 1, RULE 2). It next attempts to establish it by considering the patient's symptoms (premise 2, RULE 2).*

STEP 14

Look at second premise in RULE 2 and see if it is listed in working memory—NO

STEP 15

See if this premise exists in "THEN" part of any rule—RULE 5

STEP 16

All premises of RULE 5 are unknown and primitives, causing the following questions to be asked:

SYSTEM: Has the patient been suffering persistent headaches?
User: YES

SYSTEM: Has the patient been suffering dizziness?
User: YES

SYSTEM: Has the patient been lethargic?
User: YES

STEP 17

RULE 5 fires, which causes RULE 2 to fire, which in turn causes goal RULE 1 to also fire asserting that the infection is meningitis, causing the following display to be given.

SYSTEM: **After considering the information you have provided, I believe the infection is MENINGITIS.**

```
┌─────────────────────────────────────────────────┐
│                WORKING MEMORY                     │
│                                                   │
│  Patient known to have meningitis—FALSE           │
│  Tests run—TRUE                                   │
│  Cultures seen—TRUE                               │
│  Appearance of culture is coccus—FALSE            │
│  Patient suffering headaches—TRUE                 │
│  Patient suffering dizziness—TRUE                 │
│  Patient has been lethargic - TRUE                │
│  Suspect meningitis from symptoms—TRUE            │
│  We suspect meningitis—TRUE                       │
│  Infection is meningitis—TRUE                     │
└─────────────────────────────────────────────────┘
```

Example Review

This small example illustrates the operation of a backward-chaining system and also highlights some of the features designed into the system following the lessons learned from the MYCIN project.

Simple Goal

The system was designed to be knowledgeable about only one infection, namely meningitis, therefore only one goal was established. If you wanted the system to be capable of diagnosing other infections, you would need to write a goal for each along with their supporting rules.

Simple Questions

The session was conducted in an interactive fashion using a natural language. Questions were posed that could be answered in a YES or NO manner. However, you could design the system to accommodate the entry of string or numeric information. In general, consider using questions that require a simple YES or NO type response or a selection from some list of allowable answers. This approach is more reliable than one based on string or numeric input where user mistakes might occur.

Depth-First Search

The session maintained a focused theme, namely patient tests or patient symptoms (see STEPS 9-11). This approach is appealing to the user and occurs because of the depth-first search method employed. This is an inherent feature of most backward-chaining systems that make them attractive for applications that require user interaction.

Accommodation of User

The system offered a transparency into its reasoning by providing an explanation of **WHY** some question was asked—STEP 11. This example provided a display of the current rule being pursued with the option to the user to probe further into other rules. Most shells handle this type of query in this manner.

Display of Findings

The system displayed its final result to the user—infection is meningitis—STEP 17. This final result may only be an intermediate result along the way to some other recommendation. For example:

SYSTEM: I believe the infection is meningitis.
I will next attempt to determine a remedy for this infection.

By providing this intermediate result, the system keeps the user informed about important milestones reached, rather than simply displaying some final result.

Displays could also include context-related information from the session. For example, the term "Infection" in RULE 1 could be a variable and the final display could provide its value:

RULE 1 MENINGITIS INFECTION
IF   . . .
THEN   ?Infection = meningitis
AND   DISPLAY Conclusion

The following display function could be written that used this variable:

DISPLAY Conclusion

I believe the infection is ?Infection.

This approach permits you to write one general display, usable by other rules that conclude different infections. This offers you an efficient coding approach to displaying the system results.

Intelligent User

The example system was designed to support the intelligent user using a simple approach. By intelligent, it is meant that the user has information that can help the system. For example, rather than have the expert system initially try to determine whether the patient has meningitis (premise 2 RULE 1), the user was queried on the issue first (premise 1 RULE 1). This approach allows the user to tell the system what is known about the problem immediately, which could avoid unneeded system search.

Another way you could design the system to accommodate the intelligent user is by allowing him or her to establish the system goals. To illustrate this, consider a problem on animal identification where the system's goals are arranged in the following goal outline structure:

1. The animal is a mammal
   1.1 The mammal is a horse
   1.2 The mammal is a tiger
2. The animal is a reptile
   2.1 The reptile is a snake
   2.2 The reptile is a lizard
3. The animal is a bird
   3.1 The bird is a robin
   3.2 The bird is a finch

Using this goal structure, the system first tries to determine whether the animal is a mammal, reptile, or bird: all at level 1 of the outline. Once this classification is made, the system would try to determine the specific animal located in level 2, i.e., horse or tiger. This type of goal structure is natural to many classification problems—moving from the general to the specific.

Without any direction from the user, the system would always pursue this goal structure using the predesigned form. However, if the user already knows the general classification of the animal, for example "it is a bird," he or she would still need to answer questions that would permit the system to derive this information—a frustrating experience.

To avoid this problem, you can design the system to first ask the user if he or she knows the animal's general classification. If known, the system could avoid the pursuit of this issue and proceed to determine the specific animal. If the user doesn't know the animal's general classification, the system can default to its normal search as described in the goal outline.

You can extend this strategy to deeper levels within the goal outline structure. The user can satisfy the system's goals by simply verifying them, down to a point where help is needed in completing the problem. This technique is called "floating-the-system."

In general, you should provide the user the opportunity to tell the system what he or she knows about the problem. This allows the system to address those aspects of the problem where it can help the user and avoids the frustration caused by the pursuit of issues already known to the user.

DESIGN SUGGESTION: Design the system for an intelligent user by allowing him or her to provide known problem information.

Safety Net

The example incorporated a default display that could be presented to the user if the infection was not found to be meningitis—the ELSE part of RULE 1. This is an important feature to design into the system because without it the system would simply stop and provide no information to the user. This is a typical result you might obtain from a traditional program, i.e., "No can compute," but hardly one that you can use with an "intelligent" system. A default display in an expert system is called a **safety net** since it prevents the system from failing to report.

> **DESIGN SUGGESTION: Always provide a safety net in the system to display some default conclusion.**

The safety net can be as simple as listing some predesigned text or it may include some of the session's findings. For example, most expert systems will have milestones that it reaches when trying to establish its primary goal. A presentation of these findings can be of benefit to the user even if the top-level goal was not proven.

Consider for example the animal identification problem given in the last section. If the system was capable of identifying the animal's classification, but unable to identify the exact animal, the following display may still be of value the user:

SYSTEM: I was unable to identify the animal.
However, I believe the animal is a bird.

Ease of Expansion

In the tradition of rule-based systems, you can easily expand the system to improve its performance. One expansion technique is to make the existing knowledge **deeper.** For example, consider the first premise of RULE 5, which may be ambiguous: "patient is suffering persistent headaches." The system could be expanded to infer this premise using more reliable information, as the following rule illustrates:

IF	The patient experiences headaches each day
OR	The patient has a headache most mornings
THEN	The patient is suffering persistent headaches

A second type of expansion technique makes the system **broader** in intelligence by introducing new issues. For example, if you wanted the system to be capable of determining other infections besides meningitis, you could simply add a new goal directed toward these new infections along with supporting rules.

Documenting of Rules

Rules are written in a syntax that depends on the programming language or the expert system shell you choose for the development of the system. Often this syntax can be difficult to interpret quickly, which hinders both the debugging and maintenance of the system. For this reason, it is important that you document each rule with information that can aid in its interpretation.

At a minimum, the documentation of the rule should state what the rule can conclude from the evidence supplied in its premises. For example, the following rule states that the rule can establish a suspicion that the patient has meningitis from test results:

RULE   WE SUSPECT MENINGITIS FROM TESTS
IF   Tests were run
AND   Cultures were seen
AND   Cultures look like meningitis
THEN   We suspect meningitis from test results

There is another advantage to clearly labeling a rule. Many expert system shells maintain a library of rule titles. You can chose to display some rule from this library by selecting the appropriate title. Only with a clear rule description can you effectively use this utility.

DESIGN SUGGESTION: Document all rules, describing what each rule can accomplish.

There are several other issues that you should consider when documenting a rule which are discussed in Chapter 17.

Inference Network

When reviewing a set of rules it is often difficult to determine which rules support others during the inferencing process. Therefore, expert system designers often use an alternative way of viewing the inference process by graphically displaying the system's rules in an **inference network.**

DEFINITION 7.1: Inference network
Graphical representation of the system's rules with the premises and conclusions of the rules drawn as nodes and their supporting relation-ships drawn as links.

An inference network for the example system is shown in Figure 7.2. This network illustrates how the facts that are the conclusion of one rule serve as premises of other rules. Though the example shown in the figure is actually a tree, often nodes are connected to multiple parents, creating a graph or network structure.

Example 2: Meningitis Prescription Expert System

The previous example system diagnosed a meningitis infection. Further develop-ment of this system might involve more detailed information on meningitis or the expansion of the system to cover other infections. Another way of expanding the system is to cover additional tasks. For example, following the diagnostic task that identified some fault, the next task might naturally be one of forming a recommendation for correcting the fault. This is the approach taken in this

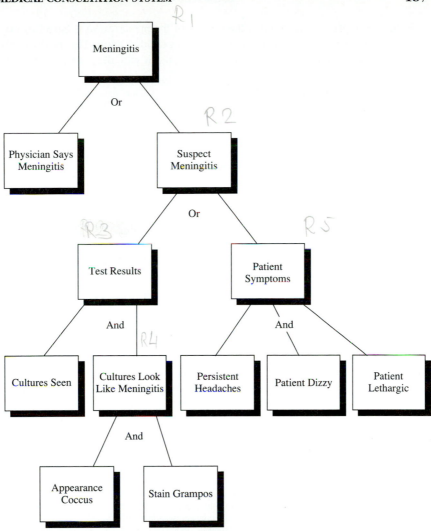

FIGURE 7.2 Inference network of meningitis identity rules.

next example where a prescription is recommended for correcting a meningitis infection.

The prescription task formulates the action needed to correct the fault identified from the diagnostic task. Prescription for a medical problem generates a therapeutic treatment recommendation for eliminating the infecting organism. In the diagnostic example system we did not identify the organisms, but simply the nature of the infection. Therefore, the prescription example system prescribes on the basis of the nature of the infection rather than on knowledge of the organisms present.

In this example we assume that the choice of the prescription is based strictly on the age of the patient—whether the patient is a child or adult. This is obviously a great over-simplification of this complex task, but it will allow us to work with a small but representative system.

The objectives of reviewing this system are:

- Continue to review backward-chaining.
- Introduce variables within goals.
- Introduce rule priorities.
- View the system's response to a **HOW** query.

Problem-Solving Approach

The rules used in the expert system are shown in Figure 7.3. The system has only one goal to prove, which we will represent in variable form ''Prescription is ?prescription,'' but with two goal rules—RULES 1 and 2. The system searches RULE 1 first because of its higher priority. Each goal rule provides a prescription on the basis of the patient's age which is established in RULE 3.

Medical Prescription Example Session

We will assume that the fact that the patient has meningitis is already known and contained in the working memory. The goal of the prescription system is to determine the proper series of drugs to prescribe.

Goal 1. Prescription is ?Prescription

RULE 1 Meningitis Prescription1
(Priority 100)
IF   Infection is Meningitis
AND   The Patient is a Child
THEN   Prescription is Number_1
AND   Drug Recommendation is Ampicillin
AND   Drug Recommendation is Gentamicin
AND   Display Meningitis Prescription 1
ELSE   Display Default

RULE 2 Meningitis Prescription2
(Priority 90)
IF   Infection is Meningitis
AND   The Patient is an Adult
THEN   Prescription is Number_2
AND   Drug Recommendation is Penicillin
AND   Display Meningitis Prescription 2

RULE 3 Age Classification
IF   The Patient's Age < 10
THEN   The Patient is a Child
ELSE   The Patient is an Adult

FIGURE 7.3   Meningitis prescription rules.

```
┌─────────────────────────────────────┐
│          WORKING MEMORY             │
│                                     │
│   Infection is meningitis—TRUE      │
└─────────────────────────────────────┘
```

STEP 1
Find rules with hypothesis in "THEN" part—RULES 1 and 2

STEP 2
Choose RULE 1 because of higher priority and look at first premise and see if it is listed in working memory—YES

STEP 3
Look at second premise in RULE 1 and see if it is listed in working memory—NO

STEP 4
See if this premise exists in "THEN" part of any rule—RULE 3

STEP 5
Look at premise in RULE 3 and see if it is listed in working memory—NO

STEP 6
See if this premise exists in "THEN" part of any rule—NO

STEP 7
This premise is a primitive, causing the following question.

SYSTEM: What is the patient's age?
User: 8

STEP 8
Rule 3 fires (patient is a child) causing Rule 1 to also fire, which updates the working memory and causes the following display.

SYSTEM: My first recommendation is the following:

AMPICILLIN
Dose: 3.8g (30ml)

GENTAMICIN
Dose: 131mg (3.2ml)

Comments: Monitor serum concentrations. Since high concentrations of penicillins can interact with aminoglycosides, do not mix these antibiotics in the same IV bottle.

```
+------------------------------------------------------------------+
|                      WORKING MEMORY                              |
|                                                                  |
|   Infection is meningitis—TRUE                                   |
|   Patient's age—8                                               |
|   Patient is a child—TRUE                                        |
|   Prescription is number_1—TRUE                                  |
|   Drug recommendation AMPICILLIN—TRUE                            |
|   Drug recommendation GENTAMICIN—TRUE                            |
+------------------------------------------------------------------+
```

COMMENT: *After reviewing the recommended drugs, the user may want to know HOW the system derived the recommendation.*

STEP 9
User: HOW

SYSTEM: **To derive goal "PRESCRIPTION IS ?PRESCRIPTION" I considered:**

> **[RULE 1]**
> **IF   Infection is meningitis   [1.1]**
> **AND   The patient is a child   [1.2]**
> **THEN   Prescription is number_1   [1.0]**
> **AND   Drug recommendation is AMPICILLIN   [1.0.1]**
> **AND   Drug recommendation is GENTAMICIN   [1.0.2]**

I already knew [1.1] "INFECTION IS MENINGITIS" is TRUE.

To derive [1.2] "THE PATIENT IS A CHILD" I considered:

> **[RULE 3]**
> **IF   The patient's age < 10   [3.1]**
> **THEN   The patient is a child   [3.0]**
> **ELSE   The patient is an adult   [3.0.1]**

To derive [3.1] "THE PATIENT'S AGE < 10" I asked you. Your answer was 8.

I then concluded [RULE 3] "THE PATIENT IS A CHILD" is TRUE.

I then concluded [RULE 1] "PRESCRIPTION IS NUMBER_1" is TRUE, and [1.0.1] "DRUG RECOMMENDATION IS AMPICILLIN" is TRUE, and [1.0.2] "DRUG RECOMMENDATION IS GENTAMICIN" is TRUE.

Example Review

The prescription example system picked up where the diagnostic system left off. Its goal is to prescribe a series of drugs to be taken by a patient suffering from meningitis. To keep the problem simple, the only issue of concern is the patient's age. Obviously in a real system you would need to consider many other factors such as allergic reactions, weight, etc.

Variable Goal

To permit the system to be easily expanded in the future to consider other prescriptions, it was designed with one variable goal to define the specific drug recommendation:

GOAL

1. Prescription is ?prescription

A real system for this problem may have several goal rules, which conclude different prescriptions. Using a variable goal statement, the system will search each goal rule and bind the value contained in the conclusion to the variable. This approach allows you to write only one goal statement while writing a set of rules for many different types of prescriptions. This approach also permits the introduction of additional prescription rules without the need to adjust the goal agenda. This in turn enhances the future maintenance of the system. It should also be mentioned that the variable in the goal statement can be written in any form, such as ?X instead of ?prescription.

Rule Priorities

Since there are two goal rules in this example—RULE 1 and RULE 2—an obvious question is, Which one will be pursued first? One technique that you can use to help the system choose is to assign the rules a "priority" or "salience."

Rule priority is a number, often in the range −1000 and 1000, which you can use to control the order in which rules are searched. For example, if two rules conclude the same piece of information, then the backward-chaining inference engine will pursue first the rule with the higher priority. In the example system, we have assigned RULE 1 with a priority higher than RULE 2, causing RULE 1 to be searched first. Other factors that can control the order of the search of rules relate to the subject of inexact reasoning which is covered in Chapter 12.

Accommodating User

This example also illustrates MYCIN's feature of explaining **HOW** the recommendation was derived (STEP 9). The system performed this function by providing a full trace of its reasoning—a style that is common among most expert system shells.

Numeric Relationships

The issue of determining whether the patient was a child or adult was handled in a simple relational fashion. That is, as RULE 3 shows, patients less than 10 years old are considered children, those 10 years of age and older are considered adults. This approach obviously has some danger since the system would recommend a series of drugs designed for an adult on a child's tenth birthday.

In general, you must be careful when considering numeric boundary conditions where dramatically different results will occur on the basis of decisions made around the boundary. Chapter 13 explores more appropriate techniques for handling boundary problems through the use of Fuzzy Logic.

DESIGN SUGGESTION: Be careful of numeric boundary decisions.

Example 3: Alternative Prescription Expert System

The past example provided a recommendation for the drugs ampicillin and gentamicin. However, as noted during the work on MYCIN (Chapter 5), the user may not like these recommended drugs for personal reasons. Therefore, the system should allow the user to drop from consideration one or both of these drugs and generate an alternative list of drugs that are acceptable to the user while still adequate for the problem. We explore this idea in this example, but to keep the problem simple, we will consider the deletion of only one of the recommended drugs.

When a drug is deleted from a prescription list and some other drug added, the new drug must meet two conditions: it must be effective and safe. For our example system, we assume that an alternative drug is effective if it comes from the same drug class as the drug deleted from the list. For the drug to be safe, we will consider only one constraint: the age of the patient. Both of these approaches are an over simplification of the problem. However, they permit us to develop a simple system that illustrates some of the important issues of the problem.

The objectives of reviewing this system are:

- Introduce complex goal structures.
- See how a user who is dissatisfied with the final recommendations can be accommodated.
- See value of rules that use variables.
- Introduce non-monotonic reasoning.
- See how an expert system can interface to a database.

Before proceeding with the example, we review the value of the last two objectives.

Non-Monotonic Reasoning

The prior examples used **monotonic reasoning.** That is, once a fact was asserted, it remained asserted. In some applications, this style of reasoning can lead to contradictions. Consider for example the following rule:

> IF   You have more than ten dollars
> THEN   You can date Kathy

If during the processing of this rule the system finds that you have more than ten dollars, then it asserts that you can date Kathy. However, if later the fact ''I have more than ten dollars'' is retracted, the system still believes that ''You can date Kathy.'' The consequence of this situation is that you are now in the embarrassing position of going to Kathy's house, but you really don't have enough money for a date.

To avoid this type of problem you would need to develop a system capable of **non-monotonic reasoning.** These systems can retract facts that are logically dependent on other facts that have been retracted. Several shells permit you to write rules with a ''logical'' condition that can automatically make a fact dependent on the facts that led to its assertion. For instance, you can rewrite the last rule as:

> IF   LOGICAL (You have more than ten dollars)
> THEN   You can date Kathy

By wrapping LOGICAL around the premise, you logically link the conclusion to the premise. Now if you retract the fact ''You have more than ten dollars,'' the fact ''You can date Kathy'' will automatically be retracted.

In general, it is possible that the retraction of a single fact can result in the retraction of all the conclusions based on that fact no matter how remote the support may be. This ability permits you to easily maintain the logical truth of the system's facts, thus avoiding potential contradictions. These types of systems rely upon a subsystem called **truth maintenance.**

Database Access

One important feature of this example system is the use of an external database. For many expert system applications, using an external database offers several advantages:

- Uses existing knowledge.
- Expert system is embedded in existing environment.
- Expert system can be designed with general knowledge.
- System maintenance is enhanced.
- Provides ready access to a large amount of information.

Uses existing knowledge   Many organizations maintain databases that contain a significant amount of information on some subject. In many applications this information can be of value to the expert system. Rather than recoding this information in the expert system, you should design the system to access it directly. In this fashion the system is embedded into existing computer practices and offers an nondisruptive introduction. Many expert system projects have failed simply because they required an organization to change existing practices.

Uses general knowledge   By accessing information from a database, the expert system can be written with *general knowledge*. For example, consider the following rule:

>IF   ?Student_GPA > ACCEPTABLE_GPA
>THEN   ?Student is acceptable

This simple rule states that if any student under consideration for enrollment has a grade point average (GPA) greater than the present acceptable value (ACCEPTABLE_GPA), then the student should be accepted. Values for both ?Student_GPA and ACCEPTABLE_GPA can be obtained from databases. That is, one database might have information on a list of students and another information on present acceptance policies. This approach offers you an opportunity of writing one general but powerful rule that can determine the acceptability of a large number of students.

Enhances system maintenance   By using rules in general form, system maintenance is greatly enhanced. Information contained in the database can be updated by the organization in their normal operating fashion with no need for changes to the expert system. If other considerations become important for making decisions, only simple changes to the expert system may be required.

Consider the prior example. If another issue later becomes important when deciding to accept a student, such as his or her SAT score, then it can easily be added to the rule. For example:

>IF   ?Student_GPA > ACCEPTABLE_GPA
>AND   ?Student SAT_SCORE > ACCEPTABLE_SAT
>THEN   ?Student is acceptable

Accesses wealth of information   Integrating an expert system with an existing database provides a wealth of information to the system. A motivation for employing a database system in any application is that it provides access to a large amount of information. This is valuable because humans often lack the ability to recall and reason with all of the relevant information on some subject. For example, physicians are aware of many drugs that can or cannot be combined, but due to the large number of available drugs, recalling all of this information may be a formidable task.

Problem-Solving Approach

The rules used in the alternative prescription expert system are shown in Figure 7.4. The following discussion goes into detail about the major problem solving steps.

Displays current drugs   The system begins with a simple display of the present recommended drugs—GOAL 1, RULE 1. It then pursues the goal of determining

```
GOALS
1. Display recommended drugs
   1.1. We have alternative drugs to consider
        1.1.1. Requested drug is effective
               1.1.1.1. Requested drug is safe
               1.1.1.2.  Try another drug
        1.1.2.  Try another drug


RULE 1   DISPLAY RECOMMENDED DRUGS
IF       DISPLAY Recommended drugs
THEN     Display recommended drugs


RULE 2   OTHER DRUG IS REQUESTED
IF       The physician wants to consider another drug
AND      The drug to be deleted is known
AND      LOGICAL (The new requested drug is known)
THEN     We have alternative drugs to consider
ELSE     STOP


RULE 3   DETERMINE WHICH DRUG TO DELETE
IF       ASK ?deleted_drug
THEN     The drug to be deleted is known


RULE 4   DETERMINE ALTERNATIVE DRUG
IF       ASK ?requested_drug
THEN     The new requested drug is known


RULE 5   NEW DRUG IS EFFECTIVE
IF       LOGICAL (Requested drug is from same class as the deleted drug)
THEN     Requested drug is effective
AND      DISPLAY ALTERNATIVE DRUG EFFECTIVE


RULE 6   DRUGS COME FROM THE SAME CLASS
CALL     CLASS
SEND     ?deleted_drug
RETURN   ?class1
CALL     CLASS
SEND     ?requested_drug
RETURN   ?class2
IF       ?class1 = ?class2
THEN     Requested drug is from same class as the deleted drug
ELSE     DISPLAY DIFFERENT DRUG CLASSES


RULE 7   NEW DRUG IS SAFE
IF       Patient's age is known
AND      LOGICAL (Patient's age is acceptable for the new drug)
THEN     Requested drug is safe
AND      DISPLAY ALTERNATIVE DRUG SAFE


RULE 8   AGE IS ACCEPTABLE FOR NEW DRUG
CALL     AGE
SEND     ?requested_drug
RETURN   Allowable_age
IF       Patient's_age >= Allowable_age
THEN     Patient's age is acceptable for the new drug
ELSE     DISPLAY TOO YOUNG


RULE 9   TRY ANOTHER DRUG
IF       LOGICAL (The physician would like to try another drug)
THEN     Try another drug
AND      RETRACT (The new requested drug is known)
AND      RETRACT (Requested drug is from same class as the deleted drug)
AND      RETRACT (Patient's age is acceptable for the new drug)
AND      RETRACT (The physician would like to try another drug)
AND      CYCLE


RULE 10  OBTAIN PATIENT AGE
IF       ASK Patient's_age
THEN     Patient's age is known
```

FIGURE 7.4 Prescription change rules.

if an alternative prescription should be considered—GOAL 1.1, RULE 2. If the premises in RULE 2 are not true, then the ELSE part of this rule is executed and the system stops.

Determines deleted drug   If an alternative drug is requested, the system asks the user from the list of currently recommended drugs which one is to be deleted. Premise 1 of RULE 2 simply asks the user if another drug is requested. Premise 2 is supported by RULE 3 and is concerned with determining which drug from the list should be deleted. RULE 3 uses the special function "ASK." The purpose of this function is to ask the user for some information, rather than to perform any logical operation. Most shells use some form of this function to acquire numeric or string information, rather than the Boolean type of information that requires the user to answer true or false. This information can be captured in a variable, such as ?deleted_drug, which can be used logically by other rules or shown in some display.

Determines substituted drug   The system next determines the new drug that the user wants substituted for the one deleted. Premise 3 of RULE 2 is supported by RULE 4, which again uses the ASK function to determine which drug should be substituted (?requested_drug). This completes GOAL 1.1.

Determines if new drug is effective   The next step is to determine whether the requested drug should be effective—GOAL 1.1.1. This goal is supported by RULE 5, which attempts to prove it by determining if the requested drug comes from the same class as the one deleted. To accomplish this, the system accesses a database called DRUGS through an external program called CLASS—RULE 6. The database is shown in Figure 7.5.

Many expert systems access information contained in a database through the use of an external program. The program can be written to supply the database information to the expert system, update the information, or append new records. All of these actions are under the control of the expert system, which makes decisions on the operation to be performed. This style of integrating an expert system with a database through the use of an external program is illustrated in Figure 7.6.

RULE 6 calls the program CLASS and sends the name of the drug to be deleted, which is captured in the variable ?deleted_drug. The program CLASS searches the database DRUGS for the record containing the name assigned to ?deleted_drug in the DRUG data field. The program CLASS then returns to the

Rec. No.	Drugs	Class	Age
1	Ampilillin	Penicillins	10
2	Ampicillin	Penicillins	15
3	Gentamicin	Aminoglycosides	20
4	Streptomycin	Aminoglycosides	25

FIGURE 7.5   Database DRUGS.

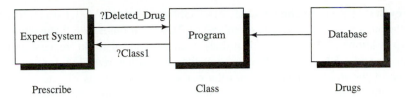

FIGURE 7.6   Database access by expert system.

expert system the name of the drug's class, captured in the variable ?class1.
RULE 6 repeats this operation to retrieve the class of the drug requested by the
user, captured in the variable ?class2. The balance of the rule simply checks to
see if the two match. If the system finds that the deleted and requested drugs
come from the same class, then it is assumed that the new drug should be effective
RULES 5 and 6 fire, and the system reports the finding to the user—RULE 5.
If no match is found, the user is informed of the mismatch—RULE 6 ELSE
part.

Determines if new drug is safe   After the requested drug is found to be effective,
the system attempts to prove that it is safe for the patient—GOAL 1.1.1.1. To
prove this, RULE 7 is pursued and the system bases its decision on the age of
the patient.

Compares ages   If the patient is older than the minimum required age for the
drug, then the requested drug is assumed to be safe. To determine this, the system
again accesses information contained in the database, this time using an external
program called AGE. RULE 8 performs this function along with making the
decision on whether the patient's age is acceptable. If the system finds that the
drug is safe, the results are reported to the user—RULE 7. If the patient's age
is too young, then the system reports this finding to the user—RULE 8, ELSE
part.

Tries another drug   In the event that the requested drug is found to be either
ineffective or unsafe, the user is offered an opportunity to try another drug—
GOAL 1.1.1.2. or 1.1.2. RULE 9 matches this goal and begins the process by
first retracting most of the session's context, and then recycles the system using
the **CYCLE** function. To accomplish the retraction, the system uses a function
called **RETRACT**, which retracts the asserted information from the working
memory and any other facts logically depended on them. The **CYCLE** function
reruns the program with all the current facts minus those retracted. Most shells
and AI programming languages have some form of the cycle retraction functions.

Remembers facts   You should also note that several facts were not retracted,
allowing them to be remembered after the system is cycled. When the system
is cycled, it will begin to again pursue the goals listed in the outline. Obviously,
we do not want the system to pursue issues already established, but to focus on
the reason the cycle occurred, i.e., try an alternative drug.

Recycles   Upon recycling, GOAL 1 is established but GOAL 1.1 was retracted. In the pursuit of this goal, only premise 3 of RULE 2 is unknown: "The requested drug is known." The system then does what we want it to do, request another drug to add—RULE 4. In this fashion, the system has recycled, remembering some of the important issues from the earlier session, and is directed to those areas that logically need to be reconsidered. At this point, the system would again check to see if the new requested drug is both effective and safe.

Alternative Prescription Example Session

We will assume that it is already known and contained in the working memory that the recommended drugs are AMPICILLIN and GENTAMICIN. The goal of the alternative prescription system is to allow the user to choose some alternative drug, which the system will then check for effectiveness and safety. The following steps illustrate the operation of the systems.

```
                    WORKING MEMORY

        Drug recommendation AMPICILLIN—TRUE
        Drug recommendation GENTAMICIN—TRUE
```

STEP 1
Goal 1.
Premise 1, RULE 1

SYSTEM: The following drugs are recommended:
              Drug1 = AMPICILLIN
              Drug2 = GENTAMICIN

STEP 2
Goal 1.1.
Premise 1, RULE 2

SYSTEM: Do you want to consider another prescription?
User: YES

STEP 3
Premise 1, RULE 3

SYSTEM: Which drug would you like to delete?
User: AMPICILLIN

COMMENT: *System binds ?deleted_drug to AMPICILLIN.*

STEP 4
Premise 1, RULE 4

SYSTEM: What drug would you like to add?
User: STREPTOMYCIN

COMMENT: *System binds ?requested_drug to STREPTOMYCIN. Goal 1.1. is satisfied and Goal 1.1.1. is pursued. The system next determines the classes of the deleted and requested drugs by accessing drug class information in the database "DRUGS" through the external program "CLASS." The system next checks to see that they come from the same class—RULE 6.*

STEP 5
ELSE, RULE 6

SYSTEM: The requested drug STREPTOMYCIN comes from the drug class AMINOGLYCOSIDES and would not be an effective replacement for AMPICILLIN which comes from the drug class PENICILLINS. To be effective, the alternative drug should come from the same drug class.

COMMENT: *Goal 1.1.1. is not satisfied, so the system pursues Goal 1.1.2.*

STEP 6
Premise 1, RULE 9

SYSTEM: Would you like to try another drug?
User: YES

COMMENT: *RULE 9 fires and a number of facts are retracted and the system is cycled.*

STEP 7
Goal 1.1.
Premise 1, RULE 4

SYSTEM: What drug would you like to add?
User: PENICILLIN

COMMENT: *The system again determines the classes of the deleted and requested drugs, and checks to see that they come from the same class—RULE 6.*

STEP 8
Conclusion, RULE 5

SYSTEM: The requested drug PENICILLIN comes from the drug class PENICILLINS and would be an effective replacement for AMPICILLIN which also comes from the drug class PENICILLINS.

COMMENT: *The system now is satisfied that the new requested drug is an effective replacement for the deleted drug. It next checks to see if the drug should be safe for the patient on the basis of the patient's age.*

STEP 9
Goal 1.1.1.1.
Premise 1, RULE 10

SYSTEM: What is the age of the patient in years?
User: 30

COMMENT: *The system now must check to see if the patient is old enough to take the drug—RULE 8. The system calls the external program "AGE" which obtains the minimum allowable age for the requested drug from the database "DRUGS."*

STEP 10
Conclusion, RULE 7

SYSTEM: The patient is 30 years old which is fine for the drug PENICILLIN
which has a minimum safe age requirement of 15 years.

Example Review

This small system is an oversimplification of the problem of prescribing alternative solutions to some given expert system recommendation. As the discussion on MYCIN in Chapter 5 illustrated, performing this task through a plan-generate-test method is a more difficult challenge. However, this small system provides insight into several typical difficulties that are often encountered in the development of an expert system.

Ease of Modification

Our small system was concerned with two points about the new requested drug: is it effective and safe? Whether you were building a small system on this problem for illustration purposes such as given here, or a large system for actual application, these two issues would be of major concern. To keep our example small, these two issues were considered using a very simple approach—see RULES 5 and 7. However, these rules are designed for easy modification if later there exists a need to increase their complexity. A key to good expert system design is to develop rules that can be easily modified to incorporate new knowledge.

To better illustrate this point consider RULE 7. This rule addressed the safety of the drug by considering only the issue of the patient's age. In a more advanced system other issues may be of concern such as toxic drug interactions, allergies, etc. To accommodate these additional concerns, you can make simple modifications to the existing example as shown by the following rule where the additions are shown in bold type:

RULE   7 NEW DRUG IS SAFE
IF   Patient's age is known
AND   Patient's age is acceptable for the new drug

AND	New drug does not produce a toxic reaction with existing drugs
AND	Patient is not allergic to the new drug
THEN	Requested drug is safe

In general, having rules that easily permit a natural expansion is an important issue in expert system design.

DESIGN SUGGESTION: Develop a rule structure that eases the natural expansion of the system.

General Knowledge

It was pointed out earlier that integrating an expert system with a database permits you to write powerful general rules that can scan the database information. This approach also greatly enhances the overall maintenance of the system since changes can be made separately to the information in the database or the decision-making knowledge in the expert system. To illustrate how the expert system's knowledge might be changed for our small example, consider the following.

The database DRUGS contains information on the acceptable minimum age requirement for safely administering drugs. This minimum age requirement may have evolved from a polling of a large number of physicians experienced in administering drugs. However, the domain expert for your project may have the opinion that others are overly conservative on the age issue for the class of drugs *Penicillins*. You might capture this belief using the following adjustment to the system:

IF	?requested_class = PENICILLINS
AND	Patient's_age $>=$ 0.8 * Allowable_age
THEN	Patient's age is acceptable for the new drug

Monotonic Reasoning

This example system was designed to accommodate the user by reconsidering the difficulty that arises when an unsatisfactory conclusion is reached. This situation occurs in this problem when the requested substitute drug is found to be either ineffective or unsafe. As shown in STEP 5, the requested drug was found to come from a different drug class, a situation that is interpreted as an ineffective alternative. The system informed the user of this result and offered the opportunity of retrying the system. The system remembered (facts were not retracted) some of the basic information supplied by the user about the patient so that it would not have to be asked again, and proceeded to request alternative information after a recycle.

Non-Monotonic Reasoning

The last section discussed how in part the example system employed a monotonic reasoning technique to the advantage of the user. However, for this application, there was also value in using a non-monotonic reasoning technique for several of the inherently logical facts.

Several rules where written that established a logical dependency between the premises and conclusions. With the firing of RULE 9 (see STEP 6) several facts were retracted along with other facts that were logically dependent on them. This step was important before the system cycled and asked the user for another drug for consideration.

This approach permits you to maintain automatically the truth of the system's facts and avoids potential contradictions. Shells that do not support non-monotonic reasoning force you to explicitly retract every fact that is required for the application.

Automobile Diagnostic System

The prior example systems on medical diagnosis illustrated the importance of an incremental development approach in the design of an expert system. The problem was solved by the sequential development of systems that addressed the tasks of infection identity, prescription selection, and prescription changes. Many problems can be divided into a series of tasks where each can be addressed by a separate expert system.

This style of expert system development also becomes important when the expertise lies with different individuals. Often a problem is solved through the cooperative effort of these individuals, each of whom solves some subpart of the problem but cooperates with the others by exchanging information. This approach to system design is called *distributed problem solving*.

When you encounter a problem in which the expertise lies with different individuals, you should consider developing separate systems that capture the knowledge and reasoning of each individual. Building each separately not only presents a more manageable development effort, but greatly eases the later maintenance of the system.

DESIGN SUGGESTION: For problems that require expertise from more than one individual, develop separate expert systems that capture the expertise of each individual.

Example 4: Automobile Diagnostics via a Blackboard

In this example we will consider a problem on automobile diagnostics where several experts are involved: a chief mechanic, an expert on automobile electrical systems, and one on fuel systems. We assume that the chief mechanic's first responsibility is to discuss the problem with the customer to assess the general nature of the auto's fault: is the problem related to the electrical or the fuel system. After accomplishing this task, the chief mechanic then turns the problem over to one of the experts on the identified faulty system. Each expert is then responsible for determining the specific fault and conveying this information to the chief mechanic. Finally, the chief mechanic determines the repair costs

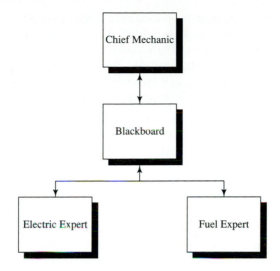

FIGURE 7.7 Automobile diagnostic expert system architecture.

involved and reports the findings to the customer. Figure 7.7 illustrates the structure built to address this problem.

As shown in Figure 7.7, three separate systems are used to capture the expertise of the three individuals: Chief Mechanic, Electrical Expert and Fuel Expert. The systems exchange information over a Blackboard structure.

The objectives of reviewing this example are:

- Introduce distributed problem solving.
- Review the design and operation of meta-rules.
- Introduce the operation of blackboard systems.
- See the use of object–attribute–values.
- See how to effectively initialize information.
- See how context can be used in displays.
- Review the display of intermediate results.
- Review "intelligent" safety nets.

Before reviewing the operation of these systems, a brief review is given on their important design features. The systems were coded using the shell LEVEL5, which incorporates all of the features needed for their development. Many of these features can also be found in other shells, which use a variation of the LEVEL5 approach.

Blackboard

When an expert system is designed to incorporate separate expert modules, a means must be made available for the modules to exchange their information. The traditional manner to accomplish this is using a structure known as a **black-**

board. The blackboard contains information posted by the various systems and used by each on a as-needed basis. LEVEL5 uses a text file approach for maintaining the blackboard and a **CHAIN** command that can be used in a meta-rule for passing control between the modules. For example, the following meta-rule could be used to pass control to a system containing expert information on an auto's electrical system, if the suspected fault is in this area:

IF   Problem seems to be with the electrical system
THEN   Determine faulty system
AND   CHAIN ELECTRICAL

Object–Attribute–Value (O-A-V)

This example also introduces the use of the object–attribute–value (O-A-V). The types of questions posed in the earlier examples have been simple ones, which were answered in a YES or NO fashion. An O-A-V provides a more powerful approach to asking questions because it allows you to display to the user a menu of possible values. When an item is chosen from the menu, the system sets this fact to TRUE and all others to FALSE. For example, given the following question and answer, the system would know the ball's color is "red" and infer it is not "blue" or "green".

Q: What is the ball's color?
     red
     blue
     green
A: red

O-A-V in Shells

Chapter 3 introduced the O-A-V fact using the following structure:

$$\text{Ball} \quad \rightarrow \quad \text{Color} \quad \rightarrow \quad \text{Red}$$
OBJECT   ATTRIBUTE   VALUE

This structure provides a clear distinction between the fact's object, attribute, and attribute value. When writing an O-A-V fact using a AI programming language such as LISP or Prolog, it is a simple matter to make the distinction in these three statement parts.

LISP: (PUTPROP 'BALL 'RED 'COLOR)
PROLOG: color(ball,red)

However, when writing an O-A-V using one of the many rule-based expert system shells currently on the market, you are more likely to find a limited version for representing this type of fact. What is most commonly found is that the shell will tie together the "object" and "attribute" part, and assign to this composite string a value.

The shells also give you two different ways of generating the O-A-V facts. Some shells require you to first define all the O-A-V facts and their possible values. In this case, when an O-A-V fact is a primitive, the system displays a question to the user containing a statement of the object-attribute part, followed by a list of their possible values. Other shells incorporate syntax within the rules such as IS, \, =, etc., to designate the fact as an O-A-V. For example, to represent an O-A-V fact pertaining to the ball's color, all of the following statements may be found:

IF   The ball's color IS red
IF   The ball's color \ red
IF   The ball's color = red

In this case, when an O-A-V fact is a primitive, the system scans all of the rules and looks for all of the values of the object–attribute statement, and presents these values in menu form to the user for selection.

Problem Solving Approach

The rules used in these expert systems are shown in Figures 7.8 and 7.9. For brevity, the Electrical Expert (see Figure 7.7) rules were omitted. The following discussion provides details on the problem solving approach used in this example.

Determines problem area   The first system that interacts with the user is the chief mechanic system. This system first pursues the goal of determining the chief mechanic's recommendation—GOAL 1. This is a variable goal using the syntax of "IS WHAT." The word "WHAT" is similar to the variable assignment such as "?prescription" used earlier. This system uses RULES 1–7 to determine the problem area and to transfer control over to the appropriate system using the command "CHAIN." The system also posts on the blackboard BLACK1.PRL specific findings that may be needed by the other systems.

Determines specific fault   The other two systems are responsible for determining the specific fault of the automobile. They use information from the blackboard, ask questions of the user, post their findings on the blackboard, then return control to the chief mechanic system.

Determines cost   The chief mechanic system then determines the cost of the repair (RULES 8–16) and reports the findings to the user (RULE 17). The final findings inform the user of the problem area, fault, and repair cost. The system can also show a safety net display in the event no fault is identified.

Automobile Diagnostic Example Session

The session begins with the chief mechanic system attempting to form a recommendation to get some other expert—GOAL 1. Two goal rules exist, RULES 1 and 2. The system pursues RULE 1 first.

```
TITLE Chief mechanic expert system

! Note - INCLUDE BLACKBOARD FILE
$BLACK1.PRL

!====================================================================
!   INITIALIZE FACTS
!====================================================================

REINIT Battery_replacement_cost = 50
AND Starter_replacement_cost = 100
AND Spark_plug_replacement_cost = 30
AND Fuel_cost = 20
AND Carburetor_rebuild_cost = 100
AND Carburetor_replacement_cost = 200
AND Fuel_filter_replacement_cost = 10
AND Fuel_line_replacement_cost = 300
AND Default_cost = 25

INIT Problem area IS unknown
AND Fault IS unknown
AND Solution IS unknown
AND Initial information is not obtained

! GOALS
1.  Chief mechanic's recommendation IS WHAT
1.1.  The cost of the repair is known
1.1.1.  Display the findings

!====================================================================
!   DETERMINE GENERAL FAULT AREA
!====================================================================

RULE  1  PROBLEM SEEMS TO BE WITH THE ELECTRICAL SYSTEM
IF     Problem seems to be with the electrical system
THEN   Chief mechanic's recommendation IS get electrical system expert
AND    Problem area IS electrical system
AND    DISPLAY NATURE OF PROBLEM
AND    CHAIN ELECTRIC

RULE  2  PROBLEM SEEMS TO BE WITH THE FUEL SYSTEM
IF     Problem seems to be with the fuel system
THEN   Chief mechanic's recommendation IS get fuel system expert
AND    Problem area IS fuel system
AND    DISPLAY NATURE OF PROBLEM
AND    CHAIN FUEL

RULE  3  STARTER DOESN'T TURN
IF     The engine's condition IS won't start
AND    The starter's condition IS doesn't turn
THEN   Problem seems to be with the electrical system

RULE  4  STARTER TURNS
IF     The engine's condition IS won't start
AND    The starter's condition IS turns
AND    The engine turns \ very slowly
THEN   Problem seems to be with the electrical system
```

FIGURE 7.8   Chief mechanic expert system.

```
RULE   5   ENGINE RUNS ROUGH
IF     The engine's condition IS will start
AND    The engine runs rough
THEN   Problem seems to be with the electrical system


RULE   6   ENGINE WON'T START BUT TURNS NORMALLY
IF     The engine's condition IS won't start
AND    The engine turns \ normally but won't start
THEN   Problem seems to be with the fuel system

RULE   7   PROBLEMS ON ACCELERATION
IF     The car hesitates when accelerated
THEN   Problem seems to be with the fuel system


!====================================================================
!    DETERMINE REPAIR COST
!====================================================================

RULE   8 FUEL COST
IF     Solution IS add fuel
THEN   The cost of the repair is known
AND    Repair cost := Fuel_cost

RULE   9 REBUILD CARBURETOR COST
IF     Solution IS rebuild the carburetor
THEN   The cost of the repair is known
AND    Repair cost := Carburetor_rebuild_cost

RULE   10 REPLACE CARBURETOR COST
IF     Solution IS replace the carburetor
THEN   The cost of the repair is known
AND    Repair cost := Carburetor_replacement_cost

RULE   11 FUEL FILTER COST
IF     Solution IS replace the fuel filter
THEN   The cost of the repair is known
AND    Repair cost := Fuel_filter_replacement_cost

RULE   12 FUEL LINE COST
IF     Solution IS replace fuel lines
THEN   The cost of the repair is known
AND    Repair cost := Fuel_line_replacement_cost

RULE   13 NO SOLUTION IS FOUND
IF     Solution IS unknown
THEN   The cost of the repair is known
AND    Repair cost := Default_cost
AND    DISPLAY NO SOLUTION

RULE   14 SHOW THE RESULTS
IF     The cost of the repair is known
THEN   Display the findings
AND    DISPLAY FINDINGS

END
```

(continued)

```
TITLE Car fuel system expert

$BLACK1.PRL

! GOALS
1. Determine the fuel system fault
        1.1. Return findings to chief mechanic

RULE 1  OUT OF GAS
IF   The engine's condition IS won't start
AND  The starter's condition IS turns
AND  Fuel gage \ doesn't move
THEN Determine the fuel system fault
AND  Fault IS out of gas
AND  Solution IS add fuel

RULE 2  CARBURETOR PROBLEM, REBUILD
IF   The engine's condition IS won't start
AND  The starter's condition IS turns
AND  Fuel gage \ does move
AND  The car will\start occasionally
THEN Determine the fuel system fault
AND  Fault IS dirty carburetor
AND  Solution IS rebuild the carburetor

RULE 3  CARBURETOR PROBLEM, REPLACE
IF   The engine's condition IS won't start
AND  The starter's condition IS turns
AND  Fuel gage   does move
AND  The car will never starts
THEN Determine the fuel system fault
AND  Fault IS bad carburetor
AND  Solution IS replace the carburetor

RULE 4  GAS FILTER
IF   The engine's condition IS will start
AND  The car hesitates when accelerated
AND  Fuel filter IS older than 1 year
THEN Determine the fuel system fault
AND  Fault IS bad fuel filter
AND  Solution IS replace the fuel filter

RULE 5  GAS LINE
IF   The engine's condition IS will start
AND  The car hesitates when accelerated
AND  Fuel filter IS less than 1 year
THEN Determine the fuel system fault
AND  Fault IS clogged fuel line
AND  Solution IS replace fuel lines

RULE 6  BACK TO CHIEF
IF   CHAIN MECHANIC
THEN Return findings to chief mechanic

END
```

FIGURE 7.9 Car fuel system expert.

STEP 1

Pursue RULE 1, premise 1. Premise 1 is unknown and supported by RULE 3. Pursue RULE 3, premise 1.

SYSTEM: Please tell me whether the engine

> won't start
> will start

User: won't start

COMMENT: *When pursuing premise 1 of RULE 3, the issue of "The engine's condition" is searched. The system displays to the user a menu of all defined values for the object-attribute-value found from scanning the rules. With the selection made by the user, the system now knows that the fact "The engine's condition is won't start" is TRUE, and the fact "The engine's condition is will start" is FALSE. Both of these values are posted on the blackboard.*

STEP 2

Pursue RULE 3, premise 2.

SYSTEM: Please tell me whether the starter

> doesn't turn
> turns

User: turns

COMMENT: *The system has failed to prove that the problem area is with the electrical system through RULE 3. It will now attempt to prove it using RULE 4.*

STEP 3

Pursue RULE 4. Premises 1 and 2 known, pursue premise 3.

SYSTEM: The engine turns

> very slowly
> normally but won't start

User: normally but won't start

COMMENT: *The system has failed to prove RULE 4 and has only RULE 5 left to prove that the problem is with the electrical system. However, premise 1 of RULE 5 is false since the value of the object–attribute "The engine's condition" was set to "won't start". The system now pursues RULE 2 in an attempt to prove the recommendation to get the fuel expert.*

STEP 4

Pursue RULE 2, premise 1. Premise 1 is unknown and supported by RULE 6. Premises 1 and 2 of RULE 6 are known, which causes RULES 6 and 2 to fire.

COMMENT: *The firing of RULE 6 causes the system to display the intermediate findings to the user and to pass control to the fuel expert system. Notice that the value of the O-A-V "Problem area" is displayed.*

SYSTEM: I believe the problem might be with the **fuel system.**

I will now check with my expert in this area.

COMMENT: *The firing of RULE 2 passes control over to the fuel expert.*

STEP 5

The fuel expert system now pursues the goal to determine the fuel system fault—Goal 1. RULE 1, premises 1 and 2 are known from the blackboard. Premise 3 is pursued.

SYSTEM: The fuel gage
doesn't move
does move

User: does move

STEP 6

RULE 1 is abandoned. RULE 2 is searched. Premises 1–3 are known and premise 4 is pursued.

SYSTEM: The car will
start occasionally
never starts

User: start occasionally

COMMENT: *RULE 2 now fires establishing the fault as a "dirty carburetor" and the solution as "rebuild the carburetor." The second goal of this system is now pursued, namely 1.1, which causes control to be returned to the chief mechanic expert system (see RULE 6). In the chief mechanic system, GOAL 1 is already established and posted on the blackboard so the system pursues GOAL 1.1 to establish the cost of the repair. RULES 8 through 16 contain this goal in their THEN part but only RULE 12 is satisfied by the "Solution" information posted on the blackboard by the fuel expert system. The system then fires RULE 12 and sets the cost of the repair to that for rebuilding the carburetor. The system then pursues the final goal, namely GOAL 1.1.1, to display the findings to the user (see RULE 17).*

SYSTEM: Thank you for letting me help you.

After working on your problem it is my belief that your car has a problem with the **fuel system.**

The specific problem is: **dirty carburetor.**

My recommendation is: **rebuild the carburetor.**

The cost for such a repair is: **100** dollars.

Example Review

In this example the shell LEVEL5 was used to develop an expert system that uses three different expert modules. This shell has the features necessary to demonstrate the key objectives of this example. Many other shells incorporate similar features, using different control statements.

Separate Systems

This example demonstrates how a number of small expert systems can be built separately that capture the expertise of various individuals, and use this knowledge in a cooperative fashion to solve some complex problem. This approach permits you to concentrate specific domain knowledge in individual expert modules which simplifies the development effort and eases the system maintenance.

Meta-Rules

Control between the different expert modules was accomplished through the use of **meta-rules.** When the context of the session indicated that some other system should continue the problem solving, then the appropriate meta-rule fired and control was passed to the system (see RULES 1 and 2 of chief mechanic system). These rules used the LEVEL5 command **CHAIN** to accomplish this task.

Display of Intermediate Findings

Before calling the other systems to continue the problem solving, the system displayed intermediate and important findings to the user using a LEVEL5 display function called **DISPLAY.** In this example, this intermediate finding was displayed using the text written in the "DISPLAY NATURE OF PROBLEM" section of the chief mechanic system. This display text captures the general problem area inferred by the system in the O-A-V "Problem area."

Unlike a conventional program that simply presents the final findings, this approach keeps the user abreast of important findings and provides a transparency to the reasoning direction. This style of programming more closely models the interaction a user might expect when consulting with a human expert.

DESIGN SUGGESTION: Provide displays to user on important intermediate findings and future direction of problem solving.

To capture information from the consultation for display, LEVEL5 permits the designer to bracket the fact of interest and embed it in the display text. For example, in STEP 4, the display that is provided comes from the following code:

DISPLAY NATURE OF PROBLEM
    I believe the problem might be with the [Problem area].
    I will now check with my expert in this area.

Blackboard

Communication between the modules was accomplished using a **blackboard.** The blackboard contains information about the problem determined by each module and used by the other modules to aid the problem solving. In this example, the blackboard exists as a separate text file called "BLACK1.PRL," and included in each module using the LEVEL5 code "$BLACK1.PRL."

O-A-V Facts

The example also demonstrated the use of object–attribute–value facts. When attempting to determine a value of a particular object–attribute, the system provided the user with a menu of all possible values obtained by scanning the rules. For example, in STEP 1 the system was attempting to prove premise 1 of Rule 3, whether the engine condition is "won't start." The object–attribute of interest was "The engine's condition." The system scanned all of the rules and found the following values for this object–attribute:

won't start, from RULE 3
will start, from RULE 5

When the user selected the value "won't start," the system also inferred that the other possible values were false, namely "will start." In this manner the system can gain additional information about the problem from only one answer.

Initializing Knowledge

The chief mechanic system included a section that initialized a set of information. This was accomplished using the "INIT" and "REINIT" commands. Both operate similarly, the difference being that those with the REINIT statement are initialized when called from some other module using the CHAIN command. Again these commands are unique to LEVEL5, but similar ones exist for other shells.

One particular value of initializing information is worth noting. All of the repair costs were represented as numeric variables within the rules and were initialized to reflect their current rates. By maintaining the cost assignments in some place separate from the rules, such as an initialization section of the program or a database, possible rate changes can be easily incorporated into the system. If the rates are used explicitly within the rules rather than implicitly through the use of variables, then when a rate change is necessary, all of the rules using this information would need to be located and adjusted.

DESIGN SUGGESTION: For information that may change, maintain the information in variable form in the rules and set the current values within the initialization section of the program or within a database.

Intelligent Safety Net

In the event no specific fault could be found, the system was designed with an *intelligent* safety net that displayed the suspected faulty system. Even if the system failed to be completely successful, it could still provide some intelligent and possibly useful information to the user. In our example, the default display could tell the user which automobile system appears to be causing the trouble, even if an exact fault could not be found.

DESIGN SUGGESTION: Provide an intelligent safety net that provides the user with some conclusion about the problem that could be derived even though a final result is absent.

SUMMARY ON BACKWARD-CHAINING EXPERT SYSTEMS

This chapter reviewed the operation of backward-chaining expert systems. Several examples were given that illustrated many of the features of this type of system. A number of design suggestions were also given to provide you with insight into developing backward-chaining systems.

The major lessons learned in this chapter were:

- Backward-chaining attempts to prove a goal by recursively moving back through the rules in search of supporting evidence.
- To ease the development and maintenance of these systems, they should be designed in modular form.
- Care should be given to provide clear final displays, including intermediate displays that keep the user informed.
- The system should be designed to allow the user to provide known information, avoiding unnecessary search by the system.
- Some intelligent findings should be provided even if the system is not totally successful.
- Database information should be used, if available, by using general rules.
- Cooperating expert system modules communicate over a structure known as a blackboard.

EXERCISES

1. Describe the basic backward-chaining process.
2. List several problems for which a backward-chaining approach would be appropriate.
3. Why is it important to design the system for the intelligent user?
4. What is the value of incorporating a variable in the goal?
5. What are the principal advantages in designing the system as a collection of individual modules?
6. Describe a problem whose tasks could best be accomplished by separate expert systems.

7. Describe a problem that requires expertise from several individuals and could best be accomplished by separate expert systems.

8. What is an inference network and what is its purpose?

9. What are the principal values of integrating an expert system with a database?

10. Assume that you have a database that contains information on employees from some company. The database contains a field that gives the employee's age and another that states whether the employee should retire. Write a general rule that can scan all of the employees and assert in the database that they should retire if they are older than 65 years.

11. What is the advantage of using variables within rules that are assigned initial values in the initialization section of the program?

12. Why should you be concerned about rules that use numeric relationships?

13. Provide an example problem that could best be managed using a blackboard structure. Discuss each expert system module and what information the modules would share within the blackboard.

CHAPTER 8

Designing Backward-Chaining Rule-Based Systems

INTRODUCTION

In this chapter we consider the steps a knowledge engineer goes through when developing a backward-chaining rule-based expert system. To illustrate this process, we consider a small problem on personal investment planning. We look at how the system's capability gradually improves through an iterative process in which the system's knowledge is expanded, tested, and refined. We will follow the design suggestions given in earlier chapters, and add a few additional ones along the way.

GENERAL DESIGN METHODOLOGY FOR BACKWARD-CHAINING SYSTEMS

Before we design any expert system, our first task is to obtain a general understanding of the problem. We want to determine the objective of the system, the major issues the expert considers, and how the expert works with available information to derive recommendations. Following this understanding, we can begin to consider actual system design approaches.

A characteristic of expert system design for any type of system, whether rule-based, frame-based or induction, is that it is a highly iterative process. A small amount of knowledge is first obtained from the expert, encoded into the system, then tested. Test results are used to uncover deficiencies in the system and become the focus for additional sessions with the expert. This cyclic process continues throughout the project as the system's knowledge grows; in an evolutionary fashion, the system's capability improves to the level of the expert. Figure 8.1 illustrates this cyclic design process.

This cyclic development style is used when building a backward-chaining system. However, the way we proceed through these cycles is unique to this type of system. Interestingly, the approach taken matches the way a backward-chaining system works. That is, we first determine the major goals and the ways these goals can be established (goal rules). Next, we look for ways of acquiring information to support the goal rules. This process naturally leads to other deeper rules that work with more primitive information. The development process, like the operation of a backward-chaining system, moves from the abstract to the specific.

There are seven major tasks you will typically perform when developing a backward-chaining system:

1. Define the problem
2. Define the goals
3. Define the goal rules
4. Expand the system
5. Refine the system
6. Design the interface
7. Evaluate the system

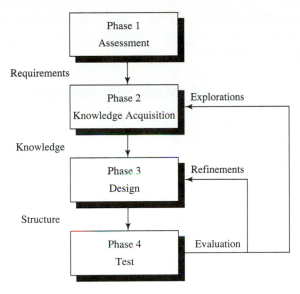

FIGURE 8.1 Rule-based system design.

However, you must recognize that these tasks are a part of a highly iterative process. You follow these steps to create a portion of the system, then repeat them a number of times until the system has been refined to the point that it provides expert performance.

Before embarking on the design of our example system, let's review the general area of financial planning and see why it is well-suited to a backward-chaining approach.

FINANCIAL PLANNING DOMAIN

Expert system development in the area of financial counseling has been very active during the past decade. Systems have been built in such areas as loan application screening (Pinson 1988), business strategy profile planning (Fowler 1990), and portfolio selection (Cohen and Lieberman 1983). Expert system developers have been attracted to these areas for several good reasons:

- The system offers real payoffs.
- The task is well-defined.
- Real experts exist.
- Many successful expert systems exist in financial counseling.

Most systems developed in the financial area use a backward-chaining inference technique. The principal reason for this is that these types of problems have solutions that fit into a finite number of independent sets. That is, though there may be a large amount of information that the expert considers, there are usually only a few possible decisions that are made. Therefore, since by its nature a backward-chaining system attempts to prove a small set of hypotheses, it is a natural choice for financial applications.

—————— TASK 1: DEFINING THE PROBLEM ——————

Your initial step on any expert system project should be to learn about the problem. Our task is to develop an expert system to assist a financial counselor with providing an investment recommendation for a client. To accomplish this, we need to learn how the financial counselor works with available information to arrive at good investment decisions. To aid us in this effort, we must first obtain information on the problem.

Reports, documents, and books are good sources of information for all expert system projects. They can provide you with a general understanding of the problem and its solution. These sources are a good starting point, but for most projects you will need the help of a real expert.

Let's assume for our problem that we were fortunate in locating an expert on financial counselling: an investment advisor at a local firm. We explain our project to her, obtain a commitment for her cooperation, and made arrangements for our first meeting.

At this first meeting we begin by asking her to provide a brief overview of investment counseling. She states there is a wide range of investment vehicles available to persons facing investment decisions, each with some benefits and drawbacks. She further states that these vehicles can be neatly classified into one of the following categories:

STOCKS

Preferred	Blue Chip	Common

BONDS

Treasury	Corporate	Municipal

MUTUAL FUNDS

Income	Bonds	Stock

SAVINGS

CD	Money Market	Savings Account

COMMODITIES

Agricultural	Prec. Metals	Oil

REAL ESTATE

Commercial	Residential	Land

While showing us this list, she explains that her job is to first determine which mixture of these categories (called a portfolio) that the investor should consider. For example, she states that she might recommend splitting the investment amount in a portfolio of 20% stocks, 40% bonds, and 40% savings. Before making a recommendation like this, she states that she must first ask the client several personal questions and some related to his or her financial state. We decide that

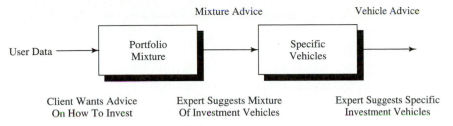

FIGURE 8.2   Investment planning problem-solving approach.

we will explore the details on these issues later. For now, we simply want a general understanding on how she provides advice to the client.

DESIGN SUGGESTION: During the problem definition stage of a project, do not interrupt the expert for problem details. Here you are looking for a general understanding of the problem and how it is solved. Details can be obtained during later discussions with the expert.

Continuing with the discussion, she states that after a portfolio decision is made, she attempts to determine which particular vehicles within each category (e.g., common stocks, treasury bonds, etc.) are best suited for the client.

Even at this early stage, this short discussion with the expert has provided us with considerable information about the problem and insight into how we might design the system. We learned about the general investment categories and specific investment vehicles within each category. We also learned about the general problem-solving approach used by the expert. We know that she uses information supplied by the client to first pick the overall portfolio, then the specific investment vehicles. Figure 8.2 illustrates this problem-solving approach.

We could continue this discussion with the expert further to obtain more details about the problem. However, we already have enough information for the next important step when designing a backward-chaining system—the goals.

―――――――― **TASK 2: DEFINING THE GOALS** ――――――――

The coding of any backward-chaining system begins with defining the system's goals. From the previous discussion with the expert, we see that our system will have two principal goals to achieve:

1. Determine portfolio mixture.
2. Determine investment vehicles within each category.

To keep our system simple, we will only address the first goal and assume that the second one could be managed in a future revision of the system.

A portfolio is simply a distribution of the investment money into one or more of the general investment categories. A real portfolio counseling system would need to consider a large number of potential portfolio recommendations. Again, to keep our problem manageable, lets assume we are only concerned about the following four:

Portfolio 1. 100% investment in savings
Portfolio 2. 60% stocks, 30% bonds, 10% savings
Portfolio 3. 20% stocks, 40% bonds, 40% savings
Portfolio 4. 100% investment in stocks

The steps that we are taking to simplify the discussion of this example are actually steps you should take when developing a real system. You should focus the design of the initial system on a small but representative part of the overall problem. Following the successful design of this small portion of the problem, you should have a system structure that is easily expandable to consider more complete issues.

DESIGN SUGGESTION: Focus the design of the original system on a small but representative part of the overall problem.

Writing a Goal Statement

Every backward-chaining system needs at least one goal to get started. For our problem, we have four different goals which we want the system to pursue, one for each portfolio. We could write four different goals or write one variable goal that instructs the system to determine the "Portfolio advice" that we seek.

Using a variable goal statement not only reduces the number of goal statements, it also permits you to add other goal rules later without the need to explicitly encode their conclusion in a goal statement. The way you write a variable goal statement will depend on the shell you choose to develop the system. Some typical forms you might find are:

Portfolio advice IS WHAT—LEVEL5
GOAL = Portfolio advice —VP-EXPERT, M.1.
Portfolio advice is ?X   —ART

———————— TASK 3: DESIGNING THE GOAL RULES ————————

Each goal in our system must have at least one rule (goal rule) that can conclude it. You design a goal rule the same way as any other type of rule. That is, you look for the necessary preconditions to satisfy the rule's conclusion. For our problem, we want to determine how the expert decides which portfolio best fits the needs of the client. The general form for all of our goal rules will look like the following:

IF   Precondition_1
AND   Precondition_2
  .   .
  .   .
THEN   Portfolio_i

The preconditions are the important issues the expert considers when deciding on a recommended portfolio. To determine these issues, we again must consult with our expert. Consider the following interaction between the knowledge engineer (KE) and the domain expert (DE):

KE: How do you pick the right investment portfolio for the client?

DE: Every investment has some risk associated with it so I want to first know something about the the client's personal and financial states. Each of these issues is important for recommending a conservative or aggressive position.

KE: So you recommend an investment on the basis of the client's personal and financial states suggesting a conservative or aggressive position?

DE: Yes.

KE: Do you ever consider other issues?

DE: Well in a sense I do. If the client only wants to invest a small amount of money, then I assume that he is really conservative, and I immediately recommend that he put all of his money in savings.

DE: How much do you consider to be a small amount?

KE: I suppose anything below $1,000.

This discussion with the expert has provided us with the principal issues considered when recommending an investment portfolio (our goal):

- Client's personal state (conservative or aggressive)
- Client's financial state (conservative or aggressive)
- Amount to invest (small or large)

Now that we know the major issues, we must next determine their relationship with a corresponding recommendation. This can be accomplished through further discussions with the expert, or you might elect to use a different technique that involves a **decision table.**

Decision Tables

Decision tables offer a knowledge acquisition technique that avoids problems normally associated with interviewing techniques.

DEFINITION 8.1: Decision Table
Table containing a series of decision factors, which label columns and represent preconditions needed to reach a conclusion, which is represented in another column. Decision factor values are placed in rows, which lead to specific conclusions.

A decision table provides an easy-to-fill-out form that the expert can use to provide the decision-making knowledge. Using this approach for our problem, we can create a decision table and present it to our expert and ask her to fill in the appropriate values. The result of this effort is shown in Figure 8.3.

INVESTMENT AMOUNT	PERSONAL STATE	FINANCIAL STATE	ADVICE
Small			Portfolio 1
	Conservative	Conservative	Portfolio 2
	Conservative	Aggressive	Portfolio 1
	Aggressive	Conservative	Portfolio 3
	Aggressive	Aggressive	Portfolio 4

FIGURE 8.3   Decision table for goal rules.

The decision factors for our goal rules are shown in the labels at the top of the first three columns. The label in the far right column is the advice provided by the expert. The specific values under this column are our goals. Each piece of advice is given only if the decision factor values for its row are true.

You should also notice in Figure 8.3 that several table values are missing. This either means that the value is not relevant (usually represented as a "*" meaning "I don't care") or that you must ask the expert for additional information to fill in the blanks.

We can now use this table to write our goal rules. If this table was large, we would need to use an "induction" tool—discussed in Chapter 16. Since this table is small, we can write the rules by simple inspection. The following rules are represented in LEVEL5 code:

Rule 1
IF   Client's_investment_amount < 1000
THEN   Portfolio advice IS 100% investment in savings

Rule 2
IF   Client's personal state suggests \ a conservative position
AND   Client's financial state suggests \ a conservative position
THEN   Portfolio advice IS 100% investment in savings

Rule 3
IF   Client's personal state suggests \ a conservative position
AND   Client's financial state suggests \ an aggressive position
THEN   Portfolio advice IS 60% stocks, 30% bonds, 10% savings

Rule 4
IF   Client's personal state suggests \ an aggressive position
AND   Client's financial state suggests \ a conservative position
THEN   Portfolio advice IS 20% stocks, 40% bonds, 40% savings

Rule 5
IF   Client's personal state suggests \ an aggressive position
AND   Client's financial state suggests \ an aggressive position
THEN   Portfolio advice IS 100% investment in stocks

Recall from the prior chapter that the use of ''IS'' and ''\'' is equivalent to the assignment ''='' found in other shells. Their purpose is simply to assign a value to a symbolic string.

Inference Network

Even in the early stages of a project it is helpful to draw an **inference network** of the rules that you collect. Recall that an inference network shows the logical relationships between pieces of information that are represented in the rules. Figure 8.4 shows the inference network for our goal rules. You can show it to your expert to confirm that you have captured the knowledge correctly, and use it as a record to refer to as you expand the system.

Testing the Goal Rules

After you have encoded the goal rules into the system, you should test the system. In general, after you have encoded any new knowledge into an expert system, you should immediately test the system.

> **DESIGN SUGGESTION: Following the encoding of any new knowledge into the expert system, you should immediately test it, using information specific to the new knowledge.**

This is particularly important during the early stages of system development when you can exhaustively test the system. That is, having only a small set of rules permits you to try out all possible combinations of answers. You can then test for the correctness and completeness of the system's knowledge. Later, when the size of the knowledge base has grown, this ability is often lost. At this point, you must rely on alternative techniques to evaluate the system, such as, the use of test cases drawn from the problem's history. We review how to evaluate large systems using test cases in Chapter 18.

Testing our goal rules would involve running the system several times for different combinations of answers. We would want to make sure that all four goals were tested and successfully established.

Search Order

Another important aspect of system testing to consider in the early stages of the project is the order in which the system searches the knowledge. When designing an expert system, we not only want our knowledge to be consistent with the

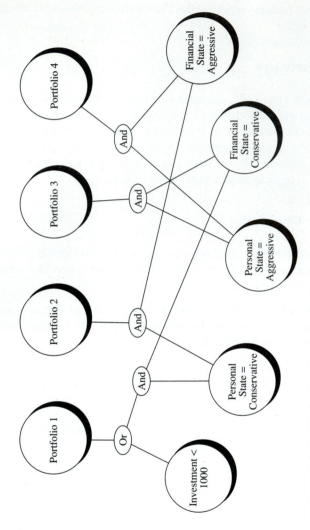

FIGURE 8.4 Goal rule inference network.

expert's, we also want the system's problem-solving approach to follow that used by the expert. To illustrate the importance of this point—a potential pitfall for our system—consider the following.

All five rules in our system conclude the same issue, namely "Portfolio advice IS . . . ," but with different values. When the system attempts to establish the goal "Portfolio advice IS WHAT," all five rules compete for attention. When we encoded the rules in our system we might have placed them in any order. A question we should ask is "In what order will the system search our rules?"

Most backward-chaining shells search competing rules in the order that they were entered. For our system, this means that RULE 1 would be searched first. Therefore, the first question asked by the system would be the amount of money the client wants to invest. We should now question whether this initial search strategy is right, wrong, or doesn't really matter.

Recall from our earlier discussion with the expert that she said a recommendation of placing the client's investment totally in a savings program would be given "immediately" if the amount to invest is small. Therefore, since the system searches this issue first, the search strategy is consistent with the approach taken by our expert. However, we were lucky because we placed RULE 1 first. Consider what would have happened if we placed it elsewhere—possibly last. The system would spend needless time asking questions when a simple and immediate conclusion could have been reached. Early testing of the system can easily uncover problems like this.

In general, you should understand how the shell you are using handles the search of the rules. If it relies on rule order, then you will need to adjust the order of the rules to accommodate any needed search constraints. Some shells permit you to assign "priority" numbers to the rules, which helps to order the search. That is, you assign higher numbers to those rules that you want searched first.

Exhaustive versus Nonexhaustive Search

You can program a backward-chaining system to perform either an exhaustive or nonexhaustive search. An exhaustive search continues to search all the rules concluding some goal, even if the goal was previously established by the firing of one of the rules. A nonexhaustive search technique stops searching after the firing of only one rule. Knowing which of these two search techniques to select for the system requires you to study how the expert solves the problem.

Consider our problem. We might want the system to make only one portfolio recommendation. For example, if we discover the client has less than $1,000, then we want the system to stop even though it is possible that the other recommendations may be valid. In this case, we would program the system to perform a nonexhaustive search.

Most shells by default perform a nonexhaustive search. Others, however, require you to use some form of a "STOP" command as an added conclusion to each rule. This approach is adequate for goal rules. However, for nongoal rules, this approach would cause the session to end prior to the system establishing its primary goal.

If our problem was to find all possible portfolio recommendations, then we would want to employ an exhaustive search technique. For example, we might want a list of recommendations, possibly rank ordered according to some degree of belief in the given portfolio meeting the needs of the client.

To enable an exhaustive search on some issue, most shells provide you a command that specifies that the issue is permitted more than one value. For example, if we wanted our system to search for all possible portfolio recommendations, we would need to tell the system that the term "Portfolio advice" can have more than one value. Depending on the shell chosen, the added statement to your program will look something like the following:

MULTIVALUED Portfolio advice

This causes the system to seek all possible values for "Portfolio advice." If we were using some inexact reasoning technique (covered in later chapters), this new command might result in the following final display:

PORTFOLIO RECOMMENDATION	BELIEF
60% stocks, 30% bonds, 10% savings	90%
100% investment in stocks	85%
20% stocks, 40% bonds, 40% savings	70%
100% investment in savings	60%

TASK 4: EXPANDING THE SYSTEM

At this point our system has five rules and can recommend four different portfolios. It is totally functional, but not very intelligent. The principal way we improve the intelligence of an expert system is to expand its knowledge. Here, two options are available to us—broadening or deepening the system's knowledge. One way we expand the system's knowledge is by giving it a *broader* understanding of the problem. That is, we teach it about additional issues. For our example, we might decide to teach it about additional portfolio mixtures. This type of expansion is fairly easy and is usually reserved for later in the project, after the system has demonstrated success.

Another way we expand the system's knowledge is by giving it a *deeper* understanding of the problem. That is, we teach it more about issues it already knows about. For our example, we would teach it how to determine the present premises in our goal rules. This is the most common expansion technique used early in the project. To appreciate why this is the case, consider the following question the system would ask given our present set of rules:

SYSTEM: Does the client's personal state suggest a conservative position?

This could be tough question for the user to answer because it requires some expertise on the problem. We would want to add knowledge to the system so that it can determine the answer to this question.

In general, during the entire development of a rule-based system, you should be looking for premises that can be expanded deeper. Ask yourself (or even better ask the user) whether the user can effectively answer the question posed by the system. If the answer is no, then add knowledge to the system that forces it to seek more primitive and reliable information.

At present, our system has three issues that can be expanded deeper:

1. Client's investment amount
2. Client's personal state
3. Client's financial state

The first one needs no further expansion since it requires the system to ask a simple question on the investment amount. The others, however, need to be expanded. To accomplish this, we will need to again consult with the expert.

When you face more than one issue that needs expanded, a good rule-of-thumb is to choose only one and focus on it during your discussion with the expert. Extracting knowledge from an expert is a far easier task when one issue is addressed at a time.

> **DESIGN SUGGESTION: Expand one issue at a time. This permits the expert to focus on a single issue and avoids problems commonly encountered when the expert is asked to address multiple issues.**

Consider for example issues 2 and 3. The first deals with "personal issues," while the other with "financial issues." If you choose to expand the first issue, and adhere to this piece of advice, you will find that the expert has little difficulty with providing you with new issues related to the concept of "personal issues." Jumping back and forth between personal and financial issues will only cause confusion.

Expanding Personal Issue

To expand on the personal issue, we have two questions to ask the expert; one for each possible issue value—conservative or aggressive:

KE: How do you determine if the client's personal state suggests a conservative position?

DE: I would suggest a conservative position if the client is old or his job is not steady. I would provide the same suggestion if the client is young, has a steady job, but has children.

Two heuristics were given that we can represent in the following rules:

Rule 6
IF   Client IS old
OR   Client's job IS not steady
THEN   Client's personal state suggests \ a conservative position

Rule 7
IF   Client IS young
AND   Client's job IS steady
AND   Client has \ children
THEN   Client's personal state suggests \ a conservative position

We now have two deeper rules to conclude one of the premises in the original goal rules. Next consider the question on the aggressive position:

> KE: How do you determine if the client's personal state suggests an aggressive position?
>
> DE: I would suggest an aggressive position if the client is young, his job is steady, but he has no children.

This new information can be captured in the following rule:

Rule 8
IF   Client IS young
AND   Client's job IS steady
AND   Client has \ no children
THEN   Client's personal state suggests \ an aggressive position

From this discussion with the expert we were able to obtain several rules to support a deeper inferencing process. However, we also uncovered several new issues that we will need to explore:

1. Client's age: young, old
2. Client's job: steady, not steady
3. Client's has children: true or false

The third one can be answered directly and would not have to be explored further. However, we should expand on the other two—again, one at a time.

Expanding Age Issue

In order to expand on the age issue we must ask the expert two questions:

> KE: At what point do you consider someone old?
>
> DE: 40 years
>
> KE: At what point do you consider someone young?
>
> DE: Anything less than 40 years

From these answers we can write the following two rules:

Rule 9
IF   Client_age < 40
THEN   Client IS young

Rule 10
IF   Client_age >= 40
THEN   Client IS old

Before proceeding with the further expansion of our system, let's take a look at a common pitfall many expert system developers fall into.

The Problem with ELSE

Many knowledge engineers have a background in traditional programming. Before moving into the ranks of knowledge engineers, these programmers were grilled in the importance of writing concise procedures: "If it can be done with one line of code instead of two do it!" When developing an expert system you are not encoding procedures, you are encoding knowledge. Often, attempts to squeeze two pieces of knowledge together in one rule can cause problems. These problems are most often found with the use of the "ELSE" statement.

To illustrate this point, consider the age issue. Given the information provided by the expert, it might be tempting to write only one rule that captures the logic of the situation:

IF   Client_age < 40
THEN   Client IS young
ELSE   Client IS old

On the surface, there doesn't appear to be anything wrong with this rule. It is a logical representation of the knowledge provided by our expert. However, its use can cause problems when the system needs expansion. For example, assume we used this rule but later decided to add the following rule that introduces a new age category:

IF   Client_age < 50
AND   Client_age >= 40
THEN   Client IS middle-age

Now, if we encounter a person of the age 45, our system would conclude that he is both "old" (from the firing of the rule with the ELSE part) and "middle-age" (the firing of our new rule). The firing of these two rules has resulted in inconsistent conclusions.

The point to recognize is that rules containing an ELSE part always fire. As you expand the system, you will need to keep account of all of the rules using an ELSE statement in order to avoid inconsistencies. Since this added effort makes it more difficult to maintain the system, rules with ELSE statements should be avoided.

DESIGN SUGGESTION: Avoid ELSE statements whenever possible.

Expanding Job Stability Issue

Recall that our expert stated that the client's job stability is an issue that she considers when making a financial recommendation. She gave us two possible values for this issue: stable or unstable. Therefore, we have two questions for her:

KE: How do you determine if the client's job is stable?

DE: I usually consider two things: the length of time that the client has worked at his present company and the level of layoffs the company is experiencing. For example, if he has worked at the company for between 3 and 10 years and layoffs are low, then I assume things are stable. In fact, if he has worked there for over 10 years, I feel things are ok.

From this answer we can write the following two rules:

Rule 11
IF   Client's length of service IS 10 years or more
THEN   Client's job IS steady

Rule 12
IF   Client's length of service IS between 3 and 10 years
AND   Layoffs at the organization IS low
THEN   Client's job IS steady

We now continue our discussion with the expert and ask the following question:

KE: How do determine if the client's job is unstable?

DE: If he has worked at the company for between 3 and 10 years and layoffs are high, then I assume things are unstable. In fact, if he has worked there less than 3 years, then I feel things aren't really stable.

From this answer we can write the following two rules:

Rule 13
IF   Client's length of service IS between 3 and 10 years
AND   Layoffs at the organization IS high
THEN   Client's job IS not steady

Rule 14
IF   Client's length of service IS less than 3 years
THEN   Client's job IS not steady

Personal State Inference Network

This completes the expansion on the personal state issue. We started with the task of obtaining a deeper set of rules that could conclude the abstract personal issue within our goal rules. Through discussions with the expert, we uncovered these rules and also discovered related issues that could be answered by the user in a reliable fashion. At this point we should add the new rules to our original inference network. Figure 8.5 shows the portion of this new network focused on the personal state issue.

If we were building a real system, we would now encode these new rules into our system and test it. This testing would focus on the personal issues to verify that we have correctly captured the expert's knowledge. However, to keep the discussion on this example system brief, we will move on to the next issue that needs to be expanded.

Expanding Financial Issue

We next consider the financial issue. We begin this effort by again consulting with our expert. We would have two questions that need to be explored—one for each possible value for the financial issue:

KE: How do you know when the client's financial state suggests a conservative position?

DE: I would suggest a conservative position if the client's total assets are less than his total liabilities. Also, if his total assets exceed his total liabilities but are less than ... let me think ... about twice his liabilities ... and ... he has kids, then I would again recommend a conservative position.

From this answer we can write the following two rules:

Rule 15
IF   Total_assets < Total_liabilities
THEN   Client's financial state suggests \ a conservative position

Rule 16
IF   Total_assets > Total_liabilities
AND   Total_assets < 2 * Total_liabilities
AND   Client has \ children
THEN   Client's financial state suggests \ a conservative position

Continuing our discussion, we ask the following question:

KE: How do you know when the client's financial state suggests an aggressive position?

DE: I would suggest an aggressive position if the client's total assets exceed his total liabilities by a factor of 2. In addition, if his total assets exceed his total liabilities, but were less than twice the amount, and he has no kids, then I would again recommend an aggressive position.

From this discussion, we can write the following rules:

Rule 17
IF   Total_assets > 2 * Total_liabilities
THEN   Client's financial state suggests \ an aggressive position

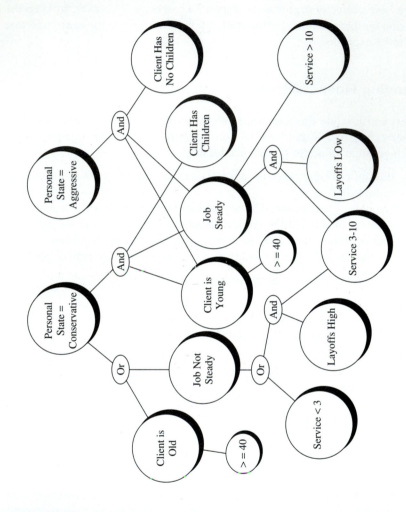

FIGURE 8.5 Personal state inference network.

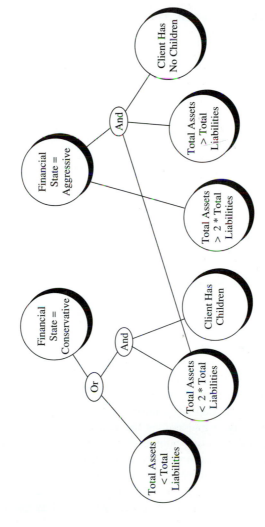

FIGURE 8.6 Financial state inference network.

Rule 18

IF	Total_assets > Total_liabilities
AND	Total_assets < 2 * Total_liabilities
AND	Client has \ no children
THEN	Client's financial state suggests \ an aggressive position

Financial State Inference Network

This completes our expansion on the financial issue. We were able to obtain a set of deeper rules for inference on the more abstract financial issue we began with in our goal rules. To maintain a record of the collected knowledge, we should add this new set of rules to our inference network. That part associated with the financial state is shown in Figure 8.6. Our next task is to refine the coding of our system.

TASK 5: REFINING THE SYSTEM

At this point, we have a fully functional system that meets our initial objectives. However, there are several additional features we can add to the system that will enhance both its performance and maintenance.

Using Variables for Numbers

Often during the development of an expert system you will need to use numbers within a rule. For example, in our problem the expert considered anyone 40 years or more to be old. We captured this heuristic in RULE 10 where this number was explicitly used within the rule. In a large rule-based system, this same number might appear in several rules scattered throughout the knowledge base. If at a later time there comes a need to change this number, you will need to locate each rule and make the appropriate adjustment. This task can often be difficult and adds to the difficulty of maintaining the system.

A better approach when using numbers within rules is to replace them with variables that are assigned values within an initialization portion of the program. This approach permits you to easily locate a variable needing adjustment and requires only a change to the variable assignment and not to the rules.

In our example system, numbers were used for the following issues:

- Client's age
- Length of service
- Relationship between assets and liabilities

We can replace the explicit use of numbers used on these issues with the following variables and their initial assignments. An example rule adjustment is also shown for each issue:

AGE ISSUE

Initialize   OLD_AGE = 40

Rule 9
IF   Client_age < OLD_AGE
THEN   Client IS young

LENGTH OF SERVICE ISSUE

Initialize   LONG_SERVICE = 10
              SHORT_SERVICE = 3

Rule 11
IF   Client's length of service >= LONG_SERVICE
THEN   Client's job IS steady

ASSET VERSUS LIABILITIES

Initialize   SAFETY_FACTOR = 2

Rule 17
IF   Total_assets > SAFETY_FACTOR * Total_liabilities
THEN   Client's financial state suggests \ an aggressive position

Intelligent Safety Net

In traditional programming applications, the programmer will usually test the code for all possible input combinations to verify its operation. This is possible because the amount of input data is often limited to a finite number of possibilities. However, when developing an expert system, you are often faced with a large number of possible input combinations, which prevents exhaustive testing of the system. In this situation, the chance may always exist that your system may not be able to reach a final recommendation.

To address this problem, you need to develop a "safety net" for your system. A safety net is simply a course of action that the system takes if it fails to reach a recommendation. It can be as complex as loading in another knowledge base that will try to correct the situation, or, as simple as a default statement displayed to the user informing him of the failure.

Another approach that you might choose to take is to provide an "intelligent safety net." By "intelligent" it is meant that the system tells the user something worthwhile about what was discovered, even though a final recommendation was not obtained.

The easiest way to accomplish this is through the goal agenda. You need to include a goal that the system will pursue only if the primary goal was not achieved. This goal would be the conclusion of a single rule that is guaranteed to fire and display the appropriate information. The premise of the rule would be a simple fact, previously asserted into the working memory, which acts only to fire the rule.

For our example system, we might elect to inform the user about the personal and financial states of the client in the safety net. To accomplish this, we would first have to make the following adjustment to our goal agenda:

1. Portfolio advice IS WHAT
2. Display default

The first goal, which we previously developed, is searched first. We need to make sure that the second goal would be pursued only in the event the first goal failed.

We next need to write the rule that displays the default text to the user:

Rule 18
IF   Recommendation is unknown
THEN   Display default
AND   DISPLAY DEFAULT TEXT

The premise of this rule would be asserted into working memory when the session begins using some form of an "INIT" statement. When this rule fires, the text associated with the statement "DISPLAY DEFAULT TEXT" would be displayed to the user. We need to design this text to inform the user that the system was unable to reach a recommendation and to provide the findings about the state of the client:

DISPLAY DEFAULT TEXT

I am sorry but I was unable to determine a portfolio that matches the needs of the client. However, on the basis of the client's personal state I would recommend a [Client's personal state suggests] and on the financial state a [Client's financial state suggests].

When this display is shown to the user, the values found for "Client's personal state suggests" and "Client's financial state suggests" would be presented. Even though the system was unsuccessful, the user may still benefit by having this information.

Providing Milestones

One way that you can accommodate the user during the consultation is to keep him or her informed about important findings and directions that the system is taking. Users are usually more comfortable with the consultation when they are kept informed.

There are several places within our system where we might elect to display intermediate findings. For example, the client's job stability assessment, his asset-to-liability comparison, etc. Assume we want to display the assessment on the client's personal state. We would need to add a statement to each rule that concluded this issue—a display statement that provided the appropriate information. Consider for example the following added statement to RULE 6 and the display statement:

Rule 6
IF   Client IS old
OR   Client's job IS not steady
THEN   Client's personal state suggests \ a conservative position
AND   DISPLAY PERSONAL STATE ASSESSMENT

DISPLAY PERSONAL STATE ASSESSMENT

After considering the client's personal issues, I would suggest [Client's personal state suggests]. I will next look into the client's financial issues.

This display not only presents the current findings, it also shows the direction the system will next take.

_____ **TASK 6: INTERFACE DESIGN** _____

The user of your expert system views the program through the systems's interface. To a large extent, the acceptance of your system will depend on how well this interface accommodates the needs of the user. Fortunately, most of the shells provide utilities to aid in the design of the interface. They permit you to tailor the design of the introductory screen, the questions asked, and the final display. It is important that you take advantage of any available utilities to design the interface to meet the needs of the user.

Introductory Display

Every expert system should have an introductory display. At a minimum, this display should tell the user about the overall purpose of the system. For example, in our application the display should tell the user that the system will provide a recommendation of a portfolio that meets the needs of the client. You might also want to tell the user a little about how you are going to accomplish the primary task. For example, in our system we might elect to explain that the system will explore both personal and financial issues to arrive at a recommendation.

Tailored Questions

Most shells ask questions automatically generated from the found primitives in the rules. For example, on the issue of "Total assets" the system might ask:

SYSTEM: Total_assets ?

Questions in this form are not only crude, they can also confuse the user leading to incorrect answers. For example, faced with such a question the user might ask "What assets do I consider?," or, "Do I enter the amount in dollars?," or, "Do I use commas when entering the number?" If questions like these occur, you can count on problems.

Fortunately, most shells permit you to tailor the questions posed to the user. You can create friendly text that includes information to solicit reliable answers. Consider for example the following revised form of the previous question:

> **SYSTEM:** Please give the total dollar amount of assets that the client owns. Include holdings in such items as bank accounts, stocks, bonds, real estate, etc. Please enter the dollar amount without commas, e.g., 150000.

Screen Directions

It is important that you provide clear directions for each screen presented to the user. State clearly any options available for the current screen and how to use them. The following sections illustrate how to provide clear screen directions at various points during the session.

Continuing the Session

Consider the simple task of continuing the session following the display of some text or graphics. Most shells require the user to press Enter or some function key to continue the session. Users will quickly become familiar with these keystroke requirements, but early on, they may need help. A short description added to the display screen informing the user how to continue is helpful. It can be as simple as

Please press ENTER to continue the session.

Asking Questions with Multiple Answers

You can also help the user when asking questions by making several options available. For example, if the question permits the user to select multiple answers from a menu of items, then a simple statement added to the screen can help. Consider for example the following:

> **SYSTEM:** What is the education level of the client? Select as many as apply, then press F4 to continue.
>
> > High school
> > College
> > Masters
> > Ph.D.

Here the user is told that he can select more than one item and also what to do when the selections have been completed.

Ending the Session

When the final display screen is presented to the user, you should clearly explain what options are available and how to select them. Typical options are:

- STOP   Stop/exit the system.
- HOW   Obtain line of reasoning that led to the conclusion.
- WHAT-IF   Change answers to prior questions to see effect on the present recommendation.
- SAVE   Save the current session.
- RESTART   Restart the session.

Consider for example the following:

> **SYSTEM:** To exit the system press F10. If you would like to restart the session press F3.

With simple directions like these, the user knows what can be done, and avoids the obvious frustration that arises if control options are not presented.

Conclusion Display

The conclusion display presents to the user the system's findings. For our example system, we would display the portfolio recommended for the client. In many applications this limited display would be sufficient. However in others, you may need to present a more in-depth report that provides the rationale behind the recommendation.

A trademark of expert systems is their ability to explain HOW a recommendation was derived. Most shells respond to this request by providing a detailed account of all the steps followed by the system. In some applications these details are necessary for the user to accept the final recommendation. However, in many other applications, the user may be satisfied with only a high-level view of the major findings that led to the final recommendation.

To accommodate users requiring only a high-level view of the reasoning, we can go back to the suggestion of reporting the milestones. By their nature, these milestones are the findings on the important issues considered by the system when attempting to determine the final recommendation. Capturing these findings and displaying them to the user along with the final recommendation will satisfy many users.

For our small system, we could write the following final display to accomplish this request:

DISPLAY FINAL RECOMMENDATION

I would recommend that the client invest the money in [Portfolio advice].
I recommend this investment because I found the client's personal state suggests [Client's personal state suggests] and financial state suggests [Client's financial state suggests].

Here the user receives both the final recommendation and some high-level reasons why the recommendation was made. Depending on the application, the depth of the reporting can be taken to any level needed by the user, including the possibility of a tabulation of the actual data entered.

------------- **TASK 7: SYSTEM EVALUATION** -------------

At this point our prototype system is complete. All of our rules are coded into the system and we assume that the interface is designed according to the recommendations given in the previous sections. We also assume that the system successfully passed tests performed with each expansion. The next step is to evaluate the system using a real test case.

This process begins by asking the expert for one of her past cases. Assume the case she provides involves a client who is 30 years old, has been with a company with a small layoff rate for 5 years, has 2 children, and wants to invest $50,000. The client also has total assets of $100,000 and total liabilities of $20,000. For this case, she recommended Portfolio 2: 60% stocks, 30% bonds, 10% savings.

Figure 8.7 is a listing of the rules in our system. The system also includes text (not shown) to support the introduction display, questioning, intermediate displays, and the conclusion display. The format for each of these displays follows earlier examples. The following interaction between the expert system and the user illustrates the operation of our system:

STEP 1
SYSTEM: Welcome to the INVESTMENT ADVISOR EXPERT SYSTEM.

   I will attempt to determine a portfolio investment for your client. I will ask you both personal and financial questions about the client. From this information, I should be able to determine either a conservative or an aggressive investment.
   Please press RETURN to begin our session.
USER: RETURN

STEP 2
SYSTEM: How much money in dollars does the client want to invest?   Please enter the dollar amount without commas, e.g., 10000.
USER: 50000

```
INIT SAFETY_FACTOR = 2  INIT OLD_AGE = 40 INIT LONG_SERVICE = 10
INIT SHORT_SERVICE = 3   INIT Recommendation is unknown

1. Advice IS WHAT
2. Display default

RULE Display default
IF Recommendation is unknown
THEN Display default
AND DISPLAY DEFAULT TEXT


!=====================================================================
!    Investment advice rules
!=====================================================================

RULE Advise 100% investment in money market - little money
IF   Client's_investment_amount < 1000
THEN Advice IS 100% investment in savings
AND  DISPLAY FINAL RECOMMENDATION

RULE Advise 100% investment in money market
IF   Client's personal state suggests \ a conservative position
AND  Client's financial state suggests \ a conservative position
THEN Advice IS 100% investment in savings
AND  DISPLAY FINAL RECOMMENDATION

RULE Advise 60% stocks, 30% bonds, 10% money market
IF   Client's personal state suggests \ a conservative position
AND  Client's financial state suggests \ an aggressive position
THEN Advice IS 60% stocks, 30% bonds, 10% savings
AND  DISPLAY FINAL RECOMMENDATION

RULE Advise 20% stocks, 40% bonds, 40% money market
IF   Client's personal state suggests \ an aggressive position
AND  Client's financial state suggests \ a conservative position
THEN Advice IS 20% stocks, 40% bonds, 40% savings
AND  DISPLAY FINAL RECOMMENDATION

RULE Advise 100% investment in stocks
IF   Client's personal state suggests \ an aggressive position
AND  Client's financial state suggests \ an aggressive position
THEN Advice IS 100% investment in stocks
AND  DISPLAY FINAL RECOMMENDATION


!=====================================================================
!    Determine client's personal state
!=====================================================================

RULE Personal conservative investments because old or job not steady
IF   Client IS old
OR   Client's job IS not steady
THEN Client's personal state suggests \ a conservative position
AND  DISPLAY PERSONAL STATE ASSESSMENT

RULE Personal conservative investments because young with children
IF   Client IS young
AND  Client's job IS steady
AND  Client has \ children
THEN Client's personal state suggests \ a conservative position
AND  DISPLAY PERSONAL STATE ASSESSMENT

RULE Personal aggressive investments because young with no children
IF   Client IS young
AND  Client's job IS steady
AND  Client has \ no children
THEN Client's personal state suggests \ an aggressive position
AND  DISPLAY PERSONAL STATE ASSESSMENT
```

FIGURE 8.7   Investment advisor rules.

```
!=========================================================================
!    Determine client's financial state
!=========================================================================

RULE Financial conservative investments because liabilities exceed assets
IF   Total_assets < Total_liabilities
THEN Client's financial state suggests \ a conservative position
AND  DISPLAY FINANCIAL STATE ASSESSMENT

RULE Financial conservative investments because not enough assets for children
IF   Total_assets > Total_liabilities
AND  Total_assets < SAFETY_FACTOR * Total_liabilities
AND  Client has \ children
THEN Client's financial state suggests \ a conservative position
AND  DISPLAY FINANCIAL STATE ASSESSMENT

RULE Financial aggressive investments because enough assets for no children
IF   Total_assets > Total_liabilities
AND  Total_assets < SAFETY_FACTOR * Total_liabilities
AND  Client has \ no children
THEN Client's financial state suggests \ an aggressive position
AND  DISPLAY FINANCIAL STATE ASSESSMENT

RULE Financial aggressive investments because plenty of assets
IF   Total_assets > SAFETY_FACTOR * Total_liabilities
THEN Client's financial state suggests \ an aggressive position
AND  DISPLAY FINANCIAL STATE ASSESSMENT

!=========================================================================
!    Determine age of client
!=========================================================================

RULE Client IS young
IF   Client_age < OLD_AGE
THEN Client IS young

RULE Client is old
IF   Client_age >= OLD_AGE
THEN Client IS old

!=========================================================================
!    Determine stability of client's job
!=========================================================================

RULE Job IS steady because of large length of service
IF   Client's_length_of_service >= LONG_SERVICE
THEN Client's job IS steady

RULE Job IS steady because of moderate service but low layoff rate
IF   Client's_length_of_service >= SHORT_SERVICE
AND  Client's_length_of_service < LONG_SERVICE
AND  Layoffs at the organization IS low
THEN Client's job IS steady

RULE Job IS not steady because moderate service but high layoff rate
IF   Client's_length_of_service >= SHORT_SERVICE
AND  Client's_length_of_service < LONG_SERVICE
AND  Layoffs at the organization IS high
THEN Client's job IS not steady

RULE Job IS not steady
IF   Client's_length_of_service < SHORT_SERVICE
THEN Client's job IS not steady
```

FIGURE 8.7   Continued

STEP 3
SYSTEM: What is the client's age?
USER: 30

STEP 4
SYSTEM: How many years has the client been with the present company?
USER: 5

STEP 5
SYSTEM: Layoffs at the organization are:
>   low
>   high
USER: low

COMMENT: *The user may have trouble answering this question. This is a typical problem found when running the system early in the project. We would need to ask the expert how she determines when layoffs are "low" or high," and add the appropriate rules to our system.*

STEP 6
SYSTEM: The client has:
>   children
>   no children
USER: children

STEP 7
SYSTEM: After considering the client's personal issues, I would suggest a **conservative position.** I will next look into the client's financial issues.

Please press RETURN to continue the session.
USER: RETURN

STEP 8
SYSTEM: Please give the total dollar amount of assets that the client owns. Include holdings in such items as bank accounts, stocks, bonds, real estate, etc.
Please enter the dollar amount without commas, e.g., 150000.
USER: 100000

STEP 9
SYSTEM: Please give the total dollar amount in liabilities that the client owes. Include such items as loans, mortgages, etc.
Please enter the dollar amount without commas, e.g., 150000.
USER: 20000

STEP 10
SYSTEM: After considering the client's financial issues, I would suggest an
aggressive position.
Please press RETURN to continue the session.
USER: RETURN

STEP 11
SYSTEM: I would recommend the client invest the money in
60% stocks, 30% bonds, 10% savings.

The major reasons why I recommend this investment is that I found
the client's personal state suggests a **conservative position** and
financial state suggests an **aggressive position.**

To exit the system press F10. If you would like to restart the session
press F3.

Session Review

The first point you should notice is that our system provides the same recommendation as made by the expert. Obtaining an agreement between the system's
findings and that of the expert is one of the critical issues when evaluating an
expert system. You should also recognize that in a real evaluation study, you
would need to use several test cases. Chapter 18 provides details on selecting
test cases for evaluating an expert system.

The next point you should also notice from this evaluation is that our system
was accommodating to the user throughout the session. The introductory display
informed the user what the system would accomplish and gave insight into how
it would be done. Questions were posed in an easy-to-follow fashion and screen
directions were provided instructing the user in the operation of the system. An
informative conclusion display was given that provided the final recommendation
and some high-level justification.

FUTURE DIRECTIONS

Now that we have built a small prototype, we should next expand its capabilities.
For example, we might encode knowledge on additional portfolios. Or, we might
elect to expand the system to recommend specific investment vehicles within
each of the general investment categories. This second point was discussed earlier
and shown in Figure 8.2 as the expert's next step in providing advice to the
client. The ease in which either of these expansion tasks can be accomplished
is greatly influenced by the flexibility of the prototype's design.

Recommending Additional Portfolios

Expanding our system to permit consideration of other portfolios will first require us to write additional goal rules. No additional goals would be needed since our system now has a variable goal statement. Each new goal rule we enter must be able to recommend one of the new portfolios.

A good starting point for writing these rules would be to refer to our present goal rules. Our expert has told us that the two major issues she considers when recommending a portfolio are the personal state and financial state of the client. Our present goal rules use these two issues with values of "conservative" and "aggressive." In order to be able to discriminate between additional portfolios, we might elect to expand on these values by introducing modifiers. For example, we might elect to use values such as: slightly conservative, moderately conservative, and very conservative. If this approach is taken, we would then need to develop a set of deeper rules that could infer these new modified values.

Another approach we could take when modifying existing goal rules to accommodate the additional portfolios involves adding additional premises that address different issues. For example, we could consider other issues such as the client's investment objectives, holding period of the investment, or even world financial conditions. This approach would also require you to write deeper rules to infer information about these new issues.

In general, when you expand your system to consider additional (but similar) goals, look first for ways you can modify the present goal rules. Modifications will usually take the form of additional values to present issues, and/or the addition of new issues. These types of modifications for our system are illustrated in bold type in the following rule:

IF	Client's personal state **new value**
AND	Client's financial state **new value**
AND	**New issue**
THEN	Portfolio advice IS **new portfolio**

Recommending Investment Vehicles

We could easily expand our system to pick the investment vehicles within each general investment category by first modifying the goal agenda so that this task will naturally follow the portfolio selection. This modification is illustrated in the following goal agenda, with the addition of the multivalued goal "Vehicle advice":

1. Portfolio advice IS WHAT
   1.1. Vehicle advice IS WHAT
2. Display default

The goal rules written to conclude this new goal (i.e., 1.1) would need to use information from the portfolio recommendation. To accomplish this, first go back to the goal rules from our earlier system and capture the general investment categories in a multivalued symbolic statement and the percentage to be invested as illustrated by the following modification to RULE1:

> IF   Client's_investment_amount < 1000
> THEN   Portfolio advice IS 100% investment in savings
> AND   Investment category IS savings
> AND   Savings_percentage = 100

Now you could write rules in the following general form to determine specific investment vehicles:

> IF   Investment category IS . . . .
> AND   . . .
>
> .   . . .
> THEN   Vehicle advice IS . . . .

The premises within these rules would address issues that can discriminate between the various vehicles within each category. The actual amount to be invested in any one vehicle would be decided using information on the amount of the total investment and the recommended percentage of the investment for the general investment category, such as "Savings_percentage."

---------- **SUMMARY ON BACKWARD-CHAINING DESIGN** ----------

This chapter reviewed the basic steps performed in the design of a backward-chaining expert system. It was shown that the design process is highly cyclic, where knowledge is collected from the expert, encoded, tested, then refined through additional interactions with the expert. Slowly the system's performance improves through each additional cycle. Besides illustrating the general design methodology for backward-chaining systems via a design example, this chapter also provided several design suggestions you should consider at several key points during the design process.

The major lessons learned in this chapter were:

- The design of a backward-chaining expert system is a highly iterative process.
- The system should be tested immediately after the introduction of new rules.
- The system should be expanded on one issue at a time.
- A decision table can be used to easily acquire decision-making knowledge from the expert.
- The use of an ELSE statement can cause system maintenance problems.

- An inference network provides a graphical record of the rules collected.
- Backward-chaining systems can be designed to perform exhaustive or nonexhaustive search.
- For rules that use numerics for relationship operations, maintain the numbers in variable form that are assigned in an initialization section of the program.
- It is important that an interface be designed to meet all of the needs of the user.

EXERCISES

1. Explain why a backward-chaining system is well suited for classification problems.
2. Why is it important to test a rule-based system immediately after the goal rules are encoded in the system?
3. During the expansion of the system, why is it important to focus on one issue at a time?
4. What is a decision table and why can it be of value during knowledge acquisition?
5. What is the problem with the use of an ELSE statement?
6. What is the value of an inference network?
7. What is the difference between exhaustive and nonexhaustive search? Explain when either technique is appropriate.
8. What is the value of representing numbers used in rules in variable form?
9. In what ways can the interface be designed to accommodate the user?
10. Expand the investor advisor system to include other portfolios.
11. Expand the investor advisor system to consider specific investment vehicles within each general investment category.
12. Develop a small backward-chaining system on a problem for which you can serve as the expert.
13. Develop an expert system that can identify an unknown animal from various observables. The system should first attempt to determine the animal's class: mammal or bird. A typical characteristic of mammals is that they have hair while birds have feathers or usually fly. Typical animals within these classes are:

MAMMALS	BIRDS
Cheetah	Ostrich
Tiger	Penguin
Giraffe	Albatross
Zebra	

Once the system has decided on the animal's class, it should then proceed to determine the identity of the animal. Features that you should consider are the animal's eating habits, its color, and body characteristics, such as size, neck length, etc. For example

```
IF      The animal is a carnivore
AND     The animal's body color is tawny
AND     The animal has dark spots
THEN    The animal is a cheetah
```

14. Use the following interaction between the domain expert and knowledge engineer to develop an expert system for providing advice to a financial client.

KE: What type of financial advice do you give?

DE: Well, the following list are the types of advice I normally give:
1. Invest the money in a savings account
2. Invest the money in both a savings account and stocks
3. Invest the money in stocks

KE: How do you determine which one to recommend?

DE: Well first, if the client's savings are not good, then I would recommend that he put his money in a saving's account. On the other hand, if his savings are good but his income is not good, then I would recommend both a savings account and stocks. Finally, if the client's income and savings are both good, then I would recommend stocks.

KE: How do determine if the client is a good saver?

DE: I usually base this on a rule of thumb. I assume that the client should have at least $5000 per dependent in savings to be considered a good saver.

KE: How do you determine if the client's income is good?

DE: If the client's job is steady and his total present income is greater than his total needed income, then I assume that his income is good.

KE: How do you determine the client's total needed income?

DE: Again, I use a rule of thumb. I first ask him for his present total income. This includes his present income from employment, stocks, bonds, savings, and anything else which provides income. By the way, this is based on yearly income. I then ask him for his base income, that is his total income by way of salaries. I then figure that the client's total income must be greater than his income from salaries plus some additional amount based on how many dependents he has. I figure this additional amount by multiplying the number of dependents by a factor of $4,000. I would also want to know if the client's job is steady before I would conclude his income is good.

KE: How would you conclude that the client's income is not good? Would it follow directly from consideration of the prior information?

DE: Pretty much so. If his job was not steady, I would certainly conclude that his income is not good due to the job's uncertainty. And, if his total present income is less than his total needed income I would then again conclude that his income is not good based on my assumption on how much I feel he should really have.

REFERENCES

Cohen, P. and M.D. Lieberman, A Report on FOLIO: An Expert Assistant for Portfolio Managers, Proceedings IJCAI-83, pp. 212–214, 1983.

Fowler, B., Planning Made Painless, Edge, vol. 3, no. 1, p. 15, January/February 1990.

Pinson, S., Multi-Expert Systems and the Evaluation of Business Risks: The CREDEX System, Expert Systems and Their Applications, 8th International Workshop, Avignon, France, EC2, Nanterre, France, vol. 2, pp. 517–538, May/June 1988.

CHAPTER 9

Forward-Chaining Rule-Based Systems

INTRODUCTION

This chapter provides a review of forward-chaining rule-based expert systems. Examples are given that provide an in-depth look at the operation of this type of system. Insight is also provided on their design, a subject that is covered in detail in Chapter 10.

REVIEW OF FORWARD-CHAINING INFERENCING

The operation of a forward-chaining system begins with initial information about the problem being asserted into working memory. You can accomplish this in a number of ways, such as by obtaining the information from a database, sensors, or asking the user. The system then scans the rules looking for ones whose premises match the contents of the working memory. If a match is found, the system *fires* the rule, places its conclusion in the working memory, and then scans the rules again. This process continues until no additional rule fires.

During a given scan of the rules, the system may locate several rules that can fire and must decide which ones to fire. In most applications, only one rule will be fired and a new cycle of the rules is begun. This process of locating rules that can fire, choosing one to fire and firing it, is called a **recognize-resolve-act** cycle.

There are several strategies used to determine which rule to fire when several compete (a process called **conflict resolution**). In the simplest application of forward-chaining, the rules are examined in order and the first one located that can fire is chosen. Another common strategy relies on rule priorities where numbers, usually between −1000 and 1000, are assigned to each rule. When rules compete for firing, the system chooses the one with the highest priority. Chapter 4 discusses other conflict resolution strategies.

The balance of this chapter reviews examples of forward-chaining expert systems. Each example illustrates the operation of a forward-chaining system and also highlights important design issues for these systems.

EXAMPLE 1: PUMPING STATION DIAGNOSTIC SYSTEM

The first forward-chaining system we review is an expert system designed to diagnose problems with a water pumping station as illustrated in Figure 9.1. The

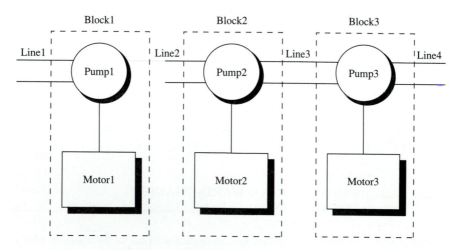

FIGURE 9.1   Water pumping station.

station is comprised of a number of blocks, each containing a pump and motor, that work in series to carry water through the various lines. We will assume that each block increases the water pressure by 50 psi. Sensors are also available that provide information on line pressures and motor currents. Nominal line pressure and motor current values are also available. The objective of the expert system is to detect and identify any fault in the operation of the pumping station.

This type of example expert system is often called an **event-driven** system. Unlike a conventional expert system that interacts with a user, an event-driven system sits there dormant and only becomes active when some special event occurs. In our example, the special event is a detected fault in the water plant.

The objectives of reviewing this example system are:

- Review forward chaining.
- See diagnostics performed in a natural three-step process.
- See how the system displays intermediate information.
- See value of final displays that incorporate intermediate findings.
- See importance of rule grouping.

Problem-Solving Approach

For this small example, we only consider the first two blocks of Figure 9.1. Rules for other blocks would follow the same approach used in this example. The rules used in the expert system are shown in Figure 9.2. The listing of the knowledge base is divided into various sections that contain rules specific to the section's task. We assume that the approach used by the forward-chaining system is to scan the rules in order and fire the first rule located whose premises match the contents of the working memory.

The problem-solving strategy used in this example follows a three-step process of fault detection, fault isolation, and fault diagnosis. Most expert systems designed for diagnostic problems follow this sequence of tasks. Some also include a fourth step called fault response, which involves the formulation of a suggested recovery procedure.

Fault Detection

Fault detection is performed by the rules in GROUP S in a simple fashion. First, the numeric readings supplied by the sensors are converted to qualitative descriptions: low or normal. Second, we assume that any fault will manifest itself in a low line pressure. Finally, we assume that faults propagate throughout the system. For example, a low pressure in Line 1 will result in low pressures in Line 2 and Line 3. Therefore, we simply have to monitor the final line pressure (Line 3 in our case) to determine if a fault exists. When a low Line 3 pressure is detected, the system informs the user that a fault exists by the display action contained in Rule 5S.

```
=============================================================
FAULT DETECTION RULES    (RULE GROUP S)
=============================================================

RULE 1S Line 1 pressure is low        RULE 6S Line 3 pressure is normal
IF   Line1 pressure < 50              IF   Line3 pressure >= 150
THEN Line1 pressure is low            THEN Line3 pressure is normal

RULE 2S Line 1 pressure is normal     RULE 7S Motor 1 current is low
IF   Line1 pressure >= 50             IF   Motor1 current < 1
THEN Line1 pressure is normal         THEN Motor1 current is low

RULE 3S Line 2 pressure is low        RULE 8S Motor 1 current is normal
IF   Line2 pressure < 100             IF   Motor1 current >= 1
THEN Line2 pressure is low            THEN Motor1 current is normal

RULE 4S Line 2 pressure is normal     RULE 9S Motor 2 current is low
IF   Line2 pressure >= 100            IF   Motor2 current < 1
THEN Line2 pressure is normal         THEN Motor2 current is low

RULE 5S Line 3 pressure is low        RULE 10S Motor 2 current is normal
IF   Line3 pressure < 150             IF   Motor2 current >= 1
THEN Line3 pressure is low            THEN Motor2 current is normal
AND  DISPLAY FAULT DETECTED

=============================================================
FAULT ISOLATION RULES    (RULE GROUP I)
=============================================================

RULE 1I Block 1 may be at fault       RULE 2I Block 2 may be at fault
IF   Line1 pressure is normal         IF   Line2 pressure is normal
AND  Line2 pressure is low            AND  Line3 pressure is low
THEN Block1 may be at fault           THEN Block2 may be at fault
AND  Block fault IS Block1            AND  Block fault IS Block2
AND  DISPLAY BLOCK PROBLEM            AND  DISPLAY BLOCK PROBLEM

=============================================================
FAULT DIAGNOSIS RULES    MOTOR PROBLEM    (RULE GROUP M)
=============================================================

RULE 1M Motor 1 may have a problem     RULE 2M Motor 2 may have a problem
IF   Block1 may be at fault            IF   Block2 may be at fault
AND  Motor1 current is low             AND  Motor2 current is low
THEN Motor1 is at fault                THEN Motor2 is at fault
AND  Suspected fault IS Motor1         AND  Suspected fault IS Motor2
AND  DISPLAY FAULT FOUND               AND  DISPLAY FAULT FOUND

=============================================================
FAULT DIAGNOSIS RULES    PUMP PROBLEM    (RULE GROUP P)
=============================================================

RULE 1P Pump 1 may have a problem      RULE 2P Pump 2 may have a problem
IF   Block1 may be at fault            IF   Block2 may be at fault
AND  Motor1 current is normal          AND  Motor2 current is normal
AND  Line1 pressure = Line2 pressure   AND  Line2 pressure = Line3 pressure
THEN Pump1 may have a problem          THEN Pump2 may have a problem
AND  Suspected fault IS Pump1          AND  Suspected fault IS Pump2
AND  DISPLAY FAULT FOUND               AND  DISPLAY FAULT FOUND

=============================================================
FAULT DIAGNOSIS RULES    LINE PROBLEM    (RULE GROUP L)
=============================================================

RULE 1L Line 2 may have a problem      RULE 2L Line 3 may have a problem
IF   Block1 may be at fault            IF   Block2 may be at fault
AND  Motor1 current is normal          AND  Motor2 current is normal
AND  Line1 pressure < Line2 pressure   AND  Line2 pressure < Line3 pressure
THEN Line2 may have a problem          THEN Line3 may have a problem
AND  Suspected fault IS Line2          AND  Suspected fault IS Line3
AND  DISPLAY FAULT FOUND               AND  DISPLAY FAULT FOUND
```

FIGURE 9.2   Pumping station rules.

Fault Isolation

Following the detection of a fault, the expert system attempts to isolate the station's block causing the problem—see RULE GROUP I. The approach we take to isolate the faulty block is based on a comparison of the block's input pressure with its output pressure. That is, if we see a block with normal input pressure but low output pressure, then we can suspect something is wrong with that block. Following the identification of the faulty block, the system informs the user of the block's identity before proceeding to diagnostics.

In general, performing an isolation task for any diagnostic task can be valuable. In our example, by first identifying the faulty block the system can concentrate its diagnostic effort on this single block rather than the entire system. In large rule-based systems, this approach can result in considerable saving of system processing time.

Fault Diagnosis

After a suspected faulty block is identified, the system attempts to determine what block component is at fault, i.e., motor, pump or line. Separate diagnostic rule groups are used for each component.

A motor problem is assumed on the discovery of a low current—see RULE GROUP M. A pump problem is assumed if the motor is operating normally but there is no pressure change across the block—see RULE GROUP P. Finally, a line problem is suspected if the motor is operating normally but the block's input pressure remains less than its output pressure—see RULE GROUP L. Here, the real suspect is a leaky output line. The block simply can't keep up with the leak, resulting in lower output pressure than would be expected.

Following the identification of any fault, the system displays the final results to the user. Though the code for this display is not shown, we assume that it is designed to display not only the suspected faulty component, but again the faulted block.

Water Diagnostic Example Session

The first step in the operation of this system involves the acquisition of the sensor readings from some data acquisition system. Assume these values were obtained resulting in the following initial state of the working memory:

WORKING MEMORY	
Line1 pressure = 50	Motor1 current = 1
Line2 pressure = 80	Motor2 current = 1
Line3 pressure = 120	

Cycles 1–5

The first five cycles involve rules from GROUP S that check the sensor readings and convert them to qualitative descriptions. From this effort, the system fires rules 2S, 3S, 5S, 8S and 10S, resulting in the following information added to the working memory:

WORKING MEMORY

Line1 pressure is normal   Motor1 current is normal
Line2 pressure is low   Motor2 current is normal
Line3 pressure is low

The firing of rule 5S means that a fault is detected and results in the following display:

SYSTEM: A fault is detected in the water's plant operation. I will next attempt to isolate the source of the problem.

COMMENT: *The system not only tells the user about present findings, it also provides information about what it is going to do next.*

Cycle 6

During this cycle, the only new rule that can fire is RULE 1I. This results in Block 1 being identified as the likely location of the faulted component. This information is added to the working memory. The firing of this rule also causes the following display to be given:

SYSTEM: I believe the fault is located in **Block1.** I will next attempt to determine the specific component within this block causing the problem.

COMMENT: *A general display (BLOCK PROBLEM) was written to show this message to the user. The system is able to capture and display "Block1" because it was established as an Object–Attribute–Fact (using LEVEL5 "IS" term). Also, the system again tells the user what it is going to do next.*

Cycle 7

During this final cycle, the system has only rules in groups M, P, and L to consider. Given the available information contained in the working memory the system fires RULE 1L, resulting in the suspected fault being identified as Line 2—output line of Block 1. The firing of this rule also causes the following display to be presented to the user:

SYSTEM: I believe the fault is located in **Block1** with the faulted component being **Line2.**

No other rules are located on the next cycle that can fire, so the system stops.

Example Review

This small example illustrates a simple forward-chaining expert system for diagnosing problems with a water pumping station. It includes several features that you should consider when designing an expert system.

Partitioned Rules

The system performed the diagnostics following a three-step process of fault detection, isolation, and diagnosis. Each step was performed by a set of rules segmented in the knowledge base to improve readability and enhance the system's maintenance. When you develop a system that involves writing rules for specific functions, or rules that are related in some other natural fashion, group them according to some common theme.

DESIGN SUGGESTION: Group together related rules and label each group clearly.

Intermediate Findings

Since the system followed a well-established sequence of tasks, it was easy to present to the user progress reports along the way. Each report stated what was observed and what the system would look into next. In most applications, you should design the system to keep the user informed on the problem solving progress. The user will obtain a better sense of the underlying important issues being discovered and will likely place more confidence in the final result reported by the system. This "design suggestion" was given in Chapter 7 on backward-chaining systems, but it also applies for forward-chaining applications.

Intelligent Safety Net

In the final display, the system reported not only the suspected fault, Line 1, but also the suspected subsystem or block, Block 1. This could be of value to the user in the event the system was unable to determine the faulted component. Simply knowing the general source of the problem may be valuable to the user.

Numeric Relationships

One of the shortcomings of this example system is that its fault detection rules (RULE GROUP S) relied on crisp numeric boundary decisions. A problem associated with this approach was noted in Chapter 7. This problem is related to the strict interpretation made by the rules using a numeric comparison. For example, RULE 2S states:

IF   Line1 pressure $>= 50$
THEN   Line1 pressure is normal

Using this rule, a Line 1 pressure of 49.99 would not be considered a normal line pressure. In fact, according to RULE 2S, this line pressure would be considered low. This strict interpretation of numeric boundaries can cause obvious problems. Chapter 13 discusses how you can avoid this problem through the use of Fuzzy Logic.

Specific Rules

Another shortcoming of this example is that the rules made explicit reference to components of the water pumping station. For example, rules were written that used the terms Line1, Motor1, etc. There is nothing really wrong with this approach, but when the same types of objects are used in similar ways, then you can enhance the coding of the system by representing the objects as variables in general rules. You will see how this is done in the next example.

EXAMPLE 2: GENERALIZED PUMPING STATION DIAGNOSTIC SYSTEM

In some expert system projects, you will be working on a problem that involves a number of similar objects. For instance, the last example considered a structure that had several motors, pumps, and lines. In this type of application, the expert will often provide general heuristics to handle problems. For example, the expert might say ''If **any** motor . . . , then . . .'' In this type of situation you should write rules that capture the general heuristics, rather than using the approach given in the last example where similar but separate rules were written for each object. This can be accomplished with the use of variables in the rules.

In this example, we reconsider the problem of water plant diagnostics. The objective of the expert system is again to detect and identify any fault in the operation of the pumping station shown in Figure 9.1. However, we will now approach the design of the expert system using variable rules. The objectives of reviewing this example system are:

- Continue review of forward chaining.
- See how variable rules can enhance the flexibility of the system and improve coding efficiency.
- See how a forward-chaining system can halt execution and ask the user a question.
- See a simple approach to fault response.

Problem-Solving Approach

Before we write the general rules that contain reference to the components within the water pumping station, we need to assert into working memory information about the structural relationships between these components. That is, for each block we need to assert information on what pump and motor belong to it, and its input and output lines. In addition, we need to assert information that describes each type of component used in our system, e.g., "Pump1 is-a pump." Finally, so that the system will know when some component is operating out of range, we need to assert the nominal sensor readings. How these assertions are used by the system will become clear when you review the general rules used in this example.

WORKING MEMORY

Block1 is-a block	Block2 is-a block
Motor1 is-a motor	Motor2 is-a motor
Pump1 is-a pump	Pump2 is-a pump
Line1 is-a line	Line2 is-a line
Line3 is-a line	
Block1 motor Motor1	Block1 pump Pump1
Block1 input-line Line1	Block1 output-line Line2
Block2 motor Motor2	Block2 pump Pump2
Block2 input-line Line2	Block2 output-line Line3
Motor1 nominal-current 1	Motor2 nominal-current 1
Line1 nominal-pressure 50	Line2 nominal-pressure 100
Line3 nominal-pressure 150	

The rules used in the expert system are shown in Figure 9.3. The rule listing is again divided into various sections related to their diagnostic task. However, the rules now include variables that generalize the diagnostic task.

General Fault Detection

Fault detection is performed by the rules in GROUP S using the same numeric relationship approach used in the previous example. However, these rules contain variables (strings beginning with "?"), that permit them to perform general fault detection across all the water lines and motors. For insight into how these rules function, consider the following general heuristic used for fault detection and RULE 1S:

FAULT DETECTION HEURISTIC: *If any line pressure drops below its nominal pressure, then you have a fault condition.*

Rule 1S Line pressure is low
IF	?Line is-a line
AND	?Line pressure ?X
AND	?Line nominal-pressure ?Y
AND	(TEST (< ?X ?Y))
THEN	?Line pressure-status low
AND	DISPLAY FAULT DETECTED

```
===============================================================
FAULT DETECTION RULES      (RULE GROUP S)
===============================================================


RULE 1S Line pressure is low
IF   ?Line is-a line
AND  ?Line pressure ?X
AND  ?Line nominal-pressure ?Y
AND  (TEST (< ?X ?Y))
THEN ?Line pressure-status low
AND  DISPLAY FAULT DETECTED

RULE 2S Line pressure is normal
IF   ?Line is-a line
AND  ?Line pressure ?X
AND  ?Line nominal-pressure ?Y
AND  (TEST ( >= ?X ?Y))
THEN ?Line pressure-status normal

RULE 3S Motor current is low
IF   ?Motor is-a motor
AND  ?Motor current ?X
AND  ?Motor nominal-current ?Y
AND  (TEST (< ?X ?Y))
THEN ?Motor current-status low

RULE 4S Motor current is normal
IF   ?Motor is-a motor
AND  ?Motor current ?X
AND  ?Motor nominal-current ?Y
AND  (TEST (>= ?X ?Y))
THEN ?Motor current-status normal


===============================================================
FAULT ISOLATION RULES      (RULE GROUP I)
===============================================================


RULE 1I Block may be at fault
IF   ?Block is-a block
AND  ?Block input-line ?Input-Line
AND  ?Block output-line ?Output-Line
AND  ?Input-Line pressure-status normal
AND  ?Output-Line pressure-status low
THEN ?Block status bad
AND  DISPLAY FAULT ISOLATED


===============================================================
FAULT DIAGNOSIS RULES      MOTOR PROBLEM      (RULE GROUP M)
===============================================================

RULE 1M Motor may have a problem
IF   ?Block is-a block
```

FIGURE 9.3 General rules for water station diagnostics.

```
AND   ?Block status bad
AND   ?Block motor ?Motor
AND   ?Motor current-status low
THEN  ?Motor status bad
AND   DISPLAY FAULT FOUND
AND   ASK Replacement premission granted
```

```
=============================================================
FAULT DIAGNOSIS RULES     PUMP PROBLEM     (RULE GROUP P)
=============================================================
```

```
RULE 1P Pump may have a problem
IF    ?Block is-a block
AND   ?Block status bad
AND   ?Block pump ?Pump
AND   ?Block input-line ?Input-Line
AND   ?Block output-line ?Output-Line
AND   ?Input-Line pressure ?X
AND   ?Output-Line pressure ?Y
AND   (TEST (= ?X ?Y))
THEN  ?Pump status bad
AND   DISPLAY FAULT FOUND
AND   ASK Replacement premission granted
```

```
=============================================================
FAULT DIAGNOSIS RULES     LINE PROBLEM     (RULE GROUP L)
=============================================================
```

```
RULE 1L Line may have a problem
IF    ?Block is-a block
AND   ?Block status bad
AND   ?Block motor ?Motor
AND   ?Motor current-status normal
AND   ?Block input-line ?Input-Line
AND   ?Block output-line ?Output-Line
AND   ?Input-Line pressure ?X
AND   ?Output-Line pressure ?Y
AND   (TEST (< ?X ?Y))
THEN  ?Output-Line status bad
AND   DISPLAY FAULT FOUND
AND   ASK Replacement premission granted
```

```
=============================================================
FAULT RESPONSE RULES     (RULE GROUP R)
=============================================================
```

```
RULE 1R Replace motor
IF    Replacement premission granted
AND   ?Block is-a block
AND   ?Block status bad
AND   ?Block motor ?Motor
AND   ?Motor status bad
```

```
AND   Motor replacement ?New-Motor
THEN  Pitch ?Motor
AND   ?Block motor ?New-Motor
AND   DISPLAY FAULT FIXED
AND   STOP

RULE 2R Replace pump
IF    Replacement premission granted
AND   ?Block is-a block
AND   ?Block status bad
AND   ?Block pump ?Pump
AND   ?Pump status bad
AND   Pump replacement ?New-Pump
THEN  Pitch ?Pump
AND   ?Block pump ?New-Pump
AND   DISPLAY FAULT FIXED
AND   STOP

RULE 3R Replace line
IF    Replacement premission granted
AND   ?Block is-a block
AND   ?Block status bad
AND   ?Block output-line ?Output-Line
AND   ?Output-Line status bad
AND   Line replacement ?New-Line
THEN  Pitch ?Output-Line
AND   ?Block output-line ?New-Line
AND   DISPLAY FAULT FIXED
AND   STOP
```

FIGURE 9.3 Continued

The first premise will bind the variable ?Line to any asserted object that "is-a line." For our example, three matches are found; one for each line asserted into working memory. The system next treats these three matches separately, where in each match, the variable ?Line is bound to a different line name, namely, Line1, Line2, and Line3. Within each separate match, this variable will remain bound throughout the balance of the rule.

The second and third premises obtain from working memory the "pressure" and "nominal-pressure" values of the bounded line variable, and binds these values to ?X and ?Y. The fourth premise performs a test to see if the line pressure is less than its nominal pressure, i.e., $?X < ?Y$. This comparison is performed with a function called "TEST" that is used in ART. Similar functions can be found in other development packages. In the event this condition is met, the fact that the matched line has a low pressure is asserted into working memory, such as "Line1 pressure-status low." For our problem, the system would check this rule three times: once for each line.

General Fault Isolation

Fault isolation in this example is performed by only one rule—RULE 1I. This rule isolates the suspected faulty block using the same idea used in the previous example—good input pressure but bad output pressure. However, we use variables to better capture the general knowledge. Consider the following general heuristic statement supplied by the expert and the rule used in this example to represent it:

> **FAULT ISOLATION HEURISTIC:** *If you notice that a block's input pressure is normal, but its output pressure is low, then the block may be faulty.*

Rule 1I Block may be at fault
IF	?Block is-a block
AND	?Block input-line ?Input-Line
AND	?Block output-line ?Output-Line
AND	?Input-Line pressure-status normal
AND	?Output-Line pressure-status low
THEN	?Block status bad

The first three premises would match all of blocks in our example, and bind the variables according to the structural information previously asserted. The final two premises perform the actual decision-making on the basis of input and output line pressures as established in the fault detection set of rules. Since we have only two blocks in our example, this rule would be checked twice. When the premise conditions have been met, the variable ?Block will be bound to the corresponding faulty block and the fact that it is faulty would be asserted into working memory, such as "Block1 status bad."

General Fault Diagnosis

Fault diagnosis is performed by the general rules shown in RULE GROUPS M (motor), P (pump), and L (line). Each of these rules contains variables and functions in the same manner discussed in the previous sections. The following heuristics were used to create diagnostic rules for each of these components. You should now be able to recognize how these rules effectively capture these heuristics.

> **MOTOR PROBLEM HEURISTIC:** *A motor with a low current is suspect.*

> **PUMP PROBLEM HEURISTIC:** *Pump problems usually result in no pressure changes across the pump.*

> **LINE PROBLEM HEURISTIC:** *When you see no problems with a block's motor, but there is some increase in pressure across the block, there may be a leak in the output line.*

Fault Response Permission

Many fault diagnostic expert systems are designed with automatic fault recovery procedures. Our system has this capability but it was designed to first ask the user for permission. Each of the rules in the diagnosis sections have as part of their conclusion a statement that asks the user for permission to replace the faulty component using the special function "ASK."

General Fault Response

The purpose of fault response is to replace the component identified as being at fault by the diagnosis rules. As stated in the last section, this task will only be performed when the user has granted permission. The rules that perform the replacement task are shown in RULE GROUP R of Figure 9.3. These rules rely upon the existence of a set of replacement parts (e.g., MotorX, PumpX, and LineX) that would need to be asserted into the working memory before the session begins.

To illustrate the operation of these rules, assume the diagnosis rules have identified that Motor1 in Block1 is bad. This information, along with the motor replacement part, is shown in the working memory given below. This information would cause RULE 1R to fire. This rule is also shown below along with a replica of it with its bound values shown in bold type.

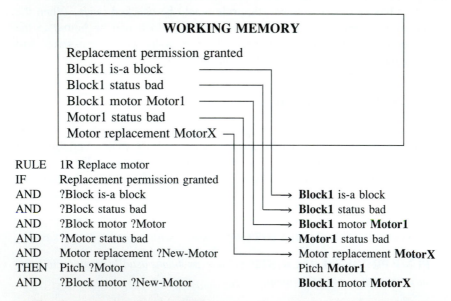

The first premise simply checks to see if permission has been granted to replace the faulted component. Since this fact is asserted in the working memory, the system continues to process the balance of the rule. The second premise searches the working memory for any assertion that can match "?Block is-a block." Several matches would actually occur here, one for each block known to the system. However, only the match associated with Block1 would survive since it is the only one that matches the next premise (its status is bad). Therefore, the second premise binds the variable ?Block to Block1, which then remains bound throughout the rule.

The third premise checks the working memory for a match for the variable ?Motor, in the fact statement "Block1 motor ?Motor." Here, Motor1 is found and bound to the variable ?Motor and used in the next premise. Following the same matching approach, the variable ?New-Motor gets bound to MotorX. Finally, the variables bound in the rule's premises are carried over to the conclusion statements resulting in the pitching of Motor1 and Block1 receiving the new motor Motor1. The other rules in the fault response section work in a similar manner.

Generalized Pumping Station Diagnostic Example Session

We first assume that the plant structural information discussed in the previous sections is already asserted in the working memory. We next assume that the following information has been asserted by the sensors:

WORKING MEMORY	
Line1 pressure 50	Motor1 current 1
Line2 pressure 50	Motor2 current 1
Line3 pressure 100	

Cycles 1–5

The first five cycles involve rules from GROUP S that check the status of the line pressures and motor currents. Following the pattern-matching approach described earlier, they assert the following information into the working memory:

WORKING MEMORY	
Line1 pressure-status normal	Motor1 current-status normal
Line2 pressure-status low	Motor2 current-status normal
Line3 pressure-status low	

The firing of rule 1S indicates that a fault has been detected resulting in the following display:

SYSTEM: A fault has been detected in the water's plant operation. I will next attempt to isolate the source of the problem.

Cycle 6

During this cycle, only RULE 1I fires with the fact "Block1 status bad" asserted. The firing of this rule also causes the following display to be given:

SYSTEM: I believe the fault is located in **Block1.** I will next attempt to determine the specific component within this block causing the problem.

Cycle 7

During this cycle, the system considers rules in groups M, P and L. Given the information contained in the working memory the system fires RULE 1P resulting in the assertion "Pump1 status bad." The firing of this rule also causes the following display and question to be presented:

SYSTEM: I believe the fault is located in **Block1** with the faulted component being **Pump1.**

SYSTEM: Do you want me to replace the faulted component?
User: YES

Cycle 8

During this cycle, rules in group R are considered. From the available information, the system fires rule 2R resulting in Pump1 being replaced with PumpX. The following display is then given and the system stops:

SYSTEM: I replaced **Pump1** in **Block1** with **PumpX.**

COMMENT: *A forward-chaining system will stop on its own when no further rules are located that can fire. However, the designer might elect to explicitly stop the system using some form of a "STOP" command. This approach can possibly avoid unneeded system processing.*

Example Review

This example considers the same pumping station diagnostic problem addressed in Example 1. It used the same heuristics but encoded them in general rules with the use of variables. This approach offers you a number of advantages when designing an expert system.

Streamlining Rules

This example illustrates how a small number of general rules containing variables can produce the same result as a large set of rules that explicitly reference the domain's objects. For instance, this example used only 8 rules to accomplish the tasks of fault detection, isolation, and diagnosis, versus the 18 rules used in Example 1 to accomplish these same tasks.

Ease of Expansion

The use of general rules allows you to easily expand the expert system. For example, if additional blocks of motors, pumps, and lines were added to the water pumping station, you would only need to assert their initial configuration information into the working memory. The existing rules could work with this new information with no need for you to modify them.

Requesting Information

Most forward-chaining systems are designed to work exclusively with information initially asserted into the working memory. Typical sources for this information are the user, a data acquisition system, or a database. In the latter two cases, procedures are written to acquire the information from the two sources and deposit it in the working memory. Control is then turned over to the expert system. If you want the system to acquire the information from the user, then you must include a **startup rule** whose only purpose is to solicit the information. This rule fires immediately when the system is started and looks something like the following:

```
IF      Get initial information
THEN    ASK . . . . . .
AND     ASK . . . . . .
  :       :
```

To set the system in motion, you need to initially assert in working memory the fact contained in this rule's premise. This would cause the rule to fire and the list of questions to be asked. Answers provided would be asserted and used by other rules in a forward-chaining fashion. In general, you can initially assert any information that is important before the session begins.

DESIGN SUGGESTION: Use a startup rule to acquire initial information from the user before the session begins.

If a startup rule is the only means used to acquire information from the user, then the user only enters the picture at the beginning of the session. However, in some applications you may need to design the system to request additional information from the user when certain events occur. This situation occurred in our example when we wanted the system to first obtain permission from the user before proceeding to the reconfiguration task—see RULES 1M, 1P and 1L. These rules included as part of their conclusion an added statement that asked for information from the user.

Another way that you can interrupt the forward-chaining process to ask the user for information is through the use of a **demon rule.** Demon rules behave like other forward-chaining rules in that they fire when their premises are satisfied by the contents of the working memory. However, they are not a part of the natural inference chain with the other rules. Their purpose is to sit dormant and fire when some special event occurs. Consider for example the following demon rule written for our example to ask the user if he wants the water plant shut down in the event a fault has been detected:

IF   ?Line pressure-status low
THEN   ASK Shut down

Since demon rules are written for special events, we usually want them to fire before other rules in the system. To accomplish this they must be assigned a priority higher than the other rules used.

DESIGN SUGGESTION: Use demon rules to monitor special events.

Stopping the System

Forward-chaining systems stop on their own when no further rules are located that can fire. This is the most common technique used to conclude the session, but not always the best way. In some applications you may need to force the system to stop, even though other rules are left to consider. In our example, we included a special command called STOP in several rules that causes the system to terminate operation. Similar commands can be found in various shells that perform the same function.

DESIGN SUGGESTION: Use some form of a STOP command to terminate the operation of the system if it is required for the application.

EXAMPLE 3: TRAIN-LOADING EXPERT SYSTEM

The next example illustrates a forward-chaining approach for a design problem. Our problem is to pack, in the most efficient manner, waiting passengers of various weights into a series of train cars. We want to minimize the number of cars needed, each of which has a maximum allowable weight. Therefore, we need to fit as many people as possible into a car without exceeding the maximum allowable weight. Another interesting constraint placed on this problem is that we would also like to pack most of the heavier people in the cars closest to the locomotive—this helps the train make any steep slopes encountered.

The objectives of reviewing this example system are:

- Review a forward-chaining system developed for a design application.
- See special structures used in design rules.
- See why a forward-chaining technique is appropriate for design applications.

Developing an expert system for a design application presents some unique problems. It requires you to use techniques that are not often found in other types of applications. An excellent review of expert systems in design applications is given by Coyne et al. (1990). Before proceeding with this example, a brief discussion of this type of system will help you to better understand the example.

Expert Systems for Design Applications

Design is the task of configuring objects under a set of constraints that generally fall into one of two categories: design requirements and design methods. The design requirements relate to choosing only those objects that meet the design goal. Design methods are associated with the design task itself, such as one part of the design can only be addressed after other steps have been completed. Consider for example XCON (McDermott 1980), an expert system for configuring DEC's VAX computer systems. XCON configures computer systems under such constraints as the customer's requirements, component specifications, available space, etc. XCON must also consider the order in which the design is put together. For example, it won't look for the place for the system's power supply until one has been chosen.

These two types of constraints associated with a design problem place special demands on the development of the expert system. The constraints associated with design requirements basically force you to use a forward-chaining approach. The constraints placed on design methods require that you write rules that include control knowledge. Let's look at both of these points in more detail.

Forward Chaining Required

Backward-chaining systems begin with well-established goals (or solutions) to prove. Because the solutions are known in advance, these systems will never recommend a solution that is not one of the original goals. Conversely, forward-chaining systems attempt to assemble new solutions. They take available information and derive logical conclusions, resulting in recommendations that may not have been expected originally.

Consider a problem of designing the layout of furniture in a room. You might have to consider such issues as what type of furniture, their sizes, which pieces best go together, etc. You could never account for all of the possible designs that could result from this problem—there could be a million solutions. This is the principal reason why forward-chaining systems are the choice for design problems. Each new problem requires a solution tailored to the design requirements.

Control Rules Required

The firing of rules in a forward-chaining system is usually controlled in a simple fashion. That is, when a rule's premises match the contents of the working memory, the rule fires. In design applications this approach will rarely work because certain tasks can only be considered after others have been completed. For example, before you could nail two boards together, you would first have to make sure you have a hammer.

To manage constraints placed on task sequencing, you need to design rules that can keep track of the state of the design and to take whatever action is necessary. To accomplish this, a design rule will usually be made up of three parts as follows:

$$\textbf{IF} <step> \textbf{ AND } <heuristic> \textbf{ THEN } <action>$$

With this structure, the information contained in the "heuristic" knowledge about the problem will only be considered when the "step" is appropriate. The "action" part might simply assert new information as conventional rules do, or it might change the action of the system, such as asserting some new step. Consider for example a rule from XCON that follows this type of structure:

> IF   Current task is assigning a power supply
> AND   Position of the power supply in the cabinet is known
> AND   Space is available in the cabinet for the power supply
> THEN   Put the power supply in the cabinet

Problem-Solving Approach

The objective of our example is to efficiently pack passengers of different weights into a series of train cars. In general, we want the system to:

- Pack the persons by decreasing weight.
- Not exceed maximum weight capacity of train car.
- Maximize the number of persons per train car thus minimizing the number of cars needed.

The rules used in the expert system are shown in Figure 9.4. The example system is comprised of a number of small rules which represent a specific task that can be accomplished if the problem state permits their operation. For example, RULE 3B would fire if the present task is to pack a large person, some large person remains to be packed, and the large person can fit in the train car currently being packed. In words, this rule reads as

> IF   Current task is pack large person
> AND   Large person is available
> AND   Large person can fit in the current train car
> THEN   Pack the large person

Similar rules exist for packing the medium and small persons. In each case, each rule also adds the person who was packed to the current car, increases the car's weight accordingly, and decreases the number of persons in the appropriate weight category.

```
============================================================
BASIC CONTROL RULES     (RULE GROUP A)
============================================================


RULE 1A Display car
IF    Task IS display present car
THEN  Display car contents
AND   DISPLAY present car
AND   Task IS start new car


RULE 2A Packing is complete
IF    Number of small persons = 0
AND   Number of medium persons = 0
AND   Number of large persons = 0
THEN  Task IS done
AND   STOP


RULE 3A Start a new car
IF    Task IS start new car
THEN  car number = car number + 1
AND   Weight of car = 0
AND   Large persons in car = 0
AND   Medium persons in car = 0
AND   Small persons in car = 0
AND   Task IS pack large person


============================================================
PEOPLE PACKING RULES     (RULE GROUP B)
============================================================


RULE 1B Pack a small person
IF    Task IS pack small person
AND   Number of small persons > 0
AND   Weight of small person + Weight of car <= Maximum weight of car
THEN  Small persons in car = Small persons in car + 1
AND   Weight of car = Weight of car + Weight of small person
AND   Number of small persons = Number of small persons - 1


RULE 2B Pack a medium person
IF    Task IS pack medium person
AND   Number of medium persons > 0
AND   Weight of medium person + Weight of car <= Maximum weight of car
THEN  Medium persons in car = Medium persons in car + 1
AND   Weight of car = Weight of car + Weight of medium person
AND   Number of medium persons = Number of medium persons - 1


RULE 3B Pack a large person
IF    Task IS pack large person
AND   Number of large persons > 0
AND   Weight of large person + Weight of car <= Maximum weight of car
THEN  Pack the large person
AND   Large persons in car = Large persons in car + 1
AND   Weight of car = Weight of car + Weight of large person
AND   Number of large persons = Number of large persons - 1


============================================================
PACKING SWITCH RULES     (RULE GROUP C)
============================================================


RULE 1C Switch from packing small person to display present car
IF    Task IS pack small person
AND   Number of small persons = 0
```

FIGURE 9.4   Train packing rules.

```
OR   Weight of small person + Weight of car > Maximum weight of car
THEN Task IS display present car

RULE 2C Switch from packing medium persons to pack small person
IF   Task IS pack medium person
AND  Number of medium persons = 0
OR   Weight of medium person + Weight of car > Maximum weight of car
THEN Task IS pack small person

RULE 3C Switch from packing large person to pack medium person
IF   Task IS pack large person
AND  Number of large persons = 0
OR   Weight of large person + Weight of car > Maximum weight of car
THEN Task IS pack medium person
```

FIGURE 9.4 Continued

The order of packing—large, medium, and small persons—is explicitly controlled by the rules that switch the task to the next appropriate one, thus following one of the constraints of the problem. For example, RULE 3C fires if the system is currently attempting to pack a large person, but none are available or the large person will not fit in the current car; then the rule switches the task to attempt to pack a medium person. In words, this rule reads as

IF   Current task is pack large person
AND   Large person is not available
OR   Large person cannot fit in the current train car
THEN   Pack the medium person

Train-Loading Example Session

Assume that the following initial conditions were asserted in the working memory.

WORKING MEMORY

Number of small persons = 4   Weight of small person = 100
Number of medium persons = 4   Weight of medium person = 200
Number of large persons = 4   Weight of large person = 300

Weight of car = 0   Maximum weight of car = 1000
Car number = 0   Task IS start new car

Cycle 1

RULE 3A fires, which starts a new car and initializes the number of people in the car and the present weight of the car to zero. It then sets the new task to "pack a large person."

Cycles 2–4

During the next three cycles RULE 3B fires, by which the number of large people in the car increases by three and the weight of the car is incremented for each additional large person. The firing of the rule also decrements the number of available large people.

Cycle 5

During this cycle RULE 3B fails to fire, since the addition of another large person would cause the weight of the car to exceed its maximum allowable weight. Therefore, RULE 3C fires creating a new task of "pack a medium person."

Cycle 6

During this cycle, RULE 2B is attempted but fails since the addition of a medium person would exceed the maximum allowable car weight. Therefore, RULE 2C fires creating a new task of "pack a small person."

Cycle 7

RULE 1B fires adding a small person to the car, increasing the car's weight accordingly, and reducing the number of available small people.

Cycle 8

The present car's weight is now equal to its maximum allowable weight. Therefore, RULE 1C fires creating a new task of "display present car."

Cycle 9

During this cycle RULE 1A fires, creating a new task of "start new car" and displaying the present contents of this first car:

> **SYSTEM: CAR NUMBER: 1**
> **Weight of car:** 1000 lbs
> **Number of large persons:** 3
> **Number of medium persons:** 0
> **Number of small persons:** 1

COMMENT: *This process continues in the same manner during the balance of the session. Eventually the number of people to be packed is reduced to zero, which causes RULE 2A to fire stopping the session. The end result of all these cycles is the number of train cars needed and the various persons within each car:*

| | Car Number | | |
	1	2	3
Weight of passengers	1000	1000	400
Number of large persons	3	1	0
Number of medium persons	0	3	1
Number of small persons	1	1	2

Example Review

This example illustrates how a small forward-chaining expert system can be effectively used for a design task. The design process proceeds from an initial state to a final state through a sequence of partial design states. At each stage, there is one rule that changes the present state of the design. Problem constraints that control this transition are a part of the rules used.

Designed to Spec

The system achieved its original goal of packing the passengers in the most efficient manner. The final design met the stated specifications, which required: minimum number of cars be used, each car packed to maximum, and the heavier individuals packed first. This was all accomplished using only a few rules that contained both heuristic and control information.

Rules in Design Systems

The rules used in this example were structured in three parts:

$$\text{IF } <step> \text{ AND } <heuristic> \text{ THEN } <action>$$

The "step" part is used to control when the rule should be considered. This part also contains heuristic information about the problem in the sense that it captures the problem solving approach used by the expert. The "heuristic" part is knowledge in the form of preconditions that must be met before the rule can fire. The "action" part changes the present state of the design or switches control to other tasks or steps.

Some expert systems developed for design applications use a different approach for controlling rule firing. These systems simply rely on rule ordering to control when appropriate rules should be considered. Though simple to design, these systems often become difficult to maintain when you must adhere to strict rule ordering.

Other systems rely on rule priorities to control when rules should be considered. A priority is a number attached to a rule that can be used to control when it will be considered. When processing a set of rules that have been assigned priority numbers, the system considers those with a higher priority first. This approach can also cause maintenance problems when it becomes difficult for you to keep track of the various priority numbers that have been used.

The approach used in this example avoids the problems just noted. Furthermore, the rules used capture the problem's knowledge directly and stand (as all good rules) as independent chunks of knowledge that can be easily read, understood, and maintained.

SUMMARY ON FORWARD-CHAINING EXPERT SYSTEMS

This chapter reviewed the basic operation of forward-chaining expert systems. Several examples were given that illustrated many of the features of these systems. These examples should provide you with insight into developing forward-chaining systems.

The major lessons learned in this chapter were:

- Forward-chaining attempts to infer all possible information from the information initially asserted into the working memory.
- A startup rule can be used to obtain initial information from the user.
- A forward-chaining system can be made to stop before all of the rules are considered using some form of a STOP command.
- Rule priorities can be used to control rule firing.
- Forward-chaining systems can be designed to provide intermediate progress reports.
- Large rule-based systems should group the rules together according to some common theme.
- Demon rules can be written to monitor for special events.
- Rules written for a design application have both control and heuristic knowledge encoded within them.
- Forward-chaining rules can be written that halt system processing and request information from the user.

EXERCISES

1. Describe the basic forward-chaining process.
2. List several problems for which a forward-chaining approach would be appropriate.
3. What is the value of incorporating a variable in a rule?
4. Why is it important to group common rules together?
5. What is an event-driven system?
6. What is the value of a demon rule? Provide an example.
7. Discuss the advantages and disadvantages of using rule priorities.

8. Discuss the value of providing the user with intermediate progress reports.

9. What information should be presented to the user in an intermediate progress report?

10. Why is a forward-chaining technique better suited than backward-chaining for design problems?

11. Discuss the rule structure used in design systems.

12. Design a forward-chaining system to pack groceries of different sizes into the least number of bags.

13. Design a forward-chaining system to control an elevator.

REFERENCES

Coyne, R.D., M.A. Rosenman, A.D. Radford, M. Balachandran and J.S. Gero, Knowledge-Based Design Systems, Addison-Wesley, Reading, MA, 1990.

McDermott, J., R1: An Expert System in the Computer Systems Domain, Proceedings AAAI-80, 1980.

CHAPTER 10

Designing Forward-Chaining Rule-Based Systems

INTRODUCTION

In this chapter, we consider how to develop a forward-chaining rule-based expert system. To illustrate the process, we consider a small problem in automobile diagnostics. We review the major steps followed when developing this example

275

system—steps that are typical of building most forward-chaining systems. We also review how to build a more advanced user interface. The types of interfaces shown in previous chapters have relied on simple textual interaction. This chapter shows how you can design a friendly and more powerful interface using graphical objects.

GENERAL DESIGN METHODOLOGY FOR FORWARD-CHAINING SYSTEMS

As with all expert system projects, the first task when developing a forward-chaining rule-based system is to obtain a general understanding of the problem. This task involves defining the project objective, the major problem issues, and ways the expert works with available information to derive recommendations.

Unlike a backward-chaining system, which starts with some goal and works back through the rules to prove the goal, a forward-chaining system starts with problem data and fires rules to infer new information. The problem data is the fuel of the system. For example, in a process monitoring application where the process contains such items as a pump and motor, you might need to consider such data as:

- pump's input/output pressure
- motor's speed/temperature

The inference engine used in a backward-chaining system provides the primary control over the system's reasoning. It takes an initial goal, establishes subgoals, and searches for relevant information to prove the goals. You simply write the rules in a form that the inference engine can use, and trust that it will be able to use them correctly.

In a simple forward-chaining system, the inference engine fires rules whose premises match information contained in the working memory. In a somewhat unpredictable fashion, the system can leap into various problem issues. In most real applications, this loose control over the firing of rules is unacceptable. You will usually need to include a premise that constrains when a rule can fire. You will see later in this chapter how this can be accomplished.

The balance of the tasks performed when designing a forward-chaining system are similar to those performed when developing a backward-chaining system. In an iterative fashion, you add knowledge to the system, test and evaluate it, and make any necessary revisions to the system. There are eight major tasks you will typically perform when developing a forward-chaining system:

1. Define the problem
2. Define input data
3. Define data-driven structure
4. Write intial code
5. Test the system

6. Design the interface
7. Expand the system
8. Evaluate the system

This chapter shows how each of these tasks is performed for an application on automobile diagnostics. Before looking at the actual design process, let's first review why this problem is well-suited for a forward-chaining approach.

AUTOMOBILE DIAGNOSTICS DOMAIN

Diagnostic problems have always been one of the more attractive applications of expert systems. One reason for this is that this type of problem is usually better understood than problems such as design or scheduling. Another reason for their attraction is that an expert system solution to a diagnostic problem will usually have tangible benefits. For example, many organizations maintain equipment whose failure can result in large costs both in terms of the equipment expense and loss due to downtimes.

Most diagnostic expert systems have used a backward-chaining approach. The principal reason for this is that most of the problems addressed had a finite number of possible faults. Each fault could then be treated as a goal and tested in a backward-chaining fashion. However, in many other diagnostic problems, the number of possible fault conditions can be very large.

Consider for example the problem of diagnosing a problem with an automobile. Here, there could be hundreds of possible fault conditions. It would be impractical—if not impossible—to treat each fault as a goal in a backward-chaining system. For this type of problem, the expert usually begins by gathering some initial information, reasons with it to pursue other important information, and finally, identifies the faulted automobile part. This style of problem solving is inherently data-driven and is best managed with a forward-chaining expert system.

TASK 1: DEFINE THE PROBLEM

As in the case with the design of a backward-chaining system, the initial design step for a forward-chaining system is to learn about the problem. For our problem, we need to learn about automobile diagnostics. To aid us in this effort, we could locate a good car mechanic who could act as our expert. However, an alternative approach exists for our problem that is common to many other diagnostic problems, and involves the use of a "troubleshooting" manual. This type of manual contains the expert's troubleshooting knowledge. In fact, it was probably written by an expert. Thus it represents an excellent source of knowledge for our project. It also offers an approach for obtaining the knowledge that should be far easier than attempting to acquire the knowledge directly from the expert. That is, it avoids the traditional problems associated with acquiring knowledge through interviews with the expert.

Before discussing an auto repair manual, let's consider these types of manuals in general.

Repair Manuals

For many diagnostic problems, e.g., automobile, plumbing, clock repair, etc., manuals exist that can aid problem troubleshooting. Most industries maintain troubleshooting manuals to aid technicians in the repair of their equipment. These manuals provide a step-by-step series of tests to isolate the problem.

Though these manuals provide a valuable source of information, they do have some shortcomings. First, the manual must be readily available. This is particularly important if the repair must be done quickly, as in a factory setting where machine downtime can be costly. Unfortunately, organizations often store hundreds of repair manuals, and the task of locating the right one can be difficult.

Second, the manual must be easy to follow. It must clearly present how to do a given test and the logical order of the various tests. Most manuals ask the reader to perform a test and then refer him or her to other sections of the manual on the basis of the test results. This can often be a tedious job for the reader, who might have to jump back and forth looking for the right spot.

Third, someone must maintain the manual. As new diagnostic information becomes available, it must be added to the manual. Simple editing of an existing manual may only add to the confusion in its use. Often, an entirely new manual must be generated.

Because of problems such as these with repair manuals, organizations are beginning to look toward expert systems for help. Simply placing the manual in electronic form can help to reduce the availability problem. The decision-making ability of the expert system also makes it simple for the system to present an easy-to-follow test sequence to the user. Finally, since an expert system's knowledge can be easily modified, the task of maintaining the manual's information is eased.

Auto Repair Manuals

Many excellent auto repair manuals are available for both the professional mechanic and the weekend tinkerer. These manuals help to identify and repair various car problems. Most manuals have a troubleshooting section that steps the reader through a series of tests to identify the problem with the car. This section is usually divided according to the principal problem, such as engine does not start, engine runs poorly, etc. Each subsection focuses on common faults associated with the primary problem.

Within each subsection, the manual will usually first provide a table or decision-tree to aid in the isolation of the faulty subsystem before proceeding to more detailed tests. For example, Figure 10.1 shows a typical decision-tree for

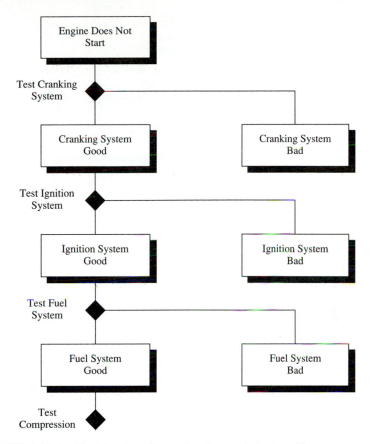

FIGURE 10.1 Decision tree for engine does not start problems.

the problem "engine does not start." As shown in the figure, tests are suggested to determine whether a given subsystem is "good" or "bad".

As illustrated in Figure 10.1, a problem of hard starting can usually be traced to a fault with either the cranking system, ignition system, fuel system, or engine compression. You should notice that this figure is heuristic in nature. That is, the order in which the various systems of the car are checked, such as cranking system, ignition system, etc., follows a path in which it is most likely to find a fault associated with an "engine does not start" problem.

The test sequence is often given in a TEST–RESULTS–PROCEED-TO table form as illustrated in Figure 10.2 for the case of starting problems. As shown in this figure, a test is suggested from which the results are used to direct the troubleshooting. For example, if the engine turns slowly or not at all after the ignition is turned on, then a cranking system problem is suspected and the troubleshooting proceeds to step 2.1.

Figure 10.3 shows the continuation of the troubleshooting for cranking system

Section 1
Starting Problems

Test	Results	Proceed To
1.1 Turn on the ignition	If engine turns slowly or not at all	2.1 Cranking system problems
	If engine turns normally	1.2

FIGURE 10.2   Starting problems troubleshooting procedures problems.

Section 1
Cranking System Problems

Test	Results	Proceed To
2.1 Put a screwdriver between the battery post and the cable clamp. Turn the headlights on high beam and observe the lights as the screwdriver is turned.	If lights brighten or not on	Bad battery connection
	If lights don't brighten	2.2
2.2 Test each battery cell with a hydrometer.	If all readings above 1.2	2.3
	If all readings are not above 1.2	Low charge
2.3 Connect jumper between battery post and starter post of solenoid. then turn on the ignition.	If starter buzzes or turns engine normally	2.4
	If starter turns engine normally	2.5
	If starter does nothing	Bad solenoid
2.4 Remove starter and place it in the starter test apparatus. Run the standard tests and compare results with starter specifications.	If starter meets specifications	2.6
	If starter does not meet specifications	Bad starter
2.5 Connect a jumper over the override switches, i.e. neutral safety switch, clutch start switch, etc. Then turn the ignition to start.	If starter operates	Bad override switch
	If starter does not operate	2.7
2.6 Remove spark plugs. Then turn engine using socket and drive on the crankshaft pulley nut.	If engine does not move	9.1 Bad engine
	If engine moves	9.4 Test engine timing
2.7 Connect a voltmeter between the starter post of the solenoid (or relay) and ground. Then turn the ignition switch to start.	If voltmeter moves	Bad ignition switch
	If voltmeter does not move	Bad or loose switch connections

FIGURE 10.3   Cranking system troubleshooting procedures.

Cranking System Repair

Problem	Repair Procedure
Bad Battery Connection	Clean Battery Terminals and Connectors - Remove and Clean the Clamp and Post - Coat the Post with Petroleum Jelly - Install and Tighten the Clamp
Low Charge	Charge the Battery - Disconnect Connectors From Battery - Connect Charger to Battery - Charge Battery Overnight - Check Battery in Morning with Hydrometer
Bad Solenoid	Disconnect Wires Connected to the Solenoid and replace it with a New One
Bad Starter	Replace or Repair Starter
Bad Override Switch	Replace Bad Override Switch
Bad Ignition Switch	Replace Ignition Switch
Bad or Loose Switch Connections	Repair or Replace Switch Connections

FIGURE 10.4 Cranking system repair procedures.

problems. Under the PROCEED TO column, either the test results lead to other steps or the identity of the fault, e.g., BAD BATTERY CONNECTION. When a fault has been identified, a repair procedure is usually provided as illustrated in Figure 10.4. An alternative way of viewing Figure 10.3 is the decision-tree shown in Figure 10.5.

Problem Specifications

There are unfortunately many possible problems with an automobile. To keep our example system small, we will focus on the problem "engine does not start"—Figure 10.1. We will also only consider problems with the "cranking

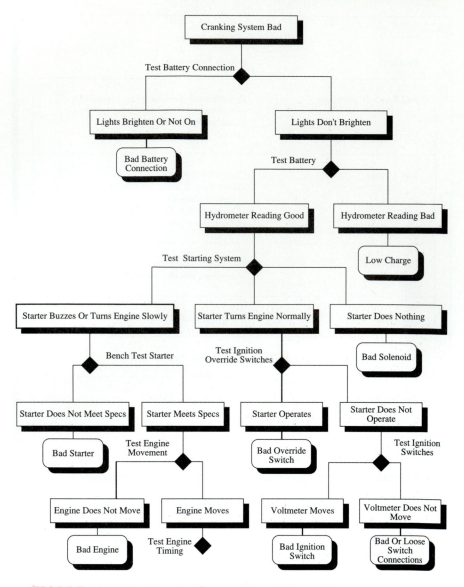

FIGURE 10.5 Decision tree for cranking system problems.

system''—Figures 10.3 through 10.5. After developing the system's structure to address this problem, we should have a good idea of how to manage other possible car problems. Our problem specifications are as follows:

- Address problems associated with ''engine won't start.''
- Address only ''cranking system'' problems.

_____ TASK 2: DEFINE INPUT DATA _____

Every forward-chaining system needs to first obtain some initial data to get started. Therefore, we need to write a rule whose only task is to ask for some information about the problem. This type of rule is often called a **startup rule.** This rule is written to automatically fire when the system starts. When it fires, it asks for problem information. For our system we want this rule to ask the user the general nature of the problem. This is accomplished with the following startup rule:

Rule 1 start diagnosis
IF   Task IS begin
THEN   ASK Car problem

To fire this rule we would first assert ''Task IS begin'' into the working memory. The function ''ASK'' causes the following question to be asked, a question that we previously tied to the expression ''Car problem'':
  What is the problem?

  Car won't start
  Car hesitates at high speeds
  Car idles rough

  . . . .

After the user selects the particular problem, the system directs the problem solving into the appropriate area.

  To keep our system simple, we will address only the first problem ''Car won't start.'' This single piece of information directs the system to consider problems that can account for this unfortunate situation. Beyond this point, unlike many other forward-chaining systems, our system remains interactive. It continues to ask questions to direct the problem solving toward the most logical conclusion.

_____ TASK 3: DEFINE DATA-DRIVEN STRUCTURE _____

In theory, a forward-chaining system works by firing rules whose premises match the contents of the working memory. For example, the following rule fires if ''A'' is true:

IF   A
THEN   Infer or do something

Using this rule, if ''A'' is true, the system either infers new information about the problem or performs some task. In small applications, this loose control of the firing of rules may provide adequate results. However, in most forward-chaining applications, you will need to include within each rule a premise that helps to control when a given rule can fire. For example:

```
IF      Task is . . . .
AND     A
THEN    Infer or do something
```

Using a rule of this form, the rule will only fire if both the rule is relevant to the current task and "A" is true. This structure helps you to maintain control over the natural forward-chaining inference process.

To illustrate this approach for our problem, consider step 2.1 of Figure 10.3. We represent the TEST portion of this step in the first premise of the rule and the RESULTS portion in the second premise. We capture in the rule's conclusion the PROCEED TO portion of the step. For example:

```
IF      Task is test battery connection   → TEST
AND     Lights don't brighten             → RESULTS
THEN    Task is test battery              → PROCEED TO
```

We use this structured approach for encoding each rule by simply following either Figure 10.3 or Figure 10.5.

TASK 4: WRITE INITIAL CODE

The purpose of the initial coding task in a forward-chaining system is to determine if we have effectively captured the problem's knowledge in a good rule structure. A good structure is one that not only provides correct results, but also a template to follow in the development of other rules. Task 3 provided our rule structure.

Since we are limiting our system to only "car won't start" problems, we need a rule to set the task to "test cranking system" first, since this is the first task considered in Figure 10.1:

Rule test cranking system
```
IF      Car problem IS car won't start
THEN    Task IS test cranking system
```

Beyond this point, the rules written would follow the structure discussed in the last section and shown in Figure 10.3. For our initial coding, we consider the problem through step 2.1 of Figure 10.3. The initial set of rules for our system is as follows (in LEVEL5 code), where the use of "IS" and "\" is equivalent to the "=" assignment found in other shells:

Rule 1 Start diagnosis
```
IF      Task IS begin
THEN    ASK Car problem
```

Rule 2 Car won't start
```
IF      Car problem IS won't start
THEN    Task IS test cranking system
```

Rule 3 Car hesitates at high speeds
IF   Car problem IS hesitates at high speeds
THEN   Task IS test fuel system

Rule 4 Step 1.1—Test the cranking system
IF   Task IS test cranking system
THEN   ASK Engine turns

Rule 5 Step 1.1—Cranking system is defective
IF   Task IS test cranking system
AND   Engine turns \ slowly or not at all
THEN   Cranking system IS defective
AND   Task IS test battery connection

Rule 6 Step 1.1—Cranking system is good
IF   Task IS test cranking system
AND   Engine turns \ normally
THEN   Cranking system IS good
AND   Task IS test ignition system

Rule 7 Step 2.1—Test the battery connection
IF   Task IS test battery connection
THEN   ASK Screwdriver test shows that lights

Rule 8 Step 2.1—Battery connection is bad
IF   Task IS test battery connection
AND   Screwdriver test shows that lights \ brighten
OR   Screwdriver test shows that lights \ not on
THEN   Problem IS bad battery connection

Rule 9 Step 2.1—Battery connection is good
IF   Task IS test battery connection
AND   Screwdriver test shows that lights \ don't brighten
THEN   Battery connection IS good
AND   Task IS test battery

—————————— **TASK 5: TEST THE SYSTEM** ——————————

Our next task is to test our small set of rules. We assume that "Task IS begin" has been initialized in the working memory. This causes the startup rule (RULE 1) to fire and the system to ask what is the problem. Here, the system searches all of the rules looking for "Car problem" values and finds RULES 2 and 3. RULE 3 was placed in the system to add an additional menu item to the question. We could later expand our system to consider fuel system problems (RULE 3) by simply adding the appropriate rules. Our system now asks the following question:

SYSTEM: What is the problem with the car?
  —won't start
  —hesitates at high speeds
USER: won't start

This answer results in the firing of RULE 2 and the assertion of "Task IS test cranking system" into the working memory. This new information causes RULE 4 to fire resulting in the following question:

SYSTEM: Please turn on the ignition.
          How does the engine turn?
          —slowly or not at all
          —normally
USER: slowly or not at all

Notice that the text for this question begins with the TEST procedure information for task 1.1 of Figure 10.2. We would need to write this text and present it to the user when this question was asked. Later in this chapter you will see how this is done.

With the answer given by the user RULE 5 fires resulting in the assertions "Cranking system IS defective" and "Task IS test battery connection." This new information causes RULE 7 to fire, resulting in the following question:

SYSTEM: Put a screwdriver between the battery post and the cable clamp.
          Then turn the headlights on high beam and observe the lights as the
          screwdriver is turned.
          What happens to the lights?
          —brighten
          —not on
          —don't brighten
USER: brighten

The basis of this question is task 2.1 of Figure 10.3. The answer given by the user results in the firing of RULE 8 further resulting in the assertion "Problem IS bad battery connection." Following this step, no other rules can fire so the system stops.

—————— TASK 6: DESIGN THE INTERFACE ——————

Now that we have a small set of rules working adequately, we next consider how to build the system's interface. Too often, attention is given to the design of the interface after most of the knowledge base has been completed. You should recognize that the interface is an extremely important component of your system. You should design it in parallel with the development of the knowledge base, and not treat it as an afterthought. The way you design and structure the knowledge base is influenced by the way you design the interface.

DESIGN SUGGESTION: Begin the design of the system's interface early in the project and develop it in parallel with the development of the system's knowledge base.

In the prior test of our system, it was seen that the interface was centered around the "ASK" function. This function was used to present questions to the user. Though the ASK function is specific to the shell LEVEL5, similar functions exist for other shells. What was not shown earlier was how this text material was put together. This section not only shows how this is done, but also shows how you can do it using a dynamic graphical interface.

Dynamic Graphical Interface

Most of the early expert systems were designed to interact with the user using only text. The system asked questions and the user responded by either typing an answer or selecting from a menu of possible answers. This style of interaction was illustrated during the testing of our system. Today, many of the shells offer a host of features to customize the interface. They provide a toolkit of various graphical items, such as: buttons, bitmaps, textboxes, meters, etc., that you can use to permit the user to observe and control the operation of an expert system— a dynamic graphical interface. This is illustrated in Figure 10.6.

This figure shows both the interface and the knowledge base for an automobile control expert system. The interface contains several graphic objects linked to various parts of the knowledge base. Objects such as the "Oil Pressure" meter, "Temperature" meter, and "Speed" slider gauge, display current values within the knowledge base. The car picture is a bitmap whose position on the screen is controlled by the "Position" value. The two "Speed Control" pushbuttons permit the user to control the speed of the car.

The knowledge base contains both information that is displayed on the interface and forward chaining rules that work with the information. For example, consider the rule that increases the car's speed:

IF   Inc Speed
THEN   Speed = Speed + 5
AND   Speed increase

When the user presses the button "Inc", the premise of this rule is set to true, causing it to fire. This action causes an increase in both the "Speed" value and the "Speed" slider gauge. The firing of this rule also causes the following rule to fire:

IF   Speed increase
THEN   Temperature = (Speed * 2) + 200
AND   Oil pressure = (Speed * 0.5) + 40

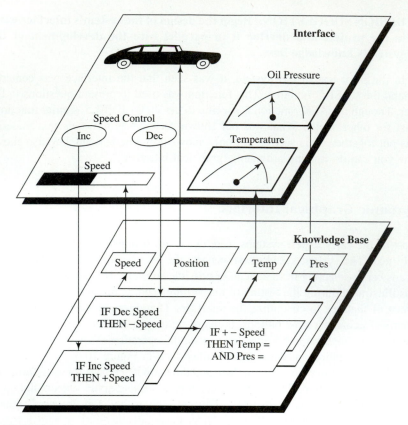

FIGURE 10.6   Automobile control interface.

The firing of this rule causes a corresponding update in the temperature and oil pressure readings in the interface.

The movement of the car across the screen is controlled by the change in the "Position" value. The car picture is a bitmap placed in the interface with corresponding X and Y coordinates that define the four corners of the bitmap. To cause left-to-right motion, a rule could be written to increment the X coordinates of all four corner coordinates. The rate of movement could be made proportional to the current speed value.

Format of Interface

Users are affected by the visual perception of the expert system's interface. Some interfaces are pleasant to view, while others are not. Some are easy to understand, while others are difficult to interpret. In this section we review ways that you can design an interface that is both pleasing and easy to follow.

The key to good interface design is *consistency*. For each screen, similar material should be consistently placed in the same locations. For example, the locations of questions and possible answers should be placed in the same spot for each screen. Using this approach permits the user to develop a mental model of where to expect information. Interfaces that vary the location of information between screens can be frustrating and confusing to the user (Mackey and Slesnick 1982).

DESIGN SUGGESTION: Place similar types of information in the same locations for each screen.

Screen Contents

There are two basic types of interface screens used in the design of an expert system: display screens and question screens. Each screen type contains information specific to its needs. The following sections discuss issues that you should cover in each screen type and the specific control functions that you should add to each screen.

Display Screens

The purpose of a display screen is to present information to the user. There are three types of display screens typically used in an expert system where you have control over the design: introduction screen, intermediate findings screen, and final display screen. Each of these screens has two principal parts: text portion and control section. The text portion is written to address the specific needs of the type of display screen. The control section provides the user with options for controlling the operation of the system. As an option, you may also want to include a title or header for the screen.

Introduction Screen

In the introduction screen, you should include a statement that explains the objective of the system. A short discussion or overview of the problem should also be given. You may also want to discuss the approach the expert system will take to solve the problem since it prepares the user for what is to follow. Another way you can help the user to be better prepared is to provide a listing of any particular material that is required during the session. For example, if later during the session the user will be required to provide information contained in some report, then informing him or her of this requirement in the introductory screen helps.

There are two typical control functions that you should provide the user in the introduction screen: a way to start the session and a way to exit. Most shells provide both of these functions. However, you often can't control the location of these functions on the screen. In later screens you may not only have a need for these same functions, but others as well. You will need to define these for the application. Since you will want to maintain consistency in the placement of all functions, it is better to define and locate these functions yourself.

Intermediate Findings Screen

The purpose of the intermediate findings display screen is to display to the user important milestones reached by the system. Consider for example an automobile diagnostic system. During the course of attempting to determine the specific problem, the system may first attempt to isolate the problem to one of the car's major subsystems, such as electrical, fuel, etc. By displaying the subsystem isolated, the major reason why, and what the system will next attempt to do, you keep the user abreast of the system's major problem solving activities.

There are three basic control functions that you should provide to the user in the intermediate findings screen: continue, exit, and restart. The "continue" function simply resumes the session. The "restart" function permits the user to restart the session in the event he or she would like to try different answers. The "exit" function is an important feature to add to all screens, which permits the user to end the session.

Conclusion Screen

The conclusion screen presents the user with the system's final recommendations or findings. The way you present this screen to the user is obviously dependent on the application. You might present a single recommendation, a list of rank-ordered recommendations, or even a form containing many of the pieces of information entered by the user and inferred by the system. In general, however, you should present what was found and some of the major reasons behind the findings. You don't have to go into the details you might find in a complete "HOW" explanation, but a repeat display of the intermediate findings can be of benefit for justifying the recommendations. The two control functions that you should explicitly add to the conclusion display are the "exit" and "restart" functions.

Question Screen

A question screen is used to obtain information about the problem from the user. This type of screen has three basic parts: text portion containing the question, answer entry part, and control section. Again, as an option, you could include a title or header for the screen.

The question's text should be written to the level of the user. If the user is a novice, unfamiliar with the terminology of the domain, you will need to avoid complex technical terms. On the other hand, if the user is skilled on the problem, you can write shorter text that includes technical terms.

Interface Screens		
Screen	Issues	Control
Introduction	System Objective Problem Discussion Session Needs	Start Exit
Intermediate Findings	What Was found Major Reason why What Will Be done	Continue Exit Restart
Conclusion	What Was Found Major Reasons Why	Exit Restart
Question	Level of User Why Question Menu vs. Text	Exit Restart

FIGURE 10.7   Interface screen design recommendations.

One option you might want to consider is to add a small text section that provides some indication why the question is being asked. As in the case of the intermediate findings screen, this approach keeps the user informed of the system's strategy.

There are two basic ways the user can respond to a question: menu selection and text entry. In general, a menu approach is preferred. It is usually easier for the user to select from a menu—particularly if a mouse is used. This approach also avoids typing errors or the entry of illegal answers. However, a menu approach requires a finite set of possible answers. If the number of possible answers is too large to fit in a reasonable size menu, or the answer cannot be anticipated (e.g., a numeric entry), then you will need to use a text entry approach.

Each question screen should provide the user with the option to "exit" the system or "restart" the system. Figure 10.7 summarizes the issues that you should cover and control functions that you should add for each screen.

System Interface

Following the advice given in the prior sections, we will now develop the interface for our automobile diagnostic expert system. The design of the introduction, intermediate, and conclusion screens is straightforward, so we will focus on the question screen.

Besides following the general recommendations given in Figure 10.7 for the design of the question screen, there are additional points we should consider given the nature of our problem. As illustrated in Figure 10.3, each "test"

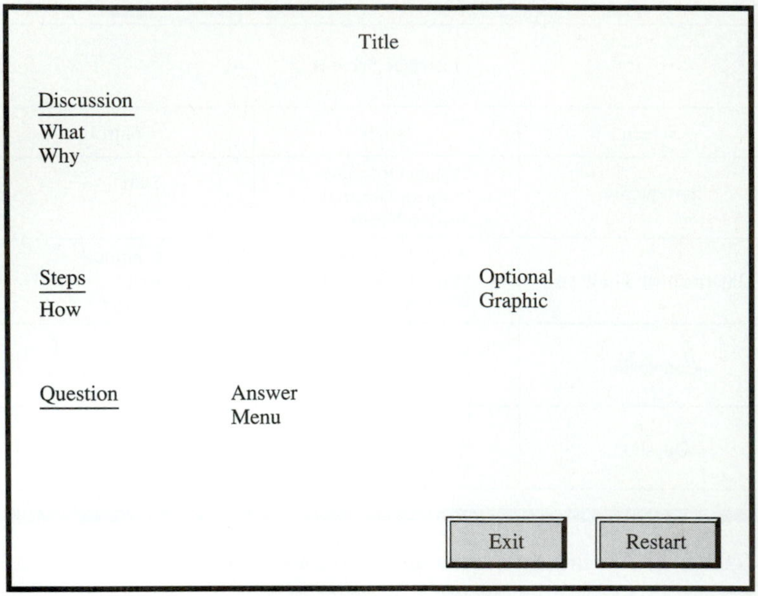

```
┌─────────────────────────────────────────────────────────┐
│                          Title                          │
│                                                         │
│      Discussion                                         │
│      What                                               │
│      Why                                                │
│                                                         │
│                                                         │
│      Steps                          Optional            │
│      How                            Graphic             │
│                                                         │
│                                                         │
│      Question           Answer                          │
│                         Menu                            │
│                                                         │
│                                                         │
│                                                         │
│                              ┌──────────┐ ┌──────────┐  │
│                              │   Exit   │ │ Restart  │  │
│                              └──────────┘ └──────────┘  │
│                                                         │
└─────────────────────────────────────────────────────────┘
```

FIGURE 10.8   Question screen template.

describes a series of steps to perform and each "result" a question with possible answers. Therefore, our question screen should contain separate sections for each. In addition, we might elect to present a graphic that illustrates how to perform the test. Using these suggestions, along with earlier recommendations, we can use the structure shown in Figure 10.8 as a template for the design of our question screen. We can design each question screen following this template to maintain consistency in our interface.

Most shells that permit you to design a complex interface screen require you to label each screen with some name. For example, you could label a screen simply "SCREEN1" or something more descriptive of the screen's contents such as "BATTERY TEST."When you want to display this screen to the user you would use some function such as "DISPLAY" or "ASK" along with the name of the screen, such as "ASK BATTERY TEST."

To illustrate the design and operation of a question screen, consider step 1.1 of Figure 10.2 and our earlier RULE 2:

Rule 2 Car won't start
IF   Car problem IS car won't start
THEN   Task IS test cranking system

When this rule fires we want to display to the user a screen with information for conducting a test on the cranking system following the format shown in Figure 10.8. To accomplish this, we can add the following rule:

Rule　Step 1.1—Test the cranking system
IF　　　Task IS test cranking system
THEN　ASK cranking system test

This rule would fire following the firing of RULE 2. The phrase "cranking system test" would be the name we associated with the screen shown in Figure 10.9. Each button in this screen is connected to a piece of knowledge in the knowledge base. For example, the button "normally" is tied to the fact "Engine turns normally." If the user pushes this button, this fact is asserted into the working memory. The control buttons "EXIT" and "RESTART" would be

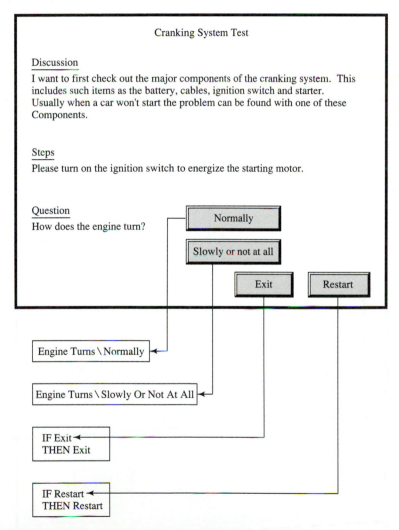

FIGURE 10.9　Cranking system test question screen.

linked to premises within rules whose firing would cause the appropriate system response.

———————— **TASK 7: EXPAND THE SYSTEM** ————————

Following the successful testing of our small set of rules, our next task is to expand the system's knowledge. For our system, this means developing additional rules beyond step 2.1 of Figure 10.3. Expansion would also include the design of the various interface screens and rules that would display the various screens. Rules that accomplish this expansion are shown in Figure 10.10. Our system is now in prototype form, ready for evaluation.

———————— **TASK 8: EVALUATE THE SYSTEM** ————————

The evaluation task is concerned with testing the prototype with some real test case. We would normally turn to our expert for the test case. However, since we used a car troubleshooting manual for the source of knowledge, we can work directly with the manual.

The end nodes of Figure 10.5 represent specific faults with the car. For a test case, we can simply choose one of these faults. To verify that our system is working properly, we can provide the appropriate answers at each decision point of Figure 10.5 and check to see if the system arrives at the same fault that we choose. For our test case, we assume that the fault is a "bad solenoid."

STEP 1

SYSTEM:

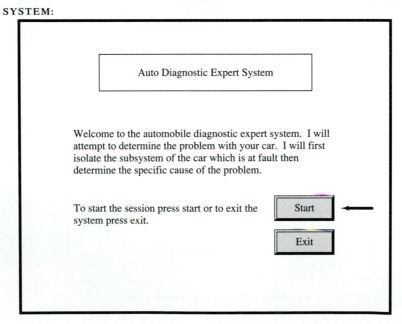

```
================================================================
SECTION S - START ''WILL NOT START'' RULES
================================================================

RULE 1S - Start diagnosis
IF    Task IS begin
THEN Task IS test cranking system

================================================================
SECTION A - TEST DISPLAY RULES
================================================================

RULE 1A - Test the cranking system        RULE 2A - Test the battery connection
IF    Task IS test cranking system         IF    Task IS test battery connection
THEN ASK cranking system test              THEN ASK battery connection test

RULE 3A - Test the battery                 RULE 4A - Test the starting system
IF    Task IS test battery                 IF    Task IS test starting system
THEN ASK Battery test                      THEN ASK Starting system test

RULE 5A - Test the starter on bench        RULE 6A - Test the ignition override switch
IF    Task IS test starter on bench        IF    Task IS test ignition override switches
THEN ASK Starter bench test                THEN ASK Ignition override switch test

RULE 7A - Test the ignition switch         RULE 8A - Test the engine movement
IF    Task IS test ignition switch         IF    Task IS test engine movement
THEN ASK Ignition switch test              THEN ASK Engine movement test
```

FIGURE 10.10 Rules for prototype system.

295

```
================================================================
SECTION B - TEST CRANKING SYSTEM - STEP 1.1 RULES
================================================================

RULE 1B - Cranking system is defective          RULE 2B - Cranking system is good
IF   Task IS test cranking system               IF   Task IS test cranking system
AND  Engine turns  slowly or not at all         AND  Engine turns  normally
THEN Cranking system IS defective               THEN Cranking system IS good
AND  ASK cranking system defective              AND  Task IS test ignition system
AND  Task IS test battery connection


================================================================
SECTION C - TEST BATTERY CONNECTION - STEP 2.1 RULES
================================================================

RULE 1C - Battery connection is bad             RULE 2C - Battery connection is good
IF   Task IS test battery connection            IF   Task IS test battery connection
AND  Screwdriver test shows that lights \ brighten   AND  Screwdriver test shows that lights  don't brighten
OR   Screwdriver test shows that lights \ not on     THEN Task IS test battery
THEN Problem IS bad battery connection
AND  ASK Battery connection defective


================================================================
SECTION D - TEST BATTERY - STEP 2.2 RULES
================================================================

RULE 1D - Battery charge is bad                 RULE 2D - Battery charge is good
IF   Task IS test battery                        IF   Task IS test battery
AND  Battery hydrometer reading IS not good       AND  Battery hydrometer reading IS good
THEN Problem IS bad battery                        THEN Task IS test starting system
AND  ASK Battery defective
```

FIGURE 10.10 Continued

```
=========================================================================
SECTION E - TEST STARTER - STEP 2.3 RULES
=========================================================================

RULE 1E - Run starter bench test          RULE 2E - Solenoid bad
IF    Task IS test starting system        IF    Task IS test starting system
AND   Starter \ buzzes                    AND   Starter \ does nothing
OR    Starter \ turns the engine very slowly  THEN  Problem IS bad solenoid
THEN  Task IS test starter on bench       AND   ASK Solenoid defective

RULE 3E - Starter turns engine normally
IF    Task IS test starting system
AND   Starter \ turns the engine normally
THEN  Task IS test ignition override switches


=========================================================================
SECTION F - STARTER BENCH TEST - STEP 2.4 RULES
=========================================================================

RULE 1F - Starter bad                     RULE 2F - Starter is good
IF    Task IS test starter on bench       IF    Task IS test starter on bench
AND   Starter \ does not meet specifications  AND   Starter \ meets specifications
THEN  Problem IS bad starter              THEN  Task IS test engine movement
AND   ASK Starter defective
```

297

```
================================================================
SECTION G - OVERRIDE SWITCH TEST - STEP 2.5 RULES
================================================================

RULE 1G - Override switch bad              RULE 2G - Starter won't operate
IF   Task IS test ignition override switches   IF   Task IS test ignition override switches
AND  Starter \ operates                        AND  Starter \ doesn't operate
THEN Problem IS bad override switch             THEN Task IS test ignition switch
AND  ASK Override switch defective

================================================================
SECTION H - ENGINE MOVEMENT TEST - STEP 2.6 RULES
================================================================

RULE 1H - Engine bad                       RULE 2H - Engine moves freely
IF   Task IS test engine movement          IF   Task IS test engine movement
AND  Engine \ does not move                AND  Engine \ moves freely
THEN Problem IS bad engine                  THEN Task IS test engine timing
AND  ASK Engine defective                   AND  ASK Perform engine timing test

================================================================
SECTION I - IGNITION SWITCH TEST - STEP 2.7 RULES
================================================================

RULE 1I - Ignition switch connections bad  RULE 2I - Ignition switch bad
IF   Task IS test ignition switch          IF   Task IS test ignition switch
AND  Voltmeter \ doesn't move              AND  Voltmeter \ moves
THEN Problem IS bad ignition switch connections   THEN Problem IS bad ignition switch
AND  ASK Ignition switch connections defective    AND  ASK Ignition switch defective
```

FIGURE 10.10 Continued

Comment: *The first screen shown to the user is the "Introduction Screen." This screen tells the user the objective of the system and provides a brief review of the problem. Assume the user selects START. This asserts "Task IS begin" into the working memory causing RULE 1S to fire, which in turn causes RULE 1A to fire displaying the next screen.*

STEP 2

SYSTEM:

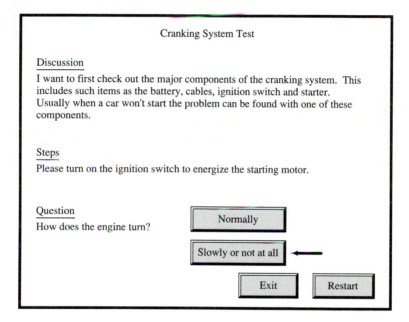

Cranking System Test

Discussion

I want to first check out the major components of the cranking system. This includes such items as the battery, cables, ignition switch and starter. Usually when a car won't start the problem can be found with one of these components.

Steps

Please turn on the ignition switch to energize the starting motor.

Question
How does the engine turn?

Normally

Slowly or not at all ⟵

Exit   Restart

Comment: *The system attempts to determine if the problem is with the "Cranking System." Assume the user selects "slowly or not at all." This asserts "Engine turns slowly or not at all" into the working memory causing RULE 1B to fire. The firing of this rule asserts "Task IS test battery connection" and displays the screen shown in step 3.*

STEP 3

SYSTEM:

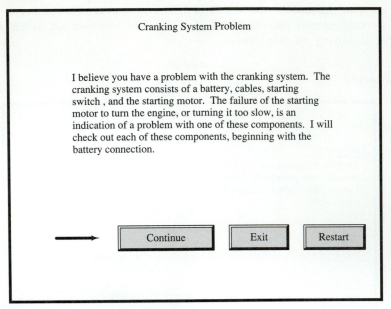

Comment: *This screen displays the intermediate finding that the problem exists in the cranking system. Assume the user selects ''CONTINUE'' to continue the session.*

STEP 4

SYSTEM:

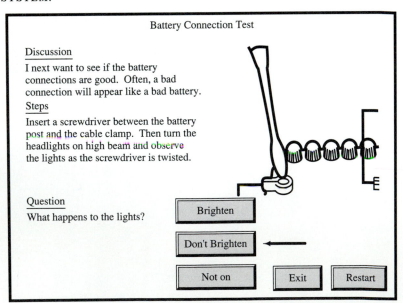

Comment: *Since in STEP 2 the fact "Task IS test battery connection" was asserted, RULE 2A fires displaying this screen. Here the system attempts to determine if the battery connections are good. Assume the user selects "Don't brighten." This asserts "Screwdriver test shows that lights don't brighten" and causes RULE 2C to fire, changing the task to "Task IS test battery." This in turn causes RULE 3A to fire resulting in the following display.*

STEP 5

SYSTEM:

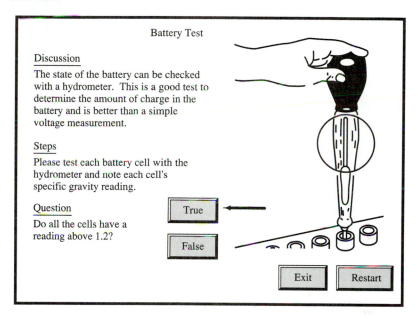

Comment: *The system asks the user to perform a hydrometer test on the battery. Assume the user selects "TRUE" resulting in the assertion of "Battery hydrometer reading IS good," which causes RULE 2D to fire changing the task to "Task IS test starting system." This in turn causes RULE 4A to fire resulting in the following display.*

STEP 6

SYSTEM:

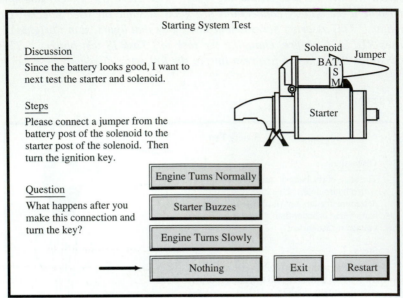

Comment: *The system asks the user to use a jumper to check out the starter system. Assume the user after performing this test finds that "Nothing" happens. This answer asserts that "Starter does nothing," causing RULE 2E to fire. This results in the following final display.*

STEP 7

SYSTEM:

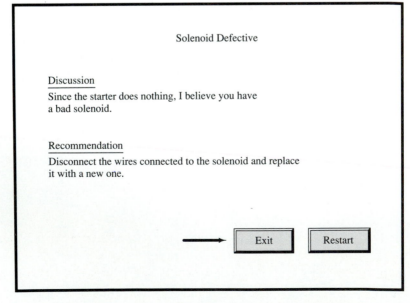

Session Review

This session illustrates a simple example of forward chaining. Facts asserted by the user caused various rules to fire, which either asserted new information or caused a new display to be presented. The control of the firing of rules was aided by the use of a state premise in the form of "Task IS . . ." A graphical interface was used to obtain information from the user by using buttons tied to various pieces of knowledge in the knowledge base. When a button was selected, its associated piece of knowledge was asserted into the working memory. The various screens were designed with consistent structure and placement of information in order to offer the user a friendly interface. Finally, and most importantly, the results of the evaluation were consistent with the decision-tree of Figure 10.5.

FUTURE DIRECTIONS

Now that we have built and successfully tested our small prototype system, our next challenge would be to continue the expansion of the system. For our problem, we could accomplish this task by simply continuing with the development of the additional steps found in our troubleshooting manual. At this point our system only addresses problems with the cranking system. We might next go on to develop rules for problems within the ignition system, fuel system, etc.

SUMMARY ON FORWARD-CHAINING DESIGN

This chapter reviewed the basic steps performed in the design of a forward-chaining expert system. The design process is highly iterative. A small amount of knowledge is initially encoded and tested. These tasks are followed by knowledge expansion and additional testing. This chapter also introduced the design of a more complex user interface. It illustrated how graphical objects contained in the interface could be used to both display knowledge base facts and control their state. The major lessons learned in this chapter were:

- The design of a forward-chaining expert system is a highly iterative process.
- The system should be tested immediately after the introduction of new rules.
- Forward-chaining inference is preferred over backward chaining if either the goals are not known a priori or their number is very large.
- Designing a backward-chaining system begins with defining the system goals, while defining initial data is the starting point for a forward-chaining design process.
- Rules used in a forward-chaining system often contain a premise that keeps track of the state of the problem solving, in order to maintain better control over the inference process.
- Design of the system's interface should begin early in the project and develop in parallel with the development of the system's knowledge base.

- A dynamic graphical interface contains graphical objects that permit the user to both observe and control the operation of an expert system.
- The key to good interface design is *consistency*. For each screen, similar material should be consistently placed in the same locations.

EXERCISES

1. Explain why a forward-chaining approach is preferred over backward chaining for problems that have a large number of possible solutions.
2. Why is it valuable to include a premise that keeps track of the state of the problem solving?
3. Obtain a car mechanic's troubleshooting manual and develop rules for problems with such systems as the ignition system, fuel system, etc.
4. Design a forward-chaining system to aid the user in tieing his shoes.
5. Computer configuration is a design task that naturally considers various components in order, e.g., processor selection, RAM selection, hard drive selection, etc. Design a forward-chaining system to accomplish this configuration task.
6. In the last problem, there may be conflicts that occur in the selection of components. For example, a RAM selection that meets the problem requirements may be incompatible with an earlier processor selection. How would you address these potential conflicts?
7. Describe the various graphical objects that can be used in an interface that provides the user with both the means to learn what is known by the expert system and ways the system can be controlled.
8. Design a graphical interface that asks a question about the temperature in the nuclear reaction in a power plant. The interface should also display the present state of the nuclear plant, e.g., operational state, containment pressure, rod positions, etc. Show how the temperature response provided by the user can impact the qualitative description of this parameter in the knowledge base.

REFERENCE

Mackey, K. and T. Slesnick, A Style Manual for Authors of Software, Creative Computing, vol. 8, 1982.

CHAPTER 11

Bayesian Approach to Inexact Reasoning

INTRODUCTION

In this chapter we review the Bayesian approach to inexact reasoning. We first explore the basic principles of probability theory to lay the groundwork for the later discussion on Bayes theorem. We also review adjustments expert system developers have made to the Bayes approach in order to better manage real-world problems. These adjustments were needed as will be shown for the development of the PROSPECTOR expert system. Examples are also provided to illustrate the theory discussed. Finally, a discussion is given on the necessary characteristics that a problem must possess in order to permit the effective use of the Bayes technique in expert systems.

PROBABILITY THEORY

Traditionally, inexact information has been treated as a problem of mathematical probability. Probability is a mathematical approach for processing uncertain information that has its roots in the 17th-century attempts by a group of French noblemen who wanted to gain an edge in gambling. In 1654, Pascal and Fermat developed the theory of classical probability that is used today for drawing numeric inferences from a body of data.

Probability theory proposes the existence of a number $P(E)$ called the **probability,** which is the likelihood of some event E occurring from a random experiment. That is, if we perform some experiment a large number of times, then we can be almost certain that the relative frequency of the event E is approximately equal to $P(E)$. The set of all possible outcomes of an experiment is called the **sample space,** which is denoted as S. Each possible outcome of the experiment is an event E and is part of the sample space.

Discrete Sample Space

Many experiments have a discrete number of outcomes. Consider for example the sample space from the experiment of rolling a die:

$$S = \{1, 2, 3, 4, 5, 6\}$$

Each event in the sample space represents a possible result of the experiment. To determine the probability of any given event from this sample space, you would perform an experiment by rolling the die a number of times denoted as N, and record the number of wins for a particular event denoted as $W(E)$. The probability of this event could then be obtained from the following equation:

$$P(E) = \frac{W(E)}{N} \tag{1}$$

Assuming a fair die, the probability of producing a given event from this sample space would be $\frac{1}{6}$, since each event is equally likely.

This is the experimental approach to defining probability. More formally, experimental probability defines the probability of an event $P(E)$ as the limit of a frequency distribution $f(E)$:

$$P(E) = \lim_{N \to \infty} \frac{f(E)}{N} \tag{2}$$

where $f(E)$ is the frequency of the outcomes of an event for N observed outcomes. This type of probability is also known as the **posteriori probability**—meaning "after the event."

Probability is a number that predicts the expected likelihood of a given event from some experiment and is constrained by the following relationships:

$$0 \le P(E) \le 1 \tag{3}$$

$$\sum_i P(E_i) = 1 \tag{4}$$

$$P(E) + P(\sim E) = 1 \tag{5}$$

where $\sim E$ represents the complement of E, that is, the event E not occurring.

Continuous Sample Space

Rather than discuss the probability of a given event or variate from a discrete set of possible outcomes, such as the possible outcomes from the roll of a die, many variates take on intermediate values in a given range of values. In these instances, we need a means of representing a variate's probability in a continuous frequency distribution. This is accomplished using a **probability distribution function.** For example, Figure 11.1 shows the probability distribution function for a person's height obtained from a group of persons.

This function can be used for predicting the likelihood of randomly choosing a person of a given height from the group of persons. For example, the probability of choosing a 6-foot person from this group would be $P(6 \text{ feet}) = 0.25$. By compiling data from a representative group on a subject of interest (e.g., person's height) you can use the distribution function for predicting the probability of a given variate occurring.

Often we will want to ask more complex questions about the likelihood of a given situation occurring which will involve several probability distribution functions. For example, consider the question "What is the likelihood of choosing both a person whose height is 6 feet and whose weight is 150 pounds?" To answer this question, you must first understand the basic rules of probability operations.

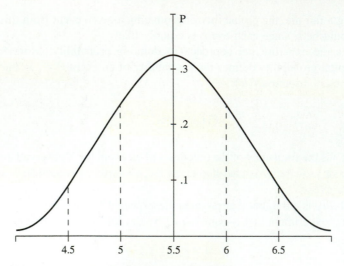

FIGURE 11.1   Height frequency distribution.

Compound Probabilities

For many problems you must consider the *combinations* of different events. You may for example want to know the probability of two different events occurring, or the probability of either of them occurring.

Intersection

For problems concerned with multiple events, we must first determine the **intersection** of the sample spaces of all of the events. From this we can then determine the **joint probability.** For example, the joint probability of two independent events A and B occurring, P(A and B), is given by the following equation:

$$P(A \cap B) = \frac{n(A \cap B)}{n(S)} = P(A)*P(B) \tag{6}$$

where $n(S)$ is a function that returns the number of elements of the entire sample space S, and $n(A \cap B)$ represents the number of elements in S which are shared by the events A and B.

Consider for example the probability of rolling an odd-numbered die and also one divisible by 3—two independent events. The different sets for this problem would be

$$S = \{1,2,3,4,5,6\}, \qquad A \cap B = \{3\}, \qquad A = \{1,3,6\}, \qquad B = \{3,6\}$$

The individual probabilities of the events A and B would be:

$$P(A) = \frac{n(A)}{n(S)} = \tfrac{1}{2} \qquad P(B) = \frac{n(B)}{n(S)} = \tfrac{1}{3}$$

It follows from equation 6 that:

$$P(A \cap B) = \tfrac{1}{2}*\tfrac{1}{3} = \tfrac{1}{6}$$

Therefore, when rolling a die, we would expect the probability of obtaining an odd-numbered die and one divisible by 3 to be $\tfrac{1}{6}$.

Union

At other times we might be concerned with determining the probability of either one or several events occurring, $P(A$ or $B)$. In this situation we are concerned with the **union** $P(A \cup B)$ of the probabilities of the two events, which is handled by the following formula:

$$P(A \cup B) = P(A) + P(B) - P(A \cap B) \tag{7}$$

Consider for example the probability of rolling an odd-numbered die (event A) or one divisible by 3 (event B)

$$P(A \cup B) = \tfrac{1}{2} + \tfrac{1}{3} - \tfrac{1}{2}*\tfrac{1}{3} = \tfrac{2}{3}$$

Conditional Probabilities

The last section was concerned with events that are independent. For example, in our die experiment the two events of obtaining an odd-numbered toss and one divisible by 3 have no effect on one another. However, events that are not mutually exclusive will influence one another. That is, knowing that one event has occurred will influence the likelihood of some other event.

The probability of an event A occurring, given that an event B has already occurred, is called the **conditional probability** and is given as

$$P(A|B) = \frac{P(A \cap B)}{P(B)} \tag{8}$$

Consider for example the probability of rolling the number 3 (event A) given that we know that one divisible by 3 has occurred (event B). We know that the probability of A is $P(3) = \tfrac{1}{6}$. However, when we weigh in the fact that a number divisible by 3 has occurred and know its probability is $P(\text{divisible by 3}) = \tfrac{1}{3}$, we find:

$$P(A|B) = \frac{n(A \cap B)}{n(S)} \bigg/ \frac{n(B)}{n(S)} = \frac{n(A \cap B)}{n(B)} \tag{9}$$

$$= \frac{\tfrac{1}{6}}{\tfrac{2}{6}} = \tfrac{1}{2}$$

Therefore, we have improved our expectation of a roll of 3 occurring knowing that one divisible by 3 has occurred, from a probability of $\frac{1}{6}$ to one of $\frac{1}{2}$.

BAYESIAN THEORY

The conditional probability $P(A|B)$ permits us to obtain the probability of event A given that event B has occurred. In many problems we are concerned with the reverse situation: What is the probability of an earlier event given that some later one has occurred? This is often referred to as the **a posteriori probability.**

A typical problem where this situation would be present is in machine diagnostics. For example, we can observe the later events in terms of machine fault symptoms, but diagnosis is concerned with the earlier events that caused the fault symptoms. In general, the *conditional* probability is forward in time, while the *a posteriori* probability is backward in time.

The solution to this problem was found by the 18th-century British mathematician Thomas Bayes, and is known as the **Bayes Theorem.** The formal definition of this theorem provides the probability of the truth of some hypothesis H given some evidence E, and is presented as

$$P(H|E) = \frac{P(H)*P(E|H)}{P(E)} \qquad (10)$$

where:

$P(H|E)$ = probability that H is true given evidence E

$P(H)$ = probability that H is true

$P(E|H)$ = probability of observing evidence E when H is true

$P(E)$ = probability of E

The $P(E)$ term in equation 10 can also be written as

$$P(E) = P(E|H)*P(H) + P(E|\sim H)*P(\sim H) \qquad (11)$$

where:

$P(E|\sim H)$ = probability that E is true when H false

$P(\sim H)$ = probability that H is false

Bayes's theorem relies on us knowing *prior probabilities* of an event, which we can use to interpret the present situation. If a rich source of prior statistical information is available, then we can determine the likelihood of some hypothesis being true, given some evidence about the problem.

The use of Bayes's theorem comes into play in the design of expert systems when you consider the structure of a typical rule:

IF E THEN H

Equation 10 can then be used to provide the probability of the hypothesis H given the evidence E. It should also be noted that this equation could be used to manage inference chains of the form

IF X THEN $E \rightarrow$ IF E THEN H

Besides establishing a probability *for* a hypothesis being true given some evidence (eq. 10), we can also find the probability *against* the hypothesis being true for the same evidence, using the following equation:

$$P(\sim H|E) = \frac{P(\sim H)*P(E|\sim H)}{P(E)} \tag{12}$$

As we will see later in this chapter, the ratio of the probability *for* a hypothesis and *against* it given the same evidence is useful in certain applications. Dividing equation 10 by 12 gives:

$$\frac{P(H|E)}{P(\sim H|E)} = \frac{P(E|H)*P(H)}{P(E|\sim H)*P(\sim H)} \tag{13}$$

Example of Bayes's Theorem

To help illustrate the use of Bayes's theorem, consider the following example. Patients with chest pains are often given an electrocardiogram (ECG) test. Test results are classified as either positive (+ECG) suggesting heart disease (+HD), or negative (−ECG) suggesting no heart disease (−HD). Assume now that a patient has produced a +ECG and we want to know how probable it is that he has heart disease, that is $P(+HD|+ECG)$. We will assume that the following probability values apply in this case, all obtained from a sample of patients complaining about chest pains:

$P(+HD) = 0.1$; 10 people out of 100 have heart disease

$P(-HD) = 0.9$; 90 people out of 100 do not have heart disease

$\qquad = 1 - P(+HD)$

$P(+ECG|+HD) = 0.9$; 90 people out of 100 who have heart disease will produce a positive ECG

$P(-ECG|-HD) = 0.95$; 95 people out of 100 who do not have heart disease will produce a negative ECG

$P(+ECG|-HD) = 0.05$; 5 people out of 100 who do not have heart disease will produce a positive ECG

$\qquad = 1 - P(-ECG|-HD)$

Therefore, from equations 10 and 11:

$$P(+HD|+ECG) = \frac{0.9*0.1}{0.9*0.1 + 0.05*0.9}$$

$$= 0.67$$

The interpretation from this result is that two-thirds the time someone with chest pains who produces a positive ECG test has heart disease.

_____ **VARIATION ON BAYES'S THEOREM** _____

In some expert system applications, developers elect to use a variation of the Bayes theorem. They introduce two new terms; **prior odds** on H and **posterior odds** on H. The prior odds on H is given as

$$O(H) = \frac{P(H)}{P(\sim H)} = \frac{P(H)}{1 - P(H)} \qquad \text{Prior} \qquad (14)$$

The posterior odds on H is given as

$$O(H|E) = \frac{P(H|E)}{P(\sim H|E)} = \frac{P(H|E)}{1 - P(H|E)} \qquad \text{posterior} \qquad (15)$$

From the definitions of the prior and posterior odds, we can now introduce two new terms: LS and LN.

Likelihood of Sufficiency

LS is called the **likelihood of sufficiency** and represents the measure of support for the hypothesis H given that the evidence E is present. LS is given in equation form as follows:

$$LS = \frac{P(E|H)}{P(E|\sim H)} \qquad (16)$$

From equations 12–16, it follows that

$$O(H|E) = LS*O(H) \qquad (17)$$

Equation 17 is often referred to as the **odds-likelihood form** of Bayes's Theorem. LS is called the likelihood of sufficiency because it represents a value that indicates how encouraging it is to our belief in the hypothesis to find the evidence present. From equation 17 it can be seen that a large LS value will transform the prior odds on H, $O(H)$, into a large value of the posterior odds on H, $O(H|E)$. In fact, as LS goes to infinity, $O(H|E)$ also goes to infinity, and by equation 15 we see that $P(H|E) = 1$ and $P(\sim HE) = 0$.

From equation 17, we can solve for LS as follows

$$LS = \frac{O(H|E)}{O(H)} = \frac{P(E|H)}{P(E|\sim H)} = \frac{\dfrac{P(H|E)}{P(\sim H|E)}}{\dfrac{P(H)}{P(\sim H)}} \qquad (18)$$

Likelihood of Necessity

LN is called the **likelihood of necessity** and represents the measure of discredit to hypothesis H if evidence E is missing. LN is given as

$$LN = \frac{O(H|\sim E)}{O(H)} = \frac{P(\sim E|H)}{P(\sim E|\sim H)} = \frac{\dfrac{P(H|\sim E)}{P(\sim H|\sim E)}}{\dfrac{P(H)}{P(\sim H)}} \tag{19}$$

or

$$O(H|\sim E) = LN*O(H) \tag{20}$$

LN is called the likelihood of necessity because it provides a number that represents how discouraging it is to find the evidence absent. In fact, if LN = 0, then $P(H|\sim E) = 0$, which means that H must be false when $E\sim$ is true. If E is not present, then we must conclude that H is false, which further means that E is necessary for H.

Rule Structure

Using LS and LN values, you can develop rules that compute their values for the rule's conclusion given the rule's evidence:

$$\text{IF } E \text{ THEN } H \text{ (LS, LN)}$$

This rule states that evidence E suggests hypothesis H with a degree specified by the factors LS and LN. Both factors are provided by the expert and are used to compute the posterior odds of the hypothesis $O(H|E)$. Both factors take on values between 0 and infinity, and the interpretation of their effect on the hypothesis can be seen in Table 11.1 (from table 4-10, Giarratano and Riley 1989).

The two equations for LS and LN must follow the following constraints:

$$\text{When LS} > 1, \text{ then LN} < 1$$

$$\text{When LS} < 1, \text{ then LN} > 1 \tag{21}$$

$$\text{When LS} = 1, \text{ then LN} = 1$$

These conditions represent mathematical constraints but may not apply to many real-world problems. For example, the expert may say that some evidence is important, that is LS > 1, but the absence of the evidence is unimportant, that is LN $= 1$. This problem is discussed in more detail in the next section.

Uncertain Evidence

In the previous rule structure,

$$\text{IF } E \text{ THEN } H \text{ (LS, LN)}$$

TABLE 11.1   Effect of LS and LN on the Hypothesis

LS	Effect on Hypothesis
0	H is false when E is true or ~E is necessary for concluding H
Small	E is unfavorable for concluding H
1	E has no effect for concluding H
Large	E is favorable for concluding H
Infinity	E is logically sufficient for H or Observing E means that H must be true

LN	Effect on Hypothesis
0	H is false when E is absent or E is necessary for concluding H
Small	Absence of E is unfavorable for H
1	Absence of E has no effect on H
Large	Absence of E is favorable for H
Infinity	Absence of E is logically sufficient for concluding H

$P(E)$ represents the probability of E being true and is used to support the hypothesis H. Establishing $P(E)$ for many problems can be difficult because the user may be uncertain in the evidence E. More generally, we can say that the evidence E is dependent upon the observed evidence E', as given by $P(E|E')$. The factor E' represents our collective belief in E. If we know the evidence with total certainty, then $E = E'$ and $P(E|E') = P(E)$, the prior probability of event E.

We can now make adjustments to our probability statements to take into account a degree of uncertainty in the evidence. The probability of H given our belief E' is given as

$$P(H|E') = P(H|E)*P(E|E') + P(H|\sim E)*P(\sim E|E') \qquad (22)$$

Equation 22 is accurate for a pure Bayesian approach and establishes the following relationships:

IF $P(E|E') = P(E)$, THEN $P(H|E') = P(H)$
IF E is true, THEN $P(E|E') = 1$, AND $P(H|E') = P(H|E)$
IF E is false, THEN $P(\sim E|E') = 1$, AND $P(H|E') = P(H|\sim E)$

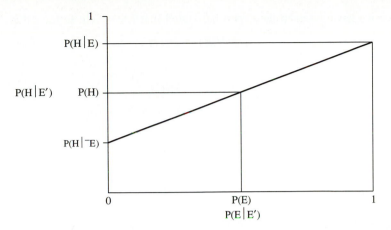

FIGURE 11.2 Bayesian relationship between P(HE') and P(EE').

These relationships in turn define a linear relationship between $P(H|E')$ vs $P(E|E')$ as shown in Figure 11.2.

A problem with equation 22 occurs for real-world problems when $P(E|E')$ equals $P(E)$, that is the observed evidence E' is in total support of the evidence E. It then follows from equation 22 that

$$P(H|E') = P(H|E)*P(E) + P(H|{\sim}E)*P({\sim}E) \tag{23}$$

or

$$P(H|E') = P(H) \tag{24}$$

For some problems an expert may say that some evidence is important, that is $LS > 1$, but the absence of the evidence is unimportant, that is $LN = 1$, violating the relationships shown in equation 21.

If $LS > 1$ and $LN = 1$, then from equation 19

$$O(H|{\sim}E) = LN*O(H) = O(H) \tag{25}$$

From equation 14 we know that the odds of H can be found by

$$O(H) = \frac{P(H)}{1 - P(H)} \tag{26}$$

It follows that

$$P(H|E') = P(H) \tag{27}$$

Using equation 27 in equation 23:

$$P(H|E') = P(H|E)*P(E) + P(H)*P(E')$$
$$= P(H|E)*P(E) + P(H)*(1 - P(E)) \tag{28}$$
$$= P(H) + P(H|E)*P(E) - P(H)*P(E)$$

Since we have assumed the expert has stated that LS > 1, it follows that

$$O(H|E) > O(H)$$

or   (29)

$$P(H|E) > P(H)$$

Therefore, the term $P(H|E)*P(E) - P(H)*P(E)$ in equation 28 must be > 0. And, from equation 28, when the expert specifies LS > 1 and LN = 1, we can conclude that

$$P(H|E') > P(H)$$ (30)

The relationship in equation 30 contradicts the expected result of equation 24, $P(H|E') = P(H)$. Under these conditions, the posterior probability of H given evidence E' is greater than it should be had the expert followed the more rigid mathematical constraint relationships of LS and LN needed to maintain an exact Bayesian model. We need some adjustment to the pure Bayesian approach to allow us to account for real-world situations.

Uncertainty Adjustment

The last section discussed how an expert might provide subjective probabilities that may lead to inconsistencies in the relationship between LS and LN. One method of avoiding this problem was proposed by Duda et al. (1976). This method relies on an ad hoc assumption that relates $P(H|E')$ to $P(E|E')$ following a piecewise linear function. This approach does not follow exactly the traditional probability theory, but provides a means that worked well in the PROSPECTOR expert system.

The $P(H|E')$ function was broken into two simple functions that could be easily manipulated and avoided the problem discussed in the prior section.

For $0 \leq P(E|E') \leq P(E)$,

$$P(H|\sim E) + \frac{P(E|E')}{P(E)}*(P(H) - P(H|\sim E))$$ (31)

For $P(E) \leq P(E|E') < 1$,

$$P(H|E') = \frac{P(H) - P(H|E)*P(E)}{1 - P(E)} + P(E|E')*\frac{P(H|E) - P(H)}{1 - P(E)}$$ (32)

Using equations 31 and 32, when the situation arises where LS > 1 and LN = 1, the value of $P(H|E')$ remains the same if $P(E|E') < P(E)$ and increases if $P(E|E') \geq P(E)$. Equations 31 and 32 are shown in Figure 11.3.

--------- **PROSPECTOR EXPERT SYSTEM** ---------

One of the most popular expert system applications which employed Bayesian decision-making was PROSPECTOR (Duda et al. 1979). PROSPECTOR is an

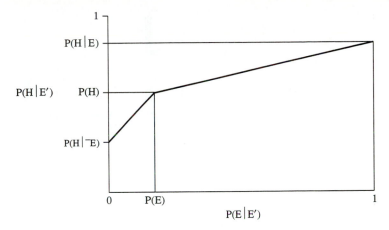

FIGURE 11.3 Piecewise linear function for partial evidence.

expert system which assists geologists in the exploration for certain types of mineral deposits. The system encodes the expertise of geologists for different mineral deposits into models that are used to determine the likelihood of a mineral being present at a given site from several observables. The system also helps in determining the best spot to drill at a favorable site.

Prospector Inference Network

Each model was represented in the system in a distinct inference network. A small portion of one of the inference networks used in PROSPECTOR is shown in Figure 11.4. Each network is composed of a set of nodes that represent evidence or hypotheses, and links that connect the different nodes together with uncertain relationships. Primitive—or askable—nodes represent evidence that must be provided by the user. For example, a question might be asked, "To what degree do you believe that the groundmass texture is aplitic?" Given this question, the user provides a numeric value that represents his belief in this statement. This information is used to support intermediate hypothesis nodes. For example, the prior evidence is in support of the hypothesis, "The groundmass is favorable for type-A porphyry copper deposit." Various intermediate nodes are used to further support the top-level hypothesis, "There is an admissible intrusive system," which is what we want to prove with this particular model.

Prospector Rules

Figure 11.4 shows the various nodes of the model, their links, and the corresponding LS and LN values between the various nodes. The links between the nodes

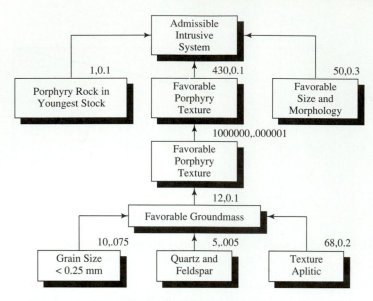

FIGURE 11.4   PROSPECTOR inference network.

form a structure similar to that found with a rule:

$$\text{If } E \text{ THEN } H \text{ (LS, LN)}$$

The term E is a node that represents some evidence and is linked to node H that represents some hypothesis. The link is uncertain, as expressed with the factors LS and LN. The network is established by the expert geologist who provides the information in each node, the links with their corresponding LS and LN factors, and prior probabilities for each node. The above example might appear in the following rule form:

IF   The groundmass texture is aplitic
THEN   The groundmass is favorable for type-A porphyry copper
        deposit   [68,0.2]

$$\text{Prior } P(E) = .001$$
$$\text{Prior } P(H) = .002$$

If E is a primitive node, then the user provides a degree of belief to E, which is used with the link's LS and LN values, along with the prior probabilities of each node, to form a level of belief in the rule's conclusion. The level of belief of H is then used to form a level of belief in the intermediate nodes connected to node H, which in turn propagates to the top-level hypothesis forming an overall belief in this hypothesis on the basis of the new information supplied by the user. The overall problem is to acquire evidence for the primitive nodes that can establish a degree of belief of the top-level hypothesis through probability propagation throughout the inference network.

PROSPECTOR used the Bayesian approach to propagate probabilities through the inference network. The form of the network was established with the help of the expert geologists who also provided prior probabilities for each node and their uncertain links to other nodes captured in the LS and LN values.

MultiPremise Rules

Thus far we have been discussing two single nodes coupled together. In the case of multiple nodes affecting a single hypothesis, the assumption of conditional independence of the evidence is made. This results in a simple method for computing the posterior probability of the hypothesis. The coupling of multiple nodes to a single hypothesis can be thought of as a multipremise rule. Each rule is composed of several premises, each providing evidence in support of the rule's conclusion. The premises could be coupled in an conjunctive or disjunctive fashion.

Conjunctive Rules

The general form of a conjunctive rule is as follows:

IF E_1 AND E_2 AND ... THEN H

All of the premises represented as evidence E_i must be true for the conclusion H to be true. In the general sense, each piece of evidence E_i is based on the partial evidence E_i'.

To propagate the probability of the rule's evidence through to the expected probability of the rule's conclusion, the PROSPECTOR team assumed the approximation used in fuzzy logic:

$$P(E|E') = \min\{P(E_i|E')\} \tag{33}$$

The min function returns the minimum value of all the $P(E_i|E')$. Once the $P(E|E')$ value is determined for a given rule from equation 33, it is used with equation 32 to determine a value for $P(H|E')$.

This is a simple approach, but has one difficulty. The $P(E|E')$ is insensitive to changes to any $P(E_i|E')$ except the minimum. Even if other probabilities increase, the $P(E|E')$ will be set at the minimum value of $P(E_i|E')$.

Disjunctive Rules

The general form of a disjunctive rule is as follows:

IF E_1 OR E_2 OR ... THEN H

For evidence probability propagation, the PROSPECTOR team assumed the following approximation:

$$P(E|E') = \max \{P(E_i|E')\} \tag{34}$$

The max function returns the maximum value of all of the $P(E_iE')$.

Updating the Odds

Within the PROSPECTOR system, the odds for each hypothesis is updated each time new evidence is provided by the user. For the case of a rule with one premise, the updated odds for H for a belief E' in the premise is given as:

$$O(H|E') = \frac{P(H|E')}{1 - P(H|E')} \tag{35}$$

Assuming conditional independence of the evidence and that all the E_i are true, then in the general case of multiple rules with uncertain pieces of evidence that update the hypothesis we have

$$O(H|E_1', E_2', \ldots, E_n') = \prod_{i=1}^{n} LS_i'*O(H) \tag{36}$$

where LS_i' is the effective likelihood ratio and is given by

$$LS_i' = \frac{O(H|E_i')}{O(H)} = \frac{P(E_i|H)}{P(E_i|\sim H)} \tag{37}$$

In a similar fashion, if all the evidence contributing to H is false,

$$O(H|\sim E_1', \sim E_2', \ldots, \sim E_n') = \prod_{i=1}^{n} LN_i'*O(H) \tag{38}$$

where

$$LN_i' = \frac{O(H|\sim E_i')}{O(H)} = \frac{P(\sim E_i|H)}{P(\sim E_i|H)} \tag{39}$$

Certainty Measure

The PROSPECTOR team also introduced a different technique for allowing the user to enter his belief about a piece of evidence. Instead of using $P(E|E')$, the term **certainty measure** $C(E|E')$ was introduced. The main reason for introducing the certainty measure was purely psychological. Most humans feel uncomfortable estimating probabilities of some piece of evidence, but are more willing to express their certainty in the piece of evidence being true or not. For example, a human might say ''I really believe that I am catching a cold,'' rather than, ''The probability of my catching a cold is 90%.''

In the PROSPECTOR system the degree of certainty in some evidence E, given the observable evidence in E', was given as $C(E|E')$ and ran from -5 to $+5$, where -5 corresponds to E being definitely false, $+5$ corresponds to E being definitely true, and 0 to the ''unknown'' situation. Therefore, one might ascribe a certainty value of 4.5 to the statement of ''I really believe that I am catching a cold.''

The certainty measure value was mapped to the probability in the evidence according to the following:

$$\text{If } C(E|E') = -5, \text{ then } P(E|E') = 0$$

$$\text{If } C(E|E') = 0, \text{ then } P(E|E') = P(E)$$

$$\text{If } C(E|E') = 5, \text{ then } P(E|E') = 1$$

In general, this certainty measure follows the same piecewise linear approach taken in equations 31 and 32 for $C(E|E')$, and is given as:

For $P(E|E') > P(E)$

$$C(E|E') = 5*\frac{P(E|E') - P(E)}{1 - P(E)} \tag{40}$$

For $P(E|E') \leq P(E)$

$$C(E|E') = 5*\frac{P(E|E') - P(E)}{P(E)} \tag{41}$$

We can determine $P(E|E')$ from equations 40 and 41 on the basis of the user-provided confidence in a piece of evidence $C(E|E')$:

For $C(E|E') > 0$

$$P(E|E') = \frac{C(E|E')*[1 - P(E)] + 5*P(E)}{5} \tag{42}$$

For $C(E|E') \leq 0$

$$P(E|E') = \frac{C(E|E')*P(E) + 5*P(E)}{5} \tag{43}$$

The posterior probability of H given E, can be evaluated from LS and the prior probability on H:

$$P(H|E) = \frac{LS*O(H)}{1 + LS*O(H)} \tag{44}$$

Similarly

$$P(H|{\sim}E) = \frac{LN*O(H)}{1 + LN*O(H)} \tag{45}$$

The updated certainty factor for the hypothesis can then be evaluated from:

For $P(E|E'_{\text{total}}) > P(E)$

$$C(H|E') = 5*\frac{P(H|E'_{\text{total}}) - P(E)}{1 - P(E)} \tag{46}$$

for $P(H|E'_{\text{total}}) \leq P(E)$

$$C(H|E') = 5*\frac{P(H|E'_{\text{total}}) - P(E)}{P(E)} \tag{47}$$

where

$$P(H|E'_{\text{total}}) = \frac{O(H|E'_1, E'_2, ..)}{1 + O(H|E'_1, E'_2, ..)} \tag{48}$$

EXAMPLE PROGRAM USING PROSPECTOR APPROACH

From the work on PROSPECTOR, a knowledge engineering language called KAS was developed (Reboh 1981). KAS is a skeletal system that is basically PROSPECTOR with the knowledge of geology removed. It offers an expert system development environment for systems that follows the structure and operation of PROSPECTOR.

To illustrate the propagation of probabilities using the PROSPECTOR approach, we will consider the following problem that could be developed using the KAS language. The problem is one of deciding whether or not to purchase a car. We will assume the hypothesis is "Don't buy." An inference network that supports this problem is shown in Figure 11.5.

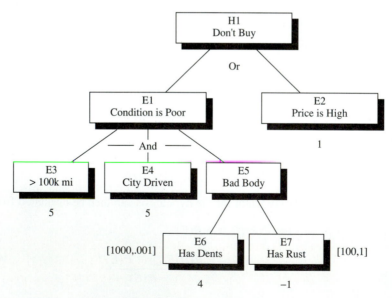

FIGURE 11.5   **Don't buy car inference network.**

The rules that form this inference network are as follows:

Rule 1

IF	The condition of the car is poor	E1
OR	The price of the car is high	E2
THEN	Don't buy the car	H1

Rule 2

IF	Mileage on the car exceeds 100k	E3
AND	The car is city driven	E4
AND	The body of the car is bad	E5
THEN	The condition of the car is poor	E1

Rule 3

IF	The car has dents	E6
THEN	The body of the car is bad	E5
	[LS = 1000, LN = .001]	

Rule 4

IF	The car has rust	E7
THEN	The body of the car is bad	E5
	(LS = 100, LN = 1]	

Both RULE 3 and RULE 4 support the hypothesis "The body of the car is bad" but with different likelihood values. Recall that the LS factor determines how much the prior odds are changed when evidence is present, while the LN factor determines how much the prior odds are changed when the evidence is absent.

In the case of RULE 3, the presence of "The car has dents" is very favorable for concluding that "The body of the car is bad" while not observing dents in the car is very unfavorable in supporting the conclusion. In the case of RULE 4, the presence of "The car has rust" is somewhat favorable in supporting the conclusion, while the absence of rust has no effect on the conclusion.

Example Session

We will assume that the domain expert has ascribed all of the prior probabilities of the evidence to be 0.1, i.e., $P(E_i) = 0.1$. The consultation session proceeds as follows: (Note: the answers to these questions are also shown next to each evidence block of Figure 11.5.)

SYSTEM: To what degree do you believe that the assumption of the car has more than 100,000 miles is appropriate? —E3

User: 5

SYSTEM: To what degree do you believe that the assumption of the car has been driven in the city is appropriate?   —E4

User: 5

SYSTEM: To what degree do you believe that the assumption of the car has dents is appropriate?   —E6

User: 4

SYSTEM: To what degree do you believe that the assumption of the car has rust is appropriate?   —E7

User: −1

SYSTEM: To what degree do you believe that the assumption of the price of the car is high is appropriate?   —E2

User: 1

CONCLUSION: My certainty in Don't buy the car is now 3.97.

Internal Operation

We will now review the internal propagation of the various probability values:

1. $C(E3|E3') = C(E4|E4') = 5$; the user observing E3' and E4' is totally certain in E3 and E4.
2. We need to find the certainty in E5, which is supported by E6' and E7'. That is, we need to find $C(E5|E4',E7')$.

     a. $O(E5)$ is found from equation 26:

$$O(E5) = \frac{P(E5)}{1 - P(E5)} = \frac{0.1}{1 - 0.1} = 0.111$$

     b. $P(E5|E6)$ and $P(E5|\sim E6)$ are found from equations 44 and 45, noting that LS = 1000 and LN = .001 for E6 → E5:

$$P(E5|E6) = \frac{LS*O(E5)}{1 + LS*O(E5)} = \frac{1000*0.111}{1 + 1000*0.111} = 0.9911$$

$$P(E5|\sim E6) = \frac{LN*O(E5)}{1 + LN*O(E5)} = \frac{.001*0.111}{1 + .001*0.111} = 1.11E - 4$$

     c.   Similarly, $P(E5|E7)$ and $P(E5|\sim E7)$ are found from equations 44 and 45, noting that LS = 100 and LN = 1 for E7 → E5:

$$P(E5|E7) = \frac{LS*O(E5)}{1 + LS*O(E5)} = \frac{100*0.111}{1 + 100*0.111} = 0.9174$$

$$P(E5|\sim E7) = \frac{LN*O(E5)}{1 + LN*O(E5)} = \frac{1*0.111}{1 + 1*0.111} = 0.1$$

     d.   The user has specified $C(E6|E6') = 4.0$. Therefore since $C(E|E') > 0$, then from equation 42:

$$P(E6|E6') = \frac{C(E6|E6')*[1 - P(E6)] + 5*P(E6)]}{5}$$

$$= \frac{4*[1 - 0.1] + 5*0.1}{5} = 0.82$$

e. The user has also specified $C(E7|E7') = -1$. Therefore since $C(E|E') < 0$ from equation 43:

$$P(E7|E7') = \frac{C(E7|E7')*P(E7) + 5*P(E7)}{5}$$

$$= \frac{-1.0*0.1 + 5*0.1}{5} = 0.08$$

f. Since $P(E6) \leq P(E6|E6') < 1$ (i.e., $0.1 \leq 0.82 < 1$), we can now find $P(E5|E6')$ from equation 32:

$$P(E5|E6') = \frac{P(E5) - P(E5|E6)*P(E6)}{1 - P(E6)} + P(E6|E6')*\frac{P(E5|E6) - P(E5)}{1 - P(E6)}$$

$$= \frac{0.1 - .9911*0.1}{1 - 0.1} + 0.82*\frac{0.9911 - 0.1}{1 - 0.1}$$

$$= 0.8129$$

g. Since $0 \leq P(E7|E7') \leq P(E)$ (i.e., $0 \leq 0.08 \leq 0.1$), we can now find $P(E5|E7')$ from equation 31:

$$P(E5|E7') = P(E5|\sim E7) + \frac{P(E7|E7')}{P(E7)}*(P(E5) - P(E5|\sim E7))$$

$$= 0.1 + \frac{0.08}{0.1}*(0.1 - 0.1)$$

$$= 0.1$$

h. We can now calculate the updated odds $O(E5|E6')$ and $O(E5|E7')$ from equation 35:

$$O(E5|E6') = \frac{P(E5|E6')}{1 - P(E5|E6')} = \frac{0.8129}{1 - 0.8129} = 4.34$$

$$O(E5|E7') = \frac{P(E5|E7')}{1 - P(E5|E7')} = \frac{0.1}{1 - 0.1} = 0.111$$

i. We can now calculate the total odds on E5 from the observations of E6' and E7' from equation 36 (note that since LN = 1, the negative response to E7 does not reduce the updated odds):

$$O(E5|E6',E7') = \frac{O(E5|E6')}{O(E5)}*\frac{O(E5|E7')}{O(E5)}*O(E5)$$

$$= \frac{4.34}{.11}*\frac{0.111}{.11}*.11 = 4.379$$

j. Next find $P(E5|E'_{total})$ from equation 48:

$$P(E5|E'_{total}) = \frac{O(E5|E6',E7')}{1 + O(E5|E6'E7')} = \frac{4.379}{1 + 4.379} = 0.814$$

k.   Since $P(E5|E'_{total}) > P(E5)$ (i.e., $0.814 > 0.1$), we can now finally find the confidence in C5 from the observations of E6' and E7' using equation 46:

$$C(E5|E6',E7') = 5*\frac{P(E5|E'_{total}) - P(E5)}{1 - P(E5)}$$

$$= 5*\frac{0.814 - 0.1}{1 - 0.1} = 3.97$$

3.   We can next determine the confidence in E1 by noting that RULE 2 is conjunctive, and by equation 33 it follows:

$$C(E1) = \min\{5.0, 5.0, 3.97\} = 3.97$$

4.   We can determine the confidence in H1 by noting that RULE 1 is disjunctive, and by equation 34 it follows

$$C(H1) = \max\{3.97, 1\} = 3.97$$

Session Review

The final figure for C(H1) represents our certainty in the hypothesis "Don't buy the car" on the basis of the user's input. The value for our confidence, $C(H1) = 3.97$, is measured on the basis of an allowable range of -5 to $+5$. Since our resultant value is close to $+5$, we would conclude in words "I would highly recommend that you do not buy the car."

You should also notice that two major factors led to this conclusion. The first factor came from the expert, when he or she specified a large LS value and a small LN value for relating the issue of "dents" to the issue of "bad body." Implied in ascribing these values was the belief held by the expert that dents in a car are a strong indication that the car has a bad body.

The second factor that led to our conclusion is that the user of the system provided a high confidence value to the observable of dents; i.e., $P(E6 = \text{dents}|E6' = \text{observed dents}) = 4$. The belief that the car had considerable dents on it propagated through to the conclusion with a high belief in the hypothesis that you should not buy the car.

In summary on this example, even though the PROSPECTOR model made a number of assumptions in forming the probability model, the resultant recommendation for the small example *appears* to provide an intelligent result.

—————— IMPORTANT PROBABILITY ISSUES ——————

Probability theory is a powerful technique for working with information that is inexact or random. It can be used in such areas as weather forecasting, financial planning, or mineral exploration. However, for this approach to be an effective technique for managing inexact reasoning in an expert system, certain conditions must be met.

Prior Probabilities Must Be Known

The use of probability theory implies the fundamental assumption that the sample space is well defined and the probabilities of each event can be obtained from a set of past data. Consider for example a medical diagnosis problem. A Bayesian approach would determine the probability of some given disease from the available evidence, using the following equation:

$$P(D|E) = \frac{P(D)*P(E|D)}{P(E)} \tag{49}$$

where:

$P(D|E)$ = probability that disease D is true given evidence E

$P(D)$ = probability that the disease D is true

$P(E|D)$ = probability of observing evidence E when disease D is true

$P(E)$ = probability that E is true

Providing reliable values for each of these probabilities is usually difficult or completely impossible, because of the large number of diseases and various symptoms that might have to be considered. In general, for many real-world problems reliable statistical information is unavailable and assumptions may generate inconsistencies in the Bayesian approach.

Probabilities Must Be Updated

Some problems involve data or information that are continually changing. In this event, an inexact reasoning technique based in probability theory will require you to recalculate all of the probability factors. This can be a time-consuming process and adds to the system maintenance effort.

Total Probability Must Equal Unity

Another problem that occurs with a strict probability approach is related to the required relationship between the probability *for* and *against* a given hypothesis. In theory we would expect

$$P(H|E) + P(\sim H|E) = 1 \tag{50}$$

Equation 50 tells us that we should expect that the probability for and against a given hypothesis, given some evidence, should add to one. However, for many problems humans are unwilling to make this assertion. Consider a situation found during the development of the expert system MYCIN as reported by Shortliffe and Buchanan (1975), where the following rule is offered to illustrate this point:

> IF   The stain of the organism is gram positive
> AND   The morphology of the organism is coccus
> AND   The growth conformation of the organism is chains
> THEN There is suggestive evidence (0.7) that the identity of the organism is streptococcus

This rule reflects the belief of an expert in the rule's conclusion, given the evidence contained in the rule's premises. The belief in the rule's relationship is captured in a numeric value of 0.7, based on a scale of -1 to $+1$, where -1 corresponds to false and $+1$ to true.

Following equation 50, we would then expect in the absence of the evidence of the rule that we would conclude to a degree 0.3 that streptococcus is not present. However, Shortliffe reports that the expert is uncomfortable in making this statement, creating a problem for developing the system along the lines of strict probability.

The problem is not with the Bayesian approach, nor with the expert; the problem is with an attempt to force a Bayesian approach on this type of problem. The fundamental problem is that while $P(H|E)$ implies a cause-and-effect relationship between E and H, there may be no such relationship between E and $\sim H$. The belief stated in the rule's relationship reflects the expert's *judgmental* belief in the relationship between the rule's premise and conclusion, and not one that meets strict probability constraints that can allow us to use the evidence in the premise to conclude anything about the unlikelihood of the conclusion.

Conditional Independence Is Required

Using a Bayesian approach also requires another assumption in order to simplify the approach for application to real-world problems. The PROSPECTOR team assumed conditional independence in the evidence to simplify the Bayesian Theorem—a constraint that may not be applicable to some problems. For example, in a medical application we may acquire evidence from the patient that he has a sore throat and a high temperature, which may be used to help infer that the patient has strep throat. However, the symptoms of sore throat and high temperature may not be independent pieces of evidence.

The assumption of conditional independence of evidence was also used by the PROSPECTOR team in forming a belief in a hypothesis that was supported by conjunctive or disjunctive rules. For conjunctive rules, the following approach was used:

$$\text{IF } E_1 \text{ AND } E_2 \text{ AND } \ldots \text{ THEN } H$$

$$C(H) = \min \{P(E_i|E')\}$$

This approach is attractive because of its simplicity but has the disadvantage of making the belief in H insensitive to any $P(E_i|E')$ except the minimum.

For disjunctive rules, another simple approach was taken from fuzzy logic to determine the belief in the hypothesis:

$$\text{IF } E_1 \text{ OR }_2 \text{ OR } \ldots \text{ THEN } H$$

$$C(H) = \max \{P(E_i|E')\}$$

Summary on Constraints

Probability theory is a well-established procedure for working with inexact information, but requires a number of preconditions or assumptions to be made before it can provide a valid approach to a given problem. Some of the important issues that must be considered are:

- A priori data about the events of the domain must be available.
- This data must be updated so that probability models can be adjusted to reflect any changes in the domain.
- The sum of the probabilities for and against a hypothesis, given some evidence, must equal one.
- Conditional independence of data must be assumed.

—————— SUMMARY ON BAYESIAN APPROACH ——————

This chapter reviewed probability theory as a technique for managing inexact reasoning in an expert system. Principally, the Bayesian technique and variations of it were explored. It was argued that when certain conditions or assumptions can be met, the Bayesian approach offers the benefit of a well-founded and statistically correct method for handling inexact reasoning.

However, in many expert system applications, we simply do not have past data on the events or models available to make accurate probability statements. For example, Shortliffe and Buchanan (1975) reported that the medical field lacked background data on a number of issues, which prevented them from using a classical probability approach. Therefore, alternative approaches were taken to deal with problems that worked with inexact knowledge for which a priori information was lacking. The two principal approaches used treated information as not inexact, but rather *uncertain* or *fuzzy*—subjects of the next two chapters.

The major lessons learned in this chapter were:

- Probability theory provides an exact approach for deriving inexact inferences.
- Bayes's theorem permits us to determine the probability of an earlier event given that some later one has occurred.
- PROSPECTOR uses rules of the form

$$\text{IF } E \text{ THEN } H \text{ (LS,LN)}$$

where LS is the "likelihood of sufficiency" and LN is the "likelihood of necessity."
- PROSPECTOR used a "certainty measure" versus a probability estimate when querying the user.
- The problem must meet several probability constraints before a Bayesian approach would be effective.

EXERCISES

1. Discuss why probability theory is an attractive approach for drawing inexact inferences.
2. List several problems where the Bayes approach would be appropriate.
3. Why did the PROSPECTOR team elect to use a "certainty measure" versus a probability estimate when querying the user?
4. What problem characteristics must be present (e.g., probability constraints) before a Bayesian approach would be an effective inexact reasoning technique?
5. Assume there are three major systems that control a nuclear power plant. Also assume that each system has a failure probability of 0.01. Determine the probability that all three systems will fail, if the failure probabilities of all three systems are independent.
6. Determine the probability of all three systems from problem 5 failing, if the failure probabilities are now considered interdependent, with the following conditional probabilities:

$$P(\text{system1 fails}|\text{system2 fails or system3}) = 0.5$$
$$P(\text{system2 fails}|\text{system1 fails or system3}) = 0.4$$
$$P(\text{system3 fails}|\text{system1 fails or system2}) = 0.3$$
$$P(\text{system1 fails}|\text{system2 fails and system3}) = 0.8$$
$$P(\text{system2 fails}|\text{system1 fails and system3}) = 0.7$$
$$P(\text{system3 fails}|\text{system1 fails and system2}) = 0.6$$

7. Given that $P(\text{all three systems fail}|\text{explosion}) = 0.8$, and the results from problems 5 and 6, assume that all three systems have failed and determine the probability that an explosion caused the event.

REFERENCES

Duda, R.O., P. Hart, and N. Nilsson, Subjective Bayesian Methods for Rule-Based Inference Systems, National Computer Conference (AFIPS Conference Proceedings), vol. 45, pp. 1075–1082, 1976.

Duda, R.O., P. Hart, K. Konolige, and R. Reboh, A Computer-Based Consultation for Mineral Exploration, SRI Report, Stanford Research Institute, 333 Ravenswood Avenue, Menlo Park, CA, Sept. 1979.

Giarratano, J., and G. Riley, Expert Systems: Principles and Programming, PWS-KENT Publishing Company, Boston, Mass., 1989.

Reboh, R., Knowledge Engineering Techniques and Tools in the PROSPECTOR Environment, SRI Technical Note 243, Stanford Research Institute, 333 Ravenswood Avenue, Menlo Park, CA, June 1981.

Shortliffe, E.H. and B.G. Buchanan, A Model of Inexact Reasoning in Medicine, Mathematical Biosciences, vol. 23, pp. 351–379, 1975.

Certainty Theory

————————— INTRODUCTION —————————

A popular alternative to probability theory for inexact reasoning in expert systems is the **certainty theory** (Shortliffe and Buchanan 1975). This theory grew out of the work on MYCIN and relies on defining judgmental measures of belief rather than adhering to strict probability estimates. This work led to the development of the certainty model, which offers a practical technique for performing inexact reasoning in many expert system applications. This chapter reviews the basic certainty theory and its evolution into practical application. It also provides examples of the theory and insight into its effective use.

————————— OVERVIEW OF CERTAINTY THEORY —————————

Experts often make judgments when solving a problem. Problem information may be suspect or incomplete, and some of the knowledge for interpreting the information may be unreliable. Yet, experts have learned to adapt to the situation and continue to reason about the problem intelligently. These difficulties are part of the normal state of affairs for many problems addressed by expert systems. The situation has driven expert system developers to search for techniques to manage inexact reasoning.

As discussed in the previous chapter, one of the earliest techniques attempted was probability theory. Though well-founded mathematically, the technique requires a statistical basis rarely found in the types of problems applied to expert systems. Consider for example a question one might encounter on a medical problem:

Does the patient have a severe headache?

How might we expect the user to answer this question? It is unlikely the user would feel comfortable answering the question as completely true or false, since the question is subjective and requires the user to make a judgment.

We might elect to permit the user to assign a number to the answer that reflects his level of belief in the answer. For example, we might use the standard probability scale of 0 to 1. However, if we obtain an answer such as 0.7, we have to ask ourselves what does it really represent and what can we actually do with it? The number has no statistical basis but is rather the user's *subjective* interpretation and is not subject to the rules of probability theory. Therefore, we could not use it to draw probability inferences through a technique such as Bayes.

We appear to be in an uncomfortable position. We are faced with a problem that contains inexact information and can't rely upon scientifically sound techniques for dealing with it. However, when you consider that expert systems are by nature heuristic problem-solvers, it seems only reasonable that we might be able to rely upon some heuristic inexact reasoning technique. This assumption turns out to be valid, as illustrated during the development of MYCIN (Shortliffe et al. 1973).

Inexact Reasoning in MYCIN

MYCIN is an expert system developed to provide advice to a physician responsible for diagnosing problems with a patient suffering from an infectious blood disease. Details on this system are given in Chapter 5. One of the principal features of this system is its ability to manage inexact information.

This is a typical problem found in many domains but it has a special significance in the medical domain because of the time constraints. In an emergency room, there is a time pressure to quickly perform the diagnosis and select the right action. For a problem with infectious blood diseases, which can be life-threatening, the types of tests the physician would like to perform can take several days to provide complete and exact results—the physician often doesn't have this time. As a result, he is often faced with the problem of incomplete information, because he may have only a few test results to work with, which come back after a few hours with some indication of what the problem might be. Therefore, for this domain in particular, there is special pressure to be able to deal with incomplete and inexact information and still come up with the best possible diagnosis.

There is also the problem of dealing with inexact inference. In medicine, as in many domains, there are very few hard and fast rules. There are a few rules where the physician might be able to say that, if he sees certain symptoms, the patient has a particular disease. However, this type of rule is usually rare. The majority of the rules used in medicine are inexact. Typically the physician will state "If I see symptoms A and B then I have some indication that we are dealing with such-and-such disease." Therefore, we have to confront the challenge of representing and using inexact inference rules.

The MYCIN development team recognized that some inexact reasoning technique would need to be incorporated into the system. They also understood that a probability approach would be inappropriate because of the inability to obtain reliable statistical information about the problem. To manage this situation, the MYCIN team decided to relax the more rigorous requirements of the classical probability technique and seek a simpler approach. They decided to first ask questions concerned with *what* they wanted the inexact reasoning technique to accomplish, rather than *how* it would be accomplished. They felt that observing how the expert works with inexact information would provide the insight needed to develop the requirements of an acceptable inexact reasoning technique.

Representing Uncertain Evidence

The MYCIN team observed that a physician working on an emergency case would often need to work with uncertain or even unknown information. They noted that under such a constraint the physician would often analyze the available information using qualitative terms or phrases such as "probably," "it is likely that. . . ," "it almost seems certain that. . . ."

For uncertain evidence, the MYCIN team decided to ascribe a certainty factor "**CF**" to the evidence, which represented the physician's belief in it. This number was given a range of -1 (definitely false) to $+1$ (definitely true). A positive value represented a degree of belief, while a negative value indicated a degree of disbelief. For example, if the physician stated that some evidence was *probably* true, a CF value of 0.6 was assigned to the evidence.

Representing Uncertain Rules

The MYCIN team also observed that the physician would often derive an inexact inference from available information. That is, given some evidence, the physician might only partially believe some conclusion. For inexact inference, it was decided to ascribe a certainty factor value to each rule. For example, consider the following rule from MYCIN:

IF   The stain of the organism is gram positive
AND   The morphology of the organism is coccus
AND   The growth conformation of the organism is chains
THEN   There is suggestive evidence that the identity of the organism is
          streptococcus CF = 0.7

Given the evidence supplied in the rule's premises, MYCIN would only partially believe in the rule's conclusion, with a level of belief reflected by the certainty factor value of 0.7. In general, rules in MYCIN were represented in the following form, where E_i represents the available evidence, H the conclusion, and CF_i the level of belief in H given the evidence:

$$\text{IF } E_1 \text{ AND } E_2 \ldots \text{ THEN } H \text{ CF} = CF_i$$

Uncertain Inferencing

It was also observed that when the physician's belief in available evidence was less than certain, then the belief in a related inference was also decreased. For example, in the prior rule that concluded that the identity of the organism is streptococcus, if the information contained in the premises were not known with certainty, that is $CF(E_i) < 1$, then the level of belief in the conclusion was reduced, namely $CF(H) < 0.7$. Techniques used in MYCIN to employ uncertain inferencing are discussed later in the chapter.

Combining Evidence From Multiple Sources

When the physician received supporting information for some conclusion from multiple sources, it was noticed that he held a higher belief in the conclusion.

Therefore, the certainty theory must also increase the belief in a conclusion receiving support from multiple rules. Consider for example the following two rules:

Rule 1		**Rule** 2	
IF	A	IF	C
AND	B	AND	D
THEN	Z CF = 0.8	THEN	Z CF = 0.7

Both rules conclude with the same hypothesis, but with different CF values and from different pieces of evidence. The firing of both rules would result in two different CF values for Z—two beliefs in Z.

The question is how do we combine these two beliefs in Z? Do we add them? Is there another formula we can use? In fact, how do we combine a "probably" with a "maybe"?

Instead of looking for some formula, the MYCIN team decided to ask, What would we like the combining function to do? That is, they decided not to concern themselves with the exact formula, but rather what kinds of properties they would like that formula to have. Two basic properties were selected:

- commutative
- asymptotic

The commutative property was important to prevent dependency on the order in which the rules were searched. For example, given our two rules, the same overall level of belief in Z should be obtained regardless of which one was considered first.

It was decided that, unless absolute proof was found for a conclusion by the firing of some rule, the combining function should asymptotically converge towards 1, but never quite reach it. That is, as confirming evidence was acquired about some conclusion, then the overall belief in the conclusion should be partially incremented.

Net Belief

It was also observed that the physician balanced his belief in a hypothesis when confronted with both positive and negative evidence. That is, during the course of acquiring evidence for a given hypothesis, at times some evidence would be found that supported it, while at other times evidence would be found that rejected it. The physician would then weigh the two to obtain a net belief in the hypothesis.

To manage this situation, the MYCIN team decided to form a net belief in a rule's hypothesis. To accomplish this, they first collected together, in a asymptotic and commutative fashion, all supporting information and called it the **measure of belief "MB"** in the hypothesis. Next, all of the information that rejected the hypothesis was collected, again in a asymptotic and commutative fashion, and was called the **measure of disbelief "MD."** The net belief or CF in the hypothesis was then found from the difference between these two values. Consider for example a situation where some of the available information supported a hypothesis H to the degree of $MB(H) = 0.8$, while other evidence supported the rejection of H producing a $MD(H) = 0.2$. In this situation the net level of belief in H would be:

$$CF(H) = 0.8 - 0.2 = 0.6$$

In words, we might say that H is *probably* true.

BASIC CERTAINTY THEORY

The last several sections provided an overview of the needs of the certainty theory model. As discussed, these needs were born out of the way a physician naturally manages inexact information. Even though it was stated that the model was not based on strict probability theory, the early attempts in the formulation of the model used a form of the theory. In this section, we review the basic certainty theory from a probability viewpoint.

The certainty theory first suggests that the prior probability of hypothesis H, $P(H)$, represents the expert's *judgmental* belief in H. The expert's disbelief, $P(\sim H)$, is then assumed according to the traditional probability constraint that states that the probability *for* and *against* a given hypothesis must equal 1:

$$P(H) + P(\sim H) = 1 \tag{1}$$

The theory next suggests that if the expert observes evidence such that the probability of the hypothesis given the evidence (called the conditional probability $P(H|E)$) is greater than the prior probability, that is, if $P(H|E) > P(H)$, then the expert's belief in the hypothesis is proportionally increased according to the ratio :

$$\frac{P(H|E) - P(H)}{1 - P(H)} \qquad \uparrow \quad INC$$

On the other hand, if the evidence produces a probability in the hypothesis that is less than the prior probability, that is, if $P(H|E) < P(H)$, then the expert's belief in the hypothesis would proportionally decrease according to

$$\frac{P(H) - P(H|E)}{P(H)} \qquad \downarrow \quad DEC$$

A central theme of this theory is that a given piece of evidence can either increase or decrease an expert's belief in a hypothesis. This idea was extended by the introduction of two new terms called **measure of belief "MB"** and **measure of disbelief "MD"**:

DEFINITION 12.1: Measure of Belief (MB)
Number that reflects the measure of increased belief in a hypothesis H based on evidence E.

DEFINITION 12.2: Measure of Disbelief (MD)
Number that reflects the measure of increased disbelief in a hypothesis
H based on evidence E.

These numbers are bounded according to the following:

$$0 \leq MB \leq 1$$

$$0 \leq MD \leq 1$$

The measures of belief and disbelief are formally defined in terms of the conditional and prior probabilities according to the following equations:

$$MB(H, E) = \begin{cases} 1 & \text{if } P(H) = 1 \\ \dfrac{\max[P(H|E), P(H)] - P(H)}{1 - P(H)} & \text{otherwise} \end{cases} \quad (2)$$

$$MD(H, E) = \begin{cases} 1 & \text{if } P(H) = 0 \\ \dfrac{\min[P(H|E), P(H)] - P(H)}{-P(H)} & \text{otherwise} \end{cases} \quad (3)$$

where:

$P(H)$ = prior probability of H

$P(H|E)$ = probability that H is true given evidence E

Since several pieces of information might be observed, some adding to the belief or disbelief in the hypothesis, a third measure is also introduced to combine the MB and MD terms into one net number that reflects the overall level of belief in the hypothesis. This net number is called the **certainty factor.**

DEFINITION 12.3: Certainty Factor
Number that reflects the net level of belief in a hypothesis given available information.

The certainty factor is computed from the MB and MD values by way of the following equation

$$CF = MB - MD \quad (4)$$

The CF value is bounded according to the following

$$-1 \leq CF \leq 1$$

A value of -1 represents "definitely false" and $+1$ "definitely true." A value of 0 represents unknown. Negative CF values represent a degree of disbelief in the hypothesis, while positive values a degree of belief in the hypothesis, as illustrated in Figure 12.1. Let's examine equations 2–4 for different cases.

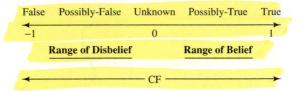

FIGURE 12.1   Range of CF values.

Case 1: Evidence Totally Confirms Hypothesis

If the available evidence E totally confirms the hypothesis H, then

$$P(H|E) = 1$$

and from equations 2 and 3 we find

$$MB(H, E) = 1$$

$$MD(H, E) = 0$$

and from equation 4 it follows that

$$CF(H, E) = 1$$

Therefore, when E totally confirms H, then according to Figure 12.1, H is considered *definitely true*.

Case 2: Evidence Totally Disconfirms

If the available evidence E totally confirms the negation of hypothesis H, then

$$P(\sim H|E) = 1$$

and from equation 1

$$P(H|E) = 1 - P(\sim H|E) = 0$$

and from equations 2 and 3 we find

$$MB(H, E) = 0$$

$$MD(H, E) = 1$$

and from equation 4 it follows that

$$CF(H, E) = -1$$

Therefore, when E totally confirms $\sim H$, then according to Figure 12.1, H is considered *definitely false*.

Case 3: Lack of Evidence

If the available evidence E is independent of the hypothesis, that is, it neither confirms nor disconfirms the hypothesis H, then

$$P(H|E) = P(H)$$

$$H \neq f(E)$$

and from equations 2 and 3 we find

$$MB(H, E) = 0$$

$$MD(H, E) = 0$$

and from equation 4 it follows that

$$CF(H, E) = 0$$

Therefore, when E is independent of H, then according to Figure 12.1, H is considered *unknown*.

Case 4: Positive Evidence

If the available evidence E partially confirms the hypothesis, then

$$P(H) < P(H|E) < 1$$

and from equations 2 and 3 we find

$$MB(H, E) = \frac{P(H|E) - P(H)}{1 - P(H)}$$

$$MD(H, E) = 0$$

and from equation 4 it follows that

$$CF(H, E) = MB(H, E)$$

Therefore, when E partially confirms H, then according to Figure 12.1, $CF(H, E)$ is in the positive range, that is, there is a level of belief in the hypothesis H.

Case 5: Negative Evidence

If the available evidence E partially disconfirms the hypothesis, then

$$0 < P(H|E) < P(H)$$

and from equations 2 and 3 we find

$$MB(H, E) = 0$$

$$MD(H, E) = \frac{P(H) - P(H|E)}{P(H)}$$

and from equation 4 it follows that

$$CF(H, E) = -MD(H, E)$$

Therefore, when E partially disconfirms H, then according to Figure 12.1, $CF(H, E)$ is in the negative range, that is, there is a level of disbelief in the hypothesis H.

Case 6: Many Confirming and One Disconfirming Source

With many sources confirming some hypothesis, the MB value converges to 1

$$\text{MB}(H, E_1, E_2, \ldots) \rightarrow 0.999$$

Next, assume only one disconfirming source of information exists, say,

$$\text{MD}(H, E_i) = 0.8$$

It then follows from equation 4 that

$$\text{CF}(H, E) = \text{MB} - \text{MD} = 0.199$$

The net result is that we have reached a very low belief in the hypothesis. The problem is that many sources of confirming information have been offset by only one piece of disconfirming information.

To help desensitize the effect of a single piece of disconfirming evidence on many confirming pieces of evidence, the original certainty factor definition shown in equation 4, was later adjusted as follows

$$\text{CF}(H, E) = \frac{\text{MB}(H, E) - \text{MD}(H, E)}{1 - \min(\text{MB}(H, E), \text{MD}(H, E))} \tag{5}$$

Using this new definition of CF for our example

$$\text{CF}(H, E) = \frac{0.999 - 0.8}{1 - \min(0.999, 0.8)} = 0.995$$

You can see that the disconfirming evidence now has only a small effect on reducing our belief in the conclusion—a result that is more consistent with human reasoning. Also note that equation 5 will likewise offset the impact of a small number of confirming pieces of information.

From these case studies, we can characterize the relationships between the probability of *H* and the MB and MD values as shown in Table 12.1.

This section introduced the concept of the certainty factor and related it to probability estimates. However, these estimates are difficult to obtain from the expert for most problems. The intent of establishing equations 2–4 is more to show how, in a general sense, $P(H)$ and $P(H|E)$ can be captured in one measure called the certainty factor, CF. Later sections discuss the concept of certainty factor in terms of a more intuitive approach to managing inexact reasoning.

DIFFICULTIES WITH PROBABILITY INTERPRETATION OF CERTAINTY FACTOR

Though the certainty factor is found by way of equations 2 and 3 which use probability estimates, you should recognize that it defies analysis as a probability measure. The following sections illustrate this point.

TABLE 12.1 Relationships between P and MB, MD, and CF

Probabilities	MB, MD, CF Values
Hypothesis True $P(H\|E) = 1$	MB = 1 MD = 0 CF = 1
Hypothesis False $P(\sim H\|E) = 1$	MB = 0 MD = 1 CF = -1
Lack of evidence $P(H\|E) = P(H)$	MB = 0 MD = 0 CF = 0
Positive evidence $P(H) < P(H\|E) < 1$	MB > 0 MD = 0 CF = MB
Negative evidence $0 < P(H\|E) < P(H)$	MB = 0 MD > 0 CF = -MD

Probability For and Against

A basic rule of probability theory is that the sum of the probability for and against a given hypothesis must be equal to 1 (see equation 1). For the certainty factor to meet the same constraint, we would expect that

$$CF(H, E) + CF(\sim H, E) = 1 \tag{6}$$

However, the following analysis will illustrate that equation 6 is not true.

$$CF(\sim H, E) = MB(\sim H, E) - MD(\sim H, E)$$

$$= 0 - \frac{P(\sim H|E) - P(\sim H)}{-P(H)}$$

$$= \frac{(1 - P(H|E)) - (1 - P(H))}{1 - P(H)} = \frac{P(H) - P(H|E)}{1 - P(H)}$$

$$CF(H, E) = MB(H, E) - MD(H, E)$$

$$= \frac{P(H|E) - P(H)}{1 - P(H)} - 0$$

Therefore,

$$CF(H, E) + CF(\sim H, E) = \frac{P(H|E) - P(H)}{1 - P(H)} + \frac{P(H|E) - P(H)}{1 - P(H)} = 0$$

or,

$$CF(H, E) = -CF(\sim H, E)$$

Therefore, for any H and E, $MB(H, E) = MD(\sim H, E)$. Clearly then the result does not follow the strict probability constraint of equation 6. The result of this analysis also shows that evidence supporting a hypothesis reduces the support to the negation of the hypothesis to an equal amount. Consider the following example which will help illustrate the impact of this result.

IF   The person is a heavy smoker
THEN   The person will get heart disease CF = 0.6

If we are absolutely sure that the person is a heavy smoker, then

MB(heart disease, heavy smoker) = 0.6
MD(not heart disease, heavy smoker) = 0.6

This result is intuitively appealing; however, it assumes a numeric result for $MD(\sim H, E)$ which may not always be correct for a given problem.

Conditional Certainty Factor

The certainty factor represents a conditional statement. However, it fails to behave like a normal conditional probability number. To illustrate this point, suppose the following information is given:

$$P(H_1) = 0.7 \qquad P(H_2) = 0.2$$

$$P(H_1|E) = 0.9 \qquad P(H_2|E) = 0.8$$

Then according to equation 2:

$$MB(H_1|E) = 0.666 = CF(H_1|E)$$

$$MB(H_2|E) = 0.750 = CF(H_2|E)$$

The result found from the certainty factor calculations would indicate a higher degree of belief of H_2 occurring than H_1, even though $P(H_1) > P(H_2)$ and $P(H_1|E) > P(H_2|E)$. This presents us with an obvious contradiction.

The moral here is not to interpret certainty factors as probabilities. While the certainty theory has some basis in the probability theory, the actual defining equations eventually developed are more *ad hoc*, and designed to mimic inexact reasoning in humans.

ed hak

——————— **PRACTICAL CERTAINTY MODEL** ———————

Over the years the certainty model has evolved into a very practical technique for managing inexact reasoning in an expert system. The concepts of the certainty theory discussed earlier—MB, MD and CF terms—are still employed, but in a very simple fashion. In the following sections we review the present form and use of the certainty model.

Uncertain Evidence

Systems that employ inexact reasoning must first find a way of representing uncertain evidence. For example, consider the statement "It will *probably* rain today." There is a degree of uncertainty associated with this statement through the use of the word *probably*.

The certainty model represents uncertain statements using CF values following the approach illustrated in Figure 12.1. That is, it maps the uncertain statement to a CF number between −1 and +1 that represents the degree of belief in the statement. For example, the prior uncertain statement would be written as

$$CF(E) = CF(\text{It will } \textit{probably} \text{ rain today}) = 0.6$$

This approach replaces the more formal probability $P(E)$ with $CF(E)$. Table 12.2 shows a typical CF value mapping for various uncertain terms.

Certainty factors are not probabilities, but are informal measures of confidence for a piece of evidence. They represent the degree to which we believe that the evidence is true. To represent this belief in the expert system, we would write the statement as an exact term, but add the appropriate CF value to it. For example:

It will *probably* rain today

or

It will rain today   CF 0.6

Uncertain Rules

Just as CF values can be attached to statements, they can also be attached to rules to represent the uncertain relationship between the evidence E given in the

TABLE 12.2   CF Value Interpretation

Uncertain Term	CF
Definitely not	−1.0
Almost certainly not	−0.8
Probably not	−0.6
Maybe not	−0.4
Unknown	−.2 to .2
Maybe	0.4
Probably	0.6
Almost certainly	0.8
Definitely	1.0

rule's premise and the hypothesis H given the rule's conclusion. The basic structure of a rule used in the certainty model is as follows:

$$\text{IF } E \text{ THEN } H \quad \text{CF(RULE)}$$

where CF(RULE) represents the level of belief of H given E. That is, given that E is true, we believe H according to

$$\text{CF}(H, E) = \text{CF(RULE)}$$

Consider for example the following rule

Rule 1
IF   There are dark clouds   —E
THEN   It will rain   —H
CF =   0.8

In words this rule would read according to Table 12.2:

"If there are dark clouds then it will *almost certainly* rain."

Certainty Propagation for Single Premise Rules

Certainty factor propagation is concerned with establishing the level of belief in a rule's conclusion when the available evidence contained in the rule's premise is uncertain. For a single premise rule, you simply multiply the CF value of the premise with the CF value of the rule

$$\text{CF}(H, E) = \text{CF}(E)*\text{CF(RULE)} \tag{7}$$

Consider for example the prior RULE 1. If we have positive evidence for the rule's premise to the degree of CF(E) = 0.5, then the established belief in the rule's conclusion is

$$\text{CF}(H, E) = 0.5*0.8 = 0.4$$

In words, this result would read according to Table 12.2:

"It *maybe* will rain."

For the same rule, if we have negative evidence for the rule's premise to the degree of CF(E) = −0.5, then the established belief in the rule's conclusion is

$$\text{CF}(H, E) = -0.5*0.8 = -0.4$$

Or, in words:

"It *maybe not* will rain."

You should notice from these two examples that the approach shown in equation 7 is consistent with the certainty theory. That is, evidence adds to either the belief or disbelief in a hypothesis.

Certainty Propagation for Multiple Premise Rules

For rules with more than one premise, the certainty factor for the rule's conclusion is established using a approach similar to that used in the PROSPECTOR system. That is, the MYCIN team assumed conditional independence of evidence in forming a belief in a hypothesis that was supported by conjunctive or disjunctive rules.

Conjunctive Rules

For conjunctive rules, the approach used in the certainty model is as follows:

$$\text{IF } E_1 \text{ AND } E_2 \text{ AND} \ldots \text{THEN } H \quad \text{CF(RULE)}$$

$$CF(H, E_1 \text{ AND } E_2 \text{ AND} \ldots) = \min\{CF(E_i)\}*CF(RULE) \tag{8}$$

The "min" function returns the minimum value of a set of numbers.
Consider the following example:

IF   The sky is dark
AND   The wind is getting stronger
THEN   It will rain
CF =   0.8

Assume that our belief in the two premises can be expressed by the following certainty values:

$$CF(\text{The sky is dark}) = 1.0$$

and

$$CF(\text{The wind is getting stronger}) = 0.7$$

Then according to equation 8, we can calculate the belief in rain from

$$CF(\text{It will rain}) = \min\{1.0, 0.7\}*0.8 = 0.56$$

According to Table 12.2, we would conclude in words "It *probably* will rain."

Disjunctive Rules

For disjunctive rules, the approach taken to determine the belief in the hypothesis is as follows:

$$\text{IF } E_1 \text{ OR } E_2 \text{ OR} \ldots \text{THEN } H \quad \text{CF(RULE)}$$

$$CF(H, E_1 \text{ OR } E_2 \text{ OR} \ldots) = \max\{CF(E_i|E')\}*CF(RULE) \tag{9}$$

The "max" function returns the maximum value of a set of numbers. Consider the past example with the premises joined conjunctively:

IF   The sky is dark
OR   The wind is getting stronger

THEN   It will rain
CF =   0.9

CF(It will rain) = max{1.0, 0.7}*0.9 = 0.9

Or in words, "It *almost certainly* will rain."

Certainty Propagation for Similarly Concluded Rules

In some applications, you will need to write multiple rules that support a hypothesis. Consider again the problem of rain prediction, but this time assume the evidence comes from two different individuals—weatherman and farmer:

Rule 1
IF   The weatherman says it is going to rain $\rightarrow E_1$
THEN   It is going to rain $\rightarrow H$
CF(RULE 1) = 0.8

Rule 2
IF   The farmer says it is going to rain $\rightarrow E_2$
THEN   It is going to rain $\rightarrow H$
CF(RULE 2) = 0.8

These two rules conclude the possibility of rain from two different sources. The CF values of the two rules have been set equal—implying equal confidence in the two sources for predicting rain.

A natural part of human reasoning is that if we obtain supporting evidence for a given conclusion from two different sources, we should feel more confident in that conclusion. For example, if both the weatherman and farmer tell us that it is going to rain, then we should feel more confident about the likelihood of rain than if only one told us. Using this idea, the MYCIN team developed a technique known as **incrementally acquired evidence** to combine belief and disbelief values established by rules concluding the same hypothesis. Consider the following two rules:

Rule 1   **Rule 2**
IF E_1 IF E_2
THEN H THEN H

The original form of the incrementally acquired evidence equation combined multiple MB or MD values (Shortliffe and Buchanan 1975):

$$MB[H, E_1 \& E_2] = 0 \quad \text{if } MD[H, E_1 \& E_2] = 1$$
$$= MB[H, E_1] + MB[H, E_2]*[1 - MB[H, E_1]] \quad \text{otherwise} \tag{10}$$

$$MD[H, E_1 \& E_2] = 0 \quad \text{if } MB[H, E_1 \& E_2] = 1$$
$$= MD[H, E_1] + MD[H, E_2]*[1 - MD[H, E_1]] \quad \text{otherwise} \tag{11}$$

Equations 10 and 11 state that the MB or MD of a newly acquired piece of evidence E_2 should be added proportionally to the value determined from the earlier evidence E_1. The new values for MB and MD are then used to update the confidence in H, namely CF = MB—MD.

In some applications it is valuable to maintain an account of the MB and MD values as they are adjusted when new information is discovered. However, in other applications, we are only concerned with maintaining a record of the updated CF value. In these applications, we can use the following equation:

$$CF_{COMBINE}(CF_1, CF_2) = CF_1 + CF_2*(1 - CF_1) \qquad \text{both} > 0$$
$$= \frac{CF_1 + CF_2}{1 - \min\{|CF_1|, |CF_1|\}} \qquad \text{one} < 0 \qquad (12)$$
$$= CF_1 + CF_2*(1 + CF_1) \qquad \text{both} < 0$$

Here, CF_1 represents the confidence in H established by one rule (e.g., RULE 1) and CF_2 the confidence in H established by another rule (e.g., RULE 2).

There are two properties of equations 10—12 that were discussed earlier as being desirable for the certainty model:

- Commutative
- Asymptotic

Commutative   The certainty model needs to be commutative to allow for evidence to be gathered in any order. That is, if more than one rule gathers information, then the combined CF value can not be dependent upon the order of the processing of the rules.

Asymptotic   The asymptotic requirement was made for two reasons. The first reflects the manner in which the physician gathers confidence about some hypothesis from multiple sources of information. If more than one source confirms a hypothesis, the physician feels *somewhat* more confident in the hypothesis. Therefore, the certainty model must incrementally add belief to a hypothesis as new positive evidence is obtained.

The second reason for requiring the certainty model to be asymptotic is to prevent the certainty value of the hypothesis from exceeding 1. That is, unless we encounter some evidence that absolutely confirms a hypothesis, we cannot be totally certain of the hypothesis. Therefore, the combining equation should converge towards 1, but never quite reach this value unless we receive absolute proof from some rule.

Consider the two rain prediction rules given earlier—RULES 1 and 2. Let's explore several test cases to examine the application of the incrementally acquired evidence technique.

Case 1: Weatherman and Farmer Are Certain in Rain

$$CF(E_1) = CF(E_2) = 1.0$$

From equation 7:

$$CF_1(H, E_1) = CF(E_1)*CF(\text{RULE } 1)$$

$$= 1.0*0.8 = 0.8$$

$$CF_2(H, E_2) = CF(E_2)*CF(\text{RULE } 2)$$

$$= 1.0*0.8 = 0.8$$

From equation 12:

$$CF_{\text{COMBINE}}(CF_1, CF_2) = CF_1 + CF_2*(1 - CF_1)$$

$$= 0.8 + 0.8*(1 - 0.8)$$

$$= 0.96$$

This example demonstrates how the certainty factor of a given hypothesis, which is supported by more than one rule, can be incrementally increased by acquiring supporting evidence from both rules. This is intuitively appealing because we should be more confident in rain after receiving additional confirmation.

Case 2: Weatherman Certain in Rain, Farmer Certain in No Rain

$$CF(E_1) = 1.0$$

$$CF(E_2) = -1.0$$

From equation 7:

$$CF_1(H, E_1) = CF(E_1)*CF(\text{RULE } 1)$$

$$= 1.0*0.8 = 0.8$$

$$CF_2(H, E_2) = CF(E_2)*CF(\text{RULE } 2)$$

$$= -1.0*0.8 = -0.8$$

From equation 12:

$$CF_{\text{COMBINE}}(CF_1, CF_2) = \frac{CF_1 + CF_2}{1 - \min\{|CF_1|, |CF_1|\}}$$

$$= \frac{0.8 - 0.8}{1 - \min\{0.8, 0.8\}}$$

$$= 0$$

This example demonstrates how the certainty factor of the prediction of rain has been set to "unknown" because one source that confirms rain is offset by another source which discounts it. In general, this example demonstrates how a "net" belief in a hypothesis is obtained by way of equation 12.

Case 3: Weatherman and Farmer Believe at Different Degrees That It Is Not Going to Rain

$$CF(E_1) = -0.8$$

$$CF(E_2) = -0.6$$

From equation 7:

$$CF_1(H, E_1) = CF(E_1)*CF(RULE\ 1)$$

$$= -0.8*0.8 = -0.64$$

$$CF_2(H, E_2) = CF(E_2)*CF(RULE\ 2)$$

$$= -0.6*0.8 = -0.48$$

From equation 12:

$$CF_{COMBINE}(CF_1, CF_2) = CF_1 + CF_2*(1 + CF_1)$$

$$= -0.64 - 0.48*(1 - 0.64)$$

$$= -0.81$$

This example demonstrates an incremental decrease in a hypothesis when more than one source of disconfirming evidence is found.

Case 4: Several Sources Predict Rain at Same Belief Level, but One Source Predicts No Rain

If many different sources confirm rain at the same level of belief, e.g., CF(Rain) = 0.8, the CF value converges towards 1:

$$CF_{COMBINE}(CF_1, CF_2, \ldots) \rightarrow 0.999 = CF_{old}$$

The term CF_{old} represents the collected belief in rain from the "old" sources of information. If a "new" source produces a negative belief in rain:

$$CF_{new} = -0.8$$

then according to equation 12 the updated belief in rain is

$$CF_{COMBINE}(CF_{old}, CF_{new}) = \frac{CF_{old} + CF_{new}}{1 - \min\{|CF_{old}|, |CF_{new}|\}}$$

$$= \frac{0.999 - 0.8}{1 - \min\{0.999, 0.8\}}$$

$$= 0.995$$

The result shows that a single piece of disconfirming evidence does not have a major impact on many pieces of confirming evidence (also see equation 5).

Certainty Propagation for Complex Rules

In some applications, you will need to write rules that contain a combination of conjunctive and disjunctive statements. Consider for example the following:

IF E_1
AND E_2
OR E_3
AND E_4
THEN H
CF = CF(RULE)

You manage certainty factor propagation for rules of this form by a combination of equations 8 and 9. For our example, the result would be

$$CF(H) = \max\{\min(E_1, E_2), \min(E_3, E_4)\} * CF(RULE)$$

———————— CERTAINTY FACTOR EXAMPLE PROGRAM ———

To illustrate the propagation of certainty factors through a set of rules, we will consider a small problem of deciding whether or not I should go to a ballgame. We will assume the hypothesis is "I shouldn't go to the ballgame." A set of rules for this problem is as follows:

Rule 1   CF(RULE 1) = 0.9
IF   The weather looks lousy   E1
OR   I am in a lousy mood   E2
THEN   I shouldn't go to the ballgame   H1

Rule 2   CF(RULE 2) = 0.8
IF   I believe it is going to rain   E3
THEN   The weather looks lousy   E1

Rule 3   CF(RULE 3) = 0.9
IF   I believe it is going to rain   E3
AND   The weatherman says it is going to rain   E4
THEN   I am in a lousy mood   E2

Rule 4   CF(RULE 4) = 0.7
IF   The weatherman says it is going to rain   E4
THEN   The weather looks lousy   E1

Rule 5   CF(RULE 5) = 0.95
IF   The weather looks lousy   E1
THEN   I am in a lousy mood   E2

Assume that the user has entered the following certainty factors for the primitives:

I believe it is going to rain, CF(E3) = 0.95
Weatherman believes it is going to rain, CF(E4) = 0.85

Also assume backward chaining is used with the goal of "I shouldn't go to the ballgame," (H1), and that the rules are exhaustively searched.

STEP 1
Pursue premise 1 of RULE 1 "The weather looks lousy"—E1.

Note that RULE 2 and RULE 4 conclude E1.

STEP 2
Pursue RULE 2

COMMENT: *The system pursues this rule first because it has a higher CF value concluding E1 than RULE 4.*

From equation 7 and the given value of CF(E3):

$$CF(E1, E3) = CF(RULE\ 2)*CF(E3) = 0.8*0.95 = 0.76$$

STEP 3
Pursue RULE 4

From equation 7 and the given value of CF(E4):

$$CF(E1, E4) = CF(RULE\ 4)*CF(E4) = 0.7*0.85 = 0.60$$

STEP 4
We now have two confirmations for E1, "The weather looks lousy," from steps 2 and 3. We now want to combine them using the incrementally acquired evidence approach.

From equation 12 and steps 2 and 3:

$$CF(E1) = CF(E1, E3) + CF(E1, E4)*(1 - CF(E1, E3))$$

$$= 0.76 + 0.60*(1 - 0.76)$$

$$= 0.90$$

STEP 5
Pursue premise 2 of RULE 1 "I am in a lousy mood"—E2.

Note that RULE 3 and RULE 5 conclude E2.

STEP 6
Pursue RULE 5

COMMENT: *The system pursues this rule first because it has a higher CF value concluding E2 than RULE 3.*

From equation 7 and step 4:

$$CF(E2, E1) = CF(RULE\ 5)*CF(E1) = 0.95*0.90 = 0.86$$

STEP 7
Pursue RULE 3

From equation 8, and the given CF(E3) and CF(E4) values:

$$CF(E2, E3 \text{ AND } E4) = \min\{CF(E3), CF(E4)\}*CF(RULE\ 3)$$

$$= \min\{0.95, 0.85\}*0.9$$

$$= 0.77$$

STEP 8
We now have two confirmations for E2, "I am in a lousy mood," from steps 6 and 7. We now want to combine them using the incrementally acquired evidence approach.

From equation 12 and steps 6 and 7:

$$CF(E2) = CF(E2, E1) + CF(E2, E3 \text{ AND } E4)*(1 - CF(E2, E1))$$

$$= 0.86 + 0.77*(1 - 0.86)$$

$$= 0.97$$

STEP 9
Return to RULE 1

From equation 9 and steps 4 and 8:

$$CF(H1, E1 \text{ OR } E2) = \max\{CF(E1), CF(E2)\}*CF(RULE\ 1)$$

$$= \max\{0.9, 0.97\}*0.9$$

$$= 0.87$$

$$= CF(\text{I shouldn't go to the ballgame})$$

In words we would conclude "I *almost definitely* shouldn't go to the ballgame."

--------------- **HEURISTIC SEARCH** ---------------

During the backward-chaining process in the prior example, on two occasions more than one rule competed for attention—see steps 2 and 6. The choice of the rule to pursue first was based on the rule with the highest CF value. This approach is sensible because the system first searches for information in the place where it might expect to find the best answer. In the area of artificial intelligence, this technique is called **best-first search.** Best-first search will look for information in those areas that are expected to provide the highest level of confidence in a rule's conclusion.

Besides simply choosing the rule with the highest CF value, a best-first search technique also provides additional support in obtaining the highest confidence in the goal being pursued. To illustrate this point, consider the following example:

Rule 1
IF   A
AND   B
THEN   C
CF = 0.8

Rule 2
IF   D
THEN   C
CF = 0.7

A system using a best-first search technique would choose RULE 1 first on the basis of its higher CF value. However, if it is found that CF(A)*0.8 < 0.7, then the system would next pursue D because of the possibility of establishing a higher level of belief in C from RULE 2. This approach is taken because of the restriction placed on establishing a belief in a rule's conclusion as was shown in equation 8. That is, CF(C) from RULE 1 can be no greater than the value already established to be below 0.7, while RULE 2 has the potential of obtaining CF(C) = 0.7. In general, a best-first search technique will always pursue those issues that can provide the highest level of belief in the goal being pursued.

CONTROLLING SEARCH WITH CF

You can explicitly control the search by referring to an issue's CF value in a relational fashion within a rule. That is, if the CF value meets certain conditions, then you can direct the search into some new area. Consider the following rule that illustrates this approach:

IF   CF(Problem is electrical system) < 0.5
THEN   GOAL = Problem is fuel system

This rule, stated in words, is "If the CF of the problem being with the electrical system is below 0.5, then set the goal to check out the fuel system." This action has the effect of switching from the search of a goal that seems unlikely, to one that might explain the problem. This type of rule is called a *meta-rule* and is used to control the search.

In general, you can use meta-rules that work with various combinations and relationships of certainty factor values. Most shells can use CF values within rules and have the ability to change the goal, using some form of this example meta-rule.

PRUNING THE SEARCH

When attempting to prove a hypothesis, an expert system must search through all of the rules that support the hypothesis. For a large set of rules, this search process can be time-consuming. Sometimes, you may want to terminate the pursuit of a goal when its level of belief has dropped to a low value. For example, MYCIN caused the current goal to be dropped when its CF value fell into the range of −0.2 to +0.2. Today's shells perform the same function using some form of a ''threshold'' command. For example, the following shells use the listed commands:

LEVEL5	—	THRESHOLD
VP-EXPERT	—	TRUTHTHRESHOLD
GURU	—	UNKNOWN THRESHOLD

Most shells provide a default threshold value that you can change at the beginning of the session. Some shells also permit you to change the threshold value during the course of the session. For example, you can write a rule that changes the threshold value prior to the pursuit of the next goal:

IF . . . THEN . . . AND THRESHOLD = #

Using this approach you can dynamically control the search effort. That is, if you want to be conservative and search for all possible information before abandoning a goal, you can set the threshold to a low value. On the other hand, if the goal to be searched is less critical, you could set the threshold to a high value to avoid unneeded search.

ASKING CF VALUES

When you employ an inexact reasoning technique, you need to design a way for the user to enter his or her level of belief to some question. The most direct way is simply to ask the user to enter a numeric from some scale. For example, using the MYCIN scale of -1 and $+1$, the following question and answer might be provided:

SYSTEM: To what degree do you believe the sky is dark?
USER: 0.6

In many applications this approach is acceptable. However, in some cases the user may feel intimidated in providing a number. In this situation, consider using a menu of qualitative terms that the user can choose from, which you then use to assign a CF value. You can use Table 12.2 as a guide. For example:

SYSTEM: Is the sky dark?

Definitely not
Probably not
Maybe not
Unknown
Maybe
Probably
Definite
USER: Probably

You would then need to write a series of rules that translate the menu selection into the corresponding CF value. For example:

IF   Sky dark = Probably
THEN   Sky condition is known
AND   CF(Sky dark) = 0.6

_____ MULTIVALUED ATTRIBUTES AND CF _____

Recall from Chapter 3 that an object–attribute–value (O-A-V) can be defined to have more than one value. When you employ the certainty model as the technique for performing inexact reasoning, you can assign each value a CF number. Consider for example the following assignments:

Sky condition = dark   CF 0.8
Sky condition = hazy   CF 0.7
Sky condition = clear   CF 0.1

Here the object–attribute "Sky-condition" has been set to three different values each with their own CF number. These CF values could have been initialized at the beginning of the session, assigned by the user, or inferred by rules. They could also be used within rules to infer CF values of another multivalued O-A-V:

IF   Sky condition = dark
THEN   Weather prediction = rain   CF 0.6
IF   Sky condition = hazy
THEN   Weather prediction = clear   CF 0.3

The firing of these two rules would lead to:

Weather prediction = rain   CF 0.48
Weather prediction = clear   CF 0.21

_____ CHOOSING UNCERTAIN ISSUES _____

When you employ an inexact reasoning technique you should recognize that not all of the issues may need to be managed in an uncertain fashion. For example, whereas an issue such as "darkness of the sky" might be uncertain, an issue such as "temperature" would not.

Most shells permit you to explicitly define which issues will be treated in an uncertain manner. For example, LEVEL5 uses the following code:

CONFIDENCE   darkness of the sky

This code causes the system to search for a CF value for the statement "darkness of the sky." Issues not declared in this manner would be considered in a Boolean fashion—either true or false.

————————— ACQUIRING CF VALUES FROM EXPERT —————————

The CF values used in the rules are a natural part of the problem's knowledge. You should think of them as artifacts of subjective terms used by the expert. When the expert discusses the problem, listen for terms or phrases like "probably," "sometimes it . . . ," "maybe." This is not only an indication that an inexact reasoning technique may be needed, but it provides the knowledge for encoding the CF values into the rules following the approach shown in Table 12.2.

DESIGN SUGGESTION: Obtain the CF values from the expert's use of qualified terms.

You should also consider avoiding the direct request of the CF values from the expert. For example, you might be tempted to ask "If the sky is cloudy, to what level do you believe it is going to rain?" Experts are usually apprehensive in providing numbers to qualify their knowledge and the results given may be misleading.

DESIGN SUGGESTION: Don't directly ask the expert for the CF values.

One final piece of advice. As you listen to the expert discuss the problem, it is very easy to miss the use of the subjective terms. Even if you are taking notes, it is likely that you will only note the major points discussed and overlook the subjective terms. Therefore, consider taping the discussion and prepare a complete transcription of the tape later. A complete transcription will uncover the subjective terms that can be used for assigning the CF values.

DESIGN SUGGESTION: Use a transcription of a tape recording of a discussion with the expert to obtain the CF values.

————————— RANKING BELIEF IN HYPOTHESES —————————

Another valuable feature of the certainty factor model is the ability to rank order a set of hypotheses according to their CF values. Consider for example an expert system designed to diagnosis problems with an automobile. The system might have knowledge of a large number of possible automobile problems, all of which would be potential goals to pursue. For a given problem, the system might arrive at varying levels of belief in the cause of the problem, as illustrated by the following list:

PROBLEM	CF
Faulty carburetor	0.87
Clogged fuel filter	0.75
Bad fuel	0.55

This approach presents the user with not only the suspected faults, but their relative likelihoods. The user may then elect to correct the fault that the system deems most likely, or use his own judgement to make a final decision.

───────── DIFFICULTY WITH DEEP INFERENCE CHAINS ──

The certainty factor propagation technique shown in equation 7 can lead to problems for deep inference chains. To illustrate this point, consider the following two rules (note that RULE 1 supports the premise of RULE 2):

Rule 1   **Rule 2**
IF A IF B
THEN B CF = 0.8   THEN C CF = 0.9

The first problem is related to probability theory. In general,

$$P(C|A) \neq P(C|B)*P(B|A)$$

However, the certainty theory model propagates the certainty value through an inference chain as independent probabilities:

$$CF(C, A) = CF(C, B)*CF(B, A)$$

Despite this problem, MYCIN was successful because most of the inference chains were short.

Another problem with deep inference chains is related to the inherent decrease in the certainty value caused by the chain. To illustrate this point, assume that the certainty in A is given as $CF(A) = 0.8$. Now consider how this value propagates through to the level of belief in C:

Rule 1   **Rule 2**
IF $CF(A) = 0.8$ ┌→ IF $CF(B) = 0.64$
THEN $CF(B) = 0.8*0.8 = 0.64$ ─┘   THEN $CF(C) = 0.64*0.9 = 0.58$

This example illustrates that the inference chain reduces the confidence in the top-level hypothesis. In general, as you create a deeper inference chain, you will encounter less of a belief in the original goal. Therefore, if you decide to use the certainty theory approach to manage inexact reasoning, avoid deep inference chains.

DESIGN SUGGESTION: Avoid deep inference chains.

───────── DIFFICULTY WITH MANY SIMILARLY CONCLUDED RULES ─────────

Earlier, it was stated that because of the nature of equation 12, if many different sources confirm a hypothesis at the same level of belief, the CF value converges towards 1. This result creates a problem since the system now assumes a belief in the hypothesis that is much higher than the value agreed upon by a number of experts. For example, all of the experts might agree that the hypothesis is *probably* true, but the system assumes that it is *definitely* true. To avoid this problem, you should refrain from using many rules that conclude the same result.

DESIGN SUGGESTION: Avoid using many rules that conclude the same hypothesis.

——————— DIFFICULTY WITH CONJUNCTIVE RULES ———————

Equation 8 offers a simple approach for combining evidence to form a certainty measure for a rule's conclusion when the premises are in conjunctive form. The technique relies on simply taking the "minimum" premise certainty value and multiplying it by the rule's certainty factor value. For many problems, this approach provides a reasonable method for managing inexact reasoning. However, problems can occur because the technique is only sensitive to information with the minimum certainty factor value. Consider the following rule and supplied premise CF values to illustrate this point.

```
IF      Sky is dark
AND     Wind is getting stronger
AND     Temperature is dropping
THEN    It will rain
CF       0.9
```

CF(Sky is dark) = 1.0

CF(Wind is getting stronger) = 1.0

CF(Temperature is dropping) = 0.1

For the given CF values, we would conclude according to equation 8:

$$CF(\text{It will rain}) = \min\{1.0, 1.0, 0.1\}*0.9 = .09$$

Or in words, according to Table 12.2, we would conclude "I *don't know* if it is going to rain." Therefore, even with complete belief in the first two premises, we are left with an unknown condition for the rule's conclusion. This result points out a potential problem with approaching certainty propagation using equation 8.

In some applications this situation is acceptable. However, if problems occur, consider writing multiple rules with fewer premises that conclude the same hypothesis and combine the collected confidence factor values by way of equation 12. Consider for example the following three rules which replace the earlier rule:

Rule 1
```
IF      Sky is dark
THEN    It will rain
CF       0.7
```

Rule 2
```
IF      Wind is getting stronger
THEN    It will rain
CF       0.6
```

Rule 3
IF   Temperature is dropping
THEN   It will rain
CF   0.6

First notice that we have set the CF values of each of these rules smaller than the earlier rule. This is a natural step since we would expect less confidence in a hypothesis given less information to work with. We can now use the previously supplied CF values for each premise along with equation 12 to obtain the overall level of belief in the conclusion by way of equation 7:

$$CF_1 = 1*0.7 = 0.7$$

$$CF_2 = 1*0.6 = 0.6$$

$$CF_3 = 0.1*0.6 = 0.06$$

Combining CF_1 and CF_2 using equation 12

$$CF_{COMBINE}(CF_1, CF_2) = 0.7 + 0.6*(1 - 0.7) = 0.88 = CF_{old}$$

Next, combine CF_{old} and CF_3:

$$CF_{COMBINE}(CF_{old}, CF_3) = 0.88 + 0.06*(1 - 0.88) = 0.89$$

Using this approach produces a dramatically different result than the earlier single rule, because it is not overly sensitive to one premise.

> **DESIGN SUGGESTION: Avoid using rules with many premises or consider splitting the complex rule into multiple rules.**

SUMMARY ON CERTAINTY THEORY

The certainty theory provides a practical alternative to probability theory for managing inexact reasoning in an expert system. It relies on ascribing judgmental belief values to uncertain statements and is suited for problems that lack a strong statistical basis. Though lacking a formal foundation, the technique offers a simple approach and produces results that are acceptable in many applications.

The major lessons learned in this chapter were:

- Certainty theory provides a judgmental approach for deriving inexact inferences.
- The "measure of belief" (MB) is a number that reflects the measure of increased belief in a hypothesis H based on evidence E.
- The "measure of disbelief" (MD) is a number that reflects the measure of increased disbelief in a hypothesis H based on evidence E.
- The "certainty factor" (CF) is a number that reflects the net level of belief in a hypothesis given available information: CF = MB − MD.
- Certainty theory uses rules of the form:

    If E Then H CF(RULE)

where CF(RULE) represents the level of belief of H given E.

- For a single premise rule:

$$CF(H, E) = CF(E)*CF(RULE)$$

- For a conjunctive rule:

$$CF(H, E_1 \text{ AND } E_2 \ldots) = \min\{CF(E_i)\}*CF(RULE)$$

- For a disjunctive rule:

$$CF(H, E_1 \text{ OR } E_2 \ldots) = \max\{CF(E_i|E')\}*CF(RULE)$$

- For a hypothesis concluded by more than one rule, the various CF values are combined using a technique called "incrementally acquired evidence."
- The CF value can be used to guide the search into areas that appear most promising.
- The CF value can be used to terminate the search if it appears unlikely to provide support for a goal. → THRESHOLD
- Hypotheses can be rank ordered according to their CF values, and presented as a list of final recommendations.

REFERENCES

Shortliffe, E.H., S.G. Axline, B.G. Buchanan, T.C. Merigan, and S.N. Cohen, An Artificial Intelligence Program to Advise Physicians Regarding Antimicrobial Therapy, Computers and Biomedical Research, vol. 6, pp. 544–560, 1973.

Shortliffe, E.H. and B.G. Buchanan, A Model of Inexact Reasoning in Medicine, Mathematical Biosciences, vol. 23, pp. 351–379, 1975.

EXERCISES

1. Discuss why certainty theory is an attractive approach for drawing inexact inferences.
2. List several problems where the certainty theory approach would be appropriate.
3. Provide an example where probability constraints would fail.
4. Discuss the advantage of maintaining separately the MB and MD values of a hypothesis.
5. For the following information and rules, determine the CF value of each conclusion.

$$CF(A) = 0.8 \qquad CF(B) = 0.7 \qquad CF(C) = -0.4$$

RULE 1		RULE 2		RULE 3		RULE 4		RULE 5	
IF	A	IF	A	IF	A	IF	C	IF	A
THEN	M	OR	B	AND	B	THEN	P	AND	B
CF =	0.8	THEN	N	THEN	P	CF = 0.7		OR	A
		CF =	0.9	CF =	0.6			AND	C
								THEN	Q
								CF =	0.8

6. Explain MYCIN's incrementally acquired evidence approach.

7. Given the following rules and information, use the incrementally acquired evidence approach to determine the level of belief that you will get the job.

> You are definitely smart.
> You may have some talent.
> You will probably accept a pay cut.
> You will definitely not move.

> IF   You are smart   THEN   You get the job   CF 0.8
> IF   You have talent   THEN   You get the job   CF 0.7
> IF   You will take a pay cut   THEN   You get the job   CF 0.6
> IF   You will move   THEN   You get the job   CF 0.5

8. Using the following rules and information, determine investment recommendations.

> CF(Interest rate low) = 0.7   CF(Interest rate high) = 0.2
> CF(Inflation low) = 0.6   CF(Inflation high) = 0.5
> CF(Employment good) = 0.6   CF(Stock prices low) = 0.4
> CF(Stock prices high) = 0.6

> R1   IF   Interest rate low   R2   IF   Interest rate high
>   AND   Inflation low   AND   Inflation high
>   THEN   Market steady   CF 0.9   THEN   Market unsteady   CF 0.8

> R3   IF   Market steady   R4   IF   Stock prices low
>   OR   Employment good   THEN   Buy stocks   CF 0.7
>   THEN   Buy stocks   CF 0.8

> R5   IF   Market unsteady   R6   IF   Bond prices low
>   AND   Employment good   THEN   Buy bonds   CF 0.6
>   THEN   Buy bonds CF 0.9

9. Discuss the advantages and disadvantages of the CF approach to managing a situation where many sources confirm a hypothesis while only one disconfirms it.

10. Discuss several ways the CF value can be used to control the search.

11. Describe a problem that has both certain and uncertain issues.

12. Describe techniques for acquiring the CF values from the expert.

13. Why should deep inference chains be avoided?

CHAPTER **13**

Fuzzy Logic

INTRODUCTION

Experts often rely on *common sense* to solve problems. We see this type of knowledge exposed when an expert describes a problem using vague or ambiguous terms. For example, the expert might state, "When the motor is running *really hot* I decrease the speed *a little*." We are accustomed to hearing a problem described in this manner, and usually have little difficulty with interpreting the use of the vague terms. However, providing a computer with the same understanding is a challenge—How can we represent and reason with vague terms in a computer?

This chapter answers the question by exploring the subject of **fuzzy logic.** We first review the basic ideas behind fuzzy logic and then look at its mathematical formalism. We then see how fuzzy logic can be employed in an expert system. The chapter also provides a structured approach for designing a fuzzy expert system and illustrates the process through the design of an example system.

OVERVIEW OF FUZZY LOGIC

Fuzzy systems have been around since the 1920s, when they were first proposed by Lukasiewicz (the inventor of reverse Polish notation) (Rescher 1969). Lukasiewicz studied the mathematical representation of "fuzzy" terms such as *tall*, *old*, or *hot*. His motivation for the work came from an understanding that these types of terms defied a truth representation in the two-valued [0,1] Aristotelian logic: true or false.

He developed a system of logic that extended the range of truth values to all real numbers in the range of 0 to 1. He used a number in this set to represent the *possibility* that a given statement was true or false. For example, the possibility that a person 6 feet tall is really tall might be set to a value of 0.9; it is *very likely* that the person is tall. This research led to a formal inexact reasoning technique aptly named **possibility theory.**

In 1965, Zadeh (1965) extended the work on the possibility theory into a formal system of mathematical logic. Possibly more important, Zadeh brought to the attention of scientists and engineers a collection of valuable concepts for working with *fuzzy* natural language terms that were almost exclusively in the hands of academic philosophers for the past forty years. This new logic tool for representing and manipulating fuzzy terms was called **fuzzy logic.**

> **DEFINITION 13.1:** Fuzzy Logic
> A branch of logic that uses degrees of membership in sets rather than a strict true/false membership.

Linguistic Variables

Fuzzy logic is primarily concerned with quantifying and reasoning about vague or fuzzy terms that appear in our natural language. In fuzzy logic, these fuzzy terms are referred to as **linguistic variables** (also called fuzzy variables).

TABLE 13.1   Examples of Linguistic Variables With Typical Values

Linguistic Variable	Typical Values
temperature	hot, cold
height	short, medium, tall
speed	slow, creeping, fast

DEFINITION 13.2: Linguistic Variable
Term used in our natural language to describe some concept that usually has vague or fuzzy values.

For example, in the statement "Jack is young," we are saying that the implied linguistic variable **age** has the linguistic value of **young.** Table 13.1 shows other examples of linguistic variables and typical values that we might assign to them.

In fuzzy expert systems, we use linguistic variables in *fuzzy rules*. A fuzzy rule infers information about a linguistic variable contained in its conclusion from information about another variable contained in its premise. For example:

Rule 1
IF   Speed is slow
THEN   Make the acceleration high

Rule 2
IF   Temperature is low
AND   Pressure is medium
THEN   Make the speed very slow

We call the range of possible values of a linguistic variable the variable's **universe of discourse.** For example, we might give the variable "speed" used in RULE 1 the range between 0 and 100 mph. The phrase "speed is slow" occupies a section of the variable's universe of discourse—it is a fuzzy set.

Fuzzy Sets

Traditional set theory views the world as black or white. That is, an object is either in or not in a given set. Consider for example a set consisting of *young* people, i.e., children. Traditional set theory would set a sharp boundary on this set and give each set member the value of 1, and all members not within the set a value of 0; this is called a crisp set. For instance, set members might consist of only those people whose age is less than 10. Using this strict interpretation, on a person's eleventh birthday their childhood suddenly vanishes.

Fuzzy logic provides a more reasonable interpretation of *young* people using a **fuzzy set.** A fuzzy set assigns membership values between 0 and 1 that reflect more naturally a member's association with the set. For example, if a person's age is 5, we might assign a membership value of 0.9, or if the age is 13, a value

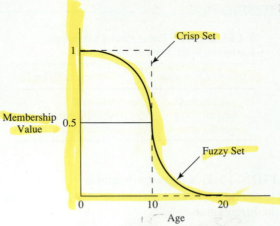

FIGURE 13.1 Fuzzy and crisp sets of "young" people.

of 0.1. In this example "age" is the linguistic variable and "young" one of its fuzzy sets. Other sets that we might consider are "old," "middle-age," etc. Each of these sets represent an *adjective* defined on the linguistic variable.

In general, a fuzzy set provides a graceful transition across a boundary as illustrated in Figure 13.1. The *x*-axis, or universe of discourse, represents a person's age. The *y*-axis is the fuzzy set membership value. The fuzzy set of "young" people maps age values into corresponding membership values. You can see from the figure that our 11-year-old person is no longer suddenly not a child. The person is gradually removed from this classification as his age increases.

Formally, we can define a fuzzy set as:

DEFINITION 13.3: Fuzzy Set
Let *X* be the universe of discourse, with elements of *X* denoted as *x*. A fuzzy set *A* of *X* is characterized by a membership function $\mu_A(x)$ that associates each element *x* with a degree of membership value in *A*.

In contrast to probability theory, which relies on assigning probabilities to a given event on the basis of prior frequencies of the event, fuzzy logic assigns values to the event on the basis of a **membership function** defined as:

$$\mu_A(x) : X \rightarrow [0, 1] \tag{1}$$

In fuzzy logic, event or element *x* is assigned a membership value by a membership function μ. This value represents the degree to which element *x* belongs to fuzzy set *A*.

$$\mu_A(x) = \text{Degree}(x \in A) \tag{2}$$

The membership value of *x* is bounded by the following relationship:

$$0 \leq \mu_A(x) \leq 1$$

A fuzzy set is an extension of the traditional set theory. It generalizes the membership concept by using the membership function μ that returns a value between 0 and 1 that represents the **degree of membership** (also called membership value) an object x has to set A.

FORMING FUZZY SETS

To represent a fuzzy set in a computer we need to define its membership function. One approach that we can use is to poll a group of people for their understanding of the term that we are attempting to represent by the fuzzy set. For example, consider the concept of a *tall* person. We could ask each of these individuals to what degree they believe a person of a given height is *tall*. After acquiring answers for a range of heights, we could perform simple averaging to produce a fuzzy set of *tall* people. We can now use this function to ascribe a belief (or membership value) to a given individual that they belong to the fuzzy set of *tall* people.

We could continue this polling to account for other height descriptions such as *short*, or *medium*. In this fashion we can obtain fuzzy sets that reflect the popular opinion of most people for each of these classifications. This point is illustrated in Figure 13.2 where fuzzy sets are shown in a piecewise linear form for the issues of three different categories of an individual's height. When we define multiple fuzzy sets on the same universe of discourse, the fuzzy literature often refers to them as *fuzzy subsets*.

By forming fuzzy subsets for various vague terms, we can ascribe a membership value of a given object to each set. Consider Figure 13.2 again. An individual

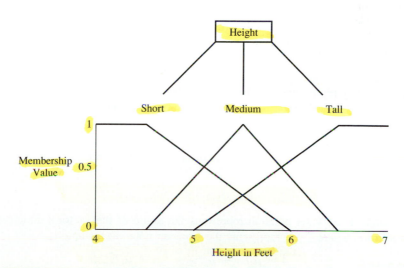

FIGURE 13.2 Fuzzy sets on height.

of a height of 5.5 feet is a member of *medium* persons with a membership value of 1, and at the same time a member of *short* and *tall* persons with a value of 0.25. This is an interesting result—a single object is considered a *partial* member of multiple sets. You will see the value of this point later when we review the operation of a fuzzy expert system.

Another approach often found in practice for forming a fuzzy set relies strictly on the interpretation of a single expert. Like the prior polling technique, you can ask the expert for his belief that various objects belong to a given set. Though this approach lacks the input from a wider audience, it does provide the expert's understanding of the concept.

A more recent approach described by Kosko (1992) relies on a neural network technique. This approach is usually seen in control type applications, where the neural network uses data on the system's operation to derive through a learning mode the form of the fuzzy set.

FUZZY SET REPRESENTATION

Prior sections introduced fuzzy sets and discussed their value in capturing quantitatively ambiguous terms used in our natural language. In this section, we introduce a formal representation of fuzzy sets.

Assume we have a universe of discourse X and a fuzzy set A defined on it. Further assume we have a discrete set of X elements $\{x_1, x_2, \ldots, x_n\}$. The fuzzy set A defines the membership function $\mu_A(x)$ that maps the elements x_i of X to the degree of memberships in $[0,1]$ (see equation 1). The membership values indicate to what degree x_i belongs to A (see equation 2). For a discrete set of elements, a convenient way of representing a fuzzy set is through the use of a vector:

$$A = (a_1, a_2, \ldots, a_n) \tag{3}$$

where,

$$a_i = \mu_A(x_i) \tag{4}$$

For a clearer representation, the vector often includes the symbol "/" which associates the membership value a_i with its x_i coordinate:

$$A = (a_1/x_1, a_2/x_2, \ldots, a_n/x_n) \tag{5}$$

As an example, consider the fuzzy set of tall people shown previously in Figure 13.2:

$$\text{TALL} = (0/5, 0.25/5.5, 0.7/6, 1/6.5, 1/7)$$

Standard fuzzy set notation represents the union of the vector's dimensions as follows; where "+" represents the Boolean notation for union:

$$A = \mu_1/x_1 + \mu_2/x_2 + \ldots + \mu_n/x_n \tag{6}$$

or

$$A = \sum_{i=1}^{n} \mu_i / x_i$$

If X is a continuous function, then the set A can be represented as:

$$A = \int_x \mu_A(x_i)/x_i \qquad (7)$$

For a continuous set of elements, we need some function to map the elements to their membership values. Typical functions used are sigmoid (see Figure 13.1), gaussian, and pi. These types of functions are smooth and can typically provide a close representation of the data that is the basis of the fuzzy set. However, these functions add to the computational load of the computer.

In practice, most applications rely on a piecewise linear fit function to represent the fuzzy set as illustrated in Figure 13.2. To capture a linear fit, we can code each fuzzy set into a **fit-vector.** For example, we can code the fuzzy set *tall* of Figure 13.2 in the vector (0/5, 0.3/5.5, 0.7/6, 1/6.5, 1/7). Mid-range fuzzy sets, such as *medium* of Figure 13.2, are usually represented by a triangular fit-vector function such as (0/4.5, 0.5/5, 1/5.5, 0.5/6, 0/6.5). Fuzzy logic development tools on the market often encode a triangular function using end-point and mid-point vector coding. For example, we could code the *medium* fuzzy set of Figure 13.2 using a vector of the form (0/4.5, 1/5.5, 0/6.5).

_____ **HEDGES** _____

Prior sections described methods for both capturing and representing vague linguistic terms quantitatively through the use of a fuzzy set. In normal conversations, humans may add additional vagueness to a given statement by using adverbs such as *very, slightly,* or *somewhat.* An adverb is a word that modifies a verb, an adjective, another adverb, or a whole sentence. Consider for example an adverb modifying an adjective, "The person is *very* tall."

If we needed to represent this new fuzzy set, we could poll the same group of people used in obtaining our earlier fuzzy set on *tall persons.* However, techniques are available for working with an existing fuzzy set to capture the impact of an added adverb. This is the subject of **hedges.**

A hedge modifies mathematically an existing fuzzy set to account for some added adverb. For example, Figure 13.3 shows the three fuzzy sets on height shown previously in Figure 13.2, along with the sets adjusted by the introduction of the term *very* derived through an operation discussed later.

To illustrate the impact of a fuzzy set modified by a hedge operation, consider a person 6 ft tall. According to Figure 13.3 we consider this individual *tall* with a belief 0.7. However, as also shown in Figure 13.3, we consider the same

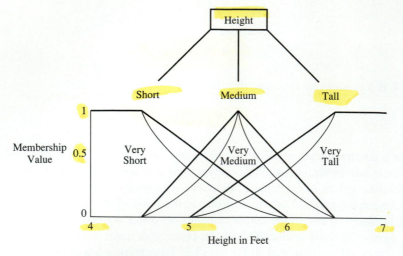

FIGURE 13.3   Fuzzy sets on height with "very" hedge.

individual *very tall* to a belief of 0.4—a reasonable result. The next sections discuss the hedges commonly used in practice.

Concentration (Very)

The concentration operation has the effect of further reducing the membership values of those elements that have smaller membership values. This operation is given as

$$\mu_{CON(A)}(x) = (\mu_A(x))^2 \tag{8}$$

Given a fuzzy set of *tall persons*, we could use this operation to create the set of *very tall persons*.

Dilation (Somewhat)

The dilation operation dilates the fuzzy elements by increasing the membership value of those elements with small membership values more than those elements with high membership values. This operation is given as

$$\mu_{DIL(A)}(x) = (\mu_A(x))^{0.5} \tag{9}$$

Given a fuzzy set of *medium persons*, we could use this operation to create the set of *more or less medium persons*.

Intensification (Indeed)

The intensification operation has the effect of intensifying the meaning of the phrase by increasing the membership values above 0.5 and decreasing those below 0.5. This operation is given as

$$\mu_{INT(A)}(x) = 2(\mu_A(x))^2 \qquad \text{for } 0 \le \mu_A(x) \le 0.5$$
$$= 1 - 2(1 - \mu_A(x))^2 \qquad \text{for } 0.5 < \mu_A(x) \le 1 \tag{10}$$

Given a fuzzy set of *medium persons*, we could use this operation to create the set of *indeed medium persons.*

Power (Very Very)

The power operation is an extension of the concentration operation.

$$\mu_{POW(A)}(x) = (\mu_A(x))^n \tag{11}$$

Given a fuzzy set of *tall persons*, we could use this operation with $n = 3$ to generate a set of *very very tall persons.*

———————— FUZZY SET OPERATIONS ————————

Intersection

In classical set theory, the intersection of two sets contains those elements that are common to both. However, in fuzzy sets, an element may be partially in both of the sets. Therefore, when considering the **intersection** of these two sets, we can't say that an element is more likely to be in the intersection than in one of the original sets.

To account for this, the fuzzy operation for creating the intersection of two fuzzy sets A and B defined on X is given as

$$\mu_{A \wedge B}(X) = \min(\mu_A(x), \mu_B(x)) \qquad \text{for all } x \in X$$
$$= \mu_A(x) \wedge \mu_B(x) \tag{12}$$
$$= \mu_A(x) \cap \mu_B(x)$$

The symbol $\wedge$ (called the logical "AND") is used in fuzzy logic to represent the "min" operation. It simply takes the minimum of the values under consideration. To illustrate this operation, consider the fuzzy sets of tall and short persons:

$$\text{TALL} = (0/5, 0.2/5.5, 0.5/6, 0.8/6.5, 1/7)$$

$$\text{SHORT} = (1/5, 0.8/5.5, 0.5/6, 0.2/6.5, 0/7)$$

According to equation 12, the intersection of these two sets is:

$$\mu_{\text{TALL} \wedge \text{SHORT}}(x) = (0/5,\ 0.2/5.5,\ 0.5/6,\ 0.2/6.5,\ 0/7)$$

When we consider the term "tall and short" it is reasonable to interpret the term as meaning "medium." With this interpretation, we would expect the highest degree of membership to be in the middle of the set, and the lowest at the set limits. This is the result we observe when we form the intersection of the "tall" and "short" fuzzy sets. This example illustrates how two fuzzy sets can be combined to form a new set. The linguistic term we might apply to this new set might be *medium height persons*.

Union

A second way of combining fuzzy sets is through their **union.** The union of two sets is comprised of those elements that belong to one or both sets. In this situation, the members of the union cannot have a membership value that is less than the membership value of either of the original sets. Fuzzy logic uses the following equation to form the union of two sets A and B:

$$\begin{aligned}
\mu_{A \vee B}(x) &= \max(\mu_A(x),\ \mu_B(x)) \quad \text{for all } x \in X \\
&= \mu_A(x) \vee \mu_B(x) \\
&= \mu_A(x) \cup \mu_B(x)
\end{aligned} \tag{13}$$

The symbol $\vee$ (called the logical "OR") is used in fuzzy logic to represent the "max" operation. It takes the maximum of the values under consideration. To illustrate this operation, consider again the two fuzzy sets of tall and short persons.

$$\text{TALL} = (0/5,\ 0.2/5.5,\ 0.5/6,\ 0.8/6.5,\ 1/7)$$

$$\text{SHORT} = (1/5,\ 0.8/5.5,\ 0.5/6,\ 0.2/6.5,\ 0/7)$$

According to equation 13, the intersection of these two sets is

$$\mu_{\text{TALL} \vee \text{SHORT}}(x) = (1/5,\ 0.8/5.5,\ 0.5/6,\ 0.8/6.5,\ 1/7)$$

The results indicate the union membership attains its highest values at the limits and its lowest at the middle of the set. A linguistic interpretation of this new set might be *not medium*.

Complementation (Not)

Given the fuzzy set A, we can find its complement $\sim A$ by the following operation:

$$\mu_{\sim A}(x) = 1 - \mu_A(x) \tag{14}$$

Given a fuzzy set of *tall persons,* this operation could be used to create the set of *not tall persons* or *medium or short persons.*

$$\mu_A(x) = \text{TALL} = (0/5, 0.2/5.5, 0.5/6, 0.8/6.5, 1/7)$$

$$\mu_{\sim A}(x) = \text{NOT TALL} = (1/5, 0.8/5.5, 0.5/6, 0.2/6.5, 0/7)$$

DERIVING ADDITIONAL FUZZY SETS

Using hedges and fuzzy set operations we can derive a variety of other fuzzy sets from existing ones. Assume for example we have a fuzzy set A of *tall persons.* We could derive a set B of *not very tall persons* from the following operation:

$$\mu_B(x) = 1 - (\mu_A(x))^2$$

To extend this idea, assume we have the fuzzy sets A of *tall persons* and B of *short persons.* We could derive a set C of *not very tall persons* and *not very short persons* from the following operation:

$$\mu_C(x) = [1 - (\mu_A(x))^2] \wedge [1 - (\mu_B(x))^2]$$

In general, we can use fuzzy operators and hedges to derive fuzzy sets that represent various linguistic descriptions and combinations of statements found in our natural language.

FUZZY INFERENCE

Fuzzy logic treats a fuzzy set as a *fuzzy proposition.* A fuzzy proposition is a statement that asserts a value for some given linguistic variable such as, "height is tall." In general, we can represent a fuzzy proposition as

Proposition: X is A

where A is a fuzzy set on the universe of discourse X. A fuzzy rule relates two fuzzy propositions in the form:

IF X is A THEN Y is B

This rule establishes a relationship or association between the two propositions.

Fuzzy expert systems store rules as fuzzy associations. That is, for the rule IF A THEN B, where A and B are fuzzy sets, a fuzzy expert system stores the association (A, B) in a matrix M (often labeled in the literature as R for *relationship*). The fuzzy associative matrix M maps fuzzy set A to fuzzy set B, Kosko (1992) calls this fuzzy association or fuzzy rule a **Fuzzy Associative Memory** (FAM). A FAM maps a fuzzy set to a fuzzy set—the fuzzy inference process.

Like other inexact reasoning techniques used in the design of an expert system, fuzzy inference attempts to establish a belief in a rule's conclusion given available evidence on the rule's premise. However, since the propositions contained in a fuzzy rule are fuzzy sets, fuzzy logic must map premise set information to conclusion set information. To accomplish this, fuzzy inference establishes an induced fuzzy set from information about a related fuzzy set.

Consider for example the fuzzy sets A—"Height is tall" and B—"Weight is heavy" related by the rule IF A THEN B.

$$\text{IF} \quad \text{Height is tall} \quad \text{THEN} \quad \text{Weight is heavy}$$

We can represent both A and B as fit-vectors and capture their relationship in the fuzzy associative matrix M. You will see how to form this matrix in later sections.

In practice, we would could use this rule to form a degree of belief that some person of a given height is heavy. Fuzzy inference does this by taking the available height information encoded in A' (a subset of A) and inducing a fuzzy set B' on B that quantitatively captures this belief. To derive the induced fuzzy set, fuzzy inference relies on **fuzzy vector-matrix multiplication.**

The two most popular fuzzy inference techniques used in practice are **max-min inference** and **max-product inference.** Before looking at these two inference techniques, you must first understand fuzzy vector-matrix multiplication.

Fuzzy Vector-Matrix Multiplication

In classical vector-matrix multiplication, we can derive a vector y given a vector x and a matrix A by:

$$\underset{1\times n}{x} \cdot \underset{n\times p}{A} = \underset{1\times p}{y}$$

$$y_j = \sum_{i=1}^{n} x_i a_{ij}$$

Fuzzy vector-matrix multiplication uses a technique known as **max-min composition** (Klir and Foger 1988), defined by the composition operator "∘". This operator performs a max-min operation on a given vector and matrix. The operation is similar to classical vector-matrix multiplication, however, we replace pairwise multiplications with pairwise minima and column (row) sums with column (row) maxima.

Consider this operation as applied to a fuzzy rule or FAM IF A THEN B, where A is a fuzzy set defined on X and B a fuzzy set defined on Y. For row fit vectors A and B represented as

$$A = (a_1, a_2, \ldots, a_n); \qquad a_i = \mu_A(x_i)$$

$$B = (b_1, b_2, \ldots, b_p); \qquad b_i = \mu_B(y_i)$$

we can define a fuzzy n by p matrix M such that

$$A \circ M = B \qquad (15)$$

and compute component b_j by:

$$b_j = \max_{1 \le i \le n}\{\min(a_i, m_{ij})\} \qquad (16)$$

To illustrate, assume $A = (.2\ .4\ .6\ 1)$ and the fuzzy matrix M is

$$M = \begin{vmatrix} .1 & .6 & .8 \\ .6 & .8 & .6 \\ .8 & .6 & .5 \\ 0 & .5 & .5 \end{vmatrix}$$

From equation 16, we can compute B as

$$b_1 = \max\{\min(.2, .1), \min(.4, .6), \min(.6, .8), \min(1, 0)\}$$

$$= \max\{.1, .4, .6, 0\}$$

$$= 0.6$$

$$b_2 = \max\{.2, .4, .6, .5\}$$

$$= 0.6$$

$$b_3 = \max\{.2, .4, .5, .5\}$$

$$= 0.5$$

Basic Ideas of Fuzzy Inference

To obtain a basic understanding of today's approaches to fuzzy inference, we need to go back and review some of the earlier ideas. Our best source for this information is the original work by Zadeh (1965).

Zadeh viewed a fuzzy set as a possibility distribution function. This function mapped elements of some universe of discourse into a number between 0 and 1 that reflected the degree of belief that some element belonged to the fuzzy set.

$$A = \text{Possibility distribution}$$

$$= \mu_A(x)$$

$$= \Pi_A$$

Zadeh also saw a need to be able to infer information on a fuzzy set B from information gained on another related one A. The approach taken to accomplish this was similar to classical conditional probability theory, where the compositional operator was used for the classical vector-matrix operation. Zadeh looked for a conditional possibility distribution matrix $\Pi_{B|A}$ such that if he composed it with the possibility distribution of A he would get back the possibility distribution of B

$$\Pi_A \circ \Pi_{B|A} = \Pi_B$$

where in general Π_A is a $1 \times n$ vector, $\Pi_{B|A}$ is a $n \times p$ matrix, and Π_B a $1 \times p$ vector. Using this approach, Zadeh could put in some information on A (labeled A'), and obtain information on B (labeled B'). He called this technique the **compositional rule of inference.**

The next question was how to form the $\Pi_{B|A}$ distribution matrix. Zadeh had an interesting approach to this question. He interpreted the components of the $\Pi_{B|A}$ matrix as pairwise implications between A and B. For example, given the fuzzy sets in fit-vector form, this matrix would appear as:

$$\Pi_{B|A} = \begin{vmatrix} a_1 \rightarrow b_1 & a_1 \rightarrow b_2 & . & . & . & . \\ a_2 \rightarrow b_1 & & & & & \\ . & & & & & \\ . & & & & & \\ . & & & & & \end{vmatrix}$$

This matrix is the same as our fuzzy associative matrix M described earlier. Over the years several implication operators have been proposed. Whalen and Schott (1983) provide an excellent review of the more popular ones. The next sections describe the two most common ones used today in the design of fuzzy expert systems.

Max–Min Inference

In max–min inference the implication operator used is *min*. That is:

$$m_{ij} = \text{truth}(a_i \rightarrow b_j) = \min(a_i, b_j) \tag{17}$$

Given two fuzzy sets A and B, we can use equation 17 to form the matrix M. We can then next use equation 16 to determine the induced vector B' from a subset of A designated as A'.

To illustrate, assume we have a universe of discourse defined on X that represents "temperature," and a fuzzy set A defined on X that represents "normal temperature." Also assume we have a universe of discourse defined on Y that represents "velocity," and a fuzzy set B defined on Y that represents "medium velocity." Finally assume we have the following fuzzy rule:

IF   Temperature is normal   THEN   Velocity is medium

or

IF A THEN B

Further assume that the fuzzy sets are represented by the following vectors, where for clarity, the vector elements are shown with their corresponding domain values:

$$\text{Normal temperature} = (0/100, .5/125, 1/150, .5/175, 0/200)$$

$$\text{Medium velocity} = (0/10, .6/20, 1/30, .6/40, 0/50)$$

We begin by forming the M matrix according to equation 17:

$$M = m_{ij} = \min(a_i, b_j)$$

$$= \begin{vmatrix} \min(0., 0.) & \min(0., .6) & \min(0., 1.) & \min(0., .6) & \min(0., 0.) \\ \min(.5, 0.) & \min(.5, .6) & \min(.5, 1.) & \min(.5, .6) & \min(.5, 0.) \\ \min(1., 0.) & \min(1., .6) & \min(1., 1.) & \min(1., .6) & \min(1., 0.) \\ \min(.5, 0.) & \min(.5, .6) & \min(.5, 1.) & \min(.5, .6) & \min(.5, 0.) \\ \min(0., 0.) & \min(0., .6) & \min(0., 1.) & \min(0., .6) & \min(0., 0.) \end{vmatrix}$$

$$= \begin{vmatrix} 0. & 0. & 0. & 0. & 0. \\ 0. & 0.5 & 0.5 & 0.5 & 0. \\ 0. & 0.6 & 1. & 0.6 & 0. \\ 0. & 0.5 & 0.5 & 0.5 & 0. \\ 0. & 0. & 0. & 0. & 0. \end{vmatrix}$$

Next, assume that the subset A' is given as

$$A' = (0/100, .5/125, 0/150, 0/175, 0/200)$$

This subset represents a crisp reading in temperature of 125 degrees. This measurement maps to a membership value of 0.5 for the fuzzy set "normal temperature." This induces a fuzzy set B' (i.e., a belief in B) that we next want to determine.

With $A' = (0/100, .5/125, 0/150, 0/175, 0/200)$, then through max–min composition (equation 16) we have

$$b_j = \max_{1 \le i \le n}\{\min(a_i', m_{ij})\}$$

$$b_1 = \max[\min(0., 0.), \min(.5, 0.), \min(0., 0.), \min(0., 0.), \min(0., 0.)]$$

$$b_2 = \max[\min(0., 0.), \min(.5, .5), \min(0., .6), \min(0., .5), \min(0., 0.)]$$

$$b_3 = \max[\min(0., 0.), \min(.5, .5), \min(0., 1.), \min(0., .5), \min(0., 0.)]$$

$$b_4 = \max[\min(0., 0.), \min(.5, .5), \min(0., .6), \min(0., .5), \min(0., 0.)]$$

$$b_5 = \max[\min(0., 0.), \min(.5, 0.), \min(0., 0.), \min(0., 0.), \min(0., 0.)]$$

$$B' = (0/10, .5/20, .5/30, .5/40, 0/50)$$

In effect, this induced fuzzy set is a clipped version of B, whose height is set by A'. This is the general effect of max–min inference as illustrated in Figure 13.4 for triangular shaped fuzzy sets. What we typically do with this induced set is discussed later under the subject of **defuzzification.**

A key point to notice from this example is the result we obtained by limiting A' to a single value. That is, we stated that our temperature reading was 125

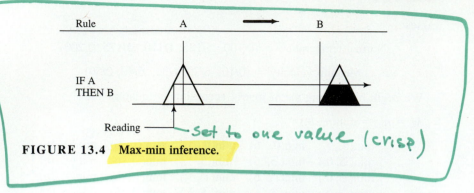

Rule   A   ⟶   B

IF A
THEN B

Reading ———— Set to one value (crisp)

FIGURE 13.4   Max-min inference.

degrees which gave us a A' fit vector of (0 .5 0 0 0) that resulted in a B' of (0 .5 .5 .5 0).

In most real-world applications of fuzzy logic systems we have a crisp value on some measurement (e.g., $x_k = 125$ degrees). With a single measurement value x_k we can use $\mu_A(x_k)$ directly with the fuzzy set representation of B, namely $\mu_B(y)$, to obtain the induced fuzzy set on B':

$$B' = \mu_A(x_k) \wedge \mu_B(y) \tag{18}$$

For instance, in our example where we assumed the temperature was 125 degrees, it follows that $\mu_A = 0.5$ and

$$B' = [\min(.5, 0), \min(.5, .6), \min(.5, 1), \min(.5, .6)] \min(.5, 0)]$$

$$= (0, .5, .5, .5, 0)$$

This is the same result obtained earlier working with the fuzzy associative matrix. Therefore, when input information is in crisp form, we do not have to calculate and maintain fuzzy matrices, but can simply work with the less demanding (from a computer overhead viewpoint) fuzzy set information.

In the event the input to a rule represents a fuzzy reading, we can still take a simple approach. Consider the rule IF A THEN B, and a fuzzy reading of A designated as A'. We can simply take the intersection of the two as our input, $\min(a'_i, a_i)$, to induce the fuzzy set B'. This approach is illustrated in Figure 13.5.

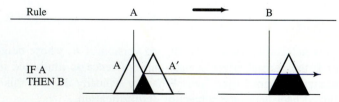

Rule   A   ⟶   B

IF A   A   A'
THEN B

FIGURE 13.5   Max-min inference for fuzzy input.

Max–Product Inference

Max–product inference uses the standard product as the implication operator when forming the components of M:

$$m_{ij} = a_i b_j \tag{19}$$

Following the calculation of this matrix, max–min composition is used to determine the induced matrix B' from some subset vector A'. To illustrate this inference technique we consider the same fit vectors used in the previous section:

$$A = (0, .5, 1, .5, 0) \qquad B = (0, .6, 1, .6, 0)$$

$$M = \begin{vmatrix} (0. \cdot 0.) & (0. \cdot .6) & (0. \cdot 1.) & (0. \cdot .6) & (0. \cdot 0.) \\ (.5 \cdot 0.) & (.5 \cdot .6) & (.5 \cdot 1.) & (.5 \cdot .6) & (.5 \cdot 0.) \\ (1. \cdot 0.) & (1. \cdot .6) & (1. \cdot 1.) & (1. \cdot .6) & (1. \cdot 0.) \\ (.5 \cdot 0.) & (.5 \cdot .6) & (.5 \cdot 1.) & (.5 \cdot .6) & (.5 \cdot 0.) \\ (0. \cdot 0.) & (0. \cdot .6) & (0. \cdot 1.) & (0. \cdot .6) & (0. \cdot 0.) \end{vmatrix}$$

$$= \begin{vmatrix} 0. & 0. & 0. & 0. & 0. \\ 0. & 0.3 & 0.5 & 0.3 & 0. \\ 0. & 0.6 & 1. & 0.6 & 0. \\ 0. & 0.3 & 0.5 & 0.3 & 0. \\ 0. & 0. & 0. & 0. & 0. \end{vmatrix}$$

Assuming again $A' = (0, .5, 0, 0, 0)$, then through max–min composition we have

$$b_j = \max_{1 \leq i \leq n} \{\min(a'_i, m_{ij})\}$$

$$b_1 = \max[\min(0., 0.), \min(.5, 0.), \min(0., 0.), \min(0., 0.), \min(0., 0.)]$$

$$b_2 = \max[\min(0., 0.), \min(.5, .3), \min(0., .6), \min(0., .5), \min(0., 0.)]$$

$$b_3 = \max[\min(0., 0.), \min(.5, .6), \min(0., 1.), \min(0., .5), \min(0., 0.)]$$

$$b_4 = \max[\min(0., 0.), \min(.5, .3), \min(0., .6), \min(0., .5), \min(0., 0.)]$$

$$b_5 = \max[\min(0., 0.), \min(.5, 0.), \min(0., 0.), \min(0., 0.), \min(0., 0.)]$$

$$B' = (0, .3, .5, .3, 0)$$

The max–product inference technique produces a scaled version of B. Figure 13.6 illustrates the general result of using this technique for triangular fuzzy sets.

Like the example used in the prior section, the A' fit-vector contained a single crisp value. Because of this limiting but typical situation found in practice, we can again make an observation that eases the computation of B'. Given that the measurement of A is x_k, we can obtain B' from

$$B' = \mu_A(x_k) \cdot \mu_B(y) \tag{20}$$

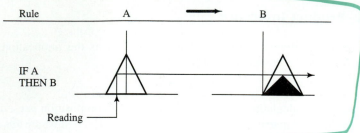

FIGURE 13.6 Max-product inference.

For our example

$$B' = 0.5 \cdot (0, .6, 1, .6, 0)$$

$$= (0, .3, .5, .3, 0)$$

As previously shown, max–min inference produces a clipped version of B. As just illustrated, the max–product inference technique produces a scaled version of B. In this sense, max–product inference preserves more information than max-min inference. When we combine induced fuzzy sets from multiple rules, as a precursor to defuzzification, this point becomes important.

--------------------- **MULTIPLE-PREMISE RULES** ---------------------

In the prior sections we have been looking at fuzzy rules that contain a single premise of the form IF A THEN B. However, in practice, we will often need to work with multiple premise rules (e.g., IF A AND B THEN C). The question we now face is how do we form the fuzzy associative matrix M for this rule?

Kosko (1992) suggests a simple answer to this question—one that is typically used in practice. Assume that fuzzy set A is defined on X, set B on Y, and C on Z. The approach relies on first defining for each premise a separate M matrix, that relates the premise to the conclusion (e.g., M_{AC} and M_{BC}). Then given some input information on the premises, A' and B', the induced fuzzy sets on C can be computed independently through composition

$$A' \circ M_{AC} = C_{A'} \tag{21}$$

$$B' \circ M_{BC} = C_{B'} \tag{22}$$

The next step is to recompose the fuzzy sets $C_{A'}$ and $C_{B'}$. The approach taken depends on whether the premises are joined conjunctively "AND" or disjunctively "OR". For premises joined in an AND fashion, the fuzzy logic intersection operator is used to join the induced fuzzy sets

$$C' = [A' \circ M_{AC}] \wedge [B' \circ M_{BC}]$$

$$= C_{A'} \wedge C_{B'} \tag{23}$$

TABLE 13.2 Computing Induced Fuzzy Sets for Multiple Premise Rules with Crisp Input Values

C'	Premise Joining	Inference
$\min(a_i, b_j) \wedge \mu_C(z)$	AND	Max–Min
$\max(a_i, b_j) \wedge \mu_C(z)$	OR	Max–Min
$\min(a_i, b_j) \cdot \mu_C(z)$	AND	Max–Product
$\max(a_i, b_j) \cdot \mu_C(z)$	OR	Max–Product

while the union operator is used for OR joined premises

$$C' = [A' \circ M_{AC}] \vee [B' \circ M_{BC}]$$
$$= C_{A'} \vee C_{B'}$$

(24)

This process can be simplified further when the inputs are crisp values. Consider the case of a single value of A defined at x_k and a single value of B defined at y_j. Given the fuzzy set membership values of $a_i = \mu_A(x_k)$ and $b_j = \mu_B(y_j)$, Table 13.2 shows simple approaches for computing C' for multiple premise rules.

Defuzzification

You have now seen two techniques for determining the induced fuzzy set B' from an estimate of A as defined by A'. In most applications, we need to take B' and obtain a crisp value. For example, earlier we worked with the fuzzy rule

IF   Temperature is normal   THEN   Velocity is medium

and used a temperature measurement to induce a fuzzy set on "normal velocity." In a control application we would want to know what specific velocity value we should use. This requires us to take the induced fuzzy set and obtain a crisp value. This is the subject of **defuzzification.**

The most popular defuzzification technique used is the **fuzzy centroid** method. This technique provides a single value y_i from B' by way of the following:

$$y_i = \frac{\sum\limits_{j=1}^{p} y_j m_{B'}(y_j)}{\sum\limits_{j=1}^{p} m_{B'}(y_j)}$$

(25)

Using this technique on our example provides us with a single velocity value. However, using it with a single rule is not very interesting because the value will always be the same—the centroid of B. In general, defuzzification is important when multiple rules conclude the same event.

Multiple Fuzzy Rules

We next consider the situation where we have n fuzzy rules or associations (A_1, B_1), . . . , (A_n, B_n). This situation leads to n matrices M_1, . . . , M_n to encode the associations or relationships between A_i and B_i.

Our interest in this set of fuzzy rules is the resultant overall belief in B given a single measurement A'. We proceed by applying A' in parallel to the bank of rules, producing an induced fuzzy set B_i' for each rule. We then sum all of the B_i' sets to form the resultant composite induced fuzzy set B', using the following standard set union operation where B is defined on domain X:

$$B' = B_1' \cup B_2' \cup \ldots B_{n-1}' \cup B_n'$$

$$= \max(B_1'(x), B_2'(x), \ldots B_{n-1}'(x), B_n'(x)) \qquad \text{for all } x \in X \qquad (26)$$

Following this union operation, we can next defuzzify the resultant B' using the centroid method. This process produces a crisp output value y_i. This entire operation is illustrated in Figure 13.7. In effect, this operation takes an input measurement of A and produces an estimate of B.

To expand on this idea, assume we want to control the velocity of some vehicle. Further assume that our decision is based on the vehicle's temperature and pressure as captured in the following rules:

IF   Temperature is normal
OR   Pressure is low
THEN   Velocity is medium

IF   Temperature is normal
AND   Pressure is normal
THEN   Velocity is low

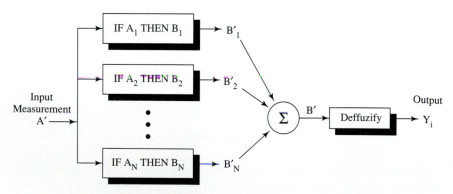

FIGURE 13.7   **Fuzzy rule system architecture.**

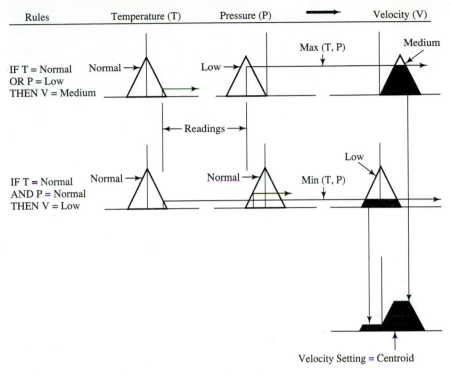

FIGURE 13.8 Max-min inference for multiple rules.

Figure 13.8 illustrates the max–min inference process for these two rules, while Figure 13.9 shows the max-product inference process. Readings of temperature and pressure are used to determine their corresponding membership values in the fuzzy sets shown. The largest value is then chosen for the disjunctive rule and the smallest for the conjunctive rule. These values are then used to either clip the inferred velocity fuzzy set (max–min inference) or scale it (max–product inference). The induced fuzzy sets on velocity are then summed (fuzzy union) and the centroid of the result found. The resultant centroid provides the desired velocity value given the input measurements.

In general, we can apply the process shown in Figure 13.7 to any number of fuzzy rules with any number of antecedent fuzzy-variable conditions.

_____ **BUILDING A FUZZY LOGIC EXPERT SYSTEM** _____

To illustrate the design of a fuzzy logic expert system we consider a problem of navigating a golf cart. We want to design a fuzzy logic system that will automatically take Kathy—an avid weekend golfer—around the golf course.

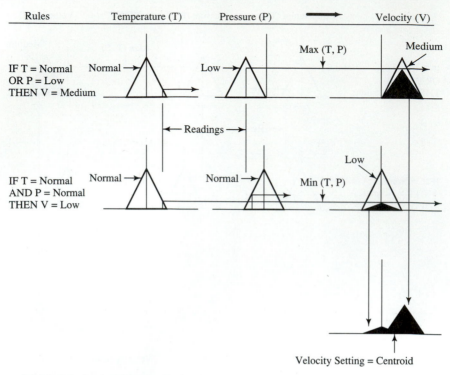

FIGURE 13.9   **Max-product inference for multiple rules.**

Kathy has had trouble controlling her cart which has led to an increase in both her anxiety and golf score. With an automatic golf cart she can relax, and hopefully better enjoy and improve her game.

There are seven major tasks you will typically perform when developing a fuzzy logic expert system:

Task 1: Define the problem
Task 2: Define the linguistic variables
Task 3: Define the fuzzy sets
Task 4: Define the fuzzy rules
Task 5: Build the system
Task 6: Test the system
Task 7: Tune the system

Task 1: Define the Problem

Like all expert system projects, we need to first obtain a source of knowledge. Usually this source is an expert on the problem. For our problem, we contact

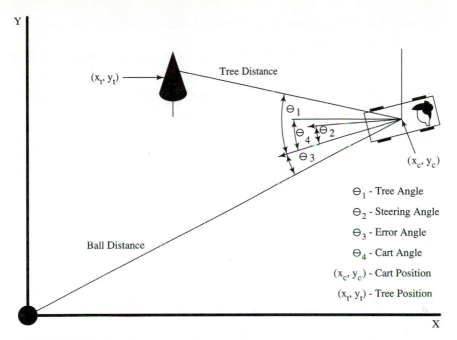

FIGURE 13.10   Cart navigation geometry.

Bob, a golf pro at a local course, who has years of experience in driving a golf cart.

Bob tells us that the basic problem is to navigate the cart in an efficient and safe fashion from some initial stationary position to the location of the golf ball. We obtain efficiency by minimizing both the distance traveled and travel time. We obtain safety by avoiding any trees along the way. To accomplish these tasks we will need to provide the fuzzy system with control over both the direction and speed of the cart. Figure 13.10 illustrates our navigation problem.

This is basically an error-nulling problem. The cart must initially steer toward the ball by nullifying the error between the angular direction of the cart and the direction toward the ball. The cart should also accelerate to some maximum allowable speed, then slow down and eventually stop when it is close to the ball; we will pick a stopping distance around 3 yards. This minimizes the error between the location of the cart and the ball's location in a quick fashion. In addition, when a tree is in the path of the cart, the cart must steer around it cautiously (i.e., slow down), then pick up speed and again steer toward the ball.

Task 2: Define Linguistic Variables

We next need to define the linguistic variables for our problem. We accomplish this task by listening to how Bob solves the problem. We want to uncover the variables that will represent our universes of discourse and the fuzzy sets that will be defined on each.

From task 1, we know that our fuzzy logic system must contend with three basic problems:

1. Control steering of cart to direct it toward the ball.
2. Control the cart's speed.
3. Control steering of cart to avoid any trees.

We next ask Bob to discuss in general how each of these problems are solved. Consider problem 1 and assume Bob provides us with the following common sense strategy for steering the cart toward the ball:

> "When the direction of the cart is away from the ball, make the cart's direction toward the ball."

In a similar fashion we obtain the expert's strategies for controlling the cart's speed:

> "When the cart is far from the ball, make the cart's speed fast."

> "When the cart is close to the ball, make the cart's speed slow."

and the cart's direction and speed:

> "When the cart is close to the tree and heading toward it, then slow the cart down and make the cart's direction away from the tree."

From this discussion we can now define our linguistic variables—the universe of discourses, and also ask our expert to define their ranges:

LINGUISTIC VARIABLE		RANGE	
Error angle	−180	to	180 degrees
Tree angle	−180	to	180 degrees
Steering angle	−45	to	45 degrees
Speed	0	to	5 yd/s
Acceleration	−2	to	1 yd/s/s
Ball distance	0	to	600 yards
Tree distance	0	to	1000 yards

Task 3: Define Fuzzy Sets

The next task involves defining the fuzzy sets on each universe. To accomplish this we again consult Bob and asked him for a list of typical adjectives used with each linguistic variable. Assume this effort resulted in the lists shown in Figure 13.11. This figure represents a vocabulary "dictionary" for the problem.

DESIGN SUGGESTION: Maintain a dictionary of terms used in the system that includes all linguistic variables and their associated adjectives.

Error Angle	Tree Angle	Steering Angle	Speed	Acceleration	Ball Distance	Tree Distance
Large Negative	Large Negative	Hard Right	Zero	Brake Hard	Zero	Close
Small Negative	Small Negative	Slight Right	Real Slow	Brake Light	Real Close	
Zero	Zero	Zero	Slow	Coast	Close	
Small Positive	Small Positive	Slight Left	Medium	Zero	Medium	
Large Positive	Large Positive	Hard Left	Fast	Slight Acceleration	Far	
				Floor It		

FIGURE 13.11 Fuzzy variables with adjectives.

We next ask Bob for information that will allow us to define the fuzzy sets for each adjective given in Figure 13.11. For example, we might first ask, ''What speed do you consider slow?'' Assume Bob provides a vague answer to this question—''around 1 to 3 yards per second.'' At this point, we can ask him to what degree he believes various speed values are ''slow''—''To what degree do you believe that 1 yd/s is slow?'' We can use similar questions for other speed values, and follow this effort with the selection of a function that reasonably maps the speed values into their corresponding belief values—we now have our first fuzzy set.

Fuzzy mapping or membership functions can have a variety of shapes depending on how the expert relates different domain values to belief values. In practice, a piecewise linear function, such as a triangular or trapezoidal shape, provides an adequate capture of the expert's belief and simplifies the computation.

We could continue this process in order to define the other fuzzy sets for the ''speed'' linguistic variable. In practice, however, once the expert has seen how the first fuzzy set is formed, he is usually able to define the other sets simply by shifting the selected mapping function over the variable's universe. However, this approach may require a small amount of narrowing or widening of the shifted function.

DESIGN SUGGESTION: Allow the expert to shift an existing fuzzy set function along the universe of discourse to account for other adjectives.

Figures 13.12 through 13.18 show the fuzzy sets for all the terms shown in Figure 13.11. Each figure also includes fit vectors for its various fuzzy sets.

One key point when defining the fuzzy sets is to make sure you have sufficient overlap in the sets to assure that every possible value establishes some fuzzy set membership value. If this is not done, the possibility will always exist that your system will be unresponsive to some value.

DESIGN SUGGESTION: Maintain sufficient overlap in adjacent fuzzy sets.

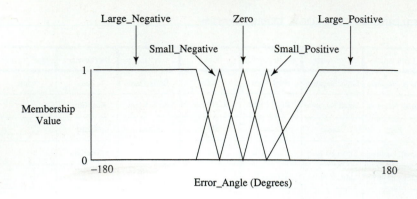

| Large_Positive | | Small_Positive | | Zero | |
X	Y	X	Y	X	Y
30	0	0	0	−30	0
90	1	30	1	0	1
180	1	60	0	30	0

| Small_Negative | | Large_Positive NEG. | |
X	Y	X	Y
−60	0	−180	1
−30	1	−60	1
0	0	−30	0

FIGURE 13.12   Fuzzy sets on error angle.

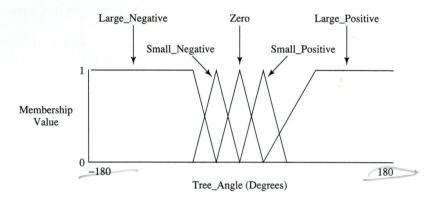

| Large_Positive | | Small_Positive | | Zero | |
X	Y	X	Y	X	Y
30	0	0	0	−30	0
90	1	30	1	0	1
180	1	60	0	30	0

| Small_Negative | | Large_Negative | |
X	Y	X	Y
−60	0	−180	1
−30	1	−60	1
0	0	−30	0

FIGURE 13.13   Fuzzy sets on tree angle.

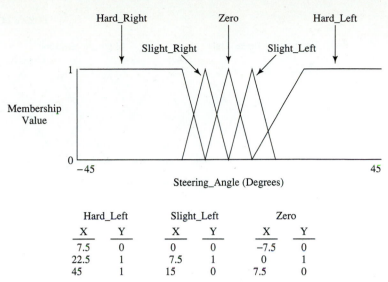

Hard_Left		Slight_Left		Zero	
X	Y	X	Y	X	Y
7.5	0	0	0	−7.5	0
22.5	1	7.5	1	0	1
45	1	15	0	7.5	0

Slight_Right		Hard_Right	
X	Y	X	Y
−15	0	−45	1
−7.5	1	−15	1
0	0	−7.5	0

FIGURE 13.14   Fuzzy sets on steering angle.

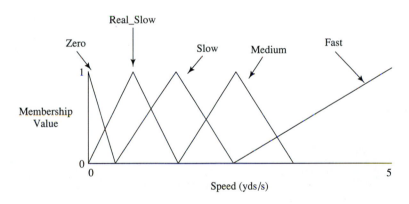

Zero		Real_Slow		Slow	
X	Y	X	Y	X	Y
0	1	0	0	0.5	0
0.5	0	0.7	1	1.5	1
		1.5	0	2.5	0

Medium		Fast	
X	Y	X	Y
1.5	0	0	0
2.5	1	2.5	0
3.5	0	5.0	1

FIGURE 13.15   Fuzzy sets on speed.

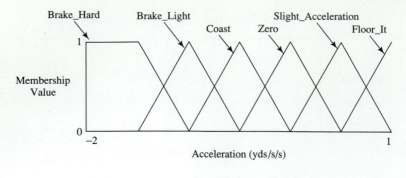

Brake_Hard		Brake_Light		Coast	
X	Y	X	Y	X	Y
−2	1	−1.5	0	−1	0
−1.5	1	−1	1	−0.5	1
−1	0	−0.5	0	0	0

Zero		Slight_Acceleration		Floor_It	
X	Y	X	Y	X	Y
−0.5	0	0	0	0.5	0
0	1	0.5	1	1	1
0.5	0	1	0		

FIGURE 13.16   Fuzzy sets on acceleration.

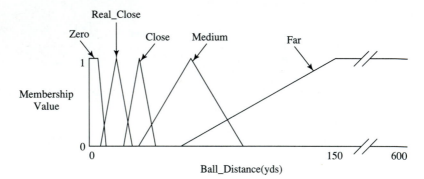

Zero		Real_Close		Close	
X	Y	X	Y	X	Y
0	1	3	0	12	0
3	1	12	1	24	1
9	0	18	0	36	0

Medium		Far	
X	Y	X	Y
24	0	60	0
60	1	150	1
96	0	600	1

FIGURE 13.17   Fuzzy sets on ball distance.

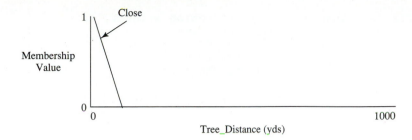

Close	
X	Y
0	1
50	0
1000	0

FIGURE 13.18 Fuzzy sets on tree distance.

Task 4: Define Fuzzy Rules

Next we need to define the fuzzy rules. To accomplish this, we ask Bob to discuss how he addresses the three primary problems: steering the cart to the ball, controlling the cart's speed, and steering the cart to avoid a tree. We also ask him to consider the use of the fuzzy adjectives previously defined. However, if other adjectives surface during this discussion, we can simply add them to our prior list and define a fuzzy set for each. The results of this effort are shown in Figure 13.19, where several fuzzy hedges and the fuzzy operator NOT are used.

It should be noted that the use of hedges in fuzzy rules should only be considered later when the system is being tuned. The initial set of rules should

```
==============================================================
Rules for steering
==============================================================

RULE 1S'- Maintain steering direction
IF   error_angle is zero
AND  tree_distance is NOT SOMEWHAT close
AND  tree_angle is NOT SOMEWHAT zero
THEN make steering_angle zero

RULE 2S - Change steering direction slightly right
IF   error_angle is small_positive
AND  tree_distance is NOT SOMEWHAT close
AND  tree_angle is NOT SOMEWHAT zero
THEN make steering_angle slight_right
```

FIGURE 13.19 Fuzzy rules for cart navigation system.

```
RULE 3S - Change steering direction slightly left
IF   error_angle is small_negative
AND  tree_distance is NOT SOMEWHAT close
AND  tree_angle is NOT SOMEWHAT zero
THEN make steering_angle slight_left

RULE 4S - Change steering direction slightly right
IF   error_angle is large_positive
AND  speed is fast
THEN make steering_angle slight_right

RULE 5S - Change steering direction hard right
IF   error_angle is large_positive
AND  speed is NOT fast
THEN make steering_angle hard_right

RULE 6S - Change steering direction slightly left
IF   error_angle is large-negative
AND  speed is fast
THEN make steering_angle slight_left

RULE 7S - Change steering direction hard left
IF   error_angle is large_negative
AND  speed is NOT fast
THEN make steering_angle hard_left


============================================================
Rules for acceleration
============================================================

RULE 1A - Brake lightly
IF   error_angle is large_positive
AND  speed is fast
THEN make acceleration brake_light

RULE 2A - Brake lightly
IF   error_angle is large_negative
AND  speed is fast
THEN make acceleration brake_light

RULE 3A - Floor it
IF   ball_distance is far
AND  speed is NOT VERY fast
THEN make acceleration floor_it

RULE 4A - Set acceleration to zero
IF   ball_distance is far
AND  speed is VERY fast
THEN make acceleration zero

RULE 5A - Slight acceleration
IF   ball_distance is medium
AND  speed is NOT fast
THEN make acceleration slight_acceleration
```

FIGURE 13.19   Continued

```
RULE  6A - Set acceleration to zero
IF    ball_distance is medium
AND   speed is fast
THEN  make acceleration zero

RULE  7A - Brake lightly
IF    ball_distance is close
AND   speed is fast
THEN  make acceleration brake_light

RULE  8A - Slight acceleration
IF    ball_distance is close
AND   Speed is zero
THEN  make acceleration slight_acceleration

RULE  9A - Brake hard
IF    ball_distance is real_close
AND   speed is fast
THEN  make acceleration brake_hard

RULE  10A - Brake lightly
IF    ball_distance is real_close
AND   speed is medium
THEN  make acceleration brake_light

RULE  11A - Coast
IF    ball_distance is real_close
AND   speed is slow
THEN  make acceleration coast

RULE  12A - Set acceleration to zero
IF    ball_distance is real_close
AND   speed is real_slow
THEN  make acceleration zero

RULE  13A - Slight acceleration
IF    ball_distance is real_close
AND   speed is zero
THEN  make acceleration slight_acceleration

RULE  14A - Brake hard
IF    ball_distance is zero
AND   speed is NOT zero
THEN  make acceleration brake_hard

RULE  15A - Coast
IF    ball_distance is close
AND   speed is medium
THEN  make acceleration coast

RULE  16A - Set acceleration to zero
IF    ball_distance is close
AND   speed is slow
THEN  make acceleration zero
```

```
==================================================================
Rules to avoid the tree
==================================================================

RULE 1T - Turn slightly left to avoid tree
IF    tree_distance is SOMEWHAT close
AND   tree_angle is SOMEWHAT zero
AND   tree_angle is SOMEWHAT small_positive
THEN make steering_angle slight_left

RULE 2T - Turn slightly right to avoid tree
IF    tree_distance is SOMEWHAT close
AND   tree_angle is SOMEWHAT zero
AND   tree_angle is SOMEWHAT small_negative
THEN make steering_angle slight_right

RULE 3T - Brake hard to avoid tree
IF    tree_distance is VERY close
AND   tree_angle is zero
THEN make acceleration brake_hard
```

FIGURE 13.19   Continued

be small and only includes fuzzy sets for the adjectives in the dictionary without any added adverbs. As you test the system, you can add adverbs to see if the system's performance improves.

DESIGN SUGGESTION: Use adverbs in the rules to tune the system's performance.

Task 5: Build System

Now that we have the fuzzy sets and rules, our next task is to build the system. This task involves the coding of the fuzzy sets, and rules and procedures for performing fuzzy logic functions such as fuzzy inference. To accomplish this task you can go in one of two ways: build the system from scratch using a basic programming language, or rely on a fuzzy logic development shell.

The C programming language is the language of choice by most developers of fuzzy logic expert systems. It offers data structures that are conducive for implementing fuzzy logic procedures. However, building a fuzzy logic system using a basic programming language requires the developer not only to code the problem's knowledge (e.g., fuzzy sets and fuzzy rules); he is also responsible for coding the fuzzy logic procedures.

A fuzzy logic shell (like all shells) provides a complete environment for building a fuzzy logic expert system. The designer is only responsible for coding the problem's knowledge—a task often accomplished by using a natural language syntax for the rules and a graphical method for defining the fuzzy sets. The most popular fuzzy logic shells available today are listed in Appendix B.

We will assume that our example system was developed using the shell CubiCalc. CubiCalc is a windows-based development tool that permits rapid prototyping of a fuzzy logic expert system. It also offers a simulation utility that allows us to easily test our system.

Task 6: Test System

After you have built the system, you will want to test it to see if it meets the specifications defined during task 1. For our system, test cases were simulated using CubiCalc's simulation utility. All test runs used the max–product inference technique.

A number of test situations exist that depend on the location of the ball, tree, and cart, and on the orientation of the cart. We will only look at two situations: no nearby tree and one with a tree in the cart's path. For both test cases we assume the ball is at coordinates (0,0).

Test 1: No Tree in Path

For the first test case we consider a situation where the tree is not in the direct path of the cart. Also, the cart is directed away from the ball at a cart angle of −45 degrees. Simulated test results are shown in Figures 13.20 and 13.21.

Figure 13.20 shows the cart's path during the test and illustrates that it had little difficulty in reaching the ball. After an initial maneuver to obtain the target,

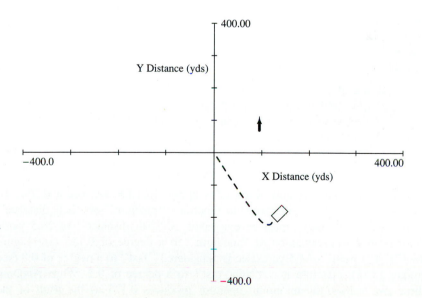

FIGURE 13.20 Cart navigation test case1.

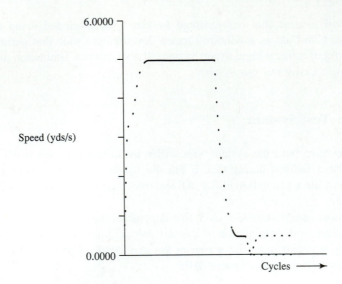

FIGURE 13.21   Cart speed test case1.

the cart followed a straight line toward the ball. No deviations from this straight line are noted due to the remoteness of the tree. The cart stops approximately 3 yards from the ball.

Figure 13.21 shows the cart's speed during the test. From a stationary position the cart quickly picks up speed to an allowable maximum value of 5 yards/second. As the cart approaches the ball it quickly decelerates. At this point the speed begins to oscillate—an undesirable situation that is discussed later.

To provide insight into the system's inference process, the simulation was paused to inspect the firing of the fuzzy rules. At the point where the simulation was paused, the following conditions existed:

—cart was 28.5 yards from ball
—cart was moving directly toward ball
—cart's speed was 4.5 yards/second
—cart was decelerating at a rate of 0.5 yards/s/s
—error angle was negligible
—tree was far away

Under these conditions only three rules apply: RULES 5A, 6A and 7A. To evaluate RULE 5A, the membership functions ''medium'' of ''ball_distance'' and ''fast'' of ''speed'' must be evaluated. A ''ball_distance'' of 28.5 yards belongs to the classification of ''medium'' to a degree of 0.125 (see Figure 13.17). A ''speed'' of 4.5 yards/sec is considered ''fast'' to a degree of 0.8 (see Figure 13.15); therefore it is ''NOT fast'' to a degree of 0.2. When ANDing these two values, the minimum operator produces 0.125 as the truth of the antecedents. Using the max–product inference technique, this value is used to

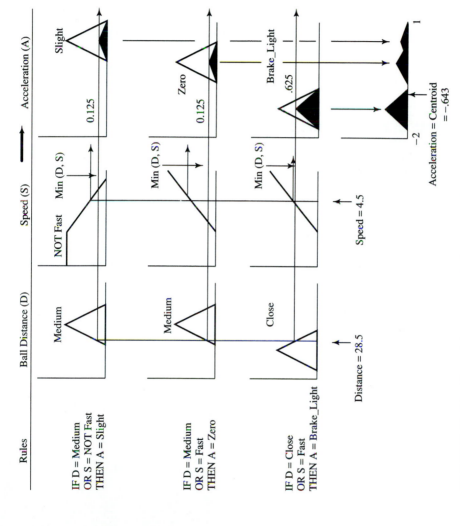

FIGURE 13.22 Fuzzy inference sample for test case1.

scale the membership function of the conclusion of RULE 5A "slight_acceleration."

When RULE 6A is evaluated, using the truth values for "medium" and "fast" found above, the antecedents again have a combined truth value of 0.125. The membership value of "zero" acceleration is scaled by this value.

When evaluating RULE 7A, the distance of 28.5 yards is considered "close" to a degree of 0.625 and the "speed" is "fast" to a degree of 0.8. Therefore, "brake_light" becomes scaled to a value of 0.625.

The parallel firing of these three rules is shown in Figure 13.22. The three induced fuzzy sets on "acceleration" are also shown combined using the union operator. A centroid of this result is then computed providing an update in the cart's acceleration. Since the final value is negative, the simulator decreases the cart's speed and the process continues.

Test 2: Tree in Path

In the next test case we consider a situation where the tree is in the direct path of the cart. Also, the cart is directed away from the ball at an angle of 60 degrees. Simulated test results are shown in Figures 13.23 and 13.24.

Figure 13.23 illustrates that the cart must first maneuver to obtain the target. The cart then follows a straight line towards the ball until it comes near the tree. At this point, it veers around the tree and then continues a straightline approach toward the ball. As in test 1, it stops approximately 3 yards from the ball.

Figure 13.24 shows that the cart once again quickly picks up speed and

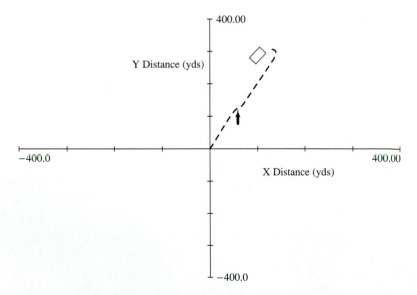

FIGURE 13.23   Cart navigation test case2.

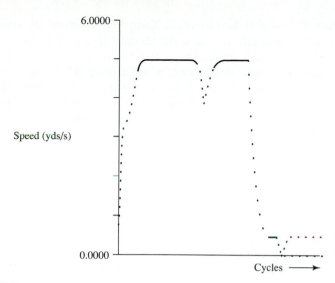

FIGURE 13.24   Cart speed test case2.

proceeds at the maximum allowable speed until it nears the tree. At this point, it slows down to cautiously move around the tree. After maneuvering around the tree it again picks up speed until it approaches the ball. Here it quickly reduces speed to prepare for stopping. Unfortunately, as was the case in test 1, the cart's speed oscillates as it nears the ball.

Task 7: Tune System

Tuning a fuzzy expert system begins with a comparison of the system's response with initial expectations. Deviations then become the focus of additional effort.

In most fuzzy expert system projects, the time spent developing the fuzzy sets and rules is small in comparison to the time spent tuning the system. Usually, the first series of fuzzy sets and rules provide a reasonable solution to the problem. This is perhaps one of the principal advantages of fuzzy logic. That is, common sense is used in forming the basis of the knowledge that tends to provide quick and reasonable results. However, obtaining more accurate results takes additional effort and becomes more of a art form.

A study of the results of our two tests shows that we meet most of the initial specifications. That is, the cart successfully reaches the ball and avoids the calamity of running into a tree. However, inspection of the speed plots indicate that we may have a problem.

Both Figures 13.21 and 13.24 show a problem when the cart is very close to the ball, because the speed continually oscillates between zero and some value. A programmer may overlook this point and be happy that the cart successfully reached the ball. However, the cart's rider Kathy may not share the programmer's delight when her teeth fall out due to the abrupt changes in speed.

To correct this problem, we need to inspect the speed control rules. Especially, we want to look at the rules that control the cart's speed as the cart comes "really close" to the ball. Rules 9A through 13A cover this situation. Rule 13A causes an increase in speed when the speed approaches zero, which initiates the oscillation. To prevent the oscillation we can eliminate this rule.

Figure 13.25 shows the cart's speed with RULE 13A eliminated for the test 1 situation. The elimination of this rule has prevented the speed oscillation. However, the simulation run now shows that the cart stops 7 yards from the ball versus the 3 yards found from the earlier simulation. In practice, we might now go back to make further adjustments to either the fuzzy sets or rules to correct this new problem.

In general, tuning a fuzzy logic system involves one or more of the following:

RULES
   - Adding rules for special situations
   - Adding premises for other linguistic variables
   - Using Adverbs through hedge operators

FUZZY SETS
   - Adding sets on a defined linguistic variable
   - Broadening or narrowing existing sets
   - Shifting laterally existing sets
   - Shape adjustment of existing sets

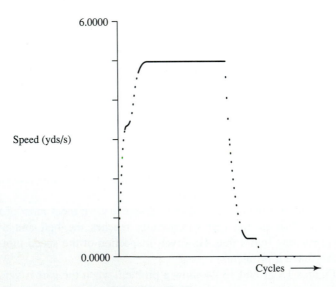

FIGURE 13.25   Cart speed adjusted rule set.

DESIGN SUGGESTION: When fine control is needed over some existing fuzzy variable, think of adding narrow fuzzy sets centered around a point of interest. In general, wide fuzzy sets provide rough control.

───────────── SUMMARY ON FUZZY LOGIC ─────────────

Fuzzy logic provides the means to both represent and reason with common sense knowledge in a computer. This ability is extremely valuable to the knowledge engineer responsible for building an expert system who is confronted with an expert that explains the problem-solving tasks in common sense terms. Vague terms or rules can be represented and manipulated numerically to provide results that are consistent with the expert.

Fuzzy logic has particular value in those control applications where it is difficult or impossible to develop a traditional control system. To date, Japan has been the leader in developing fuzzy logic control systems for such diverse applications as washing machines, video camcorders, and railway systems (Self 1990) and (Waller 1989). Market Intelligence Research Corporation (MIRC) expects total revenues for fuzzy logic-based products and neural networks combined to grow to $10 billion by 1998 (Kandel 1993). Maiers and Sherif (1985) provide 450 references to fuzzy logic applications and theory. Gaines and Kohout (1977) provide an extensive discussion and reference to fuzzy logic applications.

Key issues discussed in this chapter were:

- Fuzzy logic provides the means to represent and reason with vague or ambiguous terms in a computer.

- A linguistic variable is a term used in our natural language that describes a concept that has vague or fuzzy values. In fuzzy logic, this variable is often referred to as a *fuzzy* variable.

- Values (adjectives) of fuzzy variables are represented using *fuzzy sets*, which map set elements to a degree of belief that the element belongs to the fuzzy set.

- Hedges are mathematical operations performed on an existing fuzzy set (e.g., *tall*) to produce a new fuzzy set to account for an added adverb (e.g., *very tall*).

- The two most popular fuzzy inference techniques are max–min and max–product.

- Building a fuzzy logic expert system is an iterative process, where an initial collection of fuzzy rules and fuzzy sets is formed and later tuned to meet the project's specifications.

- Tuning a fuzzy logic expert system involves adjustments to existing rules or fuzzy sets.

_____ **REFERENCES**

Gaines, B.R. and L.J. Kohout, The Fuzzy Decade: A Bibliography of Fuzzy Systems and Related Topics, Int. J. Man-Machine Studies, vol. 9, pp. 1–68, 1977.

Kandel, A., Interview, PC AI, pp. 40–41, Mar./Apr., 1993.

Klir, G.J. and T.A. Foger, Fuzzy Sets, Uncertainty and Information, Prentice-Hall, Englewood Cliffs, N.J., 1988.

Kosko, B., Neural Networks and Fuzzy Systems, Prentice-Hall, Englewood Cliffs, N.J., 1992.

Maiers, J. and Y.S. Sherif, Applications of Fuzzy Set Theory, IEEE Trans. Systems, Man, and Cybernetics, vol. SMC-15, no. 1, pp. 175–189, Feb. 1985.

Rescher, N., Many-Valued Logic, McGraw-Hill, New York, 1969.

Self, K., Designing with Fuzzy Logic, IEEE Spectrum, pp. 42–44, Nov. 1990.

Waller, L., Fuzzy Logic: It's Comprehensible, It's Practical—And It's Commerical, Electronics, pp. 102–103, Mar. 1989.

Whalen, T. and B. Schott, Issues in Fuzzy Production Systems, Int. J. Man-Machine Studies, vol. 19, pp. 57–71, 1983.

Zadeh, L.A., Fuzzy Sets, Information and Control, vol. 8, 1965.

_____ **EXERCISES**

1. Define some typical fuzzy variables.

2. Define typical fuzzy sets for the fuzzy variables:
   temperature
   inflation
   intelligence

3. Draw each fuzzy set defined in problem 2.

4. For the fuzzy sets defined for the variable "temperature" create the modified sets using the hedge VERY.

5. Given the following fit vectors, find their union, intersection and complements.

   $(0, 0.1, 0.2, 0.8, 1)$

   $(0, 0.5, 0.5, 0.5, 0)$

6. Given fuzzy sets A and B, where $A = (.3, .8)$ and $B = (.2, .6, .5)$, use max–min composition to show that $A' = (.4, .7)$ recalls B. Discuss the significance of this result.

7. For the fuzzy sets given in problem 6, show that $A' = (.1, .3)$ does not recall B. Discuss the significance of this result.

8. Given the rule IF A THEN B, with $A = (0, .5, 1, .5, 0)$ and $B = (0, .5, 1, .5, 0)$, and $A' = (0, .5, 0, 0, 0)$, find B' using max–min inference.

9. Repeat problem 8 using max–product inference.

10. Fuzzy rules contain premises that include fuzzy variables. Each fuzzy variable is represented by a number of fuzzy sets. A fuzzy logic expert system may include a set of rules that do not account for each established fuzzy set, but can still function properly. Explain why this is the case.

11. Using the software of your choice, build the golf cart navigation fuzzy logic system described in this chapter. Run several tests on the system where for each test several rules are deleted. Provide comment on each test result.

12. Using the software of your choice, build a fuzzy logic automobile cruise control system.

13. Using the software of your choice, build a fuzzy logic system that simulates a dog attempting to catch a cat. Assume the cat is mobile, having a speed and direction.

14. Using the software of your choice, build a fuzzy logic system for the rule-based investment example system given in Chapter 8.

Frame-Based Expert Systems

―――――――――― **INTRODUCTION** ――――――――――――――――――

Chapter 3 introduced frames as one of the common methods used for representing knowledge in an expert system. In this chapter we review how a frame-based expert system uses frames combined with techniques borrowed from object-oriented programming to create a powerful tool for addressing complex problems. We will also see how general pattern matching rules can be added to the system to enhance its flexibility. Developing a frame-based system is not simply a different programming technique. It is a completely different style of programming by which we view a problem as a collection of related objects that naturally describe the problem.

―――――――――― **OVERVIEW** ――――――――――――――――――――――

History

The motivation for current work in frame-based expert systems has its roots in earlier human problem-solving studies by cognitive psychologists. These studies developed theories on how humans formed mental models that they could draw upon to aid them when solving problems. One study by Bartlett (1932) demonstrated that humans store in their long-term memory discrete knowledge structures formed from past experience that can be used for dealing with a present similar situation. Bartlett used the term **schema** to refer to one of these knowledge structures.

A schema is a unit of knowledge that contains stereotypical information about some concept. For example, if someone mentioned the word ''automobile'' to you, you would probably envision a generic form of automobile. Your mental image of it might be of a vehicle of some size, shape, etc. You possibily recognize that these features are common to the concept of a car from your experience of seeing a number of cars in the past.

In this sense, a schema is like a template that contains generic information about some concept that you could refer to for describing a given instance of the concept. For example, when confronted with a specific automobile, you can fill in specific values for its general features, e.g., its size, shape, etc.

Following the idea of Bartlett's schema, Minsky (1975) proposed a data structure for encoding in a computer typical information on some concept and coined the term **frame** to describe this structure. A frame has a name, slots with labels describing the concept's major attributes or features, and possible values for each attribute. In addition, a frame may have attached procedures that capture procedural information about the concept. When a specific instance of the concept is encountered, then the specific values related to the instance can be entered into the frame. This filled-in frame is usually given a different name, and not surprisingly, it is called an **instance.** Consider for example the following two frames that represent the concept of a "car" and an instance of it related to "your car":

CONCEPT $\longrightarrow$ INSTANCE

CAR		YOUR CAR	
DATE:	UNKNOWN $\longrightarrow$ DATE:	1957
MAKE:	UNKNOWN $\longrightarrow$ MAKE:	Chevy
COLOR:	UNKNOWN $\longrightarrow$ COLOR:	Red
WHEELS:	4 $\longrightarrow$ WHEELS:	4
STARTING:	Procedure1 $\longrightarrow$ STARTING:	Procedure1

The **CAR** frame lists the major features of "all" automobiles. Most of the features are generic; thus their values remain unknown in this frame. However, most cars have 4 wheels so it seems reasonable to set this as the default value in the **CAR** frame. In addition, starting any automobile will usually follow some set procedure, such as place the key in the ignition, give it gas, etc. This series of tasks can be captured in some procedure (e.g., Procedure1) and attached to the **CAR** frame.

The **YOUR CAR** frame represents an instance of the **CAR** frame. It inherits from the **CAR** frame its features and default values. However, it also contains feature values specific to your car. Having an instance frame inherit information from another generic frame is one of the nice features of frame-based systems— possibly not as nice as really owning a 1957 Chevy.

Frame-based expert systems encode their knowledge in frames much like the example just given. Generic concepts are captured in a frame and specific instances of the concept are represented in other frames with actual feature values. However, these systems also incorporate techniques found in object-oriented programming that add to their power and flexibility.

Object-Oriented Programming

Over the years, features were borrowed from object-oriented programming and added to frame-based systems to enhance their capabilities. Today, the areas of frame-based design and object-oriented programming share so many features that there is often some confusion in the use of the terms *object* and *frame*.

Object-oriented programmers refer to all of their data-structures as *objects*. Each object contains two basic types of information: information that describes the object and information that specifies what the object can do. In the terminology of expert systems, we would say that each object has declarative and procedural knowledge.

Object-oriented programming provides a natural way of representing real world objects. We usually view our world as being composed of objects, such as cars, flowers, bees, etc. For each of these objects, you should be able to describe them in terms of their appearance and behavior from your experience of seeing them many times. When you create an object in an object-oriented programming language, you simply give the object a name, a set of descriptive attributes, and some procedures that allow it to behave. In this fashion, creating an object-oriented program becomes an intuitive process—create an object, describe it, describe how it behaves.

In the design of frame-based systems, expert system designers refer to an object as a *frame*. This term comes out of the work of Minsky and remains part of the AI jargon. Over the years, frame-based systems have adopted most of the features found in object-oriented systems. Today, most people use the two terms interchangeably, with little harm being done except to the confused newcomer to the field.

_____ FRAME-BASED SYSTEMS _____

Let's start off with a simple definition of a frame-based expert system:

DEFINITION 14.1: Frame-Based System
A computer program that processes problem-specific information contained in the working memory with a set of frames contained in the knowledge base, using an inference engine to infer new information.

This definition is similar to that of a rule-based expert system, with the simple but important difference that frames are used to represent knowledge rather than rules. A frame provides a richer way of capturing the problem's knowledge than can be accomplished using an O-A-V triplet or a rule. It not only provides a packaged description of some object, but it also defines how the object behaves.

To illustrate the design and some of the value of representing knowledge in frames, let's consider the world of humans as shown in Figure 14.1. Each circle in the figure would be considered an object in an object-oriented system while a frame in a frame-based system. In the terminology of frame-based systems, there are *child*-to-*parent* distinctions made to express the natural relationships between frames. For example, **JACK** is a child of the parent **MEN,** while **MEN** is a child of **HUMANS.**

The frames in Figure 14.1 are organized in a hierarchical structure, moving from abstract issues at the top level toward more specific ones at lower levels. You can also link frames in other structures, such as a graph or network. Later in this chapter we will review potential benefits in these alternate structures.

At the top level of this figure we see a frame that represents the abstract concept of humans. This frame is often called a **class,** since it provides a general description of objects common to some group or class. Attached to this class frame are properties, sometimes called **slots,** which are a list of attributes common to objects from this class. All lower level frames attached to this class would inherit all of these properties. Each property has a name, a value, and possibly a set of **facets** that provide further information on the property. A facet can be

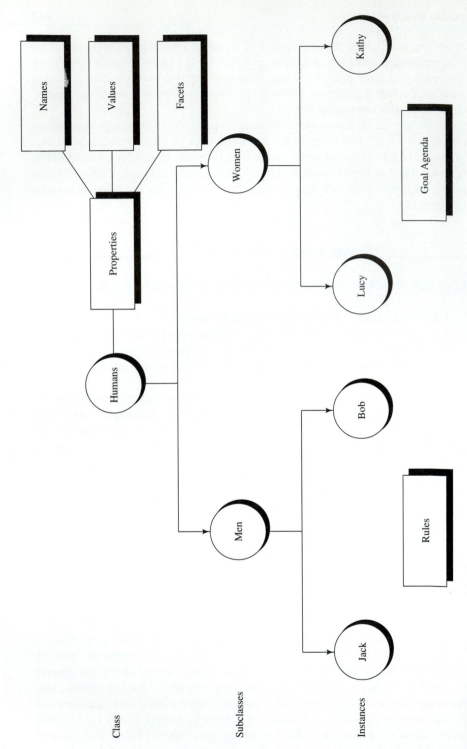

FIGURE 14.1 Frame world of humans.

used to define constraints on the property value or to execute procedures for obtaining the property value or what to do if the value changes. Because of the importance of facets, we will review this in greater detail later in this chapter.

In the middle level of Figure 14.1 we find two other frames representing somewhat less abstract concepts of men and women. Notice also that these two frames are naturally attached to their parent frame of humans. These frames are also class frames, but since they are attached to an upper-level class frame, this type of frame is often called a **subclass.** At the bottom level we find specific objects attached to their proper middle level frames. These lowest-level object frames are usually called **instances.** That is, they are a specific object or instance of their parent frame.

The terms just introduced to represent the organization of frame-based systems—class, subclass, instances (objects)—will be used throughout this chapter. However, recognizing that the reader might be using a specific frame-based shell, it is worth noting differences that might exist in the terminology. Consider for example the terms used by the following shells:

- Class, subclass, and object (Nexpert)
- Parent frame, child frame, and instance (Goldworks)
- Class, subclass, and member (KEE)

Referring again to Figure 14.1, we note that some frame-based expert systems employ a goal agenda and a set of rules. The agenda in these systems is similar to that found in rule-based expert systems. It simply provides a lists of tasks to perform. The rule set of Figure 14.1 includes powerful **pattern matching** rules that are capable of drawing inferences from the entire frame world by scanning all of the frames looking for supporting information. The next few sections discuss in detail each item of Figure 14.1.

ANATOMY OF A CLASS

As children, we learn about the world from our experience with objects within it. This experience builds our conceptual understanding of these objects. We learn what to expect in terms of their general appearance and behavior. Consider for example the world of humans.

As a child, we are likely to encounter a number of humans. From this experience, we begin to form an understanding of what to expect if we encounter a new human. For example, they should have two legs and two arms, a height constrained by some limits, and they go "Ouch" if we run over them with our tricycle. If we want to capture this conceptual understanding in an expert system, we would create a **class** frame.

DEFINITION 14.2: Class
A collection of objects that share some common properties.

A class frame contains generic information about a concept and is similar to Bartlett's schema. Like all frames, it contains a descriptive name of the concept, a set of properties that are characteristic of all its associated objects, and property values that are considered common to these objects. It may also have information describing the behavior of the concept captured in its facets. For some frame-based development shells, a class frame may also have an explicit reference to all of its associated subclasses.

To illustrate the design of a class frame, we will follow the approach taken by the shell Nexpert. Figure 14.2 shows the class frame **HUMANS** which follows the frame structure of Figure 14.1. This figure shows the frame's name, a list of properties, and some default property values which are common to all humans. Let's take a look at each property.

Most humans have two legs, so by default we assign the value of two to the **Number of legs** property. Likewise, we can make an estimate of the life expec-

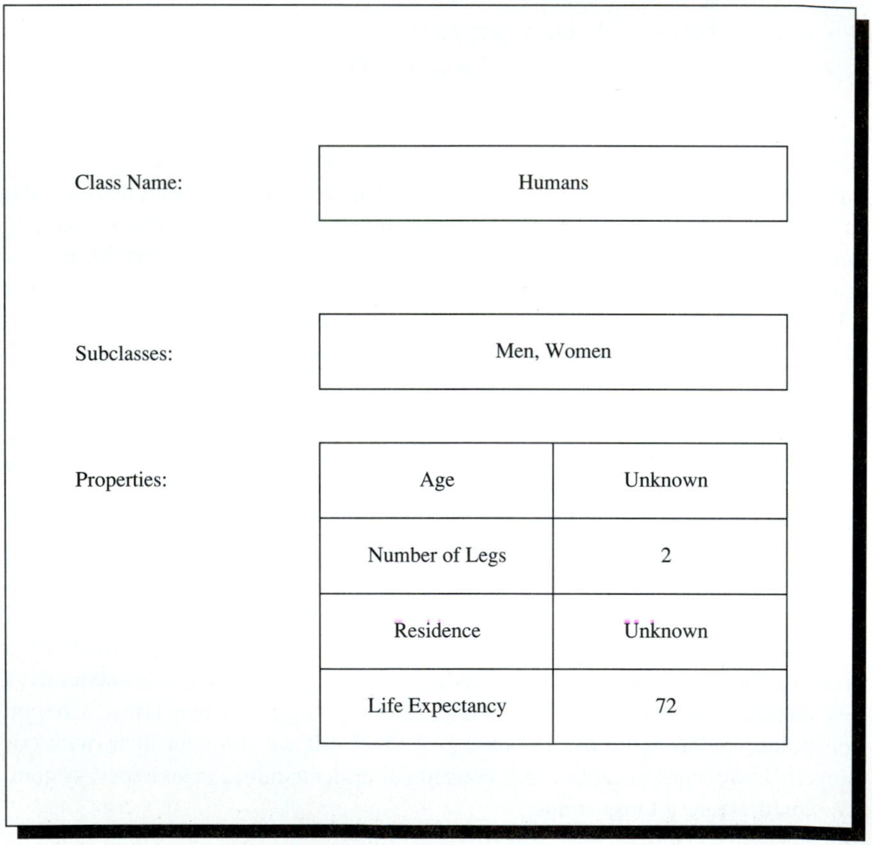

Class Name:	Humans	
Subclasses:	Men, Women	
Properties:	Age	Unknown
	Number of Legs	2
	Residence	Unknown
	Life Expectancy	72

FIGURE 14.2   Class of humans.

tancy of most humans. However, though we know that place of residence and age are common properties of all humans, it would be senseless to assign a default value for these properties for all humans.

In Nexpert, when we created the human frame of Figure 14.2, the subclasses of men and women are also created automatically. Each subclass inherits the properties and property values of its parent frame **HUMANS.** In some shells, you must first create the class frame, then assert that the subclasses exist and are children of the class.

ANATOMY OF A SUBCLASS

Subclasses are classes that represent subsets of higher level classes. In some applications you will have no need for this subclassification. Here you might simply create immediate instance objects of the upper-level class frame, e.g., Bob is a Human.

There are three kinds of class relationships that you might consider when deciding to use subclasses in your application (Rumbaugh 1988).

- **Generalization**—''Kind of'' relationship
- **Aggregation**—''Part of'' relationship
- **Association**—''Semantic'' relationship

Generalization denotes a ''kind of'' relationship between similar objects. For example, a car is a kind of vehicle, meaning that a car is a specialized subclass of the more general class, vehicle. Aggregation denotes a ''part of'' relationship between objects that share structure. For example, a door is a part of a car. Association denotes some semantic association among classes that are usually unrelated. For example, cars and houses are independent classes, but they represent things that you might own. Figure 14.3 illustrates these three types of class relationships.

For our example on the world of humans, the subclasses of men and women would represent a ''generalization'' class relationship. The class frame for **MEN** is shown in Figure 14.4.

As can be seen from this figure, the class of **MEN** has inherited all the properties from the class of **HUMANS,** with an additional property **Mustache** added to the class. Besides inheriting information from a parent, a child frame can have additional properties that are relevant only to it. This approach allows you to tailor the information in a specific frame and avoid irrelevant information in other frames. If you couldn't do this, then the only way you could have the property of **Mustache** in the **MEN** frame would be to place it in the **HUMANS** frame. However, this approach would then place this irrelevant information in the **WOMEN** frame!

A child frame will also inherit the property values from its parent unless the values are changed to reflect information specific to the object. For example,

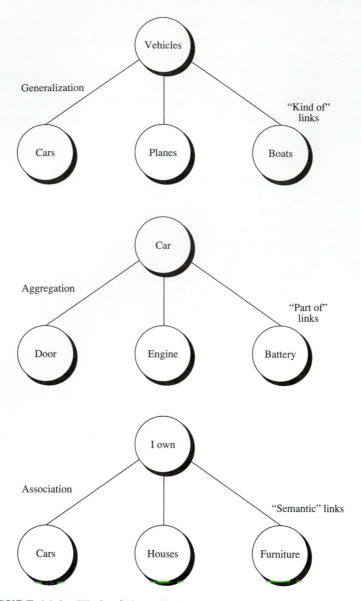

FIGURE 14.3   Kinds of class relationships.

Figure 14.4 shows a slightly lower value for **Life Expectancy** for the class of **MEN** than for the class of **HUMANS.** This implies that men are likely to have a shorter life span than all humans, which includes women. Subclasses also inherit the behavior of their parents or superclasses. That is, if any procedures were attached to the superclass facets, they would be inherited by the subclasses.

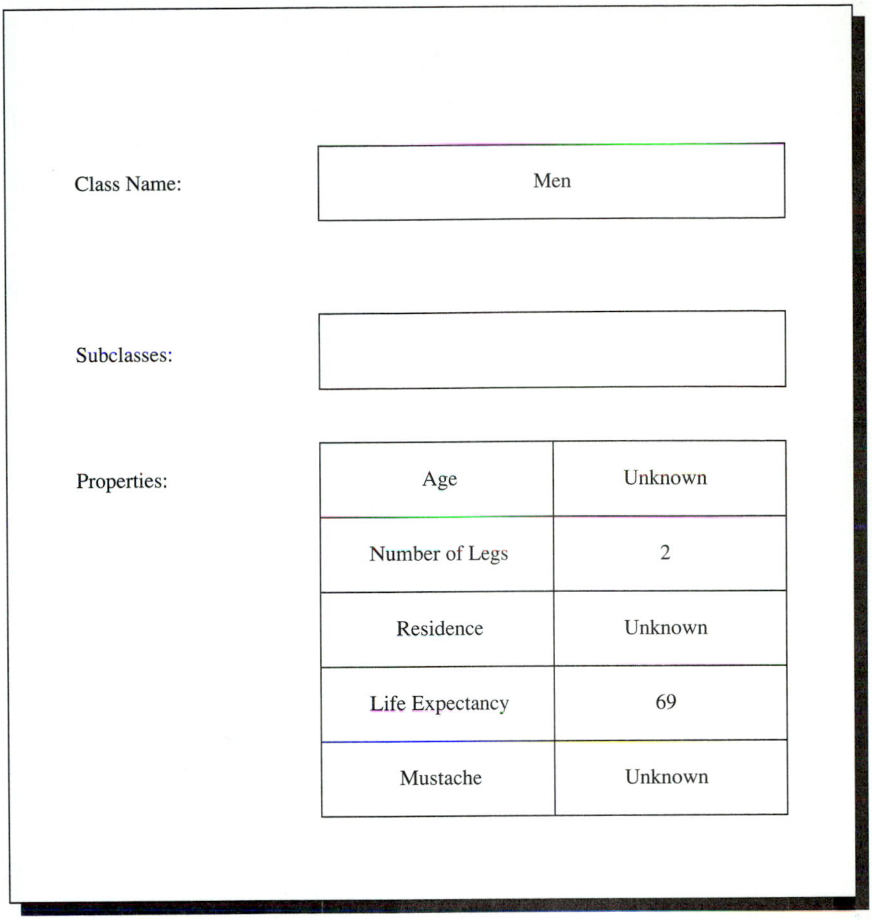

Class Name:	Men	
Subclasses:		
Properties:	Age	Unknown
	Number of Legs	2
	Residence	Unknown
	Life Expectancy	69
	Mustache	Unknown

FIGURE 14.4 Class of men.

ANATOMY OF AN INSTANCE

An **instance** frame describes a specific object from its related class. It contains all of the characteristics of the class frame, but will usually also contain information that is specific to the object.

DEFINITION 14.3: Instance
A specific object from a class of objects.

Consider for example Figure 14.5, which shows the instance **JACK.** This frame inherits all the properties from its parent **MEN** but the property values are assigned to describe the specific features of this individual. This frame could also have additional properties added if the need existed.

Object Name:	Jack	
Class:	Men	
Properties:	Age	40
	Number of Legs	1
	Residence	Pittsburgh
	Life Expectancy	85
	Mustache	True

FIGURE 14.5   Object Jack.

ANATOMY OF PROPERTIES

The **properties** used in frames describe the major features or attributes of some concept or object. These properties form a set of object-attribute-values that offer a rich representation of the object. In this section we will take a closer look at how values are assigned to these properties.

Property values are data assigned to a given property. Values can be numeric, symbolic, or Boolean. These values might be initialized when the frame is created or assigned during a session with the expert system. These values may be used and changed by rules or frames that work with the information from the session. Frames have another feature called *facets* that provide you with additional leverage over how a property value is established and controlled.

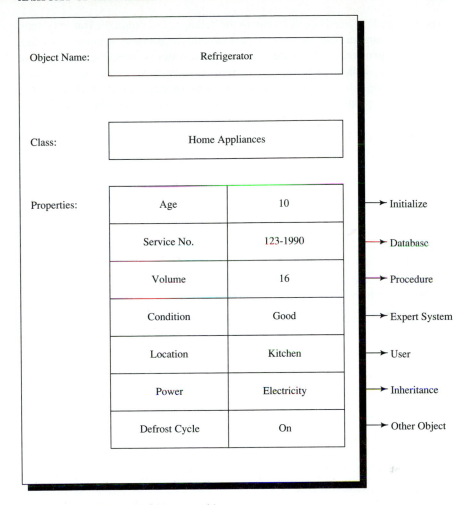

FIGURE 14.6   Refrigerator object.

Figure 14.6 illustrates the diversity of sources of property values. This figure shows a frame of a refrigerator, an instance of the class **HOME APPLIANCES.** The designer of this frame selected a number of properties to describe this object, each of which comes from a different source.

Age property—The **age** of the refrigerator is known by the designer when creating the object. Therefore, it is simply initialized at the beginning. This type of information is static and is not expected to change during the consultation session.

Service No. property—The designer has available a database file that contains the phone numbers (**Service No.**) for obtaining service for each appliance. The database offers an efficient manner for maintaining this information, since changes to phone numbers need be made only in the database and not in the frame system. New phone numbers can then be downloaded into the frame system when needed.

Volume property—The **volume** of the refrigerator is found through a procedure or *method* that calculates the volume from known dimensions. This is a convenient way for the frame to obtain this type of information. A procedure is attached to a property value, and when the value is needed, the procedure is executed.

Condition property—To determine the **condition** of the refrigerator may require some reasoning that might best be accomplished through the use of a small expert system. The designer of the frame chose to attach a command to the **condition** property value that will load an expert system when the condition of the refrigerator is needed. This expert system would pick up the consultation session, determine the condition of the refrigerator, then deposit this value into the frame and return control to the frame-based system.

Location property—To determine the **location** of the refrigerator, the user is asked. During a consultation, answers given by a user are used to update information in the frames during the consultation.

Power property—The **power** property receives its value through inheriting the value from the class of **Home Appliances.** Since most home appliances run on electricity, this value was set as the default value at the class level. If a given object would run on gas, then this property value would have to be set at the object level.

Defrost cycle property—The value for **defrost cycle** is obtained from another frame using a technique known as *message passing*. The other frame may represent the refrigerator's defrost timer, which would know when the defrost cycle is on. This other frame can then send a message to the refrigerator frame to change its **defrost cycle** property to **on.**

INHERITANCE

One of the major features of frame-based systems, one that is natural to Bartlett's view of a schema or Minsky's design of a frame, is called **inheritance.**

DEFINITION 14.4: Inheritance
Process by which the characteristics of a parent frame are assumed by its child frame.

Through this feature, a child frame inherits all of the characteristics of its parent frame. This includes all the parent's declarative and procedural knowledge. Using this feature, you can create one class frame that contains all of the generic characteristics of some class of objects, then create as many instances as needed without explicitly encoding the class level characteristics.

A valuable feature of inheritance is related to the issue of cognitive efficiency in humans. Humans will ascribe to a given concept certain features that are common to all instances of this concept. Humans will not explicitly ascribe these features at the instance level, but will assume they exist by virtue of the fact that the instance is a member of the concept. For example, the concept of humans assumes the features of legs, arms, etc., and it is implied that a specific instance of this concept, such as a person named Jack, has those same features.

Similar to the way humans economize their knowledge organization, frames allow instances to implicitly inherit features from their class. When designing an expert system using frames for representing the problem's knowledge, this ability has the practical value of easing the coding of the system. By simply designating a frame as an instance of some class, all of the class's information is automatically inherited by the instance, avoiding the need for you to explicitly encode this information.

Through inheritance, an instance inherits all of the properties, property values, and facets of its parent. In general, it would also inherit information from its grandparent, great-grandparent, etc. The instance may also have ascribed to it properties, values, or facets that it alone possesses.

Another valuable feature of inheritance surfaces if you have a need to modify information in a frame. Consider for example the need to add the property **Height** to all the instances in the world of humans example given earlier. You could simply add this new property to the frame **HUMANS,** and it will be inherited automatically by all of its instances.

Exception Handling

Inheritance is a powerful feature of frame systems, but it does pose one potential problem. As previously discussed, a child frame will inherit property values from its parent unless these values are deliberately changed in the frame. From Figure 14.4, we see that men have two legs by default (**Number of Legs** property), a value inherited from the class of **HUMANS.** Likewise, the frame **JACK** would inherit this same value. As can be seen in Figure 14.5, this value has been overwritten to reflect the unfortunate fact that Jack has only one leg. If you forgot to make this change, the system would believe that Jack, like most men, has two legs. If the system was attempting to form a activity for Jack that required him to have two legs, problems would obviously occur.

When designing a frame-based system, any frame that is an exception from the norm, must be handled explicitly. That is, if the frame has some property value unique to itself, then you must explicitly encode this value in the frame. This task is called **exception handling** and is important for both frame-based systems and semantic networks.

Multiple Inheritance

In a hierarchical frame structure such as shown in Figure 14.1, each frame has but one parent. In this type of structure, each frame will inherit information from

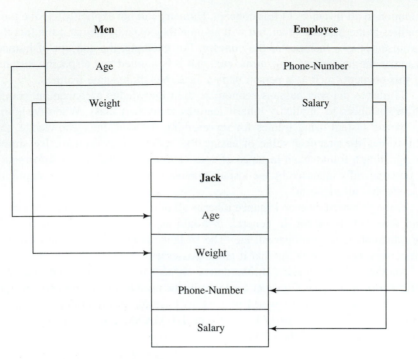

FIGURE 14.7   Multiple inheritance.

its parent, grandparent, great-grandparent, etc. At the apex of a hierarchical structure is one global class frame that describes the general world of all of the frames, and provides through inheritance information to all of the frames.

In many problems it is natural to discuss objects as they relate to different worlds. For example, **JACK** in Figure 14.5 may be discussed as being part of the world of humans and as part of the world of employees of some company. For this arrangement, the frame world structure would take on the form of a network as illustrated in Figure 14.7, where an object could inherit information from more than one parent. As you can see from this figure, the object **JACK** now inherits information from the two parents **MEN** and **EMPLOYEE.**

_____ **FACETS** _____

Frame-based systems extend the representation and control over a frame's slot or property using **facets.**

DEFINITION 14.5: Facet
Extended knowledge about a frame's property.

Facets provide you with additional control over a property value and the operation of the system. For example, facets can be used to establish an initial property value, define the property's type, or limit possible values. They can also be used to define ways of obtaining the value for the property or what to do if this value changes. A facet extends the information that the system has about a given property in the following ways:

- **Type**—Defines the type of value that can be associated with the property.
- **Default**—Defines a default value.
- **Documentation**—Provides a documentation of the property.
- **Constraint**—Defines the allowable values.
- **Minimum cardinality**—Establishes the minimum number of values a property can have.
- **Maximum cardinality**—Establishes the maximum number of values a property can have.
- **If-needed**—Specifies action to be taken if the property's value is needed.
- **If-changed**—Specifies action to be taken if the property's value is changed.

An illustration in the use of facets is shown in Figure 14.8. The figure shows an object called **SENSOR1,** a sensor from the class of temperature sensors. The object has two properties, **Reading** and **Location,** each with multiple facets.

Type facets are used to define the type of value associated with the property, i.e., numeric, string, or Boolean. For example, the **Reading** value of Figure 14.8 is defined as a numeric type. This type of facet prevents an incorrect data type from being entered into a frame by either the designer or user of the system. Recognizing the allowable data type, the system would warn the user if an invalid entry were attempted.

Default facets are used in applications where the designer wants an initial value for a given property. As can be seen in Figure 14.8, the **Location** property has a default value of **Pump1.** This simply means that this sensor is initially established to monitor the temperature of this specific pump. This type of facet is not only of value in establishing initial data, but it also permits the system to reset the property's value to this default setting, in the event a rerun of the session is performed.

Constraint facets define allowable values for the property. For example, the **Location** value would be constrained to be one of three possible values. A constraint can also be placed on numeric values, constraining the allowable range of values. Like the type facet, constraint facets can be used for truth maintenance. If a user attempts to place an unallowable value into a property, the constraint facet can detect it and respond accordingly.

Minimum and **maximum cardinality facets** establish the minimum and maximum number of values a property can have. For example, the **Location** property must have at least one but no more than one value. Property values in frames can be viewed as attribute-values in the O-A-V triplet structure. Just as

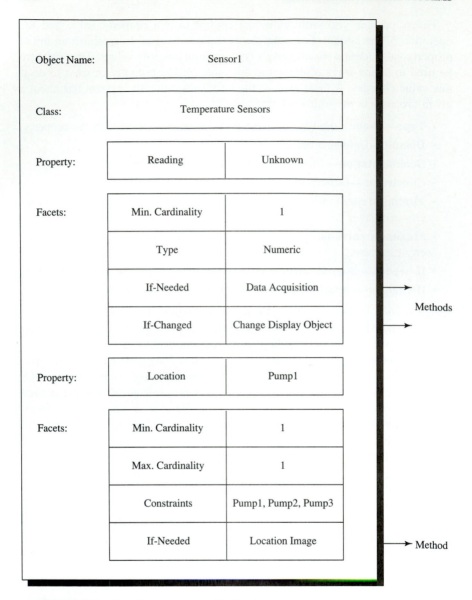

FIGURE 14.8   Sensor object with facets.

an O-A-V can be designed to be single- or multi-valued, the cardinality facet maintains control over the number of values a given property can have.

The "if-needed" and "if-changed" facets are important features of frame-based systems. You can use them to represent the behavior of various objects by attaching procedures called "methods" to an object's property.

METHODS

Let's first define a **method** and then look at some simple examples of its use through **if-needed** and **if-changed** facets.

DEFINITION 14.6: Method
A procedure attached to an object, that will be executed whenever requested.

In many applications, an object's property value will be initially set to some default value. In some applications, however, an **if-needed** method will be written in order to obtain the property's value only when it is needed. In this sense a method acts like a *demon;* it is executed only when it is needed.

Consider for example the **Reading** property of Figure 14.8. If this value is needed, the object **SENSOR1** will interrogate the data acquisition system to obtain it. Some procedural code would be written to accomplish the function. The function's name would then be referenced by this property.

In general, you can write if-needed methods to instruct the object to obtain the value by asking the user, from a database, from an algorithm, from another object, or even from another expert system. Notice that the **Location** value of Figure 14.8 is obtained by displaying an image to the user containing various pump pictures with corresponding radio buttons for selecting one.

An **if-changed facet,** like the if-needed facet, executes some method, but in this case one that performs some function in the event the property's value changes. For example, if the **Reading** property value changes, a method is executed that updates the reading of a display object representing **SENSOR1.** In general, if-changed methods can be written to perform a number of functions, such as change an object's property value, access database information, etc.

Methods designed to perform if-needed or if-changed operations can be written at a class level and inherited by all of the lower-level frames. However, a frame inheriting one of these methods can alter it to better reflect the needs of the frame.

COMMUNICATION BETWEEN OBJECTS

It was mentioned in the last section that if-needed and if-changed methods can be written that would permit objects to exchange information. For example, if an object needs information, it might obtain it from another object. Or, if one object's property value changes, it might cause a change in another object's property values. In this sense, you can make different objects communicate with one another. This feature is a trademark of both object-oriented and frame-based systems. It brings a dynamic to the system where the action of one request or change of information can cause a ripple effect by which information is exchanged throughout the system.

Object-oriented systems and some frame-based systems use a **message passing** technique to accomplish interobject communications. We will review this technique later. In the next section, we review an explicit approach towards object communications that relies upon the if-needed and if-changed facets.

Example of Interobject Communication Using Facets

The following example illustrates this style of object communication. Assume that we have three objects: refrigerator, defrost timer, and heating coil. The role of the defrost timer is to notify the refrigerator when the defrost cycle should start. When this occurs, the refrigerator in turn must signal the heating coil that it should turn its power on. Figure 14.9 shows these three objects communicating this information.

A conventional syntax used in frame-based systems for referring to an object's property within a method is:

object.property

Consider for example the premise of the rule contained in the if-changed method of the frame **DEFROST TIMER:**

IF Defrost Timer.Status = On

This premise looks at the value of the property **Status** contained in object's own frame **DEFROST TIMER.** If this value is found to be equal to ''On,'' then the rule will fire, which sets the **Status** property of the **REFRIGERATOR** object to ''Defrost,'' which in turn causes this property's method to execute. The firing of this method sets the property **Power** of the object **HEATING COIL** to ''On.'' Finally, a method is executed to change the **Status** of **HEATING COIL** to ''On.''

This example illustrates how through the use of facet methods you can make objects communicate with one another. It also shows how a change to only one property value causes a series of changes in a number of objects. Objects can influence the property values in other objects, or even itself (e.g., **HEATING COIL**).

MESSAGE PASSING

Another technique used in some frame-based systems that allows objects to communicate with each other is known as **message passing**—a standard technique in object-oriented systems.

DEFINITION 14.7: Message Passing
A signal to an object to which the object responds by executing a method.

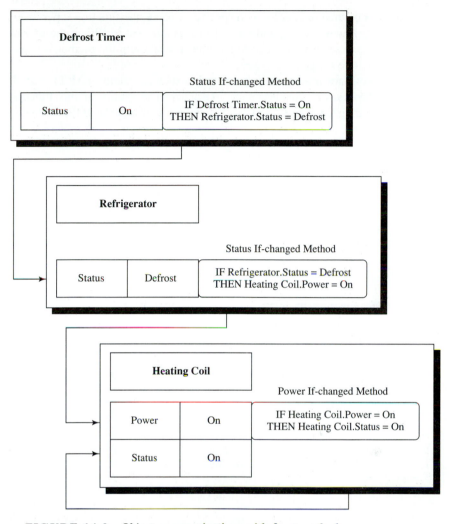

FIGURE 14.9   Object communications with facet methods.

Message passing in frame-based systems is managed in much the same way as when you place a telephone call to a friend. You might ask your friend a question or request him or her to do something. In most cases, your friend will know how to handle the message and will respond accordingly.

In frame-based systems, when an object receives a message it checks its list of methods to determine how it should respond. For example, you might send a **Draw** message to a **CIRCLE** object. When the object receives the message, it would look for a method called **Draw** attached to it, and possibly respond by drawing a circle. In some systems, such as GoldWorks, these methods are called *handlers*.

To define a method or handler, you specify its name, the function it performs, any arguments it will receive, and the object it is attached to. When the user or some other object sends a message to the object containing the method's name, the method will be triggered.

Sending messages involves using a function such as "send" (ART), "send-msg" (GoldWorks) or "SendMessage" (Kappa). The syntax of this function will vary according to the shell used, but will have some variation of the following form:

(**send** *message-name object-name arguments*)

This function contains the specific method to be executed: *message-name,* the name of the object to which the message is being sent: *object-name,* and any *arguments* needed for the execution of the method. The **send** function returns to the originator of the message the value returned by the method.

Example of Message-Passing

Figure 14.10 illustrates the operation of the **send** function. Here we see two objects representing cars owned by Bob and Jack. Each of these cars has a

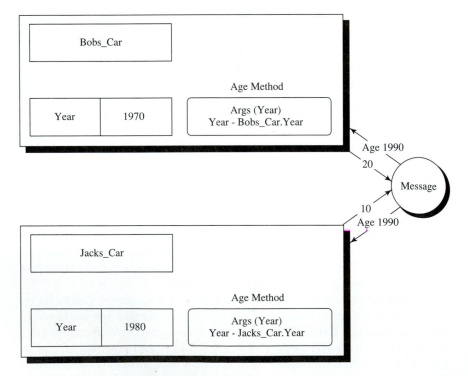

FIGURE 14.10   Object message passing.

different value for the year in which it was produced. The message sent to each of these objects is concerned with the age of the cars. The message has a label (i.e., Age) and the current year (i.e., 1990) that is needed by the corresponding methods. In response to this message, each object executes its associated method and returns its results. The exact syntax for the message sent to the object **BOBS CAR** would be:

MESSAGE	RESPONSE
(**send** Age BOBS_CAR 1990)	20

In this example, the methods were written to return a value to whatever object, or user, that sent the message. However, as in the case of if-needed or if-changed methods, methods used in message passing can be written to accomplish a variety of functions. For example, the message might result in changes to the receiving object's properties, or it might cause the object to initiate messages to other objects.

Message passing is critical for applications that naturally involve extensive interaction between objects. For example, a simulation system would require that the various objects being modeled be able to communicate their status with one another, and possibly control one another.

ENCAPSULATION

One of the features of message passing implied in the last section is that, when you send a message to an object, how the object handles the message is hidden from you. You only see the response to the message. This allows you to control the operation of the system by telling objects "what" to do, without worrying about "how" it will be accomplished. In object-oriented systems, this hiding of information is called **encapsulation.**

Consider for example that you want to modify your system's interface by adding some graphic objects. Also assume that you have available three objects called **BOX, CIRCLE** and **TRIANGLE,** each with a **Draw** method that allows each to draw shapes on the interface. By sending a **Draw** message to one of these objects, you could automatically draw the object without being concerned about the mechanics of the operation. In actual use, you might also include arguments that sized and located the objects.

INHERITING BEHAVIOR

Frame-based systems allow instances to inherit behavioral information from their class in much the same way they inherit descriptive information contained in the properties and property values. This behavioral information is inherent in class methods used either in the facets or defined for message passing. These methods are functions that individual objects can use for processing information. By placing the methods in the class level you are offered, via inheritance, an efficient way of developing the procedural code of the system.

There is, however, one small problem with this approach. Methods are often written to work with information contained in the frame's properties. To access this information, the method needs to explicitly refer to the name of the object and property.

Consider the previous example that was given in Figure 14.10. The method **Age** used in the frame **BOBS_CAR** accessed the age of the car using the statement

BOBS_CAR.Year

If you wanted this frame to inherit this method from a class, such as the class of **CARS,** you would need to explicitly refer to the frame's name in the method. If you then wanted another frame (e.g., **JACKS_CAR**) to inherit the same method, an obvious problem would occur because its method would be working with the year of Bob's car.

Writing General Methods

To allow an instance to work with methods inherited from a class, the methods must be written in a general or variable form. Most frame-based shells permit the use of some variable within the method to capture the name of the object using the method. For example, the shell will use the word *Self* or some variant to bind the name of the instance to the method, using the following syntax:

Self.property

This statement would bind the name of the object to *Self* and the object's property of interest to *property*. Consider for example writing the **Age** method of Figure 14.10 in the class of **CARS** as follows:

Args (Year): Year − Self.Year

When this method is inherited and executed by the two frames of Figure 14.10, the result would be:

Args (Year): Year − BOBS_CAR.Year
Args (Year): Year − JACKS_CAR.Year

The ability to bind variables defined at the class level is possible because of a process known as **instantiation**—a powerful feature of both object-oriented and frame-based systems. This feature greatly enhances the coding efficiency of the system and permits the system to be easily expanded.

Example of Behavior Inheritance

To further illustrate the value of behavioral inheritance, consider a small problem related to a manufacturing process. Assume your boss comes to you and wants an expert system capable of monitoring the temperature of the process at various points, and sounding an alert if something goes wrong. You were told that if any sensor reading exceeds some critical value, then the system should sound an alert. Further assume that temperature sensors are available whose readings you can access via a data acquisition system. However, you don't know how many sensors will be needed. Your job is to develop a system that will efficiently address each of these requirements.

Since the sensors share a number of common features, it would be reasonable to first create a class of temperature sensors, then later create instances for each sensor when you find out how many sensors will be used. This class frame would need to have a list of the common sensor properties and common methods that would need to be executed by each sensor. A reasonable set of common properties might be the following:

- **Name**—Name of monitoring location
- **Value**—Sensor temperature reading
- **Critical Value**—Maximum allowable temperature
- **Status**—Present state

Using the technique of writing methods with variable assignments, you could then create the class frame shown in Figure 14.11 to meet the specifications of the problem. Let's take a look at how these general methods would be interpreted at the instance level.

To obtain a value of a specific sensor, an if-needed method was designed to interrogate the data acquisition system. This method executes a function called "GET-VALUE" that uses the argument "Self.Name." This function would return the value of the sensor temperature reading and assign it to the value of the property **Value.** The if-changed method attached to this property would then check to see if this value exceeds the maximum allowable temperature reading recorded in **Critical Value.** If it does, then the object's **Status** property is set to "Alert." This in turn would cause the if-changed method of the object's **Status** property to sound an alert.

This example illustrates how methods can be assigned at the class level and used for all instances of the class. If additional temperature sensors are added to the class, they will automatically inherit these methods. If needed, these methods could be changed at the instance level to reflect specific requirements of a given sensor. By assigning methods at the class level, you are able to generalize the way all the sensors will both obtain and respond to information. This offers a natural way of developing the frame-based system and also eases the coding of the system.

RULE INTERACTION WITH OBJECTS

Many frame-based systems will employ a set of rules that interact with information contained in the frames. This type of system is often referred to as a *hybrid*

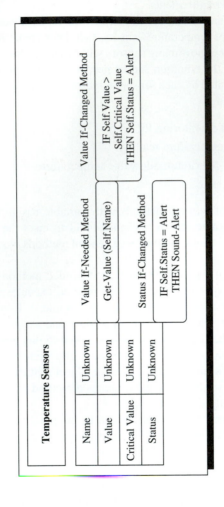

FIGURE 14.11 Class of temperature sensors.

428

system, since it combines both frames and rules for representing the problem's knowledge. To provide flexibility in scanning all of the frames, these rules will often employ *pattern matching* clauses. These clauses can contain variables that can be used for locating matching conditions among all of the frames.

The next several sections review various ways in which rules can be written to interact with frames. The different frame-based shells available all have the ability to perform the techniques that are reviewed. However, they all use different programming syntax, which may be confusing to the reader who is looking for a conceptual understanding of the techniques. Therefore, in order not to confuse the reader, we will use a "pseudo-code" approach to illustrate the techniques. This code is not far from what the shells actually use. It may not compile but it shouldn't confuse.

Frame Properties as Data

The property values of any frame can be used in a premise of a rule. Consider the following two rules, one that works with class information and another that uses information from an instance:

IF   HUMANS.Legs = 2   IF   JACK.Legs = 2
THEN Humans can walk   THEN Jack can walk

These rules look at the property **Legs** of each frame. If the value equals 2, then the rule will fire.

Modifying a Property Value

You can also use a rule to directly modify an object's property value:

IF   Jack likes to swim
THEN JACK.Sports = Swimming

If the simple fact contained in the rule's premise is true, then the frame of **JACK** has its property **Sports** set to "Swimming."

Creating a New Instance

Here's a rule that creates a new instance:

IF   Lucy is mad at Jack because he doesn't like hiking
THEN MAKE Frame BOB
                instance-of HUMANS
                WITH Sports = Hiking

This rule creates a new frame called **BOB** and makes it an instance of **HUMANS.** This frame then inherits all of the information of **HUMANS,** with a specific value of "Hiking" for the property **Sports.** Presumably, this rule makes Lucy happy because it creates a new person who shares her interests in sports.

Deleting a Frame

If you can create a new frame, it seems only fair that you can also delete one:

IF   Lucy is really mad at Jack
THEN RETRACT Frame JACK

This rule completely deletes the frame **JACK.** It also implies that the frame **LUCY** may have a property called **Overreactive.**

_____ **USING RULES WITH VARIABLES** _____

All of the previous example rules used explicit reference to specific frames and properties. In most applications, this approach would be too constraining. What is needed is a more general way of expressing rules that can apply to a number of frames. This is accomplished in frame-based systems using variables that allow you to perform complex pattern matching.

A variable is simply a symbolic string that can be bound to some piece of information. Many of the shells use a **?** symbol as the first character of the string to designate it as a variable. The entire string can be something undescriptive, such as **?X,** or something that is more descriptive of the information to which the variable will be bound, such as **?Age.**

Pattern-Matching Example

To illustrate pattern matching using variables, consider the frames of humans shown in Figure 14.12 along with the following:

Frame ?X
        instance-of HUMANS
            WITH Residence = Pittsburgh
            WITH Age = ?Age

When this pattern matching series of statements is executed, all of the frames are scanned looking for a match. The variables ?X and ?Age will match any values, but when a match is found, they are bound to the found values. The interpretation of this pattern would be "any frame that is an instance of Humans with a Residence property of Pittsburgh and an Age property of anything." For the example of Figure 14.12, two matches are found:

Frame: JACK	Frame: LUCY
instance-of HUMANS	instance-of HUMANS
Residence = Pittsburgh	Residence = Pittsburgh
Age = 35	Age = 30

The frame **BOB** failed to match since its property **Residence** was not equal to "Pittsburgh."

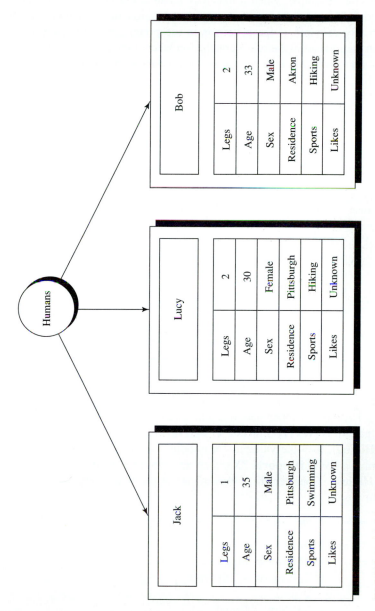

FIGURE 14.12 Human frames.

Using Matches in Rule's Conclusion

In the previous example, when a match is located, the variables ?X and ?Age are bound to their matching values for the duration of the pattern matching operation. For example, if the pattern is in the premise of a rule, the variables will retain their values in the rule's conclusion where they can be acted on further. Consider for example a rule that ages by 5 years every human who lives in Pittsburgh:

```
IF      Frame ?X
        instance-of HUMANS
            WITH Residence = Pittsburgh
            WITH Age = ?Age
THEN Frame ?X
            WITH Age = ?Age + 5
```

The premise of this rule would match every frame that was an instance of **HUMANS, Residence** in "Pittsburgh," and any age. For each match, the variable ?X would be bound to the frame's name and ?Age to the value of the property **Age.** The conclusion of the rule would take each match and modify its **Age** property by adding 5 to the bound variable ?Age; thus increasing the age of each match. As a note, if you wanted to increase the age of "everything" living in Pittsburgh (e.g., humans, cats, dogs, etc.), you could simply drop the statement "instance-of Humans."

Complex Variable Matching

In general, variables bound in one pattern of a premise can also be used for putting conditions on other patterns. For example, if the first part of a rule's premise pattern is (**WITH Sports ?X**), and this pattern is matched with (**WITH Sports Hiking**), then the variable **?X** is bound to **Hiking.** If a later pattern in the premise is (**WITH Sports ?X**), then an attempt is made to match (**WITH Sports Hiking**). Consider the following example that represents the general statement

If any man likes the same sport as any women, then the man likes the woman.

```
IF      Frame ?Person1
            WITH Sex = Male
            WITH Sports = ?Sports1
AND   Frame ?Person2
            WITH Sex = Female
            WITH Sports = ?Sports1
THEN Frame ?Person1
            WITH Likes = ?Person2
```

For the world of humans shown in Figure 14.12, the first premise of the rule would find the following matches:

MATCH 1

Frame: BOB (**?Person1**)
Sex = Male
Sports = Hiking (**?Sports1**)

MATCH 2

Frame: JACK (**?Person1**)
Sex = Male
Sports = Swimming (**?Sports1**)

When the second premise is considered, the variable ?Sports1 remains bound to the value established in the matches in the first premise. Consider MATCH1, with ?Sports1 bound to "Hiking," the following match is found in the second premise:

MATCH 1

Frame: LUCY (**?Person2**)
Sex = Female
Sports = Hiking (**?Sports1**)

This match causes the rule to fire. In the conclusion, ?Person1 remains bound to "Bob" and ?Person2 to "Lucy." The firing of the rule causes the following change to the frame **BOB**:

Frame: BOB (**?Person1**)
Likes = Lucy (**?Person2**)

The second match in the first premise binds ?Sports1 to "Swimming." After scanning all of the female frames, the second premise will find no match for ?Sports = Swimming, therefore the rule will not fire.

Creating New Instances

Using pattern matching with variables, you can create as many new instances of some class as matches found in a rule's premises. Consider for example adding a new class to our world of humans called **RESERVATIONS** with the following properties:

Frame: RESERVATIONS
Location = Unknown
Name = Unknown

You can use this new class frame to create instances of the class that match the sporting preference of various humans. Assume you want to make a reservation in Boulder for anyone who likes to hike. This could be accomplished by applying the following rule:

IF   Frame ?Person1
                WITH Sports = Hiking

THEN MAKE Frame RESERVATIONS
            WITH Location = Boulder
            WITH Name ?Person1

Using the frames of Figure 14.12, this rule would produce the following two reservations

Frame: RESERVATIONS1   Frame: RESERVATIONS2
Location = Boulder   Location = Boulder
Name = Lucy   Name = Bob

You should notice that unlike the earlier example that created a new instance, no explicit name of the created frame is given. The system places an index number at the end of the class frame and assigns this name to the new instance. If you didn't create the class **RESERVATIONS** before using this rule, the system would have assumed you wanted to create a new class frame instead of an instance.

————————— **SUMMARY** —————————

Frames provide a method for representing declarative and procedural knowledge of complex structures. They can be used to represent a problem's objects, or classes of objects, linked together in their natural association. Many expert systems today use both frame and rule representation techniques, and are often referred to as *hybrid systems*. In these hybrid systems, rules are written that interact with complex frame structures during problem solving. Key issues discussed in this chapter were:

- A frame is a data structure for representing well-understood stereotypical situations.

- A frame contains information on a given object that includes the object's name, major attributes of the object, and corresponding attribute values.

- Facets can be attached to a frame's property to provide control over the property value.

- Frames are linked together usually in a hierarchical fashion, with upper levels describing objects in the abstract and lower levels in detail.

- Upper level frames are called *class* frames and the lowest level frame an *instance* of the class.

- An instance assumes both declarative and procedural knowledge from its class through *inheritance*.

- A frame can also inherit information from more than one parent through *multiple inheritance*.

- Frames can communicate with each other through *message passing,* or using *facet* information contained in *demons.*

- Methods are procedures that represent the behavior of the object that they are attached to.

- Methods defined at the class level are inherited by instances of the class.

- General rules using variables within pattern matching clauses can be written that scan a number of frames.

━━━━━━━━ REFERENCES

Bartlett, F.C., Remembering: A Study in Experimental and Social Psychology, Cambridge University Press, 1932.

Minsky, M.L., Frame System Theory, in Thinking: Readings in Cognitive Science, P.N. Johnson-Laird and P.C. Watson, eds., Cambridge University Press, 1975.

Rumbaugh, J., Relational Database Design Using an Object-Oriented Methodology, Communications of the ACM, vol. 31, no. 4, pp. 214, April 1988.

━━━━━━━━ EXERCISES

1. Give an example frame for the concept "house." Also define several instances of this frame.

2. Discuss the relationship between object-oriented programming and frame-based systems.

3. Describe inheritance and its principal value.

4. What is exception handling? Give an example where exception handling would be important.

5. What is a facet? Give an example frame that uses various types of facets.

6. What is a method? Give an example of a frame that uses methods.

7. What is message passing? Give an example that includes several frames that communciate with each other using message passing.

8. What is encapsulation and what are its major advantages?

9. Give example frames that incorporate multiple inheritance.

10. Explain what the following rules accomplish:

```
RULE1
IF      ?Humans.Age > 50
THEN ?Humans.Status = old

RULE2
IF      You saw a new dog
THEN MAKE Frame LADDY
                instance-of DOGS
                WITH Breed = Beagle
```

RULE3
IF   Frame ?man
                WITH Status = Just married
                WITH Wife = ?wife
THEN MAKE Frame ?wife
                WITH Husband = ?man

11. Assume we have three frames describing a pump, a tank, and a pressure sensor that monitors the tank's pressure. The tank is to be maintained at a pressure of 100 psi. Define slots for each and include methods that will maintain the desired pressure.

12. Give an example rule that accomplishes each of the following:
    —Fires if a frame's property is something
    —Changes a frame's property value
    —Creates a frame
    —Deletes a frame

CHAPTER 15

Designing a Frame-Based Expert System

INTRODUCTION

This chapter describes how to develop a frame-based expert system. To illustrate the process, we will design a system to heat or cool a house (an environmental control system). We will review the major steps in developing this example system—steps that are typical when building most frame-based systems. You will see how various frame structures can be designed to best capture the problem's knowledge. You will also see how we can use basic frame-base tools such as message passing, demons, and pattern matching rules to bring these structures to life. To aid us in this effort we use the frame-based shell Kappa. Like all shells, Kappa permits you to rapidly prototype the system. It also offers most of the features found in other frame-based shells and object-oriented programming languages.

FRAMES VERSUS RULES

Earlier chapters explored the world of rule-based expert systems. It was argued that many problems are naturally expressed using IF-THEN type statements. It was also shown how this type of statement could be effectively captured and manipulated using a rule-based approach. If this is true, where does a frame-based approach offer an advantage? There is no black-and-white answer to this question. However, in the tradition of expert systems, there are rules of thumb that can help.

A rule-based system works with unrelated facts scattered throughout the knowledge base. Consider for example the following two rules:

Rule 1
IF Boiler temperature > 300
AND Boiler water level > 5
THEN Boiler condition normal

Rule 2
IF Boiler pressure < 50
AND Boiler water level < 3
THEN Add water to boiler

These rules work with various boiler facts that are isolated within the rules. In a large expert system, you could have many facts on a given object represented in many rules. If you wanted a complete picture of the object (e.g., what facts are used) you would need to scan the entire knowledge base. In this situation you need a better way to manage this information.

A frame-based system collects the related facts and represents them as slots within a single frame structure. Consider a frame that captures a description of the boiler:

Frame–Boiler
Temperature
Pressure
Water level
Condition

This frame groups the related boiler facts and presents them in an easy-to-follow manner. You can obtain a complete description of the boiler by inspecting the frame. This makes later maintenance of the system a far easier task.

A frame-based system also offers an advantage when you must work with several similar types of objects. Assume for example the problem involves several boilers. You could create one frame (class frame) similar to the previous one, then create an instance of this frame for each boiler. Through inheritance, each instance assumes the properties of its class frame. The inheritance feature of a frame-based system greatly eases both system coding and maintenance.

Another benefit of a frame-based system surfaces for problems involving similar types of objects when you need to include rules. To illustrate, consider RULE 1 and assume the problem includes several boilers. Without variables, you would need to write a separate rule for each boiler. A frame-based system permits you to use variables within the rules in the form of *pattern matching* statements, that do the work of many standard rules. You can write a single pattern matching rule that scans all of the instances of some class. Consider for example the following rule (written in the syntax of the shell Nexpert) that captures the knowledge encoded in RULE 1 in a general way:

IF ⟨Boiler⟩.Temperature > 300
AND ⟨Boiler⟩.Water_level > 5
THEN ⟨Boiler⟩.Condition = normal

In words this rule reads; "If any boiler temperature is greater than 300, and its water level is greater than 5, then its condition is normal." In operation, this rule checks every instance of the boiler class. When it finds matches for the premise statements, it sets the "Condition" slot of the matched boilers to normal.

Working with only one rule enhances the maintenance of the system. In our example you can freely add or delete boilers from the problem and do not have to touch the rules. You can also modify the rule without the need to make changes to the boiler frames.

Still another benefit of frames over rules is seen in those applications where the state of one object influences the state of another. Consider for example a control or simulation application. This type of application usually involves a large number of objects that depend upon one another. For example, the output of one object may be the input of another object. To maintain control over this situation, you need to enable the objects to communicate with one another. Frame-based systems borrow techniques from object-oriented programming, such as message-passing, to achieve this.

GENERAL DESIGN METHODOLOGY FOR FRAME-BASED SYSTEMS

Several of the basic steps taken when designing a frame-based system are similar to those followed when building a rule-based system. For example, both rely on first obtaining a general understanding of the problem. This effort provides you with insight into how to best structure the system. For a rule-based system, you obtain a general idea on how to organize the rules and structure the problem solving approach. For a frame-based system, you gain an understanding of how various objects are related and used to solve the problem. This early fact-finding also aids in the choice of the right programming language or shell for the project.

Designing either type of system is also a highly iterative process. You begin by developing a small—but representative—prototype, whose purpose is to prove the feasibility of the project. The prototype is then tested and the results used to form ideas on how to best proceed. This usually involves the expansion of the system, where you either deepen the existing knowledge (i.e., make the system smarter about what it already knows), or broaden it (i.e., make the system smarter about new issues).

The principal difference between the design of the two systems lies in how you view and work with the knowledge. For a rule-based system, you view the entire problem as being neatly represented in the form of rules. Each rule captures some heuristic on the problem. The collection of rules embodies the expert's overall understanding of the problem. Your job is to code each rule and make sure that they are logically linked to capture the expert's understanding—the inferencing.

When you design a frame-based system, your view of the problem is entirely different. Here, everything is thought of as an object. Following the first meeting with the expert, you will usually in some informal way (blackboard, notepad, etc.) list the major objects involved in the problem. These objects might be tangible things, such as boilers, pumps, etc., or abstract things, such as mortgages, leases, etc. They represent the major issues described by the expert in the earlier meetings when you are attempting to obtain a general understanding of the problem.

After identifying the objects, you will next look for ways of organizing them. This step involves collecting similar objects together in a class-instance relationship, and defining various ways that objects communicate with one another. From this effort you should be able to choose a frame architecture that best accommodates the needs of the problem. This architecture should not only provide a natural description of the problem, it should also provide the means to bring the system to life through such techniques as inheritance and message passing.

There are nine major tasks you will typically perform when developing a frame-based system:

1. Define the problem
2. Analyze the domain
3. Define the classes
4. Define the instances
5. Define the rules
6. Define object communications
7. Design the interface
8. Evaluate the system
9. Expand the system

This chapter shows how each of these tasks is performed for an application on a home environmental control system.

_____ **TASK 1: DEFINE THE PROBLEM** _____

Problem Overview

Many homes have heating and cooling systems to maintain a comfortable temperature in each room year-round. During the winter a furnace warms the house while an air conditioner cools the house during the summer months. The desired house temperature is usually maintained by the setting of a single thermostat located in one of the rooms. The homeowner sets the thermostat's mode of operation (i.e., heat or air) and the desired house temperature setting. The thermostat monitors the room temperature and turns the furnace (air conditioner) on when the temperature is below (above) the set point. This simple arrangement is usually effective but it does have some problems.

One basic difficulty with this arrangement is that it can be inefficient. Only one room temperature is monitored and used to control the temperature in the other rooms. If some rooms are vacant, the homeowner wastes energy.

Another difficulty is that large temperature variations may occur between rooms. That is, though the room where the thermostat is located may be comfortable, other rooms may be too warm or too cool. This problem can be attributed to such factors as the locations of the rooms, their insulation, etc. To avoid these types of problems, some building contractors choose to use individual heating and cooling units for each room. This is the typical arrangement found in large buildings such as hotels or apartment complexes.

Solution Overview

To demonstrate the design of a frame-based system we will build a simulator of an environmental control system. We begin the design by considering a small house. Later in the chapter, you will see that we can easily extend our system to accommodate larger buildings. This last point is a critical issue when designing a frame-based system. You want to design a structure that is easily modified to incorporate new objects or new ways of working with existing objects.

The objective of our system is to simulate the regulation of the temperature of each room in a house. We will assume that each room has its own heating and cooling units under the control of a room thermostat. Depending on whether the mode of the thermostat is set to air or heat, the thermostat turns the room air conditioner or furnace on or off to adjust the room's temperature to meet the thermostat's setting.

Let's also consider a way that we can add efficiency to our system. Assume we also want the thermostat to control the room's temperature on the basis of room occupancy. That is, we don't want to waste energy if the room is unoccupied. We therefore assume each room contains an infrared sensor that monitors whether or not the room is occupied. We could simply use this sensor to control whether the cooling or heating unit is off or on, but we will go one step further. We will allow the room temperature to deviate 5 degrees on the basis of room occupancy. For example, if the room is unoccupied and the heating (cooling) unit is chosen for operation, then the room temperature is permitted to be 5 degrees below (above) the thermostat setting. This approach improves efficiency while avoiding having someone walk into a cold or hot room. The arrangement for the environmental control system for one of our rooms is illustrated in Figure 15.1.

To keep our system simple, we assume the house has only three rooms livingroom, kitchen, and bedroom—We are limiting the scope of our problem (i.e., a feasibility study). That is, we are considering only a fraction of the number of possible rooms. However, we assume that if we can successfully show that we can control the temperature for only three rooms, we should be able to easily extend the system's capability to consider other rooms.

TASK 2: ANALYZE THE DOMAIN

Now that we have a general understanding of the problem, our next task is to study the domain in more detail. The purpose of this task is to define the problem's objects, their features and relationships, and the major events that occur. This

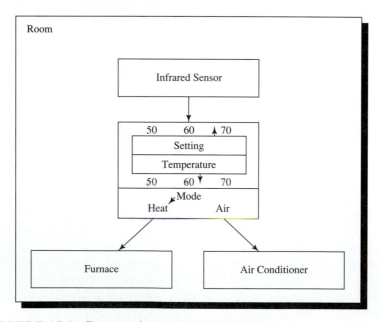

FIGURE 15.1   Room environmental control system.

task will usually be accomplished through a study of a transcript from an interview held with the expert during task 1. Chapter 17 presents formal methods for analyzing a transcript.

Task 2.1: Define Objects

The first step during the analysis task is to identify the problem's principal objects. A good place to start is to create an informal diagram on a notepad or blackboard that shows drawings of the objects. The diagram can help you identify natural relationships between the objects and can later be used to define ways the objects communicate with one another.

Begin by drawing the general or conceptual type of objects. These objects include items we can describe in general, but do not represent any specific physical object. For example, we can talk about the concept of a "room" and describe general features that are common to most rooms. You can also include in the drawing abstract items. For example, the "room temperature" represents an object that we will need to control with our system. These general objects define the class frames that we will design later.

Next draw the specific physical objects described during the problem discussion. These objects will usually be a "kind of" or a "part of" the general objects drawn. For example, a "livingroom" is a kind of "room." We can later describe the livingroom in detail, using the general information contained in the room object. These specific objects define the instances we will later design.

Figure 15.2 shows a sketch of the various objects from our problem. Also shown are lines that link related objects. Some lines form a "kind of" link. For example, "Furnace1" is a kind of "Furnace." "Part of" type links are also used; for example, "Furnace1" is a part of the "Livingroom." Links are also used to show object behavior. For example, a "Thermostat" controls a "Furnace," "Air conditioner," and "Room Temperature."

The drawing provides a broad view of the problem. It shows the major objects, their relationships, and insight into how you might design the frame architecture. We can now use the result of this work to study the problem in more detail.

Task 2.2: Define Object Features

The next step in our analysis is to describe the features of the general objects shown in Figure 15.2. These features, or properties, represent characteristics that are common to the specific objects that are linked in a "kind of" relationship. They also define the slots of our class frames.

We can characterize each room by the objects contained within it (see Figure 15.1) and whether or not it is occupied. The objects for our problem are the elements of the room's environmental control system.

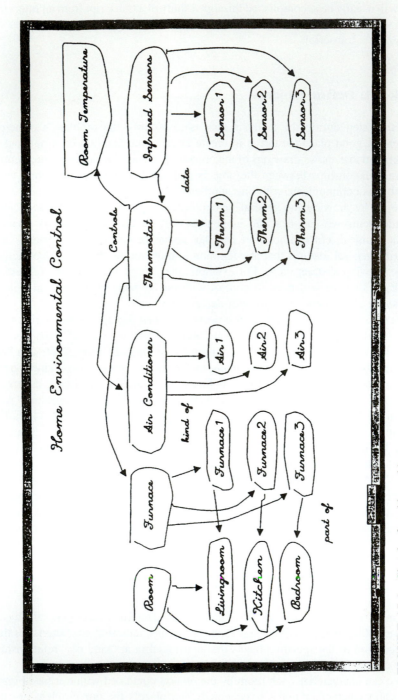

FIGURE 15.2   Sketch of problem objects.

ROOM FEATURES
Thermostat
Furnace
Air conditioner
Infrared sensor
Occupancy

Each thermostat can be characterized by its location, the objects each is connected to, and properties that describe each thermostat's state.

THERMOSTAT
Room
Furnace
Air conditioner
Infrared sensor
Mode
Setting
Temperature

We can characterize each air conditioner and furnace by its location, state (i.e., off or on), and which thermostat controls each.

AIR CONDITIONER	FURNACE
Room	Room
State	State
Thermostat	Thermostat

The infrared sensor provides occupancy (i.e., yes or no) information on a given room to the thermostat located in the room.

INFRARED SENSOR
Occupancy
Room
Thermostat

Task 2.3: Define Events

The information gathered in the previous sections provides us with a good characterization of the major objects in our problem. We should now show this information to our expert to see if we have captured the knowledge correctly. Our next task is to determine how we can use this information.

At present, we have only a static view of our problem. We know the objects and their descriptive features. We now need to study the problem further to see how we can bring this information to life. This task requires us to further analyze the transcript formed from task 1 to uncover the major events described. These events are simply a listing of activities involving the previously discovered objects. For our problem, the major events are:

- The thermostat mode of operation for each room is either heat or cool.
- When a given room is occupied the room temperature should be adjusted toward the thermostat setting.
- When a given room is unoccupied and the mode of operation is heat, then the room temperature should be adjusted toward the thermostat setting minus 5 degrees.
- When a given room is unoccupied and the mode of operation is cool, then the room temperature should be adjusted toward the thermostat setting plus 5 degrees.

This list provides us with the problem specifications and insight into which objects must communicate with one another.Knowing the problem's specifications is obviously an important point of any project. It represents the criteria against which our system's performance will be judged. It also provides the basis for formulating test cases to evaluate our system.

Most frame-based systems require objects to exchange information—communicate with one another. This is accomplished through facet actions or message passing. A review of the list of events can uncover which objects must communicate with one another, and which communication technique is best suited for the problem. This review also provides an early hint on the best selection of the frame architecture—a point discussed in the next section.

Task 2.4: Define Architecture

Our next task involves defining the frame architecture that best captures the problem's knowledge and problem solving activities. This can be a difficult task. However, you should recognize that decisions made here are only preliminary. That is, you make a good guess on some frame architecture that you believe best captures the problem's static knowledge (tasks 2.1 and 2.2), and dynamic knowledge (task 2.3). Later testing proves whether your guess was a good one.

Static knowledge is the factual information exchanged between associated frames through inheritance. This includes the inheritance of slots, default slot values, and legal slot values. Dynamic knowledge includes procedures (methods) that are activated when slot values are changed or needed, or messages are sent between objects.

A frame architecture is simply the interconnection of frames that defines some relationship between the frames. As discussed in Chapter 14, there are three types commonly used:

- **Generalization** — "Kind of" relationship
- **Aggregation**   — "Part of" relationship
- **Association**   — "Semantic" relationship

The first one, a "kind of" relationship, is the most popular first choice of frame-based designers. This choice is natural. During the early stages of system development we usually know very little about how the system will need to perform. It is only natural then to collect together similar objects and link them to a common classification—a class frame. This forms a "kind of" relationship where the objects (instance frames) inherit information from their common classification (class frame). This type of architecture is hierarchical where higher level frames are generalizations of lower level frames.

Using this approach for our problem results in Figure 15.3. We know that we have objects such as thermostats and furnaces. We can represent these general objects in upper-level class frames of our hierarchy (e.g., THERMOSTAT), with lower-level frames representing specific instances (e.g., THERMOSTAT1).

This type of architecture is a good starting point for our prototype system. We can easily add new classes or instances, or properties at the class level. However, as we develop and test the system, we will learn more about the problem and might uncover new system requirements that make this simple architecture difficult to modify. This point is explored later where different problem specifications are offered.

TASK 3: DEFINE THE CLASSES

Our next task is to encode the class frames of Figure 15.3. A class frame contains a descriptive name and a list of properties that describe a set of objects (instances) related to the class. Each class frame can also have methods that provide communication between frames. We will look at this point in a later section. For now, we will only consider the descriptive or static knowledge contained in the frame's property list.

Since this step is the beginning of system coding, you must first pick a software development tool for our project. On the language side, C++, Smalltalk, and Flavors, provide a good set of options. They are all powerful object-oriented languages and provide you with a large degree of flexibility. Unfortunately, they require as a prerequisite a mastering of the language—not always an easy task.

To ease the task of developing a frame-based system (at a small cost in flexibility) you can turn to one of the many available shells. Each shell comes with its own features and one of your jobs as the knowledge engineer is to match the problem with the right tool. For our project we will use Kappa. It offers a window-based development feature that eases the task of developing the frames. It also includes message passing, an important feature in a control or simulation application.

To create a class in Kappa you have one of two options. You can create it using a source code or a graphical approach. For example, you could create the class THERMOSTAT using the following code:

```
MakeClass (THERMOSTAT, Root)
```

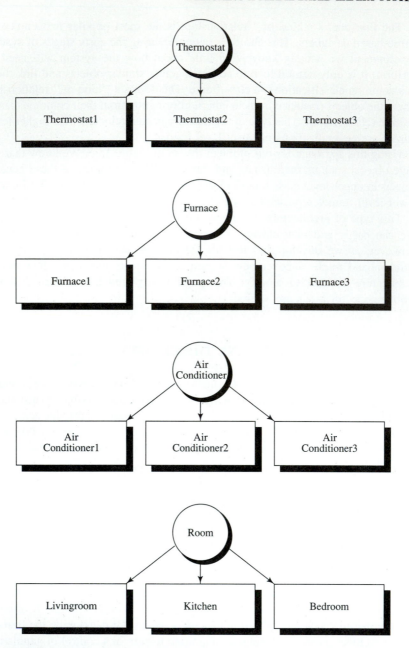

FIGURE 15.3 Frame architecture.

The function "MakeClass" creates a class and attaches it to some other frame. In this example, the class THERMOSTAT is created and attached to a default frame called "Root." This is the common attachment of new class frames. If you wanted the new class to be a subclass of some existing class, then you would replace the name "Root" with the appropriate name.

The second approach in creating a class frame is much easier and takes advantage of the mouse interface of windowing systems. Consider Figure 15.4 which shows how the "Thermostat" class is created using Kappa.

Kappa has a window called the "Object Browser" that provides a graphical display of the application's frames, including their interconnections. To create a class, you simply click the mouse on some existing frame, and select from a pop-up menu the function "Add Subclass." This action causes a new display window to be shown where you can enter the new class name and associated properties. In the example shown in Figure 15.4, the class THERMOSTAT has as a parent the system's "Root" frame. In a similar manner you could create subclasses of this new frame.

The following sections describe each class frame created with Kappa. We create a class frame for each "general" object of Figure 15.3. Their properties follow the object features described in task 2.2. A class for the object INFRARED SENSOR is not created because we will later allow the user to provide this information during the testing of the system.

Room Class

The ROOM class frame is shown in Figure 15.5. The properties describe the various objects that are common to all rooms, such as furnace, thermostat, etc., and whether or not the room is occupied. Since most of the property values will need to be defined at the instance level, we leave them blank at the class level. However, since we will later be running simulation runs on the system, we set the default condition on the room's "Occupancy" to "Unoccupied." Each time the system is reset in a manner shown later, all rooms are then assumed unoccupied.

Thermostat Class

The THERMOSTAT class frame is shown in Figure 15.6. The properties describe the objects controlled by a given thermostat (air conditioner and furnace), thermostat state information (mode, setting, and temperature), and the location of the thermostat. For purposes of later system testing, we assume various default values for all thermostats: mode = heat, setting = 68, and temperature = 65.

Air Conditioner Class

The AIR_CONDITIONER class frame is shown in Figure 15.7. The property "Room" is used to indicate in which room a particular air condition is located.

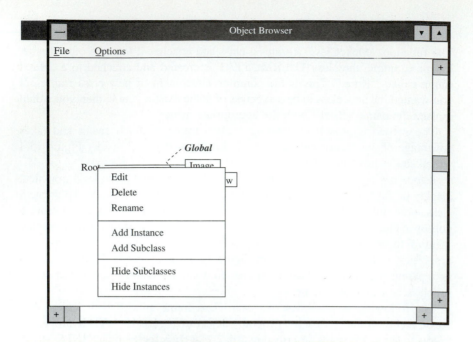

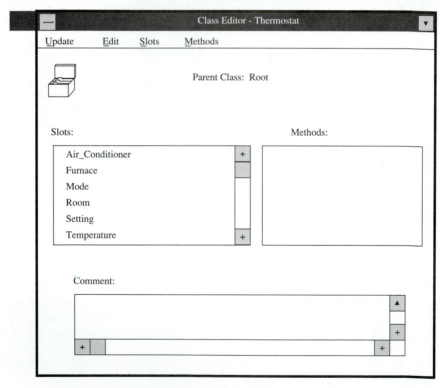

FIGURE 15.4 Creating a class frame using Kappa.

Class Name:	Room	
Properties:	Furnace	
	Occupancy	Unoccupied
	Thermostat	
	Air_Conditioner	
Methods:		

FIGURE 15.5   Room class frame.

The "Thermostat" property indicates which thermostat controls a given air conditioner. The "State" property simply indicates whether a given air conditioner is on or off. We assume by default that all air conditioners are initially off.

Furnace Class

The FURNACE class frame is shown in Figure 15.8. Its properties are the same ones found in the AIR_CONDITIONER class, and are used in the same manner. We assume by default that all furnaces are initially off.

This completes the coding of the class frames. We could now show our results to the expert to see if we have correctly captured the knowledge before proceeding to create the class instances. However, even if early mistakes or omissions are made due to the inheritance feature of frames, we can still easily correct the trouble. We simply make the necessary revisions at the class level and they are automatically recorded in all of the instances.

Class Name:	Thermostat	

Properties:	Air_Conditioner	
	Furnace	
	Mode	Heat
	Setting	68
	Temperature	65
	Room	

Methods:	

FIGURE 15.6   Thermostat class frame.

Using Facets

If it would serve the application, we could also add facet information to our class properties. Facets offer an additional way that we can control a frame's information. For example, we could specify the type of value permitted: string, numeric, or Boolean. We might also elect to constrain the allowable values. For example, we could limit the values of the ''Furnace'' slot in the class ROOM to the various furnace names that we choose, i.e., FURNACE1, FURNACE2, etc. In a similar fashion we could constrain the range of the ''Setting'' and ''Temperature'' slots of the class THERMOSTAT to values between 0 and 100. A more interesting use of the facets for our application will be seen later when we place methods in the IF-NEEDED and IF-CHANGED facets of various slots.

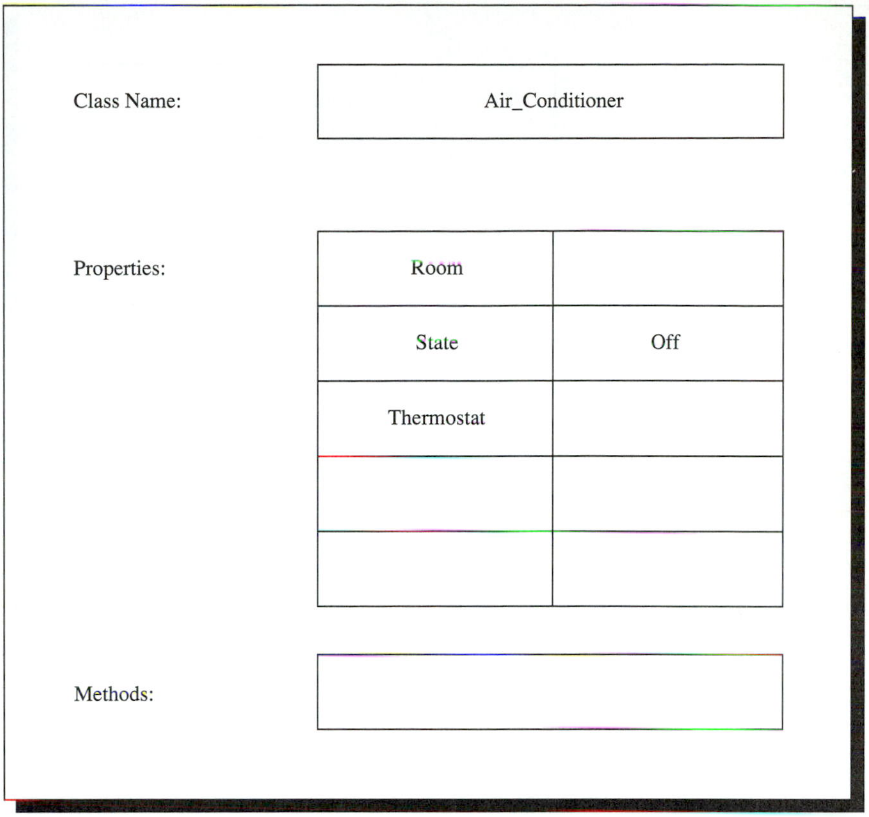

Class Name:	Air_Conditioner	
Properties:	Room	
	State	Off
	Thermostat	
Methods:		

FIGURE 15.7   Air conditioner class frame.

_____ **TASK 4: DEFINE THE INSTANCES** _____

Now that we have designed the class frames we can very easily create instances of each class. For most shells like Kappa, this task simply requires us to tell the shell that we want a new instance of some designated class. For example, we can use the following Kappa code to create the instance THERMOSTAT1 of the class of THERMOSTAT:

MakeInstance (THERMOSTAT1, THERMOSTAT)

This statement creates the instance frame THERMOSTAT1 and links it to the class frame THERMOSTAT. It also causes the class properties and methods to be inherited by the instance.

Just as a class frame could be created using Kappa's graphical technique, you can use the same approach when creating a new instance. Consider Figure 15.9 which shows how the instance THERMOSTAT1 of the class THERMOSTAT

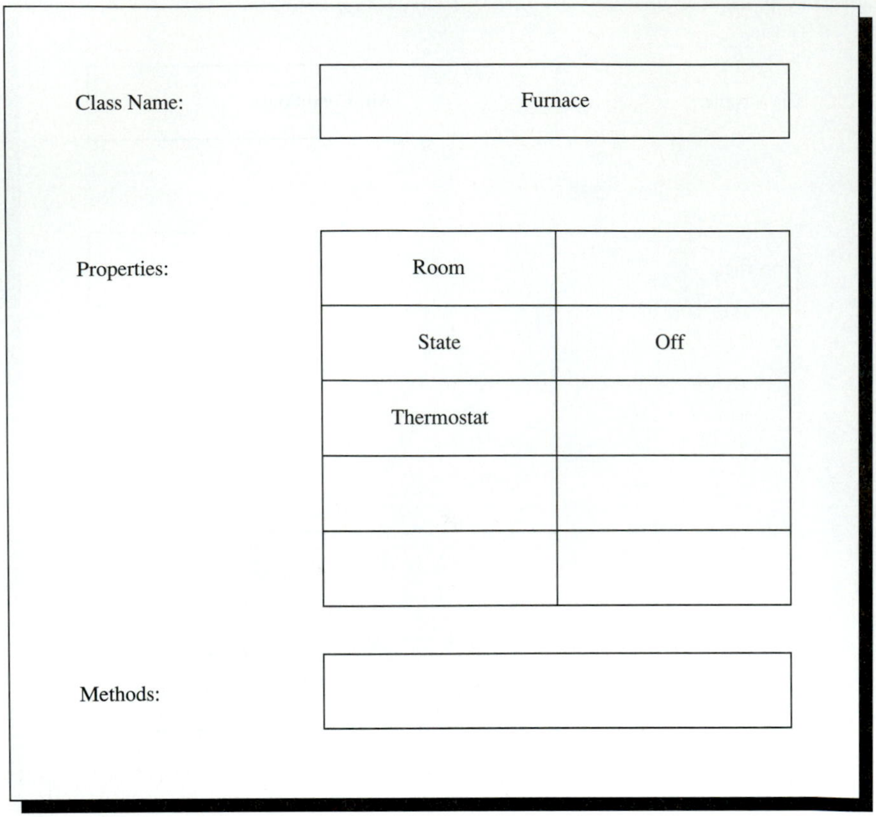

Class Name:	Furnace	

Properties:	Room	
	State	Off
	Thermostat	

Methods:	

FIGURE 15.8   **Furnace class frame.**

is created using Kappa.You simply click the mouse on the appropriate class frame and select from the pop-up menu "Add Instance." This action causes a new display window to be shown where you can name the new instance. Following this step, this new instance inherits all of the information contained in its parent frame. You could also add new properties or methods just to the instance—making them local. The following sections describe the instance frames created with Kappa following Figure 15.3.

Room Instances

In our house we have only three rooms: livingroom, kitchen, and bedroom. We need to create instances of the class ROOM for each of these rooms. These instances are shown in Figure 15.10. Each instance automatically inherits the properties of ROOM. They also all inherit an "Unoccupied" value (indicated by "*") for the "Occupancy" property. This value was assigned earlier at the class level because of our desire to have each room initially unoccupied. If for

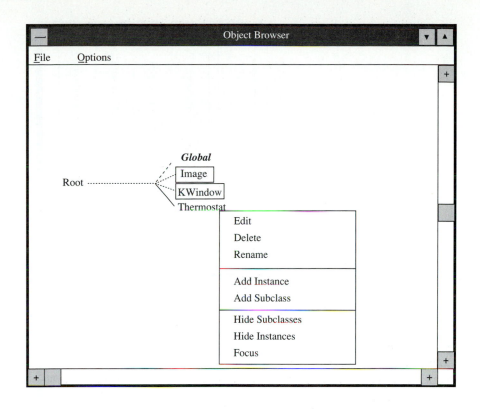

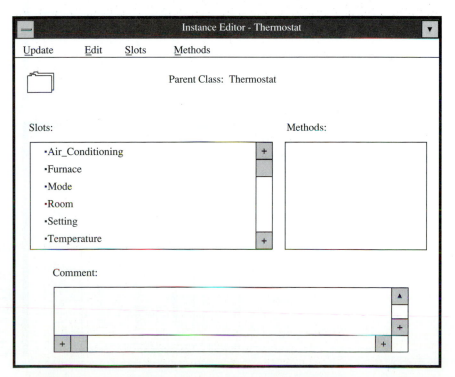

FIGURE 15.9 Creating an instance frame using Kappa.

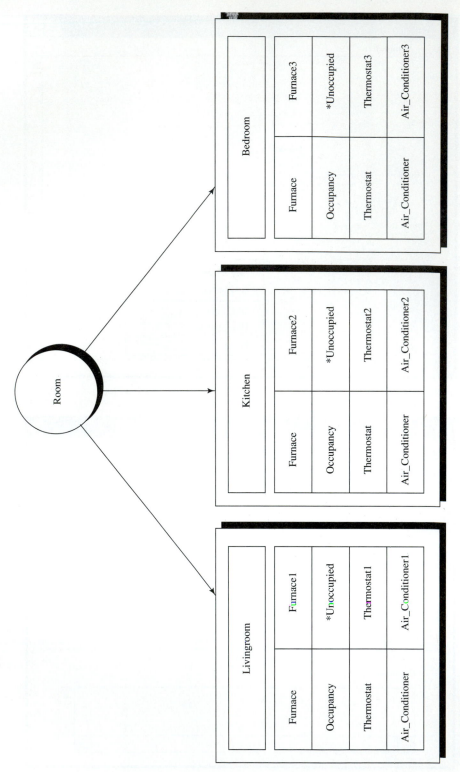

FIGURE 15.10 Room instances.

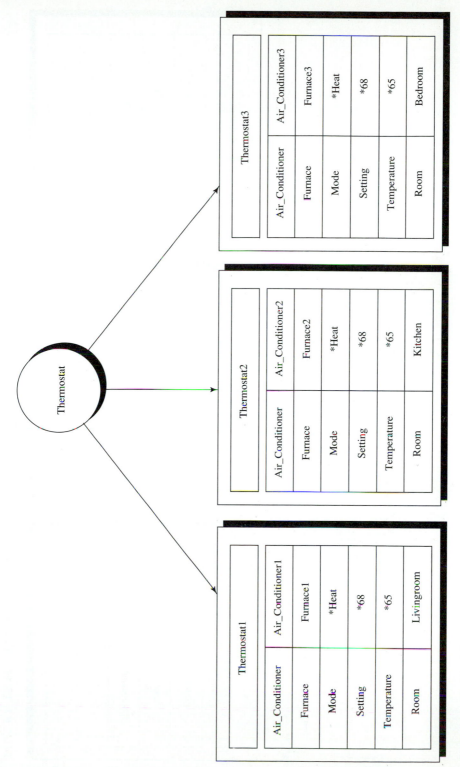

FIGURE 15.11 Thermostat instances.

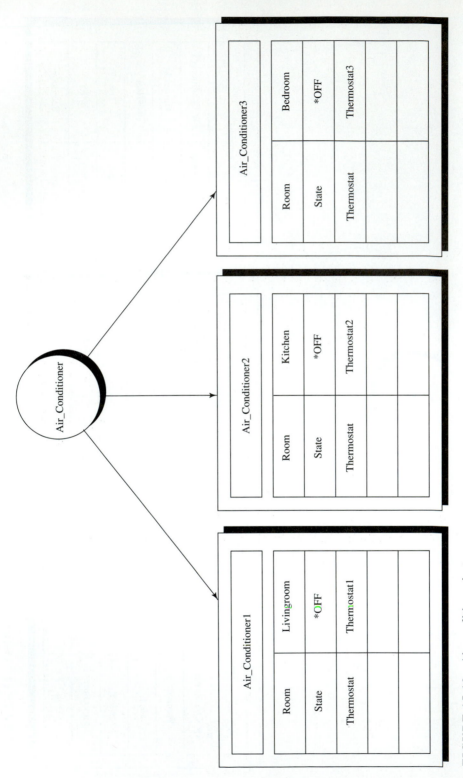

FIGURE 15.12 Air conditioner instances.

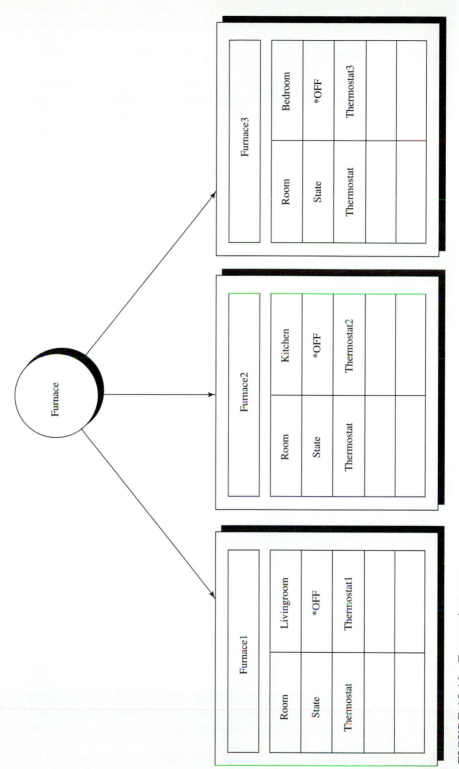

FIGURE 15.13 Furnace instances.

some reason we wanted some room to be initially occupied, we could simply overwrite the inherited value in the appropriate instance frame.

The other properties are inherited with no values and we must assign the appropriate values. For our system, we must record in each instance the name of the furnace, thermostat, and air conditioner objects located in the room. For example, the instance LIVINGROOM contains values of FURNACE1, THERMOSTAT1, and AIR_CONDITIONER1.

Thermostat Instances

Each room in our house contains a thermostat. Therefore, we must create three instances of the class THERMOSTAT (see Figure 15.11). Through the assignment of instance property values, each thermostat knows where it is located, and what furnace and air conditioner it controls. Each instance also inherits from its parent state information indicated by ''*''.

Air Conditioner Instances

Since each room contains an air conditioner, we must create three air conditioner instances (see Figure 15.12). Each air conditioner knows where it is located and which thermostat controls it. It is assumed by default that all the air conditioners are initially off.

Furnace Instances

Similar to the case of air conditioners, each room contains a furnace so we must create three furnace instances (see Figure 15.13). Like the air conditioner objects, each furnace knows where it is located and which thermostat controls it. It is assumed by default that initially all furnaces are off.

_____ TASK 5: DEFINE THE RULES _____

At this point we have created a static picture of our problem. We have classes and instances, each with slots that describe the various objects. We must now develop a way of working with this information to satisfy the problem specifications described in task 2.3—the events.

One way to accomplish this task is through pattern matching rules. These rules include variables that can be used to match select property values of each instance of a class. They enable you to write very general rules that capture the problem solving steps.

Assume for example we wanted to write a rule that performed the following function:

When a room is unoccupied, the mode of operation is heat, and the thermostat setting is 5 degrees greater than the room temperature, then turn on the room furnace.

Given the frames we created during task 4, we could use the following rule (written in Kappa):

ForAll x|THERMOSTAT

IF   x:Room:Occupancy #= Unoccupied
AND   x:Mode #= Heat
AND   x:Setting − x:Temperature > 5
THEN x:Furnace:State = ON

The syntax used in this rule needs some explanation. The function "ForAll" takes each instance of the class of THERMOSTAT, one at a time, and binds its name to the variable "x". This bound value is then applied throughout the rule. To illustrate the operation of the rule, assume the bound value is THERMOSTAT1 and refer to Figure 15.11.

The first premise checks to see if the room in which the thermostat is located is occupied. This premise first replaces "x:Room" with the name of the room, such as LIVINGROOM for THERMOSTAT1. Next, the "Occupancy" slot of this replaced value is obtained, i.e. "Livingroom:Occupancy." This premise is satisfied if this value is equal to "Unoccupied." Note that the function "#=" is used to test whether character strings are equal. The symbol "=" is used to assign values.

The second and third premises check various slot values of THERMOSTAT1. Given that all the premises are true, then the state of the furnace controlled by the THERMOSTAT1 (i.e., FURNACE1) is set to "ON." The other thermostats of Figure 15.11 would be checked in a similar manner. Other shells, such as Nexpert, GoldWorks, and ART, offer similar means for writing pattern matching rules, each with a different syntax.

Many frame-based expert systems rely strictly on pattern matching rules to direct the problem solving. Others use more of a object-oriented approach where methods tied to facets or messages are used to provide a dynamic exchange of information between frames. In some applications a combination of the two techniques is used. For our system we will only be using an object-oriented approach. Before proceeding with our design, let's explore the pros and cons of both techniques.

Object Communication vs. Rules

When designing a frame-based system, one of the more difficult decisions is to know when to use rules or one of the interobject communication techniques. Often, the choice is made on the personal preference of the designer. However, like most of the techniques available to the designer, they should be thought of as tools. The key—as always—is to pick the right tool for the job.

Advantages of Rules

As argued in earlier chapters, a rule is an independent chunk of knowledge. It takes a set of evidence contained in its premises and infers new information through actions in its conclusion. We can easily inspect it and check its correctness.

Rules also provide the means for performing deep inferencing. You can write a set of rules that takes very primitive information and infers more general information. It is also usually easy to inspect the entire set of rules to check for their correctness and consistency.

When a rule includes variables, it provides a powerful approach for capturing general problem solving knowledge. Often, the expert provides only a general description of his or her problem solving approach. For example,

"If a pump's pressure is high, but its flow rate is low, then . . ."

Using variables, you can scan all of pump instances with one rule to see if they meet the conditions of the rule.

Disadvantages of Rules

Rules provide an inefficient means for capturing knowledge that is largely procedural. They are severely limited in the types of functions they can perform, and quickly become unreadable and difficult to maintain. Methods on the other hand offer the designer a powerful and easy-to-use way of representing procedures.

It is difficult to write a set of rules that account for the propagation of changes in information. Consider for example a simulation problem. This type of problem is characterized by the interaction of the objects modeled. Often, the change to one object sets off a wave of changes that ripples through related objects. Writing rules to maintain this causal effect is difficult, and adds to the complexity of system maintenance.

Advantages of Object Communications

When we describe an object, it is often only natural to discuss how it behaves and interacts with other objects. For example, a pump produces pressure in a line while its motor is on. Since a frame-based system permits interobject communications through such techniques as IF-NEEDED and IF-CHANGED methods, or message passing, it offers a natural way of representing object behavior. Since class methods are inherited by the instances, we have an efficient way to encode procedural knowledge. System debugging and maintenance are also enhanced since changes to the methods can be made at the class level.

Encapsulation of methods within a frame keeps the details of the frame's dynamics neatly within the frame, rather than spread around a series of rules. This is especially important in large systems, where we can go to one frame to study how it behaves. This feature enhances both the debugging and maintenance tasks.

Some applications require you to write small procedures. Using a rule-based approach, you will need to write external programs for each procedure, and call them from the rules. This adds to the difficulty of both encoding and maintaining the system. A frame-based system can execute these procedures using methods attached to a frame. It is a simple task to both create and maintain these methods.

Applications such as simulation or control rely on the interaction between objects. An object might need information from some other object, or provide information to another. This exchange of information might propagate throughout the object world. It is critical in these types of applications to have available interobject communication techniques.

Disadvantages of Object Communication

Ironically, the major disadvantage of using interobject communications is a product of this last advantage. It can be difficult to debug a system where actions ripple through a large number of objects. When something goes wrong, you will need to trace back through all of the actions to locate the problem.

Another problem is the overuse of methods. Many knowledge engineers come from the ranks of traditional programmers. They are familiar and comfortable with writing procedural programs. They are then tempted to encode most of the problem's knowledge in methods.

While methods offer are excellent approach for representing procedures, they are not a good way to represent heuristics. In some cases, the designer will begin with some heuristic provided by the expert, and remap it in methods tied to various facets or messages. Not only is this inefficient, it could lead to errors if the heuristic is misrepresented. In these situations, use pattern matching rules to capture the heuristics and methods for the procedural knowledge.

———— TASK 6: DEFINE OBJECT COMMUNICATIONS ——

At this point in our design, we want to take advantage of any interobject communication techniques available with our shell that help us to meet the problem requirements. There are two ways to enable objects to communicate with one another. The first technique relies on IF-NEEDED or IF-CHANGED facets. The second technique involves messages being sent between objects. Both techniques rely on procedures (methods) being written and attached to the frame. To ease system development, always first consider defining these methods at the class level to allow them to be inherited by the instance frames. If they must be tailored at the instance level, it is a simple matter to overwrite the inherited method to suit the needs of the instance.

Facet Approach

In a facet approach, the method written is attached to either the IF-NEEDED or IF-CHANGED facet of a given frame property. This type of method is often called a *demon,* because it doesn't go into action until something happens.

The IF-NEEDED facet method is executed whenever the property value is needed. Consider for example that you wanted to write a method that enabled the frame THERMOSTAT1 to respond to a question about its location. To accomplish this, you could write the following method and attach it to the IF-NEEDED facet of the property "Room" of the frame:

THERMOSTAT1:Room

This method returns the value of the property "Room" of the THERMOSTAT1 frame. This method is simple but not very efficient since it can only be used by THERMOSTAT1.

What is needed is a way of generalizing this method so that it will work for every thermostat. To accomplish this, we need a variable that can be bound to each thermostat. Most shells provide this capability. For example Kappa uses the word *Self*. You can then write this same function for all thermostats using the following:

Self:Room

Upon inheriting this method, each thermostat instance frame can use it by instantiating its own name for the variable Self.

The last example of an IF-NEEDED facet method was not very exciting. The frame simply looked at its own value and returned it. Before leaving this subject let's look at a more interesting method.

Assume the THERMOSTAT frame had another property called "Condition" that recorded whether or not the thermostat was operating properly. If we needed to know this information, we could attach a method that loaded a rule set that performed backward chaining diagnostics on the thermostat. The following method, written in the syntax of Kappa and attached to the IF-NEEDED facet of "Condition", would accomplish this:

BackwardChain (Thermostat_OK, ThermoRules)

This method, which could be defined at the class level and inherited by all of the instances, loads the rule set "ThermoRules" that attempts to prove the goal "Thermostat_OK" in a backward chaining fashion. The method returns values of TRUE or FALSE to the "Condition" property. These rules would be written to perform certain checks on the thermostat. To enable them to work with each thermostat, the rules would need to include variables to instantiate each thermostat—an issue discussed later.

An IF-CHANGED facet method is executed whenever some property value is changed. Assume for example you wanted a method that heated a room whenever its furnace was on. To accomplish this, you could write the following method and attach it to the IF-CHANGED facet of the property "State" of the FURNACE class frame:

```
While ((Self:State #= ON))
Self:Thermostat:Temperature = Self:Thermostat:Temperature + 1
```

The first line of this method simply checks to see if the state of the furnace is on. While it is on, the second line of code is executed. The segment "Self:Thermostat:Temperature" obtains the temperature value of the thermostat located in the same room as the furnace. Consider for example FURNACE1 shown in Figure 15.13. This furnace is controlled by THERMOSTAT1. Figure 15.11 shows that the temperature of this thermostat is equal to 65 degrees by default.

If the state of this furnace changes to "ON", then the interpretation of the prior method is:

$$\underline{\text{Self:Thermostat:Temperature}} \qquad = \underline{\text{Self:Thermostat:Temperature}} + 1$$

$$\downarrow \qquad\qquad\qquad\qquad\qquad\qquad \downarrow$$

$$\underline{\text{FURNACE1:Thermostat:Temperature}} = \underline{\text{FURNACE1:Thermostat:Temperature}} + 1$$

$$\downarrow \qquad\qquad\qquad\qquad\qquad\qquad \downarrow$$

$$\text{THERMOSTAT1:Temperature} \qquad = \underline{\text{THERMOSTAT1:Temperature} + 1}$$

$$\downarrow$$

$$= \qquad\qquad 65 + 1$$

IF-NEEDED and IF-CHANGED methods provide means for objects to exchange and change information. This capability can be found in most of the frame-based development shells. To expand on this capability, some shells (such as Kappa) also provide message passing. This feature is another powerful tool in your toolbox— if available, take advantage of it.

Message-Passing Approach

Frames can talk with one another using message passing. The originator of the message defines both the frame to receive the message and the message to be executed. Syntax for message passing varies among the object-oriented programming languages and shells. Kappa uses the following form:

        SendMessage (objName, methodName, ⟨arg1, arg2, . . .⟩)

The "objName" is the name of an existing object. The "methodName" is a method defined in "objName" or any of its ancestors. The arguments (optional) are values passed to the method. The receiver of the message (objName) executes the method (methodName). This method can be defined within the object or inherited from its parent.

To illustrate the operation of message passing assume we want each of our thermostats to send a message to its furnace to turn on when the room temperature drops below some set point. To accomplish this, we can use the following Kappa code:

                    SendMessage (Self:Furnace, ON)

When this message is sent, each thermostat frame first checks to see which furnace it controls then sends it an "ON" message. The furnace frame receiving this message needs to have a method called "ON" that can interpret the message. You could define this method explicitly within each furnace frame, or more generally, at the class level.

Assume all we wanted each furnace to do upon receiving this message was to set its "State" value to "ON". This could be accomplished with the following "ON" method:

SetValue (Self:State, ON)

This is a simple message that tells the receiving furnace to turn on. In more advanced applications, we might also do other things. For example, we could send messages to other furnace components (e.g., main control or blower) to produce heat for the room. Many of the functions that we can perform with message passing could be accomplished using IF-NEEDED and IF-CHANGED facets. However, the message passing technique provides a more intuitive approach and you will find both the system development and its maintenance far easier then relying on facet exchange of information.

The next several sections show how both facet and message passing techniques can be used in our project to provide communications between our frames. Methods are defined at the various class levels that serve both techniques and provide an efficient approach for system expansion.

Thermostat

The function of the thermostat is to maintain a comfortable temperature within the room. It must also perform this function efficiently. That is, if the room is unoccupied, it must establish a room temperature 5 degrees below (above) its setting if its mode of operation is heat (air).

To accomplish this, we can provide the THERMOSTAT class frame with control over the furnace and air conditioner frames. Each instance of this class must monitor its own temperature, setting, and mode slots, and take control when any of these values change.

The easiest way to embed this control within the THERMOSTAT frame is to define a method that executes whenever the appropriate slot changes—an IF-CHANGED facet. We label this control method "Unit_control" and place it in the IF-CHANGED facet of the appropriate slots as shown in Figure 15.14. This figure also shows other methods defined for this class that are discussed later. The "Unit_control" method is shown in Figure 15.15. You should recognize that since we are defining all of these methods at the class level, they are inherited by all of the instances of the class: THERMOSTAT1, THERMOSTAT2, and THERMOSTAT3.

The purpose of the "Unit_control" method is to turn either the furnace or air conditioner on or off, on the basis of the thermostat's temperature, setting, and mode. The method consists of a set of rules as shown in Figure 15.15. Each rule sends an "ON" or "OFF" message to either the furnace or air conditioner

Class Name:	Thermostat		

			If-Changed
Properties:	Air_Conditioner		
	Furnace		
	Mode	Heat	Unit_Control
	Setting	68	Unit_Control
	Temperature	65	Unit_Control
	Room		

	Name	Body
Methods:	Air	Self:Mode = Air;
	Heat	Self:Mode = Heat;
	Init	ForAll (x|Thermostat) {ResetValue(x:Setting); ResetValue(x:Mode); ResetValue(x:Temperature);};

FIGURE 15.14 **Thermostat class with facets and methods.**

controlled by the thermostat. The responsibility for interpreting the message rests with the receiver of the message. This point is discussed later when we review the furnace and air conditioner frames.To provide an understanding of the syntax used in this method, let's consider the first rule, beginning with the first premise:

FIRST PREMISE
Self:Temperature < Self:Setting

EXAMPLE
THERMOSTAT1:Temperature < THERMOSTAT1:Setting

Class Name:	Thermostat
Method:	Unit_Control

Body:

```
{
If ((Self:Temperature < Self:Setting) And          If ((Self:Temperature > Self:Setting) And
(Self:Furnace:State #= OFF) And                    (Self:Air_Conditioner:State #= OFF) And
(Self:Mode #= Heat) And                            (Self:Mode #= Air) And
(Self:Room:Occupancy #= Occupied))                 (Self:Room:Occupancy #= Occupied))
Then SendMessage (Self:Furnace, ON);               Then SendMessage (Self:Air_Conditioner, ON);

If ((Self:Temperature < Self:Setting − 5) And      If ((Self:Temperature < Self:Setting + 5) And
(Self:Furnace:State #= OFF) And                    (Self:Air_Conditioner:State #= OFF) And
(Self:Mode #= Heat) And                            (Self:Mode #= Air) And
(Self:Room:Occupancy #= Unoccupied))               (Self:Room:Occupancy #= Unoccupied))
Then SendMessage (Self:Furnace, ON);               Then SendMessage (Self:Air_Conditioner, ON);

If ((Self:Temperature >= Self:Setting ) And        If ((Self:Temperature <= Self:Setting ) And
(Self:Furnace:State #= ON) And                     (Self:Air_Conditioner:State #= ON) And
(Self:Mode #= Heat) And                            (Self:Mode #= Air) And
(Self:Room:Occupancy #= Occupied))                 (Self:Room:Occupancy #= Occupied))
Then SendMessage (Self:Furnace, OFF);              Then SendMessage (Self:Air_Conditioner, OFF);

If ((Self:Temperature >= Self:Setting − 5) And     If ((Self:Temperature <= Self:Setting + 5) And
(Self:Furnace:State #= ON) And                     (Self:Air_Conditioner:State #= ON) And
(Self:Mode #= Heat) And                            (Self:Mode #= Air) And
(Self:Room:Occupancy #= Unoccupied))               (Self:Room:Occupancy #= Unoccupied))
Then SendMessage (Self:Furnace, OFF);              Then SendMessage (Self:Air_Conditioner, OFF);
                                                   };
```

FIGURE 15.15   Thermostat "Unit_control" method.

This premise uses the variable "Self" which is instantiated with each instance of this class, i.e., THERMOSTAT1, THERMOSTAT2, and THERMOSTAT3. This premise simply checks to see if the instantiated instance's "Temperature" is less than its "Setting."

The second premise is more embedded:

SECOND PREMISE	EXAMPLE
Self:Furnace:State #= OFF	FURNACE1:State #= OFF

In words it asks, "Is the state of the furnace controlled by this thermostat off?" To answer this question, the instantiated thermostat frame first checks its value for the slot "Furnace" then checks this frame's "State" value. For example, according to Figure 15.11, THERMOSTAT1 upon inheriting this method would ask "Is Furnace1 off?" To answer this question the slot "State" of the frame FURNACE1 is checked (see Figure 15.13).

The third premise simply asks if the mode of a given thermostat is set to heat:

THIRD PREMISE	EXAMPLE
Self:Mode #= Heat	THERMOSTAT1:Mode #= Heat

The final premise checks to see if the room in which the thermostat is located is occupied:

FOURTH PREMISE	EXAMPLE
Self:Room:Occupancy #= Occupied	LIVINGROOM:Occupancy #= Occupied

If all of these premises are found true, then an "ON" message is sent to the furnace controlled by this thermostat. We will see later that this message—not surprisingly—turns this furnace on:

CONCLUSION	EXAMPLE
SendMessage (Self:Furnace, ON)	SendMessage (Self:FURNACE1, ON)

The thermostat class frame also has a method called "Air" (see Figure 15.14). This method is used by all the thermostat instances to set their modes to air. It is executed upon the receipt of a message of "Air." In our system, this message will be sent by the user to set the mode of the environmental control of a given room. This frame also has a method called "Heat" that operates in a similar fashion (see Figure 15.14).

System Reset

When we first run the system, all of the thermostat instances inherit the default slot values in the THERMOSTAT class frame. During later testing, we will be changing these values to watch the system's performance. In order to rerun the system, we need a way of resetting the slot values to their default state.

To accomplish this, Kappa provides a function called "ResetValue" that resets a given object's slot value to the inherited value:

$$\text{ResetValue (Object:Slot\_Name)}$$

Since we have a number of slots to reset in the thermostat instances, we will create a method called "INIT" defined at the class level that resets each slot (see Figure 15.14).

The function "ForAll" takes each instance of THERMOSTAT (one at a time), and binds it to the variable "x". This bound variable is then acted on by resetting various slot values. To execute the method "INIT" we can send the following message:

$$\text{SendMessage (THERMOSTAT, INIT)}$$

Since the instances of the other classes will also need to be reset, we also need to define an "INIT" method for each class. Each method is written to reset the proper slots, following the form of Figure 15.14. We also need to send an "INIT" message to each class.

Recognizing that we will need to send four messages, one for each of our class frames, we can elect to create a single function to accomplish this task. We label this function ''Reset'' and define it as follows:

SendMessage (THERMOSTAT, INIT)
SendMessage (FURNACE, INIT)
SendMessage (ROOM, INIT)
SendMessage (AIR_CONDITIONER, INIT)

To execute this function, we can create a pushbutton display item in our system's interface that activates the function when the user presses the button. This pushbutton labeled ''Reset'' is discussed later when we explore the issue of designing our interface.

Furnace

The function of the furnace is to supply heat to a room. We therefore want to encode in the furnace class a method that continues to supply heat while the

Class Name:	Furnace		
			If-Changed
Properties:	Room		
	State	OFF	Heat
	Thermostat		
	Name		**Body**
Methods:	OFF		SetValue (Self:State, OFF);
	ON		SetValue (Self:State, ON);
	Init		ForAll (x|Furnace) ResetValue (x:State);
	Heat		While ((Self:State #= ON)) Self:Thermostat:Temperature = Self:Thermostat:Temperature + 1;

FIGURE 15.16 Furnace class with facets and methods.

furnace is on. To accomplish this we include a method called "Heat" within the IF-CHANGED facet of the slot "State" that increments the room's temperature while the furnace is on (see Figure 15.16).

The "Heat" method is controlled by a thermostat frame. As was shown in Figure 15.15, the "Unit_Control" method sends an "ON" or "OFF" message to the furnace frame. These two messages are interpreted by the furnace frame using the methods shown in Figure 15.16. Each method sets the "State" slot value of the furnace instantiated in "Self." If this assertion causes a change in value, then the "Heat" method is executed. This method continues to heat the thermostat frame named in the furnace's "Thermostat" slot, while the "State" slot value is "ON". It continues to function until the furnace frame receives an "OFF" message, which changes the "State" slot value to "OFF."

Air Conditioner

The function of the air conditioner is to cool a room. We therefore want to encode in the air conditioner class a method that continues to cool the room

Class Name:	Air_Conditioner		
			If-Changed
Properties:	Room		
	State	OFF	Air
	Thermostat		
	Name	Body	
Methods:	OFF	SetValue (Self:State, OFF);	
	ON	SetValue (Self:State, ON);	
	Init	ForAll (x|Air_Conditioner) ResetValue (x:State);	
	Air	While ((Self:State #= ON)) Self:Thermostat:Temperature = Self:Thermostat:Temperature − 1;	

FIGURE 15.17   Air conditioner class with facets and methods.

while the air conditioner is on. To accomplish this we include a method called "Air" within the IF-CHANGED facet of the slot "State" that decreases the room's temperature while the air conditioner is on (see Figure 15.17). This method operates in a fashion similar to the "Heat" method discussed in the previous section. It relies on "ON" and "OFF" methods shown in Figure 15.17, that are executed when messages are sent from the thermostat frame.

TASK 7: DESIGN THE INTERFACE

Following the coding of the system's knowledge, and before testing, we must develop the system's interface. Most frame-based shells offer a toolkit of graphical objects that you can use to tailor the interface to meet the needs of the user. Typical objects found within the toolkit are textboxes, buttons, and meters. Within the shell, each of these objects is a class frame as illustrated in Figure 15.18.

The root node "Tools" contains slots, and default values if appropriate, that are common to all of the graphical object class frames. For example, a slot of "Font Size" with a value of 12, or the slot "Location" with no default value. The various class frames have other properties that are germane to their type.

When you create a new graphical object within the interface, you are actually creating a new instance of one of these classes. You begin by selecting from the toolkit (presented as a set of icons) with a mouse the type of object you want. You are then presented with a form containing slots related to the chosen object. You can next fill in the slot values to tailor the object's display. For example, Figure 15.19 shows the form that would be presented following the creation of a new "meter" interface object. You could link this new meter to the appropriate frame (i.e., "Owner") and its slot (i.e., "OwnerSlot"). You could also tailor the meter by providing such information as its minimum and maximum values, the number of tic marks, etc. The location of the meter could also be specified explicitly within this form, or set graphically using a click-and-drag technique on the meter object within the interface.

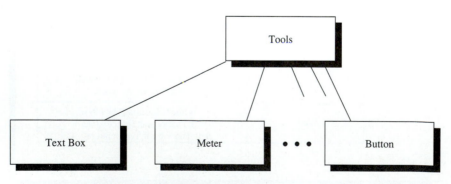

FIGURE 15.18   Interface tool classes.

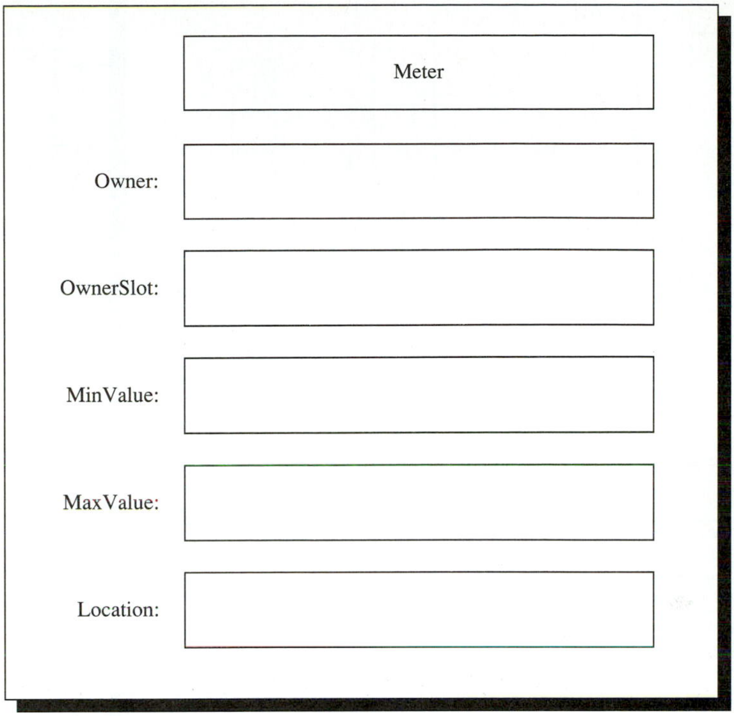

Meter

Owner:	

OwnerSlot:	

MinValue:	

MaxValue:	

Location:	

FIGURE 15.19   Meter graphical interface object form.

You can develop a graphical interface that allows the user to both observe and control the system. To permit observation, you can link the graphical object to the appropriate frame's slot. To permit control, you can link it to some predefined function that changes one or more slot values.

For our system, we want the user to both observe and control the temperature in each of our rooms: livingroom, kitchen and bedroom. The following sections show how to accomplish both of these functions. However, to keep the discussion simple, we will only consider the livingroom. The other rooms are managed in a similar fashion.

Observable Displays

We want our interface to provide the user with several displays of current knowledge base values that are important for the control of the system. For each room this includes room occupancy, mode of thermostat, state of the room's furnace and air conditioner, and the room's temperature. Figure 15.20 shows these display items (rectangles) for the livingroom, with their current values shown shaded.   The room temperature is shown using a meter display. Each

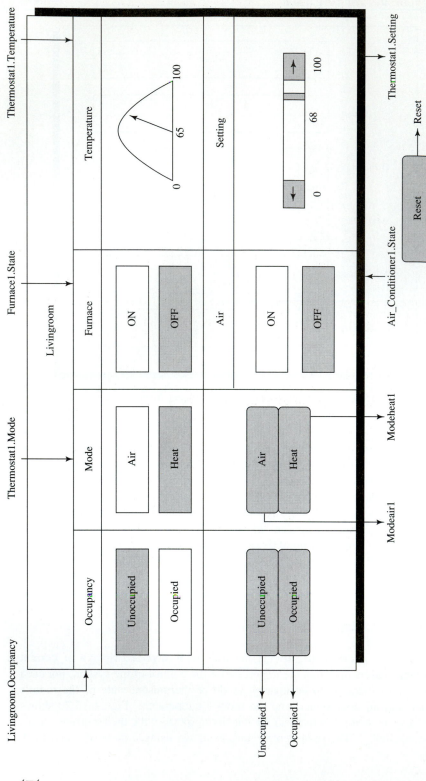

FIGURE 15.20 Part of system's interface.

display item is attached to the appropriate slot of a frame using a form of "Frame_Name.Slot_Name."

Control Displays

As in a conventional environmental control system, we want the user to be able to set the mode of operation and the desired room temperature setting. For our system, we also want the user to act as the infrared sensor that reports on the room's occupancy. To provide these control functions, we must create several interface graphical objects and link them to the appropriate functions. Figure 15.20 shows the graphical objects (pushbuttons) that provide the user with control over the livingroom temperature (illustrated as rounded rectangles). The thermostat setting is controlled using a slidebar. Also shown in the figure is a "Reset" button discussed earlier that resets all of the instances to their class level default values.

The user can specify whether the livingroom is occupied or not by pressing the appropriate button. The "Unoccupied" button is attached to a function labeled "Unoccupied1." This function sets the "Occupancy" slot of LIVINGROOM to "Unoccupied" and sends a "Unit_control" message to the THERMOSTAT1 frame:

Function—Unoccupied1
SetValue (LIVINGROOM:Occupancy, Unoccupied)
SendMessage (THERMOSTAT1, Unit_control)

The first line of this function simply sets the frame's slot value using the Kappa function "SetValue." The "Unit_control" message tells THERMOSTAT1 to make sure that the room temperature is properly adjusted for an unoccupied room.

The "Occupied" button is attached to a function labeled "Occupied1" that operates in a fashion similar to the "Unoccupied" function:

Function—Occupied1
SetValue (LIVINGROOM:Occupancy, Occupied)
SendMessage (THERMOSTAT1, Unit_control)

The user can also specify the mode of operation of the thermostat—air or heat. The "Air" button is attached to the function "Modeair1" which sends an "Air" message to the THERMOSTAT1 frame:

Function—Modeair1
SendMessage (THERMOSTAT1, Air)

This message sets the mode of operation of the thermostat to air (see Figure 15.14).

The "Heat" button is attached to a function labeled "Modeheat1" that operates in a fashion similar to the "Air" function":

Function—Modeheat1
SendMessage (THERMOSTAT1, Heat)

This message simply sets the mode of operation of the thermostat to heat (see Figure 15.14).

The user can also adjust the thermostat setting using a slidebar. This display item is attached to the "Setting" slot of the frame THERMOSTAT1.

TASK 8: EVALUATE THE SYSTEM

Our next task is to evaluate the system. We want to run several test cases to make sure that its performance meets the problem specifications. At this point, our interface would have controls for all three rooms, similar to that shown in Figure 15.20 for the livingroom. Since all three rooms should behave the same, we will limit our testing to just the livingroom.

Test Case 1

In the first test case we simply want to see if our system can effectively and efficiently control the livingroom's temperature for an unoccupied room, where the mode of operation of the thermostat is set to heat. We expect our system to maintain the room temperature 5 degrees below the thermostat setting. To test our system, we permit the user to only make adjustments to the thermostat setting display in our interface. We ask the user to perform the following tasks:

1. Increase the livingroom's thermostat setting in 1-degree increments.
2. Continue this process until setting is at 75 degrees.

To begin the test, the user presses the "Reset" button in the interface display to reset all of the instances to their class level default values. Our display now shows the following values:

> Room temperature = 65
> Furnace and air conditioner are off
> Mode is heat
> Thermostat setting = 68
> Room is unoccupied

Trace of Operation

1. The user presses the increase arrow of the thermostat slider gauge in Figure 15.20. The user can monitor the thermostat setting by viewing the numeric associated with the slider gauge.

2. With each increment, the "Setting" slot of THERMOSTAT1 likewise increments—see Figure 15.11. Each increase in this slot value also causes the IF-CHANGED method "Unit_control" to fire—see Figure 15.14.

3. Since the livingroom is unoccupied, nothing happens with the firing of this method while the "THERMOSTAT1:Setting" value remains less than "THERMOSTAT1:Temperature + 5".

4. With the continued increase in the thermostat setting, once "THERMO-STAT1:Setting" > "THERMOSTAT1:Temperature + 5", the "Unit_control" method sends a "ON" message to FURNACE1—see Figure 15.14.

5. This message sets "FURNACE1:State" to "ON"—see Figure 15.16. The interface display now shows that the livingroom's furnace is on.

6. From Figure 15.16, this "ON" value represents a change in the slot value, which causes the IF-CHANGED method "Heat" to fire.

7. "THERMOSTAT1:Temperature" now gets incremented by 1.

8. From Figure 15.14, this value change again causes the "Unit_control" method to fire, but no messages are sent under these conditions.

9. Meanwhile, the "Heat" method of FURNACE1 continues to increase the "THERMOSTAT1:Setting" value and the "Unit_control" method continues to fire. However, no messages are sent until "THERMOSTAT1:Temperature" = "THERMOSTAT1:Setting—5". The final setting of the thermostat, as set by the user, is 75 degrees. At this point, a "OFF" message is sent to FURNACE1.

10. This "OFF" message sets "FURNACE1:State" to "OFF"—see Figure 15.16. The interface display now shows that the livingroom's furnace is off.

11. This action terminates the execution of the "Heat" method.

12. System stops.

The final conditions of our system, as displayed to the user in the interface, are:

> Room temperature = 70
> Furnace and air conditioner are off
> Mode is heat
> Thermostat setting = 75
> Room is unoccupied

Discussion of Results

No changes occurred in our system while the user adjusted the thermostat setting and its value didn't exceed the room temperature by 5 degrees. This result is aligned with our requirement to maintain a lower temperature in an unoccupied room. When the user adjusted the setting to exceed this 5-degree mark, our furnace turned on. It remained on until the room temperature reached a value of

5 degrees below the thermostat setting. This result also meets one of our problem specifications.

Test Case 2

In the next test case we want to study the impact when someone walks into the livingroom. According to our problem specifications, our system should now adjust the room temperature toward the thermostat setting. To test our system on this point, we ask the user to only click on the "Occupancy" button in the display. We assume that the initial conditions of this test case are the final conditions of the previous test:

> Room temperature = 70
> Furnace and air conditioner are off
> Mode is heat
> Thermostat setting = 75
> Room is unoccupied

Trace of Operation

1. When the user presses the "Occupied" button, the function "Occupied1" is executed:

> SetValue (LIVINGROOM:Occupancy, Occupied)
> SendMessage (THERMOSTAT1, Unit_control)

The first line of this method sets a slot value. This in turn lights the "Occupied" box in the display. The second line sends a "Unit_control" message to THERMOSTAT1.

2. Under the present conditions, this method (see Figure 15.15) sends a "ON" message to FURNACE1.
3. The next several steps follow the process described in test 1. The furnace continues to heat the livingroom until the room's temperature equals the thermostat setting, at which point the system stops. The final conditions of our system displayed to the user are:

> Room temperature = 75
> Furnace and air conditioner are off
> Mode is heat
> Thermostat setting = 75
> Room is occupied

Discussion of Results

Our system appears to be working well and meeting the problem specifications. When someone walks into the living room, our infrared sensor (in this case our user) notifies our system of the event, and the furnace turns on and increases the room's temperature until it has reached the set value.

Test Case 3

Now that our furnace appears to be working properly, we next want to check out our system's control over the air conditioner. We assume that the room is initially unoccupied and the mode of operation of the thermostat is set to heat. We expect our system to maintain the room temperature 5 degrees above the thermostat setting—an efficient condition for an unoccupied room. To test our system, we ask the user to perform the following tasks:

1. Change the thermostat mode to air.
2. Decrease the livingroom's thermostat setting in 1-degree increments.
3. Continue this process until setting is at 55 degrees.

To begin the test, the user first presses the "Reset" button to reset all values to their default states:

> Room temperature = 65
> Furnace and air conditioner are off
> Mode is heat
> Thermostat setting = 68
> Room is unoccupied

Trace of Operation

1. User presses the "Air" button in the interface. This action causes the "Modeair1" function to be executed:

    SendMessage (THERMOSTAT1, Air)

2. From Figure 15.14, the "Air" method sets "THERMOSTAT1:Mode" to "Air". The interface display now shows that the livingroom's thermostat mode state is "Air".
3. The next several steps follow the process described in test 1. The user continues to decrease the thermostat setting and the IF-CHANGED method "Unit_control of THERMOSTAT1 continues to fire—see Figure 15.15. Nothing happens until the thermostat setting drops 5 degrees below the room temperature. At this point a "ON" message is sent to AIR_CONDITIONER1.
4. This message causes the method "ON" to set "AIR_CONDITIONER1:State" to "ON". Our interface display now shows that the livingroom's air conditioner is on.
5. This change of state causes the IF-CHANGED method "Air" to be executed—see Figure 15.17.

6. The "Air" method decreases the livingroom's temperature.

7. The air conditioner continues to cool the livingroom until the room's temperature equals the thermostat setting plus 5 degrees, at which point the system stops. The final setting of the thermostat, as set by the user, is 55 degrees. The final conditions of our system, as displayed to the user, are:

> Room temperature = 60
> Furnace and air conditioner are off
> Mode is air
> Thermostat setting = 55
> Room is unoccupied

Discussion of Results

Similar to the results found in test 1, this test shows that our system can effectively and efficiently cool a room. It cools the room to a point 5 degrees above the thermostat setting since the room is unoccupied.

Test Case 4

The final test case follows the theme of test 2. We want to study the impact when someone walks into the livingroom when the mode of the thermostat is air. According to our problem specifications, our system should now adjust the room temperature to equal the thermostat setting. We ask the user to only click on the "Occupancy" button in the display. We assume that the initial conditions of this test case are the final conditions of the previous test:

> Room temperature = 60
> Furnace and air conditioner are off
> Mode is air
> Thermostat setting = 55
> Room is unoccupied

Trace of Operation

1. When the user presses the "Occupied" button, the function "Occupied1" is executed. As before, this function sets the "Occupancy" slot of LIV-INGROOM to "Occupied". It also sends a "Unit_control" message to THERMOSTAT1.

2. Similar to the process described in test 2, the air conditioner continues to cool the livingroom until the room's temperature equals the thermostat setting, at which point the system stops. The final conditions displayed to the user are:

> Room temperature = 55
> Furnace and air conditioner are off
> Mode is air conditioner
> Thermostat setting = 55
> Room is occupied

Discussion of Results

Again our system appears to meet the problem specifications. When someone enters the livingroom, the air conditioner decreases the room's temperature until it has reached the set value.

—————— TASK 9: EXPAND THE SYSTEM ——————

We have now completed the initial design of our home environmental control system. However, we should view our system as a prototype, ready for expansion. The prototype is usually of narrow scope. That is, we limit the problem in some way so we can quickly build and test it. This might involve limiting the number of problem specifications or objects. However, the ones chosen should provide a good representation of the problem so that test results provide a legitimate evaluation of our design.

The purpose of the prototype is to prove the feasibility of the project and provide the justification for continuing the effort. If we have done our job right, then we should have accomplished this and have in place a structure that will ease the expansion task.

There are two basic ways that you can expand any type of expert system: you either deepen or broaden its knowledge. We will look at examples of each.

Deepening Knowledge

The task of deepening the knowledge makes the system smarter about what it already knows. In rule-based systems, this usually involves taking existing primitives and writing new rules that can infer this information. In frame-based systems, you will often look to add new objects related to existing ones. For example in our problem, you could add various furnace components such as gas control valve, blower motor, etc. You could then permit each existing furnace object to control these new elements.

You have several options available on how you could add these new elements to our system. You could follow the approach previously taken during the design of our prototype and create new classes (e.g., BLOWER_MOTOR) and instances for each element type (e.g., BLOWER_MOTOR1). This type of structure is called a *generalization*, where the instances form a "kind of" relationship with their parent frame. This approach is both simple and natural, and takes full advantage of the inheritance feature of frame-based systems.

To enable each furnace to know which elements it controls when using this approach, you would need to add new slots to the furnace class frame. For example, you could add the slot "Blower_Motor" to the class, and fill in this slot value in the FURNACE1 frame with BLOWER_MOTOR1.

Another approach for adding the new elements is to assert them as instances of existing instances. For example, you could make the new frame BLOWER_MOTOR1 an instance of FURNACE1. This type of structure is called an *aggregation,* where a new frame forms a "part of" type of relationship with its parent frame (see Figure 15.21).

This approach is attractive because it provides a visual perception of the related objects. It is also valuable because most shells have functions that provide an object with an awareness of its parent and children. You can use these functions to encode efficiently the communications between related objects.

For example, Kappa provides a function called "GetParent" that returns the name of an object's parent. Consider using this function on BLOWER_MOTOR1 of Figure 15.21:

$$GetParent\ (BLOWER\_MOTOR1) = FURNACE1$$

There are several ways you could take advantage of this function. Consider for example that BLOWER_MOTOR1 failed. Under this condition, for safety reasons, you might want to notify the furnace containing this component of the event. To accomplish this, you could send the following message:

$$SendMessage\ (GetParent\ (BLOWER\_MOTOR1),\ Blower\_failure)$$

The object FURNACE1 upon receiving this message would then take the appropriate action, such as turning off GAS_CONTROL_VALVE1.

Using the structure shown in Figure 15.21 also permits the new frames (e.g., BLOWER_MOTOR1) to inherit information from their parent (e.g., FURNACE1). For a "part of" type link, inheritance plays a minor role. The only

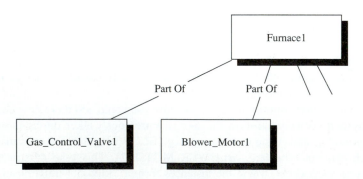

FIGURE 15.21   "Part of" type architecture for furnace components.

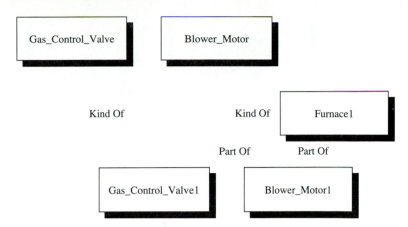

FIGURE 15.22   Multiple inheritance for furnace components.

real benefit for our problem is that the new objects know in which room they are located—the "Room" slot inherited from the furnace frames. To permit our new objects to inherit descriptive information, you could turn to multiple inheritance.

Through multiple inheritance, you link objects to more than one parent. Consider for example Figure 15.22. Here the new furnace objects are linked to both the furnace frame and their corresponding class frames. In this fashion, you create both a "part of" and a "kind of" type of link. The class frames (e.g., BLOWER_MOTOR) would contain descriptive information encoded in their slots and behavior information in methods. Using a network architecture as shown in this figure, permits you to encode efficiently both structural and descriptive problem information.

Broadening Knowledge

When you broaden the system's knowledge you add knowledge about something new. In a frame-based system, this might involve the addition of new events or new objects. The typical expansion involves the creation of new objects related to existing ones. This step is reasonable since the original prototype will usually include a sample of each object.

Consider for example the rooms currently represented in our system. Our system can control the temperature in the livingroom, kitchen, and bedroom. You might next want to expand our system to consider other possible rooms in the house.

You could begin this task by adding new instances to the ROOM class (see Figure 15.10) to account for each new room. You would then need to add new thermostat, air conditioner and furnace instances (see Figures 15.11, 15.12 and

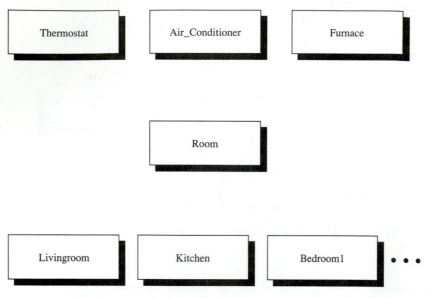

FIGURE 15.23   New system architecture.

15.13) to account for each new unit located in the new rooms. Finally, you would need to assign all the slots of the new instances appropriate values. Though this approach would work, it is not very efficient.

A better approach is to turn to a new frame architecture that will easily allow the addition of new rooms. One that will accomplish this is shown in Figure 15.23.

The major advantage of this architecture is that each new room you add automatically inherits a thermostat, air conditioner and furnace. For a large house—or consider an apartment building—this approach would be a necessity. You would need to make some minor changes to existing properties and methods, but the **knowledge** encoded in the prototype would provide the basis of this new system.

SUMMARY ON FRAME-BASED DESIGN

This chapter reviewed the basic steps performed in the design of a frame-based expert system. The major difference in designing this type of system versus a rule-based system is the view of the problem's knowledge. In a frame-based approach, you view the entire problem as being made up of objects. You seek to describe each object and form an understanding of how it interacts with other objects. Frame-based systems also offer features not found in rule-based systems, such as inheritance, facets, message passing, and pattern matching rules. These features provide you with a powerful toolkit for developing complex systems.

The major lessons learned in this chapter were:

- The transition from designing a rule-based system to a frame-based system is more than learning another programming language—it is a change of mind set. You view the problem as being composed of objects that have features and behavior.

- A frame can represent the features, state, and behavior of an object.

- The descriptive and behavioral characteristics of common objects can be represented in a class frame.

- Behavior is how an object acts or reacts to changes to its own state, or the state of other objects.

- Through encapsulation, you teach each object how to behave.

- Through inheritance, you can easily add new objects that inherit both descriptive and behavioral information from their parent class frame.

- A frame-based approach is a natural for simulation and control problems.

- Frames can be linked in a hierarchial or network fashion. The choice is guided by the application.

- You can build a frame-based system using an object-oriented language or a frame-based shell. The language approach provides maximum flexibility, but at a cost of learning the language. For quick prototyping, consider a shell approach.

- The design of a frame-based expert system is a highly iterative process.

- You should limit the scope of the prototype system—its purpose is to prove the feasibility of the project. In a frame-based design, limit the number of objects or events.

- A good way to begin the design of a frame-based system is with the use of an informal diagram that shows the problem's major objects and relationships.

- The project's events provide insight into how the objects will need to communicate with one another.

- Frame-based systems provide classes of graphical objects that can be used to tailor the interface.

—————— E X E R C I S E S

1. List and discuss advantages of representing knowledge in frames rather than in rules.
2. Discuss the advantages and disadvantages of using rules versus methods in a frame-based system.
3. Give an example problem where a hierarchial frame structure would be appropriate. Then provide an example where a network approach would be better. Explain your reasons in each case.
4. Discuss the pros and cons of using IF-NEEDED and IF-CHANGED facets to exchange information between objects versus message passing.

5. Give an example where IF-NEEDED methods used in different frames can lead to infinite loops.

6. Create a frame structure to represent various people. The structure should include several male and female individuals. All of these individuals should have some common properties, but some properties will be related to gender. This structure should be organized to best take advantage of the inheritance of common features.

7. Using the frame structure created in problem 6, add the slots "number of legs" and "handicap" to each frame in the most efficient fashion. Next, write one pattern matching rule that scans all of the frames that represent the individual people, and tells each frame if the individual is handicapped.

8. Again using the structure in problem 6, discuss how two people frames could be compared to determine if the two like each other—for example, "Bob likes Mary."

9. Discuss the advantages and disadvantages of using multiple inheritance.

10. Assume you have a problem of filling a tank with water. You have available a source of water, a pump, and a motor that operates the pump. Design a frame system using a message passing scheme that fills the tank to some given level but not beyond this level.

11. Design a frame-based system for controlling the operation of an elevator.

12. Assume you have three blocks labeled A, B, and C. Further assume block B is on top of A. You have available a robot that can be characterized completely by its hand—its location, what it is holding, etc. Design a frame-based control system to place block A onto block C.

Induction Systems

INTRODUCTION

In earlier chapters we saw that the power behind an expert system is its knowledge. We can often trace the system's success or failure to the quality of its knowledge. However, as discussed in Chapter 17, obtaining this knowledge from an expert can be a difficult task.

The knowledge engineer must be versed in the techniques of eliciting knowledge, which requires good communication skills and some understanding of the psychology of human interaction. Acquiring these skills, and being able to practice them effectively, can be difficult.

Another challenge with extracting knowledge occurs when the expert is not consciously aware of the knowledge used. A person usually becomes an expert in a domain through years of experience solving domain problems. From this experience, the expert often compiles the knowledge into quantum problem solving steps that permit efficient problem solving. In this situation, it can be difficult to decompile the expert's knowledge into a form that can be used in the expert system.

When developing a rule-based expert system, occassionally an additional difficulty is encountered where the expert is unable to communicate the knowledge in rule form. In these instances, the expert might say, "Well, it is hard to explain, but I could give you some examples." When this occurs, the knowledge engineer must use another method that can uncover the knowledge hidden in the examples, so that it can be represented in rule form.

Another difficulty occurs for expert system applications where no real experts exist. Consider for example the areas of weather forecasting and horse race handicapping. Though knowledgeable individuals exist who can predict some event, they usually rely upon past events to aid their prediction. Therefore, the domain knowledge rests in past examples, and not with human expertise. In these applications, the knowledge engineer must again use some technique that can uncover the knowledge contained within the examples.

Because of these problems associated with extracting knowledge from a human expert, techniques that can automate the process of knowledge acquisition through machine learning are extremely appealing. This chapter reviews one of these methods known as induction.

INDUCTION

Machine learning has long been recognized as an essential feature of artificial intelligence. Dietterich et al. (1981) categorize learning methods into four areas: rote learning, learning by being told, learning from examples and learning by analogy. This chapter reviews the method *learning from examples,* since it represents the most common technique used today in expert system design—a technique often called **induction.**

Definition 16.1: Induction
Inducing general rules from knowledge contained in a finite set of examples.

Induction is the process of reasoning from a given set of facts to conclude general principles or rules. For example, if I told someone that I like football, baseball, and basketball, that person might correctly conclude by induction that I like sports. Induction looks for patterns in available information to infer reasonable conclusions.

Inductive learning has been an important area of research in AI and in expert system development. Winston (1975) applied inductive learning to derive conceptual descriptions for classifying block world structures. The Meta-DENDRAL project used an induction technique to discover a set of rules for inferring chemical structures from mass spectrometry data (Buchanan and Mitchell 1978). Michalski and Chilausky (1980) showed that a combination of learning from examples and from being told could be used to form a body of knowledge for diagnosing soybean diseases in the PLANT expert system.

INDUCTION AS SEARCH

Inductive learning can be viewed as a search through a problem space for a solution to a problem. The problem space is composed of the problem's major concepts, linked together by an inductive process that uses examples of the problem.

To illustrate inductive learning and search, consider a small problem of determining a gift to purchase. Assume that the major problem concepts are *money*, a *person's age*, and *gifts*. Our problem is to determine an appropriate gift on the basis of the available money and the person's age. To keep the problem simple, we assume that we can discriminate the issues of money and age in a binary sense, that is, *money* = much or little, and *age* = child or adult. The knowledge for this problem is captured in a set of examples obtained from an expert, and is represented in the decision table shown in Table 16.1.

The concepts of money and age represent the decision factors or problem attributes. From the examples shown in Table 16.1, we can induce a search space as shown in Figure 16.1.

The search space of Figure 16.1 is also referred to as a *decision tree*, and can be used to search for a solution to our problem. For example, if we have a little amount of money to spend and we are buying a gift for a child, then we should buy a calculator.

TABLE 16.1   Decision Table for Gift Problem

Decision Factors		Result
MONEY	AGE	GIFT
Much	Adult	Car
Much	Child	Computer
Little	Adult	Toaster
Little	Child	Calculator

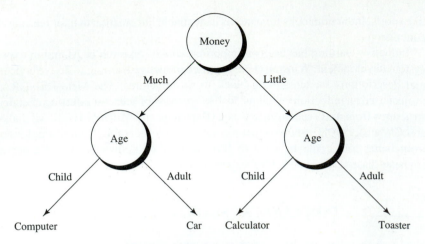

FIGURE 16.1   Search space for gift problem.

By induction, we can create a decision tree from our set of examples to use in a search process, or we can create a set of decision rules to use in our expert system. For our simple example, by induction the set of rules would be:

IF   We have much money
AND   We are buying a gift for an adult
THEN   Buy a car

IF   We have much money
AND   We are buying a gift for a child
THEN   Buy a computer

IF   We have little money
AND   We are buying a gift for an adult
THEN   Buy a toaster

IF   We have little money
AND   We are buying a gift for a child
THEN   Buy a calculator

For larger problems involving many decision factors and examples, the induction algorithm can form a small set of rules that efficiently captures the problem's knowledge.

ID3

Several induction algorithms have been developed that vary in the methods employed to build the decision tree or set of rules. Michalski (1978) and Smith et al. (1977) provide a review of these algorithms. In this chapter, we review one of the more popular induction techniques known as ID3.

ID3 is a general-purpose rule induction algorithm developed by Quinlan (1979), and is used today in most expert system shells. ID3 takes a set of problem examples and induces a decision tree. An example is a combination of decision factors, decision factor values, and actions specific to that example. For instance, an example set for weather prediction might look like that shown in Table 16.2. This example set might have come from a domain expert or from a past history of weather patterns. This set shows that four different decision factors are considered for predicting the weather: temperature, wind direction, condition of the sky, and barometric pressure.

Given this set of examples for weather prediction, ID3 can now produce a decision tree that captures the knowledge for predicting the weather. This algorithm uses a heuristic approach to generate the decision tree, which places the attributes in the nodes of the tree in a manner that can minimize the search effort in locating a solution. The algorithm can also determine if some attribute is irrelevant for predicting the final result.

Applying ID3 to the example set of Table 16.2 produces the decision tree shown in Figure 16.2, which serves to highlight several features of the ID3 induction algorithm.

Chooses most important issue first—The first feature of interest is related to the choice of the attribute *barometric pressure* as the root of the tree. When the search is begun for predicting the weather, the issue of barometric pressure will be pursued first. As can be seen from the decision tree, checking this issue first is most efficient, since two of the three possible answers will lead immediately to a prediction, therefore avoiding the need to address the issues of the condition of the *sky* or *temperature*. In general, ID3 places the most important issues nearer to the root of the decision tree.

No-data result—At times a no-data solution occurs. This indicates that the examples do not support the situation leading to this result. Encountering this

TABLE 16.2 Decision Table for Weather Prediction
(* indicates "don't care")

Decision Factors				Result
TEMPERATURE	WIND	SKY	BAROMETER	PREDICTION
Above freezing	West	Cloudy	Falling	Rain
Below freezing	*	Cloudy	Steady	Snow
Above freezing	East	Cloudy	Rising	Shine
Above freezing	*	Partly	Steady	Shine
*	*	Clear	Steady	Shine
Above freezing	South	Clear	Falling	Rain
Freezing	North	Partly	Steady	Snow

①& ②— IMMIDIATE
PREDICTION

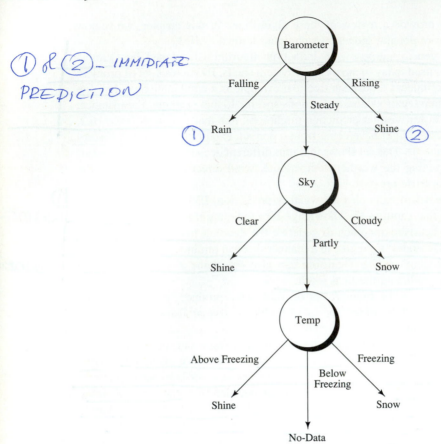

FIGURE 16.2 Decision tree for weather prediction.

situation is usually an indicator that your example set is weak and needs additional examples to support this possibility.

Excludes irrelevant factors—Another important feature of ID3 to note is that the original example set contained the attribute *wind direction*, but this issue never appeared in the decision tree. Given the set of examples, ID3 decided that this issue was irrelevant for predicting the weather. A human expert on weather prediction may be unaware that some issue is unimportant.

HOW ID3 WORKS

The ID3 algorithm is a descendent of Hunt's Concept Learning System (CLS) (Hunt et al. 1966). CLS solves single-concept learning tasks and uses the learned concepts to classify new examples. CLS can discover a classification rule or

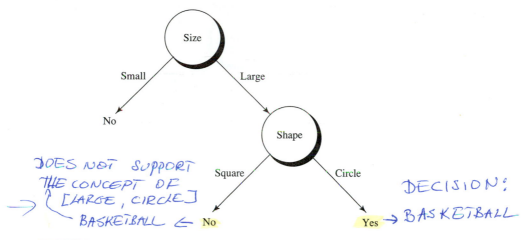

Handwritten annotations:

DOES NOT SUPPORT THE CONCEPT OF [LARGE, CIRCLE] → BASKETBALL ←

DECISION: → BASKETBALL

FIGURE 16.3   Decision tree for the concept of a large circle.

Handwritten annotation: BINARY! ONLY?

decision tree for a collection of examples belonging to two classes and use this rule to classify a new example into one of the two classes. An example is classified by starting at the root of the tree, making tests, and following branches until a node is reached, which indicates by YES or NO whether the example is in the class.

To illustrate this process, suppose we have training examples with features of *shape* {square, circle} and *size* {small, large}. Then the concept of a *basketball* (large circle) can be represented as shown in Figure 16.3, where the YES and NO nodes represent the results of following a given path through the tree. If we arrive at a YES node, then the decisions made at each earlier node are consistent with our concept of a large circle, that is, it is a basketball. If we arrive at a NO node, then our decisions do not support the concept, that is, it is not a basketball.

A new example would be classified by comparing its features with the concept representation of Figure 16.3. For instance, consider the example {large, square}. *(Handwritten: fail)* Starting with the root node *size,* we follow the branch to the *shape* node. From the *shape* node we take the square branch to the NO node, which indicates that this new example is not an example of the concept *large circle.*

Other features of the decision tree can be observed if we consider a different example {small, square}. Classifying this new example with Figure 16.3 would fail immediately following the *size* node. For this example, we would not need to consider the *shape* node, resulting in an improvement in the efficiency of the search process. In many cases, we can place a highly discriminate node at or near the root of the decision tree which will result in an improved search process.

Another feature of ID3 can be seen if we elect to treat this new example as a training example. In this case, the decision tree of Figure 16.3 is changed to reflect this new information and is shown in Figure 16.4. The updated decision tree of Figure 16.4 illustrates that decision trees are inherently disjunctive, since

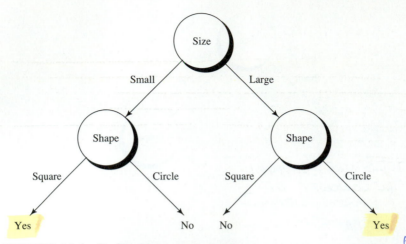

FIGURE 16.4   Updated large circle decision tree.

each branch leaving a node corresponds to a separate disjunctive case. Therefore, decision trees can be used to capture disjunctive concepts such as *large circle* or *small square*.

The ID3 algorithm can be used to generate the decision tree that captures a given concept from a set of training examples. This algorithm uses as a subroutine the CLS algorithm, which is discussed first.

CLS Algorithm

The CLS algorithm begins with an empty decision tree and iteratively builds the tree by adding decision nodes until the tree can correctly classify all of the training examples in set C. The CLS algorithm proceeds as follows (Cohen and Feigenbaum 1982):

1. If all examples in C are positive, then create a YES node and stop.
   If all examples in C are negative, create a NO node and stop.
   Otherwise, select (using some heuristic criterion) an attribute A with values $V_1, V_2, \ldots, V_n$ and create the decision node.
2. Partition the training examples in C into subsets $C_1, C_2, \ldots, C_n$ according to the values of V.
3. Apply the algorithm recursively to each of the sets C_i.

ID3 Algorithm

The ID3 algorithm closely follows the CLS algorithm with several modifications. The CLS algorithm requires that all of the training examples be available during step 1, which places a limit on the number of examples that can be effectively solved. The ID3 algorithm can work with subsets of the examples to solve more complex problems involving a large number of examples.

The heuristic used in step 1 is intended to pick the most discriminatory attribute first. Several methods can be used for estimating which attribute is the most discriminatory (Hunt et al. 1966). ID3 uses an information approach for assessing the discriminatory power for each attribute (Quinlan 1986). Given some example, the decision tree generates a message related to the class of the example. That is, if the example is related to the class YES, a message of "plus" is given. If the example is related to the class NO, then a message "minus" is given. If the probability of the plus and minus messages are respectively p^+ and p^-, then the information content of the message as measured in bits is

$$-p^+ \log_2 p^+ - p^- \log_2 p^- \qquad (1)$$

These probabilities are approximated by the relative frequencies from the set of examples C, so that p^+ is the proportion of examples in C with class "plus" and p^- the proportion with class "minus." $M(C)$ can now be defined to represent the expected information content of a message from the decision tree for a set of C example, and found from equation 1.

The problem now is to select the most discriminatory attribute. The attribute to be tested next branches to subsets C_i of C as shown in Figure 16.5. For any attribute A with attribute values V_i, the new expected information to be gained by choosing this attribute can be given as

$$B(C, A) = (\text{probability that value of } A \text{ is } V_i) * M(C_i) \qquad (2)$$

You can then apply equation 2 to each attribute and select the one that maximizes the expected information gain according to

$$M(C) - B(C, A) \qquad (3)$$

The ID3 algorithm follows these major steps:

1. Select a random subset of size W from the entire set of training examples (W is called the *window*).
2. Apply the CLS algorithm to form the decision tree or rule for the window.

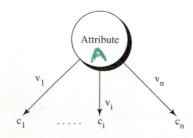

FIGURE 16.5 Attribute branching.

3. Scan the entire set of examples (not just the window) to find exceptions to the current rule.

4. If there are some exceptions, insert some of them into the window and repeat step 2; otherwise stop and display the latest rule.

This algorithm iteratively converges to a final rule that captures the concept. The purpose of step one is to form a small set of all of the examples, a *window*, because the full set of examples may be too large. This step enhances the efficiency of the algorithm.

The CLS algorithm serves as a subroutine to the ID3 algorithm. The CLS algorithm first finds the attribute (decision node) that best discriminates between positive and negative examples and partitions the data with respect to that attribute. The ID3 algorithm uses a heuristic based on the information content of a message sent from the decision tree for the given example.

After choosing the most discriminatory attribute, the data is divided into two subsets. Each subset is then partitioned in a similar way and this process is repeated until all of the subsets contain data on only one class. The final result is a decision tree that can be used to classify new examples.

ID3 Example

To illustrate the operation of the ID3 algorithm, we will consider a small rain prediction problem. Consider the set of examples *C* shown in Table 16.3. Each example is described by three attributes: *sky* {clear, cloudy}, *barometer* {falling, steady, rising}, and *wind* {north, south}. The "+" and "−" signs indicate which class the example belongs to, namely YES or NO. If the attribute *sky* is chosen first to form the root of the decision tree, then Figure 16.6 illustrates the result.

The subcollection for the value "clear" contains only examples of one class and doesn't need any further development. Developing further the attribute *barometer* provides the result shown in Figure 16.7, which shows that only the

TABLE 16.3   Decision Table for Rain Prediction

	Decision Factors			Result
	SKY	BAROMETER	WIND	RAIN
1	clear	rising	north	−
2	cloudy	rising	south	+
3	cloudy	steady	north	+
4	clear	falling	north	−
5	cloudy	falling	north	+
6	cloudy	rising	north	+
7	cloudy	falling	south	−
8	clear	rising	south	−

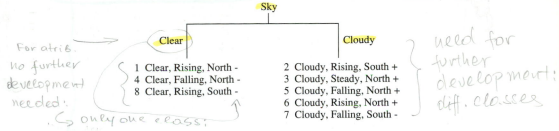

[handwritten: For atrib. no further development needed. ⤷ only one class!]

[handwritten: need for further development: diff. classes]

FIGURE 16.6 One-level tree developed for attribute "Sky."

subcollection under ''barometer falling'' needs to be expanded and is illustrated in Figure 16.8.

Figure 16.8 represents the final decision tree for the set of examples given following the ID3 algorithm. Part of the algorithm attempted to find the most discriminatory node first. In this case, the attribute *sky* was found. To illustrate how this occurred, consider the following sequence.

The collection of *C* examples contains four in class + and four in class −. According to equation 1:

[handwritten: GENERAL: NO ATTRIBUTES Set C]

$$M(C) = -\tfrac{4}{8}\log_2\tfrac{4}{8} - \tfrac{4}{8}\log_2\tfrac{4}{8} = 1 \text{ bit}$$

If we first test the *wind* attribute, we would find the one-level tree as illustrated in Figure 16.9. The information still needed for the ''North'' branch can be found from equation 1:

[handwritten: value for wind]

$$M(\text{North}) = -\tfrac{3}{5}\log_2\tfrac{3}{5} - \tfrac{2}{5}\log_2\tfrac{2}{5} = .971 \text{ bits}$$

and the ''South'' branch:

$$M(\text{South}) = -\tfrac{1}{3}\log_2\tfrac{1}{3} - \tfrac{2}{3}\log_2\tfrac{2}{3} = .918 \text{ bits}$$

Therefore, from equation 2, the expected information content is:

$$B(C,\text{''Wind''}) = \tfrac{4}{8}*.971 + \tfrac{4}{8}*.918 = .944 \text{ bits}$$

[handwritten: 5/8   3/8]

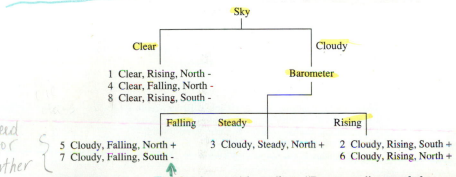

[handwritten: need for further development]

FIGURE 16.7 Two-level tree with attribute "Barometer" expanded.

One class at each branch

FINAL DECISION

```
                              Sky
              ┌────────────────┴────────────────┐
            Clear                             Cloudy
              -                           Barometer
                              ┌──────────────┼──────────────┐
                           Falling        Steady          Rising
                           Wind             +                +
                     ┌───────┴───────┐
                   North           South

        5 Cloudy, Falling, North +     7 Cloudy, Falling, South -
```

FIGURE 16.8 Three-level tree with attribute "Wind" expanded.

The information gained by using this attribute can then be found from equation 3:

WIND →

$$M(C) - B(C, \text{``Wind''}) = 1 - .944 = .0055 \text{ bits}$$

or a relatively small amount of information.

The tree for the *sky* attribute was given in Figure 16.6. The branch for the "Clear" value can provide no further information, while the "Cloudy" branch has four "pluses" and one "minus." Therefore:

$$M(\text{Cloudy}) = -\tfrac{4}{5}\log_2 \tfrac{4}{5} - \tfrac{1}{5}\log_2 \tfrac{1}{5} = .722 \text{ bits}$$

$$B(C, \text{``Cloudy''}) = \tfrac{3}{8}*0 + \tfrac{5}{8}*.722 = .45 \text{ bits}$$

and the information gained by using the attribute *sky* is:

SKY →

$$M(C) - B(C, \text{``Sky''}) = 1 - .45 = .548 \text{ bits}$$

BAR →

We can also find the expected information gained by testing the *barometer* attribute using the same method and find .156 bits. Therefore, the results indicate that the attribute *sky* should be considered first, since it appears to provide the maximum gain in expected information.

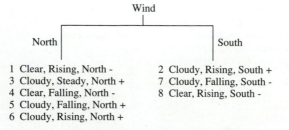

```
                         Wind
              ┌───────────┴───────────┐
            North                   South

    1 Clear, Rising, North -      2 Cloudy, Rising, South +
    3 Cloudy, Steady, North +     7 Cloudy, Falling, South -
    4 Clear, Falling, North -     8 Clear, Rising, South -
    5 Cloudy, Falling, North +
    6 Cloudy, Rising, North +
```

FIGURE 16.9 One-level tree for the attribute "Wind."

Advantages of ID3

Choosing example set—Both the CLS and ID3 algorithms perform well on single concept problems. The choice of the subset of training examples to process, the *window,* is one of its primary strengths. This method of window selection is often referred to as *exception-driven filtering.* This technique allows the program to focus on those training examples that violate its expectations, which are the examples needed to improve the representation of the concept being learned.

Chooses most discriminatory attribute first—ID3 employs an information approach to select the most discriminatory attribute first. This approach is intuitively appealing and enhances the efficiency of the system.

Limitations of ID3

Several shortcomings of the ID3 algorithm are cited by Forsyth (1989):

1. The rules are not probabilistic.
2. Several identical examples have no more effect than one.
3. It cannot deal with contradictory examples.
4. The results are therefore overly sensitive to small alterations to the training examples.

Another practical problem with decision trees is that in general, it is difficult to understand a learned concept for large decision trees. Despite some of these shortcomings, the ID3 algorithm has proven effective for producing valuable expert systems. Several of these systems are discussed later in this chapter.

DEVELOPING AN INDUCTION EXPERT SYSTEM

The major steps in developing an induction expert system include the following:

Determine objective—You must first establish the system's objective. A search through a decision tree will reach one of a finite set of decisions on the basis of the path taken through the tree. Each decision establishes some predetermined objective. For example, in our earlier gift selection problem, the objective was to pick the right gift for the person.

Determine decision factors—Decision factors represent the attribute nodes of the decision tree. These factors include problem features that you would consider to reach a final decision. For example, in the gift selection problem, we considered such factors as money, and the age and sex of the person for whom the gift is intended.

This is often the most difficult task when developing an induction system. If the decision factors chosen are poor or incomplete, the end result may be incorrect. Quinlan (1986) argues that an important learning research topic is to develop techniques that can discover a good set of decision factors.

[handwritten: & POSSIBLE VALUES FOR EACH DECISION FACTOR]

Determine decision factor values—Decision factor values represent the attribute values of the decision tree. You must generate a list of possible values for each decision factor. For example, the decision factor *money* had the values {little, lot}. When the system is run and needs information on *money,* it would offer the user a choice between *little* and *lot.*

Choosing a good set of decision factor values is important. If these values are vague or incomplete, the user may have trouble with providing answers. Consider our *little* and *lot* values. The user may find them too subjective, or might want to spend an *average* amount—a value missing from the list. It is therefore important that you involve the user early in the project to help define an effective set of values. The input the user provides will also impact how you gather and process the examples.

Determine solutions—You must determine a list of the final decisions that the system can make; these are the leaf nodes of the decision tree. For the gift system, these are the possible gifts to purchase.

[handwritten left margin: TRAINING SET ← EXAMPLE ORIGINAL]

Form example set—The examples contain the problem's knowledge and are used for intelligent decision making. These examples relate decision factor values to final outcomes, and can come from the domain expert or from a record of past events. In selecting the original example set, you should choose examples that come from a reliable source and cover a broad scope of the problem.

If the examples come from several sources, it is important to keep a record of their source. In the event the system's performance doesn't meet expectations, then the deletion of the examples from a less reliable source might improve the situation.

Create decision tree—You will need to use an induction algorithm such as ID3 to create the decision tree. In the event some decision factor doesn't appear in the induced tree, do not remove it from the original data set. Later, when other examples are added to the system, the factor may reappear when a new tree is induced. You will see this point illustrated later in the chapter.

[handwritten left margin: Same as THI in a rule-based Ex.]

Test the system—The testing step compares the predicted results of the system with actual case studies. You might choose the cases from a subset of the original examples that were not used in creation of the decision tree or use a set of future examples. Either approach is acceptable because they both use examples absent in the original design, and offer the best likelihood of uncovering system deficiencies.

Revise the system—Revising the system will usually involve adding new decision factors or factor values, or adding or deleting examples. Typical problems that occur during testing fall into one or more of the following areas: incorrect result, no result, or a contradictory result.

[handwritten left margin: Incorrect Result]

An incorrect result is simply one that differs from that expected. This problem can occur because the system's knowledge is weak, the system lacks sufficient decision factors, or the system lacks sufficient decision factor values. You may find the system weak if the knowledge source was unreliable or the example set didn't cover a broad scope of the problem. Here, you will need to find additional sources for the examples. Problems may also occur if the system is missing important decision factors or values. Here, you will need to address the granularity of existing knowledge, where existing decision factors or factor values are represented in finer detail.

A no result situation occurs when the existing set of examples can't account for the test cases's decision factor values. You can often remedy this situation with the addition of new examples.

A contradictory result occurs when more than one result is given for the same set of decision factor values. To correct this problem, you will need to add decision factors or values that can discriminate between the different results.

This section listed the major steps performed when creating a decision tree. To better illustrate this process, the next section describes the development of a small football game prediction system.

FOOTBALL GAME PREDICTION SYSTEM

Trying to predict the outcome of a football game can be both difficult and costly. Football game bettors have been wagering for years using factors that they believe are most relevant for picking the winner. Let's see if we can help the venture by developing a small induction expert system.

Objective—The objective is to build a football game prediction expert system that can predict if our team will win or lose its next game.

Decision factors—We must select the most important decision factors for predicting the winning team. This may be no easy task because there are a number of factors that we might consider. To help us, we ask an expert bettor named Harry who has placed bets for years. Harry is enthusiastic about helping us because he has been on a loosing streak for some time. In fact, he is down to his last shirt. According to Harry, the most important factors to consider are location of the game, weather, our own team's record, and the opponent's record.

Decision factor values—Harry has also provided us with a list of values for each decision factor (Table 16.4).

Solutions—The solution for this problem is a simple binary decision; we simply want to know if our team will win or lose the next game.

Examples—We need to acquire a set of examples to use for generating the decision tree. Fortunately, the season is half over and we can go back over the first eight games and get examples that include values for our decision factors. Table 16.5 lists the past examples.

TABLE 16.4   Decision Factors and Values for Football Game Prediction

LOCATION	WEATHER	OWN RECORD	OPP. RECORD
Home	Rain	Poor	Poor
Away	Cold	Average	Average
	Moderate	Good	Good
	Hot		

TABLE 16.5   Examples from First Half of Season

		Decision Factors			Result
WEEK	LOCATION	WEATHER	OWN REC.	OPP. REC.	OWN TEAM
1	Home	Hot	Good	Good	Win
2	Home	Rain	Good	Average	Win
3	Away	Moderate	Good	Average	Loss
4	Away	Hot	Good	Poor	Win
5	Home	Cold	Good	Good	Loss
6	Away	Hot	Average	Average	Loss
7	Home	Moderate	Average	Good	Loss
8	Away	Cold	Poor	Average	Win

Decision tree—We next create a decision tree (Figure 16.10) using this set of examples. The tree's decision nodes are *weather, location,* and our team's record (*own rec*). Noticeably missing from the decision tree is the factor on the opponent's record (*opp. rec*). The ID3 algorithm determined that this factor was irrelevant for predicting the outcome of the game. However, as we will see shortly, with the addition of new information this factor resurfaces—don't delete factors that don't show up in the tree; they may become important later.

Testing—We can now use the decision tree to predict if our team will win or lose future games. Harry is anxious to try out the system and wants to use it for placing his bets for the balance of the season. All he will have to do is to get the values for the decision factors for the upcoming game and see on which team he should bet. Table 16.6 shows the result of this effort.

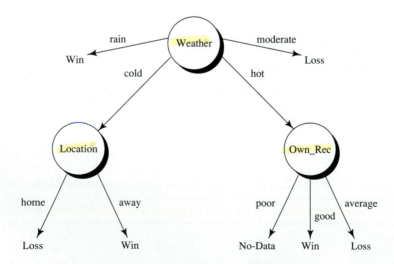

FIGURE 16.10   Football game prediction decision tree.

TABLE 16.6 Outcome Prediction and Actual Results for Second Half of Season

	Decision Factors				Results	
WEEK	LOCATION	WEATHER	OWN REC.	OPP. REC.	PRED.	ACTUAL
9	Home	Hot	Poor	Poor	No-Data	Win *
10	Home	Moderate	Good	Average	Loss	Win *
11	Away	Cold	Good	Good	Win	Win
12	Home	Hot	Good	Average	Win	Loss *
13	Home	Moderate	Good	Average	Loss	Win *
14	Away	Cold	Good	Average	Win	Loss *
15	Home	Cold	Average	Good	Loss	Loss
16	Away	Moderate	Poor	Poor	Loss	Loss

Revising—Table 16.6 shows that Harry didn't fare very well. The examples marked "*" indicate a bad prediction, and we see that only three of the final eight games were predicted correctly. Harry has just lost his last shirt.

Obviously, Harry wants to know what went wrong. He mentions that for the twelfth week, he really expected the team to win since they were playing a poorer opponent at home. The system also predicted that the team would win, but they ended up losing. Harry then remembers that several key players were absent from that game because of injuries. After discussing this issue further with Harry, we learn that another factor of concern is the team's health. We then decide to add this factor to our system with the values of {poor, average, good}.

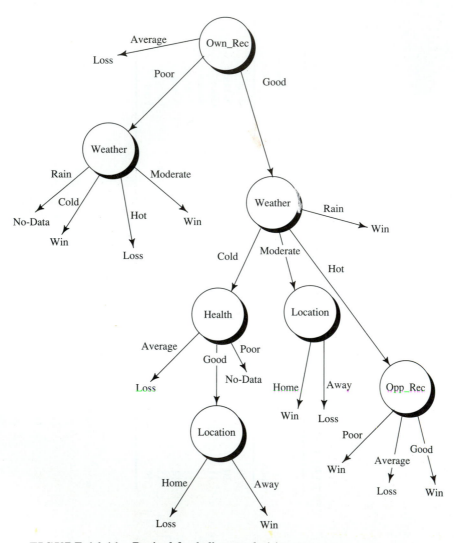

FIGURE 16.11   Revised football game decision tree.

We next have to go back over the past games and obtain a value for the team's health, and add this factor and the new examples to our system. The decision tree produced from this effort is shown in Figure 16.11. This figure shows that the opponent's record (*opp rec*) decision factor, missing earlier, has resurfaced. We can now rerun our system and compare the predicted result with the actual outcome. The results of this effort are shown in Table 16.7.

After adding the team's health-decision factor and the complete set of examples, Table 16.7 shows that the system provides excellent predictions. Harry is impressed with the system, but unfortunately it came after the season and he will have to go shirtless the rest of the winter. However, he can find comfort in knowing that he can use the system next season and already envisions himself driving a Mercedes this time next year.

SENSITIVITY STUDY

A sensitivity study for any type of system attempts to determine the influence that various system elements have on the system's behavior. For a knowledge-based system, this type of study can uncover the important pieces of knowledge. The major benefit of this study is that it draws attention toward the highly sensitive knowledge, which can aid future development efforts.

Consider the makeup of an induction system. Its knowledge elements consist of decision factors, their values, and the set of examples. A sensitivity study would investigate their influence on the system's performance. One valuable feature of an induction system developed using a software shell is the ease in which you can perform this study. Some of these shells, such as 1STCLASS, permit you to deactivate decision factors or examples without removing them from the knowledge base, then study the system's performance under these new conditions.

To illustrate, assume we wanted to know the impact of the *location* decision factor for predicting the winning team in our football game prediction system. We can deactivate this factor and then induce a new decision tree. Next, we can test the new tree against known events (see Table 16.8).

By deactivating the *location* factor, the system became confused for several examples as indicated by the "?" result. We could use this same approach to study the system's sensitivity to the other factors.

We can also study the sensitivity of the system's performance to the examples by deactivating select ones. This capability is valuable when examples come from different sources. We can deactivate those that come from one source, and see if the system's performance improves or degrades.

ADVANTAGES OF INDUCTION

Discovers rules from examples—Induction systems can discover possibly unknown rules from a set of examples. At times during the development of an

TABLE 16.7 Predicted and Actual Results for Modified System

			Decision Factors				Results	
WEEK	HEALTH	LOC.	WEATHER	OWN REC.	OPP. REC.		ACTUAL	PRED.
1	Good	Home	Hot	Good	Good		Win	Win
2	Average	Home	Rain	Good	Average		Win	Win
3	Average	Away	Moderate	Good	Average		Loss	Loss
4	Average	Away	Hot	Good	Poor		Win	Win
5	Good	Home	Cold	Good	Good		Loss	Loss
6	Good	Away	Hot	Average	Average		Loss	Loss
7	Poor	Home	Moderate	Average	Good		Loss	Loss
8	Poor	Away	Cold	Poor	Average		Win	Win
9	Average	Home	Hot	Poor	Poor		Win	Win
10	Average	Home	Moderate	Good	Average		Win	Win
11	Good	Away	Cold	Good	Good		Win	Win
12	Good	Home	Hot	Good	Average		Loss	Loss
13	Average	Home	Moderate	Good	Average		Win	Win
14	Average	Away	Cold	Good	Average		Loss	Loss
15	Poor	Home	Cold	Average	Good		Loss	Loss
16	Average	Away	Moderate	Poor	Poor		Loss	Loss

TABLE 16.8 Predicted and Actual Results for "Location" Factor Removed

		Decision Factors			Results	
WEEK	HEALTH	WEATHER	OWN REC.	OPP. REC.	ACTUAL	PRED.
1	Good	Hot	Good	Good	Win	Win
2	Average	Rain	Good	Average	Win	Win
3	Average	Moderate	Good	Average	Loss	?
4	Average	Hot	Good	Poor	Win	Win
5	Good	Cold	Good	Good	Loss	?
6	Good	Hot	Average	Average	Loss	Loss
7	Poor	Moderate	Average	Good	Loss	Loss
8	Poor	Cold	Poor	Average	Win	Win
9	Average	Hot	Average	Poor	Win	Win
10	Average	Moderate	Good	Average	Win	?
11	Good	Cold	Good	Good	Win	?
12	Good	Hot	Good	Average	Loss	Loss
13	Average	Moderate	Good	Average	Win	?
14	Average	Cold	Good	Average	Loss	Loss
15	Poor	Cold	Average	Good	Loss	Loss
16	Average	Moderate	Average	Poor	Loss	Loss

expert system, domain experts will be unable to describe their problem solving knowledge. However, they may be able to provide past examples on the problem that you can use to induce a set of decision-making rules.

Avoids knowledge elicitation problems—Induction offers a technique whereby the system's knowledge can be acquired directly through past examples. This technique can avoid problems associated with attempts to acquire the knowledge directly from the expert.

Can produce new knowledge—An induction tool can produce an expert system to guide future decisions, even though the expert may not be explicitly aware of the decision-making knowledge. This is possible because induction can uncover decision patterns that may be unapparent to even an expert on the problem.

Can uncover critical decision factors—Induction uncovers the most important decision-making factors. This advantage can lead to systems that make decisions on the basis of only a few factors, which greatly enhances the intelligence and efficiency of the system.

Can eliminate irrelevant decision factors—Often factors that initially seem important for making a final decision are found through induction to be irrelevant. This result can be revealing to the expert and aids the efficiency of the system. This result should also be considered with caution, since the addition of later examples may find that earlier exempted decision factors resurface as important considerations.

Can uncover contradictions—Due to the way examples are entered into an induction system, some shells can easily detect examples that provide contradictory results for the same set of decision factor values. Consider for instance the following examples from a pump diagnostic system:

Decision Factors		*Results*
PUMP-PRESSURE	PUMP-TEMPERATURE	CONDITION
Low	High	Pump-Leak
Low	High	Pump-Normal

An induction shell can detect contradictory results and report them to the system developer. In some cases, the contradiction may be acceptable. That is, given the decision factor values, both results may be logical. In this event, the developer can tell the shell to accept both examples.

In most cases, however, a detected contradiction indicates a problem. The problem might be a bad example, or more often, a situation where the present decision factors or values are inadequate to differentiate between results. To illustrate, consider the following.

Assume that after seeing the contradiction in the pump examples, the expert tells us that we should also consider the RPM of the motor controlling the pump. We could then ask the expert for values for this new factor that can lead to the proper results. For example:

	Decision Factors		Results
MOTOR-RPM	PUMP-PRESSURE	PUMP-TEMPERATURE	CONDITION
High	Low	High	Pump-Leak
Low	Low	High	Pump-Normal

The addition of this new decision factor illustrates not only how we can eliminate contradictions, but also how detected problems can lead to the uncovering of additional domain knowledge.

DISADVANTAGES OF INDUCTION

Often difficult to choose good decision factors—The system's effectiveness depends on choosing good decision factors. For example, what factors should you consider when developing a system to predict the winner in a football game? Often, we can trace the merit of a bettor's ability to predict correctly to the choice of the factors that they consider.

Difficult to understand rules—Most induction tools produce their results in a form of a decision tree. For complex problems, it can be difficult to understand the decision process by tracing through the tree. This tracing becomes particularly difficult when the tool is used to formulate rules for incorporation into a conventional rule-based expert system.

Applicable only for classification problems—Induction is good for problems where a set of attribute values can be classified into some expected result. For example, the problem of diagnosis attempts to classify a set of symptoms into a given fault state. Other types of problem solving paradigms, such as planning or design, are difficult to manage with an induction approach.

EXPERT SYSTEMS DEVELOPED THROUGH INDUCTION

Several successful expert systems have been developed using an induction technique. These systems may use different induction algorithms or software tools, but they all share the same feature in that the knowledge about the domain is best represented in the form of examples. The following sections provide a brief review of some of these systems.

AQ11

Michalski and others (Michalski et al. 1980) developed a program called AQ11 for diagnosing soybean diseases. The system is capable of identifying 15 different diseases. The system's knowledge was derived from 630 examples of diseased soybean plants and uses 35 decision factors. A special example selection program called ESEL was used to select 290 of the samples as training examples. ESEL attempted to select examples that were considerably different from one another. The remaining 340 examples were used for testing. Using the 290 training examples, AQ11 formulated a set of rules for classifying a new example into one of the 15 different disease categories.

In a parallel effort, the designers of AQ11 developed a rule-based system on the same problem. Knowledge for this system came from a plant pathologist. A study was then performed to compare the performance of the rule-based and the induction systems.

The 340 examples not used in the formulation of the induction system were used for the comparative testing. The rule-based system gave the correct result 71.8% of the time, while AQ11 scored 97.6%. This surprising performance of AQ11 shows that quality expert knowledge can be generated from a set of examples.

WILLARD

Severe thunderstorms in the United States annually cause loss of lives and millions of dollars in property damage. Forecasting thunderstorms is done by expert meteorologists with the National Severe Storms Forecast Center (NSSFC). This task is time consuming and involves the continuous analysis of vast amounts of data. An expert system called WILLARD was developed based on the induction technique to aid this task (Michie et al. 1984).

WILLARD was developed using 140 examples of thunderstorm weather data. The system uses a hierarchy of 30 modules, each with a single decision tree. The system queries the user about pertinent weather conditions for the area and then produces a complete forecast with supporting justification. The system characterizes the certainty of a severe thunderstorm occurrence as *none, approaching, slight, moderate* or *high,* with each prediction given with a numerical probability range. WILLARD was developed using RULEMASTER, an inductive tool for generating decision rules.

WILLARD was tested over a one-week period in late spring of 1984, in a region including west and central Texas, Oklahoma, and Colorado. During this period, five severe thunderstorms passed through this region. WILLARD's forecasts were found to compare favorable with those made by an expert meteorologist from NSSFC.

Transformer Fault Diagnosis

Transformer protective maintenance programs designed to detect early signs of transformer faults can avoid potential failure and dramatically increase the life of transformers. Traditional protective maintenance programs involve the sampling and testing of the transformer oil for signs of transformer deterioration.

The Hartford Steam Boiler Inspection and Insurance Company and its subsidiary, Radian Corporation, developed an expert system for evaluating the gas-in-oil test results (Lowe 1985). The expert system advises the engineer during the analysis of chromatographic test data for the routine test cases. The system was developed from knowledge contained in the form of past examples using the RULEMASTER rule induction tool. The system contains 27 modules, each with its own induced rule.

The system was tested using data from 900 gas-in-oil chromatographic tests, which were also evaluated by an expert. The system provided results that agreed with the expert's analyses in 90% of the cases. Lowe (1985) reported plans for automating the entry of the chromatograph test data and the automatic preparation of reports for those analyses fitting the normal diagnosis cases.

Customer Support

NORCOM, a software company located in Juneau, Alaska, markets a software product called SCREENIO. SCREENIO allows the user to design IBM PC screens for their Realia COBOL programs. NORCOM has over 500 customers for this product who will often contact NORCOM for product support. To help alleviate the workload associated with their customer support, NORCOM developed an expert system to aid their support personnel.

NORCOM had nine months of data on typical customer problems and associated solutions. They then decided to generate the expert system using the past cases as an example set. The examples contained nine decision factors and was developed in one day using the rule induction tool 1STCLASS.

In operation, this system is used by support personnel who ask the customer for values for each of the decision factors. According to NORCOM general partner John Anderson, the system has "made a major improvement in our customer support responsiveness and efficiency." Another value of the system is that entry-level personnel can use the system effectively since it leads them through the consultation.

VAX-VMS Operating System Tuning

General Research Corporation of McLean, Virginia, developed an expert system to help tune the VAX-VMS operating system (Kornell 1984). Tuning the VMS operating system is a complex and dynamic task. Over 150 parameters must be set by the system manager, and considerable adjustments and modifications are required in response to changes in system configuration and loading. Additional terminals, disks, compilers, memory and programs, as well as changes in user profiles, all affect VAX performance and require system parameter changes.

The developed system collects data on present system performance and generates a summary report. This report provides the VAX system manager with a system and user profile, as well as analyses to help answer questions posed by the expert system. The system interacts with the system manager and asks questions that lead to a recommended action, such as adjusting system parameters or user authorization values, redistribution or reducing user demand, changing user software design, or purchasing new hardware. The expert system was developed using the induction tool TIMM.

After the appropriate changes to the operating system are made, the user can measure the effectiveness of these changes by comparing the performance before and after the recommended actions are taken. Implementation of this system by General Research Corporation personnel led them to report that the expert system has made the management of the VAX-VMS operating system a more efficient task.

Predicting Stock Market Behavior

Predicting stock market behavior is a difficult challenge. Analysts use techniques such as trend analysis, cycle analysis, charting techniques or other types of historical data analysis. Each of these techniques provides the analyst with information that can be used for predicting future trends. However, each technique provides a degree of uncertainty that may make it unreliable.

Braun (Braun and Chandler 1987) developed an expert system based on the ID3 induction technique in an attempt to improve the reliability of stock market prediction. An investment analyst was used as the expert for the study. The problem chosen focused on predicting intermediate fluctuations in the movement of the market for non-conservative investors.

Twenty decision factors were chosen for producing the system. Values for these factors were determined over a time period between March 20, 1981 to April 9, 1983. Most of the information was obtained from the Wall Street Journal, while some data were found from interpretations of trend-charting techniques. Three different results were used to categorize the prediction: bullish (forecasting an upward trend), bearish (forecasting a downward trend), and neutral (indicating that either call was too risky). These predictions were interpreted for each of the 108 weeks of the study. Data was collected on the actual market movement during this period and that predicted by the expert analyst.

In tests of the stock market prediction system, the system correctly predicted the actual market movements 64.4 percent of the time while the expert analyst was correct 60.2 percent. The expert analyst was initially skeptical of any computer system. However, after reviewing the results of this study, he was impressed with both the general structure of the decision tree and with the fact that the system could correctly predict stock market movement more than 60 percent of the time.

—————— SUMMARY ON INDUCTION SYSTEMS ——————

This chapter reviewed the subject of induction, a technique for acquiring domain knowledge from examples of past events. One attraction of induction is that it avoids the often difficult task of acquiring the knowledge through interactions with a human expert. Several induction software tools are available on the market. Some of these tools are designed exclusively for rule induction, while others incorporate an induction utility along with a conventional rule-based development facility. Appendix B provides a listing of available induction expert system shells.

The important points raised in this chapter were:

- Induction forms rules or decision trees from a set of examples.
- Induction avoids the difficult process of eliciting knowledge from the domain expert.
- Induction can discover decision-making rules that are not apparent when reviewing past examples.
- Induction can provide an approach for developing an expert system when no real expert exists on the problem.
- Induction can uncover irrelevant decision factors and remove them from consideration.
- Induction can determine the most significant decision factors and use them to efficiently reach a result.
- The effectiveness of an induction expert system depends on having a good set of examples that covers a broad scope of the problem, and a good choice of decision factors.
- When a rule-based expert system is being developed, induction may be valuable for some subproblems when a set of rules cannot be directly obtained.

—————— R E F E R E N C E S

Braun, H. and J.S. Chandler, Predicting Stock Market Behavior Through Rule Induction: An Application of the Learning-From-Example Approach, Decision Sciences, vol. 8, no. 3, pp. 415–29, Summer 1987.

Buchanan, B. and T. Mitchell, Model-Directed Learning of Production Rules, in Pattern-Directed Inference Systems, D. Waterman and F. Hayes–Roth, eds., Academic Press, New York, 1978.

Cohen, P.R. and E. A. Feigenbaum, Handbook of Artificial Intelligence, vol. 3, William Kaufmann Pub., Los Altos, CA., 1982.

Dietterich, T., R. Lonclon, K. Clarkson and R. Dromey, Learning and Inductive Inference, in D. Cohen and E. Feigenbaum, eds., Handbook of Artificial Intelligence, D. Cohen and E. Feigenbaum, eds., William Kaufmann Pub., Los Altos, CA, pp. 323–525, 1981.

Forsyth, R., Expert Systems: Principles and Case Studies, Chapman and Hall Computing, New York, 1989.

Hunt, E.B., J. Marin, and P.J. Stone, Experiments in Induction, Academic Press, New York, 1966.

Kornell, J., A VAX Tuning Expert Built Using Automated Knowledge Acquisition, Proceedings of the First Conference on Artificial Intelligent Applications, IEEE Computer Society, Dec. 1984.

Lowe, R.I., Artificial Intelligence Techniques Applied to Transformer Oil Dissolved Gas Analysis, Doble Engineering Company, Insulating Fluids, 1985.

Michalski, R. and R. Chilausky, Learning by Being Told and Learning From Examples: An Experimental Comparison of the Two Methods of Knowledge Acquisition in the Context of Developing an Expert System for Soybean Disease Diagnosis, Policy Analysis and Information Systems, vol. 4, no. 2, pp. 125–260, June, 1980.

Michalski, R, Pattern Recognition as Knowledge-Guided Computer Induction, Department of Computer Science, University of Illinois at Urbana–Champaign, 1978.

Michie, D., S. Muggleton, C. Riese, and S. Zubrick, RULEMASTER: A Second-Generation Knowledge-Engineering Facility, Proceedings of the First Conference on Artificial Intelligence Applications, IEEE Computer Society, Dec. 1984.

Quinlan, J.R., Discovering Rules from Large Collections of Examples: A Case Study, Expert Systems in the Micro-Electronic Age, D. Michie, ed., Edinburgh University Press, 1979.

Quinlan, J.R., Machine Learning: An Artificial Intelligence Approach, R. Michalski, J. Carbonell, and T. Mitchell, eds., William Kaufmann Publ., Los Altos, CA., 1986.

Smith, R., T. Mitchell, R. Chestek, and R. Buchanan, A Model for Learning Systems, Heuristic Programming Project Memo HPP-77-14, Stanford University, Stanford, CA., 1977.

Winston, P., Learning Structural Descriptions From Examples, in The Psychology of Computer Vision, McGraw-Hill, New York, 1975.

--------------- **E X E R C I S E S**

1. Discuss why a rule induction technique is valuable for some domains.

2. Discuss the major advantages and limitations of induction.

3. Describe a problem (not one discussed in the chapter) where rule induction would be appropriate.

4. When the induction process produces a ''No-Data'' result, explain what this means and how it can be corrected.

5. When the induction process produces a decision tree that excludes one or more of the original set of decision factors, explain what this means and what steps should be taken.

6. Following the testing of an induction expert system, discuss the principal ways that the system should be revised to improve its performance.

7. The induction technique is only advised for classification problems. Discussed why this recommendation is given.

8. Develop an induction expert system, using ID3 or an induction shell, that can identify each of your closest relatives.

9. We want to develop an expert system to select a wine color on the basis of entree being served, the sauce on the entree, and the customer's preferred wine color. Below

is a listing of the decision factors with values and a set of examples to help decide the recommended wine color. Choose an induction software tool, enter the information, and test the system.

Decision Factors			*Results*
SAUCE	PREF-COLOR	ENTREE	COLOR
cream	red	meat	red
tomato	white	veal	white
		turkey	
		fish	
		poultry	
		other	

	Decision Factors			*Results*
	SAUCE	PREF-COLOR	ENTREE	COLOR
1	*	red	*	red
2	tomato	*	*	red
3	*	white	*	white
4	cream	*	*	white
5	*	*	meat	red
6	*	*	veal	white
7	cream	*	turkery	white
8	cream	*	poultry	white
9	tomato	*	turkey	red
10	tomato	*	poultry	red
11	*	*	fish	white
12	*	*	fish	white
13	cream	*	other	white
14	tomato	*	other	red

10. We want to create an expert system to determine if a bank customer should obtain credit for a loan. To determine whether the loan should be approved or not, we must consider the customer's credit rating, the number of years employed in the present job, and current income. Below are listed the various decision factors that must be considered along with their appropriate values. The "#.#" represents a numeric entry. Also listed is a set of examples from past test cases. Choose an induction software tool, enter the information, and test the system.

Decision Factors			*Results*
CREDIT-RATING	NO.-YEARS	INCOME	CREDIT
excellent	#.#	#.#	Approved
good			Denied
fair			
poor			

| | *Decision Factors* | | | *Results* |
	CREDIT-RATING	NO.-YEARS	INCOME	CREDIT
1	excellent	1.	25000.	Approved
2	excellent	1.	24999.	Denied
3	good	3.	30000.	Approved
4	good	3.	29999.	Denied
5	good	2.	30000.	Denied
6	fair	5.	35000.	Approved
7	fair	5.	34999.	Denied
8	fair	4.	35000.	Denied
9	poor	*	*	Denied

11. The following dialogue between a domain expert (DE) and a knowledge engineer (KE) describes a discussion for recommending a purchase of an automobile. Build an induction expert system following the dialogue. Next, identify any deficiencies in the system and correct.

KE: So you would like to design an expert system to help in selecting an automobile for a customer?

DE: Yes, we have cars of a number of sizes and want a system that can aid in selecting one for the customer.

KE: What size cars do you sell?

DE: We have sports cars, sedans, station wagons, and compacts.

KE: How do you choose one for the customer?

DE: Well, one of the first things I consider is the number of people who will be riding in the car. If more than two, then I immediately rule out a sports car.

KE: Will you always recommend a sports car if there are one or two people riding in the car?

DE: No, our sports cars are expensive and I would have to find out how much the customer can afford.

KE: So price is important?

DE: Oh yes, for example our compacts are inexpensive, the sedans moderately priced, and the station wagons are expensive.

KE: Besides price, are there other considerations?

DE: I usually also want to know if the car will mainly be used for work or not. Our compacts and sedans are a good choice for work, while our station wagons are a better choice for vacations.

12. Assume that we need to develop a small expert system that will be able to determine when a doctor has office hours. Further assume that the doctor can provide this information by categorizing his workweek in terms of days and time of day, and tells you what time slots are late (no office hours) and not late (has office hours), according to the listing below. Use an induction technique to determine if the hour is late or not late on the basis of the day and time of day.

DAYS	TIME
1. MON THROUGH THURS	1. 9 AM–2 PM
2. FRI	2. 2 PM–4 PM
3. SAT OR SUNDAY	3. 4 PM–9 AM

	TIME			
		1	2	3
	1	NOT LATE	NOT LATE	LATE
DAYS	2	NOT LATE	LATE	LATE
	3	LATE	LATE	LATE

13. For exercise 12, write a set of rules by inspection, then compare your rules to the results obtained by the induction method.

CHAPTER 17

Knowledge Acquisition

INTRODUCTION

Earlier chapters argued that an expert system gains its power from the knowledge it contains. It is therefore important that every effort be made to assure that the knowledge that goes into the system effectively captures the expert's understanding of the problem. By its nature, this is a complex task. The knowledge engineer must interact with the expert to acquire, organize and study the problem's knowledge. This task is formally called **knowledge acquisition** and remains the biggest challenge in developing an expert system.

This chapter provides an in-depth look at the knowledge acquisition process. It also discusses the most commonly used knowledge acquisition techniques and provides guidelines for effectively conducting each technique.

OVERVIEW

The objective of knowledge acquisition is to compile a body of knowledge on the problem of interest that can then be encoded in the expert system. Sources for this knowledge can be books, reports or database records. However, the most dominant source for most projects is the domain expert. Acquiring knowledge from the expert is distinguished from the more general knowledge acquisition term and is called **knowledge elicitation.**

Eliciting knowledge from an expert can involve long and tedious sessions between the knowledge engineer and the expert. The session may be an interactive discussion that involves an exchange of ideas about the problem. This style of acquiring knowledge is known as the **interview** method. Another method often used, called the **case study,** tries to uncover the knowledge by watching the expert solve a real problem.

With either method, the objective is to uncover the expert's knowledge and problem-solving skills. After accomplishing this task, the knowledge engineer codes the information into the expert system, tests the system, and uses the results

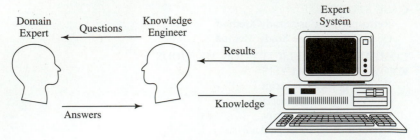

FIGURE 17.1   Knowledge elicitation process.

to plan new knowledge acquisition sessions. Figure 17.1 illustrates the knowledge elicitation process.

The process of eliciting knowledge from an expert may seem on the surface to be a straightforward and simple task. That is, if we need the knowledge for our system, why not simply ask the expert for it? However, most expert system developers have come to realize that it is not quite that simple. In fact, they have found the task to be the most difficult part of designing the expert system. Duda and Shortliffe (1983) voice their concern about this issue by stating

> *"The identification and encoding of knowledge is one of the most complex and arduous tasks encountered in the construction of an expert system. . . Thus the process of building a knowledge base has usually required a time-consuming collaboration between a domain expert and an AI researcher. While an experienced team can put together a small prototype in one or two man-months, the effort required to produce a system that is ready for serious evaluation (well before contemplation of actual use) is more often measured in man-years."*

Hayes–Roth et al. (1983) used the term *bottleneck* to describe the difficulty in knowledge acquisition

> *"Knowledge acquisition is a bottleneck in the construction of expert systems. The knowledge engineer's job is to act as a go-between to help build an expert system. Since the knowledge engineer has far less knowledge of the domain than the expert, however, communication problems impede the process of transferring expertise into the program."*

Knowledge acquisition continues to be one of the most difficult tasks in developing an expert system. Since the 1980's, the field of expert systems has turned into a cult activity. Many spin-off groups have concentrated on specific topics in the field, such as knowledge representation, inexact reasoning, machine learning techniques, etc. Fortunately, several groups have focused on developing better knowledge acquisition methodologies. From this effort, a pool of knowledge has begun to form that can help guide this process.

TABLE 17.1 Different Types of Knowledge

Types of Knowledge	
Procedural knowledge	Rules Strategies Agendas Procedures
Declarative knowledge	Concepts Objects Facts
Meta-knowledge	Knowledge about the other types of knowledge and how to use them
Heuristic knowledge	Rules of thumb
Structural knowledge	Rule sets Concept relationships Concept to object relationships

TYPES OF KNOWLEDGE

There are several elicitation techniques used to obtain knowledge from humans. Each technique has some value for obtaining certain types of knowledge. Understanding the different types of knowledge and the capabilities of the various elicitation techniques in uncovering each type, allows you to choose the proper technique.

Chapter 3 discussed the various types of knowledge used by an expert. Table 17.1 provides a list of these different types. Later in this chapter we discuss the effectiveness of different elicitation techniques in acquiring each type shown in the table.

SOURCES OF KNOWLEDGE

You may find several sources of knowledge on a project. Each can usually provide some information on the given problem and you should consider all of them during the project. Table 17.2 provides a listing of the primary sources.

Expert—The primary source of knowledge for most expert system projects is the domain expert. It is the expert's unique expertise that you are attempting to capture. However, there are additional sources of information that you should not overlook during the project.

End-user—A valuable additional source of information is the end-user. Experts will often view a problem from a low level, considering only the important

TABLE 17.2   Sources of Knowledge

Sources of Knowledge
Expert
End-user
Multiple experts
Reports
Books
Regulations
Guidelines

details. The end-user will view the problem from a high level, considering the major issues. Consulting with an end-user early in the project is of particular value when you need an initial general understanding of the problem. The end-user is also valuable later in the project in uncovering shortcomings in the system's operation.

Multiple experts—Another source of knowledge exists in other experts. Most expert system projects will use one primary domain expert in the knowledge acquisition process. This allows you to focus on the knowledge obtained from one expert and avoid the confusion created when multiple experts supply conflicting knowledge. However, at times it may be valuable to use additional experts to collect specialized knowledge on some sub-problem or to verify the knowledge collected from the single expert.

Literature—Additional sources of information may come in the form of documents such as reports, regulations, guidelines and books. At a minimum, if these documents exist, you should obtain and review them to gain an overview of the problem. These documents can also help define and clarify the terminology of the domain. They can also provide insight into the major issues you will need to address, and details on the knowledge that will eventually be used in the final system.

─────────── **KNOWLEDGE ELICITATION TASKS** ───────────

Expert system development is inherently an exploratory effort. Designers often lack an initial understanding of the problem which forces them to take a cautious approach to the project. A general understanding of the problem is first sought and used as a guide for probing for additional information. Gradually, through this iterative process of knowledge collection and analysis, they gain both an understanding of the problem and insight into its solution.

The tasks involved in knowledge elicitation create a natural cycle. The process begins with the collection of knowledge, followed by its interpretation and analy-

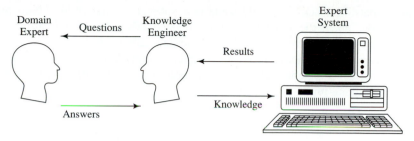

FIGURE 17.2 **Knowledge elicitation cycle.**

sis. Finally, methods are designed for collecting additional knowledge. Figure 17.2 illustrates this cyclical process.

Collect—Collection is the task of acquiring knowledge from the expert. As previously discussed, this effort is the most difficult task of the knowledge elicitation cycle. It requires you to have effective interpersonal communication skills and the ability to obtain the cooperation of the expert. Early in the project, you will first want to obtain a basic understanding of the problem. During later sessions, you will be trying to collect more specific information. This iterative style of collecting information is like a *funnel effect*—moving from the general to the specific.

Interpret—Following the collection of the information, your next task is one of interpretation. This involves a review of the collected information and the identification of key pieces of knowledge. In the early stages, the information collected will be rather general and your interest will be in defining overall problem specifications. This effort involves an informal review of the material, where, with the help of the expert, the problem's goals, constraints and scope are established. During later stages, you will use formal methods to interpret the different types of knowledge uncovered during the session.

Analyze—From studies performed during the interpretation task, the key pieces of knowledge uncovered will provide insight into forming theories on the organization of the knowledge and problem-solving strategies. During early attempts, you will identify the important concepts used by the expert. You can also determine concept relationships and how the expert uses them to solve the problem. Later sessions look at these same points in more detail, where your perception may be influenced by the chosen knowledge representation structure.

Design—Following the completion of the *collect, interpret, analyze* tasks, you should have formed some new understanding of the problem that can aid further investigations. This effort should have exposed you to new concepts and problem-solving strategies that need further exploration. All of this information provides guidance in designing new techniques for collecting additional knowledge.

Some individuals may have difficulty in accepting a knowledge acquisition cycle that has no explicit end point. In an academic sense, the development of an expert system has no termination condition. Developing an expert system is somewhat like teaching a child some new subject. As the child obtains more knowledge about the subject, he or she understands it better and can use this understanding to solve problems. In a similar fashion, an expert system can continue to improve its performance by gaining more knowledge. In a practical sense, the development cycle has an end point defined by the system's performance meeting initial specifications.

TIME REQUIREMENTS FOR KNOWLEDGE ACQUISITION

During an expert system project, the knowledge elicitation process shown in Figure 17.2 is repeated a number of times. Each task of the process requires different activities with different lengths of time to complete. Figure 17.3 shows the proportion of time that you can expect to spend on each phase of the cycle.

The collection task of the knowledge elicitation cycle involves only a short time relative to the entire cycle. Most sessions with the expert will be no more than one hour in length. However, the other phases of the cycle are time-consuming efforts.

You may have to first transcribe the information collected, which could take between four and eight hours for each hour spent collecting the information. You will then need to study the information to identify and interpret the key pieces of knowledge. This effort can take about eight hours to accomplish.

Next, you need to analyze the key pieces of knowledge identified, to determine how they fit into previously collected knowledge. This part of the process can consume up to 40 hours of effort for every hour spent collecting knowledge—a week of work from one hour spent collecting the knowledge!

Finally, this analysis can aid you in designing a new elicitation session. For example, you might discover new concepts that can be explored during the next session with the expert. This effort can take up to two days to accomplish. Figure

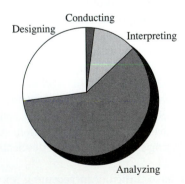

FIGURE 17.3   Knowledge elicitation task time proportions.

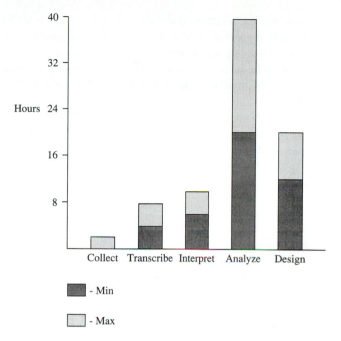

FIGURE 17.4   Time estimates for each elicitation task.

17.4 shows the estimates for the minimum and maximum amount of time that you can expect to spend to accomplish each of these tasks.

DIFFICULTIES WITH KNOWLEDGE ACQUISITION

The purpose of the collection task of the knowledge elicitation cycle is to extract the domain-specific knowledge from the expert. There are several problems inherent in this task. The source of most of these difficulties can be traced to either the elicitation technique employed or a breakdown in communications with the expert. Most expert system projects can expect to run into these difficulties at some point. However, a better understanding of the typical problems that may occur can help the effort.

Psychological View of Elicitation Problems

The field of cognitive psychology has long recognized the difficulty of eliciting knowledge from humans (Freud 1914), (Nisbett and Wilson 1977). Dixon (1981) reports that humans are not mentally conscious of many of their activities, but perform them through repetition. Humans appear to be unaware of their own mental processes when solving a problem. Similarly, Collins (1985) reports that humans may not be able to communicate their knowledge, not because they cannot express it, but because they are unaware of what knowledge they are using in the activity.

Even when a human can communicate the knowledge, there may be a problem. Bainbridge (1986) reports that there is no necessary correlation between verbal reports and mental behavior. Humans will actually do things differently from the way they explain their performance. Chomsky (1957), from work on the theory of natural language grammar, drew attention to the distinction between "competence" and "performance." He concluded that individuals frequently utter sentences that would violate their own rules of grammar owing to performance factors.

Another source of trouble in expert problem solving is related to the issue of "selective bias." Tversky and Kahneman (1973) report that an individual's judgment may be influenced by an available heuristic. They stated that

> *"A person is said to employ the available heuristic whenever he estimates frequency or probability by the ease with which instances or associations could be brought to mind."*

In other words, humans bias their approach to solving a given problem toward past experiences in solving similar problems, while possibly overlooking or ignoring information that would indicate a different approach should be taken.

It has long been recognized that a human's short-term memory is limited. Humans retain in their short-term memory only a few items related to a problem, unless they recognize a few important problem issues that they may then store in their long-term memory. Johnson-Laird and Steedman (1978) conclude in their theory of reasoning that difficulties with a human's short-term memory can explain the logical errors given by humans when attempting to explain their reasoning processes when solving past problems.

Most expert system projects rely on communication between the expert and the knowledge engineer for knowledge acquisition. The difficulty expert system designers have found in eliciting this knowledge would not be of surprise to researchers in cognitive psychology. From studies in knowledge elicitation by cognitive psychologists, several common problems surface and are shown in Table 17.3.

With this list of troubles facing the knowledge engineer, it is obvious why the simple and straightforward approach of asking the expert what knowledge is used in problem solving may often fail, and why, in general, elicitation of knowledge from experts can be prone to error. A brief review of each of the problems listed in Table 17.3 can provide additional insight into the difficulty of knowledge elicitation.

TABLE 17.3   Major Difficulties with Knowledge Elicitation

- Expert may be unaware of the knowledge used.
- Expert may be unable to verbalize the knowledge.
- Expert may provide irrelevant knowledge.
- Expert may provide incomplete knowledge.
- Expert may provide incorrect knowledge.
- Expert may provide inconsistent knowledge.

Unaware of Knowledge Used

Experts usually acquire their expertise through the experience of working on similar problems. After a period, experts may become unaware of the *deep knowledge* they use to solve the problem. Deep knowledge is formed from first principles or physical laws of the domain.

Experts compile their problem-solving knowledge into a compact form that permits them to solve problems efficiently. When asked to describe their problem-solving methods, they will often make mental leaps over important issues and have difficulty in explaining the knowledge used in detail. Experts will ascribe to intuition that which is result of a very complex reasoning process based on deep knowledge. Waterman (1986) labels this dilemma as the *knowledge engineering paradox*

> "*The more competent domain experts become, the less able they are to describe the knowledge they used to solve problems!*"

Expert system developers often refer to this situation as the *knowledge compilation* problem. One of your responsibilities is to decompile this knowledge into a form that can be studied and eventually enter into the expert system. You must be able to pick apart this intuitive knowledge, often called *shallow knowledge,* and uncover some of the deeper information. Shallow knowledge is formed from experience rather than from first principles, and is usually in the form of heuristics or rules of thumb.

To combat the knowledge compilation problem, you must be trained in knowledge elicitation techniques. This training teaches you how to identify when this trouble occurs and how to pick the proper technique to solve it. Without this training, the resultant system's knowledge may be weak or incomplete.

This problem has a further implication. Since it is rare to find an expert who is also an experienced knowledge engineer, the expert needs help to explicate the problem-solving knowledge. With the ease of expert system development offered by many of today's shells, the expert might be tempted to develop the system alone. However, without training in knowledge engineering or help from a person with this training, this is a dangerous venture.

Unable to Verbalize the Knowledge

Asking an individual to examine their own thoughts on a topic is called *introspection*. Introspection is a basic technique used in the interview method. However, many tasks do not lend themselves to verbal explanation. Manual labor efforts, such as tying a shoelace or riding a bicycle, are typical of this type of task. These tasks may be difficult to verbalize because they were learned by watching the actions of others, rather then through verbal instruction.

This dilemma has plagued cognitive psychologists for years. To solve the problem, they often have turned to studies in behaviorism to obtain a more accurate report of the mental processes. In behavior studies, psychologists attempt to obtain an understanding of the human's problem-solving knowledge by studying the human during a problem-solving session. Expert system developers refer to this technique as *case studies*.

Provides Irrelevant Knowledge

A transcript of a one-hour knowledge elicitation session can easily produce 10 pages of text. Early in the project, when you are likely to know little or nothing about the problem, you must assume everything is relevant. To do otherwise runs the risk of losing valuable information. However, staring at 10 pages of text with the understanding that you must make some sense from it, can raise the valid concern that much of this effort may end up being worthless.

There is no easy answer to this problem. In the early part of the project, you might simply ask the expert if some issue is important or not. This can eliminate irrelevant information and has the added benefit of exposing important issues that the expert could then discuss further. Later in the project, you should have a good understanding of the problem and will be better able to identify the important issues in the transcript.

Provides Incomplete Knowledge

Experts may often provide an incomplete description of their mental processes. When an expert introspects about problem-solving knowledge, he or she may often leap over some of the intuitive issues. This problem may be only a simple omission that can be easily corrected. However, if it is caused by the expert being unaware of the knowledge used (the compilation problem), the challenge can be far greater. You will likely be a novice in the domain and be unable to detect this omission. This leads to an incomplete body of knowledge in the expert system that could further lead to incorrect performance.

Having the expert system run incorrectly is often a blessing. System testing will often reveal overlooked issues and provide direction for future knowledge elicitation sessions. This is why it is often argued that the system can be a valuable aid during knowledge acquisition.

Provides Incorrect Knowledge

One problem with asking experts to verbalize problem-solving methods is that they may provide incorrect knowledge. This problem may occur if the expert lacks knowledge on some issue, or more innocently, makes a simple mistake during introspection. In either case, this problem can have a negative impact on the system's performance. Waterman (1986) gives a rather interesting suggestion on this point

> *"Don't believe everything experts say!"*

Because of this possibility, you need some way to verify the knowledge. You can often accomplish this through testing the expert system, where prior cases with known results can be compared with the system's test results. If the results differ, you can trace back through the system's knowledge and locate the incorrect knowledge that caused the difference. If the trouble arises because the expert lacks an understanding on some issue, then the use of other experts may help.

Provides Inconsistent Knowledge

One of the more frustrating experiences you may encounter occurs when the expert provides inconsistent knowledge. Just when you believe you understand some issue, along comes a contradiction. Inconsistent knowledge is often found in an expert's explanation of a problem-solving strategy. Consider for example the following statements made by an expert, that leaves you faced with a problem in not knowing what the expert does first:

> "I always first check to see if the battery is ok."

But, in a later discussion, we find the expert saying

> "I first want to find out if there are any loose wires."

Experts may also provide inconsistent knowledge when they describe the importance of certain issues. Initially, the expert might state that some issue is an important consideration, but later imply it is relatively unimportant.

Inconsistency can also surface when you ask an expert to solve some typical problem. Experts will often view a given problem as an instance of similar problems worked on in the past. Their approach in solving the problem may be influenced more by past problem solving methods, than by the current problem information. This type of approach is inconsistent because the expert provides findings that are inconsistent with the case studied.

Faced with the problems listed in Table 17.3, you need to choose a knowledge elicitation technique that can either avoid them or reduce their negative effects. Later in this chapter, we will review the ability of different knowledge elicitation techniques in avoiding these problems.

ROLES OF THE ELICITATION TEAM MEMBERS

Chapter 2 listed the various individuals involved in an expert system project and discussed the qualifications needed by each for the success of the project. In this section, we consider the roles played by these individuals in the context of knowledge elicitation.

Team Members

Forming a team of both talented and cooperative individuals is an important initial step in the knowledge elicitation process. Each of these individuals plays a role in the process and provides specific contributions. Without their contributions, either due to the individual's inability or lack of desire, the process is likely to fail. It is therefore important to choose capable and cooperative individuals for this team. In most expert system projects, the knowledge elicitation process involves three main individuals:

- End-user
- Domain expert
- Knowledge engineer

The success of the process will also depend upon the support of the organization's management, discussed in Chapter 18. Some projects include additional personnel, such as other experts or knowledge engineers, who are responsible for specialized tasks.

The next few sections discuss the primary contributions of each of these individuals to the knowledge elicitation process. Table 17.4 lists the primary responsibilities of each team member during an expert system project.

End-User

Most literature on expert systems recommends involving the end-user extensively throughout the project. Knowledge engineers recognize the importance of this point. However, in many projects the end-user is virtually ignored.

TABLE 17.4 Major Elicitation Tasks

	Elicitation Tasks
End-User	Provide problem overview
	Help define interface
	Help define explanation facility needs
	Highlight areas that need developed
	Aid in system testing
	Help define in-place operation of system
Expert	Provide primary source of knowledge
	Aid knowledge interpretation and analysis
	Aid in system testing
Knowledge Engineer	Collect the knowledge
	Interpret the knowledge
	Analyze the knowledge
	Coordinate project activities
	Maintain cooperative effort

End-users can help you during the elicitation process by providing initial insight into the problem and can help to define the system's operational requirements. They can also add to the spirit of team cooperation when they feel that their input is of value and is taken seriously. Many expert systems have been widely acclaimed for their problem-solving skills, but were never implemented because the project failed to involve the end-user.

End-User Tasks

Provide overview—At the beginning of the project, you may know very little about the problem. Even worse, you may be suffering from *meta-ignorance;* you do not know what you do not know. If your first source of information is the domain expert, you may be overwhelmed with details and become even more confused. What you initially need is a general perspective of the problem.

One of the best sources for obtaining a general understanding of the problem is the end-user. End-users perceive the problem from a much higher level than the domain expert. They can more easily explain the expected results and provide insight into the major issues that should be covered during a knowledge elicitation session.

Define interface requirements—The end-user is a valuable aid in defining the system's interface specifications. There are a number of options for any interface including menus, graphics, multiple windows, and different ways for interacting with the system such as the use of a mouse or keyboard. In many expert system projects, half of the effort can be spent on designing an acceptable interface. Generally these efforts are concerned with meeting the requirements of the end-user of the system. Therefore, it is important that you involve the end-user early and frequently throughout the project.

Define explanation requirements—An expert system can answer queries of *why* and *how*. Both of these capabilities add a transparency to the reasoning of the system and present the system in an accommodating fashion to the user. However, expert systems handle these queries differently. Most systems will simply display the current rule for the *why* query and a tracing of the rules that fired for the *how* query. This response may be adequate for the knowledge engineer during testing, however, it may be inadequate for the user. Because of this potential problem, the user is a valuable aid to you for defining the needs of the explanation facility.

Help define in-place operational requirements—You should also recognize that the user of the system may be an individual inexperienced with computers. In this situation, consideration must be given to developing a system that will accommodate the user who may be encountering a computer for the first time. Issues of how to start, work with, and terminate the system must be addressed.

Aid system development—After the prototype system is built, you may elect to consult with the end-user again to obtain further insight into problem details. One important area where the end-user can help is in establishing the proper level of the questions that the system will ask.

For example, an expert system designed to determine whether a patient is experiencing a heart attack would need to ask the user for reliable information. If the system asked

"Is the patient having a heart attack?"

the end-user may find this question too unreliable and request that the system ask a more primitive question such as

"Is the patient experiencing chest pains?"

The system would now ask a question that could be more reliably answered by the user, and use the answer to determine if the patient is having a heart attack. In general, the end-user can be a valuable aid in establishing the proper level of the system's knowledge. The level of an expert system's knowledge is often referred to as the *knowledge granularity*.

Considering the contributions of the end-user, an estimate of the amount of time the end-user can expect to spend on a one-year project is one to two months.

Expert

The expert is the primary source of knowledge for the expert system. In fact, it is the expert's knowledge and problem-solving skills that you attempt to model in the expert system. A knowledge elicitation effort attempts to extract the knowledge from the expert in a form that can be studied and used to better understand the domain and eventually be represented in the expert system. The expert can aid this effort in several ways.

Expert Tasks

Provide knowledge—The primary task of the expert is to supply his or her knowledge. This task is complicated and may require a number of knowledge elicitation sessions to complete successfully.

Aid interpretation/analysis—The knowledge elicitation session is usually recorded and transcribed later. The transcript is studied to form a better understanding of the problem and to obtain insight into areas that should be addressed in future sessions. During this study, the expert can help you uncover new concepts and problem-solving methods, and provide guidance on how this new information relates to the body of knowledge previously discovered.

Aid testing—As the project proceeds, knowledge gained through the elicitation sessions will begin to find its way into the expert system. As new knowledge is added, the system will be tested to determine its response to this new information. To verify the operation of the system, the expert may again be needed. The expert can help in determining if the existing knowledge is adequate or if changes are needed.

An estimate of time that the expert can expect to devote to a one year project is between two and four months. Figure 17.5 shows the expected range of times

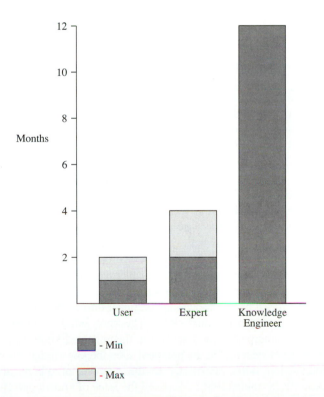

FIGURE 17.5 Expected time contribution of each team member.

for each team member, assuming the knowledge engineer spends one year on the project.

Knowledge Engineer

By its nature, knowledge engineering is an inter-disciplinary effort. The knowledge engineer must perform a range of tasks beginning with introducing the technology to individuals within an organization and ending with integrating the expert system into the workplace. Along the way, the knowledge engineer will need to play the roles of a psychologist, diplomat, and programmer.

Knowledge Engineer Tasks

The major elicitation tasks of the knowledge engineer are collecting, interpreting and analyzing knowledge. These tasks form a natural cyclic process that is repeated with each new knowledge elicitation session. Issues to pursue during a given session will depend on what you learned from prior cycles.

Collect knowledge—Collecting knowledge through elicitation involves interaction between the knowledge engineer and the expert. As discussed earlier in this chapter, there are several difficulties associated with this task. Most of these troubles relate to breakdowns in communication, therefore, the knowledge engineer must have good communication skills. Later in this chapter, you will be introduced to some of the standard elicitation techniques and guidelines for avoiding the common problems.

Interpret and analyze knowledge—After the elicitation session, the knowledge engineer must study the information and uncover the key pieces of knowledge. The knowledge engineer determines how to incorporate those pieces of information into the system's existing knowledge structures. Techniques for both interpreting and analyzing the collected knowledge are reviewed later in this chapter.

Design new session—Following the analysis task, the knowledge engineer must prepare for a new elicitation cycle. This task involves the design of an agenda that includes clarifying old issues or pursuing new ones with the expert.

Manage project—The knowledge engineer is also responsible for coordinating the efforts of the other team members to maintain productivity and interest. Assigning specific tasks, arranging meetings, and maintaining a cooperative team effort, are some of the administrative tasks required.

The tasks performed by the knowledge engineer during the elicitation process require both technical and personal skills. The knowledge engineer must have technical skills for interpreting and analyzing the collected knowledge, and programming the expert system. On the personal side, the knowledge engineer must have communication skills, sensitivity to the interests of others, and project management skills. Sviokla (1986) discussed the issue of knowledge engineering skills by stating

"The appropriate background for a knowledge engineer is not standard. Even though expert systems are at the leading edge of computer software, computer science PhDs may not always make the best knowledge engineers. Taylor, an experienced practitioner, suggests that the best knowledge engineers are an eclectic lot who come from varied backgrounds like English, philosophy, and art."

INTERVIEWING METHOD

Most elicitation methods can be categorized into two general areas: direct and indirect techniques (Olson and Rueter 1987). Direct methods involve the articulation by the domain expert of the problem-solving knowledge and primarily include interviews and case studies. Indirect methods do not rely on experts being able to articulate the knowledge. They indirectly determine what the experts must have known in order to respond the way they did to some indirect testing method. Common indirect techniques include questionnaires, repertory grid, and card sorting (Hart 1986).

The most common knowledge elicitation technique used today in the design of expert systems is the interview method. This choice is somewhat obvious because we are accustomed to solving problems by going to someone knowledgeable and asking him or her how to solve them. This allows us to quickly grasp an understanding of the problem and insight into its solution. However, if we continued in this informal manner we would soon run into problems. We might find that we are unable to acquire problem details or we could encounter situations where the expert is unable to communicate the information effectively. Effective interviewing is an art. However, there are guidelines that can be followed to improve the chances of success.

MANAGING THE INTERVIEW

Knowledge elicitation can be a time-consuming and difficult process and requires the cooperation of all the team members to be successful. The quote from John Donne, "No man is an island," captures the importance of acquiring a cooperative effort between the individuals involved in the knowledge elicitation process. Each individual's tasks are dependent on the cooperation of other team members. Without this cooperation, specific tasks cannot be completed and the entire knowledge acquisition process may fail.

Creating an environment of cooperation is primarily the responsibility of the knowledge engineer. He or she must be sensitive to the personal concerns, interests, and desires of each team member. These issues must be considered in parallel with the development of the expert system. A failure in this area may result in the loss of support from the team members, accompanied by a breakdown in the elicitation process.

Learn about the Organization and Problem

Before the first meeting, you should learn about both the problem and the sponsoring organization. Team members will interpret this effort as a show of interest in both the project and the organization. You can accomplish this background study by requesting any reports describing the problem and the organization. The study does not need to be in depth. A broad overview will allow you to discuss the project in general terms and will also introduce you to the vocabulary of the expert.

In many cases, you will do a preliminary study to identify and assess potential applications of expert systems within an organization. From this study, the problem that appears most promising will be selected for the project. In this case, you should come to the first meeting prepared to discuss the results of this study.

The First Team Meeting

Maintaining cooperation of the team members throughout the project will depend heavily on their first reaction to the project. Your management of the first meeting will have a major impact on enhancing or reducing future successes. Table 17.5 provides a list of guidelines for obtaining the initial cooperation of the team members.

Remove Fear

Recognize the problem—The first hurdle in gaining cooperation is removing any fear or resentment team members may have towards what they might perceive as an "invasion" by this new technology. People often perceive their value in terms of what functions they perform and may then view the introduction of an expert system as an "alien" device that will assume some of their responsibilities. With this loss, they see a corresponding loss in their value and status within the organization.

Improve perception of self-value—To remove fear rooted in a perception of loss of value, you should try to show how the introduction of an expert system will improve, and not decrease, this value. Like the introduction of a traditional computer or wordprocessor, team members should be taught to view an expert system as another tool they can use to ease their work and enhance their performance.

Remove Skepticism

Recognize the problem—When any new project begins, individuals involved within the organization may be skeptical. When the project involves a new technology, such as expert systems, this skepticism may only increase. These same individuals may also be concerned about the applicability of expert systems

TABLE 17.5   Guidelines for Obtaining Initial Cooperation

Remove Fear
- Convey that the expert system is not a replacement, but will be an aid to help improve present performance.
- Strip the mystery away and explain clearly what changes will occur with the introduction of the expert system.

Remove Skepticism
- Provide a brief overview of expert systems.
- Provide a brief review of successful expert system projects on similar applications.
- Provide frequent successful demonstrations of the expert system.

Establish Reasonable Goals
- Don't oversell the system.
- Explain the capabilities as well as the limitations of the system.

Promote Openness to Change
- Explain how each team member's contributions can aid in the further development and acceptance of this technology.
- Explain that only a temporary inconvenience will be experienced with the introduction of the expert system.

Provide Understanding of Expected Effort
- Describe the expected contributions of each member.
- Convey to managers a description of each team member's project tasks.

Convey Importance of Involvement
- Make the team members aware that they are an important part of the project and without their effort the project has little chance to succeed.

for the chosen project. If methods currently used within the organization have failed to solve the problem, there may be skepticism about the chances of this new technology doing any better.

Review the technology—Often, the expert system project will be the first introduction of this technology within an organization. To help erase any skepticism about the technology, provide a brief overview of expert systems. Explain clearly *what* expert systems are and *why* they can be of value. You should discuss the major characteristics of the technology and how expert systems differ from conventional programs (see Chapter 2). A brief review should also be given on past successful expert system projects, preferably ones with some relationship to the current project (see appendix C). You should also provide each member a few select introductory articles and reports on past relevant projects. The members will appreciate both the information and your consideration in providing the material.

Perform frequent demonstrations—Early attempts to remove skepticism may provide only a partial solution. Later during the project, individuals will need some positive feedback on the progress to remain convinced that the effort is worthwhile. This feedback can come in the form of successful demonstrations.

McDermott (1981) reports on this point when introducing R1 into Digital Equipment Corporation (DEC). An expert system approach to the problem of computer configuration represented an entirely different style, one that was met with skepticism by some management personnel. McDermott found the solution to the problem rested with setting reasonable goals and providing frequent successful demonstrations of the expert system. Following successful demonstrations of R1, the skepticism of individuals within DEC was replaced not with belief, but with caution and hope.

Establish Reasonable Goals

Recognize the problem—Establishing reasonable goals is important for any project. However, it is of particular importance for an expert system project where expectations may be great. Many individuals' only understanding of the technology may come from the distorted view portrayed from science fiction movies. They may have come to believe that an intelligent computer can solve almost any problem and, therefore, expect performance from the system beyond its capabilities.

Don't oversell—An initial oversell of the technology will create obvious problems later when the system does not live up to expectations. Individuals will lose interest in the project and it may be difficult to win them back. You must explain the capabilities as well as the limitations of the system to everyone involved in the project.

Promote Openness to Change

Recognize the problem—Most people are conservative by nature and prefer the status quo. In a work environment, individuals make an effort to tailor their workplace to produce a comfortable setting. They view change as an unknown, and react with fear or anxiety.

Remove the unknown—You should recognize that an individual may be reacting negatively to the change itself, and not to its effects. To address this problem you should strip the mystery away by explaining clearly what changes will occur with the introduction of the expert system. You should also convey that the changes will be positive and that the expert system is there to help and not hinder the individual's performance.

Provide Understanding of Expected Effort

Recognize the problem—It is a common problem in any project that individuals are apprehensive of getting involved when they are uncertain about their level of involvement. They become concerned that the amount of time and effort may be extensive or remove them from other important projects. They also may become concerned if their contributions are not explicitly stated as a set of tasks that management will use when evaluating their performance.

Provide a clear set of tasks—The team members must understand the objective of the project and the contributions they will be expected to make to the effort. You must convey what support they will supply and what tasks they will perform. From this information, they can estimate the amount of time and effort expected from them. You should also convey this information to the team members' managers. A clear description of their expected tasks in the early stages of the project can help alleviate most of their concerns.

Convey Importance of Involvement

Recognize the problem—One problem often encountered when introducing an expert system project is related to the perception of status among the team members. Individuals are often viewed at different levels of status within an organization. Even the labels of "expert" and "user" can shape one's view and impact the behavior of the individuals. Some members will take a strong authoritative position while others will feel inhibited and unwilling to provide suggestions.

Important contributors—To foster and encourage their involvement, you must reshape this perception and convince each member that their contributions are not only important but vital to the success of the project. The members will be more encouraged to contribute if they feel they are an important part of the effort.

Guidelines for the First Meeting

The primary objectives of the first meeting are to form a good rapport among the team members and establish credibility in the project. Accomplishing this is critical to the success of the project. Table 17.6 gives a set of guidelines for achieving these objectives.

TABLE 17.6   Guidelines for the First Meeting

- Prepare for the meeting
    Study the problem.
    Learn about the organization.
- Encourage each member to present his or her own view of the project.
- Identify and address any resistance an individual may have toward the project.
- Provide a brief review of expert system technology.
- Establish future project directions including the anticipated involvement of each member.
- Tape record the session for later review.

Preparing for the Interview

The success of any interview session will first rest with the groundwork formed by its preparation. The preparation addresses the subjects to be covered, scheduling, materials, and methods for recording the session.

Prepare Agenda

A key to a good interview is to have a clear objective of what you want to accomplish. The interview's *agenda* details how you will achieve your objective and contains a list of the major items that will be discussed during the interview. You must establish the objective and agenda first and convey them to all parties attending the interview. The agenda allows the team members to understand what you expect to achieve during the interview and gives them an opportunity to better prepare. This in turn increases the likelihood that the objective will be effectively achieved.

Scheduling

You must set up the time and location of the interview session. To accommodate the schedules of the session attendees, at least one week notice should be given to each member. In addition, the length of the session should rarely exceed one hour. This length of time both accommodates the attendees schedules and limits the fatigue that could set in with longer sessions. If you properly prepare and manage the session, this period of time should be sufficient. You should also remember an important piece of advice when arriving at the meeting:

Don't be late!

Being late not only represents an inconvenience for the other members, but it also sends a message that you may not appreciate their time or you do not take the project very seriously. Also realize that you will spend most of your effort alone. Other team members may form an opinion of your efforts away from the meeting on the basis of your actions during the meeting. If you are late for the interview, their opinion is likely to be negative, and may eventually result in the loss of their cooperation on the project.

You will normally hold the session at the expert's site. This is not only a point of accommodation but also presents a natural setting for the interview. Lincoln and Guba (1984) argue that elicitation should be carried out at a site that is natural to the activity being studied. They believe that the activity is context bound, and to study the activity outside its context is to study it removed from its meaning. This suggestion is of particular value if the knowledge you are collecting requires the expert to solve a problem that would normally be done in the workplace.

Materials List

You should also prepare a list of the materials you will use during the interview. Reports, papers, etc., should be given to each group member prior to the interview. Questions will often arise related to information discussed during earlier sessions. You will be documenting the progress of the project, including references to this collected information. It is therefore advisable to take this project documentation to each interview. If a problem arises that you can only resolve with missing documentation, frustration could set in.

You must record the information you collect during an interview. One approach is to take notes that record questions, answers, and highlights of the session. If you use a notebook record-keeping approach, there is a basic but easily forgotten list of items you will need. A notebook (with enough pages), several pens or pencils, and different colored markers for highlighting the notes. Also include a sketch pad that the expert could use for illustrating important issues.

Tape Recording

Using a notebook approach exclusively for recording the information gained during an interview has several limitations. The primary problem is that it provides an incomplete account of the session. You are likely to only note the answers to specific questions and highlights of other issues, which could lead to the loss of other important information.

Another problem with this approach is that you may miss how the expert qualifies some knowledge. The expert might say for example, "Given these conditions then I *might* believe that the pump is bad." In all likelihood, you will record this information as:

    IF   These conditions exist
    THEN   The pump is bad

Here you have lost the qualification the expert placed on this rule with the use of the word *might,* which could be important and later implemented in the expert system using some inexact reasoning approach.

Because of the limitations of simple notekeeping, most interviewers make an audio recording of the session. This approach captures the entire session for later study. When recording an interview it can be tempting to relax your attention and rely on the recording to gather the information. However, the expert may emphasize certain issues that may not receive the same emphasis during the review of the tape. It is therefore valuable to use the basic notekeeping approach to capture these important issues while also recording the session on tape. You can then focus analysis of the tape on highlighted issues.

If a tape recording approach is used, there are a few recommendations you should consider. You should record each interview on a single tape labeled with date, location, attendees and major theme of the session. Placing multiple interviews on a single tape can only cause confusion later when attempting to retrieve the information. Remember, tapes are cheap but the time lost due to poor record keeping can be costly. Also, make certain you come to each interview completely prepared. One is unlikely to forget the tape recorder; however, forgetting extra tapes or batteries is more likely and could obviously create a major problem.

Video Recording

Several expert system projects have used video equipment to record the interview session. This decision is made if it is felt that visual information is important for later interpretation and analysis efforts. A typical problem that lends itself to video recording is physical task analysis. If the expert will be performing a task that requires physical effort, study of a video tape can provide insight into problem solving that you may not capture on an audio recording.

If you decide to use a video recording approach, you should be sensitive to the violation of the natural setting discussed earlier. Most experts rarely perform their task in front of a camera and may be intimidated to some degree. This can result in behavior modification and the collection of distorted information. You should only use video recording if you cannot otherwise reliably obtain the information.

Interview Preparation Guidelines

The success of any interview session is likely to depend on the effort placed on its preparation. A well-prepared session will be more effective and efficient. Table 17.7 provides a list of guidelines you should consider in the preparation of an interview.

Beginning the Interview

The body of the interview will center on the process of knowledge elicitation. For this process to be successful, each team member must be comfortable and motivated to cooperate. The first few minutes of the meeting are therefore critical to the success of the interview.

Set Initial Tone

The initial tone for the interview should make the participants comfortable. To accomplish this, first introduce a subject of personal interest to the others. A question such as, ''How was your vacation?'' can relax the individuals and make them feel comfortable with the session. The key is to pick any subject of personal interest, but not one related to the project. Even an informal discussion centered on some project issue may not accomplish the goal of establishing a comfortable

TABLE 17.7   General Guidelines for Interview Preparation
_____

• Determine a clear objective and agenda.

• Determine who will attend.

• Provide attendees with information to be covered:
  Objective
  Agenda
  Reports, papers, etc.
  Major issues

• Determine schedule of interview.
  Give one week notice to attendees.
  Keep meeting length to one hour.
  Don't be late!

• Determine location of interview.
  Accommodate the expert
  Choose a natural setting

• Record the interview.
  Use one tape per session
  Label the tape
    Date
    Location
    Attendees
    Major theme of session
  Take notes of meeting highlights
  Use video recording only if absolutely necessary

• Bring the important material to the interview:
  Agenda
  Reports, papers, etc.
  Project documentation
  Miscellaneous supplies
    Tape recorder
    Extra batteries
    Extra tapes
    Notebook
    Sketch pads
    Pens, pencils, markers
    Coffee and donuts—if you are smart
_____

initial setting. Worse, if you bring up a project issue for discussion, it may be difficult later to redirect the conversation into the planned areas.

Review Agenda

As recommended earlier, you should provide each attendee with the session's objective and agenda prior to the interview. You can then discuss any suggestions

TABLE 17.8   Guidelines for Beginning the Interview

- Establish a comfortable setting by discussing a topic of personal interest.
- Avoid an initial subject related to the project.
- Review the session's objective and agenda.
- Resolve any misunderstandings and solicit suggestions.

or misunderstandings. This review provides a clear setting for the session and should enhance the attendee's motivation to cooperate during the session.

Table 17.8 provides a list of guidelines you should consider in beginning the interview.

Conducting the Interview

Later sections in this chapter discuss some of the most commonly used interviewing methods. Each method follows a suggested style and requires you to follow commonly recognized good interviewing practices. This section reviews several of the more important practices you should consider when conducting the interview.

Following the Agenda

You should follow the agenda as closely as possible. This practice brings order to the interview and offers the best promise for achieving the session's objective. It also offers the best chance of completing the interview in the allotted time.

Sticking to the agenda can sometimes be difficult because experts often have a tendency to wander away from the main topic into other areas. This diversion may be unproductive and cost valuable time. You must be able to recognize an unproductive deviation and gently move the conversation back to the primary agenda topic. However, you must also recognize when the expert is still trying to answer the question, but in a roundabout manner. An interruption here could be disruptive and lead to the failure to obtain the desired information.

You should also recognize that an overly strict adherence to the agenda can prevent important unexpected discoveries. Knowledge acquisition is a venture of exploration in quest of knowledge related to the problem. You may have some initial idea of where to expect to find this knowledge and form a plan to explore those areas. However, these plans must be flexible enough to allow for deviations into possibly productive areas when they appear.

Deviations from the agenda may create the obvious problem of not accomplishing the objective due to the available time. On the surface this may appear as a failure. However, if you obtain valuable information, then the interview is a success. The best rule-of-thumb to follow is

The sin is not in failing to achieve the objective, but in not obtaining some knowledge.

Types of Questions

A basic tool of the interview process is the *question*. A question can be posed to gain information about the problem or to control the interview. You must be aware of the different types of questions, what impact they can have, and how to properly pose each.

Direct Question

Direct questions are valuable when you need specific information and have the following form:

> "What does ... mean?"
> "Is ... true?"
> "What is the value of ...?"

For example

> KE: What would you consider an abnormal pump pressure?

Direct questions seek answers that have a limited number of responses. The expert may simply answer "yes" or "no," select from a limited list of values, or provide a specific value as in asking for an abnormal pump pressure.

You will normally ask direct questions later in the project when you need specific information on some previously discovered issue. Direct questions are rarely used early in the project when the objective is to gain general problem insight.

Indirect Question

Indirect questions are exploratory in nature and allow the expert to answer in a manner that is natural to his or her recall. With the use of an indirect question, you try to uncover the problem's major concepts and the general procedural knowledge used by the expert when solving the problem. Indirect questions take on the following form:

> "What issues do you consider ...?"
> "How do you determine ...?"
> "What do you look for when ...?"

For example

> KE: What issues do you consider to determine if the pump needs to be replaced?

DE: If the pump's **pressure** is low, or its **temperature** is hot, or its **age** is old, then I would replace it.

From this answer you find that the important concepts are the pump's pressure, temperature, and age. From here you could use direct questions to learn details about these concepts.

To gain insight into the general procedural knowledge, including general problem-solving strategies and general rules, an indirect question of the following form can be used

"How do you . . .?"

For example

KE: How do you determine if the pump is bad?
DE: I first check the pump's pressure and temperature. If the pump's pressure is only slightly high, but its temperature is high, then it's probably bad. Also, if it's always running hot and it's old, then it is likely bad.

From this answer you first gain information on the problem-solving strategy, i.e., first check pump's pressure and temperature. If you were not already aware of the pump's pressure and temperature being important issues, then this answer would have uncovered them. You also obtain general rules in the form:

IF   Pump's pressure is slightly high
AND   Pump's temperature is high
THEN   Pump is *probably* bad

IF   Pump is always running hot
AND   Pump is old
THEN   Pump is *likely* bad

These general rules gained from indirect questioning can be explored later through direct questioning to determine what is meant by pressure slightly high, temperature high, running hot, and pump is old. In addition, the indirect questioning approach uncovered a degree of uncertainty in the rule's conclusion: "probably bad" and "likely bad."

Probes

Often, when experts are describing some issue, they will skim over some important details. This problem typically occurs because they have compiled the knowledge, which leads them to jump over intuitive points. However, you may need these details either for your own understanding or for encoding in the expert system. For this purpose, you need to question the expert in a manner that will provide further information on the issue. This type of question is called a probe. Probe questions usually come in the form of:

"Can you explain. . .?"
"Can you discuss. . .?"

For example

KE: Can you explain why the pump's temperature is important?
DE: I am always concerned about the temperature because if the bearings are going bad, then the temperature may rise. This is a real problem for the older pumps.

This answer has uncovered more information about the causal relationship between the condition of the pump bearings and its temperature. It also uncovered a relationship between the pump's temperature and age, and a pump problem. This new knowledge is captured in the following rules:

IF   The pump's temperature is rising
THEN   The pump's bearings may be bad

IF   The pump's temperature is rising
AND   The pump is old
THEN   The pump is very likely bad

You can use probe questions to gain further insight into a specific issue. You will use them during the interview when the expert raises some issue that needs further exploration. They are injected into the interview by interrupting the expert, which unfortunately can raise problems that are discussed later in this chapter.

Prompts

Prompts are questions intended to direct the interview into some new area. You will use prompts either at the beginning or during the interview to explore a new issue. The prompt question is usually of the form:

"Can you discuss . . .?"
"Can we return to . . .?"

For example

KE: Can you discuss how to identify problems with the pump?

This question will direct the expert into the more focused area of pump diagnostics. You can then obtain the major concepts and diagnostic problem-solving strategies within this area.

Prompts establish a new direction for the interview. You can use them to explore areas of identified importance or to redirect the interview back to areas that need further elaboration. Since they cause an abrupt change, you must use them carefully. You must feel secure that the present area is unlikely to bear any additional information, before redirecting the interview into a different area.

This section discussed the basic types of questions commonly used during an interview. Each type of question has a different purpose and form. Table 17.9 shows the important aspects of these different questions.

TABLE 17.9   **Different Types of Question Commonly Used in an Interview**

Type	Purpose	Form
Direct	Obtain specific information on some known issue.	What does . . . mean? Is . . . true? What is the value of . . . ?
Indirect	Obtain general information on concepts and problem solving strategies.	What issues are considered for . . . ? How do you determine . . . ? What do you look for when . . . ?
Probes	Probe deeper into an established issue.	Can you explain . . . ? Can you discuss . . . ?
Prompts	Direct interview into a new area.	Can you discuss . . . ? Can you return to . . . ?

Good Question Design

The last several sections discussed the typical type of questions used to direct the interview. Each question type tries to elicit certain information or guide the interview in a set manner. Besides the question's purpose, another important factor you must consider is its design.

To state a good question, you must first decide exactly what information you want. Some questions ask for specific or general information, while others are more for control of the interview. A good question is short and to the point. It produces either the knowledge being sought or the needed control of the interview. When the question fails to achieve its intended purpose, then it is bad. Therefore, it is easier to discuss the issue of good question design in terms of what it should not be—a bad question.

Posing a bad question is surprisingly easy. Many of us do it everyday with a question like;

> Tony: I bet you don't want to not go?
> Karen: Ha? . . . Did you mean to ask if I want to go?
> Tony: That's what I said, right?
> Karen: Well. . .

In preparing a good question, it is important that you understand what pitfalls to avoid. Table 17.10 provides guidelines for avoiding bad questions, and thereby hopefully producing good ones.

Avoid Multiple Part Questions

It is very easy to inadvertently ask questions that address more than one issue. For example

> "Why are the pressure and the temperature of the pump. . .?"

TABLE 17.10   Guidelines for Forming a Good Question

- Avoid questions with more than one part to them.
- Avoid leading questions.
- Do not phrase questions in the negative.
- Avoid universal questions.
- Avoid the use of terms foreign to the expert.
- Watch for questions that use subjective words.

Questions like this may be confusing to the expert. The expert may wonder, "Does he want to know about the pump pressure or its temperature, or the relationship between the two?" The expert may also only discuss one issue (e.g., pressure), then forget to address the second issue raised.

Avoid Leading Questions

Leading questions imply the expected answer and reflect your possible bias on a given issue. A question such as

"Wouldn't you check the pump's temperature first?"

may be presumptuous and can lead to very little information.

Avoid Negative Questions

Negative questions can be confusing and cause difficulties with interpretation that lead to misleading results. Consider the following question

"Is it false that the water pressure is not high is not true?"

Assuming one could eventually interpret this question, would the effort be worth it, or the response trusted? In general, avoid questions that contain multiple negative terms.

Avoid Universal Questions

A universal question presumes that the issue applies to every situation, when it may only apply to some unique set of events. For example

"Do you *always* replace the pump when it is old?"

This question is severely constrained with the use of the word *always*. In general, allow the expert to establish the natural relationship between issues using an indirect question, such as "How often do you . . ."

Avoid the Use of Foreign Terms

You should avoid using terms foreign to the expert, particularly those common to expert systems. This is a very easy problem to fall into because it is natural to use terms common to the technology. For example, a question such as

"Do you also use *forward reasoning* to solve the problem?"

would cause interpretation problems for the expert. In fact, you should learn to use terms common to the expert. This allows him or her to easily interpret the meaning of the question and avoids possible confusion.

Avoid Subjective Terms

You should avoid subjective terms, such as fast, hot, or little. They cause interpretation problems and can produce misleading information. Consider the following question

"If the pump is *really hot,* do you shut it down *fast?*"

The expert may form his own interpretation of the terms *really hot* and *fast* that could be very different from your interpretation and lead to erroneous information.

Question Sequence

Each question previously discussed brings some value to the interview. In addition, you can enhance the effectiveness of these questions if you follow a general order called the *funnel sequence* (McGraw and Harbison-Briggs 1989). The funnel sequencing technique, as illustrated in Figure 17.6, addresses a particular topic by first asking general questions, then moves on to more specific questions.

This technique is a general-to-specific approach for eliciting knowledge and uses the types of questions introduced in the last few sections. You use prompts and indirect questions to obtain a broad description of the topic. These are followed by probe questions that direct the interview toward the more detailed issues. Finally, direct questions seek specific detailed information. At the comple-

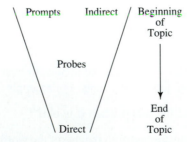

FIGURE 17.6   Funnel sequencing technique.

tion of this questioning sequence, you should have detailed information on the topic. You can then begin a new topic and repeat the funnel sequencing technique.

This technique offers two major advantages. When pursuing a new topic, answers to general questions provide a broad understanding of the topic. This provides direction to the more detailed questions asked later. General questions also offer a more relaxed introduction to the topic and are less intimidating than specific questions.

Active Listening

During the interview you should learn to be an *active listener*. Rather than simply asking questions and recording answers, you should conduct an active dialogue. In this role, you will often need to paraphrase answers provided by the expert to clarify your understanding of the response. You should also reflect about the importance of the response as it relates to your overall understanding of the problem. Finally, you should summarize for the expert what you have learned from a series of questions and ask the expert to verify your understanding.

Interruptions

A long debated issue in knowledge elicitation is the pros and cons of interrupting an expert during an answer for the purpose of obtaining more information or redirecting the discussion. On the positive side sits the advantage of clarifying an unknown issue or requesting more details when the issue is raised, rather than later during a review of the transcript. On the negative side, the interruption can disrupt the expert's train-of-thought, leading to a loss of information. You must weigh the merits of what can be gained versus the potential of what can be lost when interrupting the expert.

Interrupting an expert during a discussion of declarative knowledge may not be too disruptive. When an expert focuses on a concept and its associated details, a brief interruption to capture some details may not overly disturb the individual nor alter the thought processes to a large extent. The expert can usually answer the question and proceed where he or she left off and continue to discuss the concept. Interrupting an expert during a discussion of procedural knowledge, however, may cause more serious problems. The expert may be explaining a problem-solving strategy that is following a set sequence, where each step is discussed in the context of the other steps. An interruption during this explanation may be disruptive in that the expert loses track of the other steps and the problem's context.

The general recommendation is to proceed with a necessary interruption when the expert is explaining declarative knowledge. You should avoid the interruption, unless absolutely necessary, if the expert is explaining procedural knowledge. Often, you will need to use your own judgment on this matter and the answer may depend on the personality of the expert and the nature of the problem being discussed.

TABLE 17.11 Guidelines for Ending an Interview

- Summarize key findings.
- Review any outstanding questions raised during the interview and comment on how they will be answered.
- Review any outstanding agenda items and discuss how they will be dealt with in the future.
- Review future tasks for each team member before next meeting.
- Maintain open communication lines for aiding future tasks.
- Extend appreciation to members for their time and effort.

Ending the Interview

Studies in psychological research have shown that people most often remember the beginning and end of a session. If you perform the wrap-up of a given interview well, the team members will likely remember this and respond well to future interviews.

At the end of the session, you should review the key findings with the participants and note their comments. You should also review any outstanding questions that were raised during the interview. If some agenda items were not completed, you should discuss them and decide on how they might be addressed in the future. A brief discussion should also be given on the future direction of the project, including what tasks the team members need to accomplish, when the tasks should be completed, and when the next meeting should be anticipated. Finally, you should extend appreciation to the team members for their time and contributions to the interview. A set of guidelines for ending an interview is shown in Table 17.11.

─────────── UNSTRUCTURED INTERVIEW ───────────

Unstructured interviews are designed to allow the expert to discuss a topic in a natural manner. From this discussion, you will get a conceptual understanding of the problem and insight into the general problem-solving strategies used by the expert. This style of interviewing is usually used early in the project.

In an unstructured interview, you initially ask a general question about some broad problem issue, using a prompt or indirect question. For example, for an expert system aimed at diagnosing problems with a communications satellite, you might ask

"How do you determine when the satellite is malfunctioning?"

This type of question focuses the expert's attention at a high level of the problem, and gives a more general description. The expert can then freely choose to discuss those areas that he or she feels are most important. The discussion may eventually become more focused as the expert provides details on the more relevant issues.

Further into the interview, you may see a value in probing deeper into a given concept brought up by the expert. For example, the expert may have discussed the satellite's receiver as one of the units that commonly fail. To explore this new issue further, you may employ probe questions of the form

"Can you discuss the operation of the satellite's receiver?"

You can use probes to discover new concepts or to explore additional details of some established concept. Using probes however must be done with some caution. They may represent an interruption in the expert's discussion that can cause some difficulties with the loss of train of thought.

Example of an Unstructured Interview

The problem—Communication satellites provide the means to relay information between remote sites. Several industries have taken advantage of this ability and rely on the satellite's performance in their daily operation. Problems with the satellite can cause a loss in operation with a corresponding loss in business activities.

The solution—An expert system was developed to monitor the performance of the satellite, detect any faults, and respond by either reconfiguring the satellite or by sending information to a ground station for a request of corrective steps (Durkin 1989a).

The unstructured interview—Table 17.12 presents an example transcript of an unstructured interview taken from a session held with an expert on the

TABLE 17.12   Example Excerpt from an Unstructured Interview

KE: How do you determine when the satellite is malfunctioning? **{starter prompt}**

DE: I notice that the **messages {CONCEPT}** are garbled, or the **BER {CONCEPT, domain vocabulary}** is high **{RULE}**. This makes me sick when I think of all the money we invested in the thing and it still works worse than the radios I have at home **{irrelevant}**. And it always seems to come down to a couple of things that go wrong. The **modulator {OBJECT}** is the pits. This thing drifts off on us it seems every other day **{HEURISTIC}**. I think it mainly has something to do with its **power supply {OBJECT}**. Oh wait a minute, that **matrix switch {OBJECT}** may even be worse **{conflict}**. It hangs up on us and sometimes doesn't make a good contact **{HEURISTIC}**. The **output attenuator {OBJECT}** can on a rare occasion also cause a problem **{HEURISTIC}**, and it's actually funny when it does. Ah . . . I remember a time when . . .

KE: Excuse me, can you tell me a little more why the matrix switch is such a problem? **{prompt question}** communications satellite diagnostic project. The session begins with a general inquiry about the malfunctioning of the satellite, where the question allows the expert to answer in a general fashion. The expert suggests ''garbled messages'' and ''BER is high'' as two ways of determining if the satellite is malfunctioning. ''Messages'' and ''BER'' are identified as two new concepts. A general rule that captures the relationship between these two new concepts, and the concept of faults, would be:

> IF   Message is garbled
> OR   BER is high
> THEN   A fault exists

Encoding a rule like this in an expert system would have obvious problems. For example, how do we determine if a message is garbled or the BER is high? We would have to explore each of these issues later to obtain an understanding. Also, the term ''BER'' may be a common term to the expert, but we may need it explained.

The expert also defines an object called ''modulator,'' which can cause a satellite malfunction. He then defines another object called ''power supply,'' which is naturally linked to the modulator.

The expert continues the discussion and defines other new objects that could cause the satellite to malfunction, such as ''matrix switch'' and ''output attenuator.'' These faults are also categorized according to their likelihood, which the expert system could use in ordering the search for the faulty component. For example, since the ''output attenuator'' only rarely causes problems, we may want to consider it last.

The transcript also includes several heuristics about the operation of these objects that can guide the priority of the problem solving. For example, ''This modulator drifts off on us . . . every other day.''

In addition, the transcript shows that some of the information collected is either irrelevant, e.g., ''This makes me sick,'' or conflicting, e.g., ''Oh wait a minute.'' We also see that the expert can overlook details about an important issue, such as the matrix switch, which forces the knowledge engineer to interrupt the session and request further information on the subject.

This example illustrates how you can use the unstructured interviewing technique to gain a general understanding of the problem. Important concepts and objects emerge and a general understanding of these objects is captured in heuristics. The example also illustrates that the procedural information is given only in general terms and many details of the topics discussed are missing. Table 17.13 lists the types of knowledge obtained from this example.

Guidelines for an Unstructured Interview

An unstructured interview is exploratory in nature. You begin by asking a general question about the problem and noting the major concepts and general problem-

TABLE 17.13   Knowledge Obtained from Unstructured Interview Example

Concepts:	messages, BER
Objects:	matrix switch
	output attenuator
	modulator
	modulator power supply
Rules:	IF Message is garbled
	OR BER is high
	THEN A fault exists
Heuristics:	modulator drifts
	matrix switch sometimes doesn't make good contact
	output attenuator rarely a problem

solving methods as the expert raises them. You can use interruptions to clarify issues or terms, or to redirect the interview towards interesting areas. Table 17.14 provides a listing of some of the major points to consider when conducting an unstructured interview.

Advantages and Disadvantages of the Unstructured Interview

Advantages—The unstructured style of interviewing provides a general understanding of the problem. This is important early in the project when little is known about the problem. Important concepts, relationships, general rules, and problem-solving strategies surface with the discussion, that can guide future inquiries. It also offers spontaneity to the interview where the expert may discuss previously unknown issues.

TABLE 17.14   Guidelines for an Unstructured Interview

- Pose an initial prompt or indirect question "How do you . . . ?" or "What is . . . ?" This is called a starter prompt, which allows the expert to discuss a subject in general.

- Interrupt the session with probe questions of the form, "Why is . . . ?" or "Can you please discuss . . . ?" to explore significant issues.

- Be cautious with interruptions, particularly early in the project, when the expert may be providing valuable information that may be lost with the interruption.

- Gain an understanding of the important concepts, their relationships, and general problem-solving methods from the transcript of the session and use this information for planning future interviews.

TABLE 17.15   **Advantages and Disadvantages of the Unstructured Interview**

Advantages
- Provides a general understanding of the problem.
- Helps to identify important concepts and objects.
- Provides insight into general problem-solving methods.
- Allows for spontaneity in the interview which may give rise to previously unknown issues.

Disadvantages
- Information collected may be overwhelming, fragmented, or shallow.
- Provides very little factual information.
- Provides few details on concepts or objects.
- Provides few details on procedural information.

Disadvantages—The information collected through the unstructured interview may be overwhelming, fragmented, or shallow. The expert is likely to discuss the problem from a level of detail beyond your understanding. The expert is also likely to move quickly between different issues before clearly explaining them. Important details are glossed over, leaving you without a thorough understanding of the issue. Except for general rules or high level problem-solving procedures, which are important pieces of information to obtain early in the project, little detailed procedural information is obtained. General concepts or objects will be defined, but will be discussed with little detail. This technique is valuable for initial insight but requires training and patience. Table 17.15 lists the advantages and disadvantages of the unstructured knowledge elicitation technique.

STRUCTURED INTERVIEW

Unlike an unstructured interview, which allows the expert to define and describe any issue in an open manner, a structured interview maintains a focus on one issue at a time. This style of interviewing elicits specific details on a given issue before moving on to other points. This focus of attention on a single issue provides detailed knowledge and also uncovers related topics that can be explored. You would typically use the structured interviewing technique later in the project when you have identified the problem's key topics from reports or earlier unstructured interviews.

You would use a structured interview when you need specific information on some established topic, and know enough about the topic to pose the proper questions. For instance, consider an example from a project on crop management problems. During discussions with the expert the issue of pests has surfaced. To get more information on this subject, you might ask a probe question such as

"Can you tell me what major characteristics of the pest you use for identifying it?"

This question leads the expert into a focused discussion on the topic that should provide a list of the important pest identification characteristics. For example, the expert might indicate that issues of the pest's appearance and effect on crops are important for identification. Following this discussion, you might request more detailed information on one of these issues by probing deeper with the question

"Can you explain how you use the pest's appearance in identifying the pest?"

This question may produce a list of appearance issues, such as the pest's size, color, etc., which might then lead to the following direct question

"Can you explain the size issue?"

In this fashion, the interview probes deeper into a subject in a depth-first type fashion and uncovers important problem details. You can view a structured interviewing technique as a *concept-driven* elicitation because it probes deeper into some discovered concept.

Example of a Structured Interview

The problem—Farmers have many responsibilities when managing their crops. They must choose an appropriate crop to grow considering available resources. They are also responsible for planting, cultivating, reaping and marketing the crop. Farmers will often seek help from a regional agricultural extension service office, which maintains experts on various crops. The experts provide assistance for growing various crops and can further help with solving problems of crop management or pest infestation.

A practical problem associated with this solution is the immediate access the grower has to the regional office. Factors such as time, distance, or access during office hours, create obstacles to the grower for receiving consultation. Due to these factors, growers may decide not to seek help from the office and choose to rely on their own trial-and-error techniques.

The solution—An expert system was developed to provide readily available aid to farmers for growing and managing various crops (Durkin 1989b). The expert system can respond to most of the farmer's questions and is flexible enough to incorporate knowledge on a variety of crops.

The structured interview—Table 17.16 shows an example transcript of a structured interview taken from a session held with an expert on the crop management expert system project. Before this interview, the knowledge engineer had

TABLE 17.16   **Example Excerpt from a Structured Interview**

KE:	In a prior session you mentioned that eliminating harmful pests is important. You also said that the first step in elimination is pest identification. Can you tell me what major characteristics you consider for identifying a pest? **{focused prompt on characteristics}**
DE:	You can tell what kind of pest problem you have if you catch one of the little suckers and examine its **appearance {CONCEPT}**. Most farmers can identify the pest by looking at it, and . . . ah . . . or by inspecting the **crop damage {CONCEPT}**. Some of these guys will eat the leaves or roots **{HEURISTIC} {RULE}**. But before you try any pesticides you better be sure what it is. **{HEURISTIC}**
KE:	Can you explain how you use the pest appearance in identifying the pest? **{probe on appearance}**
DE:	You can look at the **size {CONCEPT}**, its **color {CONCEPT}**, or its **shape {CONCEPT}**. **{RULE}** Sometimes you can identify the pest from just one of these characteristics or other times you have to look at all of them. **{HEURISTIC}**
KE:	Can you explain the size issue? **{probe on size}**

determined that preventing or eliminating pests that are harmful to the crops is an important step in effective crop management. The knowledge engineer wanted to gain more information on the issue of pests. Issues such as pest damage, pest elimination, or pest identification might be covered during the interview. The transcript shown in Table 17.16 focuses on the issue of pest identification.

The session begins with a focused prompt on pest characteristics. From the expert's discussion, two new concepts surface: appearance of the pest and inspecting crop damage. "Pest appearance" would represent a subconcept of "pest characteristics." "Inspecting crop damage" would represent a new concept related to "pest identification." Viewing the appearance of the pest, and inspecting the crops for damage, would represent a general way of identifying a pest. This could be captured in general rules such as:

```
IF      The size is something
AND     The color is something
AND     The shape is something
THEN    The pest is known
IF      The leaf damage is something
OR      The root damage is something
THEN    The pest is known
```

The important knowledge captured is that we can identify a given pest from observing it, such as noting its size, color, shape, or from observing its effect, such as leaf or root damage.

This example illustrates how you can use the structured interviewing technique to identify important problem characteristics. From the initial discussion on

TABLE 17.17   Knowledge Obtained from Unstructured Interview Example

Strategies:	View the appearance of the pest first, then inspect the crops for damage.
Concepts:	Pest characteristics
	appearance
	size
	color
	shape
	Crop damage
	leaf damage
	root damage

Rules:	IF	The size is something
	AND	The color is something
	AND	The shape is something
	THEN	The pest is known
	IF	The leaf damage is something
	OR	The root damage is something
	THEN	The pest is known

Heuristics:	Some pests eat the leaves or roots.
	Before trying pesticides make sure of the identification of the pest.
	Sometimes pest identification can be done using only one pest characteristic.

some primary topic, other related concepts emerge. Each of the new concepts is discussed to reveal information about it, and to further identify additional concepts. During the discussion, general rules or strategies emerge, which you can probe further to obtain more specific rules. Heuristics also emerge that can aid in the writing of the rules or structuring the problem-solving strategies. Table 17.17 lists the types of knowledge obtained from this example.

Guidelines for a Structured Interview

To conduct the structured interview properly you must first define a list of topics to cover. Choose one of the topics and pose a prompt question to explore it. Then use a series of probing questions to explore each new topic raised by the expert. Eventually, you can gain important details by asking direct questions on the topic. Once you have the detailed information, return to some other unexplored topic and prompt the expert to discuss the subject. Table 17.18 provides general guidelines to follow when conducting a structured interview.

TABLE 17.18   Guidelines for a Structured Interview

- Choose a specific topic (focused prompt) to discuss.
- From the discussion, identify new concepts.
- Pick one of the new concepts (probe) and ask the expert to discuss it further.
- Continue this process until enough details are obtained, then return to one of the new concepts mentioned earlier and ask for further discussion.
- Gain an understanding of the important concepts and their relationships, rules, and strategies from the transcript.

Advantages and Disadvantages of the Structured Interview

Advantages—After the important issues are defined, a structured interview can be easier to prepare for and manage than an unstructured interview. The information collected is also easier to analyze since most of the information collected is related. This approach also provides more detailed information on the problem. You can explore a given concept to define new concepts accompanied with information on their natural relationships. Declarative knowledge in the form of the structure of the concept relationships emerges, i.e., hierarchical or lattice structure. You also obtain objects and their features, and probe further for specific feature values. You can also uncover general rules and problem-solving strategies involving the different concepts.

   Disadvantages—Limitations of this technique are a by product of its strength. Since the interview maintains focus on a given issue, surprises are less likely to occur than with the unstructured technique. You must be secure in your understanding of the important issues to direct the interview. Concepts or objects related to the principal topic being discussed will be discovered. However, other important issues unrelated to the main topic will not emerge during a structured interview. Like any introspective interviewing technique, this method may provide little information on procedural knowledge. The advantages and disadvantages of the structured interview knowledge elicitation technique are shown in Table 17.19.

PROBLEMS WITH INTERVIEWING

With conventional interviewing techniques, the expert discusses the problem through introspection. The expert attempts to answer questions by examining his thoughts or understanding of the issue in question. Psychological studies have

TABLE 17.19 Advantages and Disadvantages of the Structured Interview

Advantages

- Maintains a focus on a given issue.

- Provides detailed information on the issue.

- Provides insight into declarative knowledge used.

- Study of one concept can lead to the defintion of other unknown related concepts.

- Provides structural relationships of concepts.

Disadvantages

- Concepts unrelated to the interview's focus may not be found.

- You must be secure in your understanding of the important issues to direct the interview.

- Provides only weak insight into procedural knowledge such as rules or problem-solving strategies.

shown that introspection may be ineffective in obtaining a complete or reliable account of a person's problem-solving knowledge (Evans 1988). This causes a number of difficulties for the knowledge engineer when introspection is the primary method used to elicit knowledge.

Recalling procedural knowledge—One problem associated with introspective studies is the inability to recall and verbalize procedural knowledge. People can often describe and discuss their declarative knowledge; but without actually solving the problem, they have difficulty describing their problem-solving knowledge.

Ineffective long-term memory—Introspection also suffers when the individual lacks an effective long-term memory about the problem. Getting reliable information through introspection relies upon the expert remembering the important issues and reliably describing how these issues are used during problem solving. This method can obviously suffer from the expert's inability to recall the information and can further suffer from inconsistencies, inaccuracies and subjective preferences. The expert may provide lines of plausible reasoning that do not truly reflect his or her behavior.

Verbalizing manual tasks—Many problems are inherently difficult to verbalize. This may occur if the problem involves a series of physical tasks. Introspective techniques suffer from such obstacles because the task may have been mastered by watching others rather than through verbal instruction.

Verbalizing compiled knowledge—Verbalization is also difficult if the knowledge used is intuitive or compiled. Through repetition in problem solving, the expert accesses and manipulates knowledge without being aware of the details.

Asking the expert to discuss the problem through introspection may cause trouble if the knowledge has become too compiled.

Lacks context—The expert discusses a given issue divorced from any real problem, and the knowledge collected may only represent the expert's general understanding of the problem.

CASE STUDIES

Because of the limitations and difficulties with introspective interviewing techniques, the knowledge engineer will often turn to knowledge elicitation methods that focus on *case studies*. A case is an actual problem that has been solved in the past and contains both the steps taken to solve it and its final solution. There are two primary ways that a case is used during a knowledge elicitation session:

- Retrospective
- Observational

In the *retrospective* approach the expert is asked to review the case and explain in retrospect how the problem was solved. The *observational* technique involves asking the expert to solve the problem discussed in the case while you observe. In both situations, the case study focuses on a problem from the domain. This typically reveals more specific problem-solving knowledge than that obtained from interviewing techniques.

Case types—Both the retrospective and observational methods must first consider the nature of the case to be studied. There are several types of cases that can be chosen (Hoffman 1987), but the primary ones used by expert system designers are the:

- Familiar case
- Unusual case

The familiar case, also called a *typical* case, is one that is well known to the expert. Studying this type of case reveals typical knowledge used by the expert when solving the problem. This type of case is usually used early in the project where general insight is needed. The unusual case is novel or uncommon in some sense. This causes the expert to study the problem in more detail, providing deeper problem-solving knowledge. This type of case is often used later when a refinement of the system is needed.

Protocol—In cognitive psychology, the collection of information gained from an individual working on a problem is known as a *protocol*. The protocol is a record that traces the behavior of the individual while solving the problem. The protocol may be a set of notes, a tape recording, or a video of the session. The protocol may also include the verbalization of the expert "thinking aloud," as he or she describes the problem-solving tasks.

Retrospective Case Study Method

The objective of the retrospective case study method is to acquire knowledge through a review of a successfully solved past case. All of the information specific to the given case, including all findings, are given to the expert for review. In retrospect, the expert attempts to explain how the results were reached.

Directions to expert—After a case is selected for study, you ask the expert to explain how the problem was solved. The expert should review the information of the case and try to justify how the problem was solved. A simple prompt question of the following form is a good starting point.

Why was . . . (the recommendation) . . . given?

In this situation the expert is goal driven. He or she will first review the major findings of the case and then try to show how the basic problem information supports those findings. As the expert solves a case, there are several key points you should observe. Most experts will approach the case with a well-established procedure. Notice how the expert makes observations about the problem and how he or she gathers information to solve it. Also notice how the expert identifies and classifies the solutions. This will provide you with insight into the important issues and the problem-solving approach. As part of discussing the solution process, the expert will also bring to light important problem concepts.

Forming the protocol—While the expert is describing the problem's solution, you should record in the protocol the major problem-solving tasks, what information is collected during each task, how this information is used, and the various decisions made by the expert while solving the problem. Following, or possibly during the collection of this information, you can use standard interviewing questions to gain additional insight into issues raised during the problem solving. However, as previously discussed, interruptions must be used with caution since they can be disruptive to the expert's train of thought.

Example of a Retrospective Case Study

The problem—Coal mines use a ventilation system to maintain a safe level of air within the mine. The system supplies air to miners and lowers the concentration of methane and carbon monoxide to safe levels. Problems with the system can lead to unsafe conditions that can be costly in loss of lives and production.

The solution—An expert system called DUSTPRO was developed to aid coal mine managers in better controlling the mine air ventilation system (Durkin 1988). The system has knowledge about mine ventilation regulations, potential problems, and means for correcting any problem identified from specific mine conditions.

Case selection—A prior case was selected that recommended the installation of a larger main ventilation fan to improve the overall air flow throughout the mine. Mines can employ several different fans to control ventilation at various

TABLE 17.20   Example Excerpt from a Retrospective Case Study

DE: I see that this mine had to go to a much larger **main fan {result, OBJECT}**. Let me see if they recently had a **methane {OBJECT, also first one considered}** buildup . . . Um, no. . . . Now I see the problem. Look at some of these **air flow {CONCEPT, also next one considered}** numbers down there. Particularly at the face. These guys couldn't have been using any **auxiliary fans {OBJECT}** at the face. Let me see . . . Yep, they have no extra fans there. This could be one of the major reasons they were told to get a larger main fan **{HEURISTIC}** . . . it would probably have been cheaper too than buying some auxiliary equipment **{HEURISTIC}**.

locations. The main fan is the primary source of air throughout the mine, and problems with mine air circulation are often traced to this fan. Therefore, this example represents a familiar case study.

Case study—Table 17.20 shows a portion of the protocol from a session held with an expert on this project. The domain expert reviews the results of the past case and sees that a much larger main fan was recommended. This recommendation then becomes the expert's goal to prove. The expert tries to verify the recommendation in a backward sense by next looking to see if there was a history of a build up of methane, "Let me see if they recently had a methane buildup." Methane is a new object from the more general concept of mine gases. The expert identifies it as being strongly related to the final result since it was considered first.

Since the expert noted no appreciable amounts of methane, he next considered the in-mine air flows, a new concept. The expert was concerned about low flow rates, "particularly at the mine face." The word "face" was clarified later and found to be the in-mine location where the coal is being mined. Finding a low air flow at the face led the expert to believe that this issue was responsible for the recommendation. Here, the expert has tied the general issue of low air flow rates anywhere in the mine to a problem, and the specific issue of low flow at the face to the final recommendation. The first relationship establishes a general rule between the concepts of air flow rates and faults, in the form:

IF   In-mine air flow is low
THEN   A fault exists

The second relationship establishes a more specific rule between low face air flows and the recommendation for a larger fan. However, the more specific rule must also consider whether auxiliary face fans are used.

IF   No face auxiliary fans
AND   Low face air flow
THEN   Larger main fan needed

TABLE 17.21   Knowledge Obtained from Retrospective Case Example

Goals:	Single recommendation—larger main fan.
Strategies:	Methane level checked first, if no problem then check in-mine air flows particularly face air flows.
Concepts:	fans, mine gases, faults, recommendations
Objects:	main fans, auxiliary fans, methane
Rules:	IF In-mine air flow is low
	THEN A fault exists
	IF No face auxiliary fans
	AND Low face air flow
	THEN Larger main fan needed
Heuristics:	Not having auxiliary fans at the face could lead to a need of a larger main fan.
	A larger main fan may be less costly than purchasing auxiliary equipment.

This second more specific rule highlights one of the dangers of a retrospective case study. The expert suggests, ''This could be one of the major reasons they were told to get a larger main fan,'' without looking any further into the case. The expert used a bias based on prior experience that was later found to be inconsistent with this case. A later study of the case revealed other reasons for the recommendation of a larger main fan.

This example illustrates how you can use the retrospective technique to identify both declarative and procedural problem knowledge. The expert begins with the given recommendation, and in a backward fashion, identifies which problem concepts were important to establish the final results of the case, and their order of importance. From this study, concepts, rules, and problem-solving strategies emerge. However, other important concepts may have been overlooked, and details of the identified concepts found missing. Also, a review of a past case is often performed less rigorously than solving the actual problem. This approach can bias the decisions in favor of expected conditions, resulting in other important factors being overlooked. Table 17.21 lists the types of knowledge obtained from this example.

Guidelines for a Retrospective Case Study

Conducting a retrospective case study session begins with the selection of the case. A typical case can be chosen to obtain more general information about solving the problem. The choice of an unusual case causes the expert to introspect more deeply about the problem and produces more detailed information. While the expert explains how the problem was solved, the session is recorded for later study. Guidelines for performing a retrospective case study are shown in Table 17.22.

TABLE 17.22   Guidelines for Retrospective Case Study

- Choose a typical case for typical information, or an unusual one for more detailed information.

- Ask the expert to explain how he or she solved the problem.

- Record the expert's discussion for later study.

- During the expert's explanation, highlight important issues for further discussion following (or during) the session.

- Be careful of interruptions. Interrupting problem-solving tasks can be disruptive.

Advantages and Disadvantages of the Retrospective Case Study

Advantages—Like any case study, this technique obtains information in the context of a working example, thus providing better insight into problem-solving strategies. This offers a distinct advantage over conventional interviewing, which can only provide small insight into these strategies.

Another advantage of retrospection is that it does not interfere with the problem solving activity. Some cognitive psychologists argue that asking people to verbalize their problem-solving knowledge while performing a task creates an unnatural situation that influences the task performance (Evans 1988). However, retrospection requires the expert to recall from memory the information needed to solve the problem, rather than actually solving the problem. This therefore avoids the concern raised by the psychologists.

Finally, since memory recall is central to this technique, the expert will discuss the major concepts used when solving the problem. When reviewing the case, the expert will immediately explore these important concepts uncovering other related information.

Disadvantages—The major disadvantage of the retrospective case study is that it is based on a review of a past case. This involves memory recall, which can be incomplete because the expert often speculates on how the problem was solved.

Another difficulty with this technique is that it is inherently a review process. A review by its nature usually only provides a high-level view of the problem. Therefore, very few problem details are obtained.

Experts may also interpret the case as an instance of other typical cases they have solved in the past. Therefore, they may offer knowledge biased towards the more typical situation, rather than the actual one being studied. In this situation, they may state tasks performed that are inconsistent with the actual ones used during the case. The advantages and disadvantages of the retrospective case study knowledge elicitation technique are shown in Table 17.23.

TABLE 17.23 Advantages and Disadvantages of Retrospective Case Study

Advantages
- Obtains information in the context of a working example.
- Provides problem-specific information.
- Does not interfere with the problem-solving activity.
- Memory recall highlights the important issues.

Disadvantages
- May provide incomplete information.
- Provides few problem details.
- Explanations can be inconsistent with actual past behavior.

Observational Case Study Method

Many cognitive psychologists believe that the best way to discover how an expert thinks, uses available information, and arrives at solutions, is to watch people at work on a real problem (Bell and Hardiman 1989). The objective of the observational case study method is to acquire knowledge through observing the behavior of the expert during problem solving.

Directions to expert—After selecting the type of case needed (i.e., familiar or unusual), hand the expert the specific problem information and ask him or her to form a recommendation. Also ask the expert to "think aloud" while the problem is solved. Specifically, ask the expert to answer questions such as:

- What are your goals?
- What issues are important?
- How are these issues used?
- What data do you use?

Concurrent protocol—The *concurrent protocol* is the record of knowledge collected during the observational technique. You collect the knowledge concurrently with solving the problem, rather than in retrospect. However, using a "think aloud" method has been an issue of debate for years in both the areas of cognitive psychology and expert systems.

Thinking aloud—The debate centers around the question, "Does the requirement to verbalize change the thought processes involved?" (Evans 1988). Ericsson and Simon (1980) addressed this question in their studies of knowledge elicitation through "think aloud" case studies. They concluded that verbalizing during task execution had little impact on the knowledge obtained and only tended to slow down the process. They went on to emphasize the importance of collecting knowledge concurrently rather than retrospectively. They felt this approach represents the product of cognitive processes rather than self-reported descriptions.

However, Olson and Rueter (1987) argue that you must consider the task before using the "think aloud" technique. They argue that some problems, such as composing music or ones that involve perceptual-motor tasks, have no natural verbalization. They feel that forcing an individual to report on these problem-solving tasks can only lead to the collection of confusing information.

In general, if a task offers a natural opportunity for eliciting knowledge with a "think aloud" technique, then you should use it. In addition, you should use the concurrent protocol for not only identifying the important knowledge, but also for guiding future knowledge elicitation sessions that are managed in a more introspective manner using conventional interviewing techniques.

Observational Study of the Familiar Case

The familiar case approach to knowledge elicitation involves providing a problem that is typical of the ones commonly solved by the expert. When solving a typical problem, the approach taken and the knowledge used will also be typical of the domain. Common concepts, rules, and problem-solving strategies emerge during the familiar case study.

Example of a Familiar Case Study

The problem—A transformer that is not routinely serviced or checked for incipient faults may cause severe damage to itself and its surroundings. This damage can result in large costs to a company. When a transformer must be taken off line for repair, the overall operating cost to the company can range from $100,000 to $200,000 per day. Unexpected catastrophic transformer failure could cost the company as much as $1,000,000 through the damage caused to the transformer and surrounding equipment.

The solution—An expert system was developed for incipient fault detection in transformers from the study of gas levels contained in a sample of transformer oil as measured by a chromatograph (Durkin 1989c). The system can compare current gas levels with past findings to detect dangerous trends. The system can then make a recommendation to correct the problem before a transformer failure occurs.

Case selection—For the example that we will consider, the knowledge engineer wanted to obtain typical knowledge used in diagnosing transformer faults. He reviewed past test cases to find a typical one. The typical case was given to a technician who services faulty transformers. The technician was asked, "Do you see anything unusual about this case?" The answer was, "No, it's typical of the types of transformers we test around here." Equipped with a typical or familiar test case, the knowledge engineer presented the test data to the expert and asked him to make any recommendations appropriate for the given test

TABLE 17.24   Example Excerpt from a Familiar Case Study

KE:	I have here a report of the test results on a transformer recently tested by your technician. I would like you to tell me what recommendations you would make regarding any problems with this transformer. Also, as you study the report, please tell me;
	"What are your goals?"
	"What issues are important?"
	"How are these issues used?"
	"What data do you use?"
DE:	Well the first thing I want to determine if there is any problem with the transformer **{GOAL}**. There are a number of **faults {CONCEPT}** which can occur **{check later}**. Excessive buildup of certain **gases {important CONCEPT}** will usually tell me this. . . . **{RULE}**. If it doesn't, I would look at . . . **{other CONCEPTS to explore}**. Let me see . . . I see some **nitrogen** here, and a lot of **hydrogen {OBJECTS and FACTS}**. Yea, I bet this baby has got an arcing problem **{RULE and CONCEPT}**. Let me check the past records on this transformer **{STRATEGY}**. . . . This transformer has never shown this problem before **{FACT}**. Maybe its just a short term buildup which might go away if they adhere to good operating procedures **{RULE}**. I would recommend that they better control the load on this transformer **{recommendation}**, but I would like to see it retested in about . . . let me think . . . **{explore later}** 3 months **{recommendation}**.

results. In addition, the knowledge engineer asked the expert to describe the steps and knowledge used in arriving at the recommendation.

Case study—Table 17.24 shows a portion of the protocol taken from the project. The expert first states the goal pursued, "transformer problem." He further states there are several faults that can occur that can be explored later. The expert also identifies "gases" as a new concept that is important in determining if the transformer has a problem. A general rule is implied, "excessive buildup of certain gases . . . ," that relates the concept of gases to transformer faults:

IF   Excessive buildup of *certain* gases
THEN   A fault exists

This rule raises two questions: what gases, and what is excessive buildup? For now we can live with general rules like this one, but later we will have to obtain further information on these issues.

The expert also implies an alternate way of determining whether a fault exists, "If it doesn't, I would look at . . ." This identifies a new area for determining faults that can be explored later. The expert identifies important gas information: concentrations and specific gases. A semi-specific rule is given relating levels of nitrogen and hydrogen to an arcing fault:

IF   Some nitrogen exists
AND   A lot of hydrogen exists
THEN   Arcing fault exists

From this rule we can conclude that a relationship exists between the levels of nitrogen and hydrogen to an arcing fault, However, we have no understanding of "some nitrogen" or "a lot of hydrogen." Later we needed to determine possible ranges of the different gases and ascribe a particular level to the terms "some" and "a lot."

The expert identifies an additional strategy based on the study of past transformer tests to further support fault detection. A general diagnostic rule is suggested that relates present gas levels and past test data to a suspicion:

> IF   Present gas levels are something
> AND   Past gas levels are something
> THEN   I can suspect something

This rule implies that trend information is important in transformer diagnostics. It also shows that the expert system will need to have access to a database of past test results to uncover any particular trends.

This example illustrates that the study of a familiar test case can be valuable in uncovering important problem issues and general problem-solving methods. The information gained runs from the general, i.e., strategies, concepts, general rules, to the specific, i.e., objects, specific rules, data. The example also highlights other areas that the knowledge engineer can explore in later sessions. Table 17.25 lists the types of knowledge obtained from this example.

Guidelines for a Familiar Case Study

The familiar case study begins with the selection of a familiar case from the domain. The basic data or information on the case is given to the expert. The knowledge engineer asks the expert to solve the problem while "thinking aloud."

TABLE 17.25 Knowledge Obtained from Familiar Case Example

Goals:	Faults detected, recommendations given
Strategies:	Gas levels checked first, if no problem then check . . . , then past test data.
Concepts:	gases, faults, recommendations, load control, retest period
Objects:	nitrogen, hydrogen
Rules:	IF Excessive buildup of excessive gases
	THEN A fault exists
	IF Some nitrogen exists
	AND A lot of hydrogen exists
	THEN Arcing fault exists
	IF It's a short term problem
	AND Transformer correctly operated
	THEN Retest in 3 months
Facts:	Gas level data, retest time

TABLE 17.26   Guidelines for Familiar Case Study

- Choose a familiar case to study.

- Ask the expert to explain how he or she solved the problem with answers to questions such as:
    "What are your goals?"
    "What issues are important?"
    "How are these issues used?"
    "What data do you use?"

- Ask the expert to "think aloud" while solving the problem.

- Record the concurrent protocol for later study.

- During the session, highlight important issues for further discussion following (or during) the session.

The knowledge engineer records the session in a concurrent protocol for later review. Table 17.26 lists some general guidelines for conducting a familiar case study knowledge elicitation session.

Advantages and Disadvantages of the Familiar Case Study

Advantages—The principal strength of this technique is in obtaining insight into problem-solving methods typically used by the expert. Since the case is familiar to the expert, typical declarative knowledge in the form of concepts, objects, and facts emerges during the session. Using a "think aloud" technique permits the expert to introspect while performing the task. This allows the expert to provide information immediately, rather than later in a retrospective fashion. Finally, like any case study technique, the session focuses on a problem that provides problem-specific information.

Disadvantages—Since the case is typical, the expert may solve the problem using somewhat high-level expertise, possibly even relying on intuitive steps. Integrating introspection with this technique can help this situation. Another disadvantage of using a familiar case is related to the expert's bias that could produce inconsistent results. The expert may view the case as typical of those worked on in the past, and bias his or her attention towards only a few, select issues. Table 17.27 shows the advantages and disadvantages of the familiar case study knowledge elicitation technique.

Observational Study of the Unfamiliar Case

One of the difficulties mentioned in using a familiar case is the knowledge compilation problem. When solving a familiar problem, the expert will often skim over important issues, leaving large gaps in either the knowledge used or the tasks performed. If you interrupt the expert and request more explicit knowledge, he or she may only provide plausible information that does not reflect the

TABLE 17.27   Advantages and Disadvantages of Familiar Case Study

Advantages
- Expert solves a real problem.

- Obtains information in the context of a working example.

- Common concepts, rules, and problem solving strategies emerge during the familiar case study.

- Provides problem-specific information.

- The "think aloud" technique provides insight into the knowledge being used immediately rather than retrospectively.

Disadvantages
- Can miss important details unless introspection is used.

- Explanations can be inconsistent with actual past behavior.

actual methods used. This is an inherent difficulty in most knowledge elicitation methods and gives only a high level view of the expert's knowledge. This forces you to search for other methods to get more detailed information.

One way to avoid this problem is to ask the expert to solve an unfamiliar case. When faced with an unusual situation, the expert must rely more on basic knowledge to solve the problem. When explaining the problem-solving approach while working on an unusual problem, the expert will introspect more deeply and reveal more detailed information.

This approach was successfully used by the knowledge engineers who developed DIPMETER ADVISOR (Smith and Baker 1983), where they reported

"When working with familiar examples our expert does indeed appear to apply forward-chained empirical rules. . .kind of compiled inferences. Recently, however, we have participated in experiments with a number of experts from around the world. During these experiments we noted that our expert resorted to a different mode of operation when faced with a completely unfamiliar examples. He appeared to reason with underlying geological and geometric models . . . abandoning the rules."

Selecting unfamiliar case—The objective in studying an unfamiliar case is to uncover details about issues already known and to identify any other unknown issues. The case chosen must be representative of the domain. The problem should not be so rare that the expert will not consider previously known issues. However, it must be unusual enough that it requires some effort to solve.

Asking the expert for a case that meets these requirements may not work. The expert may choose a case that was difficult to solve in the past but prior experience with the case may bias the solution explanation. Therefore, one condition in selecting an unfamiliar case is that it be new to the expert. A good source for this type of case is another expert. This individual can choose a tough but representative case, but also one unknown to the expert.

Example of an Unfamiliar Case Study

The problem/solution—We will study the problem of transformer diagnostics mentioned earlier (Durkin 1989c).

Case selection—During this part of the study, the knowledge engineer wanted to probe deeper into the problem. He wanted to uncover issues that may have not surfaced earlier in the project. To accomplish this, he asked another expert to choose an unusual case. The expert chose a transformer that showed unusually high levels of combustible gases in the present test but showed no signs of these high gas levels in prior tests. The second expert commented, "It is very unusual to find a transformer which deteriorates so fast." The domain expert was asked to solve the case and to make any comments that would explain his reasoning.

Case study—Table 17.28 shows an example protocol of an unfamiliar case study taken from the project. The expert begins by examining the gas levels in the present test report. This shows that his initial strategy is data-driven. From earlier studies, the knowledge engineer found that when a fault has been identified by the expert, he looks towards other information for additional support. Therefore, the knowledge engineer concluded that the expert's problem-solving strategy is first data-driven to form a hypothesis, then goal driven to prove it.

The expert identified several objects as being important: hydrogen, methane, and acetylene. A new concept also surfaced, "combustible gases," that is related to these gases and a transformer problem. This observation led to the following rule:

IF   Percentage of combustible gas is high
THEN Transformer is ready to blow

TABLE 17.28   Example Excerpt from an Unfamiliar Case Study

KE:	I would like you to tell me what recommendations you would make with this transformer. Also, as you study the report, please tell me;
	"What are your goals?"
	"What issues are important?"
	"How are these issues used?"
	"What data do you use?"
DE:	Lot of gas **{CONCEPT}** data here **{data-driven STRATEGY}**. The **hydrogen {OBJECT}** and **methane {OBJECT}** is way up . . . so is the **acetylene {OBJECT}**. . . well somewhat. In fact, the percentage of **combustible gas {CONCEPT}** is too high . . . this baby is ready to blow **{RULE}**. Let me look at some of the past data **{STRATEGY}**. . . um . . . looks clean. I'd expect to see some combustible gases here **{HEURISTIC}**. . . something is happening really fast with this transformer **{HEURISTIC}**. Let me look at this data again **{present data}**. The **ratio {CONCEPT}** of methane to hydrogen is too high . . . let me look at some of these others.

Later, the knowledge engineer can learn how to determine the percentage of combustible gases related to other gases and obtain a clarification of the rule's conclusion, namely "ready to blow."

The expert next switched his reasoning toward the past data. He concluded it "looks clean" and became puzzled; "I'd expect to see some combustible gases here." Later, the knowledge engineer could explore why he arrived at this conclusion after reviewing the past data, but for now, he has a new rule to work with:

> IF   Present data have high levels of combustible gases
> THEN   Past data should have high levels of combustible gases

Since this transformer showed no indications of prior combustible gases, we obtain another heuristic rule:

> IF   Present data have high levels of combustible gases
> AND   Past data doesn't have high levels of combustible gases
> THEN   Transformer is deteriorating fast

The confused expert returned to study the present test data and introduced a new concept, "gas ratio." During this session he mentioned only the ratio of methane to hydrogen. Later studies may show that other gas ratios are also important in diagnosing a faulty transformer.

This example illustrates that the study of an unfamiliar test case can be valuable in obtaining more detailed information on known issues and for uncovering new issues. This technique is of particular value later in the project for discovering the more subtle aspects of the expert's reasoning and to account for the completeness of the expert system's knowledge. Table 17.29 lists the types of knowledge obtained from this example.

TABLE 17.29   Knowledge Obtained from Unfamiliar Case Example

Strategies:	Gas levels checked first, then past test data.
Concepts:	gases, combustible gases, gas ratios
Objects:	hydrogen, methane, acetylene
Rules:	IF Percentage of combustible gas is high THEN Transformer is ready to blow
	IF Present data have high levels of combustible gases THEN Past data should have high levels of combustible gases
	IF Present data have high levels of combustible gases AND Past data don't have high levels of combustible gases THEN Transformer is deteriorating fast

TABLE 17.30   Guidelines for Familiar Case Study

- Have a second expert choose an unfamiliar case.

- Ask the expert to solve the problem and answer questions such as:
  ''What are your goals?''
  ''What issues are important?''
  ''How are these issues used?''
  ''What data do you use?''

- During the session, highlight important issues for further discussion following (or during) the session.

- Use interruptions for introspection only if absolutely necessary.

- Record the concurrent protocol for later study.

Guidelines for an Unfamiliar Case Study

The first step in conducting an unfamiliar case study is to choose a case that is unusual or novel. The best source for this task is another expert. Similar to the approach taken for the familiar case study, the basic case information is given to the expert who is then asked to solve the problem while ''thinking aloud.'' The knowledge engineer records the session in a concurrent protocol for later review. Guidelines for performing an unfamiliar case study are shown in Table 17.30.

Advantages and Disadvantages of the Unfamiliar Case Study

Advantages—The major advantage of an unfamiliar case study is that it requires the expert to work with more fundamental knowledge. This helps avoid the difficulty associated with knowledge compilation. This technique also aids in uncovering previously unknown information. New details of known issues emerge as well as entirely new issues. In particular, this technique provides better insight into problem-solving strategies. Employing a ''think aloud'' technique along with the case study, provides valuable information concurrently with the session instead of reviewing the study after the fact.

Disadvantages—One major difficulty with this technique is in choosing the unfamiliar case. Thought must go into selecting a case that is unusual but still solvable. Table 17.31 shows the advantages and disadvantages of the unfamiliar case study knowledge elicitation technique.

———— COMPARISON OF ELICITATION METHODS ————

The prior sections reviewed several of the most common techniques used for eliciting knowledge from an expert. They represent a set of tools for the knowledge

TABLE 17.31   Advantages and Disadvantages of Unfamiliar Case Study

---

Advantages

- Forces the expert to use more basic knowledge, which in part helps to avoid the knowledge compilation problem.

- Obtains information in the context of a working example.

- Provides problem-specific information.

- Uncovers new details of previously known issues and can discover new issues.

- Provides better insight into problem solving strategies.

Disadvantage

- It can be difficult to choose a good unfamiliar case.

---

engineer that can be used when developing an expert system. Each technique has some value for obtaining different types of knowledge and for avoiding the common knowledge elicitation problems. Table 17.32 summarizes the capability of each technique for obtaining different types of knowledge and Table 17.33 shows their ability for avoiding elicitation problems.

A review of both tables shows that case studies in general are better than interviewing techniques for both obtaining knowledge and avoiding problems. However, you should also recognize that other considerations go into selecting

TABLE 17.32   Capability of Elicitation Technique for Obtaining Knowledge

| Knowledge Type | Interviewing | | Case Study | | | |
| | | | Retrospective | | Observational | |
	Unstructured	Structured	Familiar	Unfamiliar	Familiar	Unfamiliar
Facts	Poor	Good	Fair	Average	Good	Excellent
Concepts	Excellent	Excellent	Average	Average	Good	Good
Objects	Good	Excellent	Average	Average	Good	Good
Rules	Fair	Average	Average	Average	Good	Excellent
Strategies	Average	Average	Good	Good	Excellent	Excellent
Heuristics	Fair	Average	Excellent	Good	Good	Poor
Structures	Fair	Excellent	Average	Average	Average	Average

**TABLE 17.33   Capability of Elicitation Technique
for Avoiding Problems**

Problem Type	Interviewing		Case Study			
			Retrospective		Observational	
	Unstructured	Structured	Familiar	Unfamiliar	Familiar	Unfamiliar
Unaware of knowledge	Poor	Fair	Average	Average	Good	Excellent
Unable to verbalize knowledge	Fair	Fair	Average	Average	Average	Good
Irrelevant knowledge	Poor	Average	Average	Average	Average	Good
Incomplete knowledge	Poor	Average	Poor	Average	Average	Excellent
Incorrect knowledge	Average	Average	Poor	Average	Average	Excellent
Inconsistent knowledge	Average	Average	Poor	Fair	Fair	Excellent

a knowledge elicitation technique, such as the stage of the project or the sequence of execution of the techniques.

For example, early in the project when the intent is to obtain a general understanding of the problem and gain a rapport with the expert, an unstructured interviewing technique should be preferred over a case study approach. A structured interview might appear better than an unstructured one for gaining knowledge and avoiding problems. However, you first need some basic understanding of the problem to conduct a structured interview. Therefore, you will find more value in using this technique later in the project to probe for more detailed information.

Case studies are excellent for uncovering procedural knowledge and unknown concepts. However, you may need to follow this effort with a session incorporating an interviewing technique to explore in more detail the new information discovered.

During an expert system project, you are likely to use several different elicitation techniques. For example, while solving a case, you may ask the expert to stop and introspect about some issue that surfaces. Following the analysis of the knowledge gained from the expert using any technique, you should uncover areas that need further development. You will identify specific types of knowledge

**TABLE 17.34   General Observations
in Comparing Elicitation**

- Case studies are better than interviewing techniques for obtaining procedural knowledge.

- Structured interviews are the best choice for uncovering concepts, objects, and relationships.

- Unstructured interviews are best for obtaining insight into general concepts and problem solving methods.

- The observational case study method is, in general, better than the retrospective method for obtaining problem details and avoiding knowledge elicitation difficulties.

- Familiar case studies are best for obtaining common domain concepts and typical problem solving methods.

- Unfamiliar case studies are best for uncovering basic problem principles.

- Unstructured techniques are poor for avoiding elicitation problems.

- In general, case studies are better than interviewing techniques for avoiding elicitation difficulties.

- Unfamiliar case studies are best for avoiding elicitation problems.

that you should pursue. You should then make plans for the next session to obtain this knowledge. The knowledge elicitation process proceeds in this cyclic fashion, using different techniques to iteratively add to your understanding of the problem. Table 17.34 shows several general observations about the comparison of the elicitation techniques.

─────────── **KNOWLEDGE ANALYSIS** ───────────

Following the collection of knowledge, you must interpret and analyze the collected information. If you made a recording, the first step is to produce a transcript of the session. You must then review this transcript to identify and interpret the key pieces of knowledge. You next must analyze the pieces of knowledge to form theories on their organization—how they are related. Bell and Hardiman (1989) refer to this process of identifying and grouping key pieces of knowledge as ''chunking'' and ''sorting.''

Producing the Transcript

You should produce a complete and exact transcript of the recorded session. This avoids the possibility that you might lose some valuable information. It also uncovers subjective terms that the expert might use to qualify an issue. This becomes important if inexact reasoning is used. However, producing and analyzing a complete transcript can take considerable time and effort.

In some situations it is more practical to produce an exact transcript for only certain sections of the session. You can use notes made during the session to direct which sections you should transcribe. You should also archive the tape in case other information not transcribed is needed later.

Whether the tape is completely or partially transcribed, there are several points you should consider to maintain better record keeping of the transcription. The heading of the transcript should include general project title information, session date, location, attendees and major theme of the session. The various passages throughout the transcript should also record information important for record keeping. Specifically, each passage should contain: the tape counter number, a paragraph index number, and the name of the person speaking.

The tape counter number eases the access to the recorded message if you must review the passage at a later time. A paragraph index number is important for cross-referencing knowledge extracted from a review of the transcript with the documentation of that knowledge. During the review of the transcript, you will be highlighting specific pieces of knowledge such as rules, objects, etc. This highlighted knowledge is then recorded in the project's documentation. At times you must go back to the transcript and determine other information about the origin of this extracted knowledge. If each piece of knowledge is recorded, along with its paragraph index, then this effort is made easier. Table 17.35 shows the guidelines for transcribing a session.

Interpreting the Transcript

The interpretation phase of the elicitation cycle begins by reviewing the transcript and identifying the key pieces of knowledge, i.e., the "chunks." In general, identifying declarative knowledge is straightforward, but identifying procedural knowledge can be more difficult. Problem-solving strategies can be discussed over a wide range of the transcript, making it difficult to relate each step.

In addition to identifying key pieces of knowledge, the transcript review should also identify any issues that need further clarification by the expert. This may

TABLE 17.35   Guidelines for Producing a Transcript

Heading	Passages
Session's date	Tape counter number
Location of session	Paragraph index number
Attendees	Name of person speaking
Major theme of the session	
Project title	

occur because the expert has used a term unknown to you, or has glossed over a possibly important point.

You can use two methods to highlight the knowledge in the transcript. If you used a wordprocessor for producing the transcript, you can note the important information by using italics, underlining, or bolding techniques. You should also label each piece of identified information with the type of knowledge it represents, e.g., concept, strategy, etc. This was the approach taken in the examples provided earlier in this chapter.

The second method involves highlighting the important information with a pen, then in the right margin of the transcript you can make a note of the knowledge type. This approach is more casual and can be used for a simple typewritten version of the transcript. Table 17.36 shows the guidelines for interpreting the transcript.

Analyzing the Transcript

After you identify the "chunks" of knowledge, they need to be "sorted" and studied. This is the analysis phase of the elicitation cycle. In analyzing the transcript, you must make some sense out of the key pieces of knowledge identified during the review and interpretation of the transcript. The question is, How does this new information fit in with what is already known about the problem?

To answer this question, you must address how this new information supports or relates to previously known information. This effort involves determining how this new information is naturally linked to already known related concepts, how it adds details to established information, or how it uncovers new concepts or rules. You should also ask the expert to review the result of this analysis to confirm your findings and make any necessary adjustments.

TABLE 17.36 Guidelines for Interpreting a Transcript

- Identify the key pieces of knowledge, the "chunks."

- Use handwritten notes taken during the session to aid in identifying the key pieces of knowledge.

- If a wordprocessor is used in transcribing the information, then the important information can be noted by using italics, underlining, or bolding techniques.

- If a typewritten version of the transcript is produced, highlight the important information with a pen.

- Label each piece of identified information with the type of knowledge it represents.

- Identify any issues that need further clarification.

Recording the Knowledge

The first step of analysis is to record each new piece of information with other similar pieces discovered during earlier interviews. You should record this new information, in alphabetical order, in the *knowledge dictionary*.

The knowledge dictionary is a part of the project documentation that has sections for each type of knowledge, e.g., concepts, objects, rules, etc. Each new piece of knowledge added should also have a reference to its source. If the knowledge came from an elicitation session, you should record it with the session's date and the paragraph number of the transcript. This bookkeeping allows you to later reference the exact point where this information was obtained, which could be important for verification purposes. In Chapter 18 we review the knowledge dictionary in more detail.

Relating the Knowledge

The next analysis step involves sorting and relating the similar pieces of information collected with previously recorded information. This is a complex psychological task, since it is often difficult to relate the information in the same manner as the expert. However, even if you make mistakes, you can correct them through later reviews.

The sorting process is inherently iterative. Relationships are studied with the expert, refined, and eventually recorded in some graphical fashion. This task uncovers the natural structure and organization of the collected pieces of knowledge.

Reviewing the Knowledge

After the collected knowledge has been sorted and related, you need to review the results of this effort. You should think about what you have learned and what remains to be learned. From this review, you will see conceptual structures evolving, strategies taking shape, and rule networks growing.

With the growth of knowledge in these areas comes a better understanding of the problem and ways that you can solve it with an expert system. A large part of the review process is to highlight those areas that need further pursuit. The review process is a natural lead-in to designing the next knowledge elicitation session. Guidelines for analyzing the transcript are shown in Table 17.37.

One step in the review process should be to have the expert confirm your understanding of the knowledge collected. What you think is important and how you relate it to other knowledge is of principal concern. To accomplish this, you need a way of presenting your findings to the expert. This is the subject of the next section on representing the knowledge structures graphically.

Structuring the Knowledge Graphically

In the last section, we recommended that you relate in a graphical fashion the key pieces of knowledge discovered during the review of the transcript. Cognitive

TABLE 17.37   Guidelines for Analyzing the Transcript

- Record each new piece of information with other similar pieces of information already discovered.
- Reference each new piece of information to its source.
- Relate the piece of information to other recorded information in some graphical fashion.
- Review the body of knowledge collected with the expert to confirm the knowledge structures.
- Highlight those areas that need to be pursued and use them in designing the next knowledge elicitation session.

scientists and expert system developers have used several techniques for graphically relating knowledge. Conceptual graphs, inference networks, fault trees, and semantic networks, are some of the most common techniques used. Techniques have also been borrowed from systems analysis such as dataflow diagrams and petri nets.

All of these techniques provide visual perspectives of the important knowledge and its organization. Each technique has some advantage and limitation in providing insight into the knowledge collected and their relationships. They all share the advantage of focusing the discussion with the expert on some issue and act as a resource for gathering additional information.

Some of these techniques serve the knowledge engineer more than the expert. A semantic network for example may provide a good representation of the knowledge structures and provide the knowledge engineer a better perspective for encoding the knowledge. However, presenting a semantic network to an expert for comment can be confusing.

Any graphical technique used to represent the collected knowledge must be useful to the expert. You want to present this information to the expert for comments, verification, and possible modification. Graphs provide a visual intermediate representation of the collected knowledge before it is encoded into the expert system. They shelter the expert from the program's coding, which may be difficult to interpret. The next few sections review several techniques that help both the knowledge engineer and the expert.

Cognitive Maps

Cognitive maps are one the most common methods used for graphically displaying the natural relationships between concepts or objects. The graph is composed of nodes and arcs that link related nodes. The nodes in the graph can represent either abstract or concrete objects. Abstract objects, such as birds, computers, or cars, represent our conceptual understanding of these items. Concrete objects, such as a specific bird, are characterized by individual features of the item. The arcs in the graph link together naturally related items, e.g., specific bird node to "birds" node. The structure of the graph can be either a hierarchy or lattice.

To illustrate the properties and value of the cognitive map, we can consider a small example centered around a problem concerned with various employees within an organization. For this example, managers, engineers, and technicians, are groups of people that are all a part of an organization's employees. As such, "employees" is a concept that has features specific to the organization that are shared by the different groups (subconcepts) of people. This idea can be extended by listing specific objects under each subconcept. For example, specific individuals can be listed as managers, engineers, etc. Figure 17.7 shows a cognitive map of the employees example.

A cognitive map is similar to the design of most frame-based systems, where the structure has a class, subclasses and specific instances. Another feature that cognitive maps share with frames is inheritance. Lower level objects in the map share features from naturally related upper level objects. For example, as illustrated in Figure 17.7, all employees have an age and salary. Managers have the additional feature of "Bonus" while engineers the feature of "Job." In addition, each feature has a default value or range that is natural to the node in the map.

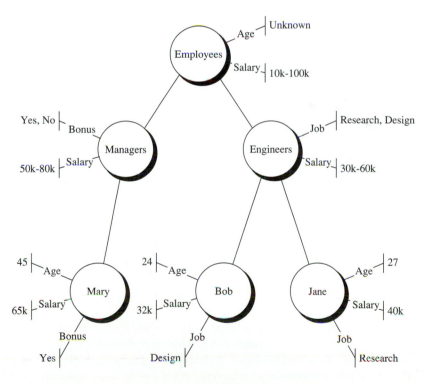

FIGURE 17.7   Cognitive map of employees.

For example, the salary for all employees is between $10k and $100k, for managers, $50k and $80k, and for Mary, a salary of $65k.

Experts have little trouble with reviewing a cognitive map. They can tell us if it makes sense or what possible changes should be considered. The expert may change certain relationships, or more importantly, add additional concepts. For example, after reviewing the cognitive map of Figure 17.7, the expert may tell us that the number of years of employment for each employee is an important consideration. This new feature can then be added to the map along with corresponding values.

Adding information is one of the principal values of a cognitive map since it represents a different way of acquiring knowledge. Unlike interviewing or case study techniques, in which the expert verbalizes knowledge from a recall of mental models, the cognitive map presents a visual picture of this model that can be discussed directly.

Inference Networks

Inference networks provide a graphical representation of the system's rules, with the antecedents and consequences of the rules drawn as nodes and their supporting relationships drawn as links. Consider for example the following set of rules for rain prediction, and the inference network for this set shown in Figure 17.8.

Rule 7

IF	Barometric pressure is falling
AND	Wind conditions indicate rain
AND	Temperature is moderate
THEN	Weather prediction is rain

Rule 8

IF	Wind is gusty
OR	Wind direction is from the east
THEN	Wind conditions indicate rain

Rule 9

IF	Wind speed is > 5 knots
THEN	Wind is gusty

Rule 10

IF	Temperature is between 60 and 80 degrees
THEN	Temperature is moderate

When reviewing and verifying a set of rules, you are concerned with both the validity of a given rule and its relationship with other rules. Verifying a rule is not too difficult. You simply locate the rule and discuss it with the expert. Verifying the rule's relationships with other rules can be more difficult.

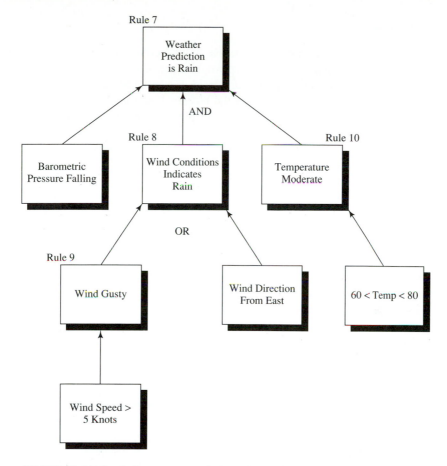

FIGURE 17.8 Inference network for rain prediction.

In the example set of rules, some of the rules are related in that they support the premises of other rules. For example, RULE 9 supports the first premise of RULE 8. Seeing this relationship for a small set of rules may not be difficult. However, relating rules scattered throughout a large set may be very difficult. This issue is of particular importance if you change a rule and are not aware of the impact of this change on related rules.

By forming an inference network you can visually see the interrelationships between the rules and better manage the review and modifications of the rules. An inference network can be valuable for maintaining a record of the rules collected through knowledge elicitation, but you must manage it carefully. During the project, you may collect hundreds of rules leading to large and unwieldy inference networks. For this reason, it is valuable to confine the inference networks to small rule sets that share some common theme.

Flowcharts

Flowcharts present a sequence of steps that will be performed. Flowcharts are a standard technique used by conventional programmers in depicting graphically the sequence of operations of the program. Blocks are drawn for specific operations, decisions, or findings. Links between the blocks show the natural order of the execution of the blocks or branches to other points within the program.

Consider the following hypothetical example of a doctor diagnosing a patient with an infectious blood disease. The interview begins with a prompt asking the doctor to discuss his approach to problem solving.

> KE: Can you please explain how you diagnose a patient with an infectious blood disease?
>
> DOCTOR: I first ask the patient to describe his or her symptoms. From this information I would then see if I could form a belief of what might be wrong.
>
> KE: What do you do if you can't form a belief?
>
> DOCTOR: I would consult some specialist.
>
> KE: What do you do if you can form a belief?
>
> DOCTOR: I would begin to ask more specific questions to confirm this belief. This might include things like . . . If I think I'm right then I would run some tests to confirm it.
>
> KE: What happens if after you question the patient, the problem doesn't look like the one you thought?
>
> DOCTOR: Well, I would see if I could form some new belief and ask more questions.
>
> KE: What do you do if you run some tests and they come back negative?
>
> DOCTOR: I would pretty much have to rethink the problem again.

The problem solving strategy described by the doctor is captured in the flowchart shown in Figure 17.9. The flowchart shows the sequence of the major steps the doctor performs and gives insight into areas that will need to be developed. It clearly shows that the expert system will be first data-driven, then goal-driven, after a hypothesis has been formed.

The primary value of flowcharting in expert system development is capturing graphically the strategies or agendas obtained through a review of the transcript. The flowchart is formed by reviewing the transcript and piecing together the various problem solving steps. Most experts have little difficulty in following the organization and operation of a flowchart, and can therefore be of value to you for verifying the results.

Another value of the flowchart is that it highlights those areas that will need to be developed in more detail. For example, from Figure 17.9 we see a need to determine a list of various hypotheses and a set of rules for confirming them. This might be the area to pursue in the next elicitation session.

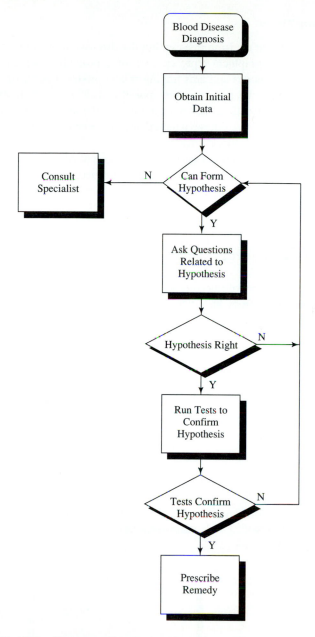

FIGURE 17.9 Flowchart for diagnosing infectious blood disease.

Decision Trees

Chapter 16 introduced decision trees within the discussion of induction systems. A decision tree is a graphical representation of a problem's search space. The tree is composed of nodes and arcs linking related nodes. Each node represents a decision issue and the arcs represent possible values for each issue. Using problem-specific information, we can trace through the tree to arrive at a solution to the problem. Figure 17.10 shows a partial decision tree for diagnosing problems with an automobile's electrical system.

A decision tree provides an easy-to-follow graphical representation of the approach used in problem solving. The important decision factors, their corresponding values and the progression through the tree for specific values can be easily understood.

Example of Knowledge Analysis

To illustrate the process of interpreting and analyzing a transcript, we will look at an example taken from an unstructured interview on the problem of crop

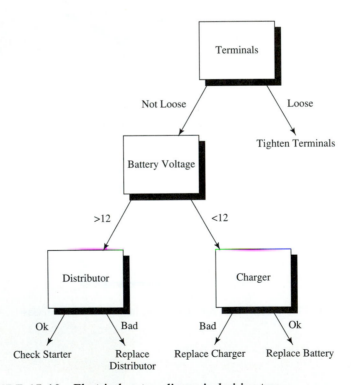

FIGURE 17.10 Electrical system diagnosis decision tree.

management (Durkin 1989b). During this interview, we wanted to obtain a general understanding of what major issues the expert considers when advising a farmer on crop management problems. We review the production of the transcript, identification of key knowledge, knowledge analysis, and knowledge display techniques.

Transcript Production

Figure 17.11 shows excerpts from the transcript. The heading of the transcript is shown with general project title information, session's date, location, attendees

---

TRANSCRIPT OF KNOWLEDGE ELICITATION SESSION

Project Title: Expert System for Specialty Crop Management

Sponsoring Organization: Department of Agriculture

Contract Number: H0127856

Date: 7/5/89

Location: Agricultural Research Center, Washington DC

Attendees: Yao-Chi Lu, Jack Durkin

Theme: Crop management problems

———— Tape counter   ———— Paragraph index number

(45 ft)   **(4)**

JD: What are the issues you consider in crop management?

(48 ft)   **(5)**

YL: Crop management problems {CONCEPT} are a major concern of the grower. Problems here result in poor **yield** {CONCEPT} and will later lead to **financial losses** {CONCEPT}. {RULE} For any crop, management problems will usually fall into one of two catagories; **cultivation problems** {CONCEPT} or **pest problems** {CONCEPT}. {RULE} Several steps are involved in cultivating a crop {STRATEGY}; **seed selection** {CONCEPT}, **soil preparation** {CONCEPT}, **sowing** {CONCEPT}, and **crop maintenance** {CONCEPT}. To obtain an effective yield from the crop, established techniques and recommended procedures should be followed for each step. Most crop problems can be traced to poor practices in one of these four steps {HEURISTIC}. In particular, if they don't know how to select good seed, I will usually spend some time with them and teach them how to pick good seed {HEURISTIC} {STRATEGY}. For the issue of pest control, I'm concerned with either **preventing** {CONCEPT} or **eliminating** {CONCEPT} the pests. If they can't prevent or eliminate the pests, then they got problems {RULE}. Pests are a particular concern when you are working with the crop's **spawn** {Q1:5}. {HEURISTIC}

FIGURE 17.11   Example transcript from interview.

PIECES OF KNOWLEDGE FROM SESSION

STRATEGIES

When looking for crop management problems, check for;
1. Crop cultivation problems
2. Pest problems

To cultivate a crop one needs to consider
1. Seed selection
    1.1 If they don't know how, teach them
2. Soil preparation
3. Sowing
4. Crop maintenance

RULES

IF	There are crop management problems
THEN	The crop will have poor yield
AND	There will be financial losses

IF	There is a cultivation problem
OR	There is a pest problem
THEN	There are crop management problems

IF	Pests can't be prevented
OR	Pests can't be eliminated
THEN	There is a pest problem

HEURISTICS

Pests are a particular concern when you are working with the crop's spawn.

Picking bad seed is a problem in cultivation.

CONCEPTS

Crop management problems	Seed selection
Crop yield problems	Soil preparation
Crop financial losses	Sowing
Cultivation problems	Crop maintenance
Pest problems	Pests
Pest elimination	Pest prevention
Crop yield	

QUESTIONS

Can you please define the term "spawn"?

FIGURE 17.12   Collected knowledge from interview.

and major theme of the session. Passages throughout the transcript are shown with tape counter numbers, paragraph index number, and the name of the person speaking.

Transcript Interpretation

During review of the transcript, key pieces of knowledge are identified (shown in Figure 17.11 in bold) and interpreted according to their knowledge type. Various concepts, rules, heuristics, and strategies are uncovered. A question was also identified, namely what is a "spawn," that can be clarified later.

Transcript Analysis

The first step in the analysis of this transcript is to collect the key pieces of knowledge identified in the review. The results are shown in Figure 17.12. This information will later be added to the knowledge dictionary in a way that permits it to be referenced to its source. This can be done by assigning the transcript data next to each piece of knowledge recorded: i.e., session date and paragraph number.

The next step is to relate each piece of information to previously recorded information. Assume in this example that no prior information was obtained and our job is to collect and organize the information in a graphical form to both study and present the findings to the expert.

The Strategies

The best place to start in the organization and display of the collected knowledge is with the procedures or strategies employed by the expert. A small flowchart that captures several of the primary steps used in solving the problem provides insight into the methods used and the issues considered by the expert.

For our example, we see there are several steps that must be performed when looking for crop management problems or cultivation problems. When addressing the issue of cultivation problems, we can represent the major steps in the flowchart illustrated in Figure 17.13.

This flowchart clearly shows the main issues that must be considered in diagnosing cultivation problems. The flowchart also shows that, besides building a diagnostic expert system, we will be responsible for building a tutoring system on the issue of seed selection. We can later review with the expert each block of Figure 17.13 and determine other necessary steps to fulfill each block's topic. Figure 17.13 illustrates this point where the issue of "crop maintenance" is shown further developed through the dashed line.

The Rules

The rules captured can be represented in the inference network shown in Figure 17.14. The inference network shows the various issues discovered during the

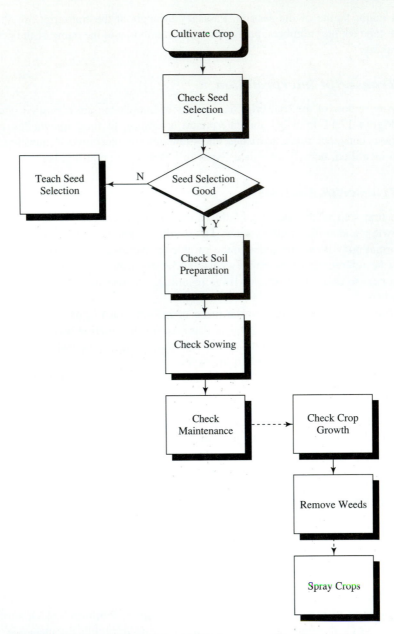

FIGURE 17.13   **Flowchart for addressing crop cultivation problems.**

review of the transcript represented as nodes and branches relating the issues as
they appear in rule form. We can later explore the primitives of the network
(e.g., cultivation problems, pest prevention, and pest elimination), to determine
ways of inferring this information.

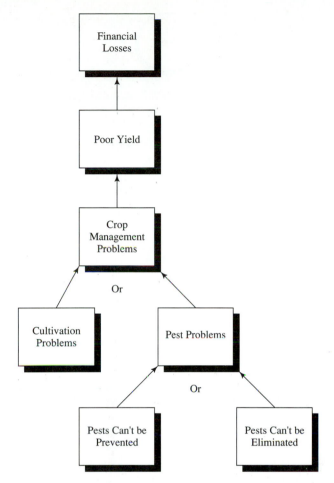

FIGURE 17.14   Crop inference network.

The Concepts

A review of the transcript uncovered several concepts that should be of interest. Consider the concept of pests. The expert did not discuss this issue in much detail, but a later discussion focused on it providing additional information. We learned that the expert was first concerned about two types of pests: fungi and predators. We later explored each type of pest to identify specific examples for each. We also uncovered general characteristics of all pests, characteristics related to each pest type, and specific features of each. From this collection of information we generated the cognitive map of the world of pests as shown in Figure 17.15.

From the collection of concepts identified in the transcript, we were also able to relate concepts as they would be used in problem solving. We know that the concept of "crop management problems" is related to the concepts of "crop cultivation" and "pest control." Figure 17.16 shows this relationship. This

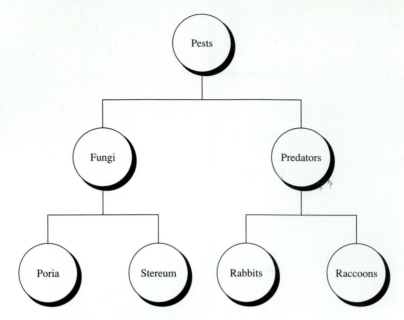

FIGURE 17.15   Cognitive map of the world of pests.

concept relationship was also seen in the rule inference network of Figure 17.14. Figure 17.16 provides a focused view of the rule network. It clearly shows that when considering crop management problems we must consider the issues of cultivation and pests.

We also have uncovered a relationship between ''crop cultivation problems'' and other concepts as shown in Figure 17.17. The issues raised in Figure 17.17 were also shown in the strategy flowchart of Figure 17.14. We can explore each

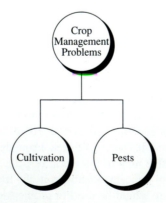

FIGURE 17.16   Crop management problems areas.

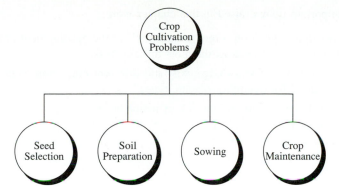

FIGURE 17.17   Cultivation problem areas.

crop cultivation problem of Figure 17.17 later to form a set of rules for each that would support the ''cultivation problem'' node of the inference network shown in Figure 17.14.

Summary of Findings

This example demonstrates the methods you should employ in reviewing the knowledge collected from an elicitation session. It also shows how you can learn from the collected knowledge and obtain insight into areas that remain to be covered. The knowledge elicitation process is cyclic; you obtain information, learn from it, and design new ways to learn more.

The next step is to design an objective for a future knowledge elicitation session. As this example shows, we gained a considerable amount of information about the problem from a very small example. Early sessions may raise more questions than provide answers. However, they offer insight into designing future sessions. In the next session we would choose one of the issues raised (e.g., pests), and focus the discussion on that issue.

—————— SUMMARY OF KNOWLEDGE ACQUISITION ——

It has long been argued that the most difficult task in developing an expert system is acquiring the knowledge from the expert. This chapter discussed this problem in detail and provided recommendations that can aid this effort. Guidelines were provided for effectively conducting an interview with the expert, the most common knowledge acquisition technique used when developing an expert system. Techniques were also offered for analyzing the collected knowledge. This analysis can uncover key pieces of knowledge and insight into further knowledge acquisition efforts.

The important points raised in this chapter were:

- Knowledge acquisition is the ''bottleneck'' in the development of an expert system because it remains the most difficult task.
- Different types of knowledge exist and different elicitation techniques are better suited for obtaining specific types.
- Knowledge elicitation involves four major tasks
  —Collection of knowledge
  —Interpretation of knowledge
  —Analysis of knowledge
  —Design of new elicitation session
- Obtaining initial cooperation requires:
  —Removing fear
  —Removing skepticism
  —Establishing reasonable goals
  —Promoting openness to change
  —Providing understanding of expected effort
  —Conveying importance of involvement
- Questions can be posed to gain information about the problem or to control the interview.Unstructured interviews provide a broad understanding of the problem and insight into the general problem solving strategies.
- Structured interviews focus on a given topic and seek to obtain specific topic information.
- Case studies require the expert to work on a real problem.
- Familiar cases are used to obtain general knowledge.
- Unfamiliar cases are used to obtain detailed knowledge.
- Knowledge analysis first involves the identification of key pieces of knowledge, then the grouping of the pieces in some natural fashion, i.e., chunking and sorting.
- Graphical representation of collected knowledge is valuable for both verification and insight into new issues to explore.

REFERENCES

Bainbridge, L., Asking Questions and Accessing Knowledge, Future Computing Systems, vol. 1, pp. 143–149, 1986.
Bell, J. and R.J. Hardiman, The Third Role—The Naturalistic Knowledge Engineer, Knowledge Elicitation: Principles, Techniques and Applications, D. Diaper, ed., John Wiley & Sons, New York, 1989.
Chomsky, N., Syntactic Structures, Mouton, The Hague, 1957.
Collins, H.M., Changing Order: Replication and Induction in Scientific Practice, Sage, London, 1985.

Dixon, N., Preconscious Processing, Wiley, Chichester, 1981.

Duda, R.O. and E.H. Shortliffe, Expert Systems Research, Science, vol. 220, pp. 261–268, 1983.

Durkin, J., DUSTPRO: A Distributed Expert System Solution to Coal Mine Dust Control, Second Annual Conference and Exposition on Expert Systems 88, Dearborn MI, April 12–14, 1988.

Durkin, J., Expert System Diagnostics for a 30/20 Gigahertz Satellite Transponder, Semi-annual report published in NASA technical series, Contract NAG3-923, March, 1989a.

Durkin, J., R. Godine, and Yao-Chi Lu, Expert System for Specialty Crop Management, The 11th International Joint Conference on Artificial Intelligence, Detroit, Michigan, Aug. 18–19, 1989b.

Durkin, J. and R. Schlegelmich, Transformer Diagnostic Expert System, LEVEL5 Third Annual Expert Systems Conference, Indialantic, Florida, Nov. 1989c.

Ericsson, K.A. and H.A. Simon, Verbal Reports as Data, Psychological Review, vol. 87, pp. 215–251, 1980.

Evans, J., The Knowledge Elicitation Problem: A Psychological Perspective, Behavior and Information Technology, vol. 7, no. 2, pp. 111–130, 1988.

Fransella, F. and D. Bannister, A Manual for Repertory Grid Technique, Academic Press, London, 1977.

Freud, S., Psychopathology of Everyday Life, Benn., London, 1914.

Hart, Anna, Knowledge Acquisition for Expert Systems, McGraw Hill, NY, 1986.

Hayes–Roth, F., D.A. Waterman, and D.B. Lenat, eds., Building Expert Systems, Addison Wesley, Reading, MA, 1983.

Hoffman, R.R., The Problem of Extracting the Knowledge of Experts from the Perspective of Experimental Psychology, AI Applications, vol. 1, no. 2, pp. 35–48, 1987.

Johnson–Laird, P.N. and M.J. Steedman, The Psychology of Syllogisms, Cognitive Psychology, vol. 10, pp. 64–99, 1978.

Kelly, G.A., The Psychology of Personal Constructs, Norton, New York, 1955.

Lincoln, Y.S. and E.G. Guba, Naturalistic Inquiry, Sage, CA, 1984.

McDermott, J., R1 The Formative Years, AI Magazine, vol. 2, no. 2, pp. 21–29, Summer 1981.

McGraw, K.L. and K. Harbison-Briggs, Knowledge Acquisition: Principles and Guidelines, Prentice-Hall, Englewood Cliffs, N.J., 1989.

Nisbett, R.E. and T.D. Wilson, Telling More Than We Can Know: Verbal Reports on Mental Processes, Psychological Review, vol. 84, pp. 231–259, 1977.

Olson, J.E. and H.H. Rueter, Extracting Expertise From Experts: Methods for Knowledge Acquisition, Expert Systems, vol. 4, no. 3, pp. 152–168, August 1987.

Smith, R.G. and J.D. Baker, The DIPMETER Advisor System, IJCAI Proceedings, pp. 122–129, 1983.

Sviokla, J.J., Business Implications of Knowledge-Based Systems, Parts I and II, DataBase, [17:4; 18:1], pp. 5–9, Summer 1986, and pp. 5–16, Fall 1986.

Tversky, A. and D. Kahneman, Availability: Heuristic for Judging Frequency and Probability, Cognitive Psychology, vol. 5, pp. 207–232, 1973.

Waterman, D.A., A Guide to Expert Systems, Addison-Wesley, Reading, MA, 1986.

——————— E X E R C I S E S

1. Explain why the knowledge acquisition process is called the "bottleneck" in the development of an expert system.

2. Describe the different types of knowledge and provide an example for each.

3. Explain the advantages and disadvantages of using multiple experts in knowledge acquisition.

4. List the different sources of knowledge and their potential value.

5. Describe the four major steps involved in knowledge elicitation and explain how they change during the course of the project.

6. List and describe the important considerations in obtaining initial cooperation on an expert system project.

7. Assume that the expert on the project arrives at an elicitation session late, and has forgotten to bring a report that was promised. What is your interpretation and reaction to this situation?

8. You have been asked to develop an expert system to replace the operator of a continuous miner—a machine used for mining coal. Your expert on the project is the operator of the machine. How do you obtain the expert's cooperation on the project?

9. You are developing an expert system to provide financial planning advice. Your expert, a financial planner, states that you can never develope a system that will perform as well as he does. How do you react?

10. You have been asked to develop an expert system to assist Blue Cross and Blue Shield in processing health claims. Prepare an agenda for your first meeting with the individuals involved on the project.

11. On an expert system project you have been offered two experts to help the system development. How do you proceed?

12. List the basic types of questions used during an interview and describe their intent. Also provide an example of each.

13. Discuss the advantages and limitations of the unstructured and structured interview techniques.

14. Describe a problem that would be suitable for an unstructured interview and one for a structured interview.

15. Explain the principal differences between retrospective and observational methods of knowledge elicitation.

16. Provide examples where either a familiar or unfamiliar case study approach would be appropriate.

17. When producing a transcript, what are the important bookkeeping issues to consider?

18. What do you believe are the important items that should be documented during an expert system project?

19. Discuss the value of the various graphical representation techniques used for analyzing knowledge.

20. How can a graphical representation be used to help the knowledge elicitation task? Provide examples.

21. For the following transcript, pick out the important pieces of knowledge, sort them, and provide graphical representations for each.

> KE: What advice would you give a farmer who was considering growing some new crop?
>
> DE: I would first want to know what the farmer is thinking of growing. . . . I would then be concerned that the farmer had the right environment for the crop. Too

often they want to grow something that they really aren't prepared to do. . . . I'd consider their amount of acreage, weather, soil conditions, . . ah . . I might even look at the lay of the land. . . . I then look at their cultivation techniques to see if they would be good for this new crop. There are a number of things that concern me here, but pests always worry me, . . . particularly for the spawn. If they run into an infestation it can really cut into their production and profit . . . After I'm satisfied that their environment is ok, I'd want to know if they even know how to grow or market the crop.

CHAPTER 18

Knowledge Engineering

————————— **INTRODUCTION** ——————————————

This chapter reviews the key ideas raised throughout the book related to expert system design and development. They are integrated into a six phase process as shown in Figure 18.1, which serves as guidance for managing an expert system project:

Phase 1: Problem assessment
Phase 2: Knowledge acquisition
Phase 3: System design
Phase 4: Testing and evaluation
Phase 5: Documentation
Phase 6: Maintenance

This is the subject of **knowledge engineering.** The field of expert systems has not yet matured to the level of conventional programming, and knowledge engineering remains more of an art form than a science. Therefore, the advice given in this chapter is just that—points to consider when developing the system.

It should also be recognized that the development effort is not as neat and clean as Figure 18.1 might suggest. Though the tasks are shown in sequence, in practice there is considerable overlap in their execution. In addition, the process is highly iterative. As information is gained from the execution of later tasks, there will be a need to return to earlier ones. As these tasks are cycled through, the system will begin to take shape. It gradually evolves from one with limited ability to one that becomes more capable due to its improved knowledge and problem-solving skills.

An interesting aspect of this iterative development process is that both the system and project personnel learn more about the problem and how best to solve it. Expert systems offer valuable solutions to real-world problems. To site a few, they can improve decision making for financial organizations, enhance productivity in manufacturing, and aid in medical diagnosis. However, one could argue that their principal value rests within the development effort—we *learn* about the problem.

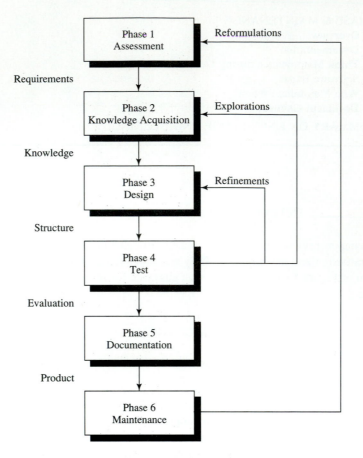

FIGURE 18.1   Phases in expert system development.

--------------- **PHASE 1: PROBLEM ASSESSMENT** ---------------

Overview

Most organizations when considering any new technology will ask the very practical questions *Will* it work? and *Why* should we try it? Since expert system technology is relatively new, answers to these questions are at best educated guesses. However, it is important that a serious effort be made to answer these questions before the project begins. Failure to do so can result in undertaking a project that has a small chance to succeed or will offer little benefit to the organization. This will further result in forming a negative view of the technology within the organization—a death sentence to future expert system projects.

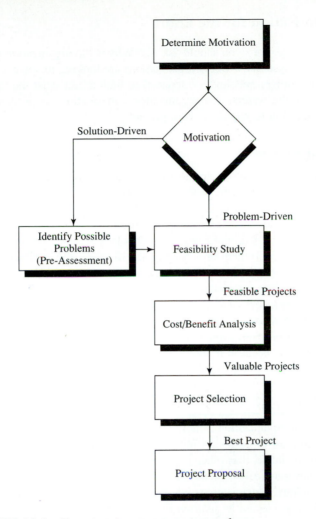

FIGURE 18.2 Expert system assessment procedure.

This section presents a methodology for assessing the applicability of an expert system to a given problem. This process is illustrated in Figure 18.2 and is structured according to the following tasks:

Task 1: Determine motivation of organization
Task 2: Identify candidate problems
Task 3: Perform feasibility study
Task 4: Perform cost/benefit analysis
Task 5: Select the best project
Task 6: Write the project proposal

Task 1: Motivation for the Effort

One of the first questions you should ask is, "Why is the organization motivated to pursue expert systems?" Some organizations are looking to solve a particular problem, while others are simply interested in finding out what the technology can do—testing the waters. The organization's motivation has a major impact on the final decision to pursue a given project.

Problem Driven

Some organizations are motivated to explore the use of a new technology out of desire to solve some specific problem. The organization may view the solution to the problem as a step toward improving profitability or productivity. An organization motivated by an existing problem can be viewed as *problem driven*.

Consider the introduction of computer technology several decades ago. Many organizations took a problem driven approach to assess the applicability of the technology. For example, computers were found to be valuable in addressing problems of labor costs associated with routine tasks such as typing or information management. Wordprocessors and database management systems soon found their place within many organizations, resulting in improved productivity and lower costs. This problem driven adoption of a new technology is attractive to many organizations because it addresses a well-defined problem, offers a clear benefit, and usually poses a small risk.

Solution Driven

In some cases, an organization is motivated to explore a new technology because of a general interest or curiosity. Individuals within the organization may have read about it, or heard that other organizations are presently using it to their advantage. They may feel it is in the best interest of the organization to investigate the new technology. Organizations interested in the general application of a new technology can be viewed as *solution driven*.

With the rapid increase in interest over the past decade in expert systems, a solution driven phenomenon has compelled many organizations to assess their applicability. These organizations are less concerned with obtaining immediate benefits, but are looking at the long-term view of maintaining a competitive position within the marketplace. They may feel that after individuals within the organization have been exposed to the technology, and have learned of its potential, future projects can produce tangible benefits. With this motivation, they are also likely to be more willing to accept higher risks.

Task 2: Identify Candidate Problems

If an organization is exploring the application of expert systems, you need to first put together a list of candidate problems that have some chance for success.

This step is done before the more formal feasibility and cost/benefit studies and is called *pre-assessment*. This task is only appropriate if the organization is exploring the technology (solution driven). If the organization has a specific problem in mind (problem driven), then you need to proceed with the next series of tasks that address the project's feasibility and desirability.

Forming the List

When forming the list of candidate problems you should seek the help of individuals within the organization. A good place to look is within middle-level management. These individuals have a global view of operations and knowledge about everyday problems. Their view is valuable because it exposes areas where the application of an expert system has the potential to provide real value to the organization.

Ask these individuals to discuss their present operations and any current problems that they may be experiencing. During this discussion, you should be looking for those tasks that require decisions to be made. This is perhaps the most revealing point. If a problem under consideration involves human decision making, it may be a candidate for an expert system approach.

Technology Demonstration

If the organization is exploring the application of expert systems, then you should view the project as more of a demonstration of the technology. Therefore, a small and relatively simple problem is more preferable than a complex one. This choice will enhance the likelihood of success and the eventual acceptance of the technology within the organization.

By small, it is meant that the scope of the problem doesn't cover a large number of complex issues. By simple, it is meant that the problem appears at first glance to be solvable.

As a guide for choosing the problem, consider what others have done in the past. For example, if prior systems have been developed for the same type of problem, then success may be likely. Also consider the problem solving paradigm. For example, many success stories exist for expert systems developed in the area of diagnostics, while it remains difficult to develop systems for planning or design tasks.

Suggestions for Choosing a Good Problem

For organizations looking to explore the technology, consider the following points:

- **Human decision making**—The problem requires human decision-making to solve.
- **Heuristic knowledge**—The expert uses rules-of-thumb gained from past experiences to guide the problem solving.

- **Judgmental knowledge**—The problem is constrained by limited or uncertain information, which requires good judgment to solve.
- **Small**—The problem is of narrow scope.
- **Simple**—Pick a problem area where expert systems have been successfully applied in the past.
- **Success likely**—You want the system to succeed recognizing that failure may doom any future interest.
- **Some value**—The solution doesn't have to be a breakthrough for the organization, but it should have some obvious value.

These recommendations don't guarantee that the project is either feasible or justified (issues covered in the next sections), but they act as an initial guide that can filter out those projects that should not receive further consideration. A problem that meets this list of recommendations will offer the best opportunity for establishing a good foothold for the technology within the organization. The interest generated by a successful first project will push the application of expert systems into more productive areas in the future.

Task 3: Feasibility Study

Before an organization will commit resources to a new project, it will want to assess the project's feasibility. The objective of any feasibility study is to determine if the project is likely to succeed. A feasibility study on an expert system project follows a two-step process.

The first step considers only those issues that are absolutely required. Here, a list of items is checked that must be met before the project would have any chance to succeed—an all-or-nothing situation. These items include the proper resources, a source of knowledge, and project personnel.

The second step considers those issues that are important for the success of the project, but which are subjective in nature and requires some judgment to assess. These issues impact the overall likelihood of successfully completing the project. They include problem features, characteristics of the people involved on the project, and deployment issues.

The following sections describe these two tasks that you will need to perform when assessing the feasibility of a given project. Figure 18.3 illustrates this process.

Project Requirements

Some of the requirements for an expert system project are the same as needed for a conventional program project. You must have the proper resources such as computers, development software, and funding. However, on an expert system project, you must also have a source of knowledge such as a human expert or

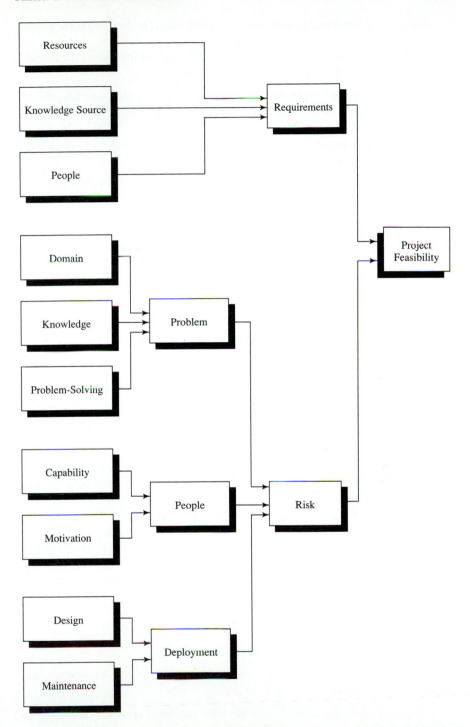

FIGURE 18.3 Expert system feasibility study.

documents, and someone talented in expert system development—the knowledge engineer.

The following list of requirements should be checked first when considering a problem for an expert system application:

- **Problem solving knowledge available**—An expert exists who has specialized knowledge on the problem or the knowledge is available in document form.
- **Knowledge engineer available**—A person is available with knowledge engineering skills.
- **Problem solution can be validated**—The expert system is testable, with results that can be compared with past test cases or other experts in the field.
- **Funding available**—Funding is available to cover the development costs.
- **System development software available**—An expert system shell or a base language is available.
- **Computer facilities available**—Computers capable of running the developed expert system software are available.

This list of requirements acts as an additional filter on the projects under consideration. Those projects making their way through the pre-assessment effort and the requirements check, can be considered further.

Project Risks

Even when a project meets the requirements check, there are other issues that can prevent the successful completion of the project. A study of these issues provides insight into the risk of the project. The potential risk associated with an expert system project is greater than with a conventional computer project. This is an inherent hazard for any new technology that is evolving rapidly. Though a large number of successful expert systems have been developed that provid clear benefits, many others have failed because the developers overlooked the project's risk (Due 1989).

For a conventional computer system project, McFarlan (1981) describes risk as exposure to possible failure to obtain expected benefits. An expert system project can fail for reasons that fall into three categories: problem, people, and deployment. These reasons, which we call feasibility issues, are listed in the following sections for each category.

Problem Feasibility Issues

Problem feasibility issues include features of the domain, the knowledge, and problem-solving tasks:

- **Expert knowledge needed**—The problem requires expertise to solve, which includes both expert knowledge and expert problem solving skills.

- **Problem solving steps are definable**—The major steps used by the expert when solving the problem can be clearly defined.
- **Symbolic knowledge used**—The type of knowledge used by the expert is symbolic in nature, rather than in the numeric form that is more commonly found in conventional programs.
- **Heuristics used**—The expert uses rules-of-thumb gained from past experiences to guide the problem solving.
- **Problem is solvable**—Expert systems are not intended to address new or novel research issues, but rather to solve problems that can currently be solved by human experts.
- **Successful systems exist**—Prior systems in the application area have been successfully built.
- **Problem is well-focused**—The overall scope of the problem is manageable, focused on an issue that is achievable by an expert system approach.
- **Problem is reasonably complex**—The problem is reasonably complex; not too easy where the effort may not be justified, or too difficult where the problem may not be manageable.
- **Problem is stable**—The knowledge and the approach to solving the problem are stable. If changes are likely to occur, then the expert system will need to be modified often.
- **Uncertain or incomplete knowledge used**—The problem requires good judgement to solve because of the uncertainty or incompleteness of the available information.
- **Non-deterministic**—In general, if the problem is deterministic in nature, then a conventional programming approach is usually the better choice.
- **Solution more of a recommendation**—The problem does not require an exact answer—rather, an educated recommendation.

People Feasibility Issues

The capability and motivation of the people involved on the project are important issues to consider when judging the project's feasibility. The major players on an expert system project are: domain expert, knowledge engineer, end-user, and management. Assessing their impact on the project's feasibility is a challenge due to the complexities of human nature. You need to consider their desires, fears, and emotions to judge whether they will effectively contribute to the project. The next several sections list the issues you should consider when evaluating each of these individuals.

Expert

The major source of knowledge for most expert system projects is a human expert. To evaluate this individual, consider the following requirements:

- **Expert can communicate the knowledge**—The expert is able to communicate the problem-solving knowledge.
- **Expert can devote time**—Developing an expert system can be a lengthy process, and it is important that the expert has the time to devote to the project.
- **Expert is cooperative**—The expert is cooperative and not hostile or skeptical of the project.

Knowledge Engineer

The knowledge engineer has many responsibilities on the project. He or she is not only the system designer, but also the project manager. There are a large number of issues to consider when evaluating the knowledge engineer's impact on the project's feasibility. The most important criteria are:

- **Knowledge engineer has good communication skills**—A large amount of the effort of the knowledge engineer is involved with eliciting knowledge from the expert. The knowledge engineer needs good communication skills to accomplish this task.
- **Knowledge engineer can match problem to software**—There are a number of programming languages and expert system development packages available for developing an expert system. The knowledge engineer should be able to choose the proper software for the application.
- **Knowledge engineer has expert system programming skills**—The knowledge engineer should have the necessary programming skills to develop the expert system.
- **Knowledge engineer can devote the time**—The knowledge engineer will spend more time on the project than any other project member. This time should be available with no conflicts from other projects.

End-User

The end-user is the individual who will eventually live with the completed system. The reaction of the end-user to the system has a major impact on the project's success. Users who are interested and involved throughout the project are most likely to respond positively to the system. The principal needs to consider when evaluating the end-user are:

- **End-user can devote time**—The end-user is available for both the development of the system and providing guidance on the design of the interface.
- **End-user is receptive to change**—Humans like the status quo and often react negatively to any type of change. If the system complicates the user's work assignments, it is likely not to be accepted. However, if the system makes the user's job easier, or frees him or her from routine or mundane tasks, it is then likely to be accepted.

- **End-user is cooperative**—The end-user's motivation on the project is important for its success. If he or she is involved throughout the project in helping to define project goals and system features, the end-user's cooperation is likely to be gained.

Management

Support from management for the project is extremely important. They have control over the allocation of funds for the project, and a loss of their support could easily lead to the termination of the project. To judge their impact on the project's feasibility, consider the following requirements:

- **Management supports the project**—Expert system development can be a lengthy and at times a high-risk venture. It is important that management be prepared to maintain support throughout the effort.
- **Management is receptive to change**—Expert systems represent a new and innovative technology, and the project can only survive if management is willing to try something new.
- **Management is not skeptical**—Any new technology, but particularly one coming under the label of "artificial intelligence," can bring out skepticism in people. It is important that management be open minded about the potential of the technology.
- **Management has reasonable expectations**—Management must not be overly optimistic nor overly pessimistic. They must understand that an expert system will perform no better than the human expert.
- **Management understands objectives**—Management needs to understand the objectives of the project and what the final result of the project will produce.

Deployment Feasibility Issues

To effectively deploy the system, you must consider several issues from the system's design to its maintenance. The important criteria to consider are:

- **System can be introduced easily**—The system can be introduced into the work environment with little disruption to present practices.
- **System can be maintained**—The system can be maintained by internal or external support personnel.
- **System not a critical-path item**—Expert systems remain a relatively new field, and as such, a high risk exists with any new project. Attempts should be made to choose a project that is not critical to other activities.
- **System can be integrated with existing resources**—For expert systems developed to work with existing software, such as databases, spreadsheets, etc., the system must be capable of integration.

• **Training available**—Since the expert system represents a new piece of software, you may need to have a training program for the end-users.

Feasibility Assessment

The prior sections discussed those issues that you should consider when assessing the feasibility of a candidate problem for an expert system project. The next task is to use some assessment method that can intelligently judge the project's feasibility. Recall also that only those problems that successfully meet all of the requirements issues would be considered.

Several investigators have developed expert system feasibility assessment strategies. One of the first efforts was the work by Prerau (1985). Prerau provided a list of issues, similar to the feasibility issues listed in the prior sections, that are important for evaluating the application of an expert system. However, no guidance was provided on how the importance of each issue could be used to arrive at a realistic feasibility assessment estimate.

A later effort by Beckman (1991) formed a list of issues to consider, then assigned each one a number that reflected its relative importance. This weighted check-list is then compared to some candidate problem, and if the problem meets an issue, it receives the issue's pre-described points. The total sum of all of the points is then used to ascribe a percentage to the feasibility of the project. This approach is illustrated in Figure 18.4 for the "problem feasibility issues" given earlier.

One shortcoming with this approach is that many issues are subjective and

PROBLEM FEASIBILITY ISSUES		
Weight	**Issue**	**Score**
1	Expert knowledge needed	
2	Problem-solving steps are definable	
1	Symbolic knowledge used	
1	Heuristics used	
2	Problem is solvable	
2	Successful systems exist	
2	Problem is well-focused	
1	Problem is reasonably complex	
1	Problem is stable	
1	Uncertain or incomplete knowledge	
1	Non-deterministic	
1	Solution more of a recommendation	
16	Total Points Total Score	
	Feasibility = Total Score / Total Points	

FIGURE 18.4   Problem feasibility assessment checklist form.

are difficult to answer in a clear yes-or-no fashion. Consider for example the issue of the problem's scope. For a given problem we might be able to comment on this issue, but it may be too constraining to be limited to a yes-or-no response. This constraint can also lead to response errors that produces a misleading feasibility assessment figure.

A different type of strategy was developed that corrects this problem (Slagel and Wick 1988). Like the prior technique, it begins by forming a list of important issues to consider. Each issue is then assigned a weight (between 0 and 10) that reflects the importance of each issue. During the evaluation of a given project, numbers (also between 0 and 10) are ascribed to each issue that reflect the degree of belief in the issue. For example, if we believe that the answer to the ''scope is small'' issue is ''somewhat,'' then an answer of 5 might be given. This value is then multiplied by the issue's weight to establish a score for the issue. All of the scores are then added and divided by the sum of the issue weights. This number is bounded between 0 and 10, and provides a project feasibility assessment estimate.

Using this approach for the issues established for each feasibility category discussed in the earlier sections results in Figures 18.5 through 18.7. The ''Weight'' values are a result of this author's consulting experience on project assessment efforts.

Each figure provides a form to evaluate a particular project category. You can collect the results from each form to obtain an overall evaluation of the project. Simply add all of the total scores and divide it by the sum of the weights from each category.

PROBLEM FEASIBILITY ISSUES				
Score	=	Weight	x	Value	Issue
		7			Expert knowledge needed
		9			Problem-solving steps are definable
		7			Symbolic knowledge used
		8			Heuristics used
		10			Problem is solvable
		8			Successful systems exist
		9			Problem is well-focused
		6			Problem is reasonably complex
		7			Problem is stable
		9			Uncertain or incomplete knowledge
		5			Non-deterministic
		6			Solution more of a recommendation
		91			
Total Score		Total Weight		Problem Feasibility = $\frac{\text{Total Score}}{\text{Total Weight}}$	

FIGURE 18.5 Problem feasibility assessment form.

				PEOPLE FEASIBILITY ISSUES	
Score	=	Weight	x	Value	Issue
					DOMAIN EXPERT
		7			Can communicate knowledge
		9			Can devote time
		7			Cooperative
		23			
Total Score		Total Weight			Expert Feasibility = Total Score / Total Weight
					KNOWLEDGE ENGINEER
		8			Good communication skills
		8			Can match problem to software
		9			Has expert system programming skill
		9			Can devote time
,		34			
Total Score		Total Weight			Knowledge Engineer Feasibility = Total Score / Total Weight
					END-USER
		6			Can devate time
		7			Receptive to change
		7			Cooperative
		20			
Total Score		Total Weight			End-User Feasibility = Total Score / Total Weight
					MANAGEMENT
		9			Supports project
		7			Receptive to change
		7			Not skeptic
		6			Reasonable expectations
		8			Understands objectives
		37			
Total Score		Total Weight			Management Feasibility = Total Score / Total Weight

FIGURE 18.6 People feasibility assessment form.

DEPLOYMENT FEASIBILITY ISSUES				
Score =	**Weight**	**x**	**Value**	**Issue**
	7			System can be introduced easily
	9			System can be maintained
	7			System not on a critical path
	9			System can be integrated
	7			Training is available
	39			
Total Score	Total Weight		Deployment Feasibility = Total Score / Total Weight	

FIGURE 18.7 Deployment feasibility assessment form.

To illustrate, assume you evaluated a candidate project that resulted in the following scores for each category:

CATEGORY	TOTAL SCORE	TOTAL WEIGHT
Problem	800	91
People	900	114
Deployment	300	39
	2000	244

Project feasibility = 2000/244 = 8.19

You can use these forms to establish feasibility values for candidate projects, and choose those with higher values to consider further. For projects with low overall values, this approach also provides you insight into what area is deficient, such as problem issues, people issues, etc.

Task 4: Cost/Benefit Analysis

At this point in the problem assessment effort, you should have a good idea if the problem (or problems) represents a candidate for an expert systems approach. The next step is to determine the expected payoff—a justification for the project.

For most projects this is usually measured in a cost/benefit analysis. The organization wants tangible evidence that shows that the investment of both time and money is justified. Under the best conditions, this can be a difficult task. When the project involves a new technology such as expert systems, the task encounters additional uncertainties.

Project Cost

The cost of developing an expert system can be high. A survey conducted in 1987 (Fried 1987) on expert system applications in the financial industry showed that the average cost for developing an expert system was $700 per rule. This figure excludes the costs of hardware, software, and the expert's time contribution to the project. An article in Forbes during the same year stated that moderate-sized expert system projects typically run $250,000 to $500,000 to complete (Simon 1987).

A more recent survey conducted on expert system applications in the service industry paints a different picture (Pepper 1991). This survey showed that most organizations actively building expert systems between 1988 and 1991 spent in total between $10,000 and $50,000. The survey also showed that principal project costs are established by labor and software expenses.

Labor expenses account for the time spent on the project by the knowledge engineer, domain expert and the end-user. Some of the early "classic" systems, such as Dendral and MYCIN, took 20 to 40 man-years to complete. Fortunately, with a better understanding of how to build an expert system—a heritage of these early systems—and with the advent of the expert system "shell," these development times have dramatically decreased. Today, most systems can be built with 1 to 3 man-years of effort.

The choice of the expert system development software is based on the nature of the problem and the organization's computer facilities. The expense of this software can range from several hundred dollars to $50,000. The price is mainly dictated by the choice of the platform—you will pay more for a mainframe implementation than a PC version.

Benefit Issues

The benefit of developing an expert system can be measured in one of four ways: improved productivity, lower costs, improved quality, or—a very intangible but important issue—improved image.

1. *Improved Productivity:*

   - **Better Decisions**—The system is capable of improving the quality of decisions.
   - **Faster Decisions**—The system reduces the time to reach a decision.
   - **Disseminates Expertise**—The system provides expertise to locations within the organization where this capability is lacking.

2. *Lower Costs:*

   - **Reduces Labor Costs**—The system reduces labor costs by allowing a possibly time-consuming task to be completed quickly or acts in place of a highly paid expert.

- **Improves Material Use**—The system improves the use of materials during manufacturing.

3. *Improved Quality:*

- **Superior Product**—The system improves the quality of the manufactured product.

- **Superior Services**—The system improves the quality of services supplied by the organization.

- **Provides Training**—The system provides training to personnel that improves their work activities.

4. *Improved Image:*

- **Innovator**—The system improves the organization's image as a leader and innovator.

The survey conducted by Pepper (1991) on expert system applications in the service industry showed that most organizations justified the effort on strategic, intangible benefits, like gaining a competitive edge (50%) or capturing and preserving scarce expertise (44%). Fewer organizations looked to benefit from cost savings. This survey indicates that most organizations are looking to explore the technology, that is, they are solution driven.

Task 5: Select the Best Project

For each problem initially selected for the assessment effort, you now have information on its feasibility and desirability. Your next task is to select one (or possibly several) to pursue in an expert system project.

The picture you now have of each possible project is both quantitative and qualitative. The feasibility study provided a number that reflects the overall feasibility estimate of the project. This number is mainly of value for comparing several projects. The cost/benefit study also provided numbers. The project's cost is usually easy to estimate, and in some cases, you can approximate the expected savings or gains to the organization. You should also have a sense of the impact that the project might have on establishing expert systems within the organization.

Knowing the organization's motivation for the project is of help on this task. If they are problem driven, you must show that the project is feasible, and that the expected benefits exceed the project's cost. Even when the organization is exploring the technology (solution driven)—a seemingly comfortable situation—you must still provide some justification for the effort. These organizations are usually more tolerant of the expected short-term gains, but they expect the project to father long-term benefits.

Task 6: Write the Project Proposal

Following the selection of a good problem, you may need to write a project proposal that documents the expected effort. This proposal should document *what* is to be done, *why* the project is important, and *how* the effort will be performed. In the discussion of each of these points, the proposal should be brief and to the point. Figure 18.8 shows the basic format found in most proposals.

Objective

The objective is a statement that defines *what* will be achieved through the effort documented in the proposal. A premium should be placed on establishing a clear and concise objective. A good rule of thumb is that if the project's objective can be stated in one sentence, then it probably is one problem. If more sentences are needed then it is likely more than one problem.

Overview

The overview provides a high-level view of the problem and proposed solution. This section should begin with a background discussion on the problem that includes:

- General nature of the problem.
- Impact the problem has on the organization.
- Review of prior attempts (if any) to solve the problem.

A general discussion should then be given on the proposed expert system effort that includes:

- General nature of the system.
- What the system will do.
- Why the system is of value.

This section might also include a review of prior expert systems developed either on the same problem or in the same general area. This brief review would enhance the reader's confidence in the likelihood of success of the project.

This section will primarily serve the interests of management within the organization. It is therefore particularly important that this section explains clearly *what* will be done and *why* it is of value. The success of winning management's support, and the subsequent funding of the project, will depend on how effectively these points are conveyed. Since this section is mainly for the consumption of management, it is often called the "executive summary."

It should also be mentioned that this section is not the place to describe in detail *how* the project will accomplish its objective. Details on how the system will be built to meet project specifications should be described later in the

PROJECT PROPOSAL

OBJECTIVE

1. Statement of what will be done.
2. One sentence for one problem.

OVERVIEW

1. High-level view of project.
2. General problem and solution discussion.
3. Provides reference to past work.
4. Explains in general what will be done.
5. Discusses why the project is of value.

PROBLEM

1. Detailed description of problem.
2. Discusses current operations and problems.
3. Describes the assessment effort.

SOLUTION

1. Discusses what the expert system will do.
2. Describes how the system will accomplish objectives.
3. Lists necessary project resources.

PLAN

1. Lists and discusses project major phases.

SCHEDULE

1. Expected time periods for project's major phases.

DELIVERABLES

1. Lists deliverable items of project.

PERSONNEL

1. Lists project personnel.
2. Provides personnel vitae.

COSTS

1. Lists project costs on various items.

FIGURE 18.8   Expert system project proposal form.

proposal. If this section contains detailed technical information, it will only serve to confuse the reader.

Problem

This section describes the problem in detail. A discussion should be given on current operations and any shortcomings in performing them (or ways of improving them). If appropriate, this section should also describe the assessment effort that led to the identification of this problem as a candidate for expert system application.

Solution

This section describes *what* the expert system will do and *how* it will accomplish the task. It should provide the reader a feeling of credibility in the proposed effort. This section should also provide a listing of necessary project resources, such as the name of the domain expert and computer hardware/software requirements. In addition, if special constraints are placed on the use of the system, such as the need for a run-time version or licensing agreements, they should be discussed in this section.

Plan

This section lists and discusses the specific tasks or phases of the project proposal. A suggested outline is to follow the phases discussed in this chapter, such as knowledge acquisition, design, etc. Within the discussion of each of these phases, details should be provided that follow the discussion given for each phase in this chapter.

Schedule

Most organizations like to see a graph that illustrates the project's schedule. This includes the expected time periods of the various phases listed in the "plan" section.

Deliverables

Include a list of items that you expect to deliver at the end of the project. The two major deliverables on the project will be the final report and the expert system software.

Personnel

This section lists the personnel who will execute the project. It includes a listing of the principal investigator and other individuals who will have responsibilities for the development or testing of the system. A short resume should also be provided for each individual. Keep the resumes focused on past work that is related to the project.

Costs

This section provides a breakdown in the project's costs that includes labor costs, material costs, etc.

Lessons Learned from R1/XCON

As a postscript to the problem assessment discussion, it is worth further exploring the issue of obtaining the support of individuals within the organization for the project. Even a technically brilliant expert system may not save a project that has been damaged from loss of support.

One of the best examples of the importance of winning support for an expert system project can be found in the work by McDermott on the development of R1 (McDermott 1981). R1, later called XCON, is an expert system developed for Digital Equipment Corp. (DEC) to aid in the configuration of VAX computer systems. DEC offers a large number of components that can be configured in a number of ways to complete a system. DEC personnel work with a client to configure the system to meet all of the client's needs. Configuring a system is a complicated and time consuming task and DEC was looking for a better solution. McDermott reported;

> *"The only reason we were asked to build the expert system was that the problem was bothering some people enough so that they were willing to try anything."*

Even though they were willing to give expert systems a try, McDermott realized the importance of not over-selling the capability of the technology. He recognized that DEC's problem was a difficult one, and if he promised more than could be delivered, he would soon lose support for the project. The capabilities as well as the limitations of the system were explained to DEC management. This factor is important in order to avoid overly optimistic expectations from a system coming with the label of "artificial intelligence."

LESSON 1: DON'T OVERSELL THE TECHNOLOGY

Explain the capabilities and limitations of expert systems.

R1 usually did what was expected of it, therefore it never made enemies. McDermott's experience convinced him that not making enemies is just as important as making friends. R1's position at DEC was tenuous enough that if a few individuals believed that it was a mistake to continue its development, the project would have ended.

Even with the willingness to try anything to solve the problem, McDermott also recognized that some individuals would be initially skeptical of the new technology. McDermott reports;

"Despite the seriousness of the problem, no one at Digital was prepared to fund the development of a knowledge-based configurer until after the demonstration version of XCON had been implemented."

He felt that until some positive results were obtained, this skepticism would remain. He recognized that even small successes from early demonstrations could stem the tide of skepticism.

LESSON 2: REMOVE SKEPTICISM

Use demonstrations to remove skepticism.

Following early successful demonstrations of the system, the skepticism of individuals within DEC was replaced not with belief, but with caution. Each successful demonstration convinced them that the system had promise.

McDermott recognized that one factor that worked to the benefit of the project was that the individuals at DEC who worked closely with the project were open to change. These individuals were receptive to a new technology and were willing to accept any small failures along the way. This situation is not always present in an expert system project, but it is an important factor for you to consider.

LESSON 3: MOTIVATE CHANGE

Establish an atmosphere conducive to change.

Any change can be initially disruptive to the operations of an organization. However, if you can convince individuals that the short-term inconvenience will result in long-term improvements, then you will have helped to create a supportive atmosphere for the project.

PHASE 2: KNOWLEDGE ACQUISITION

Overview

Following the assessment phase, your next task is *knowledge acquisition*. This task is the most difficult challenge in the development of an expert system. Because of this difficulty, Chapter 17 was devoted to the subject. In this chapter, we review the highlights of this subject.

Knowledge Acquisition Process

Knowledge acquisition is inherently a cyclical process. It follows the tasks of knowledge collection, its interpretation and analysis, and the design of methods for collecting additional knowledge.

Collection is the task of acquiring knowledge from the expert. This effort requires training in interviewing techniques. It also requires good interpersonal communication skills and the ability to obtain the expert's cooperation.

Interpretation of the collected information involves the identification of key pieces of knowledge, such as concepts, rules, strategies, etc.

Analysis involves the study of the key pieces of knowledge uncovered during the interpretation task. This effort provides insight into forming theories on the organization of the knowledge and problem-solving strategies.

Design is the task of preparing for the next meeting with the expert. Following the completion of the prior tasks, a new understanding of the problem is formed. This effort may have exposed new concepts that need further exploration. Knowledge elicitation techniques are then chosen to obtain this information during the next meeting.

Problems with Knowledge Acquisition

There are many problems with knowledge acquisition that make it a difficult task. Most of these troubles can be traced to the difficulty in extracting knowledge from an expert.

Unaware of knowledge—Through experience with solving a problem, an expert often compiles the problem-solving knowledge into a compact form, which permits efficient problem solving. If the expert is asked to describe his problem-solving methods, he will often make mental leaps over important issues.

Unable to verbalize knowledge—Many tasks are difficult to verbalize because they were learned by watching another individual perform the task. Manual labor efforts typify this type of task.

Provides irrelevant knowledge—Many elicitation sessions may be held with the expert during the project. After a time, the amount of information collected may be overwhelming. To make matters worse, much of this information may be irrelevant to the project. The task is to sift through all of this information and pick out only the important issues.

Provides incomplete knowledge—An expert may often provide an incomplete description of his or her mental processes. If the problem is a simple omission, the situation may be easily corrected. However, if it occurs because the expert is unaware of the knowledge used (compilation problem), the challenge can be far greater.

Provides incorrect knowledge—An expert may provide incorrect knowledge either because he or she is uninformed or because of a simple mistake during introspection. In either case, this leads to an incomplete body of knowledge in the expert system.

Provides inconsistent knowledge—Knowledge provided by the expert may be inconsistent with earlier statements.This problem frequently occurs when the expert provides an explanation of their problem-solving strategy.

Cooperative Team Effort

The success of the knowledge elicitation process will depend greatly on forming a team of individuals who are both skillful and cooperative. Each team member is responsible for tasks that overlap the tasks of others. Considerable interaction can be expected and it is important to nurture the sometimes fragile spirit of cooperation.

Interviewing Technique

The most common knowledge elicitation technique used today in the design of expert systems is the interview method. This technique involves a direct interaction between the expert and the knowledge engineer, where questions are asked to uncover the knowledge. To make this effort productive, the interview must be managed effectively.

Managing the interview properly requires that several points be addressed. Some of the basic ones relate to items such as preparing the agenda, scheduling the session, and preparing a materials list. Other issues are more intangible, but important to the effort. Knowing how to effectively begin, conduct, and end the interview, are important considerations for both acquiring the desired information and maintaining cooperation of the team members. Also important is knowing how to ask questions in a manner that will provide the desired information.

Different interviewing techniques exist for gaining certain types of knowledge and for avoiding some of the typical problems associated with knowledge elicitation. Chapter 17 discussed in detail the various techniques and also provided guidelines for effectively implementing each.

Knowledge Analysis

Following the interview, the collected information needs to be analyzed. The objectives of this effort are to determine what was learned and what additional issues should be pursued.

Usually a transcript is first made of a recording of the session. This transcript is then reviewed to identify the key pieces of knowledge, e.g., concepts, rules, etc. These pieces of knowledge are then analyzed to form theories on their organization and how they relate to what is already known about the problem. These pieces of knowledge are also added to the project documentation in a manner discussed later in this chapter.

One approach that can help in analyzing the collected knowledge is to record the collected information graphically. Graphical representations in the form of concept maps, inference networks, flowcharts, and decision trees can be of particular value.

PHASE 3: DESIGN

Overview

Following only a few knowledge acquisition sessions with the expert, you will have enough of an understanding of the problem to begin designing the expert system. This task starts with the selection of the knowledge representation technique and control strategy. This is followed with the selection of a software tool that best meets the needs of the problem. A small prototype system is then built to both validate the project and to provide guidance for future work. The system is then further developed and refined to meet the project objectives. This process is structured according to the following tasks:

Task 1: Select knowledge representation technique
Task 2: Select control technique
Task 3: Select expert system development software
Task 4: Develop the prototype
Task 5: Develop the interface
Task 6: Develop the product

Task 1: Selecting Knowledge Representation Technique

Ideally, you should choose a knowledge representation technique that best matches the way the expert mentally models the problem's knowledge. This approach offers the greatest likelihood of success. However, for practical reasons, you will also have to consider the organization's resources and capabilities.

The organization may already have a software tool with a given knowledge representation technique. Available resources, such as the computer the system will operate on and the amount to spend on the software, will also play deciding roles.

You can never escape these pragmatic considerations when choosing the knowledge representation technique. However, if you choose a technique to satisfy the available resources, but recognize that it is wrong for the problem, you will likely run into difficulties later due to the mismatch.

Earlier chapters described in detail the knowledge representation techniques commonly used in the development of an expert system. In addition, these chapters described when a given technique is appropriate. Let's review the highlights of these earlier discussions.

A **frame-based** approach is appropriate if the expert describes the problem by referencing important objects and their relationships, particularly if the state of one object affects other objects. This situation is found in simulation type problems or ones where causal relationships are important.

Another sign that a frame-based approach may be a good choice is that the expert considers several similar objects when solving the problem. A frame-based system can reason about similar objects using only a few pattern-matching rules that work across a class of objects. This provides an efficient approach to the coding of both the objects and the rules.

A **rule-based** approach is suitable if the expert discusses the problem primarily using IF/THEN type statements. This discussion will usually lack an in-depth description of the problem's objects, which would justify the need for a frame-based approach. Classification problems are typical of this situation where the expert tries to classify the state of some issue according to available information.

The **induction** approach is of value if past examples of the problem exist. These examples can be used to induce either a set of rules or a decision tree that captures the problem-solving knowledge. Induction can also be of value when a rule-based approach has run into problems on some issue. If a set of examples exist that address this issue, then the rules induced from this set can be incorporated into a rule-based system. Induction is also appropriate if no real expert exists on the problem, but a history of problem information is available that can be used to automatically derive decision-making procedures.

Task 2: Selecting Control Technique

Following discussions with the expert you should also have some initial insight into how the system's knowledge can best be controlled. To help this effort, ask the expert to work through a typical problem. Listen to how the expert collects information and reasons with it to solve the problem. Also listen to see if the expert uses some global strategy. That is, does he first work on one part of the problem before proceeding to other parts? Your decision on control will center on the choice of the inference technique and the goal agenda. Chapter 4 provided details for making these choices.

Forward chaining is appropriate if the expert first collects information about the problem and then sees what can be concluded. In this situation the data is driving the reasoning process. Another tip that this approach may be a good one is to look at the number of pieces of data that the expert considers versus the number of possible solutions. If the amount of data is far smaller then the number of solutions, think about trying a forward chaining approach.

Backward chaining is a good choice if the expert first considers some conclusion or goal, then attempts to prove it by searching for supporting information.

In this case, the expert is mainly concerned with proving some hypothesis or recommendation. Also, if the number of goals is much fewer than the amount of possible data, then consider a backward chaining approach.

Goal agendas capture the global problem solving approach used by the expert. The agenda may be a simple sequential series of goals to pursue, or it may be more complex, where the goals pursued can adapt to the information gained during the session. A flowchart of the expert's global problem-solving strategy will provide you with guidance for designing the goal agenda.

Problem-Solving Paradigms

Another way you can gain insight into choosing both the knowledge representation technique and the inference strategy is to review what others have done in the past for similar efforts. One approach, first suggested by Hayes–Roth et al. (1983), categorizes generic tasks into a list of problem-solving paradigms (shown in Table 18.1).

TABLE 18.1 Types of Problems Solved by Expert Systems (ADAPTED FROM Hayes–Roth et al. 1983)

Problem-Solving Paradigm	Description
Control	Governing system behavior to meet specifications
Design	Configuring objects under constraint
Diagnosis	Inferring system malfunctions from observables
Instruction	Diagnosing, debugging, and repairing student behavior
Interpretation	Inferring situation description from data
Monitoring	Comparing observations to plan vulnerabilities
Planning	Designing actions
Prediction	Inferring likely consequences of given situations
Prescription	Recommending solution to system malfunction
Selection	Identifying best choice from a list of possibilities
Simulation	Modeling interaction between system components

One idea behind this list is that experts solve problems differently, depending on the type of task. For example, a mechanic diagnosing a problem with an automobile will collect and reason with information using techniques different from those used by a financial counselor planning a client's investment strategies.

Also implied in this list is that problems sharing the same problem-solving paradigm are solved in similar ways, even though the problem areas may be considerably different. For example, a mechanic diagnosing a car uses strategies similar to a doctor diagnosing a patient.

Following these same ideas, expert system designers often choose knowledge representation and control techniques on the basis of the problem solving paradigm. These choices rely on past successes. For example, diagnostic systems have traditionally used backward chaining while control systems have relied on forward chaining. It should also be mentioned that many systems incorporate multiple paradigms. For example, a control problem may require the monitoring of sensors, sensor data interpretation, and planning of control actions.

Past attempts have been made to relate each paradigm to various features that may be desirable in the design of the expert system (Gevarter 1987, Martin and Law 1988). Following this same approach, a review was made of the past expert system projects listed in Appendix C in an attempt to match each project's problem-solving approach to the knowledge representation and control techniques employed. The result of this effort is shown in Figure 18.9.

PROBLEM TYPE VERSUS INFERENCE AND KNOWLEDGE REPRESENTATION					
PROBLEM TYPE	**INFERENCE**		**KNOWLEDGE REPRESENTATION**		
	BACKWARD	FORWARD	RULES	FRAMES	INDUCTION
Control	Low	High	High	Avg.	Low
Design	Low	High	High	Low	Low
Diagnosis	High	Low	High	Avg.	Avg.
Instruction	High	Avg.	High	Avg.	Low
Interpretation	Avg.	High	High	Low	High
Monitoring	Low	High	High	Avg.	Low
Planning	Low	High	High	Avg.	Low
Prediction	Avg.	High	High	Low	High
Prescription	Avg.	Avg.	High	Low	Low
Selection	High	Low	High	Low	Avg.
Simulation	Low	High	Avg.	High	Low

FIGURE 18.9   Problem type versus inference and knowledge representation.

The results of Figure 18.9 were compiled as follows. The various projects listed in Appendix C were studied to first determine what problem-solving paradigms were used during the effort. For each identified paradigm, a further attempt was made to determine what type of inference and knowledge representation technique was used. Following this effort, the inference and knowledge representation techniques used for each paradigm identified for all of the projects were then tabulated. This tabulation was then employed to judge if the technique was used often (High), on average (Average) or infrequently (Low). Figure 18.9 can serve as a guide in selecting the initial inference and knowledge representation techniques.

Task 3: Selecting Expert System Development Software

After you have some understanding of how to represent and control the problem's knowledge, your next task is to select the software for developing the expert system. During this effort, attempts are made to match the features of the problem with the capabilities of available software. This effort will also have to consider the practical issues of available resources and programming skills.

There are a large variety of expert system development software tools available. They range from basic programming languages to high-level development shells. They also run on a variety of computers, ranging from PCs to mainframes. Appendix B provides a catalog of the available software.

Categories of Software

Figure 18.10 shows the general classes of expert system software. This software naturally splits into the categories of languages and shells.

Typical languages used for creating a rule-based expert system are LISP, Prolog, OPS, and C. Frame-based or object systems typically use C++, Flavors, or Smalltalk. Each of these languages provides the designer the flexibility of developing the system to meet specific project specifications. However, they also require that the designer has programming skills in the chosen language.

Shells provide the designer an established environment for creating the system. They provide the knowledge representation structure, inference engine, explanation facility and interface. They may also provide specific facilities that enhance the development and debugging efforts. In general, shells can be categorized into rule-based systems, frame-based systems, induction systems, or hybrid systems. Hybrid systems are software tools that combine different knowledge representation techniques. Shells are valuable in easing the development effort and for rapidly prototyping the system. They may be more constraining than a language approach, but this is offset by the ease of system development that they offer.

Important Software Features

A number of studies have evaluated various expert system development software packages. Most of these studies list the currently available software along with

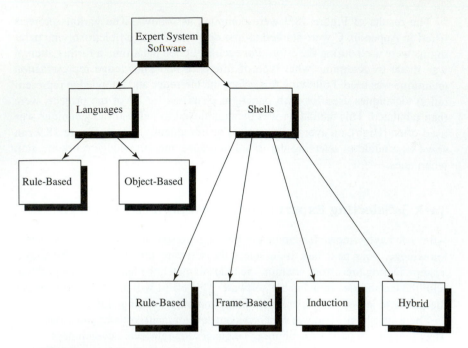

FIGURE 18.10 Expert system software categories.

a discussion of their various features. This information can help you choose the software that best matches the needs of the problem. There are many features that you should consider when reviewing the available software. We will review some of the more important ones.

General

C O S T   Costs of expert system development software vary to a large degree. Some languages and small shells can be purchased for several hundred dollars, while large hybrid tools can cost up to $50,000. The price will also vary greatly according to the chosen platform. Typically, the same software running on a mainframe or workstation can cost several times the amount for the PC version.

The expert system shell market is rapidly evolving. The power and flexibility of this software have improved while the price has decreased. This trend can be seen with the introduction of frame-based software at the PC level. For years, frame-based software was available only for mainframes or workstations, at a considerable cost. Today, you can purchase this software for the PC at a cost below $1,000. This evolution of the market has made available to a large number of knowledge engineers the opportunity to create powerful systems at a reasonable cost.

COMPUTER HARDWARE   Expert system software tools run on an variety of computers:

- Personal computers, including IBM and compatibles, and the Macintosh
- Mini and mainframes
- Workstations
- LISP machines

As previously mentioned, some shells run on different computers and will in general cost less if purchased for a smaller system. This can be of particular value in some applications where the cheaper version can be purchased initially and used to develop the prototype on the smaller system. Following successful development, the system can then be ported to the larger computer.

LICENSE   Make sure you clearly understand your legal obligations when you purchase software to develop the expert system. These obligations will impact on how you are permitted to develop and distribute the system. Software vendors have a wide range of license agreements.

When you are developing the system, most vendors will limit the use of the software to one computer. Site licenses are often available that permit the software to be used on several computers.

After the expert system is developed, you will want to distribute it to the end-users. How this is done will depend on the software purchased. Most vendors require you to purchase a distribution license. The cost of this license can vary considerably. Some vendors offer a one-time cost with unlimited distribution rights. In some cases, the vendor offers a runtime version of the software that you need to purchase for each copy distributed.

TRAINING/SUPPORT   Many organizations feel it is important that their employees receive training on the chosen software. They believe that a short but intensive course on the software will allow their employees to quickly begin work on the system, which may pay dividends in the long-term. Some vendors provide training on their product, while others rely on a third-party to provide this training.

Expert system shells can be difficult to use at times. In these situations it is important that you have someone to turn to for help. This help can come in the form of software support. Some vendors provide no assistance for their product. In other cases, support is available but only if you pay a yearly maintenance fee. In a few cases—if your lucky—assistance is free.

Developer Interface

Expert system shells offer a variety of features to aid in the design and testing of the system. We will review some of the more important ones that you should consider when selecting a shell.

CODING KNOWLEDGE   There are two ways by which shells permit the developer to code the knowledge. Some shells require the developer to write source code that captures both the knowledge and its control. This approach is very similar to the writing of standard source code for a conventional program, where a text file is created and compiled. Other shells use a ''smart'' editor approach. The shell provides the developer a template for creating rules or frames and other control type knowledge.

INEXACT REASONING   For many problems you will need to use an inexact reasoning technique. Chapters 11 through 13 described the three most common techniques used in expert system design: Bayesian, certainty theory, and fuzzy logic. Each technique offers certain advantages for a given problem.

Most of the software tools use some form of the certainty theory. A few employ Bayesian or fuzzy logic. Most tools offer only one form of inexact reasoning, but during the next decade, it is expected that they will begin offering multiple options.

RULE SETS   Earlier chapters argued the importance of designing the expert system in modular form. That is, each module should contain a set of rules designed to address one important issue on the problem. This approach not only makes designing the system easier, it also eases the testing and maintenance tasks.

Most of the tools that permit the use of separate rule sets require the developer to write individual knowledge bases that are loaded into the session when needed. In this situation, the newly loaded knowledge base may be the only one available. This approach requires the developer to include a *blackboard* that retains the session's context so it can be used by the new knowledge base.

EXTERNAL PROGRAM ACCESS   Most of the early shells were stand-alone tools. The shell-developed expert system worked exclusively with information supplied by the user. Many shells available today have an open architecture that permits the system to access and supply information to external programs. The shells can access or change information in databases or spreadsheets, such as dBASE and Lotus. They can also execute external procedural programs, such as C, Pascal, Fortran, or LISP, allowing the expert system to perform extensive numeric or symbolic computations.

DEBUGGING UTILITIES   Many of the shells provide debugging utilities to help during the design and testing of an expert system. These utilities are valuable for large knowledge bases, where it becomes difficult to keep track of what knowledge has been coded and how it is being used by the inference engine.

One common utility found in many shells is a tracing feature. This feature traces through the knowledge used during a session, using a technique very much like a *how* explanation. You can use the trace to uncover the piece of knowledge that led to a problem.

Another debugging utility (unfortunately not found in many shells) is called a consistency checker. It checks the entry of new knowledge to see if it is consistent with existing knowledge. There are several ways of checking the consistency of knowledge. To see the value of this utility, we will look at one approach. Assume the following rule exists in the knowledge base:

IF The cup contains water
THEN You can drink from it

Next assume the following rule is entered later:

IF The cup contains acid
THEN You can drink from it

A software tool equipped with a consistency checker would flag this new rule as being inconsistent with prior knowledge. The developer would then have the opportunity to correct any obvious problems. Notice in this example there is obvious trouble. However, the consistency checker may detect other apparent inconsistencies that are logically correct. In this case, the developer can simply override the warning and retain the added knowledge.

User Interface

When designing an expert system, you must also consider how the user will interact with the system. Shells provide a variety of features to tailor the interface. We will next discuss some of the more important ones to consider when selecting a shell.

QUESTIONS   Shells provide various ways of asking questions. Simple TRUE or FALSE responses or a menu of possible values may be provided. In addition, some tools allow the user to type a response to a given question.

Most shells can generate the question automatically. They use a predefined script and associate it with text related to the needed information. Though this feature alleviates the need for you to design the question, it often leads to an awkward question. Some shells permit you to write the question. You can tailor the text to present the user an easy-to-understand question.

EXPLANATIONS   One of the basic characteristics of an expert system is its ability to explain its reasoning. The system can explain *why* a question is being asked and *how* a given conclusion was reached. Most shells respond to a *why* question by displaying the current rule the system is pursuing. The response to a *how* question is usually a trace of the rules that established a conclusion.

GRAPHICS   Several shells offer a graphical user interface. These shells include a variety of graphical objects such as buttons, meters, etc., that you can use when designing the interface. The end-user can use these objects to enter information or observe system findings.

HYPERTEXT   A feature recently introduced in several shells is hypertext. Hypertext is a collection of nodes of text linked together on an associative basis. You can read the text in one node and branch to another one that has associated information. Using hypertext with an expert system has two major benefits.

First, when the user is answering a question or reviewing a final result, he or she can jump over to the hypertext node related to the material being displayed to obtain further information. For example, if the user is being asked a question, he or she can obtain information that may better clarify the question, or obtain insight into why the question was asked.

Second, due to the associative nature of a hypertext structure, the user can explore the hypertext world before returning to the expert system. This ability provides the user an opportunity to learn about the problem while using the expert system. This is a highly desirable goal since we would like the expert system to not only solve some problem, but also allow the user to learn about the domain so that the problem might be avoided in the future.

Task 4: Prototype Development

Following the selection of the software that best meets the requirements of the project, system development is begun. The details of the approach taken will depend on the type of system being developed. Chapters 8 and 10 provided details for developing rule-based systems, Chapter 14 for frame-based systems, and Chapter 16 for induction systems. In this chapter, we review some of the general development issues common to all expert systems.

Most expert system projects begin the development effort by building a small prototype system. A prototype is a model of the final system. Its basic structure, in terms of the way it represents and processes the problem's knowledge, is the same as expected in the final system. Though the prototype is only a small version of the final system and has limited ability, if properly designed, it will serve the following purposes:

- Validates the expert system approach.
- Confirms the choice of the knowledge representation technique and control strategies.
- Provides a vehicle for knowledge acquisition.

Define Global Strategy

One of the better places to start the design of the prototype is to define a global strategy. This strategy is a series of high level tasks that the system will need to perform. Consider for example a system designed to diagnose automobile problems. The expert might provide the following general approach to the problem:

1. I first look to see how the car is performing.
2. I next attempt to isolate the problem to one of the car's major systems.
3. I then try to determine the specific problem.
4. Finally, I attempt to fix the problem.

This series of tasks provides a high-level view of the problem-solving approach. Each task may require considerable decision making to accomplish. However, you should not be concerned about the details at this point. Rather, you need general insight into how you might structure the problem solving approach.

Each task in the global strategy represents a goal for the system to achieve. Collectively, they form an agenda for the system. For simple agendas such as in this example, a small list of tasks will do. For more complex agendas, you may want to create a flowchart. In either case, after the agenda is formulated, ask the expert to verify it before coding it into the expert system.

Define Knowledge Structure

During prototype development you should create a framework that accommodates future changes. A well-structured expert system will ease both the development and maintenance efforts.

Plans for maintaining the expert system begin during the prototyping phase. Many knowledge engineers think about how to maintain the system following the overall development effort. At this point, they may be staring at a complex knowledge base that is difficult to follow. This situation will severely hinder future maintenance efforts. If the system is well-structured, where the system's knowledge and control can be easily inspected and changed, then the maintenance effort will be eased.

Details on how to design a well-structured expert system were given in earlier chapters for rule-based, frame-based, and induction systems. In the next sections we consider some of the more important general issues.

Static Knowledge

A good way to begin forming the knowledge structure is to list the problem's major objects and their attributes. This step is natural for frame-based systems but is also of value for rule-based or induction ones as well. You will also want to note any relationships between objects. This effort can be aided by forming a cognitive map as discussed in Chapter 17.

This information represents the static knowledge about the problem that was compiled during the knowledge acquisition phase. During the design phase, you encode the knowledge structure into the expert system. For a frame-based system, this process is straightforward. Classes and associated objects are designed, along with corresponding attributes. For a rule-based or induction system, this information serves as a source for encoding the rules or decision tables.

Dynamic Knowledge

You should next form a good structure for the dynamic or problem-solving knowledge. This is the knowledge that will achieve each task on the agenda. The approach taken will depend on several factors, such as the chaining method, message passing, etc. The key point to keep in mind is that you want the knowledge to be easily expandable. In general, the system's knowledge is expanded by making it either deeper or broader. That is, you make the system smarter about what it already knows (deeper), or about some new issue (broader).

Details for creating a good knowledge structure for problem solving were given in earlier chapters for each type of expert system. A common theme in all of these discussions is that the structure should support a "concept-driven" expansion approach. All expert systems attempt to form an understanding of various concepts before solving the overall problem. Within each expert system, you can think of actually having multiple systems each dedicated to a given concept. If each of these seemingly embedded systems is structured well, then both expanding and maintaining the system will be made easier.

This idea is best illustrated through an example. Consider a rule taken from MYCIN:

IF   The stain of the organism is grampos
AND   The morphology of the organism is coccus
AND   The growth of the organism is chains
THEN There is evidence that the organism is streptococcus

Each premise in this rule refers to a given concept related to the organism, i.e., stain, morphology, and growth. The system would need other rules that could establish information on each concept. In a sense, the system has embedded three other expert systems, each designed around one of these concepts.

During the development of the system, each of these three systems may be developed independently. This may require you to write three different knowledge bases or simply a good partitioning of rule sets. An added benefit of this structure is that each individual system can be used for other purposes. For example, if another expert system was developed and needed to know if "the stain of the organism is grampos," the code can be directly ported to the new application. This idea is similar to the use of subroutines found in conventional programming.

Validate Project

Following the project assessment effort performed in Phase 1, you should have some idea whether an expert system approach to the selected problem should be effective. However, until the system demonstrates some success in solving the problem, there will continue to remain a degree of uncertainty. Testing the prototype can help to validate the project. Prototype testing occurs in three stages.

In the first stage, attempts are made to test the complete knowledge base for logic and consistency. The exhaustive nature of this test is only possible early in the project when the knowledge base is small. This testing uncovers deficiencies in the knowledge and reasoning strategies, and validates the choice of the knowledge representation technique and development software.

The second stage of testing is more of a demonstration of the system. Its purpose is to remove any possible skepticism for the project that might be held by individuals within the organization. Though the system will have limited capability in its prototype form, a successful demonstration on some small problem will nurture support for the project.

Eventually the prototype will mature to the point where it can attack real problems from the domain. In this stage of testing, we want to compare the system's results with those of the expert. This testing validates the system's performance and provides insight into remaining deficiencies.

These are the three primary tests performed on the prototype. There are other tests performed after the system has evolved into more of a production model. We will review all of these tests in more detail later in the chapter.

Throw Prototype Away?

One typical difficulty that may be discovered following the testing of the prototype is that the original choice of the software development tool was a poor one. For example, it may be found that the knowledge representation technique or inference method is inappropriate. If this problem occurs then a decision must be made: should you throw the prototype away and start over with another tool? In general, the answer to this question is yes.

This recommendation may at first seem unnerving, since it requires the abandonment of previously developed code. However, in the long run, the development effort will be far easier if the tool matches the features of the problem. Attempting to force an ill-chosen tool to fit a problem it was not designed to handle will only cause more trouble. You should realize that the primary purpose of the prototype is to provide an understanding of the problem and ways to solve it with an expert system. When you recode the system using another tool, you bring with you this understanding.

Vehicle for Knowledge Acquisition

As discussed several times throughout this book, the most difficult task in developing an expert system is acquiring the knowledge. In Chapter 17, dedicated to this subject, some of the common knowledge acquisition techniques are introduced and guidelines provided for effectively implementing each. Beyond the techniques introduced in Chapter 17, it is also fruitful to use the prototype system as a vehicle for acquiring knowledge.

By its nature, a prototype system is only a small rendition of the final system. The limits of its knowledge on the problem become quickly apparent during testing, where failures are the norm. With the cooperation of the expert, a postmortem study of these failures opens the door to additional knowledge. The expert can help to determine why the result given by the system is wrong, and provide insight into what knowledge is missing in the system that prevented it from reaching the correct result. In this fashion, the prototype acts as another tool the knowledge engineer can use to probe for additional knowledge.

A good example of how a prototype was used this way is XCON, which configures DEC's VAX-11/780 computer systems (McDermott 1981). The original prototype of XCON contained only a couple of hundred rules that handled about 100 different components. However, DEC has over 400 components. Therefore, XCON could only configure the simplest computer systems.

The XCON prototype was given several orders to configure and the expert was asked to comment on the results. The expert was able to point out what was unacceptable and provide insight into what knowledge the system lacked using IF/THEN type statements. For example, the expert might state "IF the system knew this THEN it would know it should be doing that." Using this information new rules were added to XCON, which eventually grew into a several thousand rule system.

Task 5: Interface Development

One pitfall many knowledge engineers fall into is waiting until later in the project to address the design of the system's interface. At this point it may be discovered that the interface cannot be designed with the existing software to satisfy the needs of the user.

Interface specifications should be defined at the beginning of the project with the cooperation of the user. Development of the interface should begin with the prototype development of the expert system. The interface should not be an afterthought, but an integral part of the expert system development process.

In later sections we will review specific points on how to design the interface to meet the needs of the user. In the following sections we review some of the general issues to consider in order to best present the interface to the user. The keys to effective interface design are:

- Consistency
- Clarity
- Control

Consistent Screen Format

The presentation of the interface is as important as the information it contains. Henkel (1984) addressed this point:

> "*The most powerful force in conjuring and maintaining the user's mental model of the computer system is the visual appearance of the user interface.*"

One of the keys to good interface design is *consistency*. Each screen usually has certain types of material to present, such as a title, questions, area for answers, and control functions. All screens should be designed so that similar material is placed in the same locations. The user will be able to develop a mental model of where to expect information. Moving on to the next screen, the user is prepared to find the needed information in the expected places. Interfaces that vary the location of information between screens can be frustrating and confusing to the user (Mackey and Slesnick 1982).

Clarity of Presented Material

As a user proceeds through a session with an expert system, a series of screens are displayed. Some of the screens ask questions, others provide explanation on the system's reasoning, and several include intermediate or final results. If the material in these screens is presented in a clear manner, the user will be receptive to the system, and the reliability of the exchange of information between the user and system will be enhanced.

Asking clear questions is the most important issue to consider. Questions that are confusing or poorly designed, can lead to errors in the user's response. This further leads to erroneous findings by the expert system—a garbagein/garbageout characteristic that expert systems share with conventional programs. Ways to avoid a poorly designed question are discussed later under the topic of testing of an expert system (Phase 4).

Providing clear explanations and results depends on the chosen development software and the needs of the application. Software capabilities on these points were discussed previously, and application requirements are reviewed later in the Phase 4 discussion.

To avoid confusion, also keep the contents of each screen simple and unfluttered. It is often a temptation to present a lengthy discussion of a question or a result, or a number of graphics to convey the information in the screen. The screen may become too "busy" and the user will loose sight of its purpose. With each screen, provide the material that is necessary to accomplish the purpose of the screen—no more and no less. During system testing, the user will be able to help on this point.

Screen Control

The user must always feel in control when consulting with an expert system. In addition, the user should not be afraid that a mistake that he or she might make could result in disastrous consequences. These two requirements place additional demands on the design of the interface.

At a minimum, make the system easy to start and exit. The exit feature should be available in every screen. Also, make it easy for the user to access system explanations and utilities. All of these can be achieved through the use of function keys or designated control areas within the interface.

Preventing the user from making a serious mistake was put very simply by Peterson (1982):

> *"Don't give the naive or careless users the weapons they need to blow themselves out of the water."*

The best way of preventing this type of problem is to give the user a restrictive and error-catching interface. This can be accomplished using a "point-and-do" interaction technique. This type of interface allows the user to point to parts or objects on the screen to select the appropriate action. Devices such as a mouse, lightpen, or a touch screen are typically used in these applications.

One benefit of a point-and-do interface is that it can avoid problems that occur from typing errors with a text-based entry interface. Another advantage is that it avoids the need for the user to remember legal responses or system commands. This allows the user to concentrate on the problem rather than the control of the system (Henkel 1984).

When designing a point-and-do interface, there are a couple of points to consider. Each object on the screen the user is permitted to select should be represented in a way that clearly indicates what action will take place following its selection. This is a typical concern when designing icons for windowing environments.

Another important point to recognize is that no matter how well you design the interface, the user might still make a mistake when selecting an item. If the item selected can cause a major event (e.g., system exit), you should design a way of detecting the event and provide the user a caution message. For example;

"Are you sure you want to. . . ."

This allows the user to back out of mistakes safely.

Screen Colors

Though not often thought of as a key issue when designing the interface, the use of screen colors can have a positive impact on the effectiveness of the interface. However, if not used properly, they can do the opposite.

Many interfaces use various colors to enhance their appeal. Colors can also help to convey information, emphasize important points, and relate spatially separate items. If used correctly, colors can offer an attractive interface and improve the system's functionality.

Colors should be pleasant and appealing, but never at the expense of clear communications. You want the user's initial focus to be on the important parts of the screen, such as the question and answer portions. Do not let colors draw attention to unimportant items on the screen (Horton 1990). Also avoid irrelevant or unnecessary colors. If the color is not relevant to the task, it can interfere with the performance of the task (Christ 1975). It is also important to limit the number of colors used to present the material. Too many colors can impede reading speed and cause difficulty with interpreting the information (Carter 1982).

Task 6: Product Development

During the development of the prototype, knowledge elicitation sessions are held and tests are run, both of which are used to uncover new information to guide the design of the expert system. With each refinement, the system capability is improved. In an evolutionary fashion, the prototype system begins to take on the form of the final system. There is no fixed point where this transition occurs; the prototype gradually evolves into a completed system.

Knowledge Refinement

A basic characteristic of an expert system is that it gains its power from its knowledge. As the system's knowledge evolves, its performance likewise improves. This evolutionary process involves either broadening or deepening the system's knowledge base. Broadening teaches the system about something it doesn't know, while deepening makes it smarter about something it already knows about.

Knowledge is made broader by adding new concepts. Consider for example taking a child to a zoo to learn about animals, and assume that she knows only about tigers and bears. If we introduce her to a lion, and teach her characteristics of this new animal, then we are broadening her knowledge about the world of animals.

We perform the same type of development in an expert system when we broaden its knowledge. In rule-based systems, rules are added that cover this new knowledge. In frame-based systems, the new concept is added by generating a new class frame.

Deepening knowledge involves adding information that supports existing knowledge. Consider again the zoo example. Assume the child knows about tigers only from reading about them. We could deepen her knowledge about tigers by teaching her new characteristics, such as their size, the sounds they make, etc.

In rule-based systems, this type of development is performed by adding rules that support existing rules. In frame-based systems, new features are added to existing frames.

Control Refinement

An early version of an expert system usually includes simple control strategies. A choice of either backward or forward chaining might be made, along with a small set of goals. This is good way of starting the design, since in the beginning you want to determine if you are going in the right direction. As the project proceeds, you will see better ways of introducing more complex control strategies.

One area where refinements in the system's control can be expected is in the goal agenda. The goal agenda provides a list of goals that the system pursues in some set sequence. During the project, you may find a need to add goals to the agenda or to refine existing ones by splitting them into finer tasks.

You may also discover that the strict sequence of a goal agenda is too constraining for the application. In this event, you may want to make the goals sensitive to the session's context. This can be accomplished through the use of meta-rules. A meta-rule can be written to establish new goals or to load other knowledge bases on the basis of discovered information.

Though you may start with a single choice of backward or forward chaining, you may find a need to switch between them. This situation usually occurs if the problem involves several tasks, some of which can be better managed by one of the inference techniques. When this occurs, you should look to structure several knowledge bases, each with its own inference technique.

Frame-based systems offer still another way of refining the control using if-changed and if-needed facets. Facets of this type are demons that take some action whenever a frame's slot value changes or is needed. You can design these demons to establish new goals or to load in new knowledge bases. This approach offers you another way to design the expert system to be adaptable to the session's context.

Interface Refinement

In the initial stages of the project the end-user will help in defining interface specifications. As the system evolves new requirements may surface. It is therefore important to keep the end-user intimately involved throughout the development process.

As the end-user works with the system, he or she can highlight deficiencies in the interface and can also provide comments on the friendliness of the system. This feedback can be used to tailor the interface to meet the needs of the user. Some of the typical points on which the end-user can provide guidance are:

- Ease of use
- Screen directions
- Questions
- Clarifications
- Results
- Interactive techniques (mouse, lightpen, etc.)

Obtaining the user's comments on these issues can be done in an informal manner, where the user is simply asked to try out the system, or in a formal manner, where some structured test format is used. We will review these points in more detail later in this chapter during the discussion of system testing.

Inexact Reasoning

Some expert systems need to use an inexact reasoning technique. However, in the early stages of the project, you should be concerned about verifying the knowledge obtained from the expert in an "exact" sense. That is, facts, rules, or frames should be coded in the system in an exact manner. Testing of the system at this point should address the correctness of knowledge in a Boolean sense. The system's results and reasoning can be more easily verified if a logical approach is taken in the encoding of the knowledge. Following this verification step, inexact reasoning methods can be used to refine the system's performance.

——————— PHASE 4: TESTING ———————

Overview

As the project proceeds the expert system will need to be periodically tested and evaluated to assure that its performance is converging toward established goals. Decisions must be made on *what* will be tested, *how* and *when* the tests will be conducted, and *who* will be involved in the tests. It is important that these decisions be made early, at a time when the original project goals are established. Planning for the tests early is important because it will have an impact on design considerations when you know what will be tested and when.

The task of evaluating expert systems is unlike that found for conventional programs where the *verification* of the software is of primary concern. Verification studies attempt to determine whether the program completely satisfies initial requirements (Adrion et al. 1982). Conventional programs usually have well-defined specifications that can be measured according to some objective standard. Expert systems on the other hand are designed for problems that do not have a clear right or wrong answer. Therefore, a "gold standard" does not exist that can be compared with the system's results (Gaschnig et al. 1983).

Because of the lack of a gold standard, the evaluation process is more concerned with system *validation* and *user acceptance* (Preece 1990). Validation efforts determine if the system satisfactorily performs the intended task (Hollinger 1989)—a relaxation of the stricter verification process. User acceptance efforts are concerned with issues that impact how well the system addresses the needs of the user. The tasks of validation and user acceptance assessment are often subjective and make the evaluation of an expert system a complex effort.

System Validation

An expert system models the decision making of a human expert. If correctly designed, the system derives the same results as the expert and reasons in a manner similar to that of the expert. Therefore, validation efforts should address the following:

- Validate the system's results.
- Validate the system's reasoning process.

Validate Results

Formal testing of an expert system usually involves the use of a test case. A test case represents some past problem that was successfully solved and includes specific problem information with corresponding results. During testing, the problem information is given to the expert system and the system's recommendation is compared with results given in the test case by an individual called the "evaluator."

On the surface this validation approach seems simple enough. That is, if the two results agree, the evaluator considers the system correct, otherwise he or she concludes the system is wrong. However, this approach assumes the test case result is "gold" and any different answer is incorrect. However, the findings of an expert represent an *expert opinion* rather than a golden result.

There are three major considerations when designing a test to validate the results of an expert system:

- Selection of the test criterion
- Selection of the test cases
- Selection of the evaluators

Selecting Test Criterion

Every project has some goal to achieve. In order to judge whether the project has successfully met its goal, a criterion is usually established against which the project is assessed.

If the organization is using the technology to address a specific problem (problem driven), then establishing a test criterion is usually straightforward. That is, the system must demonstrate that it achieves some value as measured in such factors as cost savings, productivity enhancement, product quality improvement, etc. These are very tangible issues, but they are often difficult to measure until the system has been deployed in the field.

A different approach relies on comparing the system's performance relative to that of an expert in the field. This was the technique used to evaluate MYCIN as discussed in Chapter 5. Let's review some of the more important points of this evaluation study.

Relative Comparison

MYCIN was developed to diagnose infectious blood diseases and provide an acceptable therapeutic recommendation. During evaluation studies, prior test cases of patients suffering from meningitis were studied by several experts from the Stanford School of Medicine to determine the proper therapeutic recommendation. These same test cases were also evaluated by MYCIN. All of these recommendations were then evaluated by other individuals outside of Stanford who were experts on infectious diseases. These individuals, called the evaluators, were asked to form their own recommendation for each case and then to assess the prescriptions provided by the individuals from Stanford and MYCIN. The evaluators judged the Stanford experts correct in a range of 10% to 70% of the cases, and MYCIN at 70%—MYCIN did as well, or better, than the human experts.

Establish Reasonable Goals

Another conclusion can be drawn from the evaluation of MYCIN when we consider the initial expectations of the project. The original goal was for MYCIN to be correct in 90% of the cases. However, it can be argued that this 90% figure may have been unrealistic, as reflected by the performance of the experts in the evaluation study.

In general, you should establish an acceptable performance level for an expert system aligned with the performance of human experts on the problem.

Evaluation Requires Judgement

Mistakes that expert systems make can usually be measured in a degree of error. For example, during the evaluation of MYCIN, its performance on prescribing the correct antibiotic was assessed based on classifying the given prescription into one of three categories:

Equivalent: recommendation was identical to or equivalent to that given by the evaluator.

Acceptable Alternative: recommendation was different from the evaluator, but considered to be an acceptable alternative.

Not acceptable: recommendation was considered unacceptable or inappropriate by the evaluator.

In general, when evaluating the result provided by an expert system, you will need to make a judgment call on the correctness of the result. You could proceed as the MYCIN team did and provide the evaluators with a set of possible evaluation responses, or you might elect to allow the evaluators to score the result on some numeric scale. In either case, you can use the result to judge the performance of the system, and to decide whether further development is necessary.

Selecting the Test Cases

The selection of the test material to be used when evaluating an expert system is dependent on the original project specifications. For example, many expert systems are designed to unburden a user when working on routine problems, the intent being either to free the user from the task, or to make the task easier or quicker to solve. In these applications, the test material should be past test cases that are *typical* problems from the domain. The organization may feel that if the system can solve typical problems (e.g., 90% of the cases), the project is worthwhile. They accept in this case that the other more difficult problems (10% of the cases) would need to be managed by an expert.

In other applications, the organization wants the system to solve every possible problem. In this case, you will need to collect together both *typical* test cases and ones that are *unusual*. When working on an application with these demands, it is important that you first test the system for the typical problems before trying the more difficult ones. This point is discussed later in this chapter when we consider the evolution of system testing.

Selecting the Evaluators

Selecting who will evaluate the expert system is also dependent on the original project specifications. For a system designed to aid the expert on the project, a simple choice might be to use this individual. After all, if he or she is happy with the results, the project is deemed a success.

If the system is to be used by other experts, then the selection process becomes more complicated. First, you may need to rule out the simple approach of using the project's domain expert. This approach may be challenged because the expert is testing his own knowledge that was coded in the system. Arguments can be made that the expert's view of the problem reflects his own approach, which may run counter to the view of other experts.

For this situation, you will need to seek the aid of other experts who were not associated with the project. In the ideal case, you could follow the approach taken by the MYCIN team where several independent evaluators assessed the performance of MYCIN and other experts in the field, in order to judge the system's performance. The downside of this approach is that it is difficult to obtain the cooperation of so many individuals to participate in the evaluation study. Typically what is done is that one or two other experts are asked to test the system with their own test material (double-blind test)—the system is *blind* to the test material and the evaluator is *blind* to the system's knowledge.

If the system is to be used by nonexperts, then they must be part of the evaluation team. Prior to the introduction of the system, these individuals have standard procedures they follow to solve the problem being addressed. They sit in a good position to judge the merits of the system relative to the present techniques. They can provide comments on whether the system provides better results, quicker results, etc.

Avoid Potential Bias

One aspect of the evaluation study that you may need to consider is the possible presence of bias. The evaluators, consciously or not, may be biased against a computer program that is designed to model human decision making.

The MYCIN development team experienced this problem during the early stages of testing, where the evaluators knew they were reviewing the output of a computer program. Some of their criticisms reflected a bias toward the application of computers in the medical domain, as demonstrated by the following statement made by one of the evaluators: "I don't think the computer has an adequate sense of how sick this patient is. You'd have to see a patient like this in order to judge." (Hayes–Roth et al. 1983).

Because of this bias, later tests shuffled the MYCIN results with those from human experts. The evaluators were then *blind* in the sense that they didn't know if they were reviewing the results from a computer or a human. Using this approach, the results of the evaluation showed that MYCIN did as well as any of the human experts.

This blind evaluation study was inspired by the "Turing Test" (Turing 1950), where the response of a computer along with those from a human are presented to a blind evaluator. If an evaluator cannot distinguish the computer output from that of the human, then the computer is considered as intelligent as the human. Even though this approach is simple, it is intuitively appealing and widely accepted in the evaluation of expert systems.

Validate Reasoning

Besides evaluating an expert system's result, evaluators want to know if the system is getting the right answer for the right reasons. The main reason for this is the limited number of test cases that might actually be used during evaluation studies. Even if the system is correct in these few cases, there may remain some concern that similar successes might not be achieved for other cases, unless the underlying problem-solving approach is correct. Credibility in the system is established when the evaluators are convinced that correct performance is a product of intelligent reasoning.

Two approaches can be used to validate the system's reasoning. On the macrolevel, the evaluators can study the results of various subissues that led to the final recommendation. Most expert systems are designed to form an understanding of these issues before reaching a final result. For example, a financial planning system would need to consider such issues as income stability, level of investment risk, etc., before a final plan would be formed. A review of the findings of each of these issues for a given case can add to the credibility of the system.

On the microlevel, the evaluators can trace back through all of the rules used for the case that led to the result and verify their correctness. This approach is similar to that used by the system designer during the debugging of the knowledge base.

Learning from Mistakes

Cognitive psychologists have long recognized that one of the more valuable ways that people learn new concepts is from their mistakes (Bell and Hardiman 1989).

They study why they made a mistake and determine what information is missing that prevented them from getting the right answer.

You can use this same idea when testing an expert system to improve its performance. When the system makes a mistake, allow the expert to review the results and ask him or her to tell you (1) why the answer given is incorrect and (2) why the right answer was not given. You can use the information provided by the expert to improve the expert system in two ways: correct the knowledge that led to the mistake and add the needed knowledge to reach the right answer.

Ironically, one of the best things you can have in the early stages of a project is an expert system that makes mistakes. You can use the mistakes to learn more about the problem. In this sense, system testing becomes another technique for knowledge acquisition.

To illustrate this learning process, let's consider an expert system developed to provide stock investment recommendations. Assume that the issues to consider when providing these recommendations are market status, stock area, and desired annual return. These issues are shown in Figure 18.11 as part of the problem's inference network. Next assume that the system was tested leading to the following results in the working memory and a stock recommendation:

WORKING MEMORY: Market status appears bullish
Stock area recommendation domestic business
Annual return 8% to 15%
RECOMMENDATION: Buy GM

Now assume these test results are presented to the expert for comment:

KE: Do you agree with this result?
DE: No not really, it worries me a little.
KE: Let's look at the rule that led to this recommendation.

IF   Market status appears bullish
AND   Stock area recommendation is domestic business
AND   Desired annual return 8% to 15%
THEN Recommendation is buy GM

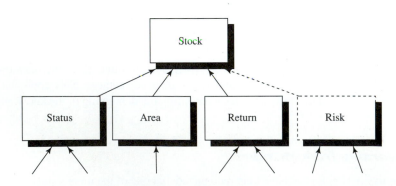

FIGURE 18.11   Stock inference network.

KE: For the information we used, do you agree that the premises should have been true?

DE: Yes.

KE: Do you agree with the rule?

DE: Almost. GM can sometimes be a risky investment. Before I would recommend it, I would want to make sure that the client was willing to take a risk.

KE: For our example, if they didn't want to take a risk what would you have recommended?

DE: Probably IBM

Through this effort we were able to find a problem with the system's knowledge and uncovered a new concept "risk" shown in dash in Figure 18.11. We could now add this new premise to the GM rule and question the expert further on the concept of risk and add the new information discovered to the knowledge base.

This example illustrates only one way where testing can aid the knowledge elicitation process. In general, using test results to probe for new information can provide several benefits:

- Discovers new concepts

- Discovers new rules

- Identifies incorrect or incomplete rules

- Identifies incorrect premises

The MYCIN development team took advantage of this idea to automate the knowledge acquisition process using a utility system called TEIRESIAS (Davis 1979). TEIRESIAS was designed to interact with the user during testing to learn from mistakes. The system can locate and correct the knowledge that led to a mistake, and can also automatically add new knowledge that would lead MYCIN to the correct response.

User Acceptance

Perhaps the ultimate test of an expert system is *Will it be used?* The technical merits of the system may soon be forgotten if the system is not accepted by the end-user. Therefore, a major part of any expert system evaluation study must address the needs of the user. Some of the more important issues that you will need to consider to evaluate the degree of user acceptance are:

- Ease of use

- Clarity of questions

- Clarity of explanations

- Presentation of results

- System utilities

Ease of Use

When you are caught up in developing the technical features of the expert system, an easy item to forget is to present the system in an easy-to-use fashion. Users are typically apprehensive about using a new piece of software. Some of the typical questions they ask are:

- How do I start the program?
- How do I obtain explanations?
- How do I access utilities?
- How do I exit the program?

If the interface is designed properly, the user will have little difficulty in obtaining answers to these questions. If the user runs into trouble, you will need to make changes to the interface. However, the choice of the expert system development tool may restrict your ability to address these questions.

Most tools come equipped with fixed methods for performing each of these functions. If they are inadequate, you may not be able to change them. It is therefore important to match the needs of the user with the interface features of the software tool.

Another important user acceptance issue is the system's speed of operation. Expert system development tools are written in different languages and run in the interpreted or compiled mode. Along with the choice of the computer, the choice of the software will have an impact on the speed of execution of the program. You will want to make certain that the execution time does not introduce undesired performance.

Most user interfaces rely on a conventional typewriter keyboard. In some cases, the user may be an inexperienced typist and may not be motivated to learn the skill. As an option, you may want to consider other interface techniques such as a mouse, lightpen, or a touch screen. However, again available options are tool dependent.

Clarity of Questions

The performance of an expert system is strongly dependent on the information it receives from the user. If the information is incorrect, the system's results will likewise be in error. Therefore, it is important that the design of the system's questions solicit reliable answers.

The user can help identify problems with the questions during system testing. Ask the user to comment on any difficulty he or she has in answering the questions. Also, watch the user. If there is a hesitation in providing the answer, it may indicate the question is confusing or difficult to interpret.

To illustrate some of the typical pitfalls that can occur in the design of a question, and ways that they can be avoided, consider the following examples.

EXAMPLE 1: The I don't understand some term question.

Q: Is the decay function coefficient 5 nepers?

A: What is a neper?

COMMENT: This is a problem because the user doesn't understand the term "neper."

RECOMMENDATION: Avoid terms that are foreign to the user or provide further explanation of the question.

EXAMPLE 2: The I don't know how to answer question.

Q: Is the car's charging system operating normally?

A: I don't know.

COMMENT: This is a stumbling block because the user cannot determine this information.

RECOMMENDATION: This is a typical difficulty commonly found in the early stages of the project when the system has limited domain knowledge. Correct this problem by developing the system further so that it can infer the answer by asking other questions.

EXAMPLE 3: The vague question.

Q: Is the motor's temperature hot?

A: ?

COMMENT: The question is vague because of the use of the word "hot."

RECOMMENDATION: Avoid subjective or ambiguous terms unless you are employing an inexact reasoning technique that can manage them.

EXAMPLE 4: The unbounded question.

Q: Is the water pressure
   rising
   falling

A: Its steady, but how do I tell you?

COMMENT: The user has the answer but the question doesn't permit the answer to be given.

RECOMMENDATION: When using a menu of possible answers, provide all possible answers.

EXAMPLE 5:   The double-negative question.

Q: Is it false that the water pressure is not high?

A: ?

COMMENT: This question is confusing and takes time to interpret.

RECOMMENDATION: Ask clear questions without negations.

Clarity of Explanations

Many expert system applications require that the user be provided explanations on the system's reasoning. This includes explanations of "why" some question is being asked and "how" some conclusion was reached. Both of these explanations provide the user with insight into the system's reasoning that can add to the user's trust in the final result.

To accommodate the user's need for effective explanations, during the testing of the system you should ask him or her to comment on any shortcomings. Unfortunately, most expert system development tools provide little flexibility in modifying the explanation facility. If major changes are needed, you may have to consider a different tool or a base programming language where flexibility exists to tailor the explanations.

Presentation of Results

There are a variety of ways of presenting the final results to the user. The approach can be as simple as presenting a single recommendation. In other applications, the user may want multiple recommendations, possibly rank-ordered. In addition, if the system employs some inexact reasoning technique, then the recommendation may need to be accompanied with a numeric reflecting the level of belief in the result. During system evaluation, make sure the system's presentation of the final results is clear and meets the user's needs.

User Questionnaire

Most expert system projects use informal methods to evaluate the user acceptance. Designers cover the issues discussed in the prior sections, relying on comments provided by the user during the use of the system. In some cases, designers use a formal approach that employs a user-questionnaire to document user responses to system testing (Berry and Hart 1990).

A user-questionnaire includes a listing of the important system features that the user considers when evaluating the expert system. The user is asked to judge the acceptability of each feature. There are two basic ways the user's opinion can be solicited: closed questions and open questions (Berry and Hart 1990).

A closed question provides the user a selection of responses to judge the acceptability of some feature. For example, the user could judge a given feature as poor, weak, average, good, or excellent. This approach can easily incorporate a numeric weighting scheme that could provide an overall score for the system.

In an open question approach, the user is asked to provide comments on the acceptability of each feature. This approach has the potential for eliciting more information than the closed question approach, but requires more time to complete and lacks a numeric scoring opportunity.

If you decide to use a questionnaire approach to judge the user's acceptance of the expert system, then a combination of the closed and open question methods may be helpful. You can ask the user to judge each feature on some subjective weighting scale, and as an option, provide any comments felt appropriate. There are several ways you can approach the design of a user questionnaire. Figure 18.12 is offered as a starting point.

Evolution of Testing/Evaluation

Much of the early work on expert systems treated system evaluation as one of the final project steps. Often, shortcomings found during the evaluation study were impossible to correct due to the size and complexity of the knowledge base. In recent years, there has been a trend toward an integration of the design and evaluation tasks, with an appreciation that evaluation should occur throughout the project. Today, most knowledge engineers treat expert system testing and evaluation as a continual and evolutionary process. The process begins with an informal test of the initial prototype, and becomes increasingly more formal as the system is refined.

In the next several sections we review this evolutionary evaluation process. In particular, we consider the important issues to evaluate at each stage of the process.

Stage 1: Preliminary Testing

Immediately following the development of the prototype, an informal test of the system should be conducted that evaluates the complete knowledge base. This test should apply all possible combinations of answers to the questions asked by the system. System-derived solutions should then be verified for each set of answers.

This type of test not only provides an early verification of the system's performance, it can also uncover the following:

- Unachievable goals
- Unachievable intermediate conclusions
- Unused rules
- Conflicting rules
- Unachievable or unnecessary premises
- Poor reasoning strategies

USER QUESTIONNAIRE		
FEATURE	**EVALUATION**	**COMMENT**
Ease of use		
Starting the system		
Obtaining explanations		
Help facilities		
Interface technique		
Exiting the system		
Nature of questions		
Clarity of terms		
Answers complete		
Clarity of questions		
Nature of explanations		
WHY explanations		
HOW explanations		
Presentation of results		
Easy to follow		
Complete		
System utilities		
Easy to access		
Complete		
General considerations		
Speed of system		
System is useful		
Provide any general comments about the system		

FIGURE 18.12   User acceptance questionnaire.

Performing a complete test of the system's knowledge is usually possible only during early stages when the system is small. Later, when the knowledge base grows, it becomes virtually impossible to test all the possible answers to the questions. To illustrate the extent of this problem, consider the following.

An expert system called LOAN PROBE was developed to assist with evaluating the collectability of general commercial real estate loans (Ribar et al. 1991). In practice, the average number of questions asked is between 100 and 120. This leads to 2×5^{100} possible answers for their system. The designers estimate the time it would take to build test cases, run them, and analyze the results to be 45,000 years! This situation is typical of most expert systems. Unless you have this time, you will have to rely upon test cases to sample the performance of the expert system.

One way that you can ease the task of testing the complete knowledge base is to design the system using several separate modules. Each module would be designed to address some subproblem and would contain its own knowledge base and inference technique. Each module can then be tested separately. This approach not only makes it easier to test the entire system, it also permits you to continue to perform a complete test later in the project as the system grows.

Preliminary testing also assesses the choice of the knowledge representation and inference schemes, and the choice of the development software. Issues to consider during this stage of testing are:

- Study the complete knowledge base.
- Uncover deficiencies in the knowledge and reasoning strategies.
- Validate knowledge representation and inference approach.
- Validate choice of software.

Stage 2: Demonstration Testing

Following further development of the prototype, a demonstration of the system should be given to individuals within the organization. The objective of this demonstration is to validate the expert system approach. This demonstration does not have to show expert performance, but rather illustrates that it can be achieved.

An important benefit of a successful demonstration is that it can revitalize interest in the project. Early enthusiasm for the project may have burned off and given way to some degree of indifference. When the team members can see the system taking shape through a successful demonstration, they will be more motivated to continue the effort (McDermott 1981).

Since you want the demonstration to be well received, you should consider several points when preparing it. First, you must recognize the capabilities as well as the limitations of the system at this stage of its design. This will help define the scope of the demonstration. For example, you might choose to show the system's capability in solving only one small task, for a system being designed to solve many tasks.

Another suggestion is to "show off" the system features that you believe are impressive and illustrate intelligent problem solving. Assume for example your system uses some inexact reasoning technique. If the demonstration shows how the system can derive an unanticipated result from the supplied information using this technique, the demonstration will be technically impressive.

You should also recognize the importance of the system looking good. Individuals will view your system through its interface. Therefore, it is important that the design of the interface, even early in the project, be well thought out.

Feedback from the individuals at the demonstration provides general guidance for future efforts. You will know from their comments if you are moving in the right direction to meet original expectations. The specific points that you should address during a demonstration are:

- Choose a problem of limited scope within the capabilities of the system.
- Use demonstration to validate the expert system approach.
- Show off major system features.
- Design interface to accommodate needs of the user.

Stage 3: Informal Validation Testing

At some point during the project, the system will be complete enough to be tested against real problems from its domain. Here, the objectives are to determine how effective the system is in solving the problems and to uncover system deficiencies. Since this will be the system's first exposure to real problems, a good choice of test material is *typical* past test cases.

This type of test case easily uncovers obvious problems in the system's knowledge. That is, when the system can't solve a typical problem, you can usually locate either existing faulty knowledge or missing knowledge.

With the help of the expert, this testing also uncovers problems with the system's reasoning. The expert can study an audit trail of the system's reasoning when solving the case, and provide comment on how he may have proceeded differently.

If the application requires it, this testing also evaluates the system's ability to interface to databases or external procedural programs. The testing also includes the evaluation of the user interface—a task that should be included in every test stage. During this stage of testing, some issues to consider are:

- Select typical past test cases.
- Evaluate system's ability in solving typical cases.
- Identify system deficiencies.
- Obtain comments from user on the interface.

Stage 4: Refinement Testing

After the system has proven capable of handling the typical cases, you should turn your attention to more difficult or unusual test cases. Even if the original intent of the system is to manage only typical situations, these tests push the system to consider more complex problems. The result of this effort is usually a refinement of the system's knowledge and control.

This type of test is often difficult for the system, and usually results in failure. However, through failure you may discover previously unknown knowledge, which you can add to the system to improve its performance. This approach is aligned with the philosophy of TEIRESIAS (Davis 1979), discussed earlier in the chapter. Issues to consider during this testing are:

- Select unusual past test cases.
- Evaluate system's ability in solving unusual cases.
- Uncover deficiencies in system's knowledge and control.
- Identify system deficiencies.

Stage 5: Formal Testing

The testing tasks discussed in the prior stages are mainly intended to serve the design process. Test results uncover system deficiencies that provide direction for system development. The next stage of testing involves the formal evaluation of the expert system. Here, the objective is to determine how well the system can be expected to meet initial project goals.

Comment: *This is a laboratory test. It provides information for estimating the system's expected success when deployed.*

To perform this test three items are necessary: (1) test material, (2) test criteria, and (3) test evaluators. Guidelines for selecting these items were provided in earlier sections. Specific points to address during this testing stage are:

- Select past test cases.
- Define test criteria.
- Select the evaluators.
- Run the system for each test case.
- Ask evaluators to judge system's performance for each test case.
- Obtain comments on the interface.
- Identify system strengths and deficiencies.

Stage 6: Field Testing

All the tests discussed in the prior stages are performed in the laboratory. For laboratory tests, it is possible to exert a large degree of control over the evaluation process. You can pick what to evaluate, how to conduct the test, and who to involve. However, when the system is deployed into the field, there will always be some degree of uncertainty in the performance and acceptability of the system. The accuracy of an expert system can decrease dramatically when moved from the laboratory to the field. Therefore, you should consider the system's deployment as an additional test.

During a field test, the system is deployed into the work environment and exposed to the types of problems that it was originally designed to address. The principal objective of this test is to determine if the system meets its original goals, and if not, what additional efforts are needed. This test involves both the further validation of the system and assessment of the user's acceptance.

Designing test criteria for a field test of an expert system is not trivial. Very few systems have undergone formal field testing, leaving the literature void of established guidelines. The task is also complicated by the diverse intent of expert systems where performance indicators vary. At best we can discuss only the general issues that should be considered.

First, test criteria for the field test must be established. This is a list of performance indicators against which the system can be evaluated. Many of points considered during the laboratory evaluation of the system might be used.

The primary source of information for forming this list is the original project specifications. The test should be designed to assure that points of interest are measured. For example, if the intent of the system is to reduce the time to perform some task, then the system's processing time becomes an important test criterion.

Issues on how the system is used and behaves are also likely considerations. You may for example want to determine the number of times the user accepted the system's advice, the user's confidence in the advice, or the time it took for the user to obtain the advice. These issues are important to evaluate the user's community acceptance of the system. An end-user will be helpful with forming criteria on this point.

The system's performance may also be measured indirectly, by assessing its affect on the organization. Points to consider are items such as, cost savings, productivity enhancement, and product or service quality improvement. To illustrate, consider the following examples.

OCEX (Herrmann 1990) is an expert system that checks orders for medical products by providing instructions on how to proceed with each order, such as corrective instructions for incorrect orders. The system produced considerable savings by reducing order processing time. It was calculated that OCEX saves Hewlett-Packard about $350,000 per year.

RBEST (Braunwalder and Zaba 1990) determines the cause of disk drive failures during environmental stress tests. The system provided a 20-fold increase in the production rate of disk drives by reducing diagnosing times. The system was evaluated according to the following criteria:

- Time spent on diagnosing disk drives.

- Time spent on fixing disk drives.

- Number of units identified with no faults that would have been determined faulty with present procedures.

During the field test evaluation study, some organizations use a control group. Individuals within the control group solve the problem using standard procedures, while others in a "test group" use the expert system to solve the same problem. A comparison of the performance of the two groups is then used as an evaluation measure. Ribar et al. (1991) report on this approach when testing LOAN PROBE, an expert system that evaluates commercial loans.

The duration of the field test is another factor to consider. In some cases, it takes a period of time before the system is accepted and used in practice. Until the system is routinely used, it may be difficult to access its impact on the organization.

Another problem that could occur is related to what is known as the *Hawthorne* effect (Roethlisberger and Dickson 1939). Studies have shown that human performance may improve simply because something new has been introduced and the performance is monitored. For example, it was found in one study there was an improvement in the productivity of workers in a factory when the lighting level was increased, and then a further improvement when the lighting was decreased. To avoid the Hawthorne effect, it is necessary to ensure that the observed effects are a result of the expert system, and not a result of the change itself. You can accomplish this by delaying the system evaluation until it has been in place for some period of time.

Issues covered during the field testing stage are:

- Define test criteria for the field test.
- Determine if the system meets its original goals when applied to real problems.
- If applicable, consider using a control group of users.
- Determine user acceptance.
- Consider field test time issues.

PHASE 5: DOCUMENTATION

Overview

As an expert system project matures, the quantity of knowledge collected from the expert grows. After a time, you may find the amount of information overwhelming. To handle this situation, you will have to decide early in the project on some approach for effectively documenting this information.

This documentation serves as your personal diary of the project. It should contain all the material collected during the project that you need to reference for developing the system. If properly designed, it will also serve the later tasks of maintaining the system and writing the project's final report.

You could rely on a paper form of documentation, however, it will be more useful if placed in electronic form because you will be able to easily make changes to the information, and copy it into reports. You could also take advantage of a *hypertext* technique, as discussed later in the chapter. The following sections provide guidelines for designing this documentation.

What Needs to be Documented?

During an expert system project, information that you need to retain and record in the documentation serves three primary purposes:

- Reference for developing the expert system
- Reference for writing the final report
- Reference for maintaining the expert system

During the development effort, you will need to turn to this documentation often for recording new information or studying previously discovered information. Since most projects require a final project report, the information recorded in the documentation serves as a valuable source for this effort. Following the deployment of the expert system, the system will need to be maintained. To accommodate each of these efforts, you should document the following:

- Knowledge
- Knowledge graphs
- Source code
- Tests
- Transcripts
- Glossary of domain specific terms
- Reports

The documented knowledge includes the individual rules, frames, strategies, etc. Knowledge graphs are illustrations of the relationships between the different pieces of knowledge, such as inference networks, cognitive maps, etc. The source code is a listing of the code used in the expert system. This includes both the expert system's code and any code associated with external procedural programs or databases. The test documentation includes a description of each test. This includes the purpose of the test, individuals involved, and findings. Transcripts are a written version of recordings made during each knowledge elicitation session. The glossary contains terms that are specific to the problem domain. Finally, the reports include those provided by the organization on the problem and technical references on past expert system studies that were used during the project.

How to Organize the Documentation?

Besides containing the information listed in the last section, the documentation should be organized to ease the system development, report writing and system maintenance. To accomplish this, the documentation should meet the following specifications:

- Easy entry of new knowledge
- Easy access and modification of old knowledge

- Easy access to related information
- Easy replication of material for report writing

One of the better ways to organize the documentation to meet these specifications is in the form of a book. This approach offers a natural style where individual sections are reserved for common material, such as tests, transcripts, etc. This organization is inherently easy to follow because we are accustomed to following a book structure. This approach is also of value if the documentation is placed in electronic form for on-line review. A book style organization also aids later report writing where much of the information can be copied over to the report.

This style of organizing the project's material follows that found in most books. It contains a title, a table of contents of each section, a body that contains sections on such items as project assessment and tests, and finally a location for references and appendices.

One section in the body of the documentation that is unique to an expert system project is called a *knowledge dictionary*. This section contains information on the pieces of knowledge collected during the project such as rules, objects, and strategies. Later in this chapter we will review how to design this dictionary to meet the documentation specifications.

Often during an expert system project you will have a need to search through the document for related information. For example, you might be reviewing some object and would like to know which rules use it. One approach you might take to aid this effort is to include an index of terms in the documentation. As in a book, this index would include the important project topics, with referral to other important subheadings.

Creating an index for the document can be time consuming. Some auto-indexing software tools exist that can make this effort easier. Therefore, you will have to make a judgment call on whether the effort justifies the value obtained.

One particular value in having an index surfaces if you incorporate a *hypertext* utility to support navigation through the document. Later in this chapter we will study how to create and organize the project's documentation using a hypertext approach. But first, let's briefly review hypertext and how you might benefit by using it when designing the documentation.

Hypertext

A basic problem with reviewing information in any document is the difficulty in identifying relationships between pieces of information stored in separate locations. For example, when reading some topic in a book, you may have difficulty in locating related material located elsewhere in the book. This problem occurs because a book provides a linear presentation of the material, which moves through a subject in a set sequence. Attempts to locate related material are limited to a review of the book's index.

To ease the browsing of related information in a document that has been placed in electronic form, some designers today adopt a hypertext technique.

The idea of hypertext was first introduced by Bush (1945) as a method for structuring associative links between text. Nelson (1965) called this technique "hypertext" and studied its implementation on a computer.

Hypertext can be defined as the creation and representation of links between related pieces of information (Parsaye et al. 1989). The structure contains nodes each of which includes a piece of information. Nodes that are related in some fashion are linked together. In some applications the nodes contain graphics or sounds, resulting in a structure called *hypermedia*.

You can use a hypertext structure to read information on one subject, then navigate through other nodes to learn about related information. To illustrate, consider the following example.

Assume you were reading a book about Africa and came across the word "elephant." If a hypertext link was formed from this word to text describing an elephant, you could access it and read about elephants. At this point you might learn that elephants live in "India." This word could be linked to information elsewhere in the book, or possibly even within another book. After navigating through all of the information of interest, you could then return to the original subject of Africa and continue its review.

In general, hypertext offers the reader an ability to easily obtain associative information. It also provides the reader the freedom to choose the sequence of the information to review.

Using Hypertext in Expert System Documentation

One approach of using hypertext to help document an expert system project relies on the documentation's index (Durkin 1991). The index serves as a portal to related information on some subject. By forming hypertext links between index items and the appropriate parts of the documentation, this approach allows an easy structure to build and use. Figure 18.13 shows an example of this approach.

The reviewer is first seen examining a rule entitled "RECEIVER FAULT." Words shown in the rule in bold type have associated with them hypertext links to other information. In this example, the reviewer wants to explore the term "BER." To accomplish this he selects this term (using a mouse) that links him to the term BER contained in the documentation's index. At this point, he can choose one of several references to this term as listed under the BER index. In this case, the reviewer choses to locate the reference of this term in some transcript. This selection is made by clicking on the "TRANSCRIPT" option which produces a new selection window containing a list of relevant transcript dates. Choosing one of these the reviewer is presented with the transcript containing the item of interest. The user can review the discussion of this term within a context that can better describe the term. As can also be seen from this example, the transcript could contain other terms of interest (e.g., ATTENUATOR) that could be referenced in a similar fashion.

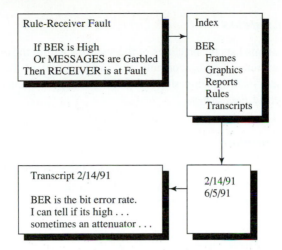

FIGURE 18.13   **Hypertext linking of expert system documentation.**

In general, hypertext can make an expert system project's documentation dynamic. You can easily browse through the material for review or verification. Most expert system projects do not rely upon this utility, but it is one that you should consider because of its added flexibility.

Guidelines for Designing the Documentation

In the following sections we review the material that should be documented during an expert system project. Also offered are guidelines for recording the material in each section of the document. Included with the discussion within each section are areas where hypertext could be of benefit. The contents of the project's documentation should include the following:

- Table of Contents
- Project Proposal
- Knowledge Dictionary
- Source Code
- Tests
- Transcripts
- Project Personnel
- Glossary
- References
- Index

Table of Contents

The table of contents lists the headings of the sections within the documentation. It provides a reference for the contents and organization of the document. If hypertext is used, each heading should be linked to its associated part of the document to permit easy access.

Project Proposal

You should include a copy of the project proposal within your documentation. You may need to refer to it periodically throughout the project, and it will be a valuable source of material for writing the final report.

Knowledge Dictionary

Conventional programming projects use data dictionaries for documenting collected information. In expert system projects, the different types of knowledge collected (e.g., rules, frames, etc.) are recorded in a document called the *knowledge dictionary* (McGraw and Harbison–Briggs 1989).

The dictionary reserves different sections for the recording of each type of knowledge. Within a section, each piece of knowledge should be given a descriptive title that can be used for recording it alphabetically. When you document each piece of knowledge, you should include all of the information that will be needed for both developing and maintaining the system. This includes information that clearly describes the piece of knowledge and its relationship with other pieces recorded elsewhere in the dictionary. It also includes bookkeeping data that reference each piece of knowledge to its transcript source, such as transcript date and paragraph number.

Some of the information recorded is simple boilerplate data that is used for general bookkeeping. This might include the project's title, name of the funding organization, date recorded, etc. Other information is more technical and includes programming code, knowledge base names, etc. It is also important that you record a natural language translation of the code's syntax for the following reason.

During knowledge elicitation sessions, you will often need to review with the expert information contained in the knowledge dictionary. If this information is presented to the expert in the software's syntax, he or she is likely to find it incomprehensible. It may even require you to spend time interpreting the meaning of the code—time that you cannot afford. It is therefore advisable that you record each piece of knowledge in both its formal programming syntax and a natural language translation. This will also aid individuals who must later maintain the system.

The following sections review the different parts that should be included in the knowledge dictionary. Guidelines and templates are also offered for recording each type of knowledge.

Rule Section

The rule section contains information on all the rules used in the expert system. You should consider dividing this section into subsections, where each contains a set of rules related to some topic or function.

Document each rule with a descriptive title. This is important because most project documentations maintain a list (alphabetically arranged) of the rules by title. When you need to inspect a rule, you can refer to the list. In addition, many shells maintain a similar list for inspecting the rules.

When writing the rule's title, use the name of the "object" of the rule's conclusion as the first word. This approach is valuable because you will usually seek a rule on the basis of concluded information. The balance of the title should refer to information contained in the rule's premises. Consider for example a rule designed to conclude meningitis from laboratory test results with the following title:

RULE TITLE: Meningitis diagnosis from laboratory tests

This title provides both a description and a source of reference for the rule by capturing as the first word the object of the conclusion, that is "Meningitis." This practice allows you to quickly locate the rule of interest. Rule numbering should be avoided because it is nondescriptive and causes problems when additional rules are added or deleted, where renumbering would be required.

As previously discussed, it is valuable to document the relationships between the pieces of knowledge—particularly if hypertext is used. When documenting the rule, consider recording its relationship to such items as what rule set it belongs to and its inference network and transcript.

Two versions of the rule should be documented: coded form and natural language form. The coded form serves the system development and debugging tasks. The natural language form accommodates the expert's review of the rule.

You should also document any information obtained from the expert or reports that further describes the rule. This description should include the rule's purpose and any constraints associated with its operation. You will also need to record basic information such as who coded the rule, date of coding, etc. Figure 18.14 shows a template for documenting a rule. Guidelines for entering information in this form are:

- Provide a descriptive rule name.
- State where the rule came from, who coded it, when it was coded, and the related transcript.
- Give rule priority and certainty factor if appropriate.
- Reference appropriate inference network and rule set.
- Provide both a natural language and coded form of rule.
- Provide a description of the rule that includes its purpose, constraints, and any comments by expert.

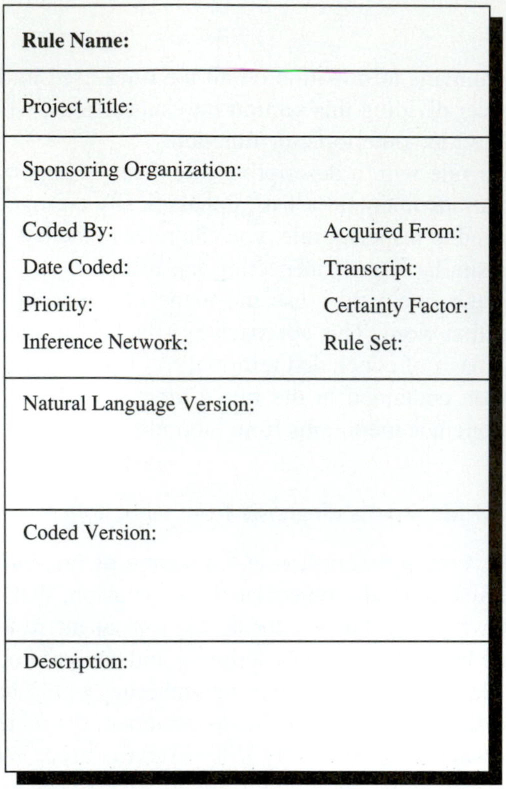

Rule Name:

Project Title:

Sponsoring Organization:

Coded By: Acquired From:

Date Coded: Transcript:

Priority: Certainty Factor:

Inference Network: Rule Set:

Natural Language Version:

Coded Version:

Description:

FIGURE 18.14   Rule documentation form.

Flexibility is added to the review of the rule if the form shown in Figure 18.14 incorporates a hypertext capability. The "Transcript" and "Inference Network" slots can be linked to associated information. Specific objects written in the natural language version of the rule can also be provided by hypertext links to other information. This point was discussed earlier and illustrated in Figure 18.13. A hypertext link could also be used to display upon request the coded version of the rule, which is maintained in another section of the document. This would avoid the need to type in the code for each rule, and gives new meaning to the term "reusable code."

Object Section

The object section contains information on all the frames used in the expert system. This section might be divided into subsections, where each contains a set of objects related to some concept or class.

Each object documented should contain information on how it fits into the overall knowledge structure and specific information about its own properties.

Structural information is provided by documenting the object's parents and children. A reference to a cognitive map containing the object will also permit the reviewer to obtain further structural information.

Property information is the important feature of the object. Each property may have both static and dynamic information attached to it. Static information includes its name, description, value type (e.g., numeric, Boolean, etc.), value constraints (e.g., range, choices, etc.) and default value. If the property is inherited from one of the object's parents, you may also want to record this for reference.

Dynamic information includes how to obtain a value for the property (IF-NEEDED) and what to do if the value changes (IF-CHANGED). These dynamic values are managed using demons that should be documented in both their natural language and coded forms. Figure 18.15 shows a template for documenting an object. Guidelines for entering information in this form are:

- Provide a descriptive object name.
- State where the object came from, who coded it, when it was coded, and the related transcript.

Object Name:	
Project Title:	
Sponsoring Organization:	
Coded By:	Acquired From:
Date Coded:	Transcript:
Parents:	Children:
Cognitive Map:	Object Set:
Property: Value: Constraints: Type: If-Needed: If-Changed:	
Property: Value: Constraints: Type: If-Needed: If-Changed:	
Description:	

FIGURE 18.15   Object documentation form.

- Provide the object's parents and children if appropriate.
- Reference appropriate cognitive map and object set.
- Provide complete information on each property.
- Provide a description of the object that describes its purpose and includes the expert's comments.

If hypertext is used, there are several points on this form that you might consider linking to other information. The "Parents" and "Children" slots could be linked to the associated objects. Likewise, the "Cognitive Map" slot could be linked to the graph displaying the relationships of this object to other ones. Linking the "IF-NEEDED" and "IF-CHANGED" slots to their corresponding demons may be of particular value. These demons are likely to be functions written in some programming syntax. Using a link to obtain this information would avoid the need to type in this code.

Graph Section

Chapter 17 discussed the value of representing graphically the knowledge collected from elicitation sessions. It also showed that the typical graphical techniques used on an expert system project are flowcharts, cognitive maps, and inference networks. These graphs offer the best approach for representing strategies, object relationships, and rule associations. Your knowledge dictionary should contain a separate section for each of these graphs.

You can also link these graphs to associated information elsewhere in the documentation using a *hypermedia* technique. Like hypertext, this technique connects related nodes. In this case, however, one of the nodes is a graph. This graphical node could be an entire graph, or only one part of the graph. For example, within a cognitive map you could link one of the map nodes to its associated class frame.

Source Code

All of the source code developed needs to be documented. This includes listings of each knowledge base, procedural programs, and the listing and structure of all databases used. Each of these different types of listings should be placed in separate sections. In addition, each should have a descriptive name and a brief discussion of its function and operation.

Tests

During the course of the project, tests will be periodically conducted to both validate the system and to determine the adequacy of the system's interface. The results of these tests should be documented. This documentation is important for recording the development of the system and for later reporting on the system's

Test:
Project Title:
Sponsoring Organization:
Date: Location:
Attendees:
Objective:
Problem Discussion:
Session Trace:
System Evaluation:
Interface Evaluation:
Comments:

FIGURE 18.16   Test documentation form.

performance. Figure 18.16 shows a template for documenting these tests. Guidelines for entering information in this form are:

- Provide a name for the test that describes its intent.
- Give the date and location of the test.
- List the attendees.
- Give a short description of the test's objective.
- Provide a discussion of the problem.
- Give a session trace (questions/answers/conclusions).
- Discuss evaluation of system and interface.
- Provide comments by expert and end-user.

Transcripts

As argued in Chapter 17, a recording should be made of each knowledge elicitation session and later transcribed. Your documentation should have a record of each transcript. Even if only notekeeping is used, you will need to retain a record of each session. Guidelines for producing the transcript were given in Chapter 17.

Project Personnel

Provide a listing of all individuals involved on the project. This listing should include the name of the person, with his or her title, address, and phone number. This is a simple list to compile and is valuable if you need to contact one of the individuals.

Glossary

During the project you will likely be exposed to a number of terms that are common to the problem area but are new to you. You should keep an alphabetically ordered record of these terms to reference when needed.

References

Keep a record of all the material referenced during the project (e.g., books, reports, etc.). This material may be related to the problem, the organization, or past expert system studies.

Index

An index provides a source of related information for some subject. It is a valuable feature of any documentation scheme, but is of particular value if you incorporate a hypertext technique. As was illustrated in Figure 18.13, the index can be used as a portal for obtaining associated information on some subject through hypertext links.

Final Report

For most expert system projects you need to write a final report. There are variations of what will be presented in this report that depend on the organization for whom the work was done. The following sections discuss the typical information reported on an expert system project. The contents of the project's final report should include the following:

- Title Page
- Table of Contents

- Executive Summary
- Project Overview
- Program Description
- Test Results
- Summary
- References
- Bibliographies
- Appendices

Title Page

In addition to the title itself, the title page should include the author's name, sponsoring organization, contract number, name of the organization performing the work, and the report's date.

Table of Contents

The table of contents provides a listing of the contents of the report and a way of locating subject information. It shows the reader the main points covered within the report and the organization of the report. For sections listed with subheadings, the subheadings should be shown indented. All headings should also include page number reference. Since most reports do not have an index, the table of contents is the only aid to the reader for locating material.

Executive Summary

The executive summary is a brief overview of the project. It is intended for executives or managers of the organization. These individuals are not necessarily oriented in the project's technical issues, but have a broader concern for the organization. They review the executive summary in order to judge the value of the work and to obtain help in their decision making. Therefore, the executive summary should condense the main information within the report to a point where it clearly explains **what** was done and **why.** A good executive summary is short but still provides a good overview of the project.

You should begin this section with a general discussion of the nature of the problem. For example, you might describe how presently the problem takes considerable time to solve, or requires an expert to solve it who is not always available. Next, an argument should be made on why an expert system approach was taken. In layman's terms, discuss how the system can be used by the organization to address the previously described problem. Finally, the executive summary should explain the benefits of the system. This discussion might describe how the system should improve productivity, profitability, or the organization's competitive position in the marketplace.

The executive summary should be written after the body of the report is completed. It should be concise, confined to one or two pages, and should highlight the key points raised in the report. Points to cover in the executive summary are:

- State project objective.
- Provide general discussion of problem.
- Discuss why an expert system approach was taken.
- Describe in general how the expert system solves the problem.
- State benefits of system.

Project Overview

This section provides an overview of the project and touches on many of the same points covered in the executive summary but in greater detail. You may elect to use subheadings here to better present the material to the reader.

This section should begin with a background discussion of the problem. It should clearly define the problem and further describe the impact the problem has on the organization. If a problem assessment effort was made (Phase 1), then results of the study should also be given.

You should next discuss why an expert system was felt to be the best approach to the problem. This discussion is likely to touch on the typical benefits that expert systems bring to a project, as described in Chapter 2. If similar types of systems have been built in the past, they should be referenced and briefly described.

A general description of the organization and operation of the expert system should next be given. Several block diagrams that capture a high-level view of these issues can be very valuable to the reader. Included with this discussion should be a listing and justification of the software tools used and the choice of the computer platform.

Finally, a brief discussion should be given on the testing and evaluation of the system. This discussion should state the value of the system and offer arguments on how it meets the project's objective. Points to cover in this section, that could be managed by subheadings, are as follows:

- Give problem background.
- Provide justification for expert system approach.
- Give discussion of system organization and operation.
- Review system's evaluation.
- State value of expert system.

Program Description

This section provides a detailed description of the design and operation of the expert system. Because of the complexity of this discussion, you will want to organize this section in a manner that presents the material in an easy-to-follow manner.

One approach that can help is to first provide a general overview of the system's operation, which includes specific tasks that it performs. These tasks should be discussed in their natural sequence, with possible reference to a flow-chart depicting a high-level view of the overall problem-solving approach. During this discussion, refer to any knowledge bases or external programs used during a given task. Later in this section, you can explain the programming details associated with each task. Usually, readers can better follow these details when they are placed within the context of an overall problem-solving description.

The initial overview should also provide a description of the overall structure of the expert system. This includes a listing of each program module used in the design of the complete system, such as different expert system modules, proce-dural programs, and databases. It should also include a discussion on the relation-ships between these different modules. Block diagrams are extremely helpful in explaining this organization. Points to cover in the overview part of this section are:

- Provide a description of the system's operation.
- Give a flowchart depicting a high-level view of the overall problem-solving approach.
- Provide a description of the overall structure of the expert system.
- Show a block diagram that illustrates the relationships of the various pro-gramming modules.

The balance of this section should discuss in detail each program module mentioned in the overview. To aid this effort, you may want to use individual subsections dedicated to each module. Begin each subsection with a brief overview of the program. State the program's objective and provide a general description of the program's structure and operation. You should next describe in detail how the program functions, presenting strategies used, how the system obtains information, what it does with results, and so on. Flowcharts, cognitive maps, and inference networks aid this discussion. Place source coding in the report's appendix and only refer to it in the discussion. Points that you should cover in each subsection are:

- State the program's objective.
- Provide a general description of its operation.
- Describe how the program functions.
- Use graphics to aid describing the operation and structure of the program.

Test Results

Each test conducted during the project should be included in the final report. These serve as the raw data that support your conclusions. Use separate subsections for each test discussion.

During the discussion of each test, first provide the objective of the test, then a brief description of the test. If a past case was used as the source of the test material, then a brief discussion of the case should follow. All information supplied to the expert system during the test must be noted. A final review should also be included that summarizes the findings. This would include a discussion on the evaluation of the system's performance and interface. To aid the reporting of these tests, you should refer to the test information contained in the knowledge dictionary. Specific points that you should cover in this section are:

- State the test's objective.
- Provide a brief description of the test.
- If a test case is used, then describe the case details.
- List test data supplied to system.
- Describe evaluation of system's performance and acceptability of interface.

Summary

The summary discusses in a concise manner the key points covered in the report. It should provide a short description of the problem, how the expert system addresses it, and the benefits the system provides the organization. Finally, recommendations should be given on future directions. Specific points that you should cover in the summary are:

- Provide a brief description of the problem.
- Describe how the expert system addresses the problem.
- List clearly the benefits of the expert system.
- Give recommendations for future work.

References

This section provides a list of reports, books, journals, etc., referenced in the body of the report. It allows the reader to reference (and possibly order) material used in the report.

Bibliographies

Beyond the material referenced within the report, there may be material used during the project that should be listed in the bibliography. It may also be valuable to produce a second bibliography that includes basic articles on expert systems and ones related to similar past projects. Often, this may be the first introduction of this technology within the organization. Therefore, reference to background material will represent a valuable source of information for the organization.

Appendices

Information placed in the appendices is important but peripheral to the body of the report. This information supports the report and is used more for reference by the interested reader. Each appendix should be labeled with a letter of the alphabet and a descriptive title. Typical information found in the appendices of a report on an expert system project will include the following.

Glossary—The glossary contains terms commonly used in both the problem area and expert systems. You should organize the terms alphabetically, possibly dividing the problem terms from those related to expert systems into two sections. A glossary is especially important if the report will be read by managers who may not be versed in some of the technical language used within the report.

Source Code—This section includes the listing of the expert system's source code. Since your knowledge dictionary will have a similar section, you can simple copy it over to the final report.

User Manual—The user may need a guide for operating the expert system. This guide should touch on the simple aspects of how to start and stop the system. It should also provide detailed instructions on the full use of the system, including information on how to answer questions, obtain explanations, etc. To enhance this guide, you may want to include a tutorial. This tutorial should step the user through the operation of the system, in a way that exercises the important features of the system.

PHASE 6: MAINTENANCE

Overview

The final phase of the project is system maintenance. This task follows the deployment of the system into the field where it is used routinely by the users. However, calling it the final phase may be misleading.

Most expert systems contain knowledge that is evolving over time. The organization using the system may acquire new products and equipment, or change procedures for working with existing resources. This changing state requires appropriate modifications to the system. Consider for example a system developed at Allstate Insurance Company.

Allstate developed an expert system to assist in processing no-fault insurance claims based on the New York State Workmen's Compensation Board Schedule of Medical Insurance Fees (Rauch–Hindin 1988). The system processes the simpler claims and thus alleviates some of the workload. It also processes a claim in a timely manner, which avoids penalties assessed by the state for late claims.

One of the problems that Allstate faced was the ever-changing nature of the schedule set by the state of New York for processing claims. There were periodic addendums to the schedule, and once every six years, there was a major update. This required Allstate to assign the developers the further responsibility of maintaining the system on a regular basis.

As an expert system is used, deficiencies may also be discovered. Users may find the system difficult to use, or may uncover omissions. They may also discover a "moth" in the system (a bug). The term "bug" was coined during World War II, when a team of Harvard University researchers puzzled by the shutdown of an early computer removed a moth stuck in an electric relay.

Maintaining any type of software can be costly. A study performed by General Motors showed that 70% of the life-cycle cost of a program is consumed by its maintenance (Rauch-Hindin 1988).

Given the likelihood of needed system changes and their associated costs, an effective maintenance program needs to be established for every expert system project. Users need a way to report problems they encounter, and individuals with knowledge engineering skills must be available to make the changes. There must also be a way to manage the maintenance effort to assure that the task is accomplished effectively.

In the following sections, we review the major issues to consider when putting together an expert system maintenance program. These sections also provide guidelines to accomplish the task.

Documentation

The most important ingredient of a good maintenance program is the project's documentation. If it is complete and well organized, then individuals charged with maintaining the system will have an easier job. Guidelines for creating the documentation were given in the Phase 5 discussion.

Think Maintenance during Design

Plans for system maintenance should be made at the beginning of the project. Knowing how the system will need to be maintained is informative when the system is designed. That is, you can design a system architecture that is accommodating to maintenance personnel. A major pitfall of many past projects has been the postponement of formulating maintenance plans until the end of the project (McGraw and Harbison–Briggs 1989).

Earlier chapters provided guidelines for developing rule-based systems, frame-based systems, and induction systems. If these guidelines are followed, not only will they help the development effort, but also the later maintenance of the system. The following sections discuss some of the more important design issues to consider, which will impact the later maintenance of the system.

Modular Structure

To aid maintenance efforts, the system's knowledge should be organized in a manner that permits rapid access to parts of interest and allows easy modification. This is a common theme when organizing procedural code in a conventional program, where code modularity is important.

In an expert system, this can best be achieved by segregating the system's knowledge into individual modules, where each is designed to address a specific subtask. These modules allow easy assess on a function basis, and are usually small enough to permit easy inspection and change.

Separate Knowledge From Information

Some organizations look to apply an expert system using information common to everyday business decision making. This information might include product statistics, equipment inventory data, or personnel records. The expert system processes this information using its knowledge coded in the knowledge base. From a maintenance standpoint, it is better for these types of problems if the system's decision-making knowledge is kept separate from the information.

One method of separating the two involves placing the information in a database and writing the knowledge using variable rules. In this fashion, if changes are needed to only the information, simple changes can be directly made to the database. Also, if the way decisions are made changes, the appropriate rules can be located and modified.

Another method for separating knowledge from information involves placing the information in frames that are scanned by a set of variable rules. This approach offers a benefit similar to the database approach, in that either the knowledge or information can be accessed and changed separately.

Meta-Rules

Another design issue that impacts the maintenance of the system is the use of meta-rules. Meta-rules add to the flexibility in controlling the system's reasoning. For example, you could write a meta-rule that establishes a new goal on the basis of the session's context. However, they can make the maintenance effort more difficult.

When there is a need to review the operation of an expert system, most knowledge engineers will begin by inspecting the goal agenda. It provides a high-level view of the system's operation, and if trouble occurs, a review of the agenda can help isolate that part of the knowledge base causing the problem. However, a meta-rule is buried within many other rules and the knowledge engineer may not even be aware that it exists.

It would be unfair to recommend excluding meta-rules from the system because of this potential maintenance problem. But there are a couple of points to consider that can help.

First, you need to make the maintenance personnel aware that meta-rules exist and where they are located. This boils down to good documentation practices. Second, you need to make the meta-rules easily accessible. This can be accomplished by grouping them together in a separate rule-set.

Software Issues

The choice of software used to develop the expert system will also have an impact on the maintenance task. Of concern here is the programming talent needed, system portability, modification utilities, and new releases. Let's take a look at each of these as they affect the maintenance effort.

Programming Skills

As discussed earlier in this chapter (Phase 3), the choice of development software can range from base languages up to large hybrid tools. Individuals charged with maintaining the system would need to have as a prerequisite programming skills in the chosen software. In general, it requires far more training to learn a base language than an expert system development tool. In either case, however, you will need to have the maintenance personnel trained on the software prior to implementing the maintenance program.

System Portability

Portability of an expert system across different computers gives an organization the flexibility to move the system to other existing computers, or to upgrade to more powerful ones when they become available. In general, systems developed using a base language can be ported easily, while ones developed using a shell may be limited to certain computers or operating systems. If you believe software portability will be an important consideration in the future, then consider this factor in your choice of the development software.

Modification Utilities

Modifying the knowledge in an expert system isn't as simple as throwing in a few rules as new knowledge is discovered. The system's knowledge is highly interrelated, and to change even one rule you must know its logical link to other rules. This situation places special demands on the development interface to restrict modifications to allowable changes.

Several software tools provide utilities that can guide you through the process of adding new knowledge to the system. One utility of value discussed earlier in the chapter is a *consistency checker*. This utility checks each new rule entered with other rules presently in the system for logical consistency and possible contradictions. This not only avoids difficulties with the system's knowledge, it also eases the system maintenance.

Maintenance Agreement

Most software vendors provide, as an optional purchase, a maintenance agreement with their software. This agreement usually covers the cost of support and any new releases. It can be valuable for the long-term support of the system's maintenance. However, you will need to make a judgment call as to whether the cost is justified.

If you feel that maintenance personnel will often need to turn to the vendor for help in maintaining the system, the maintenance agreement is probably worth the cost. In addition, you should recognize that most vendors do not support outdated releases. If you intend to upgrade the system with each new release, then the purchase is highly recommended. You will obtain continual support and improved software at a fraction of the cost of purchasing the software without the agreement.

Who Maintains System?

Deciding who is to maintain the system is an important decision when putting together an expert system maintenance program. The individual(s) must have the capabilities to perform the task and clearance by the organization.

The developer of the system is the first obvious choice. This individual has both knowledge engineering skills to perform the task and experience with the system. However, this individual may be more valuable on other new projects.

The organization may elect to choose others who have less or no experience with either the system or expert system development. If this approach is taken, then the organization assumes the responsibility of training the individuals. This approach was taken by DEC following the development of XCON.

DEC established a group of people to maintain XCON. Since XCON was developed using OPS, these individuals first needed training in the language. This process took on average about three months to complete. A by-product of this approach was that eventually a dedicated AI group of individuals proficient in expert system design was established within DEC, who were able to extend the capability of XCON to consider the configuration of other types of computer systems.

Organizations that have the expert system developed by outside contractors or consultants may look toward these individuals to maintain the system. Unfortunately, they may find that the well has run dry. A survey conducted by Pepper (1991) on expert systems in the service industry found that not one respondent who had their system developed with outside help was happy with the follow-up support.

A lesson to be learned from past experiences is that it is important for organizations to developed the in-house ability to both develop and maintain an expert system. If the project is sourced out to a contractor, the organization should assign an individual(s) to the project to not only monitor it, but also to learn from it so that future maintenance will be achievable.

For security purposes, it is important that only designated individuals be allowed to maintain the system. The reason for this recommendation should be obvious when you consider the possible damage that can be done if an unauthorized individual is given access to the system. Each piece of knowledge in the system has a possible impact on the system's final result. One small change can lead to a totally different result. Consider for example the following simple change to a rule in a financial investment system:

OLD RULE	NEW RULE
IF Desired return > 15%	IF Desired return > **10%**
AND Market is bull	AND Market is bull
THEN Advise high-risk stocks	THEN Advise high-risk stocks

In this example, a change was made to the percentage of desired return as a condition for recommending high-risk stocks. This change may have been made by an unauthorized person with good intentions. However, when the client loses his shirt from bad advice, he will gain little comfort from your explanation of the innocence of the mistake—you will probably be staring at a law suit (Tuthill 1991).

Document Changes

It is extremely important to keep good records on any changes made to the system. If this isn't done, it is very easy to lose track of the system's knowledge. Figure 18.17 is offered as a template for performing this documentation. Each

```
┌─────────────────────────────────────────┐
│              Maintenance Form            │
├─────────────────────────────────────────┤
│  Project Title:                          │
├─────────────────────────────────────────┤
│  Sponsoring Organization:                │
├─────────────────────────────────────────┤
│  Modified By:            Date Modified:  │
├─────────────────────────────────────────┤
│  What Was Modified:                      │
│                                          │
│                                          │
├─────────────────────────────────────────┤
│  Why Was It Modified:                    │
│                                          │
│                                          │
├─────────────────────────────────────────┤
│  Discussion:                             │
│                                          │
│                                          │
└─────────────────────────────────────────┘
```

FIGURE 18.17   Maintenance documentation form.

time the system is modified, the following critical pieces of information should be documented:

- What was modified.
- Who performed the modification.
- When the modification was made.
- Why the modification was made.

——————————— **SUMMARY ON KNOWLEDGE ENGINEERING** ————

This chapter reviewed the major tasks performed in the design and development of expert systems. This subject is commonly referred to as knowledge engineering. Six phases were offered as a structured methodology for managing an expert system project.

The major lessons learned in this chapter were:

- There are six major phases followed when developing an expert system, which are often performed in parallel and cycled through several times before the project is complete.
- An organization's motivation for pursuing an expert system project is important when assessing the project.
- Problem, people, and deployment issues are important when assessing the project's feasibility.
- Expert system testing involves the validation of the system's results and its reasoning process.
- System testing is conducted throughout the project, becoming increasingly more formal as the project proceeds.
- The project's documentation is important for both developing and main-taining the expert system.
- A *knowledge dictionary* contains the important pieces of knowledge collected during the project such as rules, objects, etc.
- The system should be designed to ease the later maintenance tasks. All changes made to the system during maintenance should be clearly docu-mented.

——————————— **R E F E R E N C E S**

Adrion, W.R., M.A. Branstad, and J.C. Cherniavsky, Validation, Verification and Testing of Computer Software, ACM Computing Surveys, vol. 14, no. 2, pp. 159–192, June 1982.

Beckman, T.J., Selecting Expert System Applications, AI Expert, pp. 42–48, Feb. 1991.

Bell, J. and R.J. Hardiman, The Third Role—The Naturalistic Knowledge Engineer, in Knowledge Elicitation: Principles, Techniques and Applications, Dan Diaper, ed., John Wiley & Sons, New York, 1989.

Berry, D.C. and A.E. Hart, Evaluating Expert Systems, Expert Systems, vol. 7, no. 4, pp. 199–207, Nov. 1990.

Braunwalder, K. and S. Zaba, RBEST: An Expert System for Disk Failure Diagnosis During Manufacturing, in Practical Experience in Building Expert Systems, M. Bramer, ed., John Wiley & Sons, New York, 1990.

Bush, V., As We May Think, Atlantic Monthly, vol. 176, pp. 101–108, 1945.

Carter, R.C., Search Time with a Color Display: Analysis of Distribution Functions, Human Factors, vol. 24, pp. 302–312, 1982.

Christ, R.E., Review and Analysis of Color-Coding Research for Visual Displays, Human Factors, vol. 17, pp. 542–570, 1975.

Davis, R., Interactive Transfer of Expertise: Acquisition of New Inference Rules, Artificial Intelligence, vol. 12, pp. 121–158, 1979.

Due, R.T., Determining Economic Feasibility: Four Cost/Benefit Analysis Methods, Journal of Information Systems Management, pp. 14–19, Fall 1989.

Durkin, J., FIDEX: An Expert System for Autonomous Satellite Diagnostics, Second NASA Space Communications Technology Conference, Cleveland, Ohio, Nov. 1991.

Fried, L., The Dangers of Dabbling in Expert Systems, Computerworld, pp. 65–72, June 29, 1987.

Gaschnig J., P. Klahr, H. Pople, E. Shortliffe, and A. Terry, Evaluation of Expert Systems: Issues and Case Studies, in Building Expert Systems, Hayes–Roth, F., D.A. Waterman, and D.B. Lenat, eds., Addison-Wesley, Reading, Mass., 1983.

Gevarter, W.B., The Nature and Evaluation of Commercial Expert System Building Tools, IEEE Computer, pp. 24–41, May 1987.

Hayes-Roth, F., D.A. Waterman, and D.B. Lenat, Building Expert Systems, Addison-Wesley, Reading, Mass., 1983.

Henkel, P., The Elements of Friendly Software Design, Warner Books, New York, 1984.

Herrmann, F., OCEX-Order Clearing Expert System, in Practical Experience in Building Expert Systems, M. Bramer, ed., John Wiley & Sons, New York, 1990.

Hollinger, E., Evaluation of Expert Systems, in Topics in Expert System Design, G. Guida and C. Tasso, eds., Elsevier North-Holland, pp. 377–416, 1989.

Horton, W., Designing & Writing On-Line Documentation, Help Files to Hypertext, John Wiley & Sons, New York, 1990.

Mackey, K. and T. Slesnick, A Style Manual for Authors of Software, Creative Computing, vol. 8, 1982.

Martin, A. and R. Law, Expert System for Selecting Expert System Shells, Information and Software Technology, vol. 30, no. 10, pp. 579–586, Dec. 1988.

McDermott, J., R1 The Formative Years, AI Magazine, vol. 2, no. 2, pp. 21–29, Summer 1981.

McFarlan, F.W., Portfolio Approach to Information Systems, Harvard Business Review, pp. 142–150, Sept.–Oct. 1981.

McGraw, K. and K. Harbison-Briggs, Knowledge Acquisition: Principles and Guidelines, Prentice-Hall, Englewood Cliffs, N.J., 1989.

Nelson, T.H., The Hypertext, Proceedings of the World Documentation Federation, 1965.

Parsaye, K., M. Chignell, S. Khoshafian, and H. Wong, INTELLIGENT DATABASES: Object-Oriented, Deductive Hypermedia Technologies, John Wiley & Sons, New York, 1989.

Pepper, J., We're Off to Seize the Wizard: The Revolution in Service Automation, ServiceWare Inc., Verona, PA, 1991.

Peterson. D.E., Screen Design Guidelines, in Tutorial, End User Facilities in the 1980's, J. A. Larson, ed., IEEE, 1982.

Preece, A.D., Towards a Methodology for Evaluating Expert Systems, Expert Systems, vol. 7, no. 4, pp. 215–223, Nov. 1990.

Prerau, D.S., Selection of an Appropriate Domain for an Expert System, AI Magazine, vol. 6, no. 2, pp. 26–30, Summer 1985.

Rauch–Hindin, W.B., A Guide to Commercial Artificial Intelligence: Fundamentals and Real-World Applications, Prentice-Hall, Englewood Cliffs, N.J., 1988.

Ribar, G., F. Arcoleo, and D. Hollo, Loan Probe: Testing a Big Expert System, AI Expert, pp. 43–49, May 1991.

Roethlisberger, F. and W. Dickson, Management and the Worker, Harvard University Press, Cambridge, Mass., 1939.

Simon, R., The Morning After, Forbes, pp. 164–168, Oct. 19, 1987.

Slagel, J. and M. Wick, A Method for Evaluating Candidate Expert Systems Applications, AI Magazine, pp. 45–53, Winter 1988.

Turing, A.M., Computing Machinery and Intelligence, Mind, vol. 59, 1950.

Tuthill, G., Legal Liabilities and Expert Systems, AI Expert, pp. 45–51, March 1991.

───────── E X E R C I S E S

1. Discuss why expert system development is considered an iterative process.

2. Discuss the major differences between the development effort of a conventional program and an expert system.

3. If you were to walk into an organization and attempt to sell them on expert system technology, how would you proceed?

4. How does an organization's motivation impact project assessment?

5. An expert system is being designed to assist help-desk operators with managing calls related to problems with computer systems sold by the organization. How should the performance of the system be evaluated?

6. Blue Cross and Blue Shield must verify health care claims at a rate of 66,000 per month. Discuss how an expert system would be of value to them.

7. Several nations have agreed to stop underground nuclear testing. How can an expert system be built to verify that these countries are adhering to this agreement? How would you validate the operation of such a system?

8. A firm has asked you to build an expert system to diagnosis problems with one of their production lines. They have also told you to use the expert system development tool that they have previously purchased. What is your response?

9. You have been asked by the Department of the Navy to develop an expert system that can identify the type of torpedo launched by an enemy. The Navy knows the types of information needed to make this identification, but have been unable to apply this information in a conventional program approach. What types of problems might you expect when developing this system?

10. When writing an expert system project proposal, what issues would you consider are the most important for winning the contract?

11. Why do some expert systems fail? Several articles have been written on the subject, but most attribute the reason(s) to points discussed in this chapter. Provide a few reasons that are typical of past failures.

12. Discuss ways in which you can design an expert system that will aid later system maintenance.

13. Why is rapid prototyping considered important when developing an expert system?

14. What are the major design considerations that can help the later maintenance effort?

15. Discuss possible legal liability issues for an expert system project.

16. You have been asked by a company to design an expert system to assist in responding to chemical spill emergencies. What possible legal liabilities might be associated with this project?

17. What is the difference between software verification and validation?

18. Why is it important to validate an expert system?

19. Discuss qualitative and quantitative techniques for validating an expert system.

20. Like any project, an expert system project should be documented. Discuss the specific items that should be documented in an expert system project that are unlike those found in other projects.

21. This chapter discussed how hypertext could be used to help document an expert system project. Describe how it might be used to enhance the operation of an expert system.

22. Discuss how to organize the documentation of an expert system project.

23. What is a knowledge dictionary? Also, describe its contents.

24. If you promise to maintain an expert system that you developed, what possible ''headaches'' might you expect?

25. If you were a manager within an organization responsible for an expert system project, how would you put together a maintenance program for the system?

26. Discuss security issues for an expert system project.

27. Critics of expert systems often state that they are only procedural programs written in IF-THEN structures—structures that are also found in procedural programs. How would you respond to this criticism?

Glossary of Expert System Terms

Abduction   An uncertain inference.

Abstraction   Technique of using generic assumptions concerning an object or event during reasoning.

Act   One of the tasks in the recognize–resolve–act cycle of forward chaining systems, which fires a chosen rule.

Active value   A slot value of a frame that can change during a consultation automatically by invoking a procedure when program data is changed.

Agenda   1. A means for organizing goals in an expert system. 2. A list of rules (called a conflict set) that have been ''recognized'' as able to fire during a forward chaining recognize–resolve–act cycle.

Agenda-based system   A system that uses an agenda as a means for controlling the execution of rule sets.

AKO   A Kind Of. A link to establish a-kind-of relationship between objects and classes.

Algorithm   A set of step-by-step instructions for accomplishing a task.

Alternative worlds reasoning   Reasoning based on what-if strategies, where multiple solution paths are taken on the basis of alternative decisions.

Analogical reasoning   A method of reasoning where two separate concepts have some type of resemblance. One is well understood and the other possesses similar characteristics. The technique permits other information to be inferred from the similarity between the two.

Ancestor   An upper level class frame in a frame hierarchy that is related to a lower level frame.

AND   A logical operator used in a rule that implies that all statements joined with an AND must be true before the rule's consequent is considered true.

Antecedent   A condition in a rule's premise.

Approximate reasoning   Inexact reasoning employing techniques such as probability theory, fuzzy logic, or certainty factors.

Arc   A directed link between nodes.

ART   A large hybrid expert system development tool by Inference Corp.

Artificial intelligence   A field of study in computer science that pursues the goal of making a computer reason in the same manner as humans.

Assertion   A fact derived during reasoning.

Assumption-based system   A technique used in belief-revision systems to keep track of the origin of propositions.

Assumption-based truth maintenance   Hypothetical reasoning. Reasoning in parallel with truth maintenance support where all solutions are found and an evaluation function is used to find the best solution.

Attribute   A property of an object. For example, a ball has the attributes of "color" and "radius."

Audit trail   The record of reasoning steps taken by an expert system to reach a conclusion.

Axiom   A statement assumed to be true.

Backward chaining   An inference control strategy. In a rule-based system, backward chaining begins with a goal and tries to prove it to be true by proving the premises of a rule that contains the goal as its conclusion. The premises of this rule (also called a goal rule) are considered "subgoals," which the system tries to prove are true by pursing other rules that contain the subgoals as conclusions. Eventually, this backward chaining sequence reaches premises that are not supported by other rules, and the user is then ask to verify the truth of the premise statement. These are called "primitive rules." Also called goal-driven search.

Bayes theorem   A statistical technique for managing inexact reasoning in an expert system.

Before demon   A procedure that is executed before a frame's slot value is obtained or changed.

Best-first search   Search technique that uses knowledge about the problem to guide the search. It guides the search toward the solution nodes of the problem space.

Bidirectional reasoning   Control strategy that switches between forward and backward chaining.

Bidirectional rule   Rule that can be used in either forward or backward chaining.

Bidirectional search   Search technique that starts at both ends of a search space and meets in the middle.

Binary tree   A tree in which each node has only two children.

Binding   The process of assigning a value to a variable.

Blackboard   An expert system design where several independent expert systems share information in a common working memory. Architecture used by HEARSAY.

Blind search   A search technique that makes no use of knowledge to search the problem space. Will find a solution, if it exists, but at a cost of time due to the exhaustive nature of the search.

Boolean logic   A means of reasoning that asserts facts as either true or false, and includes logical connectors such as AND, OR, and NOT to join propositions.

Branch   Connection between nodes in a tree.

Breadth-first search   Search technique that looks for a solution along all of the nodes on one level of a problem space before considering nodes at the next lower level.

Brute-force search   A method of search that attempts all possible paths in a search space to find a solution.

C   A low-level, efficient, general-purpose programming language, originally developed at AT&T's Bell Labs along with the UNIX operating system.

C++   An object-oriented extension of the C language.

CAD   Acronym for computer-aided design. Using a computer for design.

CAI   Acronym for computer-aided instruction. Using a computer for teaching.

Cardinality   A facet in frame-based systems that restricts the number of values a slot can have.

Case-based reasoning   Theory in AI that proposes that the elements of human memory are based on specific historical events or "cases." A problem is compared to a set of previous examples (cases) and the case most similar to the problem is used as the basis for solving the problem.

Causal reasoning   Reasoning based on cause–effect relationships between the problem's objects.

Certainty   Degree of confidence or belief in a fact or relationship.

Certainty factor   A number assigned to a fact or rule to indicate the confidence one has in the fact or in the rule's relationship. Used in the MYCIN expert system and differs from conventional probability coefficients.

Certainty theory   A technique of inexact reasoning based on the degree of belief or disbelief in a statement formed by propagating certainty factors through a set of rules.

Child   Object that inherits characteristics from a parent object or class.

Class   A collection of objects that share common properties.

Classification   A problem-solving method that associates a set of categories with possible problem solutions.

Clause   A conditional statement held in the premise part of a rule.

CLOS   Common Lisp Object Standard. A standard form of Lisp for developing an object-oriented program.

Cognition   The mental process of knowing. Having knowledge.

Cognitive economy   The organization of knowledge in structures that permit easy recall.

Cognitive map   Graphical representation showing the natural relationships between concepts or objects.

Cognitive science   The study of human problem-solving processes.

Combinatorial explosion   A condition that occurs when attempting to solve large complex problems using search techniques. This trouble mainly arises if the problem space is large and exhaustive search techniques are used. Expert systems can often avoid this difficulty by using knowledge to focus the search and attempt to obtain an acceptable solution rather than an optimum one.

Common Lisp   A dialect of Lisp that is accepted as the standard version of Lisp.

Common sense   A general source of knowledge that humans possess on solving real-world problems obtained through experience.

Common-sense reasoning   Human decision making using common-sense knowledge. This type of knowledge is often highly compiled.

Compiled knowledge   Domain experts often solve problems without being able to explain their problem-solving techniques and the knowledge used in the problem solving. This type of knowledge is called ''compiled.'' During knowledge acquisition, the knowledge engineer must be able to decompile this knowledge in order to enter it into the expert system.

Concept   An expert system's representation of an idea or object.

Confidence factor   Similar to certainty factor.

Conflict resolution   Technique of resolving the problem of multiple matches in a rule-based system during inferencing. When more than one rule can fire during a cycle, a conflict arises and a decision must be made on which rule will be allowed to fire.

Conjunction   The logical AND that joins two propositions in a rule.

Consequent   The conclusion of a rule.

Consistency Property of a system of rules where all deductions are logically consistent.

Constraint-based reasoning Method of reasoning where conditional statements are used to constrain the problem-solving approach.

Consultation paradigms General types of problem solving techniques.

Context The state of the solution as captured in the working memory at any point during the consultation.

Context tree Tree arrangement of context related objects or rules.

Contradiction Condition where the antecedents of two rules are the same while the consequents are different.

Control A procedure, explicit or implicit, that determines the overall order of problem-solving activities in an expert system.

Control agenda Series of goals to pursue that establishes the high-level reasoning strategy of an intelligent system.

Control strategy Method used by the inference engine to order the rules during the system's reasoning.

Cooperating knowledge bases Specialized expert systems that independently work on subproblems but support and interact with each other via a blackboard.

DARPA An agency of the U.S. Government, the Defense Advanced Research Projects Agency.

Data abstraction Method of constructing data types that can be used to represent higher-level concepts.

Data driven Inferencing method where data is obtained and the system determines what it can conclude from this information. Also called "forward chaining."

Decision support system A class of software for helping make decisions.

Decision table Table containing a series of decision factors that label columns and represent preconditions needed to reach a conclusion that is represented in another column. Decision factor values are placed in rows that lead to specific conclusions.

Declarative knowledge Descriptive or factual knowledge.

Deduction Coming to a conclusion by the process of reasoning deductively.

Deductive reasoning Reasoning from the general to the specific.

Deep knowledge Basic knowledge coming from first principles or physical laws of the domain.

Defuzzication Process of converting a fuzzy value into a crisp value.

Degree of membership   The likelihood, expressed as a number from 0 to 1, that a particular object belongs in a fuzzy set.

Demon   A procedure activated by the changing or accessing of a given slot value.

Demon rule   A rule that fires whenever its premises match the contents of the working memory.

DENDRAL   Rule-based expert system used to determine the structure of an organic chemical compound using data acquired from mass spectrometers and nuclear magnetic resonance instruments.

Dependency-directed backtracking   Backtracking guided by dependency records during problem solving to the point where failure occurred.

Depth-first search   A search technique that explores each branch of a search space to its full vertical length, then proceeds using some chosen rule of search such as from left to right. Each branch is searched for a solution; if none is found, a new vertical branch is searched using the same rule of search.

Diagnostic paradigm   Problem-solving approach requiring the identification of symptoms or characteristics of a situation in order to determine the problem and corresponding solution.

Disjunction   The logical OR that joins two propositions in a rule.

Distributed problem solving   Problem-solving architecture that includes a network of systems that interact to solve the problem.

Domain   The problem area. Examples are medical diagnostics, VAX configuration, and so on. Expert systems work on well-focused domains.

Domain expert   A person who possesses the skill and knowledge to solve a specific problem in a manner superior to others.

Domain-specific knowledge   Knowledge about the problem area.

EMYCIN   An expert system shell derived from work on MYCIN.

Encapsulation   The hiding of data and procedures within an object.

Entropy   A measure of the disorder of a system. The entropy of the universe tends to increase.

Epistemology   Study of the nature of knowledge.

Equivalent   Expressions in logic that have the same truth values.

Evaluation function   Procedure used to determine the value of a proposed path through a problem space.

Event-driven reasoning   Reasoning initiated by some event. Used in expert systems with demon rules that monitor for the event.

Exhaustive search   A search technique where every possible path through a problem space is examined.

Existential quantifier   For some variable X there exists some object that could instantiate the variable.

Expectation-driven reasoning   Control strategy that employs current data and decisions first to formulate hypotheses about yet unobserved events and second to allocate resources to activities that confirm, disconfirm, or monitor the expected events.

Experiential knowledge   Knowledge gained from experience solving the problem. Typically consists of rules of thumb (shallow knowledge) in contrast to first principles (deep knowledge).

Expert system   A computer program designed to model the problem-solving behavior of a human expert.

Explanation   Information provided to justify course of reasoning or conclusion. WHY is used to explain why a particular question is being asked and HOW is used to explain the line of reasoning that led to a certain conclusion.

Facet   Extended knowledge about a frame's property, such as its type, range, or what procedures to execute if the value is needed or changed.

Fact   A declarative assertion or statement that has the property of being either true or false.

Fact base   The collection of facts gathered during an expert system session. Also called a working memory.

Fault tree   A tree diagram containing an ordered representation of faults that may be found in a system.

Fire   To activate the conclusion of a rule if the premises are true.

First principles   Basic theory of the domain used to solve the problem rather than rules of thumb.

FLAVORS   An object-oriented programming language written in LISP.

Forward chaining   Inference strategy where conclusions are drawn by first looking at the facts or data on the problem. Also known as data-driven search. In a rule-based expert system, forward chaining begins by asserting certain facts, seeing what rules can fire based on these assertions, picking a rule to fire, then cycling. This process is continued until a goal is reached or no additional rules can fire.

Frame   A knowledge representation method that associates an object with a collection of features. Each feature or attribute is stored in a slot with a corresponding attribute value, or method for acquiring the value. Frames can be abstract in the sense of a class (e.g., class of women) or more specific in the sense of an instance of the class (e.g., Betty). An instance can inherit attributes from its associated class.

Frame-based system A computer program that processes problem-specific information contained in the working memory with a set of frames contained in the knowledge base, using an inference engine to infer new information.

Fuzzy logic A branch of logic that uses degrees of membership in sets rather than a strict true/false membership.

Fuzzy reasoning Method of working with inexact information. Works with subjective or poorly understood concepts to determine an adequate solution. Quantifiers are defined as possibility distributions that carry linguistic labels, such as *short*, *very short*, or *extremely short*, for characterizing the height of a given person.

Fuzzy set Degree of membership distribution for membership of some object in a linguistic variable set.

Garbage collection The process of gathering and eliminating unneeded or discarded data in LISP processing in order to create more memory for additional processing.

Generalization Process of deriving an abstract principle from data.

General problem solver (GPS) An early AI system that separated problem-solving methods from knowledge about the problem.

Generate and test A problem-solving method that involves first the generation of possible solutions followed by a test that evaluates, prunes, accepts, or rejects the solutions generated.

Goal A hypothesis to prove in an expert system. Also, a node in a search space containing a solution.

Goal driven An inference technique that begins with a goal or hypothesis and works backward through the rules in an attempt to prove the goal. Also called backward chaining.

Goal outline A menu containing a series of goals and subgoals to be pursued by an expert system.

Goal regression Method used in planning systems to avoid subgoal interactions. A procedure of solving one subgoal at a time and checking to see that a newly solved subgoal does not conflict with one previously solved.

Granularity The level of detail of knowledge in a rule or frame.

Handler Procedure that is invoked by sending a message to an object or frame. Similar to a method.

Heuristic Knowledge, often expressed as a rule of thumb, that guides the search process.

Heuristic search   Search technique that uses heuristic knowledge about a domain to help pick the path most likely to lead to a solution and thereby reduces the search effort.

Hierarchy   Knowledge rank organized from abstract or general knowledge to more specific knowledge. Powerful knowledge representation scheme used in frame-based expert systems.

HOW   Explanation on "how" the system derived a conclusion.

Hybrid system   A system that combines several different knowledge representation techniques.

Hypertext   The organization of information in nodes connected by associated links.

Hypothesis   A statement that is subject to verification or proof. A goal in a goal-driven expert system.

Hypothetical reasoning   Form of reasoning that makes assumptions about the problem. It maintains several lines of reasoning active at one time, which provides a what-if type search approach.

ICAI   Intelligent Computer-Aided Instruction. Instructional software that uses AI techniques.

ID3   A machine-learning algorithm used in induction expert systems that formulates a decision tree from a set of examples.

If-changed demon   A procedure attached to a frame's property slot that is executed whenever the property's value changes.

If-needed demon   A procedure attached to a frame's property slot that is executed whenever the property's value is needed.

Implication   A logical expression relating a condition to a conclusion.

Induction   Inducing rules from knowledge contained in a set of examples.

Induction system   An expert system that has knowledge contained in the form of examples. An induction system builds rules or a decision tree from the examples.

Inductive reasoning   Reasoning from the specific to the general.

Inference   The process of deriving new information from known information.

Inference engine   Processor in an expert system that matches the facts contained in the working memory and the domain knowledge contained in the knowledge base, to draw conclusions about the problem.

Inference network   Graphical representation of the system's rules with the antecedents and consequences of the rules drawn as nodes and their supporting relationships drawn as links.

Inferential flow analysis   Knowledge elicitation technique that attempts to determine the cause–effect relationships in a problem.

Inheritance   Process by which the characteristics of a parent frame are assumed by its child frame.

Instance   A specific object from a class of objects.

Instantiation   The process of assigning a specific name or value to a variable. An individual with a given age is an instantiation of the more general object ''person.''

Intelligence   The ability to acquire and apply knowledge to solve a problem.

Interpreter   The inference engine in an expert system.

IS-A   A link used in semantic networks and frame-based systems, which establishes a ''kind-of'' relationship between linked nodes or frames.

KEE   A large hybrid expert system development tool using rules and frames available from IntelliCorp.

Knowledge   A collection of facts, rules, and concepts used to reason with.

Knowledge acquisition   The process of acquiring, organizing, and studying knowledge.

Knowledge base   Part of an expert system that contains the domain knowledge.

Knowledge-based systems   Systems whose performance depends on encoded knowledge.

Knowledge dictionary   Part of an expert system project documentation that catalogs the pieces of knowledge discovered during the project.

Knowledge elicitation   The process of acquiring knowledge from a domain expert to enter into the knowledge base of an expert system.

Knowledge engineer   A person who acquires the domain knowledge, and builds and tests the expert system.

Knowledge engineering   The process of building an expert system.

Knowledge granularity   Level of knowledge that can be reliably provided by the user of an expert system.

Knowledge representation   The method used to encode knowledge in an expert system's knowledge base.

Learning   The process of gaining knowledge and understanding through education or experience.

Linguistic variable   A common term used in our natural language to describe some concept, such as ''the temperature is *very hot*,'' or ''the person is *tall*.''

LISP   Programming language based on list processing. Most widely used language by American AI researchers.

Logic   A system of reasoning based on the study of propositions and their analysis in making deductions.

Logic-based system   A system employing formal logic as its primary representation.

Machine learning   Study of techniques that will allow a computer to learn from experience.

Maximum cardinality   Establishes the maximum number of values a frame's property can have.

Means–ends analysis   A method for controlling search. The current state and the goal state are first obtained. A procedure is then selected and used to reduce the difference between these two states. The result is a new state that is closer to the goal state. Process is then repeated until the current state is the goal state. Also called the "General Problem Solver or GPS."

Membership function   A formula used to determine the degree of membership of some object to some fuzzy set. The formula is a representation of the fuzzy set.

Message   A signal to an object, to which the object responds by executing a method.

Meta-knowledge   Knowledge in an expert system that explains how the system is controlled or reasons. Knowledge about knowledge.

Meta-rule   A rule that describes how to control the problem-solving process.

Method   Procedure attached to a frame's slot that defines how the slot's value is to be obtained.

Minimum cardinality   The minimum number of values a frame's property can have.

Model-based reasoning   A method of reasoning that draws conclusions about the state of a modeled system exposed to a set of simulated data.

Modus ponens   Rule of logic that asserts that if we know A is true and A implies B, then we can assume B is true.

Monotonic reasoning   Method of reasoning that assumes once a fact is asserted it cannot be altered during the course of the reasoning.

Multiple inheritance   The ability of an object or frame to inherit information from multiple parents.

Multiple lines of reasoning   A problem-solving method in which a number of possibly acceptable approaches to find a solution are explored in parallel.

Multivalued attributes An attribute that can have more than one value.

MYCIN A classic expert system developed to diagnose infectious blood diseases and help a doctor recommend the appropriate treatment. A backward chaining rule-base expert system.

Natural language interface Part of expert system that allows the user to communicate with the system in a natural language such as English.

Nonmonotonic reasoning Method of reasoning that allows changes in reasoning for changes in a given fact. It allows for both the retraction of the given fact and all the conclusions formed from the fact.

NOT Logic operator used to represent the negation of a statement.

O-A-V Object–attribute–value.

Object A physical or conceptual item that has a collection of related attributes that describe it. See "Frame."

Object-oriented programming A programming method that supports knowledge represented in the form of "objects" or "frames" that communicate with each other using "messages."

OPS A programming language derived from LISP for building rule-based expert systems.

OR A logical operator used in a rule that implies that if any statement joined with an OR is true, then the rule's consequent is considered true.

Paradigm An example or model of a set of related things.

Parallel processing Simultaneous processing, as opposed to conventional sequential processing.

Plausible reasoning Reasoning that is inexact because either the knowledge or available information is uncertain.

Polymorphism A characteristic of object-oriented programming or frame-based systems in which a given message may be interpreted and acted upon differently between objects or frames.

Predicate A statement about the subject of a proposition.

Predicate calculus A programming language or logic system where statements about objects and their relationships are made. Each element in the predicate calculus is an object and the statements are called predicates. It is an extension of propositional calculus.

Premise A statement in the IF part of a rule that must be satisfied before the rule's conclusion is accepted.

Primitive   Premise of a rule that is not supported by any other rule.

Probability   A number representing the likelihood of a given event occurring. Most expert systems use confidence factors rather than probability numbers.

Problem space   A tree or graph containing nodes and branches used for searching for a solution to a given problem. The nodes represent possible problem states and the branches possible paths between states.

Problem solving   The process of seeking a solution to a given problem. Most problem-solving techniques used in expert systems focus on goal- or data-driven search techniques. Goal outlining or goal procedure programs greatly enhances an expert system problem-solving approach.

Procedure   A well-structured way of performing a given task.

Production   Term used by cognitive psychologists to describe a rule.

Production system   A model of human problem solving where problem situations contained in the short-term memory are combined with productions in the long-term memory to infer new information.

Prolog   A programming language based on the predicate calculus. A popular AI language outside of the United States.

Property   An attribute or feature of an object or frame.

Proposition   A declarative assertion or statement that has the property of being either true or false.

Propositional calculus   Logical system for reasoning. Conclusions are obtained from a series of statements according to the processing of rules.

PROSPECTOR   An expert system for helping to find ore deposits.

Pruning   Reducing the alternatives in a problem space during search when it appears that continual search in the pruned area will be fruitless.

Qualitative reasoning   A way to describe phenomena in terms of causal, compositional, or subtypical relationships among objects or events.

R1   An expert system designed for configuring VAX computer systems.

Reasoning   The process of working with knowledge, facts and problem-solving methods to draw conclusions or inferences.

Recognize–resolve–act cycle   A procedure used in forward-chaining rule-based expert systems. During the "recognize" step, rules are examined to see if their premises are true based on the facts in the working memory. These rules are then placed in a "conflict set." The "resolve" step chooses a rule from the conflict set using a conflict resolution scheme. During the "act" step, the rule chosen from the resolve step is fired.

Repertory grid   A technique used during knowledge elicitation. It relies on relating and differentiating various objects discovered during the elicitation session.

Resolution   Inference strategy used in logical systems to determine the truth of an assertion.

Rule   A method of representing knowledge consisting of premises and a conclusion. IF the premises are true, THEN the conclusion is also true.

Rule-based system   A computer program that processes problem-specific information contained in the working memory with a set of rules contained in the knowledge base, using an inference engine to infer new information.

Rule of thumb   A rule based on good judgment, gained from experience rather than first principles. Often called *shallow knowledge*.

Rule set   A set of rules that relate to some common concept or function.

Runtime version   Software that allows the running of an expert system developed by some software tool, but prohibits modification of the system or further system development.

Salience   A number assigned to a rule to represent its priority related to other rules.

Schema   A data structure that represents a stereotyped situation, event, or object. Typically found in expert systems represented in frames or scripts.

Script   A sequence of naturally followed events.

Search   A process of problem solving where a set of possible solutions is sought by traversing a problem space.

Search space   See problem space.

Semantic network   A method of knowledge representation using a graph made up of nodes and arcs, where the nodes represent objects and the arcs the relationship between the objects.

Shallow knowledge   Knowledge based on good judgment rather than first principles. Often called a *heuristic*.

Shell   An expert system development package that has all the facilities for building an expert system minus the domain's knowledge.

Slot   A component of a frame. Describes a particular attribute or relationship of the frame.

Slot value   A value or method for obtaining the value of a slot in a frame.

Specificity   One of the criteria used by conflict resolution in forward chaining, which chooses a rule to fire from a set of competing rules, on the basis of the number of premises.

State space   A graphic representation of all of the potential problem states of a given problem.

Subclass   A class that inherits information from a parent class. Usually used to divide a higher level class into natural divisions before defining specific instance frames.

Superclass   An upper-level class of some subclass or object.

Symbol   An alphanumeric pattern that represents some object characteristic or event of a problem.

Symbolic programming   Manipulating symbols that represent objects and their relationships.

Taxonomy   Classification of objects that are alike.

TEIRESIAS   A knowledge acquisition program built during the development of MYCIN. Interacts with the domain expert following a consultation in which a difficulty has occurred. Can work with the domain expert to modify the system to correct the mistake.

Temporal reasoning   Reasoning about problem states as they evolve over time.

Theorem prover   Program that begins with a goal and searches for implications (rules) whose conclusions will prove the goal.

Threshold   A numeric that must be exceeded before some action is taken.

Tracing   A mechanism in most expert systems that provides an ordered listing of the knowledge used to arrive at a conclusion. Used to explain "how" a conclusion was reached.

Truth-maintenance system   A belief-revision system that maintains a record of what caused a fact to be inserted into the working memory, and can thereby retract the fact if its dependent information is no longer true.

Turing test   A test to determine if a computer program has intelligence. A human working in a closed room converses over a computer terminal with "something." If the human cannot tell if the "thing" he is conversing with is a human or a computer, then it is assumed that the program is intelligent.

Uncertainty   The level of belief in a given fact either given by the user of an expert system or derived by the system. Also see certainty.

Unification   A rule of inference in logic that is used to unify two formulas to produce a clause.

Universal quantifier   A statement that indicates that a statement is true for all values in the problem.

Value   A quantity or quality that describes an attribute.

Variable rule A rule that contains one or more variables that can be used to match various facts inserted into the working memory. Usually used to scan instances of a given class frame.

Viewpoint Ability of an expert system to reason about alternatives. Also called "multiple worlds."

WHY Explanation on "why" the system is pursuing a line of reasoning.

Working memory That part of an expert system that contains the known facts of a given session with an expert system.

APPENDIX B

Catalog of Expert System Development Software

EXPERT SYSTEM SHELLS

FUZZY LOGIC DEVELOPMENT TOOLS

LISP

OBJECT ORIENTED DEVELOPMENT SOFTWARE

OPS

PROLOG

EXPERT SYSTEM SHELLS

1st-CLASS
Trinzic Corp.
101 University Ave.
Palo Alto, CA 94301
(415) 328-9595
PRICE: $2,495 for IBM PC/XT/AT and
DEC VAX
KNOWLEDGE REPRESENTATION: table-form
INFERENCE: induction

ACE
Knowledge Associates, Ltd.
302 W. 259th St.
Riverdale, NY 10471-1908
PRICE: Contact vendor
KNOWLEDGE REPRESENTATION: rule-based
INFERENCE: forward and backward
chaining

ADS
Trinzic Corp.
101 University Ave
Palo Alto, CA 94301
(415) 328-9595
PRICE: $9,000 for IBM PC/XT/AT, PS/
2; $70,000–$80,000 for IBM main-

frames, depending on operating
system
KNOWLEDGE REPRESENTATION: rule and
frame-based
INFERENCE: forward and backward
chaining

Advisor-2
Expert Systems International
1700 Walnut St.
Philadelphia, PA 19103
(215) 735-8510
PRICE: $695 for IBM PC/XT/AT, DEC
VAX, MicroVAX, Sun and Apollo
workstations
KNOWLEDGE REPRESENTATION: rule-based
INFERENCE: forward and backward
chaining

AIM
Abtech Corp.
503 Dale Ave.
Charlottesville, VA 22903
(804) 977-0686
PRICE: $1,495 for IBM and Mac
KNOWLEDGE REPRESENTATION: rule-based

INFERENCE: forward and backward chaining

Arity Expert
Arity Corp.
29 Domino Dr.
Concord, MA 01742
(508) 371-1243
PRICE: $295 for IBM PC/XT/AT and PS/2
KNOWLEDGE REPRESENTATION: frame-based
INFERENCE: backward chaining and induction

ART (Automated Reasoning Tool)
Inference Corp.
5300 W. Century Blvd.
Los Angeles, CA 90045
(213) 417-1243
PRICE: $30,000 for Apollo, HP, Sun, DEC
VAX, Symbolics, and Explorer workstations
KNOWLEDGE REPRESENTATION: rule and frame-based
INFERENCE: forward chaining

ART-IM (Automated Reasoning Tool-IM)
Inference Corp.
5300 W. Century Blvd.
Los Angeles, CA 90045
(213) 417-1243
PRICE: $8,000 for IBM PC/AT, PS/2
KNOWLEDGE REPRESENTATION: rule and frame-based
INFERENCE: forward chaining

Auto-Intelligence 1.26
IntelligenceWare Inc.
9800 S. Sepulveda Blvd.
Los Angeles, CA 90045-5228
(213) 417-8896
PRICE: $490
KNOWLEDGE REPRESENTATION: rule-based
INFERENCE: backward chaining

Crystal
Intelligence Environments
P.O. Box 388

Chelmsford, MA 01824
(508) 256-6412
PRICE: $995 for IBM PC/XT/AT MS-DOS versions; $1,995 for OS/2 versions
KNOWLEDGE REPRESENTATION: rule-based
INFERENCE: forward and backward chaining and induction

Decision Expert
Digital Equipment Corp.
290 Donald Lynch Blvd.
Marlboro, MA 01752-4790
(508) 490-8052
PRICE: $7900 for DEC VAX
KNOWLEDGE REPRESENTATION: table-form
INFERENCE: induction

ESP Advisor
Expert Systems International
1700 Walnut St.
Philadelphia, PA 19103
(215) 735-8510
PRICE: $695 for IBM PC/XT/AT, DEC VAX, MicroVAX, Sun, and Apollo workstations
KNOWLEDGE REPRESENTATION: rule-based
INFERENCE: forward and backward chaining

ESP Frame Engine
Expert Systems International
1700 Walnut St.
Philadelphia, PA 19103
(215) 735-8510
PRICE: $695 for IBM PC/XT/AT, DEC VAX, MicroVAX, Sun, and Apollo workstations
KNOWLEDGE REPRESENTATION: frame-based
INFERENCE: forward and backward chaining

Expert Controller
Umecorp (formerly Ultimate Media Corp.)
45 San Clemente Dr.
Corte Madera, CA 94925
(415) 924-6700
PRICE: $10,000 for IBM PC/AT

KNOWLEDGE REPRESENTATION: frame-based

INFERENCE: forward and backward chaining and set logic

EXSYS EL
EXSYS Inc.
P.O. Box 11247
Albuquerque, NM 87192
(505) 256-8356
PRICE: $175 for IBM PC/XT and PS/2; $600 unlimited runtime license, $2,500 and up for DEC VAX and some UNIX machines
KNOWLEDGE REPRESENTATION: rule-based, optional frame extension
INFERENCE: forward and backward chaining

EXSYS Professional
EXSYS Inc.
P.O. Box 11247
Albuquerque, NM 87192
(505) 256-8356
PRICE: $995 for PCs, $1,000 unlimited runtime license, $2,500 and up for DEC VAX and some UNIX machines
KNOWLEDGE REPRESENTATION: rule-based
INFERENCE: forward and backward chaining, optional frame extension

Flex
Logic Programming Associates Ltd
Studio 4 Royal Victoria Patriotic
Trinity Road, SW18 3SX, United
  Kingdom
44 81 871-2016
PRICE: $1000–$2000 for PCs
KNOWLEDGE REPRESENTATION: rule and frame-based
INFERENCE: forward and backward chaining

Goldworks
Gold Hill Computers Inc.
26 Landsdowne St.
Cambridge, MA 02139
(617) 621-3300
PRICE: $8,900 for 386 PCs, $7,900 for Macintosh II, $9,900 for Sun 3, 4, and 386i

KNOWLEDGE REPRESENTATION: rule and frame-based and object oriented

INFERENCE: forward and backward chaining

Guru First Step
Micro Data Base Systems Inc.
P.O. Box 6089
Lafayette, IN 47903-6089
(800) 344-5832
PRICE: $895 IBM PC
KNOWLEDGE REPRESENTATION: rule-based
INFERENCE: forward and backward chaining, mixed forward and backward chaining, and induction

Guru
Micro Data Base Systems Inc.
P.O. Box 6089
Lafayette, IN 47903-6089
(800) 344-5832
PRICE: $7,000 IBM PC/XT/AT, PS/2, DEC VAX, and Sun work station single-user systems, $9,900 for LAN version
KNOWLEDGE REPRESENTATION: rule-based
INFERENCE: forward and backward chaining, mixed forward and backward chaining, and induction

Intelligence/Compiler
IntelligenceWare Inc.
9800 S. Sepulveda Blvd.
Los Angeles, CA 90045-5228
(213) 417-8896
PRICE: $495; $7,500 for DEC VAX
KNOWLEDGE REPRESENTATION:
INFERENCE: forward and backward chaining and inexact logic

Kappa-PC
IntelliCorp
1975 El Camino Real West
Mountain View, CA 94040
(415) 965-5500
PRICE: $495 for IBM PC
KNOWLEDGE REPRESENTATION: rule and frame-based and object oriented
INFERENCE: forward and backward chaining

KBMS
Trinzic Corp.
101 University Ave.
Palo Alto, CA
(415) 326-9595
PRICE: $9,000 for IBM PC, DEC VAX
and Sun
KNOWLEDGE REPRESENTATION: rule and
frame-based
INFERENCE: forward and backward
chaining

KDS
KDS Corp.
934 Hunter Rd.
Wilmette, IL 60091
(708) 251-2621
PRICE: $1,795 for IBM PC/XT/AT and
Apollo workstations
KNOWLEDGE REPRESENTATION: rule and
frame-based
INFERENCE: forward and backward chain-
ing and induction

KEE (Knowledge Engineering Environment)
IntelliCorp
1975 El Camino Real West
Mountain View, CA 94040
(415) 965-5500
PRICE: $9,900–$30,000 for DEC VAX,
Sun, Apollo, Symbolics, micro-
Explorer and Explorer workstations,
IBM PC RT, Compaq 80386 and HP
machines
KNOWLEDGE REPRESENTATION: frame-
based and object oriented
INFERENCE: forward and backward
chaining

KES (Knowledge Engineering System)
Software Architecture & Engineering
Inc.
1600 Wilson Blvd. #500
Arlington, VA 22209
(703) 276-7910
PRICE: $4,000 for PCs, $10,000 for Sun
−4, $7,000 for Apollo and other Sun
machines

KNOWLEDGE REPRESENTATION: frame-
based
INFERENCE: forward and backward
chaining

Knowledge Craft
The Carnegie Group
5 PPG Pl.
Pittsburgh, PA 15222
(412) 642-6900
PRICE: $10,000–$70,000 for 386
machines, DEC VAX, MicroVAX,
Sun 3 and 4, Symbolics, and Explorer
workstations
KNOWLEDGE REPRESENTATION: frame-
based
INFERENCE: forward and backward
chaining

KnowledgerMaker
Knowledge Garden Inc.
473A Malden Bridge Rd. RD2
Nassua, NY 12123
(518) 766-3000
PRICE: $199 for IBM PC/XT/AT
KNOWLEDGE REPRESENTATION: table-form
INFERENCE: induction

KnowledgerPro
Knowledge Garden Inc.
12 Technology Drive #8
Setuaket, NY 11733-4049
(518) 246-5400
PRICE: $595 for IBM PC/XT/AT
KNOWLEDGE REPRESENTATION: rule-based
INFERENCE: forward and backward
chaining

LASER
Bell Atlantic Knowledge Systems
Group
34 Washington Rd.
Princeton Junction, NJ 08550
(609) 275-4545
PRICE: $900–$25,000 for Sun, DEC
VAX, IBM RT-PC, PS/2, IBM 9370,
and Macintosh II
KNOWLEDGE REPRESENTATION: frame-
based

INFERENCE: forward and backward
chaining

Level5
Information Builders Inc.
1250 Broadway
New York, NY 10001-3782
(914) 347-6860
PRICE: $295 for IBM PC/XT/AT and
Macintosh, $19,200 for DEC VAX
KNOWLEDGE REPRESENTATION: rule-based
INFERENCE: backward chaining

Level5 Object
Information Builders Inc.
1250 Broadway
New York, NY 10001-3782
(914) 347-6860
PRICE: $995 for IBM PC/XT/AT and
Macintosh
KNOWLEDGE REPRESENTATION: rule and
frame-based
INFERENCE: backward and forward
chaining

LogicTree
CAM Software
750 N. 200 West, Ste. 208
Provo, UT 84601
(801) 373-4086
PRICE: $495 for IBM PC/XT/AT and
PS/2
KNOWLEDGE REPRESENTATION: table-form
INFERENCE: induction

M.1
Cimflex Technology Corp.
1810 Embarcadero Rd.
Palo Alto, CA 94303
(415) 424-0500
PRICE: $5,000 for IBM PC/XT/AT site
licenses
KNOWLEDGE REPRESENTATION: rule-based
INFERENCE:

M.4
Cimflex Teknowledge
1810 Embarcadero Rd.
Palo Alto, CA 94303
(800) 285-0500

PRICE: $995 for IBM PC
KNOWLEDGE REPRESENTATION: rule-based
INFERENCE: forward and backward
chaining

MacSMARTS
Cognition Technology Corp.
565 Wheeler St.
Cambridge, MA 01238
(617) 492-0246
PRICE: $195 for Macintosh
KNOWLEDGE REPRESENTATION: table-form
INFERENCE: induction

MacSMARTS Professional
Cognition Technology Corp.
565 Wheeler St.
Cambridge, MA 01238
(617) 492-0246
PRICE: $495 for Macintosh
KNOWLEDGE REPRESENTATION: table-form
INFERENCE: induction

Nexpert Object
Neuron Data
444 High St.
Palo Alto, CA 94301
(415) 321-4488
PRICE: $995–$8,000 for development
system on IBM PC/XT/AT, Macintosh, DEC VAX, 386 machines, PS/2,
Sun, Apollo, HP, and other UNIX platforms; $750 for run-time version
KNOWLEDGE REPRESENTATION: rule and
frame-based
INFERENCE: forward and backward
chaining

OPS83
Production Systems Technologies
5001 Baum Boulevard
Pittsburgh, PA
PRICE: $1,950 for MS DOS version;
$2,950 for OS/2 version; $3,950 for
UNIX System V version
KNOWLEDGE REPRESENTATION: rules
INFERENCE: forward chaining

Personal Consultant
Texas Instruments Corp.
P.O. Box 1444
Houston, TX 77251
(800) 847-2787
PRICE: $495 for IBM PC/XT/AT; $95
 for run-time disk
KNOWLEDGE REPRESENTATION: decision
 tree
INFERENCE: backward chaining

Personal Consultant Easy
Texas Instruments Corp.
P.O. Box 1444
Houston, TX 77251
(800) 847-2787
PRICE: $495 for IBM PC/XT/AT
KNOWLEDGE REPRESENTATION: rules
INFERENCE: forward and backward
 chaining

pLogic
pLogic Knowledge Systems, Inc.
23133 Hawthorne Blvd.
Torrance, CA 90505
(213) 378-3760
PRICE: $495 for IBM PC/XT/AT; $95
 for run-time disk
KNOWLEDGE REPRESENTATION: table-form
INFERENCE: induction

ProKappa
IntelliCorp
1975 El Camino Real West
Mountain View, CA 94040
(415) 965-5500
PRICE: $14,450 for HP 9000, Sun, RS/
 6000
KNOWLEDGE REPRESENTATION: rule and
 frame-based and object oriented
INFERENCE: forward and backward
 chaining

ReMind
Cognitive Systems Inc.
220-230 Commercial St.
Boston, MA 02109
(914) 347-6860
PRICE: $3,000 for IBM PC
KNOWLEDGE REPRESENTATION: rule and
 frame-based and object oriented
INFERENCE: forward and backward
 chaining

Superexpert
Softsync Inc.
162 Madison Ave.
New York, NY 10016
(212) 685-2080
PRICE: $199.95 for IBM PC/XT/AT and
 Macintosh
KNOWLEDGE REPRESENTATION: table-form
INFERENCE: induction

TIMM
General Research Corp.
1900 Gallows Rd.
Vienna, VA 22182
(703) 506-5166
PRICE: $1,900 for IBM PC; $19,000 for
 mainframes
KNOWLEDGE REPRESENTATION: table-form
INFERENCE: induction

VP-Expert
Paperback Software Inc.
2830 Ninth St.
Berkeley, CA 94710
(415) 644-2116
PRICE: $349 for IBM PC/XT/AT
KNOWLEDGE REPRESENTATION: rule-based
INFERENCE: forward and backward chain-
 ing and induction

─────────── **FUZZY LOGIC DEVELOPMENT TOOLS** ───────────

BOOLE
URSIC Computing
5210 Trafalger Place
Madison, WI 53714
(608) 241-0651
PRICE: $95 for IBM PC

CubiCalc
Hyperlogic Corp.
1855 E. Valley Pkwy Ste. 210
Escondido, CA 92027
(619) 746-2765
PRICE: $495 for IBM PC

Manifold Editor
Fuzzy Systems Engineering
12223 Wilsey Way
Poway, CA 92064
(619) 748-7384
PRICE: $250 for IBM PC

RT/Fuzzy
Integrated Systems Inc.
3260 Jay Street
Santa Clara, CA 95054

(408) 980-1500
PRICE: $5,000, for UNIX and VMS work-
stations

TILShell
Togai Intralogic Inc.
30 Corporate Prk Ste. 107
Irvine, CA 92714
(714) 975-8522
PRICE: $3000 for IBM PC

LISP

Allegro CL
Franz Inc.
1995 University Ave.
Berkeley, CA 94704
(510) 548-3600
PRICE: contact vendor

CLOE
Symbolics Inc.
6 New England Executive Pk
Burlington, MA 01803
(617) 221-1356
PRICE: $4,000 for IBM PC Windows

FranzLISP
Fort Pond Research
15 Fort Pond Road
Acton, Mass. 01702
(508) 263-9692
PRICE: $99 (interpreter) $199 (compiler)
for Macintosh

GCLisp
Gold Hill Inc.
26 Landsdown St.
Cambridge, MA 02139
(617) 621-3300
PRICE: $350 for IBM PC

IBUKI Common Lisp
IBUKI
PO Box 1627
Los Altos, CA 94022
(415) 961-4996
PRICE: $700 for PC, $2,800 for IBM, Sun,
HP, SGI

Lucid Common LISP
Lucid Inc.
707 Laurel St.
Menlo Park, CA 94025
(415) 329-8400
PRICE: $2,495 for PC, $4,400 for SPARC,
Apollo, HP and Sun

Macintosh Common LISP
Apple Computer Inc.
20525 Mariani Ave.
Cupertino, CA 95014
(800) 282-2732, (408) 996-1010
PRICE: $495

muLISP-90
Soft Warehouse Inc.
3660 Waialae Ave Suite 304
Honolulu, HI 96816-3236
(808) 521-4119
PRICE: $400 for IBM PC

NanoLISP
Microcomputer Systems Consultants
PO Box 6646
Santa Barbara, CA 93160-6646
(805) 967-2270
PRICE: $100 for IBM PC

Poplog
Computable Functions Inc.
35 South Orchard Drive
Amherst, Mass. 01002
(413) 545-1249
PRICE: $749 for PC/SCO UNIX and Macin-
tosh, $4,500 for SPARC and VAX VMS

Procyon Common Lisp
ExperTelligence Inc.
5638 Hollister Ave., Suite 302
Goleta, CA 93117
(805) 967-1797
PRICE: $2,700 for DOS/Windows and
  Macintosh

Star Spphire Common LISP
Sapiens Software Corp.
P.O. Box 3365
Santa Cruz, CA 95063-3365
(408) 458-1990
PRICE: $99 for PC

Software Engineer
Raindrop Software Corp.
833 Arapaho, Suite 104
Richardson, TX 75081
(214) 234-2911
PRICE: $249.95 for DOS/Windows

Top Level Common LISP
Top Level Inc.
100 University Drive
Amherst, Mass. 01002
(413) 549-4455
PRICE: $687 for UNIX

OBJECT ORIENTED DEVELOPMENT SOFTWARE

Borland C++
Borland International
1800 Green Hills Rd POB 660001
Scotts Valley, CA 95067-0001
(408) 439-1607
PRICE: $495 for IBM PC

GCLisp Developer
Gold Hill Inc.
26 Landsdown St.
Cambridge, MA 02139
(617) 621-3300
PRICE: contact vendor, for IBM PC

Prog. Workshop C++
Apple Computer Inc.
20525 Mariani Ave.
Cupertino, CA 95014
(408) 996-1010
PRICE: contact vendor

Smalltalk/V Windows
Digitalk
9841 Airport Boulevard

Los Angeles, Calif. 90045
(213) 645-1082
PRICE: $499 for IBM PC

Turbo C++
Borland International
1800 Green Hills Rd.
POB 660001
Scotts Valley, CA 95067-0001
(408) 439-1607
PRICE: $100 for IBM PC

Turbo C++ for Windows
Borland International
1800 Green Hills Rd.
POB 660001
Scotts Valley, CA 95067-0001
(408) 439-1607
PRICE: $150 for IBM PC

OPS

CLIPS
COSMIC, The University of Georgia
382 E. Broad St.
Athens, GA 30602
(404) 542-3265
PRICE: $490 for IBM PC, Macintosh, and
  DEC VAX

DEC OPS5
Digital Equipment Corp.
111 Locke Drive
Marlboro, MA 01748
(508) 480-5225
PRICE: contact vendor

OPS5/PC
J Soft Inc.
21414 W Honey Land
Lake Villa, IL 60046
(312) 856-3645
PRICE: $195 for IBM PC

OPS83
Production Systems Technologies Inc.
5001 Baum Boulevard
Pittsburgh, PA 15213
(412) 683-4000
PRICE: contact vendor

PROLOG

AAIS Prolog
Advanced AI Systems Inc.
PO Box 39-0360
Mountain View, CA 94039-0360
(415) 948-8648
PRICE: $298 for Macintosh

Active Prolog Tutor
Amziod
40 Samuel Prescott Drive
Stow, MA 01775
(508) 897-5560
PRICE: $65 for IBM PC

ALS Prolog Professional
Applied Logic Systems
P.O. Box 90
University Station
Syracuse, NY 13210-0090
(315) 471-3900
PRICE: $499 for IBM PC and Macintosh,
$799 for 386-based PCs under DOS or
SCO UNIX

Arity Prolog Professional Compiler
Arity Corp.
29 Domino Dr.
Concord, Mass. 01742
(508) 371-1243
PRICE: $650 for IBM PC

BIM Prolog (SPARC)
BIM
Kwikstraat 4
Everberg B-3078, Belgium
(01132) 27 595 925
U.S. Distributor: The Shure Group
1514 Pacific Ranch Dr.
Encinitas, Calif. 92024
(619) 944-0320, (800) 627-6564
PRICE: $7,500

Cogent Prolog
Amziod
40 Samuel Prescott Drive
Stow, MA 01775
(508) 897-5560
PRICE: $199 for IBM PC

Delphia Prolog
Delphia
27 Ave. de la Republique
38170 Seyssinet, France
(01133) 76 266 894
U.S. Distributor: Arity Corp.
29 Domino Dr.
Concord, Mass. 01742
(508) 371-1243
PRICE: $10,000 for Sun3, SPARC, Apollo,
HP 9000, and VAX VMS

IF Prolog (SPARAC)
InterFace GmbH
Garmischerstr. 4/V
Munich D-8000, Germany
(01149) 89 510 860
U.S. Distributor: Oasis
2 32nd Ave.
Waltham, Mass. 02154
(617) 890-7889
PRICE: $1,999 for DOS, $5,400 for Macin-
tosh and microVAX, $7,200 for HP,
$6,300 for SPARC and IBM RS/6000,
$10,200 for DECstation

LPA 386-Prolog
Logic Programming Associates Ltd.
Logic Programming Associates Ltd
Studio 4 Royal Victoria Patriotic
Trinity Road, SW18 3SX, United
Kingdom
44 81 871-2016
PRICE: $2,000 for IBM PC

PDC Prolog
Prolog Development Center
568 14th St., N.W.
Atlanta, Ga. 30318
(800) 762-2710
PRICE: $299–$2,000

Quintus DOS Prolog
Quintus Corp.
2100 Geng Rd.
Palo Alto, Calif. 94303
(415) 813-3800
PRICE: $325–$1,695 for IBM PC

Quintus Prolog Development System
Quintus Corp.
2100 Geng Rd.
Palo Alto, Calif. 94303
(415) 813-3800
PRICE: $10,000 for Sun, Sparc

Quintus MacProlog
Quintus Corp.
2100 Geng Rd.
Palo Alto, Calif. 94303
(415) 813-3800
PRICE: $1,295 for MAC

Catalog of Expert System Applications

This appendix contains brief summaries of selected expert systems from a variety of application areas. Also provided is a reference for each system, permitting access to more detailed information on a system of interest. Listed are 200 of the 2500 systems uncovered during the survey discussed in Chapter 1.

Agriculture

AIDECS furnishes control for a bioregenerative, closed ecological life support system in all areas from planning of agricultural management to control of environmental conditions. The system deals with control over two widely different time scales: scheduling crop planting and harvesting over the extended horizon needed to ensure maintenance of the CO_2/O_2 and other gas balances (typically involving units of weeks, months and years), and controlling environmental parameters such as temperature and humidity to be properly correlated with crop requirements and external weather conditions (typically involving units of hours and days). The system was developed at Kansas Univ., Lawrence, KS.

Kim, T. and B.P. Zeigler, AIDECS: An AI-based, distributed environmental control system for self-sustaining habitats, Artificial Intelligence in Engineering, vol. 5, no. 1, pp. 33–42, January 1990.

AQ11 incorporates knowledge of plant environment and disease symptoms to provide advice on the diagnosis of soybean disease. The system considers issues such as the month of year, temperature, plant height, and condition of the plants. Rules, generated from an induction technique, represent the knowledge by directly displaying the diagnostic expertise provided to the system. The system was developed at the University of Illinois.

Michalski, R.S. and R.L. Chilausky, Learning by being told and learning from examples: An experimental comparison of two methods of knowledge acquisition in the context of developing an expert system for soybean disease diagnosis, Policy Analysis and Information Systems, no. 2, 1980.

BULBFLY assists in the management of wheat bulb fly in the United Kingdom. The system provides recommendations on strategic and practical options for management of wheat bulb fly. BULBFLY gives comparative costs of the various treatments recommended, ecological and biological information of the pest, details of cultural control practices, and general advice on the safe use of insecticides. The system was developed at Imperial College, Berkshire, UK.

Jones, T., et al., An expert system for management of Delia Diparctata (Diptera: Anthomyiidae) in UK, Journal of Economic Entomology, vol. 83, no. 5, pp. 2065–2072, 1990.

OMAX provides 24-hour-a-day crop management advice to cotton farmers to suggest a daily strategy for irrigation, fertilization, and for applying defoliants and cotton boll openers. Its advice is based on weather reports, soil characteristics, pest damage, and growth and development predictions by the FORTRAN simulation model GOSSYM. Sensors in the cotton fields automatically report weather conditions to the system, and Comax reevaluates its recommendations daily. Knowledge is represented as rules. The system was developed by The Crop Simulation Research Unit at Mississippi State.

McKinon, J.M. and H.E. Lemmon, Expert systems in agriculture, Computers and Electronics in Agriculture, vol. 1, no. 1, 1985.

??ID is an expert system for fertilizer prescription. A lack of extension officers and a shortage and rapid turnover of research and regional management staff involved in plantation nutrition was seen as a problem in the Cape Province. Opportunities for increasing timber production by addition of fertilizers were being missed and wrong decisions were being made. To improve the situation ENID was built to aid the manager's decision making, to provide an easily accessible source of otherwise hard to obtain information on fertilization. The system, based on a synthesis of all available information, runs on microcomputer and questions the manager about his/her options and local conditions, and makes recommendation based on the responses. The program is quick, interactive and can be interrogated about the reasons for its decision. It is readily updated as new information becomes available and will provide an increasing knowledge base for fertilizer decisions. The system was developed at the University Canterbury, Christchurch 1, N.Z.

??yn, T.W., D.C. Grey, and D.G.M. Donald, ENID: An expert system for fertilizer prescription in the Cape Province of South Africa, South African Forestry Journal, vol. 0, no. 151, pp. 71–77, 1989.

??nARs provides evaluation of the financial health of a farm business. It is designed to operate from a minimum dataset and to provide an initial assessment of the overall financial health of the business. FinARS was built using INSIGHT 2+ and runs on IBM-PC compatible computers. FinARS can be used as a tool for teaching financial analysis concepts to students, county agents, lenders, and farmers. It can also be used as a diagnostic tool for farmers (or by extension agents or lenders working with farmers) to provide an initial interpretation of their firm's financial situation, diagnose its potential problems, and provide suggested alternatives for improving the firm's financial situation. FinARS consists of four basic components—liquidity, solvency, and profitability, and an overall integrative, evaluation component. Each component utilizes a decision tree structure; financial ratio information, standards, rules of thumb, and trend information are used to structure the decision rules. The system was developed at the University of Florida.

Boggess, W., P. Van Blokland, and S. Moss, FinARS: A financial analysis review expert system, Agricultural Systems, vol. 31, no. 1, pp. 19–34, 1989.

LUCVAR provides advice to a farmer on the best lucerne (alfalfa) varieties to grow. The system considers information supplied from the user on such issues as the use of the crop, soil conditions, and the amount to be spent. Besides providing recommendations, the system also provides information on the effective growing of the crop, cultivation, and pest control. The system is rule based and uses backward chaining. LUCVAR was designed using the ESP Advisor tool set. It was developed at the Agricultural Research Centre, Tamworth, Australia.

Lodge, G. and T. Frecker, LUCVAR: A computer-based consultation system for selecting lucerne (alfalfa) varieties, Expert Systems, vol. 6, no. 3, pp. 166–177, Aug. 1989.

MUSH is an expert system developed to aid farmers in the management of crops. To effectively grow and manage any crop, a grower must have knowledge in a variety of areas. For assistance, the grower will often consult with one of the available regional agricultural extension service offices, which maintains experts on various crops. However, factors such as time, distance, access during office hours, etc., create obstacles to the grower for obtaining help. MUSH was developed to provide readily available assistance in the following areas of crop production: crop management problem diagnosis, financial planning, and crop management tutoring. The system also provides sources of references to obtain additional information on various crop topics. The system interplays diagnostics with tutoring so that after a problem is solved, the user is tutored on how to avoid the problem in the future. Hypertext and interactive graphics are used extensively, which serves to enhance the system's interface and effectiveness. The Shiitake mushroom was chosen as a test case for this expert system because it offers an excellent marketing potential, and relatively few human experts exist who are capable of assisting growers with this crop. The system was built using a traditional rule-based approach using KnowledgePro and runs on an IBM or compatible PC. The system was developed at the University of Akron, Akron, OH.

Durkin, John, Ronald Godine, and Yao-Chi Lu, Expert system for specialty crop management, AI Applications in Natural Resource Management, vol. 4, no. 3, pp. 48–56, Summer, 1990.

XLAYER provides management advice to northeastern commercial poultry layer managers. It has demonstrated ability to diagnose and estimate economic and associated losses and recommend remedial management action for over 80 individual production management problems significantly affecting flock profitability. The XLAYER program, containing over 400 production rules and running on IBM-compatible personal computers, possesses diverse diagnostic capabilities consistent with those of poultry management experts in nutrition, housing and equipment, disease, marketing, economic, and human-induced management areas. The system was developed at Oregon State University, Corvallis, OR.

Schmisseur, E., J. Pankratz, and M. Gehman, XLAYER: An expert system for layer management, Poultry Science, vol. 68, no. 8, pp. 1047–1054, 1989.

Business

AUTHORIZER'S ASSISTANT (AA) aids in credit card application processing for American Express. It helps credit authorizers sort through 12 databases to determine whether or not to approve individual charges. AA does a heuristic search of the databases to arrive at a recommendation. The system cuts the time needed to process credit card customers' purchase authorization requests, minimizes losses from bad credit decisions, and improves human authorizers' overall business performance. The system is implemented in ART on an IBM mainframe. It was developed by Inference Corp.

Rothi, J.A. and D.C. Yen, Why American Express gambled on an expert data base, Information Strategy: The Executive's Journal, vol. 6, no. 3, pp. 16–22, Spring 1990.

BA, Bidder's Associate, aids in the preparation of bids for a jet-engine parts manufacturing company. The company receives a request for quotation (RFQ) and estimates the cost to manufacture the parts and the price that will win the bid. BA is case-based and was developed on a 386-based PC using C and a text-based windowing graphics interface. BA allows the user to enter information from the RFQ, select relevant similarity features, and rate their relative importance. The user can retrieve similar past bids and compare the highest scoring (most similar) bids to the new bid. The retrieved bid information is then used in the construction and cost estimation of the new bid. The system was developed by Stottler Henke Associations Inc., Belmont, CA.

Stottler, R.H., Case-based reasoning for bid preparation. AI Expert, vol. 7, no. 2, pp. 44–49, Mar. 1992.

BERT, Bank ExpeRT, assists bank examiners in evaluating the financial condition of banks. The Office of the Comptroller of the Currency (COC), is responsible for evaluating the financial condition of over 4,400 nationally chartered banks. The COC currently has 2,800 bank examiners that analyze banking data, prepare bank status reports, and conduct on-site inspections at troubled banks. BERT downloads all the data from COC's Amdahl mainframe onto the examiners' PC and then begins analyzing the data. The system considers 2,000 decisions and reduces them to five overall conclusions that are presented with narrative comment. The analysis takes about six minutes per bank. In tests, its conclusions matched those of the field testers 90 to 95 percent of the time. The system was implemented using GURU.

Osborn, P. and W. Zickefoose, Building expert systems from the ground up, AI Expert, vol. 5, no. 5, pp. 28–35, May 1990.

CARMA, Computer-Assisted Real Estate Market Analyst, assists in the evaluation of the real estate market. The system is rule-based, uses a backward-chaining strategy, and consists of ten different rule modules. The system was implemented using EXSYS and Lotus 1-2-3. CARMA asks questions related to the area under consideration, such as population and employment trends, household incomes, and housing demands. It then uses Lotus to calculate financial ratios to aid in producing its overall evaluation of the real estate market.

Holmes, W.T. and M.E. Warkentin, The computer-assisted real estate market analyst: A knowledge-based real estate market analyst. Proc. of the 1989 Conference of the Northeast Decision Sciences Institute, 1989.

ELOISE, English Language–Oriented Indexing System for EDGAR, assists personnel at the U.S. Securities and Exchange Commission (SEC) with detecting unusual security transactions. EDGAR consists of a storage system for SEC filings that are received directly from filling companies. ELOISE analyzes the SEC filing documents using natural language processing techniques to detect the presence of certain predefined patterns and concepts. The system was developed using KEE and runs on a Symbolics LISP machine. It was developed at Arthur Andersen and Co.

Behan, Joe, Overview of Financial Applications of Expert Systems, Proceedings of IEEE Computer Society, WESTEX-87: Proceedings—Western Conference on Expert Systems, Anaheim, CA, pp. 223–229, June 2–4, 1987.

ESCAPE, Expert System for Claims Authorization and Processing, is used in the validation process for incoming warranty program checks at the Ford Motor Company. The system helps Ford dealers determine if a given vehicle is covered under warranty for the work proposed. The system checks each incoming claim and attaches an error code to any that are not valid. It verifies that the vehicle type, production date, mileage, part and labor costs, and other data are appropriate for the warranty coverage indicated by the submitting dealer. If the mileage is too high, if the vehicle line is not eligible for the specific policy, or if any other error conditions are identified, the claim can not be validated. ESCAPE was developed using ART-IM/MVS and runs on an IBM 3090 mainframe. It was developed by Ford Motor Co. and Inference Corp.

Bunney, W., et al., Ford Motor Company's system for claims authorization: Escape, The 1990 Second Annual Conference, Innovative Applications of Artificial Intelligence, 1990.

FOLIO offers consultation in the area of portfolio selection by defining a client's investment goals and suggesting a means for attaining these goals. The system first determines the client's objectives then suggests percentages of each fund that should meet these goals. FOLIO was designed to make recommendations for dividend-oriented (low-risk stocks) and commodity-sensitive (higher-risk stocks) investments. The system is rule based and uses forward chaining. It was developed at Stanford University.

Cohen, P. and M.D. Lieberman, A report on FOLIO: An expert assistant for portfolio managers, Proceedings IJCAI-83, pp. 212–214, 1983.

HELDA is a help-desk assistant that supports customer service calls for software problems. Helda is composed of 32 knowledge bases containing 3,500 rules. It contains two expert systems: ACE and SADAR. ACE automates problem description by guiding the user through a series of questions that establish what the caller was trying to do and what problems occurred. SADAR uses the results of ACE and searches for a past problem that is similar in description to the current one. SADAR also uses confidence factors to reflect the similarity between the current and past problems. The system was implemented using ADS and runs on an IBM 3084 mainframe. Cost savings for the first year were $1.5 million. The system was developed at Cincom Systems, St. Louis, MO.

Kilhoffer, A. and C. Wisely, HELDA: The help-desk assistant, AI Expert, vol. 5, no. 2, pp. 57–59, Feb. 1990.

INSURANCE RISK ASSESSMENT APPLICATION: An expert system was developed to assist an insurance company with determining the risk of underwriting life insurance policies. The source of knowledge for the system was the Lincoln National Life Underwriting Manual, which contains assessment rules for almost 500 diseases. The system has three main modules: documentation analysis and additional information requirements for professional and sport activities assessment, and assessment of diseases declared by the client. The system considers the client's blood pressure, weight, urine analysis, diabetes mellitus, myocardial infarct, and coronary diseases. It uses both rules and frames to code the knowledge, and employs a backward-chaining strategy. The system was implemented using PC PLUS on an IBM PC. The system was developed by Seguros America, Mexico.

Vargas, D., An expert system for risk assessment in an individual's life, in Operational Expert System Applications in Mexico, F.J. Cantu-Ortiz, ed., Pergamon Press, 1991.

LENDING ADVISOR assists bank loan officers with loan applications for lending to companies with $5 to 150 million in revenues. The system assesses the company's loan history, cash flows, and managing and marketing strengths. It then performs financial projections and calculates a risk assessment for the loan. The system is rule based, employs forward chaining, and was developed by Syntelligence for Wells Fargo Bank and First Wachovia Bank, using their own expert system shell called SYNTEL, which has its origin in the KAS shell. It runs on an IBM mainframe.

Hart, Peter, Amos Barzily, and Richard Duda, Qualitative reasoning for financial assessments: A prospectus, AI Magazine, vol. 7, no. 1, pp. 62–68, Spring 1986.

Objective Financial System assists financial planners with preparing a financial plan for individuals with low or middle incomes starting at $30,000. The system makes recommendations on income tax planning, living expenses, debt management, personal residence, education funding, general insurance management, retirement planning, estate planning, life insurance, and general investments. It is rule based and makes extensive use of databases to hold the current market data. The system runs on the DEC PDP-11 series of computers and was developed at Objective Financial Systems, Inc., Columbus, OH.

Behan, Joe, Overview of financial applications of expert systems, Proceedings of IEEE Computer Society, WESTEX-87: Proceedings—Western Conference on Expert Systems, Anaheim, CA, pp. 223–229, June 2–4, 1987.

RAP, Relocation Allowance Planner, is an expert system that assists government employees who need to interpret and apply the Federal Travel Regulations for relocation purposes. A person who is intending to relocate can interact with the system beforehand to find out whether he is eligible for a relocation allowance, which kinds of expenses are covered, and the amounts that are considered reasonable. It is rule-based system implemented on a DOS-based microcomputer. The inference engine is written in Arity PROLOG and the user interface is written in Microsoft C. The system was developed at the National Center for Toxicological Research (NCTR) and the University of Arkansas.

Berghel, H., et al., An expert system for government regulations, PC AI, vol. 4, no. 6, pp. 50–53, November/December 1990.

STOCK MARKET PREDICTION APPLICATION: an expert system was developed using an induction technique to improve the reliability of stock market prediction. The problem chosen focused on predicting intermediate fluctuations in the movement of the market for nonconservative investors. Information for the system was obtained from the Wall Street Journal, and from interpretations of trend-charting techniques. Three different results were used to categorize the prediction: bullish (forecasting an upward trend), bearish (forecasting a downward trend), and neutral (indicating that either call was too risky). The system used the ID3 algorithm to induce its knowledge base.

Braun, H. and J.S. Chandler, Predicting stock market behavior through rule induction: An application of the learning-from-example approach, Decision Sciences, vol. 8, no. 3, pp. 415–29, Summer 1987.

TAXADVISOR appraises financial condition of estates valued at over $175,000 and suggests strategies for estate and tax management. The system provides advice on insurance purchases, retirement actions, transfer of estate, and gift and will issues. It is rule based and uses backward chaining. The system was developed at the University of Illinois, Champaign-Urbana.

Michaelsen, R., A knowledge-based system for individual income and transfer tax planning, PhD Thesis, University of Illinois, Accounting Dept., Champaign-Urbana, 1982.

TAXPAYER SERVICE ASSISTANT (TSA) helps assistors provide advice to taxpayers on tax law topics. The US Internal Revenue Service (IRS) employs 5000 assistors to answer telephone inquiries from taxpayers. TSA serves these assistors by improving the correctness and completeness in answers provided to the over 18 million calls on tax laws that are received yearly. The system was developed at Internal Revenue Service, Washington, DC.

Beckman, T.J., An assistant expert system: Assisting assistors in assisting taxpayers. Antonisse, H.J., Benoit, J.W., and Silverman, B.G. (eds.), Proceedings of the Annual AI Systems in Government, Washington, DC, IEEE Comput. Soc. Press, Washington, DC, pp. 210–217, March 1989.

UNIK-FCST, UNIfied Knowledge-ForeCaST, assists with making adjustments in statistical forecasting of the demand for oil products. Time series models have served as a highly useful forecasting method, but are deficient in that they merely extrapolate past patterns in data without taking into account expected future events and other qualitative factors. To overcome this limitation, forecasting experts in practice judgmentally adjust the statistical forecasts. UNIK-FCST learns from historical judgmental adjustments through generalization and analogy, reasons based on similar cases, and composes and decomposes the impacts of simultaneous judgmental events nonmonotonically. The system was developed at Korea Advanced Institute of Science and Technology, Seoul, Korea.

Lee, J., et al., UNIK-FCST: Knowledge-assisted adjustment of statistical forecasts, Expert Systems with Applications, vol. 1, no. 1, p. 3949, 1990.

Chemistry

CHROMATOGRAPHY TEST DESIGN APPLICATION: an expert system was developed for designing a chromatograph test. The expert system recommends specifications for the column system, optimizes the operating conditions, performs peak identification and quantitation on line, and diagnoses the hardware system. The system was developed at Dalian Inst. Chem. Phys., Acad. Sinica, Dalian, Liaoning, China.

Lu, P. and H. Huang, Expert system for chromatography, Journal of Chromatography, vol. 452, pp. 175–190, 1988.

METALS AND ALLOYS IDENTIFICATION APPLICATION: An expert system was developed to identify common metals and alloys. The user is asked to supply information on density, color, hardness, and simple chemical tests that can be performed by nonmetallurgists in a nonlaboratory setting. If sufficient information is available, the system will positively identify the metal or alloy. If there is not sufficient information, the system will provide a list of possible metals in order of likelihood. The system is rule based and employs backward chaining. The system was implemented using EXSYS and was developed at General Electric.

Anthony, T.R., The Metals Analyst: An expert system for identifying metals and alloys, GE Corporate Research and Development Report No. 85CRD181.

SECS presents possible techniques for synthesizing complex organic molecules. It uses the structure of a target structure supplied by the chemist and generates a plan to create it from basic building block molecules. The system uses a backward-chaining scheme and was implemented in FORTRAN on a PDP-10 and IBM 370. The system was developed at the University of California, Santa Cruz.

Wipke, W. Todd, Glen I., Ouchi, and S. Krishnan, Simulation and evaluation of chemical synthesis-SECS: an application of artificial intelligence techniques, Artificial Intelligence, vol. 11, 1978.

SYNCHEM2 is an expert system for organic synthesis discovery that uses graph embedding. Graph embedding (subgraph isomorphism) is an NP-complete problem of great theoretical and practical importance in the sciences, especially chemistry and computer science. SYNCHEM2 searches for synthesis routes of organic molecules without the online guidance of a user. The system was developed at State Univ. of New York, Stony Brook, NY.

Benstock, J.D., D.J. Berndt, and K.K. Agarwal, Graph embedding in SYNCHEM2, an expert system for organic synthesis discovery, Discrete Appl. Math. (Netherlands), vol. 19, pp. 45–63, March 1988.

X-RAY ANALYSIS APPLICATION: an expert system was developed to analyze X-rays to determine the chemical content of materials. The system automatically performs the interpretation of large numbers of X-ray spectra obtained by electron probe microanalysis of single particles. The system is rule based and employs forward chaining. The system was implemented using OPS5 and was developed at the University of Antwerp, Universiteitsplein 1, B-2610 Wilrijk/Antwerp, Belgium.

Janssens, K., et al., The development process of an expert system for the automated interpretation of large EPMA data sets, Chemometrics and Intelligent Laboratory Systems, vol. 4, no. 2, pp. 147–162, 1988.

Communications

ACE, the Automated Cable Expert, is an expert system designed to direct preventative maintenance activities in a local telephone network. It helps telephone companies reduce the incidence of phone cable failures. ACE selects equipment for maintenance by analyzing historical data, and suggests maintenance that should be performed to reduce the likelihood of cable related problems. The system examines two databases: the Cable Repair Administrative System and the Trouble Repair Evaluation and Administration Tool. ACE frees the limited number of expert cable analysts who would need to examine this large amount of data. It is a rule-based system that processes information drawn from the databases in a forward-chaining fashion. The knowledge base and inference engine are written in FRANZ LISP and OPS4, and the system runs on a VAX 11/780. It was developed at AT&T Bell Laboratories, Whiffany, N.J.

Vesonder, Gregg, et al., ACE: An expert system for telephone cable maintenance, Proceedings IJCAI-83, pp. 116–121, 1983.

COMEX selects the proper communication channel (HF, VHF, UHF, satellite, telephone) for the desired communication application (voice, data). It also selects the equipment, the proper path (direct, relay), and the equipment to use (modem, radio, antenna). It finally selects the equipment operating parameters as well as the frequency and communications protocol. The system uses information supplied by the user and from external utility programs such as frequency management programs. COMEX is a fuzzy logic–based system that employs several knowledge bases that communicate over a blackboard. The system runs on an IBM-PC.

Schneider, M., J. Perl, and A. Kandel, COMEX—An autonomous fuzzy expert system for tactical communications networks, in Fuzzy Expert Systems, A. Kandel, ed., CRC Press, 1991.

HEARSAY is a speech understanding system. The system consists of a set of cooperating independent processes, each representing a source of knowledge.

The knowledge is used either to predict what may appear in a given context or to verify hypotheses resulting from a prediction. The system was developed at Carnegie-Mellon University.

Reddy, D.R., L.D. Erman, R.D. Fennell, and R.B. Neely, The HEARSAY speech understanding system: An example of the recognition process, IJCAI-73, Stanford University, pp. 185–93, 1973.

ITAPAC Assistance System (IAS) assists network operators with managing and controlling the Italian public packet-switched network (ITAPAC). The heart of IAS is an expert system that implements the network management knowledge provided by experts and uses it for advising the network operators. The system continuously monitors the network in real time through a connection with the Network Control Center, and as soon as an anomaly is detected, it warns the operator about the problem and its severity. Upon request, it can also provide information about the detected anomaly and can suggest smart corrective actions deduced from expert rules. The system was developed at CSELT, Turin, Italy.

Giovannini, F. and C.F. Rossi, Expert systems for the management of the Italian public packet-switched network, CSELT Technical Reports (Centro Studi e Laboratori Telecomunicazioni), vol. 18, no. 4, pp. 279–282, Aug. 1990.

NETMAN is a knowledge-based program that uses a machine learning technique, knowledge-based learning, in the domain of Network Traffic Control. NETMAN's task is to maximize call completion in a circuit-switched telecommunications network. NETMAN learns from its own experiences and by observing the actions of other agents. NETMAN is one of the components of ILS (Integrated Learning System), which contains implementations of several learning paradigms working together to improve problem-solving performance. NETMAN combines two machine learning paradigms: Explanation-Based Learning and Empirical Learning. The system was developed at GTE Lab Inc., Waltham, MA.

Silver, Bernard, NetMan: A learning network traffic controller, Proceedings of the 3rd International Conference on Industrial and Engineering Applications of Artificial Intelligence and Expert Systems—IEA/AIE 90, Charleston, SC, pp. 923–931, July 15–18, 1990.

Computer Systems

ALCA assists sales personnel with the task of configuring a costumer's local area network. The system is able to generate all feasible LAN/WAN configuration possibilities automatically and to pick the most appropriate solution to solve the customer's needs, while specifically addressing open systems inerconnection (OSI) standards. ALCA is based on a centrally updated knowledge base of various local area networking products and their interconnection possibilities. ALCA also allows querying to find out protocol interfaces supported by a particular product/service. The system is frame based and was developed at AT&T Bell Laboratories, Homdel, NJ.

Lirov, Y., S. Prakash, and S. Ravikumar, ALCA: Automated local area networks configuration aid, Expert Systems: The International Journal of Knowledge Engineering, vol. 8, no. 3, pp. 171–181, August 1991.

COMPUTER INTRUDER DETECTION APPLICATION: TRW Inc. has developed a security system for their credit information database. The system is a data driven, front-end expert program that has the ability to update its responses from the database. The system develops a user profile that is updated daily. Suspected violations are discovered by making statistical comparisons between the accumulated inquiry patterns and the daily patterns. TRW uses the system to monitor access lines to trap violators. As more information is available on each user's habits the expert system becomes more accurate. The suspected violations are also reviewed by the system administrator to remove any accidents caused by chance, such as by a customer's broken computer.

Tener, William, Intruders beware: Artificial intelligence system based on patterns, Credit World, vol. 77, ISSUE-2, pp. 31–34, Nov.–Dec., 1988.

CRIB identifies computer hardware and software faults. The system isolates the fault to a subunit level. It can also backtrack and consider other subunits, if the originally suspected subunit is later found not to be at fault. The system models the computer as a hierarchy of subunits in a semantic net. The system was developed by the merged efforts of International Computers Limited, the Research and Advanced Development Centre, and Brunel University.

Addis, T.R., Expert systems: An evolution in information retrieval, International Computers Limited (ICL) Technical Journal, May 1980.

??? provides novice users with help in using the VAX/VMS operating system. The expert system follows the user's responses ???? questions and volunteers its help when it believes that the user would benefit from advice. The user need not ask for help or ???ise an error condition. The advisor recognizes correct yet efficient command sequences and helps the beginner become more proficient by indicating how these tasks may be done more efficiently. The system was developed at the University of Pennsylvania.

???rager, J. and T. Finin, T., An expert system that volunteers advice, AAAI-2, Carnegie-Mellon University, pp. 339–340, 1982.

???? assists in the selection of appropriate applications and application environments for expert-systems technology. ES is a useful tool for assisting an ADP manager who is inexperienced with expert-systems project selection. Selection criteria based on a literature survey were verified and weighted by knowledge engineers and AI project managers. It was learned that successful expert-systems projects require both the proper problem environment (business factors) and problem form (technical approach). The system was implemented using PRO-LOG. The system was developed at MITRE Corp., McLean, VA.

???avid, G.A. and D. Yeh, An expert system for selecting appropriate domains for expert systems, Third Annual Expert Systems in Government Conference Proceedings, Washington, DC, IEEE Comput. Soc., (Cat. No. 87CH2467-9), pp. 260–265, Oct. 19–23, 1987.

FIDES, Fuzzy Intelligent Differential Equation Solver, assists a finite element programmer by automatically defining the finite element mesh. Users only need specify the most essential data that define their problem, such as an ordered list of points, the boundary conditions, and the differential equation coefficients. FIDES then provides a suitable finite element triangular mesh for the finite element computer program MANEP. MANEP is a two-dimensional finite element program for solving second order self-adjoint elliptic partial differential equations, and can treat linear and various types of nonlinear problems. FIDES is based in fuzzy logic. It was developed in LISP and runs on a VAX 11/780.

Friedman, M. and A. Kandel, On the design of a fuzzy intelligent differential equation solver, in Fuzzy Expert Systems, A. Kandel, ed., CRC Press, 1991.

MAXITAB is an expert interface to the statistical package MINITAB. This system provides guidance in the processes of data analysis and interpretation. Statistical packages provide the users with relatively easy-to-use and powerful mechanics of data analysis, but up to now they do not provide much help with the design and strategies of the analysis. As such, there is a risk of misuse of these packages by statistically inexperienced users. MAXITAB was designed to support this category of users in statistical evaluations.

Chowdhury, S., O. Wigertz, and B. Sundgren, A knowledge-based system for data analysis and interpretation, Methods of Information in Medicine, vol. 28, no. 1, pp. 6–13, Jan. 1989.

PROUST, Program Understander for Students, finds nonsyntatic bugs in PAS-CAL programs written by novice programmers. When students compile a program successfully, PROUST is automatically invoked to analyze it. PROUST reports any bugs that are in the program to the student. It is designed to find every bug in most beginner's programs. PROUST is apable of correctly identifying all of the bugs in over 70 percent of the programs that students write. The system is written in LISP and runs on a VAX 11/750 and an IBM PC. The system was developed at Yale University.

Johnson, W.L. and F. Soloway, PROUST, Byte, pp. 179–190, April 1985.

RA, Relation Assistant, assists in the design of relational databases for microcomputer users. The system asks for very simple input but produces a well-designed database structure. Microcomputer users can safely use the RA's output to build their databases properly and not have to worry about inconsistencies and anomalies in their databases. RA is implemented in PROLOG on IBM compatible personal computers. The system was developed at Cleveland State University, OH.

Hao-Che Pu, Automating relational database design for microcomputer users, Collegiate Microcomputer, vol. 9, no. 4, pp. 231–236, Nov. 1991.

YES/MVS oversees the operation of the MVS operating systems. The system performs the following major tasks: maintains adequate job entry queue space, handles network communications, schedules batch files, responds to hardware errors, monitors subsoftware systems, and monitors overall system performance. The system utilizes rule-based knowledge representation and forward-chaining inferencing. It is implemented in OPS5 and was developed at the IBM T.J. Watson Research Center.

Griesmer, J.H., et al., YES/MVS: A continuous real time expert system, Proceedings AAAI-84, 1984.

Education

ACES assists graduating students majoring in either electrical engineering, computer engineering, or computer science, with deciding upon an area of specialization. The system can also prescribe a list of graduate schools that match the student's qualifications, location desired, and the area of specialization decided by the system. ACES was implemented using Personal Consultant on an IBM/AT microcomputer. It was developed at Miami University, Coral Gables, FL.

Geffin, S., T. Burges, and B. Furht, The expert system for career planning: ACES, Microcomput. Appl., vol. 6, no. 3, pp. 71–77, 1987.

ATEC is an intelligent tutoring system that assists in the training of air traffic controllers, without subjecting them to the hazards of real conditions where a single mistake could prove disastrous. The system is part of the Intelligent Simulation Training System (ISTS) project. ISTS approaches the problem by combining a computer-based graphic simulation of a radar scope intelligent tutoring module, and an expert system that represents the knowledge of an expert air traffic controller (ATC). A variation of the ATEC system could alternatively be used in connection with a real radar scope to assist a working controller in everyday decisions. The system was developed at the Department of Computer Science, Embry-Riddle Aeronautical University, Daytona Beach, FL.

Ransom, A., A. Kornecki, A. Gonzalez, P. Bauert, and R. Phinney, Simulation based expert for ATC training, Simulation Environments and Symbol and Number

Processing on Multi and Array Processors, Proceedings of the European Simulation Multiconference, Nice, France, pp. 211–216, June 1–3, 1988.

COACH TRAINING ASSISTANT APPLICATION: an expert system was developed to assist a coach with training athletes. The system models selected aspects of a master coach thereby providing the novice coach with insights into the game that would normally take years to acquire. It includes access to a laser videodisc that permits the portrayal of the skills and tactics, training progressions, and other information used by the master coach so that the technical complexity inherent in physical movement can be controlled, verbally described, and graphically presented to the user. The system was developed at Calgary University, Alberta, Canada.

Vickers, J.N. and G.E. Kingston, Modelling the master coach: Building an expert system for coaching, Proceedings of the International Conference on Computer Assisted Learning in Post-Secondary Education, Calgary, Alberta, Canada, pp. 207–212, May 5–7, 1987.

COURSE SCHEDULING APPLICATION: an expert system was developed to assist academic department chairmen in the preparation of semester course schedules. Input includes the credit hour load and the number of preparations for each faculty member, a list of courses to be offered, and the number of sections of each course. Data on room availability, faculty time and course preferences, and faculty qualifications enable the system to build a schedule that satisfies a large number of constraints. The system was developed at Northwest Missouri State University, MO.

McDonald, Gary and Merry McDonald, An expert system solution to a constraint satisfaction problem in academic administration, Proceedings of the 1990 Symposium on Applied Computing (IEEE), Fayetteville, AR, pp. 161–163, Apr. 5–6, 1990.

DIGITS is an intelligent computer-aided instruction system for the tutoring of an introductory course in digital electronics. DIGITS functions by guiding the student towards the discovery of issues in the tutorial material. DIGITS was implemented in ADA at Case Western Reserve University in Cleveland, OH.

Khatibi, F. and W.L. Schultz, DIGITS: An intelligent tutoring system using the ADA programming language, Proceedings of AIDA-87, Third Annual Conference on Artificial Intelligence, and ADA, Fairfax, VA, Oct. 14–15, 1987.

GUIDON is an intelligent tutoring system in the area of medicine. The system is an adaption of MYCIN, which offers the student a tutor for medical diagnosis. GUIDON provides the student a medical case to solve and checks the student's understanding using the original diagnostic rules used in MYCIN. The student asks questions to gather important data and proposes hypotheses. The system then compares the student's behavior to the expert behavior as modeled within MYCIN's rules. It also intervenes when the student requests help or when the student runs into trouble. The system is rule based and is implemented in LISP.

Clancey, W.J., GUIDON, Journal of Computer-Based Instruction, vol. 10, no. 1, pp. 8–14, 1983.

LEARNING DISABILITY APPLICATION: An expert system was developed to assist a child with a learning disability. When a child is experiencing learning difficulties the exact nature of the child's problems must be determined in order to plan a successful instructional program. This system guides the teacher through the various stages of diagnosing learning disabilities. Specifically, it works to assist in the assessment of reading problems. The system is implemented in LISP and was developed at the University of Saskatchewan, Canada.

Colbourn, M.J., An expert system for the diagnosis of reading difficulties, in Proceedings of British Computer Society Expert Systems Group Technical Conference on the Theory and Practice of Knowledge Based Systems, Brunel University, pp. 52–55, September 1982.

MENTONIEZH is an intelligent tutoring system in geometry that coaches and corrects a student during two stages of problem solving: figure drawing and proof building. The system uses a plan recognition method, which deduces, from the problem's space research and the student's inputs, the underlying intention, and can also detect intention shifting. It relies on the classical architecture of an ITS. The expert of the domain—a set of geometry rules together with an inference engine—can solve exercises in different ways and distinguish the student's erroneous or unuseful inferences. The pedagogical model is used to conduct the interaction between the student and the system, to give explanations if the student applies an erroneous reasoning, and to provide him with clues when in deadlock. The system was developed at RISA/INRIA, Rennes, France.

Py, D., MENTONIEZH: An intelligent tutoring system in geometry, Artificial Intelligence and Education, Proceedings of the 4th International Conference on AI and Education, Amsterdam, The Netherlands, pp. 202–209, May 24–26, 1989.

QUEST, Qualitative Understanding of Electrical System Troubleshooting, is an intelligent tutoring system in the area of electric circuit troubleshooting. The system can help in predicting component behavior, designing or modifying a circuit to exhibit certain behaviors, listing faults consistent with some behavior, and locating faults. The system can handle any type of circuit, given its topological description. It simulates the circuit behavior using a qualitative model that is the basis of its explanations during instruction.

White, B.Y. and J.R. Frederiksen, QUEST: Qualitative understanding of electrical system troubleshooting, ACM SIGART Newsletter, no. 93, pp. 34–37, 1985.

STEAMER simulates and explains the operation of the Navy's 1078-class frigate steam propulsion plant to aspiring naval engineers. The system simulates various plant components, such as valves, switches, etc., that the user can adjust and observe the impact on the plant's overall operation by observing changes in such items as pressures, temperatures, etc. Knowledge representation is accomplished in a object-oriented scheme using FLAVORS. The system was developed via the collaboration of the Naval Personnel and Research Center and Bolt, Beranek, and Newman.

Williams, M.D., J.D. Hollan, and A.L. Stevens, Human reasoning about a simple physical system, in Mental Models, D. Genter and A. Stevens, eds., Erlbaum, Hillsdale, N.J., pp. 131–153, 1983.

Electronics

AI-TEST is an expert system for functional fault detection and isolation in electronic equipment. Its main features include probabilistic diagnostic assessment and effective management of the testing process including goal-oriented test evaluation and selection. Together with detailed documentation of the unit under test (UUT), AI-TEST essentially provides an intelligent electronic service manual that guides the user through the diagnostic process. The system was developed at Tel Aviv University, Israel.

Ben-Arie, D., A case history with AI-TEST: An expert system for electronic trouble shooting, Proceedings AUTOTESTCON '87, IEEE International Automatic Testing Conference, Bridging Standards to Advancing Technology (Cat. No. 87CH2510-6), San Francisco, CA, pp. 363–369, Nov. 3–5, 1987.

ANALOG IC DESIGN APPLICATION: an expert system was developed to assist in analog IC design. Due to the nonlinear nature of the analog design process, iterations are always necessary to achieve accurate and reliable designs. The system combines a knowledge-based approach with a conventional circuit simulator for the iterative design process. The system is capable of optimizing circuit topologies, as well as circuit element geometries, to better satisfy the performance specifications. Circuit reconstruction is achieved through circuit primitive replacements and design equation substitutions. Circuit primitive and critical nodes are processed before layout generation to minimize undesired parasitic effects. Layout parasitics can be included optionally in the design of optimization step. The system was developed at the University of Southern California, Los Angeles, CA.

Sheu, B., et al., Flexible architecture approach to knowledge-based analogue IC design, IEEE Proceedings, Part G: Electronic Circuits and Systems, vol. 137, no. 4, pp. 266–274, Aug. 1990.

AUTORED assists in the CAD design of VLSI circuits. It offers an approach for understanding CAD electronic circuit diagrams via knowledge-based recognition and interpretation. AUTORED can recognize various types of bipolar, junction FET, and MOSFET transistors in an electronic circuit diagram. The system identifies transistor categories, orientations, types, and connection structures. The system was implemented on a minicomputer under RSX operating system. The system was developed at the University of Florida.

Tou, J.T., C.L. Huang, and W.H. Li, Design of a knowledge-based system for understanding electronic circuit diagrams, Proceedings of the First Conference on Artificial Intelligence Applications, Denver, Colo., IEEE/AAAI, 1984.

CIRCUIT DIAGRAM INTERPRETATION APPLICATION: an expert system was developed to automatically interpret circuit diagrams. Circuit diagrams are characterized by symbols, connections, and text. The system performs the automatic extraction of a description from a circuit diagram. The system consists of two major parts, one for the line interpretation and one for the text interpretation. A decision tree containing the a priori knowledge about the form of symbols controls the interpretation of lines while the text interpretation is controlled by both the results of the line interpretation and a set of finite state automata defining the denotations. The system is implemented in FORTRAN and was developed at the University of Erlangen, West Germany.

Bunke, H., Automatic interpretation of lines and text in circuit diagrams, in Pattern Recognition Theory and Applications, J. Kittler, K.S. Fu, and L.F. Pau, eds, D. Reidel, pp. 297–310, 1982.

DEDALE assists with the diagnosis of analog circuits. DEDALE allows the fast and intelligent identification of circuit faults. For diagnosis, the system relies on structural and functional descriptions of the defective circuit, a circuit diagram and layout drawing, a parts list, and information resulting from electrical tests. The system was developed at Electron. Serge Dassault, Saint-Cloud, France.

Muenier, M. and P. Deves, DEDALE: An expert system for analog circuit maintenance, Knowledge Based Concepts and Artificial Intelligence: Applications to Guidance and Control (AGARD-LS-155), Ottawa, Ont., Canada, pp. 311–312, Sept. 10–11, 1987.

DIGITAL FILTER DESIGN APPLICATION: An expert system was developed to assist with the design of digital filters. The system is capable of deriving a set of transfer function coefficients from a set of points that are sketched by the user. The user specifies a design by sketching (using a mouse) a curve that approximates the desired magnitude plot. The system then operates on the set of points that define the curve to determine the design parameters, computes the transfer function, and finally produces a magnitude plot. The system was developed at New Mexico University, Albuquerque, NM.

Margo, V. and D.M. Etter, An expert system for digital filter design, Proceedings of the 33rd Midwest Symposium on Circuits and Systems, Calgary, Alta., Canada, IEEE (Cat. No. 90CH2819-1), vol. 2, pp. 997–1000, Aug. 12–14, 1990.

EQUAL: Given a circuit topology, the system can construct by qualitative causal analysis a description of the mechanism by which the circuit operates. This mechanism is then parsed by a grammer for circuit functions. It uses a theory of common-sense understanding of the behavior of electronic circuits. The system is based on the intuitive qualitative reasoning electrical engineers use when they analyze circuits. This intuitive reasoning provides a great deal of important information about the operation of the circuit, which although qualitative in nature describes important quantitative aspects of circuit functioning (feedback path, stability, impedance and gain estimates, etc.). The system was developed at Xerox PARC, Calif.

De Kleer, J., How circuits work, Artificial Intelligence, vol. 24, pp. 205–280, 1984.

ICFAX, Integrated Circuit Failure Analysis Expert System, aids in the analysis of failed integrated circuits. ICFAX captures a substantial portion of the procedural knowledge necessary to successfully analyze CMOS integrated circuit failures. ICFAX is designed to apply generically to all types of CMOS ICs. ICFAX also contains general information on how to analyze components as well as product specific information, including schematics, layout plots, product specifications, and fabrication data. The expert system centralizes textual and graphical knowledge about failure analysis, increasing the analyst's productivity and ability to determine the failure. The system was designed using LEVEL5 Object on an IBM PC. The system was developed at Sandia National Laboratory, Albuquerque, NM, and is available to U.S. companies through R&D agreements with Sandia.

Henderson, Christopher L. and Jerry M. Soden, ICFAX: An integrated circuit failure analysis expert system, Proceedings of the International Reliability Physics Symposium, Las Vegas, NV, IEEE Electron Devices Soc., IEEE Reliability Soc., (IEEE cat no. 91CH2974-4), pp. 142–151, Apr. 9–11, 1991.

KAFKA assists in the troubleshooting of personal computer boards. The system determines which component in the board should be replaced. It uses model-based reasoning by employing knowledge about the description of the board, and heuristic knowledge that describes the board's behavior. The system is implemented in CLEOPATRA, a knowledge representation language developed at Olivetti. This language is an object-oriented approach that permits the computer boards to be represented at various levels of detail, i.e. pins, components, and circuits. The system was developed at Olivetti Systems and Networks, Cupertino, CA.

Iacono, G., G. Butera, and P. Scaruffi, A model-based heuristic approach to board troubleshooting, ESD/SMI Second Annual Expert Systems Conference, Detroit, MI, pp. 249–256, Apr. 12–14, 1988.

OPGEN plans the sequence of instructions to be followed by a technician for assembling PC boards. Working with information supplied from CAD generated schematics and a list of parts, OPGEN generates operation sheets for the placement of the parts on the board. The system uses both frames and rules, and was developed at Hazelton Corp.

Frail, R.P., and R.S. Freedman, Opgen revisited: Some methodological observations on the delivery of expert systems, Proc. of the Expert Systems in Government Symposium, IEEE Computer Society, pp. 310–317, Oct. 1986.

Engineering

Amethyst diagnoses problems in rotating machines. Rotating machines, such as pumps, compressors, fans, etc., all produce vibrations as they rotate. These vibrations occur due to imperfections in the bearings, the mounting of the equipment, the shape of the shaft, buildup on the blades, etc. AMETHYST addresses all of these problems using a spectral analysis of the vibration data to determine the nature of the fault. The system is rule based, employs backward chaining, and was implemented using the shell CRYSTAL. The system runs on an IBM PC. It also interfaces to the IRD database, which contains component vibration information. The VIOLET software package is used to access and control the database for spectral data storage. The system was developed at Intelligent Applications Ltd., West Lothian, Scotland, UK.

Milne, R., AMETHYST: Automatic diagnosis of rotating machinery faults, in Operational Expert System Applications in Europe, G.P. Zarri, ed., Pergamon Press, 1991.

CONCRETE DAM RISK ASSESSMENT APPLICATION: An expert system was developed to assist in the field inspection of existing concrete dams for purposes of risk assessment. The symptoms and failure modes identified by the expert system along with the required knowledge and procedures are organized in a structured knowledge tree. The instantiation of the frames and firing of the rules for each consultation traces part of the inference tree contained in the structured knowledge tree. Interaction between nearly decomposable problems are executed with meta-knowledge procedures, shared rule groups, and active values. The system was developed at Minnesota University, Minneapolis, MN.

Frank, B.M. and T. Krauthammer, Development of an expert system for preliminary risk assessment of existing concrete dams, Eng. Comput., vol. 3, no. 3, pp. 137–48, 1988.

FINITE ELEMENT ANALYSIS APPLICATION: An expert system was developed to assist in finite element (FE) analysis to analyze deformations and stresses in physical structures. In order to design a numerical model of a physical structure, it is necessary to decide the appropriate resolution for modeling each component part. Choosing the appropriate resolution, or FE mesh, requires considerable expertise. The inductive logic programming algorithm called Golem was used to form PROLOG rules for this mesh generation expert system.

Dolsak, Bojan and Anton Jezernik, Mesh generation expert system for engineering analyses with FEM, Computers in Industry, vol. 17, No. 2,3, pp. 309–315, Nov. 1991.

LSC, Line Safety Code, reviews architectural designs for conformance with the Line Safety Code of the National Fire Protection Association. The system uses building design information as supplied by a CADD system. LSC stores design information in frames. It reviews this information to make sure the design is consistent with the important fire safety standards. The system integrates frames, rules, and algorithmic procedures. It is implemented in KEE on a TI Explorer.

Lathrop, J., ed., Life Safety Code Handbook, National Fire Protection Assocation, Worcester, Mass., 1985.

OHCS, Oil Hydraulic Circuit-Simulator, assists engineers with designing hydraulic circuits. OHCS integrates four processes of expert reasoning, designing, analysis, and drawing inspection. OHCS employs various kinds of AI technologies such as time-state reasoning, qualitative reasoning, hypothetical reasoning, constraints propagation technique, TMS, ATMS, and symbolic algebraic manipulation. The system is able to apply the expertise of the designers to generate circuit designs as well as CAD drawings that meet specifications. The system uses both rules and frames. OHCS runs on a Symbolics LISP machine and is implemented in ART. It was developed at Kayaba Industry Co., Ltd., Kanagawa, Japan.

Nakashima, Y. and T. Baba, OHCS: Hydraulic circuit design assistant: A knowledge-based system for Kayaba Industry Co., Ltd., Proceedings of the First Annual Conference on Innovative Applications of Artificial Intelligence, Stanford, Calif., American Assoc. Artificial Intelligence, Menlo Park, Calif., March, 1989.

RADIOGRAPHIC IMAGE NDT DIAGNOSIS APPLICATION: An expert system was developed to assist in the analysis of data from radiographic image nondestructive testing (NDT). The system classifies and evaluates the defect against quality assurance requirements of the inspection process. The system is based on a hierarchical frame-based knowledge representation technique and employs backward chaining. The system also uses certainty factors for inexact reasoning. The system was developed at the University of Surrey, Surrey, UK.

Kehoe, A. and G.A. Parker, An IKB defect classification system for automated industrial radiographic inspection, Expert Systems: The International Journal of Knowledge Engineering, vol. 8, no. 3, pp. 149–156, August 1991.

RETWALL designs earth-retaining structures. The system first selects a set of general design descriptors based on interpretations of the desired performance in terms of site conditions. It then selects a design based on an implicit cost criterion and refines the properties of the structure such as its geometry, dimensions, and reinforcement. RETWALL is rule based and uses both forward and backward chaining.

Hutchinson, P., M. Rosenman, and J. Gero, RETWALL: An expert system for the selection and preliminary design of earth retaining structures, Knowledge-Based Systems, vol. 1, no. 1, pp. 11–23, 1987.

SACON eases structural analysis by suggesting specific analysis strategies. The system uses knowledge about stresses and deflections of the structure under different load conditions to determine the appropriate strategy. SACON is designed to identify the type of numerical analysis, the needed modeling detail, and specific analysis data required. Decisions are constructed on the basis of material behavior, relations between geometry and structural behavior, measures of the importance of time and temperature changes, and user-supplied specifics such as characteristics of the spectrum of analysis types, the relation between accuracy and model detail on the structure, its mechanical loadings, and its temperature states. The system is rule based, employs backward chaining, and was implemented using EMYCIN. The system was developed at Stanford University.

Bennett, J., L. Creary, R. Engelmore, and R. Melosh, A knowledge-based consultant for structural analysis, Computer Science Dept., Stanford University, Stanford, Calif., Sept. 1978.

SEAPP assists petroleum engineers with analyzing well test data. It provides a reservoir model that predicts the behavior of the reservoir, which allows the engineer to plan oil extraction methods that maximize the well's oil production. The system's choice of the model is based on a pressure-derivative curve derived from the well test data. SEAPP uses both rules and frames, and was implemented using NEXPERT OBJECT on a DEC workstation. The system was developed at SOFTTEK, Mexico.

Meade, Y., SEAPP: An integrated expert system for well test analysis, in Operational Expert System Applications in Mexico, F.J. Cantu-Ortiz, ed., Pergamon Press, 1991.

SPERIL assesses the damage to a structure following an earthquake. The system uses an inexact inference technique based on fuzzy logic and certainty factors to obtain a rational solution. The fuzzy set theory and the production system with certainty factor are employed jointly in the inexact inference to deal with the continuous nature of the damage state and to attain the modularity of uncertain knowledge. The system is implemented in C on a PDP 11/45. It was developed at the University of Tokyo and Purdue University.

Ishizuka, M., K.S Fu, and J. Yao, Inexact inference for rule-based damage assessment of existing structures, IJCAI-81, Vancouver, pp. 837–842, 1981.

Environmental

ACID RAIN ANALYSIS APPLICATION: An expert system was developed to assist with acid rain analysis. Data from several large governmental collections are uploaded to an IBM PC/AT. These data cover watershed aquatic chemistry, sensitivity to acidity, volume of water discharge from subregions, acid deposition, and various geographical parameters. The query language is map based, and the analysis package uses a special-purpose spreadsheet. Several functions that are currently in use as discriminants in assessing the state of a particular watershed are built in. Feedback from the analysis is via map coloring returned to the map subsystem through a built-in spreadsheet function. The system was developed at National Water Research Institute, Burlington, Ont., Canada.

Fraser, A.S., D.A. Swayne, J. Storey, and D.C. Lam, An expert system/intelligent interface for acid rain analysis, Proceedings of the 1987 Summer Computer Simulation Conference, Montreal, Que., Canada, pp. 483–487, July 27–30, 1987.

BIOSPHERE CONTROL APPLICATION: An expert system was developed to control the environment in a biosphere. Biosphere 2 is an experiment in closed-system ecology and is intended to demonstrate the viability of materially closed ecosystems where water, air, and food are recycled. Its complex ecosystems require a sophisticated, reliable control and monitoring system to ensure the success and safety of both the ecosystems and the inhabitants of Biosphere 2. The expert system controls temperature, humidity, and air velocities. It was developed using G2. The architecture of the expert system-based nerve system comprises five major levels: environmental sensing and response, local control and data acquisition, supervisory monitoring and control of subsystems, telecommunications, and global monitoring. Distributed control systems for each of seven biomes are monitored by two other G2-based expert systems.

Stewart, Rocky L., Biosphere 2 nerve system, Communications of the ACM, vol. 34, no. 9, pp. 69–71, Sept. 1991.

DELAQUA, Deep Expert system LAke water QUAlity, combines AI and simulation methods to support decision making in water quality control of lakes and reservoirs. It contains a knowledge base (PROLOG 2), a data base (dBASE III+) and a simulation system (FORTRAN 77) by which the following decision aids can be made available: derivation of recommendations for operational control of undesired impacts on raw water quality by algal blooms or pathogen germs; classification of raw water quality by means of legal standards; drawing of analogy conclusions by the use of measured and simulated water quality data of reference waters; predictions of raw water quality under changing control strategies, and environmental conditions of lakes and reservoirs. The expert system was implemented on an IBM-PC. It was developed at Dresden Univ. Technol., Dresden.

Recknagel, F., et al., DELAQUA—A prototype expert system for operational control and management of lake water quality, WATER SCI. TECHNOL., vol. 24, no. 6, pp. 283–290, 1991.

EXPRES, EXpert system for Pesticide Regulatory Evaluation Simulations, was designed to aid regulatory personnel in their assessment of the potential for pesticides to contaminate groundwater. The system consists of existing simulation models coupled with a knowledge-based system. The numerical models are used to simulate the transport and transformation of pesticides in the unsaturated zone. The knowledge-based system guides the user through the choice of all the necessary information for characterizing the physical, climatic, hydrogeological, pedological, and agricultural settings of typical agricultural regions across Canada required by the pesticide model, as well as aiding the user with the model predictions. The sytem was developed at National Water Research Institute, Canada Centre Inland Waters, Burlington, Ontario.

Crowe, A.S. and J.P. Mutch, Assessing the migration and transformation of pesticides in the subsurface: The role of expert systems, Water Pollution Research Journal of Canada, vol. 25, no. 3, pp. 293–324, 1990.

FIRE PRESCRIPTION DESIGN APPLICATION: An expert system was developed to assist with the design of fire prescriptions. Prescribed fire is used to manipulate forest ecosystems to accomplish a variety of resource management objectives. To develop prescriptions that successfully achieve these objectives, managers use information from a variety of sources. This rule and frame-based expert system integrates this technical and heuristic information, and interprets it for application. Site data and the manager's objectives for treating the site with prescribed fire are inputs to the expert system. The system develops a fire prescription: ranges of acceptable fire effects, a description of the desired fire treatment, and a range of conditions under which to burn to achieve the desired treatments and effects. The system was developed at Intermountain Research Station, Forest Service, U.S. Department of Agriculture, Missoula, Mont.

Reinhardt, E., A.H. Wright, and D.H. Jackson, An advisory expert system for designing fire prescriptions, Ecological Modelling, vol. 46, nos. 1–2, pp. 121–133, 1989.

FOREST FIRE RESOURCE DISPATCHING APPLICATION: An expert system was developed to assist with the dispatching or resources during a forest fire. The dispatch of water bombers and fire-fighting crews to newly reported fires is an important task carried out by modern regional forest fire management centers. The problem of bomber dispatch involves the use of aircraft of varying speeds, cost, and fire-fighting effectiveness. Candidate aircraft for dispatch can be situated at remote attack bases or at ongoing fires. The problem of crew dispatch also involves candidate crews situated at remote attack bases or at ongoing fires, but unlike bomber dispatch, helicopter transport must be arranged. A transport helicopter must be flown to the specific crew's location and then to the fire. A helicopter is permitted a second trip to pick up an additional crew. The bomber- and pre-dispatch problems have both been formulated as dynamic FORTRAN programming algorithms within the expert system. The expert system defines the desired bomber force and number of crews to be dispatched to a specific fire. The system was developed at Petawawa National Forestry Institute, Canadian Forestry Service, Chalk River, Ont.

Kourtz, P., Two dynamic programming algorithms for forest fire resource dispatching, Canadian Journal of Forest Research, vol. 19, no. 1, pp. 106–112, 1989.

HAZARD computes the carcinogenic risk of environmental chemicals on the basis of the carcinogenic potential of chemicals and the probability of exposure. The system contains information on the chemical structure and exposure information on a limited number of high-priority chemical carcinogens. It screens hazard potentials of environmental chemicals on the basis of structure–activity relationships in the study of chemical carcinogenesis. The system analyses the current state of known structural information about chemical carcinogens and predicts the possible carcinogenicity of untested chemicals. The system was developed at Battelle Institute, Federal Republic of Germany.

Gotttinger, H.W., HAZARD: An expert system for risk assessment of environmental chemicals, Methods of Information in Medicine, vol. 26, no. 1, pp. 13–23, 1987.

HAZARDOUS MATERIAL IDENTIFICATION APPLICATION: assists in assessing an accident scene involving the release of hazardous materials. The system can determine with limited data from accident locations the specific chemical released (or at least the class of chemicals involved) and then exercise the appropriate hazard prediction models. It contains facts and rules about hazardous chemicals and their physical and chemical characteristics and possible scenarios of behavior dependent on the release and environmental conditions. The system uses this information and the responses to a set of interactively entered data to identify the chemical. The system was developed at Technol. Management Systems Inc., Burlington, MA.

Rao, P. and P. Raj, Expert system interface to hazard prediction models, Journal of Hazardous Materials, vol. 25, no. 1–2, pp. 93–106, 1990.

HERMES, Heuristic Emergency Response Management Expert System, is an intelligent aid to a member of a chemical emergency response team. The system consists of a real-time advisor, which gives suggested actions according to a sketch-pad description of the accident scene and any information that can be determined about the emergency situation. Using incident case data, fundamental knowledge such as properties of chemicals, and experiential knowledge in managing chemical spills, the system makes risk estimates and suggests procedures for containment and corrective actions. HERMES includes a sophisticated interface to facilitate the communication between the user and the knowledge base. The system was developed by Alberta Research Council. HERMES was written using the knowledge engineering shell Goldworks and HALO graphics primitives on the COMPAQ 286 and 386 machines with 5–13MB memory.

Mendoza, M., et al., HERMES: An expert system for emergency response management, Proc. of Technical Seminar on Chemical Spills, Calgary, Alberta, Canada, pp. 1–4, 1989.

OIL SPILL RESPONSE APPLICATION: An expert system was developed to assist in forming an adequate response to an oil spill at sea. Timely and adequate response in case of an incident causing oil spillage in the sea is crucial in order to minimize damage to the environment and the impact on the economic and social welfare of the people residing in the area affected. The decision-making problem in oil combatting is a complex one, attempting to balance the potentially high cost of oil spill damage and the high cost of cleaning operations. This expert system addresses these problems and was implemented using PC PLUS. The system was developed at Ege University, Izmir, Turkey.

Orhun, Emrah and Onur Demirors, PC plus based oil pollution combating system, Proceedings of the 14th Annual Energy-Sources Technology Conference and Exhibition, Houston, TX, Expert Systems and Applications American Society of Mechanical Engineers, Petroleum Division (Publication) PD, vol. 35, Publ. by ASME, pp. 25–28, Jan. 20–23, 1991.

Geology

DIPMETER uses dipmeter logs to infer subsurface geological structure. The system uses rock conductivity measurements made at various depths within the borehole along with geological knowledge encoded in rule form to infer structures. The system uses forward chaining and is implemented in LISP on a XEROX workstation. It was developed by Schlumberger-Doll Research.

Davis, R., et al., The dipmeter advisor: Interpretation of geologic signals, Proceedings IJCAI-81, pp. 846–849, 1981.

DRILLING ADVISOR reduces down time in the drilling process of oil rigs by recognizing and resolving problems caused by the drill bit becoming lodged within the borehole. The system is rule-based and uses backward chaining. The system is implemented in S.1 and was developed by the merged efforts of Teknowledge and Societe Nationale Elf Aquitaine.

Elf-Aquitane and Teknowledge, The drilling advisor, Fundamentals of Knowledge Engineering, Teknowledge Report, Teknowledge Inc., Palo Alto, CA, 1983.

FERRET-EMI interprets electromagnetic probe readings of the earth to determine the conductivity of the soil. It also provides information on the layering of the soil, the depths and distribution of groundwater, and the presence of objects in the ground. Rules are used to represent the knowledge and both forward and backward chaining are used for inferencing. The system is implemented in C on an IBM/AT PC. The system was developed at APROTEC GmbH, Frankfurt am Main, West Germany.

Hofmann, J., R. Konnecke, and G. Schmidt, PC based expert systems for signal and image interpretation in geophysics and medicine, Artificial Intelligence and Advanced Computer Technology Conference/Exhibition, Rhein-Main-Halle, Wiesbaden, West Germany, TCM Expositions, Liphook, UK, 1986, pp. 16, September 1986.

SEA interprets seismic data from Norway's regional seismic array, NORESS, for underground nuclear weapons test ban treaty verification. Three important aspects of the expert system are that it emulates the problem-solving behavior of the human seismic analyst, it acts as an assistant to the human analyst by automatically interpreting and presenting events for review, and it enables the analyst to interactively query the system's chain of reasoning and manually perform an interpretation. The system was developed at the University of California, Livermore, CA.

Mason, C.L., R.R. Johnson, R.M. Searfus, and D. Lager, SEA—An expert system for nuclear test ban treaty verification, Proceedings of the Australian Joint Artificial Intelligence Conference, J. Gero and F. Sudweeks, eds., Sydney, NSW, Australia, Univ. Sydney, Sydney, NSW, Australia, pp. 11–25, November 1987.

SEISMIC SIGNAL INTERPRETATION APPLICATION: A rule-based interpretation expert system for seismic images was developed. The system consists of two substructures: a texture analyzer and an intelligent interpreter. The texture analyzer adapts the "texture energy measurement" method to extract discriminant features from the texture-like signal image. The intelligent interpreter is made up of a knowledge database, a reasoning engine, and a parallel region growing controller. Forward chaining is used to control the knowledge, which is represented in rules. The system also incorporates an inexact reasoning capability through the use of certainty factors. The system is implemented in C on a VAX 8600 and was developed at the University of Pittsburgh.

Zhen Zhang and M. Simaan, A rule-based interpretation system for signal images, Proceedings of the SPIE—The International Society for Optical Engineering, vol. 635, pp. 280–287, 1986.

Image Processing

ACRONYM is an image understanding expert system that does symbolic reasoning on two-dimensional images using three-dimensional models. The system uses three separate rule-based expert systems: a system that predicts geometrically invariant features to look for in the image; a system that obtains descriptions of possible image features, and a system that uses the descriptions from the second system to find constraints and check the consistency of the results. The three systems are iterated in order to obtain a finer detail interpretation of the image.

Brooks, R.A., Model-based three dimensional interpretations of two dimensional images, IEEE Trans. on PAMI, vol. 5, pp. 140–150, Mar. 1983.

CALAP assists in the interpretation of aerial images in the area of mapping and terrain analysis. The system has knowledge on the principles of physiography and geomorphology. Given information about the general area where the image was taken, CALAP moves sequentially through decision trees associated with locating and delineating landforms expected to be found in the region. The system is implemented in OPS5 and was developed at U.S. Army Engineer Topographic Laboratories.

Leighty, R., The AI research environment at the U.S. Army Engineer Topographic Laboratories, Proc. of the Army Conf. on Application of Artificial Intelligence to Battlefield Information Management, Washington, DC, pp. 37–44, Jan. 1984.

IMAGE SEGMENTATION APPLICATION: An expert system was developed for a robotic vision application that performs the segmentation of images of natural scenes in order to understand their content. The system is a rule-based expert system. It includes general knowledge about low-level properties of processes to segment the image into uniform regions and connected lines. In addition to the knowledge rules, a set of control rules are employed. These include meta-rules that embody inferences about the order in which the knowledge rules are matched. They also incorporate focus of attention rules that determine the path of processing within the image. Furthermore, an additional set of higher level rules dynamically alters the processing strategy. The system was developed at McGill University, Canada.

Nazif, A.M., and M.D. Levine, Low level image segmentation: An expert system, IEEE Transactions on Pattern Analysis and Machine Intelligence, PAMI-6, 5, pp. 555–577, September 1984.

MATERIAL DEFECT DETECTION APPLICATION: An expert system was developed that detects and categorizes defects in digitized images of materials characterized by complex texture patterns. The system performs two major tasks: image segmentation and defect classification. Segmentation is done in two steps. First, individual texture samples are isolated. Second, a pyramid linking scheme is used to locate defects in each sample. This pyramid linking scheme can be fine-tuned to various textures and to the size of the defects to be detected. The defect classification method is dependent on the material being analyzed. The system was developed using a hierarchical defect classification scheme for analyzing wood. The hierarchy incorporates a shape descriptor, size, and textural descriptors of individual defects. The system was developed at the University of Tennessee, Knoxville, TN.

Brzakovic, D., et al., Approach to defect detection in materials characterized by complex textures, Pattern Recognition, vol. 23, nos. 1–2, pp. 99–107, 1990.

VISION LEARNING APPLICATION: A vision system that can be trained to learn about objects automatically was developed. It learns its rules by examples. The vision system learns the shape features of an object for use in a binary tree classifier. At each node of the tree a feature and threshold value are selected by maximizing a modified version of the Kolmogorov–Smirnoff distance based on the training samples. The resulting binary tree classifier is suitable for real-time applications, inasmuch as traversing the tree involves only a simple comparison at each node. The system was developed at Oakland University.

Haskell, R.E. and B. Mirshab, Learning shape features using a binary tree classifier, CAD/CAM Robotics and Factories of the Future. 3rd International Conference (CARS and FOF '88) Proceedings, Southfield, MI, pp. 188–92, vol. 3, 1989.

Information Management

BROWSER heuristically searches a database containing information on U.S. Navy aircraft with little or no human intervention. The formation of databases containing information on mechanical systems for troubleshooting purposes has become increasingly popular and important. Examination of these databases by humans can be very costly. BROWSER searches the database guided by models and heuristics looking for interesting patterns or configurations. The user is then notified of the existence of these patterns. The system is implemented in LISP on a DEC-10. It was developed at the University of Illinois at Urbana-Champaign.

Dankel, D.D., Browsing in large databases, IJCAI-79, Tokyo, vol. 1, pp. 188–190, 1979.

CHEMICAL DATABASE INTERROGATION APPLICATION: An expert system was developed to aid in information retrieval from a chemical database. The system uses psychological similarity between data. The similarity relationships between data are derived from a database that is based on a set-theoretic model of psychological similarity. These relationships are represented in the computer as a network. The generalization function enables propagation of information obtained from user similarity responses over the network. Using the generalization function, the computer determines the generic kind of question it should next pose to the user. Through this question/answering process, the knowledge-based system aids the user in specifying requests for relevant data, as well as in retrieving data from the database. The system was developed at the University of Virginia and Kyoto University, Japan.

Nakamura, K., A.P. Sage, and S. Iwai, An intelligent data-base interface using psychological similarity between data, IEEE Transactions on Systems, Man and Cybernetics, SMC-13, vol. 4., pp. 558–568, July/Aug. 1983.

EP-X assists with bibliographic information retrieval of environmental pollution literature. The system actively assists users in defining or refining their topics of interest using a semantically based search technique. It does so by applying search tactics to a knowledge-base describing topics in a particular domain and a database describing the contents of individual documents. To support semantically based search, the system's knowledge base consists of frames (to represent stereotypic topics and the relationships among concepts), semantic primitives, and parent–child relationships (in the form of tangled hierarchies) and triggers for semantic primitives. The database consequently consists of frame instantiations. The system was developed at Ohio State University, Columbus, OH.

Smith, P., et al., In search of knowledge-based search tactics, Proceedings of the Twelfth Annual International ACM SIGIR Conference on Research and Development in Information Retrieval, Cambridge, MA, Publ. by ACM, pp. 3–10, June 25–28, 1989.

FASTPATH is a system for automated classification, association, and routing of free-format text documents. The system uses as input the output of the TMC INDEXER program. The INDEXER takes machine readable natural language text and produces indexes that are used by FASTPATH. FASTPATH is used by BDM Corp. to analyze information from the Commerce Business Daily (CBD) after it was indexed by the INDEXER. The system is able to recommend to BDM which CBD announcements to bid on, by comparing each announcement with BDM's history on similar contracts and available personnel skills. The system also automatically produces a document of the recommended CBD announcement, related corporate experience, and resumes of project personnel. The system was developed at BDM Corp., McLean, VA.

Morrison, W., K. Tatalias, and T. Woteki, FASTPATH, Artificial Intelligence and Advanced Computer Technology Conference/Exhibition, Rhien-Main-Halle, Wiesbaden, Germany, Sept. 23–25, 1986.

FLEXICON is a litigation support system developed for the effective retrieval of legal documents by legal and paralegal professionals. It includes a text analysis and processing component, processing raw text and intelligently extracting key information in the form of electronic headnotes. It also includes an innovative nonboolean search and retrieval mechanism. As well, it provides many features that improve legal research such as a menu-driven interface, thesauri, relevance feedback, and retrieval by topic. The system was developed at British Columbia University, Vancouver, BC.

Gelbart, D. and J.C. Smith, Beyond Boolean search: FLEXICON, a legal text-based intelligent system, Third International Conference on Artificial Intelligence and Law, ACM, Oxford, UK, pp. 225–234, June 25–28, 1991.

LUNG CANCER INFORMATION RETRIEVAL APPLICATION: a rule-based expert system was developed that allows a microcomputer user to obtain staging, prognostic, and therapeutic information relevant to patients with lung cancer. The user interacting with the system is asked sequential questions regarding the characteristics of the tumor of a particular patient, the nodal status, the presence or absence of metastasis, how the staging information was derived (clinically or at surgery), the tumor cell type, and the therapeutic options being considered (different surgical procedures, radiotherapy, chemotherapy, and others). The system selects the appropriate answers and displays the stage of the tumor and relevant prognostic information. The user can change all or some of the conditions (i.e., therapeutic options) and compare the results of the various "WHAT-IF" simulations. The system is rule based, employs backward chaining, and was implemented using EXSYS. The system was developed at Cedars-Sinai Medical Center, Los Angeles, Calif.

Marchevsky, A. M., Expert systems for efficient handling of medical information: I. Lung cancer, Analytical and Quantitative Cytology and Histology, vol. 13, no. 2, pp. 89–92, 1991.

NEWS WIRE MONITORING APPLICATION: an expert system was developed that scans news wire text in real time and triggers an alarm when topics previously chosen by a user are found. A natural language interface allows the user to specify topics. The system filters incoming text with a simple keyword search and then parses sentences further to derive primitive knowledge structures corresponding to user selections. The system was implemented on a Symbolics computer.

Clippinger, J.H., An Artificial Intelligence System for the Realtime Monitoring and Analysis of Textual Information, Proceedings of the Trends and Applications Conference, Washington D.C.: IEEE Computer Society, pp. 65–67, 1983.

Law

AREST, the Armed Robbery Eidetic Suspect Typing expert system, aids in the investigation of robberies. AREST is used by the investigator to provide a list of possible robbery suspects upon which the investigative effort may be focused. Victim/witness descriptions from robberies are compared against this knowledge base and a list of both probable and possible suspects is prepared. The system aids in the investigation of robberies by making faster and better decisions, and by providing needed suspect information in a timely fashion. The system was developed at the University of Oklahoma.

Holloway, B., J. Karasz, and A. Badiru, Knowledge elicitation for expert systems in the law enforcement domain, Computers and Industrial Engineering, vol. 17, pp. 90–94, 1989.

CARES, Computer Assisted Risk Evaluation System, helps caseworkers develop profiles and risk assessments for child abuse. The system helps the caseworker by estimating risk to a child based on telephone hotline data, and by evaluating risk and creating education strategies for changing abusive behavior in families. CARES can be used on any 286- or 386-based PC that runs DOS and has 1 Mbyte of memory. Its user interface is based on PASCAL, and its Inference Engine is based on LISP. The system was developed at TA Roberts & Assoc's Expert and is helping the Marion County (IN) Department of Public Welfare handle child abuse and neglect cases.

Expert system offers relief for child abuse, Computerworld, p. 37, July 29, 1991.

EVIDENT determines admissibility of evidence under the U.S. federal rules. It is an expert system developed for helping the law student learn admissibility of evidence under the federal rules. According to many law students, the law class of "evidence" is extremely difficult because the student must remember all the rules of evidence and be able to analyze a situation and know when the various rules and their exceptions apply, and how. It is a backward chaining rule-based system. The system was designed using the shell EXSYS at George Washington University, Washington, DC.

Liebowitz, J. It's clearly evident, isn't it? (Legal expert systems), Expert Systems for Information Management, vol. 1, no. 2, pp. 126–138, Summer 1988.

FinCEN, Financial Crimes Enforcement Network, assists personnel at the U.S. Treasury Department with investigating transactions over $10,000 in order to identify and trace transactions that may involve illegal activities. The system is also used by the IRS, Postal Inspection Service, the Federal Reserve, and U.S. Customs. The system is rule-based and runs on an Apollo workstation.

Robb, D.W., Computer center tracks criminals by their finances, Government Computer News, vol. 66, April 30, 1990.

FLEXICON is a litigation support system developed for the effective retrieval of legal documents by legal and paralegal professionals. It includes a text analysis and processing component, processing raw text and intelligently extracting key information in the form of electronic headnotes. It also includes an innovative nonboolean search and retrieval mechanism. In addition it provides many features that improve legal research such as a menu-driven interface, thesauri, relevance feedback, and retrieval by topic. The system was developed at British Columbia University, Vancouver, BC.

Gelbart, D. and J.C. Smith, Beyond Boolean search: FLEXICON, a legal text-based intelligent system, Third International Conference on Artificial Intelligence and Law, ACM, Oxford, UK, pp. 225–234, June 25–28, 1991.

GREBE determines if a particular case has an existing precedent. GREBE uses both general legal rules and specific explanations of precedents to evaluate legal predicates in new cases. GREBE assesses the similarity of a new case to a precedent of a legal category by attempting to find a pattern of relations in the new case that corresponds to the facts in the precedent. The system was developed at the University of Texas, Austin, TX.

Branting, L.K. Representing and reusing explanations of legal precedents, Proceedings of the Second International Conference on Artificial Intelligence and Law, Vancouver, BC, Canada, ACM, New York, pp. 103–110, June 1989.

LDS analyzes product liability cases to determine defendant liability, overall case worth, and settlement amount. The system helps both researchers and litigators understand better how claim evaluation takes place, since it provides a basis for generating and organizing hypotheses about litigator's methods for making settlements. LDS is rule based and is implemented in ROSIE. The system was developed at The Rand Corporation.

Waterman, D.A. and M. Peterson, Rule-based models of legal expertise, Proceedings of the First Annual National Conference on Artificial Intelligence, 1980.

Link Analysis System assists the Criminal Investigation unit at the IRS in gathering and interpreting information for criminal investigations. The IRS has databases containing information on bank transactions and U.S. Customs records. The system identifies items from different databases that relate to a specific person or event and draws diagrams that illustrate the relationships between the individual and the items, including any other entity related to the transaction. Its main use is to assist Special Agents with their investigation when an individual or group is already under suspicion for criminal tax behavior. The system was implemented on a Symbolics workstation and was developed at the IRS.

The Spand Robinson Report on Artificial Intelligence, John Wiley, vol. 5, no. 4, April 1989.

Manufacturing

ALUMINUM FOIL ROLLING FLATNESS CONTROL APPLICATION: An expert system was developed for automatic flatness control in aluminum foil rolling production. The system adjusts the target shape pattern according to the material characteristics and the operating conditions, and has shown ability to improve all kinds of aluminum foil throughout a one-year trial in the operational rolling process. The system was developed at Kobe Steel, Ltd., Tokyo, Japan.

Konishi, M., et al., Expert system for flatness control in aluminum foil rolling, Research and Development (Kobe Steel, Ltd.), vol. 40, no. 3, pp. 23–25, July 1990.

BLAST FURNACE HEAT CONTROL APPLICATION: An expert system was developed for blast furnace heat level control. It consists of two parts, namely, the prediction system for blast furnace heat level and the action guidance system for controlling the blast furnace heat level. The prediction system uses two prediction models. One is the rule-based model for short-term heat level variation and the other is the statistical model for long-term heat level variation. These models are combined using fuzzy inferences, so that a new prediction system can be realized for both short- and long-term heat level variation. The action guidance system is an expert system that determines the appropriate action variables and their values according to the results of the prediction model. The system is effectively employed at Kakogawa Works no. 1 blast furnace and Kobe Works no. 3 blast furnace as a guide for furnace operators. The system was developed at Kobe Steel Ltd., Tokyo, Japan.

Matsuda, K., et al., Expert system for blast furnace heat level control, KOBELCO Technology Review, no. 10, pp. 43–46, Mar. 1991.

Callisto assists in scheduling tasks of a manufacturing process. The system schedules the activities to accomplish the task, monitors the status of related activities to determine both plan and schedule changes required to meet goals, and manages change in orders. As the design engineer is considering a design based on the availability of parts or components, the system can advise the engineer on parts, enabling the designer to reconsider a design based on an updated inventory. Callisto uses both frames and rules to represent knowledge. The system was developed at DEC.

Rauch-Hindin, W.B., A Guide to Commercial Artificial Intelligence: Fundamentals and Real-World Applications, Prentice-Hall, 1988.

CONTINUOUS CASTER STEEL MILL SCHEDULING APPLICATION: a fuzzy logic–based expert system was developed for on-line monitoring and reactive scheduling of continuous caster steel mill manufacturing. A continuous caster steel mill takes raw material such as scrap, pig iron, and refined ore through a sequence of processes to produce slabs of steel to meet orders with specified quality and composition. The system first forms an ''area schedule'' based on steel orders and time constraints. A ''reactive scheduler'' then converts this area-level schedule into an operational control plan using fuzzy heuristics and resource allocation techniques. The system then monitors the manufacturing process and makes adjustments to the plan as needed adjustments are detected. The system was implemented using Concurrent Real Time OPS5 and C++ on a Macintosh. It was developed as a collaborative effort of individuals from Carnegie Mellon University, University of Kentucky, and Pyromet Automation Services, Pittsburgh, PA.

Paul, C.J., et al., An intelligent reactive monitoring and scheduling system, IEEE Control Systems, vol. 12, no. 3, pp. 78–86, June 1992.

CPMAPS II, Computer Programmed Manufacturing and Assembly Planning System, assists in the manufacturing of printed circuit boards (PCBs) at Northern Telecom Canada Ltd. The system uses a hierarchical design approach based on two levels. At the first level, the design and engineering constraints applicable to PCBs are considered. At the second level, workplace constraints and capabilities that affect the plan are considered. The system interacts with manufacturing databases and determines process plants to assemble through-hold and surface-mount electronic components of the board. The system is frame based, was implemented using KEE on a SUN 3 workstation, and was developed at Northern Telecom Canada Ltd.

Dagnino, A., Knowledge-based and object-oriented approaches to process planning at Northern Telecom, in Operational Expert System Applications in Canada, C.Y. Suen and R. Shinghal, eds., Pergamon Press, 1991.

GREASE aids in the selection or design of products that extend the life of machines used in a manufacturing process. It can also improve the quality of the material being manufactured. The goal of GREASE is to find the best trade-off between the price of the product and the amount that it extends the life of the manufacturing machine. In addition, a number of other constraints on the product may be imposed by the raw material being used in the manufacturing process, the manufacturing operation, and by the operators of the machines. GREASE was developed at the Intelligent Systems Laboratory of Carnegie-Mellon University, in cooperation with Gulf Oil.

Fox, M., P. Spirtes, D. Correga, and J. Mogush, GREASE: A system for the selection and design of products that extend machine life, SIGART Newsletter, Number 92, pp. 57–58, April 1985.

INS assists with scheduling jobs in a job-shop environment. INS uses a blackboard control structure along with opportunistic planning methods to solve scheduling problems in a job shop. Using a blackboard control structure makes it possible for local schedulers representing entities such as materials, men, and machines to communicate with each other to avoid conflicts. The system was developed at Johnson C. Smith Univ., Charlotte, NC.

Choi, J.U. and T.A. Byrd, Blackboard model implementation in a knowledge-based job-shop scheduling system, Second International Conference on Computers and Applications, Beijing, China, IEEE Comput. Soc., (Cat. No. 87CH2433-1), pp. 605–611, June 23–27, 1987.

IREX assists in the selection of industrial robots in a work environment. The system is comprised of three basic parts. The first part examines several proposed applications where automation is desired and chooses the one best suited for automation using a robot. The second part uses rules to select the configuration, drive, programming type, and playback type. The third section of the expert system examines a data base of robots and selects the five best robots for the application based on the users specifications of that job. The system was implemented in KEE and later transferred to the Keystone environment on a PS-2 Model 80. The system was developed at the University of Louisville, Louisville, KY.

Gardone, B.A. and R.K. Ragade, IREX: An expert system for the selection of industrial robots and its implementation in two environments, Proceedings of the 3rd International Conference on Industrial and Engineering Applications of Artificial Intelligence and Expert Systems—IEA/AIE 90, Charleston, SC, pp. 1086–1095, July 15–18, 1990.

LIMA, Logistics Inventory Management Assistant, assists Unisys spare parts inventory analysts in developing an action plan on a part-by-part basis to maintain inventory levels within a target zone. LIMA is a PC-hosted tool, incorporating business presentation graphics, statistical analysis, "what if" capabilities, and expert assistance from a PROLOG knowledge base. Data provided to LIMA are extracted from a large mainframe database of parts usage. The expert system component guides the analyst through a data validation process, generates an action plan to cover the planning period and engages the analyst in a planning dialogue. The system was developed at Unisys Corp., Paoli, PA.

Lipshutz, M., et al., LIMA: A logistics inventory management assistant, Proceedings of the 7th IEEE Conference on Artificial Intelligence Applications, Miami Beach, FL, pp. 393–397, Feb. 24–28, 1991.

MASTER PRODUCTION SCHEDULING APPLICATION: an expert system was developed to perform master production scheduling for the manufacturing of integrated circuits. Master production scheduling is a broad planning activity, which controls and coordinates the subsequent phases of a typical manufacturing scheduling process, including manufacturing resource planning, finite scheduling, dynamic scheduling, and dispatching. Such a plan stretches over a long period. It normally plans for about six to thirty-six months using sales forecasts, results of the production plans of the previous periods, production environment constraints, and management production goals. The system was designed to improve the productivity of the human master scheduler and help him arrive at decisions of better quality as a result of evaluating various scenarios. The system was developed at Gintic Inst. of CIM, Singapore.

Niew, B., et al., Knowledge based master production scheduler, First International Conference on Expert Planning Systems, Brighton, England, IEE Conference Publication, no. 322, pp. 88–93, June 27–29, 1990.

PACIES generates part codes for the selection of small part feeding and orienting devices for use in automatic assembly. The system embodies the specific knowledge and experience of human experts to determine a part code consistent with the UMASS coding system to facilitate the handling and orienting of small parts for use in automatic assembly. The system is rule based and was implemented on an IBM/PC using micro-PROLOG. The system was developed at GM Tech. Center, Warren, MI.

Chen, YuTong and R.E. Young, PACIES: A part code identification expert system, IIE Trans., vol. 20, no. 2, pp. 132–136, June 1988.

PWA Planner, Printed Wiring Assemblies Planner, is a rule-based system for preparing assembly plans for the manufacture of printed wiring assemblies (PWAs) via automatic component mounting machines. PWA Planner uses a forward planning procedure. It starts from a design blueprint and a bare printed wiring board. It then mounts components on the board until the completed PWA is reached. The final assembly plan includes a component assignment diagnostic file, a process plan, and automatic mounting machine program files. PWA Planner is written in PROLOG and was developed at Purdue University, West Lafayette, IN.

Chang, Tien-Chien and J. Terwilliger, A rule based system for printed wiring assembly process planning, Int. J. Prod. Res. (UK), vol. 25, no. 10, pp. 1465–82, Oct. 1987.

ROBOT TASK PLANNING APPLICATION: An expert system was developed for the planning of robot tasks in a robotic assembly environment. The system is a hierarchical planning and execution system that maps user-specified 3D part assembly tasks into various target robotic work cells, and executes these tasks efficiently using manipulators and sensors available in the work cell. One level of this hierarchy, the Supervisor, is responsible for assigning subtasks of a system-generated Task Plan to a set of task specific Specialists and online coordination of the activity of these Specialists to accomplish the user-specified assembly. The design of the Supervisor is broken down into five major tasks: resource management, concurrence detection, task scheduling, error recovery, and interprocess communications. The system was implemented on a VAX 11/750. It was developed at Rensselaer Polytech. Inst., Troy, NY.

Moed, M.C. and R.B. Kelley, An expert Supervisor for a robotic work cell, Proc. SPIE, Intelligent Robots and Computer Vision, Sixth in a Series, Cambridge, MA, vol. 848, pp. 502–507, Nov. 2–6, 1988.

TRANSFORMER PRICE ESTIMATING AND DESIGN APPLICATION: an expert system was developed to assist in the manufacture of distribution transformers. It provides a production price estimation and design guidelines. The system is able to provide price quotes and bids, and details on the transformer design. It also generates parts lists automatically. The system uses several knowledge bases that communicate over a blackboard. It uses rules, frames, and neural networks. The system was implemented using PROLOG and was developed on an IBM PC. The system was developed at Sistemas Inteligentes, Monterrey, Mexico.

Pena, R., A general expert system for the design of capital goods, in Operational Expert System Applications in Mexico, F.J. Cantu-Ortiz, ed., Pergamon Press, 1991.

WELDING SEAM TRACKING APPLICATION: An expert system was developed for tracking three-dimensional seams in unstructured environments for robot welding applications. The integrated control system of the adaptive, real-time, intelligent seam tracker includes a high-level control module which uses rule-based heuristics and model-based reasoning to interact with the joint in real time. It may be integrated with an expert welding knowledge base for on-line control of welding process parameters. The low-level control module allows seam tracking with correct torch orientation using a sensor and image analysis.

Nayak, N., An integrated system for intelligent seam tracking in robotic welding, thesis (Ph.D), Pennsylvania State University, University Park, PA, 1989.

WOOD TRUSS FABRICATION APPLICATION: an expert process planning system, based on the Semi-intelligent Process Selector (SIPS) expert system shell, is linked with an industrial robot arm to perform fixed plant cutting and assembly operations (wood truss fabrication). The operational protocol of this system involves providing truss design input to the process planner via a file of truss feature parameter frames. This planner, which is resident on a TI Explorer workstation, generates the fabrication sequence and transfers this sequence to a robot control program that is resident on a separate microcomputer. The system was developed at the University of Maryland, College Park, MD.

Bernold, L.E. and E.E. Livingston, A prototype for intelligent computer integrated wood truss fabrication, ROBOT. AUTON. SYST., vol. 6, no. 4, pp. 337–349, 1990.

Mathematics

AM carries on simple mathematics research: defining and studying new concepts under the guidance of a large body of heuristic rules. The 250 heuristics communicate via an agenda mechanism, a global priority queue of small tasks for the program to perform and reasons why each task is plausible (e.g., "Find generalizations of 'primes', because 'primes' turned out to be so useful a concept"). Each concept is an active, structured knowledge module. One hundred very incomplete modules are initially supplied, each one corresponding to an elementary set-theoretic concept (e.g., union). This provides a definite but immense space that AM begins to explore. In one hour, AM rediscovers hundreds of common concepts (including singleton sets, natural numbers, airthmetic) and theorems (e.g., unique factorisation). The system is implemented in LISP on a PDP-10. It was developed at Stanford University and Carnegie-Mellon University.

Lenat, D.B., Automated theory formation in mathematics, IJCA/-77, MIT, vol. 2, pp. 833–842, 1977.

ExMat is a rule-based expert system for analyzing matrices and systems of linear equation. ExMat allows the user to enter a coefficient matrix and the right-hand side vector of the system. Based on rules derived from the subject area of matrix theory and matrix numerical analysis, ExMat provides an expert analysis of the system. The analysis includes solvability of the systems, and the calculations of the proper inverse and solution of the system. The procedural knowledge of ExMat consists of a list of action rules determining the needed numerical procedure. ExMat provides a significant improvement over standard numerical libraries in the sense that it uses its built-in analysis to select the appropriate numerical method. The system was developed at Louisville University, KY.

Imam, I.N. and A.S. Elmaghraby, An expert system for matrix analysis (ExMat), Conference Proceedings: 1988 IEEE SOUTHEASTCON, (Cat. No. 88CH2571-8), Knoxville, TN, pp. 535–536, Apr. 11–13, 1988.

EXPERIPLAN selects and applies statistical analyses to experimental or observational research studies in medicine, biology education, and psychology. A research study is a proposed hypothesis describing the relationhip between observed variables. It is based on observed characteristics (variables) of individual subjects. EXPERIPLAN selects an appropriate statistical analysis from the hypothesis and the variables' properties. It contains tutorial components that explain the analysis using the original hypothesis variables, and describe empirical relationships between variables. EXPERIPLAN contains information on eight predefined variables (IQ, Sex, Age, Education, etc.) and their empirical relationships. The system is implemented in LISP on a 64 K Kaypro 4 computer. It was developed at Northwestern Medical School, Chicago.

Schreiner, J., EXPERIPLAN: An expert system that selects statistical analyses for research studies, SIGART Newsletter, no. 89, pp. 27–28, 1984.

MACSYMA performs symbolic manipulation of algebraic equations. It solves a variety of mathematical problems dealing with areas such as limits, solution of equations, and symbolic integration. The system employs a number of knowledge bases that can be chosen for a particular problem. The system is implemented in LISP and was developed at MIT.

Martin, W.A. and R.J. Fateman, The MACSYMA system, Proceedings of the Second Symposium on Symbolic and Algebraic Manipulation, pp. 59–75, March 1971.

PLANE GEOMETRY APPLICATION: an expert system was developed that solves plane geometry problems at the junior high school level. In order to solve some kinds of plane geometry problems, it is necessary to introduce auxiliary lines. Human experts can quickly introduce these lines using knowledge obtained by their experiences, and can solve the given problems easily. But these problems are very difficult for inexperienced students. The system, which is written in the PROLOG language, can generate auxiliary lines automatically if these lines are necessary to solve the appropriate problems. It does not generate auxiliary lines at random, but generates only effective lines to solve the problems. The system is rule based and was implemented on a VAX 8200. It was developed at Seikei Univ., Tokyo, Japan.

Yamazaki, M. and Y. Iida, Inductive generation of auxiliary-lines in geometry, Technology Reports of the Seikei University, no. 49, pp. 39–56, Jan. 1990.

Medicine

AI/LEARN is an educational videodisc system designed to teach clinical observational skills and reasoning in medicine. The AI/LEARN system uses a learning conditions approach to teaching. To teach visual concepts, the system uses the principle of exemplar/nonexemplar pairs and immediate feedback. To teach If-Then problem solving it uses the format of minicases with delayed feedback. The software to operate the system has been custom developed and is domain independent. The result is a prototype of a new authoring package for videodisc teaching that operates on IBM compatible microcomputers. The medical domain selected for this prototype system was rheumatic diseases; the knowledge used to teach reasoning skills is derived from the knowledge base of an expert system: AI/RHEUM.

Mitchell, J.A., et al., AI/LEARN: An interactive videodisc system for teaching medical concepts and reasoning, Journal of Medical Systems, vol. 11, no. 6, pp. 421–429, December 1987.

ATTENDING analyzes and critiques a physician's plans for anesthetic management for hypothetical surgical operations. The system studies the plan and assesses the risks involved and presents its findings in a form of English text. To critique a physician's plan, the system knows about the various risks involved in a patient's anesthetic management. It compares these risks against one another to evaluate risk tradeoffs. The system then discusses the risks and benefits of the plan with the physician. The system was developed at the Yale University School of Medicine.

Miller, P. L., Medical plan-analysis: The ATTENDING system, Proceedings IJCAI-83, pp. 239–241, 1983.

BABY monitors newborn intensive care unit on-line patient data, discerns irregularities, and offers corrective solutions. The system monitors data, looks for significant patterns, and suggests further evaluations. BABY also tracks the clinical status of the newborns and can answer questions about each patient. BABY uses a Bayesian probabilistic method for handling uncertainty, similar to the method used in PROSPECTOR. The system is rule based and uses forward chaining. The system is implemented in PASCAL and was developed at the University of Illinois, Champaign-Urbana.

Rodewald, L.E., BABY: An expert system for patient monitoring in a newborn intensive care unit, M.S. Thesis, Computer Science Dept., University of Illinois, Champaign-Urbana, 1984.

BLUE BOX assists physicians in the control and care of depressed patients by diagnosing the type and degree of the depression. The system uses information of patient symptoms, family history, and knowledge about psychiatry and drugs to suggest either a drug treatment program or hospitalization. The system represents knowledge in rules and was developed at Stanford University.

Mulsant, B. and D. Servan-Schreiber, Knowledge engineering: A daily activity on a hospital ward, Computers in Biomedical Research, vol. 17, pp. 71–91, 1984.

BREAST CANCER DIAGNOSIS APPLICATION: an expert system was developed for early detection of breast cancer. The system conducts a conversation with a woman who is anxious about breast cancer. The conversation is divided into two parts: one is listening to the woman's symptoms regarding the breast then giving advice, the other is an explanation of breast cancer and how to detect it in its early stages. After listening to the woman's symptoms, the system presents its conclusion and suggests courses of action the woman should take. The system is written in PROLOG on an IBM PC. The system was developed at the Dep. Epidemiol., Clin. Res. Inst., Kanagawa Canc. Cent., 54-2 Nakao-cho, Asahi-ku, Yokohama-shi, Kanagawa Prefect. 241, Japan.

Morio, S., et al., An expert system for early detection of cancer of the breast, Computers in Biology and Medicine, vol. 19, no. 5, pp. 295–306, 1989.

BTDS, Brain Tumors Diagnostic System, assists a physician in the diagnosis of brain tumors. BTDS consists of an expert system and a learning system. The former can help diagnosticians in judging the causes of brain tumors according to computed tomography pictures, and the latter, based on a revised inductive learning method, is especially suitable in the case of brain tumors. By applying the proposed learning mechanism, the initial knowledge base can be constructed and new rules can be learned from noise data in the process of inference. The system was developed at the Nat. Chiao-Tung Univ., Hsin-Chu, Taiwan.

Wang, C.H. and S.S. Tseng, A brain tumor diagnostic system with automatic learning abilities, Proceedings of the Third Annual IEEE Symposium on Computer-Based Medical Systems, Chapel Hill, NC, pp. 313–320, June 3–6, 1990.

CASNET/GLAUCOMA recognizes and prescribes remedies for disease states related to glaucoma. Its reasoning procedures interpret the findings of a patient in terms of a causal-associational network (CASNET) model that characterizes the pathophysiological mechanisms and clinical course of treated and untreated diseases. Strategies of specific treatment selection are guided by the individual pattern of observations and diagnostic conclusions. Knowledge is represented in a causal-association network. The system is implemented in FORTRAN and was developed at Rutgers University.

Szolovits, P. and S.G. Pauker, Categorical and probabilistic reasoning in medical diagnosis, Artificial Intelligence, vol. 11, pp. 115–144, 1978.

CENTAUR interprets pulmonary test results to determine the presence and severity of possible lung disease in a patient. The system uses information on the amount of gas in the lungs and the rate of flow of gas in and out of the lungs to make its decisions. A frame and rule combination is used to represent the system's knowledge, and certainty factors are included to permit inexact reasoning. The system is implemented in LISP and was developed at Stanford University.

Aikins, J.S., Prototypical knowledge for expert systems, Artificial Intelligence, vol. 20, pp. 163–210, 1983.

DIET is a dietary recommendation expert system developed for dietitians. The system uses dietary information on patients obtained from five categories: demographics, laboratory results, medical conditions, medications, and eating characteristics to make dietary plans. To combine the effects of each condition, a composition approach is adopted to find the most appropriate diet. The system is implemented in OPS5 and was developed at Cheng Kung Univ., Tainan, Taiwan.

Kao, C. and K.J. Hwang, A dietary recommendation expert system using OPS5, Proceedings 1987 Fall Joint Computer Conference—Exploring Technology: Today and Tomorrow, Dallas, TX, IEEE Comput. Soc., (Cat. No. 87CH2468-7), pp. 658–663, Oct. 25–29, 1987.

DXPLAIN assists a physician in diagnosing a patient's illness. It uses information based on the patient's symptoms, physical exam, and laboratory tests results. It uses about 4,700 descriptors to score the possibility of one or more diseases using knowledge on about 2,000 potential diseases. It presents a list of suspected diseases, rank ordered according to its suspicion. The system was developed at Massachusetts General Hospital, Boston, MA.

Barnett, G., J. Cimino, and J. Hupp, DXPLAIN: An evolving diagnostic decision support system, Journal of the American Medical Association, vol. 258, pp. 67–74, 1987.

EEG ANALYSIS SYSTEM: an expert system was developed for the automated detection of spikes and sharp waves in the EEG for the detection of epileptiform activity. The system consists of two distinct stages. The first is a feature extractor, written in the conventional procedural language Fortran, which uses part of previously published spike-detection algorithms to produce a list of all spike-like occurrences in the EEG. The second stage, written in OP55, reads the list and uses rules incorporating knowledge elicited from an electroencephalographer (EEGer) to confirm or exclude each of the possible spikes. Information such as the time of occurrence, polarity, and channel relationship is used in this process. A summary of the detected epileptiform events is produced, which is available to the EEGer in interpreting the EEG. The system was developed at the Dev. Med. Physics and Bioengineering, Christchurch Hosp., Private Bag, Christchurch, New Zealand.

Davey, B., et al., Expert system approach to detection of epileptiform activity in the EEG, Medical & Biological Engineering & Computing, vol. 27, no. 4, pp. 365–370, 1989.

Hematex assists in the interpretation of full blood counts and blood smears in a hematology laboratory using information supplied by Technicon H1 blood cell analyzers. The H1 enables a technologist or hematologist to evaluate a patient's blood picture through the interpretation of a combination of numeric results, morphology flags, cytograms, and histograms. By combining this information with the visual evaluation of blood smears, a large number of hematologic diseases can be diagnosed. Heamatex extracts information from the H1 and then interprets it, in order to facilitate with the diagnosis of a particular blood disorder. The system was developed at the University of the Orange Free State, Bloemfontein, South Africa.

Tolmie, C., et al., Expert system for the interpretation of full blood counts and blood smears in a hematology laboratory, Artif. Intell. Med., vol. 3, no. 5, pp. 271–285, Oct. 1991.

HEPAR assists with the diagnosis of disorders of the liver and biliary tract. The patient's disorder is assessed in two stages. In the first stage, available data from medical interview, physical examination, and simple laboratory tests are used to determine whether the disorder is hepatocellular or biliary obstructive in nature, and whether benign or malignant features are present. In the second stage, the system produces a subset of possible diagnoses out of a set of more than 80 disease categories, using additional data from supplementary tests. The system is rule based and was developed at the University of Amsterdam.

Lucas, P. and A. Janssens, Development and validation of HEPAR, an expert system for the diagnosis of disorders of the liver and biliary tract, Med. Inf. (London), vol. 16, no. 3, pp. 259–70, July–Sept., 1991.

OBCONSULT is an expert system for the management of high-risk pregnancies. The system requests user inputs such as indications (i.e., primary symptoms), test results, patient history, and prior complications. The system reviews this information using a set of rules developed by medical staff and provides recommendations for further testing and periodic reassessment and suggests a diagnosis. The intended uses of the program are as a consultant to OB/GYN physicians who are not specialists in handling high-risk pregnancies and as an educational tool. The system was implemented using VP-Expert on a PC. The system was developed at Biomedical Engr. Program, Hartford Graduate Center, CT.

Donohue, B., et al., OBCONSULT: A prototype knowledge-based system for the management of high risk pregnancies, Proceedings of the 12th Annual International Conference of the IEEE Engineering in Medicine and Biology Society, Philadelphia, PA, pp. 1324–1325, Nov. 1–4, 1990.

VM monitors the condition of postsurgical patients in an intensive care environment. VM maintains a set of patient-specific expectations and goals for future evaluation. The system examines the patient history and type of surgery to establish ranges of expected behavior. It identifies an alarm condition if these ranges are exceeded and suggests corrective actions. It is expectation driven and uses the current and past patient history to establish guidelines for patient measurements. The guidelines are used to dynamically establish upper and lower limits for comparison with each new measurement from the monitoring system. It responds with suggestions to clinicians and periodic summaries. VM is rule based and uses forward chaining. It checks that information previously acquired is still valid for making conclusions, and cycles through the rule set each time new information is available. VM is implemented in LISP and was developed at Stanford University.

Fagan, L., Ventilator manager: A program to provide on-line consultative advice in the intensive care unit, Report HPP-78-16, Computer Science Dept., Stanford University, Stanford, Calif., Sept. 1978.

WEANPRO, WEANing PROtocol, assists respiratory therapists and nurses in weaning post-operative cardiovascular patients from mechanical ventilation in the intensive care unit. The knowledge contained in WEANPRO is represented by rules and is implemented in M.1 by Teknowledge, Inc. WEANPRO will run on any IBM-compatible microcomputer. Test results of the system revealed that it significantly decreases the number of arterial blood gas analyses needed to wean patients from total dependence on mechanical ventilation to independent breathing using a T-piece.

Tong, David A., Weaning patients from mechanical ventilation. A knowledge-based system approach, Computer Methods and Programs in Biomedicine, vol. 35, no. 4, pp. 267–278, Aug. 1991.

Meteorology

ARCHER identifies meteorological phenomena from their signatures on Doppler radar. Probabilities that phenomena under study could be any one of a number of possible meteorological archetypes (i.e., stereotyped phenomena such as convective cells or gust fronts) are determined by comparing current evidence with stored meteorological knowledge. The system was developed at NOAA/Environmental Science Group, Boulder, CO.

Moninger, W.R., ARCHER: A prototype expert system for identifying some meteorological phenomena, Journal of Atmospheric and Oceanic Technology, vol. 5, no. 1, pp. 144–148, February 1988.

CONVCTIV assists in the prediction of severe thunderstorms in the area of northeast Colorado and adjacent areas. A large body of meteorological data is collected constantly and available to meteorologists through computer systems such as PROFS (Program for Regional Observing and Forecasting Services). Such programs provide a meteorologist with the data needed to develop a good weather forecast. However, often there is a limited time frame in which to make a prediction and some problems, such as severe thunderstorm prediction, require highly specialized and complex knowledge. To address this problem, an expert system was built to help use the data available to predict severe thunderstorms. External programs were used extensively to handle the necessary complex mathematical calculations. The system was designed to be used by someone who is a knowledgeable meteorologist. The system can make predictions on thunderstorm likelihood and severity. The system is rule based and employs backward chaining. The system was implemented using EXSYS and was developed at NOAA, Colorado State University, Fort Collins, CO.

Weaver, J.F. and R.S. Phillips, Mesoscale thunderstorm forecasting using RAOB data, surface mesonet, in Mesoscale Analysis and Forecasting Incorporating Nowcasting, B. Battrick and E. Rolfe, eds., Proceedings of an International Symposium, Vancouver, BC, Canada, ESA, Noordwijk, Netherlands, pp. 327–331, August, 1987.

HAIL PREDICTION APPLICATION: An expert system was developed that predicts the production of hail from an existing and observed thunderstorm on the Colorado high plains. The system uses Doppler radar and a product Z_{DR} derived from this data as input. Output from the system is a classification of the thunderstorm for the production of hail ranging from nonsignificant to severe. In some cases the user is alerted to the likelihood of tornadoes and/or strong winds. The system was developed by the U.S. National Weather Service.

Merrem, F.H., Two expert systems used in weather forecasting, Expert Systems in Government Symposium, McLean, Virginia, IEEE Comput. Soc. Press, Washington, DC, pp. 458–459, October 1986.

METEOR is a rule- and frame-based system for short-term severe storm forecasting. Initial predictions are based on interpretations of contour maps generated by statistical predictors of storm severity. To confirm these predictions, METEOR considers additional quantitative measurements, ongoing meteorological conditions and events, and how the expert forecaster interprets these factors. Meteorological events are derived interpreting human observations of weather conditions in the forecast area. This task requires a framework that supports inferences about the temporal and spatial features of meteorological activities. To accommodate the large amounts of different types of knowledge characterizing this problem, a number of extensions to the rule and frame representations were developed. These extensions include a view scheme to direct property inheritance through intermingled hierarchies and the automatic generation of production system rules from descriptions stored in frames when they are needed. The system was developed at Alberta University, Edmonton, Alberta, Canada.

Elio, R. and J. De Haan, Representing quantitative and qualitative knowledge in a knowledge-based storm-forecasting system, International Journal of Man–Machine Studies, vol. 25, no. 5, pp. 523–547, November 1986.

RAIN PREDICTION APPLICATION: an expert system was developed for predicting regional heavy rain. The system can accept, recognize, analyze, explain, understand, use, appreciate, and refine the forecasting knowledge in MKL (Meteorological Knowledge Language) taught by meteorologists. The MKL language is good for describing meteorological knowledge and can represent almost all forecasting knowledge, thus enabling the system, with a great range of knowledge, to raise the processing abilities. The system was developed at the Inst. Atmos. Phys., Acad. Sinica, Beijing, People's Rep. China.

Dai, Honghua, et al., An expert system for predicting the regional heavy rain, Adv. Atmos. Sci., vol. 4, no. 4, 1987.

WILLARD determines the possibility of severe thunderstorms occurring in the central United States region. The system uses information supplied by a meteorologist about present weather conditions, coupled with knowledge about weather prediction gained from past examples. WILLARD's knowledge was formed using the induction shell Rulemaster. The system was developed at Radian Corporation.

Michie, D., S. Muggleton, C. Riese, and S. Zubrick, RULEMASTER: A second-generation knowledge-engineering facility, Proceedings of the First Conference on Artificial Intelligence Applications, IEEE Computer Society, Dec. 1984.

Military

ACIM is an expert system that assists helicopter pilots in flying their aircraft. ACIM integrates information from numerous aircraft systems and determines what, when, where, and how information should be provided to the pilot. The system is implemented in KEE on the TI Explorer workstation. ACIM was developed at Boeing Military Airplane Company, Wichita, KS.

Martz, S., C. Leininger, and J. Ducas, Advanced helicopter cockpit information management, pp. 1–8, 1987.

ACOUSTIC SIGNAL INTERPRETATION APPLICATION: An expert system was developed to assist a sonar operator in the identification of acoustic sources. The system extracts features such as line families or interference patterns from raw acoustic data. It then uses a rule-based approach to match these features with known classes of vehicles. This matching process is performed using a Dempster-Shafer inexact reasoning approach that permits matches to be rank ordered. The system was developed at Defence Research Establishment Atlantic, Nova Scotia, Canada.

Hughes, R. and J. Maksym, Acoustic signal interpretation: Reasoning with non-specific and uncertain information, Pattern Recognition, vol. 18, no. 6, pp. 457–483, 1985.

ADRIES, Advanced Digital Radar Imagery Exploitation System, is a test bed for research on extracting information from radar imagery. The system is capable of producing interpretations of possible military situations given the radar imagery, terrain data (maps or digital terrain databases), and other tactical data. The system is model based and employs a Bayesian probabilistic inference network. Models represent knowledge of the organization and formations of military units. The system can use these models with terrain information to determine the likelihood of the presence or absence of certain types of enemy forces. The system contains a distributed set of objects that communicate through message passing. The system was developed at Advanced Decision Support Systems, Mountain View, CA.

Levitt, T., et al., Terrain knowledge elicitation for ADRIES, Part II, Contract DACA76-86-C-0010, Decision Support Systems, Mountain View, CA, Oct. 1987.

BATTLE determines allocations for a set of weapons to a set of targets, In the system, each resource is a military weapon and each task to which a resource can be allocated is firing at a military target. An evaluation function is used to determine the expected reduction in target value for the applied weapon. After the calculation of individual effectiveness values, portions of an allocation tree are constructed to determine good allocation plans for a set of weapons. It was designed for use by the U.S. Marine Corps' Marine Integrated Fire and Air Support System. BATTLE represents its knowledge in rules and performs inexact reasoning using PROSPECTOR-like certainty factors. The system was developed at the Naval Research Laboratory, Washington, DC.

Slagle, J. and M. Gaynor, Expert system consultation control strategy, Proceedings AAAI-83, pp. 369–372, 1983.

EPES assists F-16 pilots for in-flight emergencies. In an emergency situation, the system first warns the pilot of the event, recommends corrective procedures, then automatically takes control if corrective action is not taken. The primary goal of the system is to maintain the aircraft's speed, heading, and altitude. The knowledge base for EPES includes parts, goals, and rules, and implements emergency procedures from an F-16 flight manual. Semantic network and rule-based knowledge representation strategies are employed within the system. The system is implemented in LISP on a LISP machine and was developed at Texas Instruments.

Anderson, B.M., N.L. Cramer, M. Lineberry, G.S. Lystad, and R.C. Stern, Intelligent automation of emergency procedures in advanced fighter aircraft, Proceedings of the First Conference on Artificial Intelligence Applications, IEEE Computer Society, Denver, CO, December 1984.

ESL aids the military intelligence analyst in performing the Indications & Warning task: assimilating hundreds of incoming reports, and predicting where and when an armed conflict might erupt next. The system currently contains 60 condition/action rules and 170 other frames that deal with the sorts of objects and processes that are being reported on. It employs a two-dimensional blackboard to accommodate reports from very different sources, to efficiently trigger relevant rules, and to keep the human analyst abreast of the situation. The system is implemented in LISP on a Xerox workstation. It was developed at California University and Stanford University.

Lenat, D.B., A. Clarkson, and G. Kiremidjian, An expert system for indications and warning analysis, IJCAI-83, Karlsruhe, vol. 1, pp. 259–262, 1983.

FORCE AGENT is an adaptive simulation model that simulates ground, air, and naval warfare in both conventional and nuclear settings. The system is adaptive because it permits three rule-based modules to examine the current state of affairs as the simulation proceeds, allowing those modules to alter the course of events. The system was developed at the Rand Corp., Santa Monica, CA.

Shukiar, H., The Rand strategy assessment center system perspective, Conf. of Soc. for Computer Simulation, Boston, MA., pp. 1–22, July 23–26, 1984.

HANNIBAL monitors enemy communication and performs a battlefield situation assessment. The system uses data about the location of the communications and signal characteristics such as the frequency, modulation, channel class, etc. HANNIBAL is rule based within a blackboard structure. The system is implemented in AGE and was developed at ESL.

Brown, H., J. Buckman, R. Engelmore, D. Harrison, and C. Pfefferkorn, Communication intelligence task—HANNIBAL demonstration, Report, ESL, Inc., Sunnyvale, Calif., 1982.

Intelligent Weapon Suggestion System is a research expert system built to assist the Weapons Department Head on board a naval warship in making accurate and efficient decisions in critical battle situations. The system receives preprocessed sensor input, determines what contacts are present, performs target analysis and correlation based upon the current tactical situation, and suggests the most effective weapon(s) to deploy against various hostile targets. Simulation results have shown that the system can provide timely decision support in a time-critical combat environment. The system was implemented using KEE and was developed at Naval Postgraduate School, Monterey, CA.

Weng, W.I., Rule-based weapon suggestion system for shipboard three dimensional defense, Master's thesis, Naval Postgraduate School, Monterey, CA., Dec. 90.

MINEPLAN, Minefield Planner Expert System, assists Navy personnel with laying mines. Minefield planning requires consideration of a number of factors: mine actuation, enemy target factors, potential mine countermeasures, aircraft delivery factors, etc. A large search space of possible solutions exists that requires analysis of factors such as placement of the minefield, number and type of mines, mine settings, etc. The system was developed at the Naval Surface Warfare Center, White Oak, MD.

Rock, D., et al., AI and the military: Time for a standard, AI Expert, vol. 5, no. 8, pp. 56–64, Aug., 1990.

PILOT'S ASSOCIATE is an intelligent flight simulator. The system is interfaced to symbolic processors that act as the flight simulator. The system consists of a VAX-11/780 driving a full, six-degree-of-freedom simulator linked by Ethernet to three Symbolics LISP machines. On the LISP machines are expert systems performing situation assessment, tactics and route planning, and intelligent pilot–vehicle interface. The system was developed at Lockheed.

Broadwell, M.M. and D.M. Smith, Interfacing symbolic processes to a flight simulator, Proceedings of the 1986 Summer Computer Simulation Conference, San Diego, CA., pp. 751–755, 1986.

Mining

CHOOZ aids mine managers in underground manpower planning activities. It automatically compiles work crews, premium work lists, and suggests strategies for deploying a work force for the maximum productivity. The system is written in Turbo PROLOG on an IBM PC. It was developed at Tanoma Coal Co., N.V., Indiana, PA.

Britton, S., Computer-based expert system aids underground mine planning, Coal Age, pp. 69–70, Jan. 1987.

DUSTPRO provides advice to a coal mine operator for the control of the mine ventilation system to minimize a miner's exposure to respirable dust. Respirable dust is the primary cause of black lung disease. The system uses information about available ventilation equipment and control procedures, coupled with mine ventilation regulations, to provide recommendations for reducing dust levels within the mine to assure a safe working environment. The system uses a distributed problem-solving approach, where 30 separate expert systems designed for specialized activities address the ventilation problem and communicate their results over a blackboard structure. The system was designed using the shell LEVEL5 on an IBM PC. It was developed at the U.S. Bureau of Mines, Pittsburgh, PA.

Durkin, J., DUSTPRO: A distributed expert system for coal mine dust control, ESD/SMI Second Annual Expert Systems Conference, Detroit, MI, pp. 377–385, Apr. 12–14, 1988.

ECAS, Emergency Control Advisory System, assists mining personnel with mine emergency management following a disaster. The system is capable of diagnosing the likely causes of the problem and advising mine management of optimum choices before the arrival of the rescue team. It is also capable of providing the rescue team guidance. The resultant system can also be used for training mining personnel and rescue teams in correct procedures under emergency or hazard conditions. The system was developed at the National Energy Research, Development and Demonstration Council, Canberra, Australia.

Aubrey, J., et al., Development of an expert system for hazard/emergency control and training, National Energy Research, Development and Demonstration Council, Canberra, Australia, Report No. 143, Dec. 1990.

FACE-BOSS aids the face-boss (section foreman) in a coal mine. The face-boss has to juggle resources and manpower in order to satisfy mine management's demand for increased productivity while meeting federal (and other) safety regulations. FACE-BOSS codifies the activities of the face-boss into a collection of hierarchical subtrees that reflect the reasoning process employed by expert face-bosses in the field. It was developed at West Virginia University.

Reddy, Y.V., R.S. Nutter, R.S. Raman, N.A. Reddy, and A.W. Butcher, Intelligent mine management system, SIGART Newsletter, Number 92, p. 95, April 1985.

FANPRO assists in the diagnosis of vane-axial fans. Aerodynamic stall of vane-axial fans is both an operational problem and a safety concern. While deep stall is relatively easy to detect, the diagnosis of a partial stall is often more difficult. Its transient nature and the fact that its symptoms can mimic electromechanical problems of the fan and fan drive assembly, or vice versa, compound the difficulty of making a timely and accurate diagnosis. FANPRO has been developed to aid in the diagnosis of these problems. The system was developed at Pennsylvania State University, University Park, PA, in collaboration with the U.S. Bureau of Mines Research, Pittsburgh Research Center, Pittsburgh, PA.

Kohler, Jeffery L., Edward D. Thimons, and Fred N. Kissell, Diagnosis of fan stall and electromechanical problems of the fan using knowledge-based expert systems, Proceedings of the 5th US Mine Ventilation Symposium, West Virginia Univ. Morgantown, WV, pp. 566–572, May 3–5, 1991.

Power Systems

ALFA predicts short-term demand for electricity based on daily, weekly, and seasonal variations of load, as well as holidays, special events, and load growth. The system is rule based. ALFA is in operation at the Energy Management System Center at Niagara Mohawk Power Corporation in upstate New York, generating, in real time, hourly load forecasts for up to 48 hours in advance. ALFA uses an extensive 10-year historical database of hourly observations of 12 weather variables and a rule base that takes into account daily, weekly, and seasonal variations of load, as well as holidays, special events, and load growth. The system includes a satellite interface for the real-time acquisition of weather data. ALFA is written in LISP and runs on a large IBM mainframe computer.

Jabbour, K., J.F.V. Riveros, D. Landsbergen, and W. Meyer, ALFA: Automated load forecasting assistant, IEEE Transactions on Power Systems, vol. 3, no. 3, pp. 908–914, August 1988.

ARGUS, Alarm Response Guidance and Usage System, was designed to promote more effective response to alarms in a power plant control room by providing detailed information to the control room operator on both the cause of the alarm and the actions required to respond to the situation. ARGUS will read plant data, process this data through the existing alarm response procedures logic, and display the resultant diagnosis of the condition to the operator. Any actions required to alleviate the alarmed condition will also be displayed to the operator. The system was developed at Westinghouse Electr. Corp., Pittsburgh, PA.

Lipner, M., et al., Alarm response guidance and usage system (for power stations), Proceedings of the American Power Conference, Chicago, IL, pp. 342–5, April 23–25, 1990.

DIAREX, is a real-time expert system designed to diagnose nuclear power plant failure and offer recommendations for corrective action. Its main goal is to diagnose the anomalous transients affecting plant operation, e.g. a reactor scram, then provide corrective recommendations in real time. The system uses rules described in the process representation language PRL. It was developed at Nippon Atomic Industry Group Company, Japan.

Naito, N., A. Sakuma, K. Shigeno, and N. Mori, A real-time expert system for nuclear power plant failure diagnosis and operational guide, Nuclear Technology, vol. 79, pp. 284–296, Dec. 1987.

EFD, Early Fault Detection, detects faults in a nuclear power plant before the traditional alarm limits are reached. The system directs the operator to the fault and provides extra time to take action. EFD detects small changes in process parameters, measured as deviations between calculated reference measurements from mathematical models and actual plant values. The system was developed at the NRC as part of the OCED Halden Reactor project.

Haugset, K., The development of an advanced computerized control room, Post-Graduate Seminar on Computers in Nuclear Power Stations, Winterthur, Switzerland, Nov. 28–30, 1988.

ELECTRIC POWER SYSTEM DIAGNOSTIC APPLICATION: an expert system was developed to identify faulted sections of a power system and to interpret protection apparatus operation. The expert system is capable of identifying bus faults, line fault sections, and fault sections in the common area of a specific bus and line. The expert system also identifies the status of the circuit breakers involved in the faulted area and indicates the type of relay that operated. The system was developed at Clemson University, SC.

Johns, M., A.A. Girgis, and R. Schalkoff, Development of an expert system for identification of faulted sections in a transmission system, Proceedings of the Nineteenth Southeastern Symposium on System Theory, Clemson, SC, IEEE Comput. Soc., (Cat. No. TH0180-0), pp. 121–124, Mar. 15–17, 1987.

ELECTRIC POWER SYSTEMS OVERLOAD APPLICATION: an expert system was developed that supports the operator of a control center in decision making during emergency operation of an electric power system. The system is focused on the elimination of abnormal operating conditions caused by excessive power flow in certain lines. The control objective is to return the line flows to their normal limits by acting on the synchronous generators. The knowledge necessary to solve the overload problem is formulated with regards to the most feasible methods for online applications. KEE was used for the development and implementation of the knowledge base. The procedure for alleviating line overloads is translated into a set of production rules, which are interpreted by the inference engine. The system was developed at Genoa Univ., Italy.

Delfino, B., G.B. Denegri, M. Invernizzi, A. Canonero, and P. Forzano, An expert system for alleviating overloads in electric power systems: general concepts and applications, Proceedings of the Fourth Conference on Artificial Intelligence Applications, San Diego, CA, IEEE Comput. Soc., (Cat. No. 88CH2552-8), pp. 299–304, Mar. 14–18, 1988.

GIO, Gas In-Oil analyzer, is an on-line diagnostic expert system for the automatic sampling/analysis of insulation oil in oil-filled equipment such as the oil transformer. The system performs three methods of diagnosis: diagnosis by gas pattern analysis, diagnosis by specific gas detection, and diagnosis by insulation oil property deterioration. The system was developed at Fuji Electr. Eng. Co. Ltd., Japan.

Ito, K., T. Harada, and T. Kagawa, Implementation of on-line/sensor-based diagnosis expert, J. Jpn. Soc. Artif. Intell. (Japan), vol. 1, no. 2, pp. 211–18, 1986.

NUCLEAR POWER PLANT TRANSIENT IDENTIFICATION APPLICATION: a hybrid system was developed that couples rule-based expert systems using fuzzy logic, to pretrain artificial neural networks (ANN) for the purpose of transient identification in nuclear power plants. The system also uses a model-based approach in order to work with the many aspects of the transient and to determine the state of the system based on the interpretation of potentially noisy data. The expert system performs the basic interpretation and processing of the model data to pretrain the ANNs. Having access to a set of neural networks that typify the general categories of transients, the rule-based system is able to perform identification functions. Membership functions—condensing information about a transient in a form convenient for a rule-based identification system characterizing a transient—are the output of neural computations.

Tsoukalas, L., et al., Hybrid expert system, Proceedings of the American Power Conference, Chicago, IL, vol. 53, pp. 1206–1211, Apr. 19–May 1, 1991.

TRANSFORMER FAULT DIAGNOSIS APPLICATION: An expert system was developed to aid in the diagnosis of faulty electrical transformers. One of the most reliable techniques for testing the condition of a transformer is the gas-in-oil method. This method measures the concentration of various gases in a sample of oil taken from the transformer using a gas chromatograph. The results are then evaluated by an expert to judge the condition of the transformer. This expert system can automatically obtain information from the chromatograph and information on past tests from a database. The system then reasons with this information to determine if a fault is suspected and recommends steps to correct the fault. The knowledge in the system was obtained from the domain expert in the form of heuristic rules and works with gas level concentrations in a form of fuzzy sets. The system runs on a PC and was developed using the expert system shell INSIGHT2+. The system was developed at the University of Akron, Akron, OH.

Durkin, J. and R. Schlegelmich, Transformer diagnostic expert systems, LEVEL5 Third Annual Expert Systems Conference, Indialantic, Florida, Nov. 1989.

Science

BACON.5 is an expert system that discovers empirical laws. The system represents information at varying levels of description, with higher levels summarizing the levels below them. The system applies a small set of data-driven heuristics to detect regularities in numeric and nominal data. These heuristics note constancies and trends, leading it to formulate hypotheses, define theoretical terms, and postulate intrinsic properties. Once the program has formulated a hypothesis, it uses this to reduce the amount of data it must consider at later times. A simple type of reasoning by analogy also simplifies the discovery of laws contained in symmetric forms. These techniques have allowed the system to rediscover the ideal gas law, Kepler's third law of planetary motion, Coulomb's law, Ohm's law, Galileo's laws for the pendulum and constant acceleration, Snell's law of refraction, conservation of momentum, Black's specific heat law, and Joule's formulation of conservation of energy. The system is implemented in OPS and was developed at Carnegie University.

Langley, P., G.L. Bradshaw, and H.A. Simon, BACON.5: The discovery of conservation laws, IJCAI81, Vancouver, vol. 1, pp. 121–126, 1981.

GAMMA assists nuclear physicists in identifying the elemental composition of unknown substances. Gamma ray activation spectra are used by nuclear physicists to identify the elemental composition of unknown substances. Neutron bombardment causes some of the atoms of a sample to change into unstable isotopes, which then decay, emitting gamma radiation at characteristic energies and intensities. By identifying the unstable isotopes, the composition of the original substance can be determined. GAMMA has been developed to perform this function. It is based on the generate-and-test paradigm. The system was developed at Yale University and Schlumberger-Doll.

Barstow, D.R., Knowledge engineering in nuclear physics, IJCAI-79, Tokyo, Vol. 1, pp. 34–36, 1979.

GENESIS assists research geneticists with the analysis of a DNA's molecular structure. The system determines the order within the DNA chain of the four different bases: adenine, cytosine, guanine, and thymine. One common technique for determining the order involves labeling one end of the chain with a radioactive element. Enzymes are then used to cut the chain by dissolving one of the bases. The remaining initial piece of the chain, which is labeled by the radioactive element, can then be measured to determine its length. This process is repeated until the sequence of the bases is determined along the complete DNA chain. GENESIS includes seven different expert systems that aid this testing method. The system is commercially available from Intellicorp, Mountain View, CA.

Harmon, P., R. Maus, and W. Morrisset, Expert Systems: Tools & Applications, John Wiley, 1988.

GSS, General Surveillance System, monitors the operation of an accelerator in a high-energy physics laboratory to assure safe conditions. The system uses sensor data that provides information on such items as inflammable gases, smoke, temperatures, etc., to detect a potential problem and avert a possible accident. The system is rule based and event driven, and was implemented using GENESIA II on a VAX. The system was developed at CERN/ECP, Geneva, Switzerland.

Chevrier, F., Safety controlled by an expert system on experimental sites in high energy physics, in G.P. Zarri (ed.) Operational Expert System Applications in Europe, Pergamon Press, 1991.

MOLGEN offers intelligent advice to a molecular geneticist on how to organize and sequence laboratory tools such as techniques for changing DNA material, techniques for determining the biological consequences of changes, instruments for measuring effects, chemical methods for inducing or inhibiting changes, and other tools, in order to achieve an experimental goal. MOLGEN is also intended to check user experiment plans for feasibility, and to provide an extensive knowledge base for interrogation. The system is rule based and implemented using KEE on a Xerox 1108. It was developed at Stanford University.

Feigenbaum, E.A., The art of artificial intelligence: Themes and case studies of knowledge engineering, IJCAI-77, MIT, vol. 2, 1977.

Space

AMPS, the Autonomously Managed Power System, is an expert system for power management on the space station. AMPS consists of four basic components: scheduler, resource manager, fault diagnosis, and power distributor. All of these components are under the control of a high-level supervisor module. AMPS was developed by Lockheed of Palo Alto, CA, using ART.

Nguyen, T.A. and W.C. Chiou, Cooperating expert systems for space station power distribution management, SPIE, vol. 729, pp. 7–10, 1986.

APEX, the Autonomous Power Expert System, is an expert system designed to monitor the power system on Space Station Freedom. This system detects faults by comparing expected values to measured operating values. It demonstrates the ability to handle three different types of fault states: inconsistent faults, active faults, and incipient faults. It was developed at NASA Lewis Research Center using KEE on a TI Explorer II workstation.

Quinn, T. and J. Walters, Autonomous power expert system advanced development, Fourth Annual Workshop on Space Operations Applications and Research, NASA Publication 3103, vol. 1 pp. 383–390, June 26–28, 1990.

Booster Flight Controller Expert assists flight controllers with diagnosing problems on the Space Shuttle. The system can detect failures and provide control recommendations to the flight controller. It can also run simulations to analyze various control maneuvers. During ascent or entry, the flight controller has less than 20 seconds to detect a problem, analyze it, and take action. The expert system has demonstrated the ability to correctly identify all known booster failure scenarios, and simulate additional potential ones, in a few seconds. The system was implemented using G2 and was developed at NASA.

Pohle, G., Data acquisition for G2 using RTDS, Proc. Gensym Users Society Annual Meeting, Houston, TX, Mar. 6–8, 1991.

CLEAR, the Communications Link Expert Assistance Resource, is a fault isolation expert system for the Cosmic Background Explorer (COBE) mission operations room. The system assists personnel during periods of real-time data acquisition by isolating faults in the spacecraft communication link and providing advice on how to correct them. The system was developed by NASA Goodard Space Fight Center using CLIPS.

Hughes, P., CLEAR: Automating control centers with expert system technology, Third Annual Workshop on Space Operations Applications and Research, NASA Publication 3059, pp. 289–293, June 25–27, 1989.

FIDEX, Fault Isolation and Diagnosis EXpert system, was developed for communication satellite diagnostics. FIDEX is a frame-based system with an architecture that integrates a frame hierarchy that describes the transponder's components, with other hierarchies that provide structural and fault information about the satellite. FIDEX also includes an inexact reasoning technique and a primitive learning ability. Inexact reasoning was an important feature for this system due to the sparse number of sensors available to provide information on the satellite's performance. FIDEX can determine the most likely faulted component under the constraint of limited information. FIDEX learns about the most likely faults in the transponder by keeping a record of past established faults. This permits the system to search first for those faults that are most likely to occur, thus enhancing search efficiency. FIDEX also has the ability to detect anomalies in the sensors that provide information on the transponder's performance. This ability is used to first rule out simple sensor malfunctions. The expert system was designed with a generic structure and features that make it applicable to other types of space systems. The system was implemented using NEXPERT OBJECT on an IBM PC and was developed at the University of Akron.

Durkin, John, Donald Tallo, and Edward Petrik, FIDEX: An expert system for satellite diagnostics, Space Communications Technology Conference, Onboard Processing and Switching, Nasa Lewis Research Center, Cleveland, OH, Nov. 12–14, 1991.

L*STAR performs real-time monitoring of telemetry from the Pointing and Control System of the NASA Hubble Space Telescope. It aids ground personnel in maintaining the health and safety of the spacecraft. In order to handle asynchronous input and perform in real time, the system consists of three or more separate processes that run concurrently and communicate by way of a message-passing scheme and can reside on the same or different computers. The data management task gathers, compresses, and scales the incoming telemetry data before sending them to the other tasks. The inferencing task consists of a proprietary high-performance inference engine written in C. It uses the telemetry data to perform a real-time analysis of the state and health of HST. It was implemented on a set of VAXes and MicroVAXes and uses DECNET mailboxes as the message-passing mechanism. The system is rule based and was developed by Lockheed of Sunnyvale, CA.

Dunham, L., T. Laffey, S. Kao, J. Schmidt, and J. Read, Knowledge-based monitoring of the pointing control system on the Hubble Space telescope, Third Conference on Artificial Intelligence for Space Applications, Part 1, NASA Conference Publication 2492, pp. 95–100, Nov. 2–3, 1987.

LES, Load Enable Scheduler, is an expert system that schedules/reschedules the payloads for the space station power system. The system begins by generating a baseline schedule in the form of event lists. It can then reschedule the loads in response to changing constraints that require a reconfiguration. The system was implemented on a LISP workstation in LISP.

Geoffory, A.L., Power resource management scheduling for scientific space platform applications, 22nd Intersociety Energy Conversion Engineering Conference, Phila., Pa, vol. 1, Aug. 10–14, 1987.

MTS-EXPERT was developed to monitor the Galileo mission telemetry system. It is capable of regularly going through large volumes of data to identify, diagnose, and isolate faults. The system includes the capability of temporal reasoning, uncertainty management and intelligent graphic user interfaces. It was developed at JPL with the use of ART on a Sun3/160 workstation.

Mouneimne, S., Mission telemetry system monitor: A real-time knowledge-based system, Goddard Conference on Space Applications of Artificial Intelligence, NASA Publication 3009, pp. 207–212, May 24, 1988.

PI-in-a-Box was developed to assist astronauts aboard the Space Station Freedom in the performance of experiments. The system monitors data from the experiment and suggests proper actions during the experiment. The system is able to detect that a particular data set reveals some unexpected behavior of the system under study that warrants a repetition of the experiment or a change in the set of experiments that are to follow. The system was implemented initially using NEXPERT OBJECT on an IBM PC and later converted to CLIPS. It was developed at NASA-Ames.

Haymanne-Haber, G., An expert system to advise astronauts during experiments: The protocol manager module, Third Annual Workshop on Space Operations Applications and Research, NASA Publication 3059, pp. 187–194, June 25–27, 1989.

RENDEZVOUS was designed to control the rendezvous vehicle during proximity operations. Fuzzy sets are used to model the human capability of common-sense reasoning in decision-making tasks and are integrated with expert systems to create a system that performs comparably to a manned system. The system was developed at NASA Johnson Space Center.

Lea, R., Automated space vehicle control for rendezvous proximity operations, Goddard Conference on Space Applications of Artificial Intelligence, NASA Publication 3009, pp. 59–66, May 24, 1988.

Transportation

ADVANCED DISPATCHER is an expert system control system for elevator dispatching. The system was designed to work in buildings with one or more goups of elevators. Each group could consist of two to eight elevator cars. The system continually monitors the traffic in the buildings through various sensors, providing passenger counts that are analyzed using a statistical analysis technique. Forecasting techniques that make use of current and past traffic patterns are then used to predict traffic originating and terminating at different floors for the next several minutes. Dispatching algorithms are then selected to serve predicted traffic efficiently. Dispatching involves multistage decision making. The system performs intelligent simulations of elevator operation to learn which dispatching strategy would provide the desired performance. The system was developed at Otis Elevators, Farmington, Conn.

Kameli, N. and K. Thangavelu, Intelligent elevator dispatching systems, AI Expert, vol. 4, no. 9, pp. 32–37, Sept. 1989.

AIR TRAFFIC CONTROLLER APPLICATION: An expert system was developed that provides advice to air traffic controllers on the optimal tactics for resolving predicted aircraft conflicts. The system combines computational algorithms with rule bases containing the knowledge and experience of controllers in the air traffic environment. The hybrid nature of the system is based on a design approach involving a decomposition of the overall sequence of logical decisions required to resolve the predicted conflict into a global inferencing algorithm. The system was developed at Carleton Univ., Ottawa, Ont., Canada.

Bowen, B.A., An expert system for aircraft conflict resolution in dense airspaces, Knowledge Based Concepts and Artificial Intelligence: Applications to Guidance and Control (AGARD-LS-155), Ottawa, Ont., Canada, pp. 4/1–13, Sept. 10–11, 1987.

AIRPORT STAFF SCHEDULING APPLICATION: an expert system was developed for scheduling the job assignments for the servicing staff at an airport. The system produces the schedule (called a master roster) according to constraints associated with requirements, and the availability and capability of the staff. The system is rule based and is implemented in C on an IBM PC. It can configure a schedule of 400 staffs in less than a minute. The system was developed at the University of Hong Kong.

Chow, K.P. and C.K. Hui, Knowledge-based approach to airport staff rostering, in Operational Expert System Applications in the Far East, J.K. Lee et al., eds., Pergamon Press, 1991.

AUTONOMOUS LAND VEHICLE NAVIGATION APPLICATION: An expert system was developed to navigate an autonomous land vehicle (ALV) along roads using a vision system. The ALV vision task consists of hypothesizing objects in a scene model and verifying these hypotheses using the vehicle's sensors. Object hypothesis generation is based on the local navigation task, the a priori road map, and the contents of the scene model. Verification on an object hypothesis involves directing the sensors toward the expected location of the object, collecting evidence in support of the object, and reasoning about the evidence. Constructing the scene model consists of building a semantic network of object frames exhibiting component, spatial, and inheritance relationships. The control structure is provided by a set of communicating rule-based systems implementing a structured blackboard. Each rule system contains the rules for defining the attributes of a particular class of object frame. The system was developed at Maryland University, College Park, MD.

Dickinson, S.J. and L.S. Davis, An expert vision system for autonomous land vehicle road following, Proceedings CVPR '88: The Computer Society Conference on Computer Vision and Pattern Recognition, Ann Arbor, MI, IEEE Comput. Soc., (Cat. No. 88CH2605-4), pp. 826–831, June 5–9, 1988.

AUTONOMOUS UNDERWATER VEHICLE NAVIGATION APPLICATION: An expert system was developed for the simulation of autonomous underwater vehicle (AUV) navigation. The system performs mission control functions. The simulator utilizes an interactive mission planning control console and is fully autonomous once initial parameters are selected. The system was implemented using KEE on a LISP workstation. It was developed at U.S. Naval Postgraduate School, Dept. of Computer Science, Monterey, CA.

Zyda, Michael J., et al., Three-dimensional visualization of mission planning and control for the NPS autonomous underwater vehicle, IEEE Journal of Oceanic Engineering, vol. 15, no. 3, pp. 217–221, July 1990.

BUS ROUTING APPLICATION: a bus routing expert system was developed for rural school districts. It generates routes aiming to reduce the number of busses required and the fleet traveling distance by an expert system approach. It also allows planner participation in the process. It was developed on microcomputer hardware and is combined with a powerful low-cost mapping software to create a system capable of importing and updating digitized road maps. The system was developed at the University of Alabama, Tuscaloosa, AL.

Chen, Der-San and Henry A. Kallsen, Bus routing system for rural school districts, Proceedings of the 12th Annual Conference on Computers and Industrial Engineering, Orlando, FL, Computers & Industrial Engineering, vol. 19, no. 1–4, pp. 484–488, Mar. 12–14, 1990.

GATES assigns gates to arriving and departing flights at New York's John F. Kennedy International Airport. The system uses flight information and knowledge about current constraints to possible gate assignment schedules. GATES is a constraint-satisfaction expert system. To make its decisions, it uses two types of production rule: permissive rules and conflict rules. Permissive rules determine when it's appropriate to consider a particular gate for a particular flight, and permit the system to search the next level of rules to obtain an assignment. Conflict rules determine when particular flights cannot be assigned to particular gates. System operators can modify schedules by retracting rules, adjusting tolerances, and deleting information. GATES is a rule-based system implemented in PROLOG on a PC. The system was developed at North Texas State University.

Brazile, R. and K. Swigger, GATES: An airline gate assignment and tracking expert system, IEEE Expert, pp. 33–39, Summer 1988.

Safety Bag is part of an electronic railway interlocking system that maintains railway safety and reliability. The system is designed with an Interlock Processor and a Safety Bag channel. The system checks each command to make sure that it conforms with safety standards and the present state of the railway. Safety Bag checks all the instructions that are generated by the Interlock Processor due to a command issued by the signalman and due to a command to line up the route. It generates instructions that are required reaction on input events, such as to set signals from free to stop when a track becomes occupied or a switch loses the correct position. The system is rule based and is implemented in the rule-based language PAMELA. The system was developed at ALCATEL Austria.

Klien, P., The safety-bag expert system in the electronic railway interlocking system ELEKTRA, in Operational Expert System Applications in Europe, G.P. Zarri, ed., Pergamon Press, 1991.

APPENDIX D

Expert Systems Bibliography

This appendix provides a list of valuable references categorized into the following subject areas:

- Building an Expert System
- Frame-Based Expert Systems
- Induction Systems
- Inexact Reasoning
- Introduction to Expert Systems
- Knowledge Acquisition
- Knowledge Engineering
- Knowledge Representation

Students should be encouraged to read select references as the expert system course discusses each area.

Building an Expert System

Attarwaia, F.T. and A. Basden, A Methodology for Constructing Expert Systems, R&D Management, vol. 15, no. 2, pp. 141–149, 1985.

Feigenbaum, E.A., Knowledge Engineering: The Applied Side of Artificial Intelligence, Tech Rep. STAN-CS-80-812 (HPP-80-21), Dept. of Computer Sci. Stanford University, 1980.

Frieling, M., J. Alexander, S. Messick, S. Rehfuss, and S. Shulman, Starting a Knowledge Engineering Project: A Step-by-Step Approach, The AI Magazine, pp. 150–164, Fall 1985.

Haley, P. and C. Williams, Expert System Development Requires Knowledge Engineering, Computer Design, pp. 83–88, Feb. 15, 1986.

Hill, H., A Methodology for Building Expert Systems, National Computer Conference, pp. 7–12, 1987.

Sagalowicz, D., Development of an Expert System, Expert Systems, vol. 1, no. 2, pp. 137–141, 1984.

Smith, R.G., On the Development of Commercial Expert Systems, The AI Magazine, pp. 61–72, Fall 1984.

Williams, C., Expert Systems, Knowledge Engineering and AI Tools—An Overview, IEEE Expert, vol. 1, no. 4, pp. 66–70, 1986.

Frame-Based Expert Systems

Aikens, J.S., A Representation Scheme Using Both Frames and Rules, in Rule-Based Expert Systems, B.G. Buchanan and E.H. Shortliffe (eds.), Addison-Wesley, pp. 424–440, 1984.

Bobrow, D.G. and T. Winograd, An Overview of KRL, a Knowledge Representation Language, Cognitive Science, vol. 1, no. 1, pp. 3–46, Jan. 1977.

Fikes, Richard and Tom Kehler, The Role of Frame-Based Representation in Reasoning, Communications of the ACM, vol. 28, no. 9, pp. 904–920, Sept. 1985.

Goldstein, I. and S. Papert, Artificial Intelligence, Language, and the Study of Knowledge, Cognitive Science, vol. 1, no. 1, Jan. 1977.

Kempf, Renate and Marilyn Stelzner, Teaching Object-Oriented Programming with the KEE System, Sigplan Notices, OOPSLA '87 Proceedings, vol. 22, no. 12, pp. 11–25, 1987.

Minsky, M., A Framework for Representing Knowledge, in The Psychology of Computer Vision, P. Winston (ed.), McGraw-Hill, pp. 211–277, 1975.

Stefik, M.J., D.G. Bobrow, S. Mittal, and L. Conway, Knowledge Processing in LOOPS: Report on an Experimental Course, Artificial Intelligence, vol. 4, no. 3, pp. 3–14, Fall 1983.

Stefik, M.J., An Examination of a Frame-Structured Representation Systems, in Proc. of the 6th Intern. J. Conf. on Artificial Intelligence, Tokyo, Japan, pp. 845–852, Aug. 1979.

Winston, P., Representing Knowledge in Frames, Chapter 7, Artificial Intelligence, Addison-Wesley, pp. 181–187, 1977.

Induction Systems

Buchanan, B. and T. Mitchell, Model-Directed Learning of Production Rules, in Pattern-Directed Inference Systems, D. Waterman and F. Hayes-Roth (eds.), Academic Press, New York, 1978.

Braun, H. and J.S. Chandler, Predicting Stock Market Behavior Through Rule Induction: An Application of the Learning-From-Example Approach, Decision Sciences, vol. 8, no. 3, pp. 415–29, Summer 1987.

Cohen, P.R. and E.A. Feigenbaum, Handbook of Artificial Intelligence, vol. 3, Morgan Kaufmann Pub., Los Altos, CA., 1982.

Dietterich, T., R. Lonclon, K. Clarkson, and R. Dromey, Learning and Inductive Inference, in Handbook of Artificial Intelligence, D. Cohen and E. Feigenbaum (eds.), Morgan Kaufmann Publishing, Los Altos, CA, pp. 323–525, 1981.

Durkin, J., Induction Via ID3, AI Expert, vol. 7, no. 4, pp. 48–53, Apr. 1992.

Durkin, J., Designing an Induction Expert System, AI Expert, vol. 6, no. 12, pp. 29–35, Dec. 1991.

Forsyth, R., Expert Systems: Principles and Case Studies, Chapman and Hall Computing, New York, 1989.

Kornell, J., A VAX Tuning Expert Built Using Automated Knowledge Acquisition, Proceedings of the First Conference on Artificial Intelligent Applications, IEEE Computer Society, Dec. 1984.

Hunt, E.B., J. Marin, and P.J. Stone, Experiments in Induction, Academic Press, New York, 1966.

Lowe, R.I., Artificial Intelligence Techniques Applied to Transformer Oil Dissolved Gas Analysis, Doble Engineering Company, Insulating Fluids, 1985.

Michalski, R. and R. Chilausky, Learning by Being Told and Learning From Examples: An Experimental Comparison of the Two Methods of Knowledge Acquisition in the Context of Developing an Expert System for Soybean Disease Diagnosis, Policy Analysis and Information Systems, vol. 4, no. 2, pp. 125–260, June 1980.

Michalski, R., Pattern Recognition as Knowledge-Guided Computer Induction, Department of Computer Science, University of Illinois at Urbana-Champaign, 1978.

Michie, D., S. Muggleton, C. Riese, and S. Zubrick, RULEMASTER: A Second-Generation Knowledge-Engineering Facility, Proceedings of the First Conference on Artificial Intelligence Applications, IEEE Computer Society, Dec. 1984.

Quinlan, J.R., Discovering Rules From Large Collections of Examples: A Case Study, Expert Systems in the Micro-Electronic Age, D. Michie (Ed.), Edinburgh University Press, 1979.

Quinlan, J.R., Machine Learning: An Artificial Intelligence Approach, R. Michalski, J. Carbonell, and T. Mitchell (eds.), Morgan Kaufmann Publ., Los Altos, CA.

Smith, R., T. Mitchell, R. Chestek, and R. Buchanan, A Model for Learning Systems, Heuristic Programming Project Memo HPP-77-14, Stanford University, Stanford, Cal., 1977.

Winston, P., Learning Structural Descriptions From Examples, in The Psychology of Computer Vision, McGraw-Hill, New York, 1975.

Inexact Reasoning

Bandler, W., Probabilistic Versus Fuzzy Production Rules in Expert Systems, Int. J. Man-Machine Studies, vol. 22, pp. 347–353, 1985.

Bonissone, P., Editorial: Reasoning With Uncertainty in Expert Systems, Int. J. Man-Machines Studies, vol. 22, pp. 241–250, 1985.

Dubois, D. and H. Prade, On the Combination of Uncertain or Imprecise Pieces of Information in Rule-Based Systems, Int. J. Approx. Reasoning, vol. 2, no. 1, pp. 65–87, Jan. 1988.

Gaines, B., The Fuzzy Decade: A Bibliography of Fuzzy Systems and Closely Related Topics, Int. J. Man-Machine Studies, vol. 9, pp. 1–68, 1977.

Giarratano, J. and G. Riley, Expert Systems: Principles and Programming, PWS-KENT Publishing Company, 1989.

Guilamo, P.J., Fuzzy Logic Allows Creation of Precise Process Controllers, EDN, pp. 201–204, April 15, 1987.

Gupta, M.M. and T. Yamakawa (eds.), Fuzzy Logic in Knowledge-Based Systems, Decision and Control, Elsevier Science Publishing Company, 1988.

Gupta, M.M. and T. Yamakawa (eds.), Fuzzy Computing: Theory, Hardware, and Applications, Elsevier Science Publishing Company, 1988.

Gupta, M.M., A. Kandel, W. Bandler, and J.B. Kiszka (eds.), Approximate Reasoning in Expert Systems, Elsevier Science Publishing Company, 1985.

Kandel, Abraham, Fuzzy Mathematical Techniques with Applications, Addison-Wesley, 1986.

Karwowski, W. and A. Mital (eds.), Applications of Fuzzy Set Theory in Human Factors, Elsevier Science Publishing Company, 1986.

Klir, G. and T. Folger, Fuzzy Sets, Uncertainty, and Information, Prentice-Hall, 1988.

Lamberti, D. and W.A. Wallace, Presenting Uncertainty in Expert Systems: An Issue in Information Portrayal, Information Management, vol. 13, no. 4, pp. 159–169, Nov. 1987.

Lecot, K., Control Over Inexact Reasoning, AI Expert, pp. 32–43, 1986.

Mamdani, E.H. and B.R. Gaines (eds.), Fuzzy Reasoning and its Applications, Academic Press, 1981.

Neapolitan, R.E., Models for Reasoning Under Uncertainty, Applied Artificial Intelligence, vol. 1, no. 4, pp. 337–366, 1987.

Negoita, C.V., Expert Systems and Fuzzy Systems, Benjamin Cummings, 1985.

O'Leary, D.E., Soliciting Weights or Probabilities From Experts for Rule-Based Expert Systems, International Journal of Man-Machine Studies, vol. 32, no. 3, pp. 293–301, March 1990.

Pang, D., J. Bigham, and E. Mamdani, Reasoning with Uncertain Information, IEE Proc. vol. 134, no. 4, pp. 231–237, July 1987.

Rauch, H., Probability Concepts for an Expert System Used for Data Fusion, The AI Magazine, pp. 55–60, Fall 1984.

Schwartz, T.J., Fuzzy Systems in the Real World, AI Expert, pp. 29–36, August, 1990.

Shortiffe, Edward and Bruce G. Buchanan, A Model of Inexact Reasoning in Medicine, Mathematical Biosciences, vol. 23, pp. 351–379, 1975.

Tonn, B.E. and R.T. Goeltz, Psychological Validity of Uncertainty Combining Rules in Expert Systems, Expert Systems, vol. 7, no. 2, pp. 94–101, May 1990.

Whalen, Thomas and Brian Schott, Issues in Fuzzy Production Systems, Int. J. Man-Machine Studies, vol. 19, pp. 57–71, 1983.

Whalen, T. and B. Schott, Alternative Logics for Approximate Reasoning in Expert Systems: A Comparative Study, Int. J. Man-Machine Studies, vol. 22, pp. 327–346, 1985.

Whalen, T. and B. Schott, Issues in Fuzzy Production Systems, Int. J. Man-Machine Studies, vol. 19, pp. 57–71, 1983.

Zadeh, L.A., Fuzzy Sets, Information and Control, pp. 338–353, 1965.

Zadeh, L.A., K. Fu, K. Tanaka, and M. Shimura (eds.) Fuzzy Sets and Their Applications to Cognitive and Decision Processes, Academic Press, 1975.

Zadeh L.A., Management of Uncertainty in Expert Systems, Theory and Application of Expert Systems in Emergency Management Operations, Proc. of a Symposium Held at the Department of Commerce, Wash. DC, pp. 24–25, Apr. 1985.

Introduction to Expert Systems

Bell, M.Z., Why Expert Systems Fail, J. Opl. Res., vol. 36, no. 7, pp. 613–619, 1985.

Davis, R., B. Buchanan, and E. Shortliffe, Production Rules as a Representation for a Knowledge-Based Consultation Program, Artificial Intelligence, vol. 8, pp. 15–45, 1977.

Davis R. and J. King, An Overview of Production Systems, Machine Intelligence, vol. 8, pp. 300–322, 1977.

Durkin, J., Introducing Students to Expert Systems, Expert Systems: The International Journal of Knowledge Engineering, Oxford, UK, vol. 7, no. 2, May, 1990.

Emrich, M.L., Expert Systems Tools and Techniques, Oak Ridge National Laboratory Report ORNL/TM-9555, August 1985.

Gevarter, W.B., An Overview of Expert Systems, NASA Report NBSIR 82-2505, May 1982.

Harvey, J.J., Expert Systems: An Introduction, Electrical Communication, vol. 60, no. 2, pp. 100–108, 1986.

Hayes-Roth, F., The Knowledge-Based Expert System: A Tutorial, IEEE Computer, pp. 11–28, September 1984.

Hayes-Roth, F., Rule-Based Systems, Communications of the ACM, vol. 28, no. 9, pp. 921–932, September 1985.

Mayers, W., Introduction to Expert Systems, IEEE Expert, pp. 100–109, Spring 1986.

Michie, D., Expert Systems, The Computer Journal, vol. 23, no. 4, pp. 369–376, 1980.

Miller, A., Expert Systems, IEEE Potentials, pp. 12–15, October 1986.

Murphy, T.E., Setting up an Expert System, The Industrial Control Magazine, pp. 54–60, March 1985.

Nau, D.S., Expert Computer Systems, IEEE Computer, vol. 16, no. 2, pp. 63–85, Feb. 1983.

Quinlan, J.R., An Introduction to Knowledge-Based Expert Systems, The Australian Computer Journal, vol. 12, no. 2, pp. 56–62, May 1980.

Shahla Yaghmai, N. and J.A. Maxin, Expert Systems: A Tutorial, Journal of the American Society for Information Science, vol. 35, no. 5, pp. 297–305, 1984.

Teschler, L., Stripping the Mystery from Expert Systems, Machine Design, pp. 68–74, April 25, 1985.

Thompson, B.A. and W.A. Thompson, Inside an Expert System, BYTE, pp. 315–330, April 1985.

Winfield, M.M., Expert Systems: An Introduction for the Layman, Computer Bulletin, December 1982.

Knowledge Acquisition

Bainbridge, L., Asking Questions and Accessing Knowledge, Future Computing Systems, vol. 1, pp. 143–149, 1986.

Bainbridge, L., Verbal Reports as Evidence of the Process Operators's Knowledge, Int. J. Man-Machine Studies, vol. 11, pp. 411–436, 1979.

Bell, J. and R.J. Hardiman, The Third Role—The Naturalistic Knowledge Engineer, Knowledge Elicitation: Principles, Techniques and Applications, Dan Diaper (ed.), John Wiley & Sons, New York, 1989.

Boose, J.H., A Knowledge Acquisition Program for Expert Systems Based on Personal Construct Psychology, Int. J. Man-Machine Studies, vol. 23, pp. 495–525, 1985.

Boose, J.H., Rapid Acquisition and Combination of Knowledge From Multiple Experts in the Same Domain, Proc. Second Conf. on Artificial Intelligence Applications, Miami, Fla, pp. 461–466, December 1985.

Boose, J.H. and J.M. Bradshaw, A Knowledge Acquisition Workbench for Eliciting Decision Knowledge, Proc. Twentieth Hawaii Conf. on System Sciences, pp. 450–459, 1987.

Butler, K.A. and J.E. Corter, The Use of Psychometric Tools for Knowledge Acquisition: A Case Study, in Artificial Intelligence and Statistics, W. Gale (ed.), Reading, MA: Addison-Wesley, 1986.

Chomsky, N., Syntactic Structures, The Hague: Mouton, 1957.

Collins, H.M., Changing Order: Replication and Induction, in Scientific Practice: London: Sage, 1985.

Cook, N.M. and J.E. McDonald, A Formal Methodology for Acquiring and Representing Knowledge, Proc. of the IEEE, vol. 74, no. 10, pp. 1422–1430, October 1986.

DeGreef, P. and J. Breuker, A Case Study in Structured Knowledge Acquisition, International Joint Conference on Artificial Intelligence, Los Angeles, CA, vol. 1, pp. 390–392, August 1985.

Diaper, D. (ed.), Knowledge Elicitation: Principles Techniques and Applications, John Wiley & Sons, New York, 1989.

Ericsson, K.A. and H.A. Simon, Verbal Reports as Data, Psychological Review, vol. 87, pp. 215–251, 1980.

Evans, J., The Knowledge Elicitation Problem: A Psychological Perspective, Behavior and Information Technology, vol. 7, no. 2, pp. 111–130, 1988.

Fellers, J.W., Key Factors in Knowledge Acquisition, Computer Personnel, vol. 11, no. 1, pp. 10–24, May 1987.

Fransella, F. and D. Bannister, A Manual for Repertory Grid Technique, Academic Press, London, 1977.

Friedland, P., Acquisition of Procedural Knowledge From Domain Experts, Proc. Seventh Int. J. Conf. on Artificial Intelligence, Vancouver, British Columbia, pp. 856–861, 1981.

Gaines, B.R., An Overview of Knowledge Acquisition and Transfer, Int. J. Man-Machine Studies, vol. 26, no. 4, pp. 453–472, April 1987.

Gammack, J.G. and R.M. Young, Psychological Techniques for Eliciting Expert Knowledge, in Research and Development in Expert Systems, M.A. Bramer (ed.), London, UK: Cambridge Univ. Press, pp. 105–112, 1985.

Grover, M.D., A Pragmatic Knowledge Acquisition Methodology, Proc. 8th Joint Conf. Artificial Intelligence, pp. 436–438, 1983.

Hart, A., Knowledge Acquisition for Expert Systems, McGraw-Hill, New York, 1986.

Hart, A., Knowledge Elicitation: Issues and Methods, Computer-Aided Design, vol. 17, no. 9, pp. 455–462, November 1985.

Hayes-Roth, F., P. Klahr, and D.J. Mostow, Knowledge Acquisition, Knowledge Programming, and Knowledge Refinement, The Rand Publications Series, R-2540-NSF, Santa Monica, CA, May 1980.

Hoffman, R.R., The Problem of Extracting the Knowledge of Experts from the Perspective of Experimental Psychology, AI Applications, vol. 1, no. 2, pp. 35–48, 1987.

Johnson, L. and N.E. Johnson, A Knowledge Elicitation Method for Expert Systems Design, System Research and Info. Science, vol. 2, no. 3, pp. 153–166, 1987.

Johnson-Laird, P.N. and M.J. Steedman, The Psychology of Syllogisms, Cognitive Psychology, vol. 10, pp. 64–99, 1978.

Kahn, G., S. Nowlan, and J. McDermott, Strategies for Knowledge Acquisition, IEEE Trans. on Pattern Analysis and Machine Intelligence, vol. PAMI-7, no. 5, pp. 511–522, September 1985.

Kelly, G.A., The Psychology of Personal Constructs, Norton, New York, 1955.

Lincoln, Y.S. and E.G. Guba, Naturalistic Inquiry, California: Sage, 1984.

McGraw, K. and K. Harbison-Briggs, Knowledge Acquisition: Principles and Guidelines, Prentice Hall, 1989.

Michalski, R.S. and R.L. Chilausky, Knowledge Acquisition by Encoding Expert Rules Versus Computer Induction From Examples—A Case Study Involving Soybean Pathology, Int. J. Man-Machine Studies, vol. 12, pp. 63–87, 1980.

Mittal, S. and C.L. Dym, Knowledge Acquisition from Multiple Experts, The AI Magazine, vol. 6, no. 2, pp. 32–36, Summer 1985.

Nisbett, R.E. and T.D. Wilson, Telling More Than We Can Know: Verbal Reports on Mental Processes, Psychological Review, vol. 84, pp. 231–259, 1977.

Olson, J.R. and H.H. Rueter, Extracting Expertise from Experts: Methods for Knowledge Acquisition, Expert Systems, vol. 4, no. 3, pp. 152–168, August 1987.

Quinlan, R., Discovering Rules From Large Collections of Examples: A Case Study, in Expert Systems in the Microelectronic Age, D. Michie (ed.), Edinburgh Univ. Press, Edinburgh 1979.

Rolandi, W.G., A Practical Approach to Knowledge Engineering, AI Expert, pp. 60–65, April 1988.

Shaw, M.L. and B.R. Gaines, Interactive Elicitation of Kowledge From Experts, Future Computer Systems (UK), vol. 1, no. 2, pp. 151–190, 1986.

Smith, R.G. and J.D. Baker, The DIPMETER Advisor System, IJCAI Proceedings, pp. 122–129, 1983.

Sviokla, J.J., Business Implications of Knowledge-Based Systems, Parts I and II, DataBase, [17 : 4; 18 : 1], pp. 5–9, Summer 1986, and pp. 5–16, Fall 1986.

Tversky, A. and D. Kahneman, Availability: Heuristic for Judging Frequency and Probability, Cognitive Psychology, vol. 5, pp. 207–232, 1973.

Waldron, V.R., Interviewing for Knowledge, IEEE Trans. on Professional Communications, vol. PC29, no. 2, pp. 31–34, June 1986.

Welbank, M., A Review of Knowledge Acquisition Techniques for Expert Systems, BTRL, Ipswich: Martlesham Consultancy Services, 1983.

Wright, G. and P. Ayton, Eliciting and Modeling Expert Knowledge, Decision Support Systems, vol. 3, no. 1, pp. 13–26, 1987.

Knowledge Engineering

Attarwaia, F. and A. Basden, A Methodology for Constructing Expert Systems, R&D Management, vol. 15, no. 2, 1985, pp. 141–149.

Feigenbaum, E.A., Knowledge Engineering: The Applied Side of Artificial Intelligence, Tech Rep. STAN-CS-80-812 (HPP-80-21), Dept. of Computer Sci., Stanford University, 1980.

Fidelak, M. and F. Victor, Verification of production systems (expert systems), Janicki, R. and Koczkodaj, W.W. (eds.), Computing and Information, Proceedings of the International Conference, Toronto, Ontario, Canada, North-Holland, Amsterdam, Netherlands, pp. 371–378, May 1989.

Frieling, M., J. ALexander, S. Messick, S. Rehfuss, and S. Shulman, Starting a Knowledge Engineering Project: A Step-by Step Approach, The AI Magazine, pp. 150–164, Fall 1985.

Haley, Paul and Chuck Williams, Expert System Development Requires Knowledge Engineering, Computer Design, pp. 83–88, Feb. 15, 1986.

Hill, H., A Methodology for Building Expert Systems, National Computer Conference, pp. 7–12, 1987.

Lehner, P.E., Toward an Empirical Approach to Evaluating the Knowledge Base of an Expert System, IEEE Transactions on Systems, Man and Cybernetics, vol. 19, no. 3, pp. 658–662, May/June 1989.

Sagalowicz, D., Development of an Expert System, Expert Systems, vol. 1, no. 2, pp. 137–141, 1984.

Smith, Reid, On the Development of Commercial Expert Systems, The AI Magazine, pp. 61–72, Fall 1984.

Williams, C., Expert Systems, Knowledge Engineering, and AI Tools—An Overview, IEEE Expert, vol. 1, no. 4, pp. 66–70, 1986.

Knowledge Representation

Barlett, F.C., Remembering, Cambridge: CUP, 1932.

Barr, A. and E.A. Feigenbaum (eds.), The Handbook of Artificial Intelligence, vol. 1, Morgan Kaufman Pub., 1981.

Erman, L.D., The HEARSAY-II Speech Understanding System: Integrating Knowledge to Resolve Uncertainties, Computing Surveys, vol. 12, no. 2, pp. 213–253, June 1980.

Minsky, M.L., Frame System Theory, Thinking: Readings in Cognitive Science, P.N. Johnson-Laird and P.C. Watson (eds.), Cambridge: CUP, 1975.

Minsky, M.L., A Framework for Representing Knowledge, The Psychology of Computer Vision, Patrick Henry Winston, ed., New York: McGraw-Hill Book Company, 1975.

Newell, A. and H.A. Simon, Human Problem Solving, Englewood Cliffs, N.J. Prentice-Hall, 1972.

Quillian, M.R., Semantic Memory, Semantic Information Processing, M.L. Minsky (ed.), Cambridge, Mass.: MIT Press, 1968.

Sources of Additional Information

Expert System Books
Journals and Magazines
Newsletters
Abstracts and Indexes

Expert System Books

A Comprehensive Guide to AI and Expert System
R. Levine, D.E. Drang, and B. Edelson, McGraw-Hill, 1986.

A Fuzzy Prolog Database System
D. Li and D. Liu, John Wiley, 1990.

A Guide to Commercial Artificial Intelligence
W.B. Rauch-Hindin, Prentice-Hall, 1988.

A Guide to Expert Systems
Donald A. Waterman, Addison-Wesley, 1986.

A Perspective on Intelligent Systems: A Framework For Analysis and Design
L. Kohout, Chapman and Hall, 1990.

A Practical Guide to Designing Expert Systems
S.M. Weiss and C.A. Kulikowski, Rowman & Allanheld, 1984.

AI Theory and Applications in the VAX Environment
Michael Stock, McGraw-Hill, 1988.

An Introduction to Expert Systems
Jay Liebowitz, McGraw-Hill, 1988.

An Introduction to Expert Systems: Knowledge-Based Systems
R.J. Mockler and D.G. Dologite, Macmillan, 1992.

Analysis of Fuzzy Information
J. Bezdek, ed., CRC Press, 1987.

Application of Expert Systems, Volume II
J. Quinlan, ed., Addison-Wesley, 1989.

Application of Expert Systems, Volume I
J. Quinlan, ed., Addison-Wesley, 1987.

Applications of Fuzzy Set Theory in Human Factors
W. Karwowski and A. Mital, Elsevier, 1986.

Applying Expert Systems in Business
D.N. Chorafas, McGraw-Hill, 1985.

Artificial Intelligence in Business
Paul Harmon and David King, John Wiley, 1985.

Artificial Intelligence and the Design of Expert Systems
George Luger and William A. Stubblefield, Benjamin/Cummings, 1989.

Artificial Intelligence: Structures and Strategies for Complex Problem Solving
George Luger and William A. Stubblefield, Benjamin/Cummings, 1992.

Artificial Intelligence and Expert Systems
S. Savory, Ellis Horwood Limited, Halsted Press, John Wiley, 1988.

Artificial Intelligence: A Knowledge-Based Approach
M.W. Firebaugh, Boyd and Fraser, 1988.

Artificial Intelligence: Its Role in the Information Industry
P. Davis, Learned Information, 1991.

Artificial Intelligence, Simulation and Modeling
L. Widman, K. Loparo, and N. Nielsen, John Wiley, 1989.

Blackboard Systems
R. Engelmore, ed., Addison-Wesley, 1989.

Building Expert Systems
Frederick Hayes-Roth, Donald A. Waterman, and Douglas B. Lenat, Addison-Wesley, 1983.

Building Expert Systems: A Tutorial
J. Martin and S. Oxman, Prentice-Hall, 1988.

Building Large Knowledge-Based Systems
Douglas B. Lenat, Addison-Wesley, 1983.

Building Your First Expert System
T. Nagy, D. Gault, and M. Nagy, Ashton-Tate, 1985.

Build Your Own Expert System
C. Naylor, Halsted Press, 1983.

Catalogue of Artificial Intelligence
A. Bundy, ed., Springer-Verlag, 1990.

Competent Expert Systems: A Case Study in Fault Diagnosis
E.T. Keravnou and L. Johnson, McGraw-Hill, 1987.

Computer Systems That Learn: Classification and Prediction Methods from Statistics, Neutral Nets, Machine Learning and Expert Systems
S. Weiss and C. Kulikowski, Morgan Kaufmann, 1991.

Coupling Symbolic and Numerical Computing in Expert Systems
J.S. Kowalik, ed., Elsevier, New York, 1985.

Crash Course in Artificial Intelligence and Expert Systems
Louis E. Frenzel, Howard W. Sams & Co., 1987.

Creating Expert Systems for Business and Industry
Paul Harmon and Brian Sawyer, John Wiley, 1990.

Decision Support and Expert Systems
E. Turban, Macmillan, 1988.

Decision Support Models and Expert Systems
D. Olson and J. Courtney, Macmillan, 1992.

Designing and Implementing Your Own Expert Systems
Beverly and W. Thompson, Byte/McGraw-Hill, 1985.

Designing Expert Systems: Guidelines and Techniques
Paul Kline and Steven Dolins, John Wiley, 1989.

Designing and Programming Personal Expert Systems
C. Townsend and D. Foucht, Tab Books, 1981.

Designing Systems: A Guide to Selecting Implementation Techniques
Paul Kline and Steven Dolins, John Wiley, 1989.

Developing and Managing Expert Systems: Proven Techniques for Business and Industry
D. Prerau, Addison-Wesley, 1990.

Developing Business Expert Systems with LEVEL5
D. Burker, Macmillan, 1988.

Developing Expert Systems for Business Applications
J. Chandler and T. Liang, Macmillan, 1990.

Developing Expert Systems: A Knowledge Engineer's Handbook for Rules and Objects
Edmund Payne and R. McArthur, John Wiley, 1990.

Developing Knowledge-Based Systems Using 1ST-CLASS
Christopher Ruth, McGraw-Hill, 1988.

Developing Knowledge-Based Systems Using an Expert System Shell
R. Mockler, Macmillan, 1992.

Developing Knowledge-Based Systems Using EXSYS
Christopher Ruth, McGraw-Hill, 1988.

Developing Knowledge-Based Systems Using VP-Expert
D.G. Dologite, Macmillan, 1992.

Developments in Expert Systems
M. Coombs, ed., Academic Press, Orlando, Fla., 1984.

Encyclopedia of Artificial Intelligence, Second Edition
S. Shapiro ed., John Wiley, 1992.

Expert knowledge and Explanation
Charles Ellis, John Wiley, 1989.

Expert Systems
Paul Harmon and David King, John Wiley, 1984.

Expert Systems: A Clear Guide to The Facts
Alex Goodall, Expert Systems International, Oxford, England

Expert Systems A Practical Introduction
P. Sell, John Wiley, 1985.

Expert Systems, A Decision Support Approach
M. Klein and L.B. Methlie, Addison-Wesley, 1990.

Expert Systems and Applied Artificial Intelligence
E. Turban, Macmillan, 1992.

Expert Systems Architectures
L. Johnson and E.T. Keravnou, Kogan Page, 1989.

Expert Systems and Fuzzy Systems
C. Negoita, Benjamin/Cummings, 1985.

Expert Systems, Concepts and Examples
Alty and Coombs, NCC Publications, Manchester, England 1984.

Expert Systems Design and Development Using VP-Expert
S. Friederich and M. Gargano, John Wiley, 1989.

Expert Systems for Business
B. Silverman, ed., Addison-Wesley, 1987.

Expert Systems for Engineering Design
M.D. Rychener, ed., Academic Press, 1988.

Expert Systems for Engineers
J.N. Siddall, Marcel Dekker, 1990.

Expert Systems: Human Issues
D. Berry and Anna Hart, Chapman and Hall, 1990.

Expert Systems in Data Processing: Applications Using IBM's Knowledge Tool
J. Hellerstein, D. Klein, and K. Milliken, Addison-Wesley, 1990.

Expert Systems: Knowledge, Uncertainty and Decision
I. Graham and P. Jones, Chapman and Hall, 1988.

Expert Systems: Principles and Case Studies
R. Forsyth, Chapman and Hall, 1989.

Expert System Programming: Practical Techniques for Rule-based Systems
Ken Pedersen, John Wiley, 1989.

Expert Systems: Techniques, Tools and Applications
P. Klahr and D. Waterman, eds., Addison-Wesley, 1986.

Expert System Technology: Development and Application
Robert Keller, Yourdon Press, 1987.

Expert Systems: Tools and Applications
Paul Harmon, Rex Maus, and William Morrissey, John Wiley, 1988.

Fuzzy Computing: Theory, Hardware, and Applications
M.M. Gupta and T. Yamakawa, North Holland, 1988.

Fuzzy Controllers: An In-Depth Assessment
R. Miller and T. Walker, Richard K. Miller, Norcross, Ga., 1991.

Fuzzy Expert Systems
Abraham Kandel, CRC Press, 1991.

Fuzzy Mathematical Techniques with Applications
A. Kandel, Addison-Wesley, 1986.

Fuzzy Reasoning and its Applications
E.H. Mamdani and B.R. Gaines, Academic Press, 1981.

Fuzzy Sets and Their Applications to Cognitive and Decision Processes
L. Zadeh, K. Fu, K. Tanaka, and M. Shimura, Academic Press, 1975.

Knowledge Acquisition
James F. Brule, McGraw-Hill, 1989.

Knowledge Acquisition for Expert Systems
Anna Hart, McGraw-Hill, 1986.

Knowledge Aided Design
M. Green, ed., Academic Press, 1992.

Knowledge-Based Design Systems
R. Coyne, M. Rosenman, A. Radford, M. Balachandran, and J. Gero, Addison-Wesley, 1990.

Knowledge-Based Programming
E. Tyugu, Addison-Wesley, 1988.

Knowledge-Based Systems in Artificial Intelligence: Two Case Studies
R. Davis and D. Lenat, McGraw-Hill, 1980.

Knowledge-Based Systems for Management Decisions
Robert J. Mockler, Prentice-Hall, 1989.

Knowledge-Based Systems for Strategic Planning
Robert J. Mockler, Prentice-Hall, 1989.

Knowledge-Based Systems in Engineering
Clive L. Dym and Raymond E. Levitt, McGraw-Hill, 1991.

Knowledge Acquisition: Principles and Guidelines
K. McGraw and K. Harbison-Briggs, Prentice-Hall, 1989.

Knowledge Elicitation: Principles, Techniques and Applications
Dan Diaper, John Wiley, 1989.

Knowledge Representation for Decision Support Systems
Lief B. Methlie and R.H. Sprague, Jr., eds., Elsevier, New York, 1985.

Knowledge Systems and Prolog: A Logical Approach to Expert Systems and Natural Language Processing
Walker, Adrian et al., ed., Addison-Wesley, 1987.

Induction: Processes of Inference, Learning, and Discovery
Holland, John H., et al., MIT Press, 1986.

Inductive Acquisition of Expert Knowledge
S. Muggleton, Addison-Wesley, 1990.

Intelligent System Design: Integrating Hypermedia and Expert System Technologies
Larry Bielawski and Robert Leward, John Wiley, 1990.

Introduction to Artificial Intelligence and Expert Systems
Dan W. Patterson, Prentice-Hall, 1990.

Introduction to Expert Systems
Peter Jackson, Addison-Wesley, 1990.

Introduction to Expert Systems: The Development and Implementation of Rule-Based Expert Systems
James P. Ignizio, John Wiley, 1991.

Manager's Guide to Expert Systems Using Guru
Clyde W. Holsapple and A.B. Whinston, Dow Jones-Irwin, Homewood, Ill., 1986.

Managing Artificial Intelligence and Expert Systems
D. DeSalvo and J. Liebowitz, Yourdon Press, 1990.

Management Expert Systems
C.J. Ernst, ed., Addison-Wesley, 1988.

Manufacturing Intelligence
P. Wright and D. Bourne, Addison-Wesley, 1988.

Neural Networks and Fuzzy Systems: A Dynamic Systems Approach to Machine Intelligence
B. Kosko, Prentice-Hall, 1992.

Operational Expert System Applications in Canada
C. Suen and R. Shinghal, Pergamon, 1991.

Operational Expert System Applications in Europe
Gian Piero Zarri, Pergamon, 1991.

Operational Expert System Applications in Mexico
J. Francisco, Pergamon, 1991.

Operational Expert System Applications in the Far East
Jae Kyu Lee, et al., Pergamon, 1991.

Operational Expert System Applications in the United States
J. Liebowitz, Pergamon, 1991.

Practical Experience in Building Expert Systems
Max Bramer, John Wiley, 1990.

Principles of Artificial Intelligence and Expert Systems Development
David W. Rolston, McGraw-Hill, 1988.

Principles of Expert Systems
P. Lucas and L. Gaag, Addison-Wesley, 1990.

Probablistic Reasoning in Expert Systems
Richard Neapolitan, John Wiley, 1990.

Programming Expert Systems in OPS5
Lee Brownston, Robert Farrell, Elaine Kant, and Nancy Martin, Addison-Wesley, 1985.

Programming in Prolog
Clocksin, W.F. and C.S. Mellish, Springer-Verlag, Berlin, 1981.

Prolog and Expert Systems
K. Bowen, McGraw-Hill, 1991.

Prolog to Expert Systems
W. Leigh, McGraw-Hill, 1987.

Putting Expert Systems into Practice
Robert G. Bowerman and David E. Glover, Van Nostrand Reinhold, 1988.

Readings in Expert Systems
D. Michie, ed., Science Publishers, 1982.

Readings in Machine Learning
J. Shavlik, ed., Morgan Kaufmann, 1990.

Readings in Planning
J. Allen (ed.), Morgan Kaufmann, 1990.

Readings in Uncertain Reasoning
G. Shafer (ed.), Morgan Kaufmann, 1990.

Real-Time Expert Systems Computer Architecture
Robert F. Hodson and Abraham Kandel, CRC Press, 1991.

Reasoning Under Incomplete Information in AI
Lea Sombie, John Wiley, 1990.

Representation of Commensense Knowledge
E. Davis, Morgan Kaufmann, 1991.

Rule-Based Expert Systems
B. Buchanan and E. Shortliffe, eds., Addison-Wesley, 1984.

Smalltalk-80: The Language and its Implementation
Adele Goldberg and David Robson, Addison-Wesley, 1983.

Standards and Review Manual for Certification in Knowledge Engineering: Handbook of Theory and Practice
M. White and J. Goldsmith, Systemware Corp., Rockville, Md., 1989.

Structured Induction in Expert Systems
A. Shapiro, Addison-Wesley, 1987.

The AI Business: The Commercial Uses of Artificial Intelligence
P.H. Winston and K.A. Prendergast, eds., MIT Press, 1984.

The AI Workbench: BABYLON
T. Christaller, et al., Academic Press, 1992.

The CRI Directory of Expert Systems
G. Smart and J. Langeland-Knudsen, Learned Information, 1986.

The Reliability of Expert Systems
Erik Hollnagel, John Wiley, 1989.

The Rise of the Expert Company
E. Feigenbaum, P. McCorduck, and H. Nii, Times Book, 1988.

Uncertain Information Processing in Expert Systems
P. Hajek, T. Havranek, and R. Jirousek, CRC Press, 1991.

Understanding Expert Systems
Mike Van Horn, Bantam Books, 1986.

We're Off to Seize the Wizard: The Revolution in Service Automation
J. Pepper, ServiceWare Inc., Verona, Pa., 1991.

Journals and Magazines

Artificial Intelligence
Elsevier Science Publishing Co.,
Journal Information Center
P.O. Box 882
Madison Square Station
New York, NY 10159
(212) 633-3750

AI Expert
Miller Freeman
600 Harrison St.
San Francisco, CA 94107
(415) 905-2382

AI Magazine
American Association for Artificial Intelligence
445 Burgess Drive
Menlo Park, CA 94025
(415) 328-3123

AI Source Book and AI Trends
Relayer Group
8232 E. Buckskin
Scottsdale, AZ 85255
(602) 585-8587

Artificial Intelligence for Engineering Design, Analysis and Manufacturing
Academic Press Inc.
1250 Sixth Ave.
San Diego, CA

Cognitive Science
Ablex Publishing Corporation
355 Chestnut Street
Norwood, NJ 07648

Engineering Applications of Artificial Intelligence
Pergamon Press
395 Saw Mill River Road
Elmsford, NY 10523

Expert Systems Journal
Learned Information
Woodside, Hinksey Hill
Oxford, OX1 5AU, U.K.

Expert System User Magazine
Cromwell House
20 Bride Lane
London, EC4 8DX, U.K.

Expert Systems with Applications
Pergamon Press
395 Saw Mill River Road
Elmsford, NY 10523

Knowledge Acquisition
Academic Press Inc.
1250 Sixth Ave.
San Diego, CA

IEEE Expert
345 East 47th Street
New York, NY 10017

Intelligence
P.O. Box 20008
New York, NY 10025

Intelligent Tutoring Media
Learned Information
Woodside, Hinksey Hill
Oxford, OX1 5AU, U.K.

International Journal of Man–Machine Studies
Academic Press
24–28 Oval Road
London, NW1 7DX, England

Journal of AI in Education
Association for the Advancement of Computer Education
P.O. Box 2966
Charlottesville, VA 22902

Knowledge Engineering
Richmond Research
P.O. Box 336
Village Station
2001 Varick St.
New York, NY 10014

Law, Computers & Artificial Intelligence
Triangle Journals Ltd
PO Box 65, Wallingford
Oxfordshire, OX10 0YG, U.K.

PC AI
3310 West Bell Rd.
Suite 119
Phoenix, AZ 85023

Newsletters

AI Trends Newsletter
DM Data, Inc.
6900 East Camelback Road
Scottsdale, AZ 85251

*AISB Quarterly, Newsletter of the Society for the Study of Artificial Intelligence
and Simulation of Behavior*
Institute of Educational Technology
The Open University Walton Hall
Milton Keynes, MK7 6AA, England
(quarterly newsletter)

Applied Artificial Intelligence Reporter
Intelligence Computer Systems Research Institute
P.O. Box 1308-EP
Fort Lee, NJ 07024
(monthly newsletter)

Artificial Intelligence Markets
AIM Publications
P.O. Box 156
Natick, MA 01760
(monthly newsletter)

Canadian AI Newsletter
Canadian Artificial Intelligence Society
243 College Street
Toronto, Canada M5T 2Y1

Cognizer Report
Cognizer Co.
7276 Beaverton-Hillsdale Hwy
Portland, OR 97225
(monthly newsletter)

Expert Systems Strategies
Cutter Information Corp.
1100 Massachusetts Ave.
Arlington, MA 02174-9990

Advanced Technology for Developers
High-Tech Communications
103 Buckskin Court
Sewickley, PA 15143
(412) 741-7699

Machine Intelligence News
Oyez International Business Communications Ltd.
56 Holborn Viaduct
London, EC1A 2EX, England
(monthly newsletter)

SIGART Newsletter, ACM Special Interest Group in Artificial Intelligence
Association for Computing Machinery
11 West 42nd Street
New York, NY 10036
(quarterly newsletter)

The Artificial Intelligence Report
Artificial Intelligence Publications
95 First Street
Los Altos, CA 94022
(monthly newsletter)

The Spang Robinson Report
3600 West Bayshore Rd.
Palo Alto, CA 94303

Abstracts and Indexes

Artificial Intelligence Abstracts
DESCRIPTION: Contains abstracts and citations to AI publications. Sources include books, journals, and proceedings from the computer sciences, philosophy, and linguistics. Published bimonthly.
SOURCE: Blackwell, Oxford, U.K.

Artificial Intelligence Abstracts
DESCRIPTION: Contains indexes to AI publications organized by subject, source, industry, and author. Sources include books, journals, and conference proceedings. Published 10 times a year.
SOURCE: EIC Intelligence, New York, N.Y.

Computer and Control Abstracts
DESCRIPTION: Contains abstracts and citations of computer applications. Sources include books, journals, and conference proceedings. Published monthly.
SOURCE: Institute of Electrical Engineers (INSPEC), Piscataway, N.J.

Computer and Information Systems Abstracts Journal
DESCRIPTION: Contains indexes, bibliography, and abstracts of journals and conference proceedings. Published monthly.
SOURCE: Cambridge Scientific Abstracts, Bethesda, Md.

Computer Literature Index
DESCRIPTION: Provides citations and synopses. Sources include books, journals, and conference proceedings. Published quarterly.
SOURCE: Applied Computer Research Inc., Phoenix, Ariz.

Computing Reviews
DESCRIPTION: Provides reviews of computer literature. Sources include books, journals, and conference proceedings. Published monthly.
SOURCE: Association for Computing Machinery, New York, N.Y.

Microcomputer Index
DESCRIPTION: Provides indexes, citations, and abstracts, primarily of the microcomputer literature. Also provides book reviews, product announcements, product development, and software evaluation. Published bimonthly.
SOURCE: Database Services Inc., Palo Alto, Calif.

Index